AF666751

Michael Koch, Andreas Butz, Johann Schlichter (Hrsg.)

Mensch und Computer 2014 – Tagungsband

Weitere empfehlenswerte Titel

Mensch-Maschine-Interaktion
Andreas Butz, Antonio Krüger, 2014
ISBN 978-3-486-71621-4, e-ISBN 978-3-486-71967-3

Prozessführungssysteme
Michael Herczeg, 2014
ISBN 978-3-486-58445-5, e-ISBN 978-3-486-72005-1,
Set-ISBN 978-3-486-79087-0

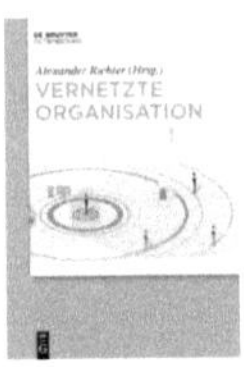

Vernetzte Organisation
Alexander Richter (Hrsg.), 2014
ISBN 978-3-486-74728-7, e-ISBN 978-3-486-74731-7,
Set-ISBN 978-3-486-98957-1

Informatik und Gesellschaft
Andrea Kienle, Gabriele Kunau, 2014
ISBN 978-3-486-73597-0, e-ISBN 978-3-486-78145-8

i-Com, Zeitschrift für interaktive und kooperative Medien
Jürgen Ziegler (Ed.)
ISSN 2196-6826

Mensch und Computer 2014 – Tagungsband

14. Fachübergreifende Konferenz für Interaktive und Kooperative Medien
Interaktiv unterwegs – Freiräume gestalten

Herausgegeben von
Michael Koch, Andreas Butz, Johann Schlichter

DE GRUYTER
OLDENBOURG

Herausgeber

Prof. Dr. Michael Koch
Universität der Bundeswehr München
Fakultät für Informatik
Institut für Softwaretechnologie
Werner-Heisenberg-Weg 39
85577 Neubiberg
michael.koch@unibw.de

Prof. Dr. Johann Schlichter
Technische Universität München
Institut für Informatik
Boltzmanstr. 3
85748 Garching
schlichter@in.tum.de

Prof. Dr. Andreas Butz
Ludwig-Maximilians-Universität München
Institut für Informatik, Lehrstuhl für
Mensch-Maschine-Interaktion
Amalienstr. 17
80333 München
butz@ifi.lmu.de

ISBN 978-3-11-034415-8
e-ISBN (PDF) 978-3-11-034448-6
e-ISBN (EPUB) 978-3-11-039661-4
Set-ISBN 978-3-11-034449-3

Bibliografische Information der Deutschen Nationalbibliothek
Die Deutsche Nationalbibliothek verzeichnet diese Publikation in der Deutschen Nationalbibliografie; detaillierte bibliografische Daten sind im Internet über http://dnb.dnb.de abrufbar.

Ein Unternehmen von Walter De Gruyter GmbH, Berlin/Boston
Lektorat: Dr. Gerhard Pappert
Herstellung: Tina Bonertz
Titelbild: Fachbereich Mensch-Computer-Interaktion der Gesellschaft für Informatik
Druck und Bindung: CPI books GmbH, Leck
♾ Gedruckt auf säurefreiem Papier
Printed in Germany

www.degruyter.com.

Inhaltsverzeichnis

Vorwort

Innovative und vernetzte Computertechnologien haben in den letzten Jahren entscheidend dazu beigetragen, dass Menschen nicht nur an Desktop-Rechnern mit verschiedenen Informationsdiensten und vor allem über solche Dienste miteinander interagieren können. Auch und gerade unterwegs, haben neue Gerätetypen mit neuen Benutzungsschnittstellen völlig neue Freiräume für IT-Nutzer geschaffen.

Die Fachtagung Mensch und Computer 2014 in München nimmt diese technologischen Entwicklungen zum Anlass, um unter dem Motto „Interaktiv unterwegs – Freiräume gestalten" Beiträge deutschsprachiger Forscher zur Entwicklung von Interaktionskonzepten vorzustellen und kritisch zu diskutieren.

Die „Allgegenwärtige Mensch-Computer Interaktion" wurde 2014 auch von der Gesellschaft für Informatik als eine der fünf „Grand Challenges" der Informatik vorgestellt. Motivierend für die Bedeutung war dabei, dass der persönliche Erfolg und die gesellschaftliche Stellung von Menschen zunehmend von der erfolgreichen und wirkungsvollen Beteiligung an computergestützten Kommunikations- und Informationsangeboten abhängig ist. Gleichzeitig werden die technischen Systeme, ihre Struktur, Funktionalitäten und Interaktionsformen komplexer, obwohl oder gerade weil die Systeme durch Miniaturisierung, Vernetzung und Einbettung immer weniger sichtbar und damit auch immer weniger (be)greifbar sind. Diese zunehmende Allgegenwärtigkeit und Komplexität bei gleichzeitig abnehmender Sichtbarkeit dieser Technologien erschwert es insbesondere für die Breite der Bevölkerung, diese mühelos und erfolgreich verstehen und nutzen zu können.

Um eine breite Zugänglichkeit allgegenwärtig nutzbarer Kommunikations- und Informationsdienste zu erreichen, sind insbesondere zwei Herausforderungen zu lösen: Erstens ist eine intuitive Benutzbarkeit zu ermöglichen. Dies beinhaltet neben der nahtlosen Integration verschiedenster Komponenten der Benutzerschnittstelle und dem Eingehen auf die mentalen Modelle der Nutzer auch eine Anpassung der Benutzerschnittstelle auf den einzelnen Benutzer oder auf die Gruppe von Benutzern. Zweitens muss den Nutzern eine Absehbarkeit der Folgen von Interaktionen ermöglicht werden. Dies beinhaltet es auch den Nutzern ökonomische, soziale und individuelle Möglichkeiten und Risiken beurteilbar bewusst zu machen.

Der vorliegende Tagungsband enthält wissenschaftliche Beiträge zu den auf der Tagung präsentierten Fachvorträgen und Kurzbeiträgen (Postern) und liefert damit verschiedene Perspektiven aus den Bereichen Forschung und Praxis. Die Beiträge des UPA-Teils der Tagung erscheinen in einem eigenen Tagungsband. Weiterhin wird noch ein Workshopband herausgegeben, der die Beiträge der wissenschaftlichen Workshops sowie der Systemdemonstrationen und Industriebeiträge dokumentiert.

Alle Beiträge sind auch in der Digital Library des Fachbereichs Mensch-Computer-Interaktion unter http://dl.mensch-und-computer.de/ verfügbar.

Die 28 Langbeiträge des wissenschaftlichen Teils sind in einem doppelt-blinden Begutachtungsverfahren aus insgesamt 68 Einreichungen ausgewählt worden. Gleiches gilt für die Kurzbeiträge. Wir danken an dieser Stelle sowohl den Einreichern für die Erstellung der Beiträge als auch dem am Ende dieses Bandes aufgelisteten Programmkomitee für die Begutachtung und Auswahl der auf der Tagung vorgestellten Beiträge.

München, im Juli 2014

Michael Koch, Andreas Butz, Johann Schlichter

Langbeiträge

M. Koch, A. Butz & J. Schlichter (Hrsg.): Mensch und Computer 2014 Tagungsband, München: Oldenbourg Wissenschaftsverlag, 2014, S. 3-14.

Auswirkungen von Gamification in Enterprise Collaboration Systems

Petra Schubert, Ludwig Paulsen, Johannes Hager

Forschungsgruppe Betriebliche Anwendungssysteme, Universität Koblenz-Landau

Zusammenfassung

Dieser Beitrag behandelt Gamification als Ansatz für die Förderung der Akzeptanz und Nutzung von Kollaborationssystemen. Über einen Zeitraum von fünf Monaten wurden die Auswirkungen von Gamification-Elementen auf Projektengruppen an zwei Universitäten untersucht. Für die Datenerhebung wurden Fragebögen, persönliche Interviews und Eventlogs eingesetzt. Die Ergebnisse zeigen, dass Gamification eine sehr erfolgreiche Maßnahme sein kann, der Einsatz der spezifischen Elemente allerdings gut geplant und auf den Organisationskontext und die verfolgten Ziele abgestimmt werden muss. Vor allem die kompetitiven Gamification-Elemente, die einen direkten Vergleich zwischen Benutzern in einem öffentlichen Forum erlauben, stellten sich als potenziell „problematisch“ heraus. Individuelle Elemente, die den Fortschritt eines Benutzers ohne direkten Vergleich mit Anderen zeigen, wurden als „unproblematischer“ empfunden. Besonders beliebt waren Elemente, die ein Feedback auf das eigene Verhalten und die inhaltlichen Beiträge nur dem betroffenen Benutzer selbst anzeigen.

1 Motivation und Forschungsschritte

Enterprise Collaboration Systems (ECS) sind betriebliche Anwendungssysteme und unterstützen die Zusammenarbeit von Mitarbeitern im Unternehmen. Die neuste Form dieser Kollaborationssysteme, Enterprise Social Software (ESS), transferiert die Möglichkeiten von Social Media in den Unternehmenskontext (Schubert & Williams 2013). Aber die Einführung dieser „Social“ Software läuft nicht immer so erfolgreich ab wie vom Management erhofft. Das Thema „Adoption“ (Richter & Stocker, 2011) und speziell die Förderung der Akzeptanz und der Nutzung von ECS (Diehl et al. 2013) beschäftigen die akademische Welt bereits solange es diese Systeme gibt. Gamification, der Einsatz von spielerischen Elementen in Business Software, könnte ein erfolgversprechender Ansatz zur Förderung der Nutzung von ECS sein. Vor diesem Hintergrund war es interessant zu untersuchen, wie eine Gamification-Software sich auf die Arbeit von Individuen in Projektteams auswirken würde. Unsere Probanden waren Studierende an zwei Universitäten in Ost- und Westdeutschland, die im Rahmen ihres Studiums eine Projektarbeit durchführen mussten. Die Benutzung der Kollaborationsplattform wurde als zusätzliche Lernerfahrung empfohlen, war aber nicht die eigentliche Aufgabe des Projekts. Den Teilnehmern wurde kein expliziter Hinweis auf die vorhandenen Gamification-Komponenten gegeben. Es gab keinerlei Hinweise darauf, dass die Lehrenden die Gamification-Ergebnisse für die Notenbildung heranziehen würden. Die Gamification-Elemente waren ohne Erläuterungen auf der Plattform vorhanden und wurden standardmäßig angezeigt. Tabelle 1 gibt einen Überblick über den Forschungsaufbau.

Zeitraum	01.10.2013-28.02.2014 (5 Monate, Wintersemester)
Teilnehmer	Studierende an zwei deutschen Universitäten in Ost-/Westdeutschland
Enterprise Collaboration System (ECS)	IBM Connections (Hersteller: IBM)
Gamification-Software	Kudos Badges (Hersteller: ISW)
Aufgabe der Teilnehmer	Projektarbeit in Gruppen von 3-4 Studierenden. Jeder Gruppe stand eine „Community“ auf der ECS zur Verfügung
Formen der Datenerhebung	Fragebögen (35), Team-Interviews (6), Eventlogs, Interviews mit Softwarehersteller (1)
Formen der Datenauswertung	Qualitative Analyse, SPSS

Tabelle 1: Steckbrief Forschungsaufbau

Abbildung 1 zeigt die Forschungsschritte. Zunächst wurden unter Einbezug existierender Literatur die Forschungsfragen und der Fragebogen entwickelt. Die Gamification-Elemente wurden auf der ECS installiert, so dass sie allen Teilnehmern an beiden Standorten zur Verfügung standen. Am Ende der Projektzeit wurde eine Befragung durchgeführt, an der 35 Personen teilnahmen. Anschließend wurden die Fragebögen in einer ersten Version ausgewertet. Die Ergebnisse warfen für die Forscher einige Fragen auf, die in sechs Gruppeninterviews mit den Teilnehmern besprochen wurden. Um weitere Erfahrungswerte in die Studie einzubeziehen, wurde ein Workshop mit dem Softwarehersteller an seinem Firmensitz durchgeführt. Hier wurden die Ergebnisse aus der Studierendenbefragung mit den Ergebnissen aus Kundenprojekten verglichen.

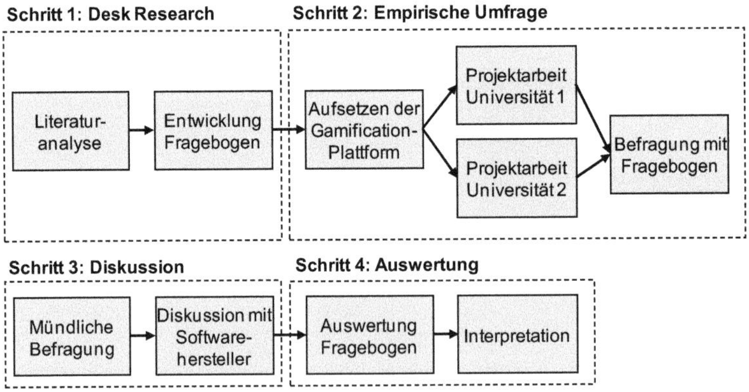

Abbildung 1: Forschungsschritte

Das folgende Paper *fokussiert auf die Auswertung der schriftlichen Befragung* der Teilnehmer. Die Ergebnisse der Analyse der Eventlogs konnte aus Platzgründen nicht erfolgen.

Das verbleibende Paper ist wie folgt organisiert: Das folgende Kapitel enthält eine Beschreibung von Gamification in der Literatur sowie eine Vorstellung der eingesetzten Gamification-Elemente. Im Anschluss werden die Ergebnisse der schriftlichen Befragungen vorgestellt und diskutiert. Den Abschluss bildet das Fazit mit einer Zusammenfassung der Ergebnisse.

2 Literatur und Gamification-Software

Der Begriff Gamification stammt aus dem Englischen und bedeutet wörtlich „Spielifizierung". Dieser Begriff ist jedoch nicht geläufig, obgleich er sehr gut den Charakter von Gamification beschreibt — nämlich die „Spielifizierung von Nicht-Spielen". Es geht also darum, irgendetwas, das normalerweise nicht als Spiel angesehen wird oder im Kontext von Spielen betrachtet wird, um Spielmechanismen anzureichern. Diese Annäherung an den Begriff Gamification wird durch die existierenden Definitionen gestützt: „Gamification is the use of game design elements and game mechanics in non-game contexts." (Domínguez et al. 2012)

Diese Definition beschreibt sehr gut den Kern des Konzeptes Gamification. Eine andere Definition geht noch weiter und umfasst darüber hinaus auch das *Ziel des Einsatzes* von Gamification: „Gamification ist die Verwendung von spieltypischen Mechaniken außerhalb reiner Spiele, mit dem Ziel, das Verhalten von Menschen zu beeinflussen." (Breuer 2011)

Der Aspekt der „Beeinflussung" ist für den Einsatz in Business Software interessant, da dies ein wichtiger Aspekt in Softwareeinführungsprojekten ist. Ein weiterer wichtiger Aspekt, das sogenannte „User Engagement", also die „Partizipation" (vgl. auch Koch et.al. 2013), wird in der folgenden Definition von Deterding et al. (2011) betont: "Gamification" is an informal umbrella term for the use of video game elements in non-gaming systems to improve user experience (UX) and user engagement."

Zusammenfassend sind die folgenden drei Aspekte für Gamification von Business Software entscheidend: Das Schaffen eines *Spielcharakters* (und damit einer gewissen Anreiz-/ Spaßkomponente), *Beeinflussung* des Benutzerverhaltens und *Partizipation* (z.B. Anreiz zur aktiven Beteiligung).

Gamification wird häufig im Kontext von Software und zunehmend auch im Kontext von Business Software verwendet. „Gamification is 75% Psychology and 25% Technology." (Kumar & Herger 2013) Die beiden Aspekte werden in den folgenden zwei Abschnitten näher erläutert.

Motivationstheorie (*Psychologie-Aspekt*)

Mit Hilfe der klassischen Motivationstheorien (vgl. u. A. Maslow 1943, Alderfer 1969 und Heckhausen & Heckhausen 2010) können Mechanismen für Gamification konzipiert werden oder bestehende Mechanismen auf ihre Effektivität argumentativ untersucht werden. Beispielsweise könnte argumentiert werden, dass Gamification nur dann greift, wenn eine gewisse Mindestanzahl an Ebenen in der Maslow'schen Bedürfnishierarchie (vgl. Maslow 1943) befriedigt werden (so geschehen in Koch et al. 2013). Im vorliegenden Beitrag liegt der Fokus nicht auf der argumentativen Herleitung der Wirksamkeit der Mechanismen, sondern auf einer empirischen Untersuchung der Auswirkungen von Gamification, die zeigen soll, wie Softwarenutzer in einer Arbeitsumgebung (Projektarbeit) auf Gamification-Elemente reagieren.

Business Software und Enterprise Collaboration Systems (*Technologie-Aspekt*)

Die hier vorgestellte Studie untersucht das Verhalten von Benutzern in sogenannten Enterprise Collaboration Systems (ECS). Diese repräsentieren die oben erwähnten 25% Technologie von Gamification. Wir verstehen ECS als "moderne" Form von Groupware: „Enterprise Collaboration Systems are an emergent or more modern form of groupware enriched by the possibilities of the latest developments in technology (e.g. Web 2.0)." (Schubert & Williams 2013, S. 224) Der hier gewählte Begriff des „Systems" umfasst sowohl Hardware als auch Software. Der Softwareteil wird in neueren Publikationen meist als „Enterprise Social Software" (ESS) bezeichnet.

Spielelemente und Softwareumgebung

In der dieser Arbeit zugrunde liegenden Untersuchung haben die Probanden das Gamification Tool Kudos® und das Enterprise Collaboration System IBM Connections® verwendet. Die Spielelemente, die Kudos® bietet, werden im Folgenden beschrieben.

Kudos Leaderboards

Kudos Leaderboards sind Community-Ranglisten, in denen die aktuelle Platzierung aller Mitglieder einer Community angezeigt wird. Der Rang des Nutzers basiert auf einem Punktesystem. Diese Punkte werden für die Ausführung von Events vergeben. Dies sind beispielsweise: Beiträge in Foren, Wiki-Einträge, Blog-Posts, das Anlegen von Aktivitäten (Todos), der Upload von Dateien, das Geben von Empfehlungen, etc.

Kudos Badges, Kudos Missions, Achievement Levels

Kudos Badges sind Abzeichen (engl. Badges), die der Plattformnutzer als Belohnung für das Erreichen verschiedener Ziele bekommt. Einfache Abzeichen lassen sich schon für den Upload eines Profilfotos erlangen. Schwerer zu erreichen ist bspw. das „Schreibe 100 Forenbeiträge"-Abzeichen. Zusammengefasst werden die Abzeichen in sog. Kudos Missions. Diese Missionen bestehen aus einem Block von Badges. Erst wenn alle Badges aus einem Block erlangt wurden, ist die jeweilige Kudos Mission abgeschlossen. *Achievement Levels* sind ein weiterer Gamification-Baustein von Kudos. Diese Level reichen vom „Newbee" (Neuling), bis zur „Hall of Fame", in welche nur die Power-User von IBM Connections einziehen können. Um ein Level zu erreichen, wird eine bestimmte Anzahl von Punkten benötigt, die wie bei der Rangliste durch Aktivitäten im System gesammelt werden können.

Profile Progress

Ein weiteres Feature ist der *Profile Progress*. Er gibt an, wie weit die Profilangaben eines Nutzers bereits ausgefüllt sind und zeigt ihm auch, durch welche Maßnahmen der Profilfortschritt (=Profile Progress) vorangetrieben kann. Sobald ein bestimmter Fortschrittstipp erfüllt wurde, wird ein neuer Tipp eingeblendet. Auf diese Weise wird der Benutzer schrittweise an die Aufgaben und Möglichkeiten seines *Social Profiles* herangeführt (cascading information). Ziel solcher Nutzerprofile ist ein effizienteres Networking. Durch die Bereitstellung aussagekräftiger Informationen können Benutzer schneller relevante Beziehungen knüpfen und Experten für bestimmte Themen im Unternehmen finden.

Kudos Thanks, Kudos Awards

Kudos Thanks werden gegenseitig zwischen den Community-Mitgliedern vergeben. Die Thanks haben spezifische Namen und können zum Dank für die darin beschriebene Leistung an einen anderen Nutzer verliehen werden (z.B. „Diligence! For working hard and achieving the goal.“). Thanks werden erfahrungsgemäß zwischen Kollegen und von Vorgesetzten an Teammitglieder vergeben – aber nicht in die andere Richtung, da dies als Einschleimerei gedeutet werden könnte.

Verwandte Arbeiten und Zusammenfassung

Verschiedene empirische Untersuchungen haben gezeigt, dass Gamification sich auf die Anwender eines „gamifizierten“ Systems auswirken kann und somit in der Lage ist, Personen in ihren Handlungen zu beeinflussen. In ihrer Literaturanalyse „Does Gamification Work? – A Literature Review of Empirical Studies on Gamification“ untersuchen Hamari et al. (2013) die wichtigsten empirischen Studien im Bereich Gamification. Auf Grund ihrer Untersuchungen kommen sie zu dem Schluss, dass Gamification positive Effekte und Vorteile hervorrufen kann. Bisherige Studien beschäftigten sich in unterschiedlichsten Kontexten mit Gamification. Beispielsweise in Bereichen wie Bildung (Cheong et al. 2013), Handel (Hamari et al. 2013) und intra-organisationale Anwendungen (Farzan et al. 2008). Im Zusammenhang mit Enterprise Gamification, dem Einsatz von Gamification-Elementen in Unternehmen (Werbach & Hunter 2012), lassen sich bisher nur sehr wenige Untersuchungen finden. Die vorhandenen Studien zu Enterprise Gamification beziehen sich z.B. auf die Intranetanwendung Beehive von IBM (Farzan et al. 2008; Thom et al. 2012). Diese zeigten signifikante Veränderungen des Nutzerverhaltens. Dies äußerte sich durch eine gesteigerte Beitragsanzahl, sowie eine geminderte Qualität der Beiträge nach der „Gamifizierung“.

Gamification im Kontext von Enterprise Collaboration Systems ist ein junges Konzept. Definitionen, Begriffsabgrenzungen und Klassifikationsansätze für Spielmechanismen wurden bereits vorgenommen. Auch die wissenschaftlichen Zusammenhänge mit den Ursprungsdisziplinen Motivationslehre und Softwareergonomie wurden, wie oben ausgeführt, untersucht. Es gibt darüber hinaus bereits einige empirische Studien, die wiederum in Metastudien ausgewertet wurden. Studien im Kontext von Business Software bzw. ECS konnten im Rahmen der Literaturrecherche keine gefunden werden.

3 Studienergebnisse

Das folgende Kapitel präsentiert die Ergebnisse der *Auswertung der Fragebogen-basierten Umfrage*. Die Ergebnisse der komplementären mündlichen Befragungen sowie eines Gesprächs mit dem Softwarehersteller über seine Erfahrung mit Kunden flossen teilweise in die Interpretation und in das Fazit mit ein. Die Auswertung der Eventlogs stand zum Zeitpunkt der Publikation noch aus.

Der Fragebogen wurde den Teilnehmern mit dem Online-Tool LimeSurvey zur Verfügung gestellt und mit Hilfe der Statistiksoftware SPSS ausgewertet. Der Fragebogen ist auf Nachfrage von den Autoren erhältlich. Am häufigsten wurden ein- und zweidimensionale 5-Punkte-Likert-Skalen verwendet. Außerdem wurden Entscheidungsfragen und offene Fragen gestellt. Die Prozentzahlen ergänzen sich nicht immer zu 100%, da die Fragen nicht zwingend beantwortet werden mussten.

An der Umfrage nahmen insgesamt 35 Personen teil. Davon waren 57% männlich und 40% weiblich. Über 90% der Befragten gaben an, dass sie bereits Erfahrungen im Umgang mit Kollaborationstools haben. Davon schätzen sich rund 58% „eher erfahren" oder „sehr erfahren" ein. Insgesamt lässt sich erkennen, dass der Großteil der Teilnehmer bereits Erfahrungen mit Kollaborationsumgebungen hatte; nur ca. 9% der Teilnehmer hatten „wenige" oder „überhaupt keine" Erfahrungen. Gute Voraussetzungen für die Beantwortung der Gamification-Fragen im Fragebogen bildeten die Antworten auf die Fragen nach der Wahrnehmung der elementaren Gamification-Features von Kudos (hiermit sind Rangliste, Abzeichen, Profilfortschrittsanzeige gemeint, wie sie im vorherigen Kapitel beschrieben wurden). Sowohl die Rangliste, als auch die Abzeichen wurden von ca. 95% der Befragten wahrgenommen. Die Profilfortschrittsanzeige haben alle Umfrageteilnehmer bemerkt.

Es wurde eine Kombination aus expliziten und impliziten Fragen verwendet, um herauszufinden ob Gamification Auswirkungen auf Motivation und Partizipation der Nutzer hat. Außerdem wurden die in Kudos vorherrschenden Gamification-Elemente (Rangliste, Abzeichen, Profilfortschrittsanzeige) einer Einzelbetrachtung unterzogen, um Unterschiede in der Auswirkung der verschiedenen Features zu erkennen.

Ergebnisse zu Motivation und Partizipation

Die Anwendermeinung zur Motivationsförderlichkeit von Gamification fällt eher positiv aus. Nur ca. 6% antworteten, dass sie Gamification „überhaupt nicht" als motivationsfördernd empfanden. Ca. 34% der Befragten sehen zumindest ein geringes bis mittleres Potenzial zur Motivationsförderung. Über 57% stufen Gamification als förderlich bis sehr förderlich für die Motivation ein. Geantwortet wurde auf einer 5-Punkte-Likert-Skala von „überhaupt nicht" motivationsfördernd bis „sehr stark" motivationsfördernd.

Die Untersuchung zeigt, dass beim größten Teil (ca. 43%) die Motivation zur Teilnahme auf IBM Connections durch Kudos gestiegen ist. 40% der Befragten gaben an, dass es zu keiner Motivationsveränderung durch Kudos kam. Ungefähr 12% gaben im Gegenzug an, dass ihre Motivation durch Kudos gesunken sei. Bei 5,7% der Teilnehmer sogar „stark". Die Antwor-

Das natürliche Verständnis von Gamification bezieht sich eher auf die öffentlich sichtbaren Elemente (im oberen Bereich der Matrix dargestellt). Dieselben Funktionsweisen, die Rankings, Badges und Social Recognition öffentlich sichtbar bieten, können auch „privat“ in der Form von anonymen Rankings, Missions oder Social Analytics verfügbar gemacht werden.

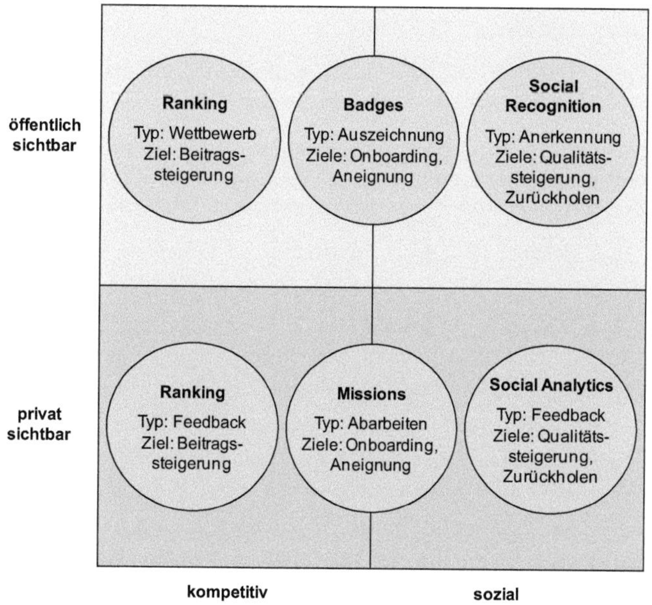

Abbildung 2: Gamification-Typen und mögliche assoziierte Ziele

Unternehmen, die eine Einführung von Gamification in Erwägung ziehen, sollten zuvor gezielt die einzuführenden Typen und die damit assoziierten Ziele abwägen. Funktionen, die nur für den einzelnen Benutzer sichtbar sind, können durchaus ähnliche Effekte erzielen wie öffentlich sichtbare Elemente, sind aber weniger „riskant“ und weniger im Blickpunkt des Betriebsrats. Auch sollten Gamification-Elemente gezielt nach der aktuellen Reifephase der Plattformeinführung ausgewählt werden und können so z.B. gezielt das Onboarding (Einstieg in die Plattform), die Aneignung (Akzeptanzsteigerung), die Steigerung von Beitragsmenge und –qualität (aktive Nutzung der Plattform) oder das Zurückholen von Benutzern nach einer festgestellten Abwesenheit unterstützen (vgl. Abbildung 2).

Bei Spielen gibt es in der Regel Sieger und Verlierer. Allerdings möchte man in einem Unternehmen keine „Verlierer“ haben. Deshalb müssen Game-Designer Gamification-Elemente sehr gezielt und konfigurierbar entwickeln. Unternehmen müssen sie passend zu ihren Zielen und ihrer Unternehmenskultur einsetzen. Was in dem einen Unternehmen funktioniert, muss nicht zwangsweise auch im nächsten funktionieren. Vor allem in Deutschland ist die Ausgangssituation für Gamification nicht ideal. Das fehlende Bedürfnis nach Wettbewerb, der Wunsch nach Schutz der Privatsphäre und enge Gesetzgebung (Betriebsrat) ermöglichen die Einführung von Gamification-Elemente nur in einem speziell abgesteckten Rahmen.

Literaturverzeichnis

Alderfer, C. P. (1969). An empirical test of a new theory of human needs. *Organizational behavior and human performance*, 4(2), S. 142-175.

Breuer, M. (2011). Was ist Gamification? URL: http://intelligent-gamification.de/2011/05/11/was-ist-gamification/, zuletzt abgerufen am 11.03.2014.

Cheong, C., Cheong, F. & Filippou, J. (2013). Quick Quiz: A Gamified Approach for Enhancing Learning. *Pacific Asia Conference on Information Systems (PACIS)*, 2013.

Deterding, S., Sicart, M., Nacke, L., O'Hara, K. & Dixon, D. (2011). Gamification. using game-design elements in non-gaming contexts. In PART 2 of the *Proceedings of the 2011 annual conference extended abstracts on Human factors in computing systems*. S. 2425-2428.

Diehl, R., Küttner, T. & Schubert, P. (2013). Introduction of Enterprise Collaboration Systems: In-depth studies show that laissez-faire does not work, *Proceedings of the Bled Conference*, 2012.

Domínguez, A., Saenz-de-Navarrete, J., De-Marcos, L., Fernández-Sanz, L., Pagés, C., & Martínez-Herráiz, J. J. (2012). Gamifying learning experiences: Practical implications and outcomes. *Computers & Education*, 63, 380-392.

Farzan, R., DiMicco, J. M., Millen, D. R., Dugan, C., Geyer, W., & Brownholtz, E. A. (2008a). Results from deploying a participation incentive mechanism within the enterprise. *Proceedings of the SIGCHI Conference on Human Factors in Computing Systems,* S. 563-572.

Hamari, J., Koivisto, J., & Sarsa, H. (2014). Does Gamification Work? – A Literature Review of Empirical Studies on Gamification. *Proceedings of the 47th Hawaii International Conference on System Sciences*, Hawaii, USA, January 6-9, 2014.

Heckhausen, J. & Heckhausen, H. (2010): Motivation und Handeln, 4. Auflage. Berlin. Springer.

Koch, M.; Ott, F. & Oertelt, S. (2013). Gamification von Business Software – Steigerung von Motivation und Partizipation. Schriften zur soziotechnische Integration, Band 3. München: Forschungsgruppe Kooperationssysteme, Universität der Bundeswehr München.

Kumar, J. M. & Herger, M. (2013). Gamification at Work: Designing Engaging Business Software. Aarhus, Denmark, The Interaction Design Foundation. ISBN: 978-87-92964-06-9. Book available online at http://www.interaction-design.org/books/gamification_at_work.html

Maslow, A. H. (1943). A theory of human motivation. *Psychological Review*, 50(4), 370.

Richter, A. & Stocker, A. (2011). Exploration & Promotion: Einführungsstrategien von Corporate Social Software, Konferenz Wirtschaftsinformatik, Zürich, 2011.

Schubert, P. & Williams, S. P. (2013). The Concept of Social Business: Oxymoron or Sign of a Changing Work Culture? *Proceedings of the 26th Bled eConference*, S. 1–14.

Thom, J., Millen, D.R. & DiMicco, J. (2012). Removing Gamification from an Enterprise SNS. *CSCW'12*, February 11–15, 2012, Seattle, Washington, USA, S. 1067-1070.

Werbach, K.; Hunter, Dan (2012): For the win: How game thinking can revolutionize your business. Wharton Digital Press, 2012.

M. Koch, A. Butz & J. Schlichter (Hrsg.): Mensch und Computer 2014 Tagungsband, München: Oldenbourg Wissenschaftsverlag, 2014, S. 15-24.

Gamification: Auswirkungen auf Usability, Datenqualität und Motivation

Christian Zagel, Freimut Bodendorf

Friedrich-Alexander Universität Erlangen-Nürnberg, Lehrstuhl für Wirtschaftsinformatik im Dienstleistungsbereich

Zusammenfassung

Mit dem Einsatz von Spielelementen im spielfremden Kontext wird die Methode der Gamifizierung derzeit als universelles Mittel zur Prozessoptimierung diskutiert. Ziel dieser Arbeit ist es, Verbesserungspotenziale durch Einsatz von Gamifizierung in RFID-basierten Prozessen, insbesondere der RFID-basierten Bestandserfassung, aufzudecken. Neben einer argumentativen Herleitung der Methodeneignung wird ein konkretes Gamifizierungs-Konzept vorgestellt. Die Ergebnisse von Fokusgruppenstudien und Laborexperimenten mit mehr als 13.800 Leseoperationen zeigen eine deutliche Steigerung der Bedienbarkeit, Datenqualität sowie Mitarbeitermotivation. Abhängig vom Grad der Gamifizierung erhöht sich jedoch auch die Zeit, welche pro Prozessiteration benötigt wird.

1 Motivation

Viele der bisherigen Denkansätze zur Optimierung von Prozessen im Groß- und Einzelhandel beschränken sich auf die Reduktion der anfallenden Kosten: halb- oder vollautomatisierte Prozesse sollen beschleunigt, Mitarbeiter eingespart, oder die Leistung pro Mitarbeiter erhöht werden. Diese Vorgehen verfolgen das Prinzip der harten Leistungssteigerung und vernachlässigen den menschlichen Faktor als die Hauptkomponente der Serviceerstellung (Coffey 1999). Nach weitgehender Ausschöpfung der traditionellen Methoden zur Prozessverbesserung müssen neue Ansätze gefunden werden. Einer dieser Ansätze betrachtet den Mitarbeiter als wertvolle Komponente der Dienstleistungserstellung: Gamifizierung. Die Methode wird als Mittel angesehen, Abläufe durch Beeinflussung der Denkweise sowie der Aufgabenwahrnehmung zu verbessern.

Gamifizierung beschreibt die Verwendung spieltypischer Elemente im spielfremden Kontext mit dem Ziel der Motivationssteigerung und Generierung von User Experience (Deterding et al. 2011). Obwohl erste Ansätze bis ins späte 19. Jahrhundert zurück reichen (Stampfl 2012),

The first step was the identification of requirements that a good gamification concept has to fulfill. Based on Breuer's (2011a) theoretical elaborations and in accordance with Bartle (1996), a gamification concept was created that specified certain game mechanisms appealing to specific types of players. Based on this gamification concept, the information architecture and interaction concept were developed, serving as a foundation for the visual design.

2 Gamification Concept

According to Deterding (2011), gamification can be seen as the use of game design elements in non-game contexts. Zichermann and Cunningham (2011) define gamification as the process of game thinking and game mechanics to engage users and solve problems. Gamification hence uses game mechanisms in a non-game context to bind users and to animate them to solve problems. This means, gamification combines a marketing element with problem solutions, turning discouraging, hard, and boring tasks into easier, interesting, and motivating problem solving. But it is important that the user enjoys engaging with a product's user interface (UI) and is fully immersed in the activity. This state is called a *flow* (Csikszentmihalyi, 2008). Breuer (2011a) mentions different requirements to achieve flow. At first objects have to be defined clearly. The user shouldn't be overburdened nor underchallenged. At next the user needs quick and clear feedback. And at least bothersome influence factors should be avoided.

If gamification is applied intelligently and efficiently, users will have a high level of motivation to engage in the game. Various factors can motivate people. External factors, such as rewards (extrinsic motivation), as well as internal motivation, such as achieving the users' individual goals (intrinsic motivation), can stimulate a user to act. As Zichermann and Cunningham argue, both forms are legitimate forms of motivation (Zichermann & Cunningham 2011, pp. 27ff.). However, if someone has been motivated extrinsically once, he has to be rewarded repeatedly to stimulate and maintain motivation, while internal motivation is long-lasting and does not rely on outside factors.

2.1 Types of gamers

The challenge with gamification is to design it in a way so that the user thinks he is pursuing a self-imposed objective. The way to get the user to think and act accordingly is to mix extrinsic and intrinsic motivation incentives. However, different types of gamers are motivated differently. Bartle identifies four types of game players located in the four corners of a two-dimensional axis (Figure 1). The type of player depends on whether a player is focused on *playing* or the *world*, and whether a player type rather tends to *act* or *interact*. These four types of game players are ideal types. In reality, a *Socializer* can also feature characteristics of a *Killer*, *Explorer*, or *Achiever*.

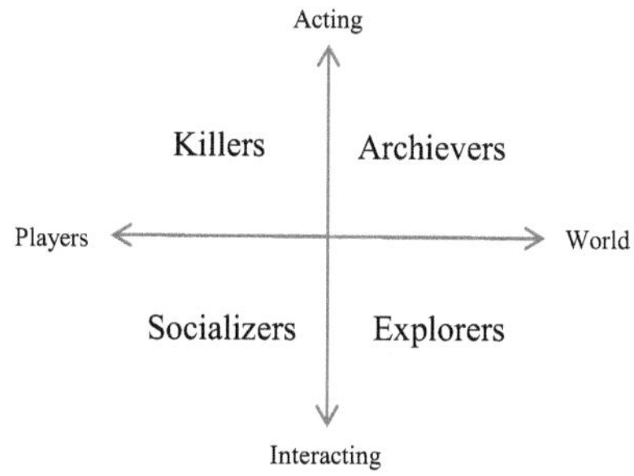

Figure 1: The four types of players according to Bartle (1996).

2.2 Game mechanisms

To motivate a player, certain stimuli have to be translated into specific game mechanisms. Specifically, these mechanisms have to support a user in achieving his set of goals, provide clear feedback on the user's progress, interconnect users with similar objectives, and generate flows (Breuer 2011b). Basic game mechanisms are *points*, a key measure for a player's mastery of the game, but also *levels*, *high-score* lists, *badges*, and *challenges*.

Based on Bartle's types of gamers, a number of game mechanisms reflecting motivational features for every individual type of player were compiled. This guarantees that a broad variety of people will be motivated by the game mechanisms. According to Wodke (2013), the following game mechanisms were included in the concept: *systems of points*, *systems of level and hierarchy*, *high scores and statistics*, *social interaction,* and *systems of achievements*.

Among different kinds of *points*, experience points are very important. These are points that accumulate with achieved tasks. They are hence different from pay points in the sense that they cannot be exchanged for goods in the context of the game. It is also possible to receive reputation points by receiving ratings from other players.

The *level system* should also be well conceived, because it represents the afore-mentioned points. Levels give the player a good impression of where to position his expertise and experience, and the corresponding points display how far away he is from stepping up to a higher level (cf. von Ahn & Dabbish 2008).

The main bulk of points is often achieved by completing *challenges* which become more difficult the further players progress in the game. It is important that the player is neither over-burdened nor under-challenged in any way. To create challenges, time limits to solve certain tasks are often used. They set clear, achievable, and non-trivial objectives. If the challenges are well chosen, the user is likely to put more effort into certain tasks (cf. von Ahn & Dabbish 2008).

High scores show the user's name and amount of points, sorted according to the number of points all the players in the list have accumulated. One can differentiate between non-discouraging high scores and infinite high scores. Non-discouraging high scores position new users in the middle of the hierarchy, no matter what level they have. Below them, all their friends are listed that do not have as many points as they do. Also, new users can see the distance left to draw and overtake users immediately above. When the player is among the top 10 or 20, the list can be displayed "normally" (reflecting the real order), listing all players in one list, beginning with the first (Zichermann & Cunningham 2011, p. 50). The risk is that players feel demotivated when they lose their position on the list or do not improve. One solution is to split up the long list in order to alleviate discouraging effects (Zichermann & Cunningham 2011, pp. 51ff.).

3 Design Concept

In the inDAgo-project a user centered design approach based on ISO 9241 (DIN, 2010) is used. To gather valuable information about the target group a context analysis was conducted. This enables to model *personas* and *scenarios* on which the design concept relies. Personas are fictitious people with, nevertheless, very specific characteristics. They act as users of a certain product in the context of scenarios (Pruitt & Adlin, 2005). Scenarios narratively describe typical situations in which personas interact with a product as realistic as possible. For the purpose of illustrating a typical use-case for the HelpMe app, we have created two personas: Nils Bauer and Rosemarie Herzig.

3.1 Central personas

Nils Bauer is a helper persona. Nils is 25 years old and has been studying in the city of Darmstadt for three years. Although he did not grow up in Darmstadt, he knows his way around very well. Before he started his studies, he completed his alternative national service in a senior-citizens home where he experienced at first hand the everyday problems of elderly people. Because he would like to stay involved in helping the elderly, he has registered with the inDAgo network some time ago.

Rosemarie Herzig is the persona of a senior citizen. Since her husband passed away, 85 year-old Mrs. Herzig lives in her apartment near Darmstadt by herself. Because her grand children live in the vicinity, they often visit her. She uses a wheeled walker to support herself when moving around. When Mrs. Herzig goes into town, she takes it with her on the bus or tram. Her children have given her a mobile phone as a present which she does not use though. Because her typewriter got broken, her grandchildren have given her a computer which she used to register on Facebook. Her posts can be followed at *http://blog.indago-projekt.de/rosemarie.html.*

3.2 Example scenario

Nils is in the town center of Darmstadt. His smart phone notifies him that he has just received a message from the HelpMe app. On the display he is informed that he was just granted 1 helper point because he has been available for five consecutive hours now. On the whole, Nils has already collected 21 points. A few minutes later the app alerts him that someone is in need of help. Nils sees on his display that Rosemarie Herzig requires assistance and that he is only a few minutes of walk away from her. So he decides to accept the call.

According to the app, he is not the only potential helper in the vicinity, but as he is the first to accept he receives 3 helper points. The app guides him to Mrs. Herzig's current location in the western part of Darmstadt. As this is thc first time Nils has accepted a call from this part of the town, he receives 2 extra points. Having arrived at Mrs. Herzig's position, he helps her carry home her heavy shopping. Afterwards, Nils confirms in the app that he has completed helping Mrs. Herzig and enters a short description of what he helped her with. The app indicates to Nils that he has just completed a new achievement since this is the first time he has helped someone with heavy shopping. Nils sets off to attend a lecture.

On his way, his app notifies him that Mrs. Herzig has rated his help positively, giving him a thumbs-up rating. This new rating elevates Nils level from the level *First Aider* to *Good Soul* because he has accumulated sufficiently many helper points, has been available for a sufficiently long time, has offered his help often enough, and has received sufficient thumps-up ratings from different parts of the city. He is now able to post his level promotion on platforms such as Facebook or Twitter. Having arrived at the lecture theatre, Nils switches his status from *available* to *not available*.

4 Prototype

Based on scribbles, wireframes and low-fidelity prototypes, an HTML prototype was created using the wireframing and prototyping software Axure. In contrast to a low-fidelity prototype, an HTML prototype is nearly completely functional, i.e. all interaction elements react to the user's input. The prototype can be viewed under the following URL: *http://share.d.com/YXP7YF*.

The prototype altogether consists of 11 different screens that can be separated into two categories. The first category contains screens that are accessible and functional only if the user is available to help others (cf. subsection 4.1). These screens allow the user to view statistics and cultivate contacts. Besides, the user can switch between six different views via corresponding menu items: *home*, *town*, *friends*, *points*, *badges*, and *settings* (cf. Figures 2-6). The second category provides screens that can be only viewed while the user is in the process of helping as described in subsection 4.2.

4.1 Screens while being available

The *home screen* is the screen the user accesses first when opening the HelpMe app. The screen quickly and clearly displays information about the helper, his contacts, and the town he is helping in. In the top part of the screen, the user can view his profile picture, name, current level, received ratings as well as the name of the town. Below this information, the user can view a newsfeed providing information about his activities, the activities of his friends, or the activities of other helpers. The user can also filter the feed so that for instance only his activities or ratings are displayed, or solely the activities of his friends. Furthermore, any helper can send messages from here to the community of helpers in his city. In this way the helpers within a community can communicate with each other. Summarizing, the home screen provides a clear overview of relevant information and enables the user to access all areas of the app without opening the menu (Figure 2).

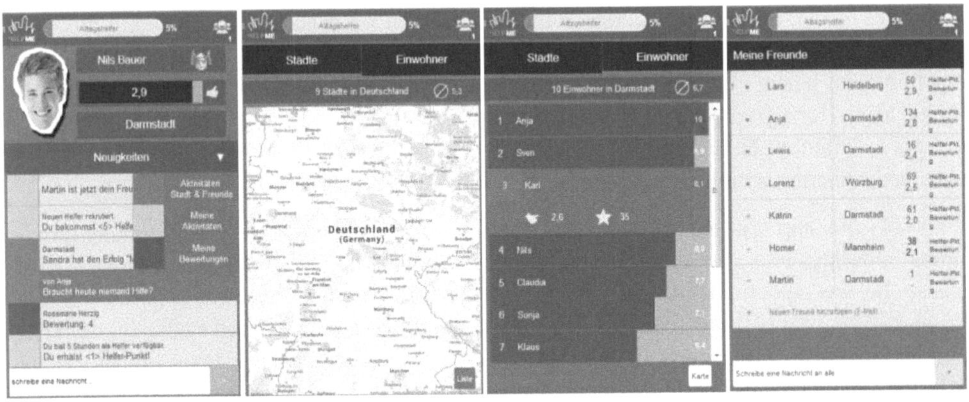

Figure 2: The "home screen" (left), the two tabs of the "town screen" (middle) and the "friends screen" (right).

The *town screen* (Figure 2) displays all information concerning the helper's town. The screen is split up into two areas which can be switched via tabs. The first tab, the town-related part, provides a comparison of different cities. On a heat map, the user can view all the towns in his home country in which the HelpMe app is used. Differently colored and sized markers give the user a good impression about where people, on the average, have offered their help most frequently. The heat map can be transformed into a list displaying a high score of towns. This list is calculated from the average number of residents' ratings, the number of helpers' activities, and the number of helpers in the town.

The second tab on the town screen, the residents-related part, refers to all the helpers located in the user's city. In this view, the user can look at a map displaying all helpers currently assisting another person. The helper is represented by a level-specific icon. This view can be changed in order to display a high score list of all helpers in the user's city which is calculated from the number of helper's activities, points, and rankings. Opening a list item provides detailed information about a user's ranking and number of points.

On the *friends screen* (Figure 2) the user can add friends to his list, delete them from it, or stay in contact with other friends. The list provides information about the current status of a friend, that is to say whether the user is currently available to offer help or not. Clicking on the friend's name opens the chat function enabling the user to send and receive messages, or to view previously received or written messages. At the bottom of the friend list, a button is provided by which the user can add new contacts or invite his friends to the helper network via email. To delete a friend from the list, the user simply has to swipe the screen from right to left and confirm the deletion of a contact afterwards. If no friend is selected, a user can send a status update to his friends if required, as done in many common social networks.

The *points screen* (Figure 3) provides the user with a quick overview of his current level, the number of gathered points, and the ratings from people he has helped so far. This information, either culminated or averaged, is displayed at the top of the screen. Below this screen section, a scrollable dashboard-like list summarizes all previous activities. While scrolling, one list item in the middle of the screen is always focused yielding the following information: the name of the person that was helped as well as the date of the activity is displayed in the left half of this list item. On the right hand side, the points received for an activity are shown. Moreover, a thumb icon (either pointing up, down, or to the side) shows the user how the help seeking person has subjectively rated the quality of his help.

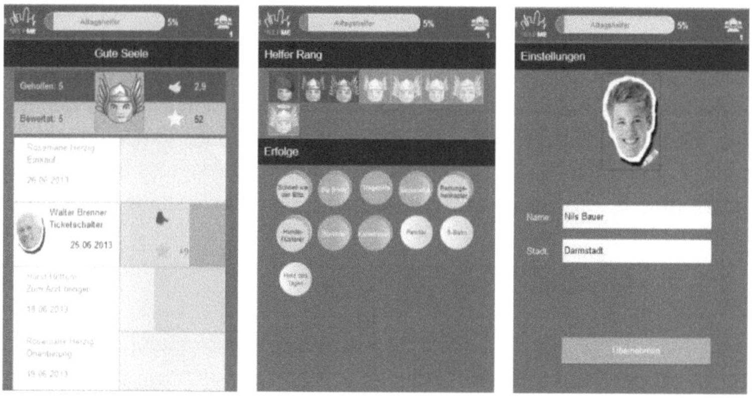

Figure 3: "Points screen" (left), "badges screen" (middle), and the "settings screen" (right).

The *badges screen* (Figure 3) lists the user's achievements and mastered levels over time. Those levels that have not been reached yet are shaded. Below all available achievements are listed. Since an achievement is attained in three consecutive steps, up to three circular badges per entry are displayed on top of each other. The individual levels differ in their color. Clicking onto a certain mastered rank or achievement opens up an info box displaying the achievement's title and requirements. When the user clicks on a rank or achievement which has not been completed yet, the title of the achievement as well as the needed progress to reach the next level are displayed in percentage points. It is important to note that the user does not know how many activities or points remain to reach the next level.

In the *settings screen* (Figure 3), the user can change his profile picture, name, and town. When a user enters a new city, the full name of the town is filled in by means of autocomplete. In the future it is planned to offer the user more possibilities for adjusting certain settings. A possible scenario could be, for example, to allow the user to change the screen design according to his individual taste.

offer their help simply for the sake of the game, and not for the objective of helping the elderly. If a player received a call for help from a part of the town in which the user has already fulfilled his quota of helping, the user would not have the incentive to help anymore, because he would not gain anything in the context of the game.

Other elements were already omitted early in the development stage. Detailed statistics, for example, are difficult to integrate usefully into a mobile app. An idea for the future is to create an additional online platform on which users can view statistics and use other features of the app, such as the chat function. The challenge of consciously omitting such functions is to find a suitable way to motivate a gamer in the first place. Why should a user fitting the profile of an *Achiever* try to accumulate achievements when he does not know how to do that? On a more general level, this problem addresses the question how to motivate players permanently, especially highly experienced users. How far can the app's system be extended to ensure its long-term success? These challenging issues require further in-depth work. Furthermore a next step is to evaluate the additional value of gamification in this app.

References

Ahn, Luis von & Dabbish, Laura (2008). *Designing games with a purpose*. In: Communications of the ACM. Vol. 51(8), August 2008, pp. 58-67.

Bartle, R. (1996). *Hearts, Clubs, Diamonds, Spades: Players Who Suit MUDs*. In: Journal of MUD Research 1(1), 1996.

Breuer, Markus (2011a): *Flow - mehr als Gamification*. URL (retrieved March 31st, 2014): http://intelligent-gamification.de/2011/05/06/flow-mehr-als-gamification

Csikszentmihalyi, Mihaly (2008): *Flow: Das Geheimnis des Glücks*. Stuttgart 2008: Klett-Cotta.

Deterding, Sebastian (2011): *Gamification: Toward a Definition*. In: CHI 2011 Workshop Gamification: Using game design elements in non-game contexts. Vancouver, Canada, 2011, pp. 12-15. URL (retrieved March 31st, 2014): http://gamification-research.org/wp-content/uploads/2011/04/02-Deterding-Khaled-Nacke-Dixon.pdf

DIN (2010): Ergonomics of human-system interaction - Part 210: Human-centred design for interactive systems (ISO 9241-210).

Peters, E., Pritzkuleit, R., Beske, F., & Katalinic, A. (2010). Demografischer Wandel und Krankheitshäufigkeiten. Bundesgesundheitsblatt-Gesundheitsforschung-Gesundheitsschutz, 53(5), 417-426.

Pruitt, J.; Adlin, T.: The persona lifecycle. Keeping people in mind throughout product design. Amsterdam, Boston: Elsevier, 2005.

Wodtke, Christina (2013): *No Stinking Badges: Better Lessons from Game Design*. URL (retrieved March 31st, 2014): http://de.slideshare.net/cwodtke/stinkingbadges6-1212a

Zichermann, Gabe & Cunningham, Christopher (2011): *Gamification by Design. First edition*. Sebastopol 2011: O'Reilly Media.

M. Koch, A. Butz & J. Schlichter (Hrsg.): Mensch und Computer 2014 Tagungsband, München: Oldenbourg Wissenschaftsverlag, 2014, S. 35-44.

Employing Blended Interaction to Blend the Qualities of Digital and Physical Books

Christoph Gebhardt, Roman Rädle, Harald Reiterer

Human-Computer Interaction Group, University of Konstanz

Abstract

This paper presents Integrative Workplace, a system which blends the qualities of digital and physical sources by augmenting physical books with properties of digital books and vice versa. On the base of Blended Interaction, we designed a system which helps users to interact with the new and unfamiliar functionality of augmented documents and apply it to accomplish a real world task. In a user study, law students employed Integrative Workplace to work on a legal case. The positive feedback of participants indicated that we managed to design a system which is usable in a professional context. Furthermore, the study revealed evidence that participants apply Conceptual Blending to understand user interfaces and that digitally well-established concepts are a part of users' reality. These findings resonate with the theoretical foundation of Blended Interaction. The results of this user study encourage us to continue to use Blended Interaction in the design process of novel user interfaces with an unfamiliar functionality.

1 Introduction

In the Living Lab of the *Blended Library* (Heilig, Rädle, & Reiterer, 2011) we develop and investigate new user interface and interaction concepts to support research processes in the physical library of the future. It was designed and set up according to the needs of library users, which were extracted from an online questionnaire. The questionnaire was sent out to students and staff of the University of Konstanz. As a result of the questionnaire, we identified that most library users still experience the media disruption between digital and analog sources as a problem in their workflow. Participants complained about the costly process of digitizing quotes from printed sources or handwritten notes. A participant, for instance, stated: "ultimately everything is digitally written." For this reason many participants require a "full digitization of all library texts." One participant summarized the advantages of working with digital texts on electronic devices as "clean working, fast search and easily shareable with others". In contrast, other participants highlighted the importance of printed documents for their working practices. In their opinion, it is easier to compare the contents of several books spread on a desk than on digital devices. Furthermore, they value books for possibilities like the "fast skimming of pages to get a short overview", the better reading comfort as well as the easy marking and annotating of text. Also in research there are different works which highlight these qualities of paper documents for knowledge work and require to mimic them with electronic devices (Kidd, 1994; Sellen & Harper, 2003). For these reasons, our work aims to bridge the media disruption, not by a full digitization of printed sources, but by merging the qualities of physical and digital sources in the context of the working practices of library users. We want to create a consistent method of working with digital and physical sources by giving physical books qualities of digital books and vice versa. In contrast to related works, we do not focus on advancing the interaction possibilities of paper. But focus on a user-centered interaction design. Based on the design framework *Blended Interaction* (Jetter, Reiterer, & Geyer, 2014), we designed a system considering humans' general skills and common sense knowledge to blend the qualities of digital and physical sources in an easy to understand and operate manner.

In the following, we introduce the design framework Blended Interaction and we present how we applied Blended Interaction to understand and sharpen the design of Integrative Workplace. We conclude with the results of our user study and a summary.

2 Blended Interaction

The goal of Blended Interaction is to enable a user-centered design of natural interactions in interactive spaces[1]. The framework tries to advance Mark Weiser's vision (Weiser, 1991) to create an "invisible" ubiquitous computing "that provides us with the great powers of digital computation in an unobtrusive manner, so that we are freed to use them without thinking and 'mental gymnastics' and to focus beyond computers on new goals" (Jetter et al., 2014). For that purpose it draws on the principles of *Reality-based Interaction* (Jacob & Girouard, 2008) and of *Conceptual Blending* (Fauconnier & Turner, 2002). Reality-based Interaction attempts to make human-computer interaction similar to the interaction with the real world. By drawing on humans' pre-existing knowledge and skills, the mental effort required to operate a system is reduced and users are free to focus on the actual task without their cognitive flow being interrupted by cumbersome interactions. Jacob et al. also highlight "the ability to go beyond a precise imitation of the real world" (Jacob & Girouard, 2008) as the source of the power of using computers. A guideline to design intuitive but expressive user interfaces is "to give up reality only explicitly and only in return of other desired qualities" (Jacob & Girouard, 2008) of the digital world. In contrast to Reality-based Interaction, Blended Interaction not only applies users' natural skills and pre-existing knowledge of the real world but also considers digital well-established concepts in the design of new user interfaces. As humans spend more and more time in the digital world, we cannot consider human thinking free from digital influences anymore and need to take them into account when designing new interaction concepts.

[1] For a more detailed description of Blended Interaction see (Jetter et al., 2014).

Conceptual Blending theoretically explains how human thinking subconsciously creates a new concept through projection from two existing input concepts. Therefore human mind connects the two input concepts on the base of a generic space. The generic space contains basic level concepts which are common to both inputs (e.g. both inputs are containers). On base of these commonalities, human mind blends both input concepts in an output concept that has a new and emergent structure which is not available from the inputs alone. Blended Interaction uses this process of indirect projection to theoretically explain that user interfaces only need to share selected aspects of reality for users to be able to understand and operate a new interaction design. This enables us to use computational power to go beyond what is possible in the real world by keeping a natural and intuitive interaction. In addition, Blended Interaction introduces the four domains of design as different perspectives on the interaction design to holistically support a certain task:

Individual Interaction: The goal is an intuitive handling by applying pre-existing skills and knowledge of the real and the digital world.

Social Interaction: A system should facilitate the social interaction between users having a common task and support collaborative working.

Workflow: Designers should consider the organizational workflow of a certain task and better supporting it in the interaction design.

Physical Environment: The architecture of a room and the form factors of digital devices (shape, display size) should be adjusted according to a certain task.

3 Applying Blended Interaction

In a first step, to limit the design domain, we analyzed different scientific disciplines and chose legal research for its clearly structured and systematic methodology. To understand legal working practices, a survey with law students who wrote a seminar paper in the summer semester break of 2012 (N=14) was conducted and the Blended Library questionnaire was re-evaluated, only considering participants with a background in jurisprudence (N=70).

In the following chapters we analyze the results of this initial study in relation to the Blended Interaction domains of design. We will demonstrate how the framework guides the design process from the context analysis to the implementation of the interaction design. The social interaction domain of Blended Interaction is not addressed due to the fact that writing a legal paper mostly involves single person working.

3.1 Physical Environment

In legal work it is frequently necessary to compare opinions from different sources. For this reason, students who are working on a legal case have numerous opened books on their desks. They place them next to each other and, if space is limited, they also pile them to even have more information at a glance (Figure 1).

Figure 1: Two workplaces of law students with numerous piled and side by side situated books.

In contrast, digital devices do not facilitate this method because, as law students mentioned, on typically sized displays it is possible to at most place two documents beside each other. Additionally, some participants complained about the problem of losing track of the opened documents on their computers. On a digital device it is difficult to match a just read text passage to a source without looking for its title as all documents look similar and disappear behind the same icons. As opposed to this, the position of a physical book on a desk simplifies a subconscious mapping of a text passage to the according book without needing to know the title of a source. In terms of designing the physical environment, this highlights the importance of space for legal work. Law students need to have the possibility to clutter a tabletop with books, notes or other artifacts as it helps them to compare between sources and to keep an overview over the gathered information. Also in literature, the possibility to lay out information in space is an often cited need of knowledge work (Kidd, 1994; Sellen & Harper, 2003). For this reason a huge tabletop forms the base of the physical environment. Using a projector to augment the table with digital contents enables us to equip the physical environment with an infinite digital landscape (Figure 2).

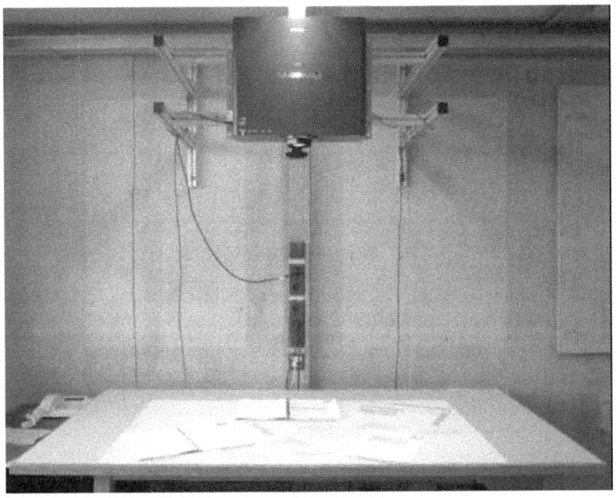

Figure 2: Physical environment of Integrative Workplace

Therefore, in the digital world, users are not constraint to the size of the tabletop, but are able to acquire as much space as needed. By designing our physical environment as it is, we blend a physical tabletop with a digital landscape. In the prospective of legal work, this opens up new methods. Law students can now situate physical and virtual documents next to each other and thus cross-read between digital and analog sources (similar to (Deininghaus & Möllers, 2010)). According to our goal to create a consistent method of working with digital and physical sources, users are also able to spatially arrange, move and pile digital documents in the same way as physical documents.

3.2 Individual Interaction

As already mentioned, excerpting information from analog sources with today's technologies still means additional working steps and thereby the interruption of the cognitive flow. For this reason, we want to blend the easy excerpting of text from digital sources with printed documents (similar to (Wellner, 1991)). To facilitate a consistent working method for electronic and printed texts, we use the same pen and the same interaction technique to excerpt text in printed and digital documents. In addition to (Steimle, 2009), who firstly introduced this approach, our system enables a consistent real-time feedback on interactions with both, digital and physical documents (Figure 3).

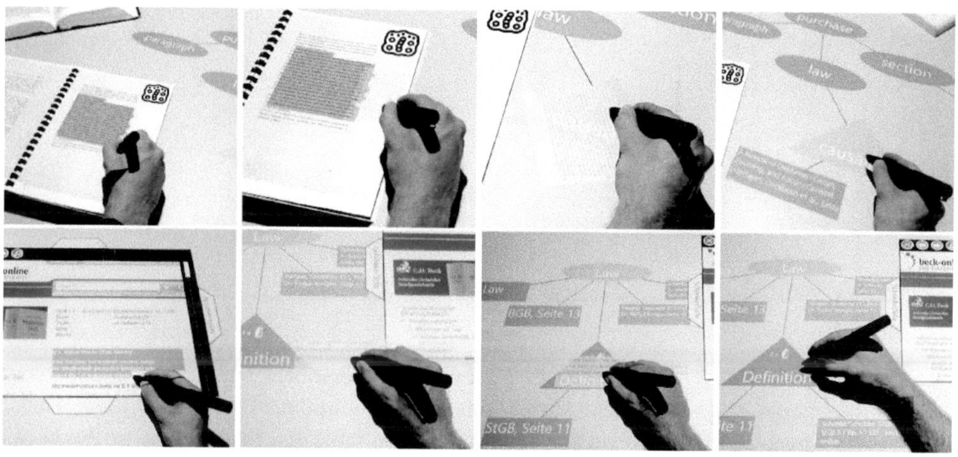

Figure 3: Selecting, dragging and dropping text of a physical book (on top) and of a digital document (on bottom).

With a digital pen users can select text, as they would do in mouse operated applications. For instant user feedback, the projector highlights that text successively. The pen can be used to drag a copy of the selected text and drop it at a desired location on the tabletop. In terms of Blended Interaction, the strongly developed body skill of using a pen in combination with the digitally well-established concept of (text) selection on electronic devices, blends the computational power used to digitize printed text in an easy to understand and to use manner.

By using bimanual pen and touch interaction a new challenge arises. Because on digital devices pen and touch are not restricted to their inherent functionality, it is necessary to define an easy to understand way to differentiate between interactions which can be performed by the pen and interactions which are performed using touch. This is a controversially discussed topic in research with different approaches to handle it (Frisch, Heydekorn, & Dachselt, 2010; Hinckley et al., 2010). As recommended by Hinckley et al., we take the behaviors that people already exhibit when working with pen and paper as foundation for our pen and touch gestures: using the pen to write or draw and touch to manipulate. In terms of Blended Interaction, we used pen and touch as the first input space and the computational power, for example to dynamically align digital documents or to recognize shapes and handwritten text, as second input space. The common generic space that a pen is used to write or draw and touch to manipulate keeps it easy to understand and to operate the additional expressive power.

3.3 Workflow

The analysis of the workflow of law students revealed that the index of a book is often used as a starting point for a literature review by taking a catchword of a legal record to find relevant information. Participants also emphasized full-text search in digital documents as one of the major benefits of using computers. For this reason, we want to augment physical documents with a digital full-text search.

Figure 4: Full-text search in physical documents

In Integrative Workplace, a full-text search in a physical document highlights the matching words on the opened pages. Full-text search was already introduced in FACT (Liao, Tang, Liu, Chiu, & Chen, 2010). However, an interactive scrollable list to the right of the book displays the matching words per page for the entire book (Figure 4).

The context analysis also made clear, that law students would value the possibility to save excerpts from physical and digital documents at one place to have all information at a glance. In our prototype this place is the tabletop. By dropping them on it, excerpts of physical and digital sources are saved as textual items which can be arrange in a mind map. We chose a mind map as graphical visualization because it leaves users the structural freedom to decide how they arrange items. In this way, beside their usual way of working linearly, law students also can draw, for example, an arboreal visualization which matches their approach when working at a civil law case.

Analyzing their workflow, it appeared that law students often search for excerpted text passages to reread them in context. Therefore we designed the reference backtracking function which guides users to the original page of an excerpt of both, digital and physical sources. In case of a digital source, applying a hold gesture on a text item displays the according webpage and highlights the excerpted passage (Figure 5, b). When backtracking to a physical source, the source's title is displayed on the tabletop after the hold gesture was performed (Figure 5, a1). If then, the according source is placed on the desk, the book is augmented with an arrow, which indicates the direction to flip pages for finding the original page of an excerpt (Figure 5, a2). On the original page the excerpted passage is highlighted (Figure 5, a3). This functionality, to our knowledge, is not offered by related works.

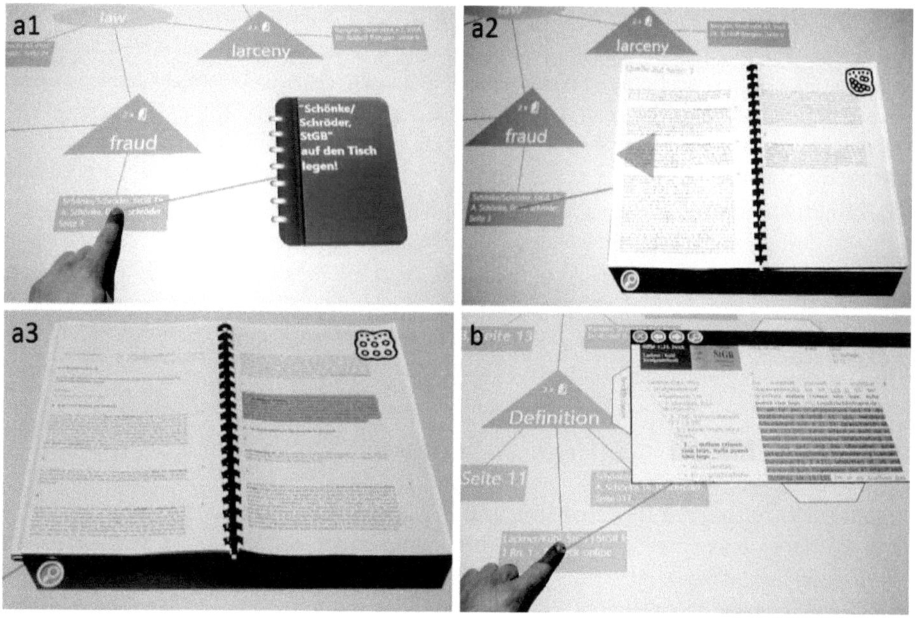

Figure 5: Backtracking from a mind map text item to its physical (a) or digital (b) source.

In contrast to related works, Integrative Workplace allows using the digital functionalities of physical books (excerpting, full-text search, backtracking to source) on any number of books in parallel. To be able to evaluate our proposed future interaction design we mimicked digitally manipulable physical books with a technical approach similar to (Dachselt & AL-Saiegh, 2011). Extending their approach, our system works with multiple freely moveable documents.

4 User Study

To evaluate our interaction design, nine law students (three females, six males) were asked to work on a legal case in the area of German criminal law with the help of Integrative Workplace. After a short introduction into the system and a training phase, the participants had 30 minutes to work on the case. During this time they were asked to think aloud. In a screening, we ensured that they had sufficient skills in legal working[2]. In the following, the three main findings of our user study are presented.

4.1 System Design

All participants perceived the functionality of Integrative Workplace as futuristic and beyond what they think computers can offer. This became apparent in the reactions during the introduction to the system (e.g., "nice invention", "I'm amazed"). With the study, we want to determine if our design helps users to understand and interact with the new and unfamiliar functionality. Therefore we asked the participant to fill the System Usability Scale (Brooke, 1996), as a good design can be seen as the base of a good usability. The analysis revealed a SUS Score of 66.94 giving the system an adjective usability rating in between OK and GOOD and classifying it as marginally acceptable (Bangor, Kortum, & Miller, 2008). To investigate if users appreciate the features of Integrative Workplace, we asked the participants about the biggest advantage of the system. The two most frequently named responses were the easy copying of text from physical books (four participants) and the possibility to deposit excerpted text from digital and physical sources in one place (four participants). Because both features come with blending the qualities of digital and physical books, this can be seen as further indication that our design enables an intuitive usage of the new computational power.

As "the usability of any tool or system has to be viewed in terms of the context in which it is used" (Brooke, 1996) the detected SUS score, to a certain extent, reflects the appropriateness of Integrative Workplace for legal work. To further investigate what effect our design has on juristic working practices, we asked students if Integrative Workplace supports legal work. On a five point Likert scale (1 = "I agree", 5 = "I disagree"), they answered the question positively with an average value of 1.78. Asked for a reason, the participants most frequently named the high clarity over excerpts as all are saved at one place (five participants). One problem of the design of Integrative Workplace, which was revealed by the study, is that a mind map is not a beneficial visualization in matters of legal work. Most participants suggested to somehow design a linear visualization as it better fits juristic working practices: "In law, there is a distinct evaluation order of legal issues. It is not possible to reflect this order with a mind map".

4.2 Users Apply Conceptual Blending in User Interfaces

In the observations of the participants, we found evidence that humans apply Conceptual Blending to understand new functionality in user interfaces. All three participants, who applied a full-text search in physical books, tried to open book pages by touching the digital visualization which displays the matching words per page. These incidents highlight that the participants did not distinguish between the digital visualization and the physical book but rather perceived both as one unity. Trying to understand the unfamiliar UI, the participants

[2] On average they studied 6.3 semester (SD=2.9 semester) and wrote 3.4 seminar papers (SD=1.2 seminar papers).

draw on their knowledge of the digital world, that on electronic devices touching a label representing a certain page normally opens the according page, and conceptually blend it with the physical book. For them, this naturally results in a blend which offers, although not existent, the functionality that book pages can be flipped by touching a digital visualization. The incidents highlight that Blended Interactions approach of applying Conceptual Integration to design interactions is a logical conclusion as humans do so themselves.

4.3 Digital Concepts are Part of Users' Reality

A design decision which caused interaction problems is using the pen to write or draw and touch to manipulate. Although we adapted this behavior from reality, seven out of nine participants tried, for example, to move a mind map item with the pen or to draw a mind map item using a finger. One participant stated: "I didn't know when I had to use the pen and when the finger". Similar findings have been made in literature (Frisch et al., 2010; Matulic & Norrie, 2012). Through the proliferation of tablets and smartphones "people are gradually developing a habit of using their fingers for all kinds of interactions, including quite a few that one would think would be more adequately performed with a pen" (Matulic & Norrie, 2012). In terms of Blended Interaction, this is a nice example, which shows that digitally well-established concepts became a part of the users' reality and that it is necessary to consider them when we want to design interfaces which are intuitive to use and easy to understand.

5 Conclusion

This work presents a user interface which is blending the qualities of digital and physical sources in the context of jurisprudence. Using Blended Interaction's four domains of design, we analyzed legal working practices to implement a system which supports legal work by augmenting physical sources with qualities of digital sources and vice versa. To prove our design we conducted a user study with nine law students who worked on a legal case. The enthusiastic reactions of the participants revealed that the functionality of our system was beyond what they thought computers can offer. Still we found strong indications that our interaction design managed to combine the qualities of physical and digital sources in a way users can understand and interact with the new and unfamiliar functionality. Furthermore, the positive feedback of participants regarding the support of legal working practices indicated that we managed to design a system which is usable in the context of a real world task. In terms of the theoretical foundation of Blended Interaction, incidents of the user study give evidence that users apply Conceptual Integration when interacting with a new user interface. In addition, the misuse of pen and touch indicates that digital well-established concepts became a part of humans' reality and need to be considered in the design of new user interfaces. These results and a good performance of the system in the System Usability Scale encourage us to continue to use Blended Interaction in the design process of novel user interfaces. In future work, we intend to use Integrative Workplace to conduct a systematic evaluation that examines how digital desks might change knowledge work practices and its outcomes compared to tools used at nowadays desks (Gebhardt, Rädle, & Reiterer, 2014).

References

Bangor, A., Kortum, P. T., & Miller, J. T. (2008). An Empirical Evaluation of the System Usability Scale. *International Journal of Human-Computer Interaction, 24*(6), 574–594.

Brooke, J. (1996). SUS-A quick and dirty usability scale. *Usability Evaluation in Industry.*

Dachselt, R., & AL-Saiegh, S. (2011). Interacting with Printed Books Using Digital Pens and Smart Mobile Projection. *MP2 Workshop at CHI 2011.*

Deininghaus, S., & Möllers, M. (2010). Hybrid documents ease text corpus analysis for literary scholars. In *Proc of ITS'10* (pp. 177–186).

Fauconnier, G., & Turner, M. (2002). *The Way We Think: Conceptual Blending and the Mind's Hidden Complexities.* Basic Book.

Frisch, M., Heydekorn, J., & Dachselt, R. (2010). Diagram editing on interactive displays using multi-touch and pen gestures. In *In Proc. of Diagrams '10* (pp. 182–196).

Gebhardt, C., Rädle, R., & Reiterer, H. (2014). Integrative Workplace : Studying the Effect of Digital Desks on Users ' Working Practices. In *Proc. of CHI'14 EA* (pp. 2155–2160). ACM Press.

Heilig, M., Rädle, R., & Reiterer, H. (2011). Die Blended Library: Benutzerorientierte Verschmelzung von virtuellen und realen Bibliotheksdiensten. In *Benutzerorientierte Bibliotheken im Web: Usability-Methoden, Umsetzung und Trends.* Berlin: De Gruyter Saur.

Hinckley, K., Yatani, K., Pahud, M., Coddington, N., Rodenhouse, J., Wilson, A., … Buxton, B. (2010). Pen + touch = new tools. In *Proc. of UIST '10* (pp. 27–36). New York, USA: ACM Press.

Jacob, R., & Girouard, A. (2008). Reality-based interaction: a framework for post-WIMP interfaces. In *Proc. of CHI'08* (pp. 201–210). ACM Press.

Jetter, H., Reiterer, H., & Geyer, F. (2014). Blended Interaction: Understanding Natural Human-Computer Interaction in Post-WIMP Interactive Spaces. *Theme Issue on Designing Collaborative Interactive Spaces, Personal and Ubiquitous Computing.*

Kidd, A. (1994). The marks are on the knowledge worker. In *Proc. of CHI '94* (pp. 186–191). ACM.

Matulic, F., & Norrie, M. (2012). Empirical evaluation of uni-and bimodal pen and touch interaction properties on digital tabletops. In *Proc. of ITS '12.* ACM Press.

Sellen, A., & Harper, R. (2003). *The myth of the paperless office* (p. 239). Cambridge, London: The MIT Press.

Steimle, J. (2009). Designing pen-and-paper user interfaces for interaction with documents. In *Proc of TEI'09* (pp. 197–204).

Weiser, M. (1991). The computer for the 21st century. *Scientific American, 3*(3).

Wellner, P. (1991). The DigitalDesk calculator: tangible manipulation on a desk top display. In *Proc. of UIST '91* (pp. 27–33).

M. Koch, A. Butz & J. Schlichter (Hrsg.): Mensch und Computer 2014 Tagungsband, München: Oldenbourg Wissenschaftsverlag, 2014, S. 45-54.

MyMovieMixer: Ein hybrider Recommender mit visuellem Bedienkonzept

Katja Herrmanny, Sandra Schering, Ralf Berger, Benedikt Loepp, Timo Günter, Tim Hussein, Jürgen Ziegler

Universität Duisburg-Essen

Zusammenfassung

In diesem Beitrag stellen wir ein neuartiges, auf direkter Manipulation beruhendes Bedienkonzept für komplexe hybride Empfehlungssysteme anhand des von uns entwickelten Film-Recommenders MyMovieMixer vor. Der Ansatz ermöglicht es den Nutzern, ein hybrides Recommender-System mit einem komplexen Zusammenwirken verschiedener Filtermethoden durch interaktive und visuelle Methoden intuitiv zu steuern. Gleichzeitig wird die Transparenz der Empfehlungsgenerierung deutlich erhöht. Die Ergebnisse einer empirischen Evaluation des Systems zeigen, dass der Ansatz in Bezug auf Usability, User Experience, Intuitivität, Transparenz, wahrgenommene Empfehlungsqualität und somit letztlich im Hinblick auf die Nutzerzufriedenheit vielversprechend ist.

1 Einleitung

Durch das Internet haben Nutzer heutzutage einen nahezu unbegrenzten Zugang zu Informationen, gleichzeitig kommt es aber auch zu einer wahren Informationsüberflutung durch täglich neue Inhalte. Eine damit einhergehende Herausforderung für Entwickler von Empfehlungssystemen (kurz Recommender) ist es, die Informationsmenge, die dem Nutzer präsentiert wird, so einzugrenzen, dass sie seinen individuellen Präferenzen bestmöglich entspricht (Ricci et al., 2010). Heute gängige Recommender verwenden zumeist vorab gewonnene Nutzerprofile und voll automatisierte Empfehlungsmethoden, was für den Nutzer zu einem minimalen Interaktionsaufwand und – bei guter Passung – geringer kognitiver Belastung führt (Pu et al., 2012). Allerdings sind sie meist auch wenig flexibel und nicht oder nur eingeschränkt durch den Nutzer steuerbar. Oft mangelt es zudem an einer nachvollziehbaren, transparenten Empfehlungsgenerierung (Tintarev & Mastoff, 2010), was sich negativ auf Akzeptanz und Vertrauen in die Empfehlungen auswirken kann (Xiao & Benbasat, 2007). Weiterhin ist in vielen Situationen kein Nutzerprofil verfügbar (Cold-Start-Problem) oder die Nutzer wünschen keine Speicherung ihrer Präferenzen. In der Vergangenheit lag der Fokus der Forschung überwiegend auf der Optimierung der Empfehlungsalgorithmen, obwohl der Anteil, zu dem diese über den Erfolg eines Recommenders entscheiden, zunehmend schwindet (Konstan & Riedl, 2012). Die typischerweise offline ermittelte Passung der Empfehlungen mit den Nutzerpräferenzen lässt sich durch verbesserte Algorithmen nur noch marginal steigern (Pu et al., 2012). Zuletzt rückte daher die Frage der User Experience zunehmend in den Vordergrund (Knijnenburg et al., 2012), denn für den Anwender sind außer der Präzision der Empfehlungen und der Aufwandsminimierung bei der Suche oft weitere Aspekte von gleicher oder eventuell sogar höherer Bedeutung: So wünschen sich Nutzer eine aktivere Rolle im Empfehlungsprozess (Xiao & Benbasat, 2007) und sind häufig zufriedener, wenn sie den Recommender beeinflussen können. Dafür nehmen sie weniger präzise Vorschläge und sogar zusätzlichen Aufwand in Kauf (Konstan & Riedl, 2012). Die Berücksichtigung der Bedürfnisse und Zufriedenheit des Nutzers ist daher von großer Bedeutung.

Der vorliegende Beitrag stellt einen neuartigen Ansatz vor, der Nutzern die Möglichkeit bietet, die Empfehlungsgenerierung zu steuern, die Wirkung verschiedener Empfehlungsmethoden und deren Kombination zu explorieren und den Prozess besser nachvollziehen zu können. Die exemplarisch für das Anwendungsfeld der Filmempfehlungen konzipierte, implementierte und evaluierte Anwendung *MyMovieMixer* verbindet eine visuelle Darstellung verschiedener Filtermethoden mit direkten Interaktionsmöglichkeiten durch ein Drag-and-Drop-Konzept und nutzt diverse Feedback-Mechanismen zur Transparenzsteigerung: Dem Nutzer stehen verschiedene Kriterien zur Verfügung, mit denen er seine Wünsche hinsichtlich der vorzuschlagenden Filme angeben kann. Zur Empfehlungsberechnung nutzt MyMovieMixer einen hybriden Ansatz, bei dem die Ergebnisse der für die verschiedenen Kriterien genutzten Empfehlungsverfahren verrechnet und darauf basierend Vorschläge angezeigt werden. Um die Verständlichkeit bei komplexen, hybriden Empfehlungssystemen zu gewährleisten, ist es wichtig, dass der Nutzer den Ursprung der Empfehlungen kennt und die Kombination der Recommender nach seinen Wünschen konfigurieren kann (Parra et al., 2014). Eine solche Möglichkeit erhält der Anwender bei MyMovieMixer über Slider, mit denen er die Gewichtung der einzelnen Kriterien jederzeit modifizieren kann. Die Arbeit zeigt somit einen Lösungsansatz auf, dem Nutzer eine intuitive Steuerung eines hybriden Recommenders und eines komplexen Zusammenspiels von Filtermethoden zu ermöglichen.

2 Visuelle, interaktive Empfehlungsgenerierung

Der Einsatz interaktiver Methoden in Empfehlungssystemen ist ein bislang wenig untersuchtes Gebiet, dessen Potenzial aber zunehmend erkannt wird. So geben manche etablierte Systeme dem Anwender die Möglichkeit der Verfeinerung von Ergebnismengen basierend auf dem Prinzip des Relevance Feedback (Salton & Buckley, 1997). Während sich durch die Anwendung dieses Prinzips auf Recommender die wahrgenommene Kontrolle steigern lässt, werden dabei die bestehenden Interessensprofile der Nutzer zumeist lediglich weiter verfeinert. Solche langfristig gesammelten Informationen über die Nutzerpräferenzen sind als Eingabe für viele Empfehlungsalgorithmen von zentraler Bedeutung, obwohl dies etwa erschwert, auf situative Bedürfnisse zu reagieren. Auch mangelt es häufig an Daten für den aktuellen Nutzer, um akkurate Vorschläge zu generieren. Diesem Cold-Start-Problem durch vermehrten Einfluss des Nutzers zu begegnen, wird bisher jedoch selten in Betracht gezogen.

Kritikbasierte Recommender (Chen & Pu, 2012) steigern die Interaktivität, indem sie den Anwender die Empfehlungen nach ihrer Erzeugung bezüglich bestimmter Features bewerten lassen. Dies beruht auf der Annahme, dass es leichter fällt, die präsentierten Items zu kritisieren als selbst ein Suchziel zu formulieren. Durch die Kritik kann der Nutzer die Empfehlungsmenge jederzeit beeinflussen und kontinuierlich sein Suchziel verfeinern, indem er z. B. explizit Interesse an günstigeren Produkten äußert. Die Verwendung mehrerer, dynamisch ausgewählter Features kann seine Effizienz dabei weiter steigern (McCarthy et al., 2005). Meist beruhen die Features auf einer eingeschränkten Menge vorab modellierter Dimensionen, teilweise aber auch, wie etwa bei *MovieTuner* (Vig et al., 2011), auf einer großen Menge von durch die gesamte Nutzerbasis vergebenen Tags, die automatisch vom System gewählt und präsentiert werden. Dies erlaubt es, explizit Empfehlungen von z. B. Filmen mit mehr Action zu verlangen. Meist kommen Tags jedoch unabhängig von anderen inhaltlichen Kriterien zum Einsatz. Eine individuelle Auswahl und Gewichtung, um sie in kombinierter Form in den Empfehlungsprozess einfließen zu lassen, ist so bis dato nicht möglich.

Zhang et al. (2008) konnten zeigen, dass visuelle Unterstützung und direkte Interaktion mit den Inhalten in kritikbasierten Recommendern positiv in Bezug auf Nachvollziehbarkeit, wahrgenommene Nutzerfreundlichkeit und Interaktionsaufwand bewertet werden. Bisher existieren aber nur wenige Ansätze, die Empfehlungssysteme mit interaktiven visuellen Darstellungen kombinieren. *SmallWorlds* von Gretarsson et al. (2010) stellt eine graphbasierte interaktive Visualisierung für einen in Facebook eingebetteten Recommender dar, welcher dem Nutzer das Äußern seiner Präferenzen erleichtern und die Transparenz des eingesetzten Empfehlungsalgorithmus erhöhen soll. Entsprechend zeigte sich der Empfehlungsprozess als leichter verständlich und die Zufriedenheit der Anwender konnte gesteigert werden.

Insbesondere hybride Empfehlungssysteme (Burke, 2007), bei denen das Zusammenspiel mehrerer Algorithmen oft zu präziseren Vorschlägen führt, sind bisher kaum vom Nutzer steuerbar. *TasteWeights*, ein interaktiver und hybrider Recommender von Bostandjiev et al. (2012) ist ein erster Schritt in diese Richtung. Die dynamische Aktualisierung der Präferenzen für genau diejenigen Items, die zur Empfehlungsgenerierung herangezogen werden, sowie die Exploration mit Hilfe direkter und visuell gestützter Interaktionsmöglichkeiten werden dabei als wesentliche Unterstützung im Empfehlungsprozess herausgestellt. Obwohl primär auf die Gewichtung des Einflussgrades der Informationen aus verschiedenen sozialen Netzen beschränkt, konnte die wahrgenommene Güte der Empfehlungen und das Verständnis für ihr Zustandekommen gesteigert werden. Mit *SetFusion* zeigen Parra et al. (2014) wie sich ein nach einer klassischen Strategie (Burke, 2007) arbeitender hybrider Recommender vom Anwender beeinflussen lässt. Das für Konferenzen konzipierte System erlaubt es, die drei verwendeten Empfehlungsalgorithmen per Slider individuell zu gewichten. Die Änderungen wirken sich allerdings nicht unmittelbar auf die Ergebnisliste aus. Weitergehende Interaktionen wie eine gezielte Verfeinerung der Vorschläge oder die Gewichtung inhaltlicher Aspekte sind nicht vorgesehen. Der eingesetzte inhaltsbasierte Algorithmus erwartet zudem ein persistentes Nutzerprofil. In Nutzerstudien zeigte sich jedoch bereits ein als hoch empfundener Grad an Kontrolle. Dabei erschienen die Empfehlungen durch eine Visualisierung der Ergebnismenge und Erklärungen, welche Methoden für ihr Zustandekommen verantwortlich waren, nachvollziehbar. Zudem ließ sich ein gesteigertes Engagement der Nutzer verzeichnen. Die tatsächliche Empfehlungsqualität wurde allerdings nicht weiter betrachtet.

Insgesamt existieren bislang nur wenige, häufig limitierte Ansätze, welche Explorationsmechanismen mit Recommendern integrieren, die Interaktivität des Empfehlungsprozesses erhöhen und die Kontrolle des Nutzers steigern. Neben der Konzentration auf die Algorithmen ist in der Literatur oft eine Abhängigkeit von langfristigen Nutzerprofilen zu bemerken. Gestaltungshinweise zu Empfehlungssystemen weisen u. a. deshalb auf eine Minimierung des Aufwandes bei der initialen Präferenzerhebung sowie auf eine möglichst unterhaltsame und attraktive Gestaltung hin, um den Nutzer zu mehr Eingaben zu motivieren (Pu et al., 2012). Auch sind Erklärungen der Vorschläge ein Mittel, um die wahrgenommene Effektivität des Recommenders, die Zufriedenheit, den empfundenen Einflussgrad, die Akzeptanz und schließlich das Vertrauen in das System zu erhöhen (Pu et al., 2012). All dies verdeutlicht, dass interaktive, visuell unterstützte Empfehlungssysteme noch großes Potenzial bieten.

3 Die Anwendung MyMovieMixer

Mit MyMovieMixer haben wir unter Berücksichtigung der zuvor beschriebenen Aspekte ein webbasiertes Empfehlungssystem implementiert, um Anwendern in verschiedensten Nutzungsszenarien (z. B. Filmabende, Suche nach einem Geschenk) Spielfilme aus dem Bestand des MovieLens-Datensatzes[1] vorschlagen zu können. Da sich das System flexibel für verschiedene Situationen eignen sollte, bei denen sich wechselnde Stimmungen, Personenkonstellationen und Rahmenbedingungen auf die Empfehlungen auswirken können, basiert deren Berechnung ausschließlich auf explizit und ad-hoc während der Nutzungssitzung formulierten Präferenzen. Langfristige Profile sind somit nicht nötig. Die explizite Formulierung der Eingaben ist an klassische Produktfilter angelehnt, geht jedoch durch den Einsatz von Empfehlungsalgorithmen darüber hinaus. Das System zielt dabei auf eine Erhöhung der Nachvollziehbarkeit und Kontrolle durch den Nutzer ab, indem die resultierenden Vorschläge stets vollständig auf visuell wahrnehmbare und direkt manipulierbare Elemente der Benutzeroberfläche zurückgeführt werden können.

3.1 Benutzerinteraktion

Die grafische Nutzerschnittstelle besteht aus drei Bereichen (s. Abbildung 1): Die linke Seite enthält eine Reihe voneinander unabhängiger Widgets, über die der Nutzer seine Präferenzen angeben kann. Beispielsweise können über das Genre-Widget ein oder mehrere bevorzugte Genres gewählt werden. Die Kriterien zur Präferenzeingabe werden innerhalb der Anwendung konsistent durch rechteckige Kacheln, bestehend aus Titel und grafischem Hintergrund, repräsentiert. Die Kacheln sind innerhalb der Widgets angeordnet. Möchte ein Nutzer von einem oder mehreren Widgets Gebrauch machen, so zieht er per Drag and Drop darin enthaltene Kacheln in den mittleren Bereich (Arbeitsbereich) und verwendet diese so als Kriterium für die Empfehlungen. Es ist möglich, mehrere Kriterien aus einem Widget zu nutzen (beispielsweise mehrere gewünschte Schauspieler). Im mittleren Bereich verfügen die Kacheln

[1] MovieLens-10M-Datensatz (http://grouplens.org/datasets/movielens/)

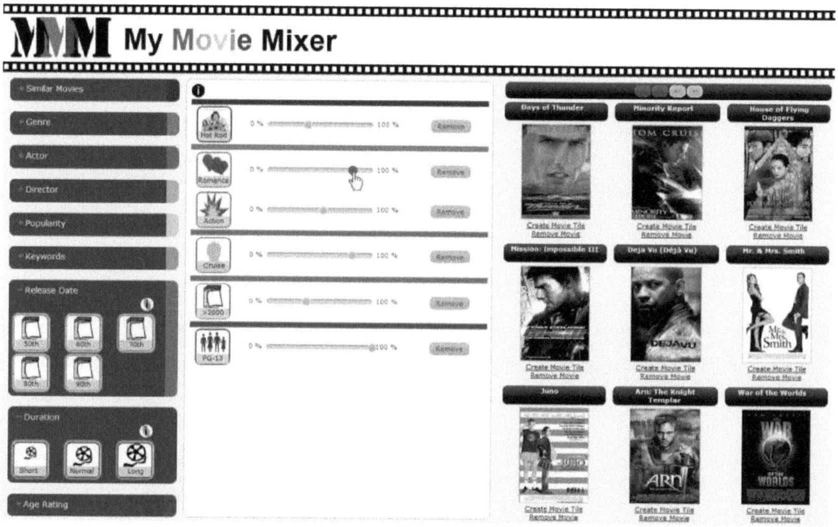

Abbildung 1: Oberfläche von MyMovieMixer: Links die Widgets, deren Kacheln in den mittleren Bereich gezogen werden können. Rechts die nach jeder Interaktion automatisch aktualisierten Empfehlungen.

dann zusätzlich über einen Slider, um dem jeweiligen Kriterium einen Stellenwert für die Empfehlungsgenerierung zuzuweisen. Auf diese Weise kann ausgedrückt werden, dass die Erfüllung eines bestimmten Kriteriums zwar grundsätzlich wünschenswert, dabei im Vergleich zu anderen Kriterien aber mehr bzw. weniger wichtig ist.

Da die zuvor genannten Eingaben, einschließlich der Manipulation der Slider, eine Aktualisierung der Ergebnisse (rechte Seite) auslösen, kann der Nutzer geeignete Wertebereiche für Slider-Einstellungen explorativ erlernen. Darüber hinaus können durch Anklicken einer Empfehlung Filmdetails sowie Erklärungen zu deren Zustandekommen, d. h., welche der Kriterien berücksichtigt werden konnten, als Dialogfenster abgerufen werden. Dies soll die Transparenz erhöhen und zugleich die Anwender befähigen, wie in kritikbasierten Recommendern gezielt mit Feedback zu reagieren und die zugrundeliegenden Kriterien auf- bzw. abzuwerten, um wahlweise mehr oder weniger auf diese zutreffende Vorschläge zu erhalten.

3.2 Algorithmische Umsetzung

Als lose gekoppeltes Hybridsystem (Burke, 2007) behandelt MyMovieMixer alle Kriterien zunächst unabhängig voneinander. Für jeden Film m und jedes Kriterium c_i wird ein Wert zwischen 0 und 1 ermittelt, welcher den Grad angibt, mit dem m das Kriterium erfüllt. Abhängig von der Art des Kriteriums geschieht die Berechnung des Erfüllungsgrades auf unterschiedliche Weise: Für ein Kriterium der Art „Film soll ähnlich zu Film x sein" wird beispielsweise ein Item-basierter Recommender herangezogen, der die berechnete Ähnlichkeit von m zu x auf den Bereich [0;1] abbildet. Andere Kriterien greifen zur Berechnung des Erfüllungsgrades hingegen auf Fuzzy Logic (Zadeh, 1965) zurück. Als Beispiel sei hier ein präferiertes Jahrzehnt (z. B. 1990er) genannt: Ein Film von 1993 erfüllt dieses Kriterium vollständig und wird dementsprechend auf 1 abgebildet. Ein Film von 1989 sollte aber nicht komplett unberücksichtigt bleiben, wie es bei binärer Logik der Fall wäre. Daher wird gemäß der Fuzzy Set Theory eine unscharfe Erfüllungsfunktion verwendet, die bei knapper Verfehlung des Kriteriums immer noch einen gewissen, wenn auch niedrigeren Erfüllungsgrad (beispielsweise 0.5) zuweist. Darüber hinaus nutzt MyMovieMixer eine Reihe weiterer, inhaltsbasierter Empfehlungsverfahren: So wird die Suche über Tags unterstützt, wobei die Relevanz eines Tags in Bezug auf einen Film durch die Anwendung der TF-IDF-Heuristik (Baeza-Yates & Ribeiro-Neto, 1999) ermittelt wird. Zudem ist eine binäre Filterung z. B. nach Genres und Regisseuren möglich. Schließlich liegt für einen Film m und jedes Kriterium c_i eine Relevanz $r_i(m, c_i)$ im Bereich [0;1] vor.

Um die aggregierte Gesamtrelevanz r für einen Film gemäß aller Kriterien zu ermitteln, werden die einzelnen Relevanzwerte mit Hilfe der angegebenen Gewichte w_i (die Einstellungen der Slider in Abbildung 1) als gewichtetes Mittel über alle Kriterien zusammengeführt (s. Formel 1).

$$r(m, c_1, \dots, c_n, w_1, \dots, w_n) = \frac{\sum_{i=1}^{n} w_i \cdot r_i(m, c_i)}{\sum_{i=1}^{n} w_i} \quad (1)$$

Abschließend wird gemäß der Gesamtrelevanz absteigend sortiert und die Filme mit dem höchsten Wert werden dem Nutzer präsentiert. Tabelle 1 illustriert die Formel anhand eines Beispiels: Gewünscht wird ein Film von Steven Spielberg (Kriterium c_1 mit Gewicht w_1=100) aus den 1990er Jahren (Kriterium c_2 mit Gewicht w_2=50). Im Sinne einer übersichtlichen Darstellung sei angenommen, dass nur drei Filme in der Datenbasis vorkommen.

Film	$r_1(m, c_1)$ *(Regie)*	$r_2(m, c_2)$ *(Jahr)*	$r(m, c_1, c_2, 100, 50)$
Indiana Jones 3 (Spielberg, 1989)	1.0	0.5	0.833
Jurassic Park (Spielberg, 1993)	1.0	1.0	1.000
Pulp Fiction (Tarantino, 1994)	0.0	1.0	0.333

Tabelle 1: Beispiel zur Verrechnung einzelner Relevanzwerte für einige Filme

4 Evaluation des Ansatzes

Bei der Entwicklung von MyMovieMixer verfolgten wir einen nutzerzentrierten Entwicklungsansatz, bei welchem insgesamt drei Nutzerstudien prozessbegleitend durchgeführt wurden. Im Folgenden wird über die letzte dieser Studien berichtet, bei der in einer summativen Evaluation die Interaktions- und Manipulationsmöglichkeiten mit dem System im Hinblick auf die folgenden Fragestellungen untersucht wurden.

1. Wie ist das Nutzungserleben?
2. Welche Probleme zeigen sich während der Nutzung von MyMovieMixer?
3. Wie nehmen die Nutzer die Interaktions- und Manipulationsmöglichkeiten wahr?
4. Ist das System MyMovieMixer intuitiv zu bedienen und schnell erlernbar?
5. Wie benutzerfreundlich ist das System MyMovieMixer insgesamt?
6. Wie wird die Qualität der generierten Empfehlungen wahrgenommen?

4.1 Studienaufbau und Datenerhebung

Die Evaluation wurde als Laborstudie mit mehreren Nutzeraufgaben konzipiert. Insgesamt umfasste die Stichprobe 30 Personen (14 w) im Alter von 21 bis 67 Jahren (M=28, σ=10.18), die Mehrzahl von ihnen Studierende (83.3 %). Die erste Aufgabe der Probanden bestand in einer freien Exploration des Systems. Sie sollten dabei MyMovieMixer unter der Annahme nutzen, dass sie einen Film sehen möchten, aber noch nicht wissen, welchen. Nach dieser Aufgabe bewerteten die Teilnehmer in einem Fragebogen die Intuitivität der Bedienung. Nachfolgende Aufgaben umfassten die Erstellung von Kacheln, die Berücksichtigung vorgegebener Präferenzen in unterschiedlicher Anzahl und deren Gewichtung. Auch die Manipulation der Ergebnisse und die Betrachtung des Feedbacks, wie die empfohlenen Filme den eingegebenen Kriterien entsprechen, wurden fokussiert. Durch diese Szenarien wurde sichergestellt, dass die Probanden alle relevanten Funktionen des Systems nutzten. Während der Interaktion erfolgte ein Think Aloud mit einer Verhaltensbeobachtung durch die Versuchsleitung. Außerdem wurde die Bearbeitungszeit erfasst. Im Anschluss an die Aufgabenbearbeitung beantworteten die Probanden weitere Fragebogen-Items. Dabei wurde zunächst die Erlernbarkeit, Verständlichkeit und kognitive Anstrengung bezüglich der Nutzung der Widgets, Kacheln und Slider sowie der Interaktion mit den Filmempfehlungen und der Detailanzeige erfragt. Des Weiteren enthielt der Fragebogen Items zur Erfassung der wahrgenommenen Qualität der Empfehlungen. Außerdem setzten wir die *System Usability Scale* (SUS; Brooke, 1996), den *User Experience Questionnaire* (UEQ; Laugwitz et al., 2008) sowie selbst generierte Items zum Gesamteindruck und zur Nutzungsabsicht ein.

4.2 Ergebnisse

Nach der ersten, explorativen Benutzung von MyMovieMixer gaben die Probanden auf einer positiv gepolten Skala von 1 bis 5 an, sich gut zurechtgefunden zu haben (M=3.63, σ=1.16). Die Intuitivität wurde bei der initialen Nutzung im Mittel mit 2.87 (σ=0.97) bewertet. Die nach Vollendung aller Aufgaben erhobenen Ergebnisse zeigen sehr hohe Werte in Bezug auf Erlernbarkeit und Verständlichkeit der Interaktion mit den verschiedenen Funktionen von MyMovieMixer sowie eine geringe kognitive Belastung (s. Tabelle 2).

	Widgets, Kacheln und Slider		**Ergebnis- und Detailanzeige**	
	M	σ	*M*	σ
Erlernbarkeit	4.53	0.819	4.37	0.809
Verständlichkeit	4.07	0.828	4.27	0.980
geringe kogn. Anstrengung	4.13	1.008	4.27	0.944

Tabelle 2: Beurteilung der Funktionen hinsichtlich Erlernbarkeit, Verständlichkeit und kognitiver Anstrengung

Das Zustandekommen der Filmempfehlungen wurde dem Großteil der Probanden klar: Lediglich 4 Probanden (13.3 %) gaben an, dies nicht nachvollziehen zu können, was zum einen mit einer fehlenden Darstellung der Gewichtung der Kriterien in der Film-Detailanzeige begründet wurde, zum anderen damit, dass relevante Filme zu weit hinten in der Ergebnisliste erschienen. Die Qualität der Empfehlungen wurde dennoch sehr positiv mit einem Mittelwert von 4.17 (σ=0.42) bei positiver Polung auf einer Likert-Skala von 1 bis 5 bewertet.

Auch die Usability wurde mit einem Wert von durchschnittlich 77 % auf der SUS positiv bewertet. In Bezug auf die User Experience lagen die durchschnittlichen Bewertungen deutlich im positiven Bereich der siebenstufigen, bipolaren Skala (−3 bis 3) des UEQ ($M=1.94$, $\sigma=0.35$). Außerdem bewerteten die Teilnehmer den Umgang mit dem System auf einer Likert-Skala von 1 bis 5 durchschnittlich als eine spannende Erfahrung ($M=4.13$, $\sigma=0.90$).

Die Auswertung der Ergebnisse des Think Aloud, der Beobachtung sowie der Zeitmessung während der Interaktion mit MyMovieMixer zeigte, dass die meisten Probanden nach einer kurzen Orientierungsphase selbstständig die Interaktionsmöglichkeiten ausprobierten. Der Testung der Systemfunktionalitäten – insbesondere der Widgetleiste sowie dem Drag and Drop der Kacheln – schenkten sie dabei viel Zeit ($M=11.4$ min, *Range*=5–26 min). So erhielten sie bereits in der ersten Aufgabe einen Überblick über die wichtigsten Funktionalitäten. Die folgenden Aufgaben wurden zielgerichteter und deutlich schneller bearbeitet. Es zeigte sich, dass die Funktionen insgesamt schnell und ohne Hilfe der Versuchsleitung gefunden und verstanden wurden. Darüber hinaus wurde beobachtet, dass die Probanden die Drag-and-Drop-Funktionalität zusätzlich zu den bisher implementierten an weiteren Stellen in der Interaktion vermuteten, etwa zum Ziehen einer Filmempfehlung in den Arbeitsbereich.

5 Diskussion und Fazit

Wie eingangs herausgestellt, bilden grafische Visualisierungen, Interaktionsmöglichkeiten und Empfehlungstransparenz wichtige Kriterien für die Nutzerzufriedenheit bei Recommendern. Jedoch mangelt es an konkreten Umsetzungen solch visueller und interaktiver Lösungen. Besonders für komplexe hybride Recommender existieren derartige Bedienkonzepte bis zum jetzigen Zeitpunkt noch nicht. Mit MyMovieMixer haben wir ein visuelles Interaktionskonzept umgesetzt, welches den aufgezeigten Limitationen bisheriger Ansätze entgegenwirken soll. Da Erklärungen der Vorschläge die wahrgenommene Effektivität, die Zufriedenheit, den empfundenen Einflussgrad, die Akzeptanz sowie das Vertrauen in das System erhöhen können (Pu et al., 2012), sollte der Empfehlungsprozess dabei für den Nutzer transparent sein. Durch die interaktive Darstellung geht die in der Evaluation ermittelte hohe Empfehlungsqualität wie nach Zhang et al. (2008) mit gesteigerter Nachvollziehbarkeit einher. Durch direkt auf Aktionen erfolgendes Feedback und die unmittelbare Anpassung der Empfehlungen sollte zudem die empfundene Kontrolle des Nutzers erhöht werden.

Mehr Interaktions- und Kontrollmöglichkeiten können allerdings zu einem Mehraufwand bei der Nutzung führen. Die vorgestellten Evaluationsergebnisse zeigen jedoch, dass MyMovieMixer im Allgemeinen als intuitiv und angenehm zu bedienen bewertet wurde. Dabei konnte eine hohe Empfehlungsqualität erreicht werden und die Nutzer empfanden die Vorschläge als gut nachvollziehbar. In Bezug auf *Fragestellung 1* weisen sowohl die Ergebnisse des UEQ als auch die des Think Aloud und der Verhaltensbeobachtung auf ein positives Nutzungserleben hin. Aufgrund der Beobachtung, dass die langen Bearbeitungszeiten der ersten Aufgabe nicht auf Probleme, sondern auf die intensive Exploration des Systems durch die Teilnehmer zurückzuführen sind, ist anzunehmen, dass der Umgang mit dem System den Nutzern Spaß gemacht und ihr Interesse geweckt hat. Dies deckt sich mit den Angaben der

Probanden, dass der Umgang mit dem System eine spannende Erfahrung gewesen sei. *Fragestellung 2* beleuchtete etwaige Probleme bei der Nutzung von MyMovieMixer: Insgesamt traten wenige Probleme auf. Optimierungen sind im Hinblick auf eine konsequentere Umsetzung des verwendeten Drag-and-Drop-Prinzips jedoch empfehlenswert. Hinsichtlich des Interaktionskonzepts der Anwendung (*Fragestellung 3*) wurden von den Teilnehmern im Rahmen des Think Aloud die direkte Manipulation, die grafische Visualisierung der Empfehlungskriterien als Kacheln und das Drag and Drop als eine der hauptsächlichen Interaktionsmethoden positiv hervorgehoben. Mit *Fragestellung 4* wurden die intuitive Bedienbarkeit und die Erlernbarkeit von MyMovieMixer untersucht. Die Beobachtungsergebnisse zeigen einen recht selbstverständlichen, anfangs von Exploration geprägten und später zielgerichteten Umgang mit dem System. Dieser Eindruck der intuitiven Handhabung und der einfachen Erlernbarkeit deckt sich mit den Fragebogen-Ergebnissen. Im Hinblick auf *Fragestellung 5* konnte die Benutzerfreundlichkeit des Systems durch die zuvor diskutierten Fragestellungen und die Ergebnisse der SUS gezeigt werden. Die Qualität der Empfehlungen (*Fragestellung 6*) wurde sehr positiv bewertet. Auch wurde die Darstellung, auf welchen Kriterien diese basieren, als transparent wahrgenommen.

Der Ansatz scheint also in Bezug auf Usability, User Experience, Intuitivität, Transparenz und somit letztlich im Hinblick auf die Nutzerzufriedenheit vielversprechend zu sein. Durch das visuelle Konzept konnte eine unterhaltsame, attraktive Gestaltung erreicht werden, was nach Pu et al. (2012) die Nutzer zu mehr Eingaben motiviert. Gleichzeitig wurde der zu leistende kognitive Aufwand als gering bewertet, was sich u. a. durch die Verwendung von Kacheln als Repräsentation für Kriterien und die Interaktion mittels Drag and Drop begründen lässt. Das Drag-and-Drop-Prinzip sollte jedoch noch umfassender und konsequenter eingesetzt werden, etwa beim Hinzufügen empfohlener Filme als Kriterium oder für das Löschen gewählter Kriterien. Weiterhin ist denkbar, die initial in den Widgets angezeigten Kacheln unter Verwendung von Empfehlungsalgorithmen an vorherige Nutzereingaben anzupassen. In zukünftigen Studien planen wir zudem eine detailliertere Untersuchung der Empfehlungsqualität sowie der möglichen Berücksichtigung weiterer relevanter Aspekte, wie z. B. Diversität und Serendipität.

Insgesamt erlaubt das vorgestellte Bedienkonzept für hybride Recommender auf situative Bedürfnisse zu reagieren, ohne langfristige Nutzerprofile zu benötigen. Dadurch wird auch das weitverbreitete Cold-Start-Problem umgangen, da sämtliche Eingaben ad-hoc erfolgen. Zudem bietet die konsistente Visualisierung der Suchkriterien viele Vorteile und hat sich besonders zur Steigerung der Transparenz bei den Empfehlungen bewährt. Die einfach gehaltene Darstellung ermöglicht es dem Anwender dabei in Anlehnung an kritikbasierte Recommender, die Empfehlungen anhand zahlreicher Kriterien kontinuierlich seinem Suchziel anzupassen, ohne dass MyMovieMixer dabei zu komplex oder unübersichtlich wirkt. Durch das angewendete Prinzip der losen Kopplung ist es zudem möglich, beliebige Widgets und somit beliebige Recommender und Filtermethoden zu integrieren.

Danksagung

Wir bedanken uns bei Jennifer Frantz und Katharina Lattenkamp für die Mitarbeit im Entwicklungsprozess von MyMovieMixer.

Literaturverzeichnis

Baeza-Yates, R. & Ribeiro-Neto, B. (1999). *Modern Information Retrieval*. New York: ACM.

Bostandjiev, S., O'Donovan, J. & Höllerer, T. (2012). TasteWeights: A visual interactive hybrid recommender system. In *Proc. RecSys 2012*. New York: ACM. 35–42.

Brooke, J. (1996). SUS – A quick and dirty usability scale. *Usability Evaluation in Industry*, 189–194.

Burke, R. (2007). Hybrid web recommender systems. In P. Brusilovsky, A. Kobsa & W. Nejdl (Hrsg.), *The Adaptive Web. Methods and Strategies of Web Personalization*. Berlin: Springer. 377–408.

Chen, L. & Pu, P. (2012). Critiquing-based recommenders: Survey and emerging trends. *User Modeling and User-Adapted Interaction, 22*(1-2), 125–150.

Gretarsson, B., O'Donovan, J., Bostandjiev, S., Hall, C. & Höllerer, T. (2010). SmallWorlds: Visualizing social recommendations. *Computer Graphics Forum, 29*(3), 833–842.

Knijnenburg, B. P., Willemsen, M. C., Gantner, Z., Soncu, H. & Newell, C. (2012). Explaining the user experience of recommender systems. *User Mod. and User-Adapted Interaction, 22*(4-5), 441–504.

Konstan, J. A. & Riedl, J. (2012). Recommender systems: From algorithms to user experience. *User Modeling and User-Adapted Interaction, 22*(1-2), 101–123.

Laugwitz, B., Held, T., & Schrepp, M. (2008). Construction and evaluation of a user experience questionnaire. In *HCI and Usability for Education and Work*. Berlin: Springer. 63–76.

McCarthy, K., Reilly, J., McGinty, L. & Smyth, B. (2005). Experiments in dynamic critiquing. In *Proc. IUI 2005*. New York: ACM. 175–182.

Parra, D., Brusilovsky, P. & Trattner, C. (2014). See what you want to see: Visual user-driven approach for hybrid recommendation. In *Proc. IUI 2014*. New York: ACM. 235–240.

Pu, P., Chen, L. & Hu, R. (2012). Evaluating recommender systems from the user's perspective: Survey of the state of the art. *User Modeling and User-Adapted Interaction, 22*(4-5), 317–355.

Ricci, F., Rokach, L. & Shapira, B. (Hrsg.). (2010). *Recommender Systems Handbook*. Berlin: Springer. 1–35.

Salton, G. & Buckley, C. (1997). Improving retrieval performance by relevance feedback. In *Readings in Information Retrieval*. Morgan Kaufmann. 355–364.

Tintarev, N. & Masthoff, J. (2010). Designing and evaluating explanations for recommender systems. In Ricci, F., Rokach, L., Shapira, B. & Kantor, P. B. (Hrsg.), *Recommender Systems Handbook*. Berlin: Springer. 479–510.

Vig, J., Sen, S. & Riedl, J. (2011). Navigating the tag genome. In *Proc. IUI 2011*. New York: ACM. 93–102.

Xiao, B. & Benbasat, I. (2007). E-commerce product recommendation agents: Use, characteristics, and impact. *MIS Quarterly, 31*(1), 137–209.

Zadeh, L. (1965). Fuzzy sets. *Information and Control, 8*(3), 338–353.

Zhang, J., Jones, N. & Pu, P. (2008). A visual interface for critiquing-based recommender systems. In *Proc. EC 2008*. New York: ACM. 230–239.

M. Koch, A. Butz & J. Schlichter (Hrsg.): Mensch und Computer 2014 Tagungsband,
München: Oldenbourg Wissenschaftsverlag, 2014, S. 55-64.

The facilitator's perspective on IT support in innovation workshops

Sabine Schön[1], Alexander Richter[2], Michael Koch[1], Gerhard Schwabe[2]

Cooperation System Center, Bundeswehr University Munich[1]
Department of Informatics, University of Zurich[2]

Abstract

Supporting collocated meetings has always been an important field for CSCW. However, whereas solutions for video conferencing and presentation have been widely adopted, IT support to mutually edit artefacts has not yet found its way into practice. To contribute to a better understanding of the situation, we investigate perceived benefits and barriers of IT support using the example of interactive phases in innovation workshops. We conducted an interview study with professional facilitators of innovation workshops and found that existing technologies are perceived as disturbing in several ways. Consequently, we identify open issues and implications for the design of future solutions.

1 Motivation

A company's strategic position in the competitive market depends upon its ability to continuously fascinate customers with novel products and services. In their endeavour to innovate, companies have to address a variety of challenges. For example, in early phases[1] it is necessary to reduce the complexity of innovative projects and to foster information exchange, as well as shared understanding (Hauschildt & Salomo 2007). Corporations employ professional facilitators to guide teams through this process. Workshops play a key role in this context and are used as a central method to unite interdisciplinary skills (Katzenbach & Smith 2003). Especially in interactive phases of these workshops, facilitators use many tools, such as posters and post-its, to reduce complexity and foster interaction (Nielsen 2012). In the 1990s, Group Support Systems (GSS) have been extensively discussed as a means to support facilitators of different kinds of workshops with an electronic moderation toolkit (e.g. Nunamaker et al. 1991). However, actual meeting support is still mostly limited to analogue tools, including post-its and pens. These tools are easy to use and their benefit is obvious (Nebe et al. 2011). If technology is used, it is mostly presentation

[1] In this paper, we understand early phases of innovation processes as activities that include problem identification, idea generation and development of new concepts like business models and service strategies.

software, such as Powerpoint. Moreover, some studies have focused on providing solutions to mutually edit digital artefacts, like post-its, in collocated meetings (e.g. Hilliges et al. 2007). They have also not yet been adopted in the vast majority of workshops. Since most studies, which identify reasons for or against the use of IT, are predominantly related to the classical use of desktop computers (e.g. Alavi 1993, Aiken et al. 1994, Mark et al. 1997), it has been postulated that due to the availability of tablets, smartphones or large screens in "Collaborative Interactive Spaces", the conditions should be re-examined (Jetter et al. 2012).

Since the facilitators are the major promoters or demoters of the use of new technology in workshops, we would like to contribute to that research by analysing the reasons facilitators use IT (or not), using innovation workshops as application domain. Thereby, we demonstrate open issues, research opportunities and implications for the design and development of IT support[2], which overcomes barriers and exploits benefits that favour the necessary value for practical use. After reviewing related work in Section 2, we first will describe our empirical approach (Section 3). We have conducted a series of 17 interviews to identify perceived benefits and barriers. We present our results in Section 4 and discuss these in Section 5. Finally, we provide a summary, outline limitations and future work in Section 6.

2 Related Work

Various studies in the 1990s, have shown how GSS support collocated meetings. Nunamaker et al. (1991) point out that the parallel and anonymous input options in electronic meeting support can encourage participants to increase participation. A structured meeting process with the help of GSS can foster focusing on key issues and avoids unproductive behaviour. The automatic documentation of cooperation subsequently allows a better understanding of the content (Nunamaker et al. 1991). In that context, Krcmar et al. (2001) stated that the linkage to previous results and their further development is easier through the reusability. Alavi (1993) showed that the verbal exchange is not replaced by GSS, but increases instead. Notwithstanding these positive assessments of the impact of GSS, there are critical voices. Aiken et al. (1994) identified that the use of GSS can impose effort and consume time, especially for less technology-savvy participants. Furthermore, according to Mark et al. (1997), structural requirements by GSS can restrict facilitators and participants in their interaction. Most early work on GSS assumed a technological determinism; that an application or feature could impose a certain effect on the group. Since the mid 1990s this was replaced by the notion that a skilled facilitator can use GSS to trigger such an effect (Schwabe 1995). A GSS does not only provide him with a set of tools, e.g. for brainstorming, but it also gives him absolute control over the participants' computer. The reliance on skilled facilitators positioned GSS in a niche, as professionally facilitated workshops are rare compared to informal group work or meetings. Nonetheless, researchers are striving to replace the facilitator by engineering a workshop practice once and then letting participants to

[2] In the following, we will use this general term to describe IT tools comprising software and hardware components aiming to support collocated collaborative work (e.g. creating and editing shared artefacts like post-its).

instantiate this practice themselves (Kolfschoten & Vreede 2007). However, those efforts do not explain why GSS did not find their way into practice and can be regarded as mostly forgotten in its key customer group. More recent studies assume the main reason of resistance is that the collaboration artefacts are presented inappropriately. They thus strive to improve the quality of the digital artefacts (e.g. digital post-its). Herrmann and Nolte (2010) showed that the use of large vertical, interactive projection screens helps the participants to see their contributions at a glance and put artefacts into structural relationship. The additional use of mobile devices gives participants the opportunity to contribute content in parallel and therefore support various stages of cooperation (Herrmann & Nolte 2010), such as the discussion with the facilitator as well as phases with parallel input. However, Hilliges et al. (2007) stated that using single-user systems in a collaborative setting entails the risk that the attention of the participant's decreases. Streitz et al. remarked already in 1999: the computer should stay in the background.

Whilst a few studies demonstrate the potential of IT support, there is still a lack of studies that explain why it is not used to work together in practice. The need for a better understanding of factors that prevent but also motivate use seems to be reinforced by the fact that recently a couple of new technologies have the potential to support innovation workshops in new ways. As an example, Haller et al. (2010) presented the NiCE Discussion Room, which consists of a multi-touch wall display in combination with tangible menus, laptops and paper interfaces. The authors identified that in using paper interfaces, the participants felt more inclined to contribute. Also Scott et al. (2003) advise the integration of physical objects because they allow users to apply the years of experience they have accumulated. Geyer et al. (2011) present a user interface with hybrid post-its that have both a physical and digital representation. They offered the capability to retrieve images by placing a physical note into a certain space. This was very well perceived among participants and triggered lively discussions. Although the research resulted in a stream of commercial products, they are still rarely applied in interactive phases of innovation workshops. Why? Before we discuss this in more detail, we will briefly introduce our methodology.

3 Method

By aiming to develop an innovative and purposeful artefact in a specified problem domain, in our case innovation workshops, our research approach is based on the design science paradigm (Hevner 2004). Taking into account Gregor & Hevner (2013), our goal is to improve existing artefacts and provide a solution that favours the necessary value for practical use. In this paper, we present the first activity of design science according to Peffers et al. (2007): Problem identification and motivation. In this way, we identify open issues, reveal research opportunities and implications for the design of future solutions.

To contribute to a better understanding of the current situation, we investigate perceived benefits and barriers of commercial IT support using the example of interactive phases in innovation workshops. We conducted a qualitative interview study with six female and eleven male facilitators who design and conduct international innovation workshops. Since facilitators typically decide on the use of visual tools and have extensive knowledge about different types of workshop participants, they represent our key stakeholders. After 17 interviews, the addition of further interviewees promised no new information (Hennink 2011). The selected facilitators work as freelancers, employees or managers in Germany and Austria. 14 of the respondents work as external facilitators in consulting firms or innovation agencies and two as internal facilitators in international companies. One participant facilitates innovation workshops in the university environment. The interviewees were between 27 and 59 years old and all regularly use computers and mobile devices, except for one participant. Twelve interviews were conducted personally and five by telephone. The interviews were recorded with the consent of the participants. The time frame of an interview was between 30 and 60 minutes. The interviews have been conducted in a semi-structured way (Schultze & Avital 2011) to come close to an open discussion. An interview guide helped to maintain the structure (Bryman & Bell 2007).

In the first part of the interviews, respondents were asked to report on their last typical innovation workshop. Thus, we gained insights into the working practices and the examples acted as specific application reference for further questions. Using the guidelines ensured that certain characteristics, such as structure, objectives, tools, location, duration, preparation and follow-up, were discussed. This allowed us to determine whether commercial IT support was already in use in interactive phases. This was the case with two respondents, while several reported that they had tried such tools for this application. Following the approach of Stacey and Vincent (2011), we enriched our interviews with multimedia data to get in-depth answers. We introduced web-based, real-time collaboration software, which was specially developed for the support of innovative processes[3]. Thus, the facilitators received an exemplary impression of software that could be used in interactive phases. Following this, the facilitators were asked which added value they see in the use of such software. To collect data, whether and how new (touch-based) user interfaces affect the usage decision, the facilitators were presented three videos, each showing alternative control concepts for the use of real-time collaboration software to mutually edit digital post-its[4]. After each video, the facilitators were asked if and why they would or would not use it in their workshops. At the beginning or after the survey, metadata such as age, work experience, use of digital devices, company, company size and position were collected. The interviews were transcribed and coded sentence by sentence according to the open coding scheme of Corbin and Strauss (2008). Afterwards axial coding (Corbin & Strauss 2008) helped us to group categories to more high-level ones. Next we will present our results based on these generated categories.

[3] Rapid Modeler is a team software for business design that allows participants to mutually edit digital post-its on a shared workspace to design, e.g. business models or service strategies (www.rapidmodeler.de).

[4] (a) Laptop per person with one joint projection, (b) one joint interactive tabletop and tablet per person, (c) one interactive wall-mounted screen and mobile device (laptop, tablet or smartphone) per person

4 Results

We begin by describing perceived benefits of use, as indicated by facilitators. As we learned from the interviews, the documentation of innovation workshops is complicated for facilitators. Results produced with tools like post-its must be digitized. An IT tool that helps to automatically document results as well as the development process was considered as beneficial by the facilitators. Compared to working with paper tools, IT support offers the possibility to include external content, such as images and videos, which can serve as a source of inspiration. Moreover, different dimensions can be imaged, as there are more ways to store and link information. The interviewed facilitators were eager to improve the interaction among the participants, to stimulate them to contribute or discuss more. Furthermore, the fact that the use of IT allows supporting innovation processes without media change in synchronous and asynchronous collocated or remote collaboration is seen as beneficial. Although most of the interviewed facilitators perceived these benefits, barriers of use nonetheless outweigh them and led to a negative usage decision. In the following, we describe the barriers stated by the facilitators. All of them allude to the fear that the IT support used disturbs their workshops, due to (a) external influences, (b) complexity and (c) parallelism. Additionally, facilitators fear to change their (d) way of designing workshops.

a) Most interviewees reported the predominant fear that their participants might be distracted by *external influences* and lose focus. If personal mobile devices are used, private and business applications like email or instant messaging might disturb the workshops. Since they cannot control this, the facilitators sometimes even require turning off all digital devices during the course of a workshop[5]. It is the only way to ensure the full and undisturbed concentration as well as the development of group dynamics. Since most workshops take place at external facilities such as hotels, often only a projector is available. Thus, many facilitators mentioned the problem of transporting all tools.

b) Many facilitators explained that they were concerned that the attention of participants may be deflected by the use of IT due to *complexity*. The coexistence of shared and private working areas, such as large interactive screens and mobile devices, represents a barrier for interaction, since attention is away from the shared workspace. This influence on their attention occurs also when writing on post-its, but this activity is considered faster and easier, since no additional editing options (e.g. colour) are provided. It is feared that once attention is directed to the input device, the content of the workshop is moved into the background[6]. The facilitators believe that "pen and paper" is a pure tool because the usage is not only simple but also boring. Moreover, facilitators fear a loss of focus due to malfunctions and usability complications. The risk remains high that less technology-savvy participants would be excluded. For facilitators however, the balanced participation and equality of the participants is essential. Not only may the loss of focus of the participants

[5] "But just on the other hand, it is more my motto, when people come to workshops, then I do not need them to sit in front of a screen, that's what they already do the whole week, right?"(I5)

[6] "I'd currently be concerned that the technology is in the foreground too much and is not a pure tool [...] it must then be a tool, a tool, and without a big wow effect or gimmick." (I2)

cause concern, but also the risk of complications during setup. Compared with handing out paper and pens, the initial setup of an IT tool presents a challenge[7].

c) By offering next to the analogue communication channel a second digital channel, the facilitators fear that once the attention is *directed to the digital channel*, the parallel activities in the group are no longer perceived. So it can happen that discussions fail because the contributions of others will not be noticed. In these terms, the biggest concern is that, finally, the personal interaction is replaced by the digital. However, in the perception of the facilitators the bundling of attention of all participants is an important prerequisite for successful workshops. The facilitators fear they could lose track and contributions would remain unnoticed[8]. In this case, the fundamental rules for cooperation would have to be communicated in advance, which constitutes an additional effort for facilitators.

d) Several facilitators mentioned that they cannot imagine the use of IT, because the tools are too inflexible for use in their *own facilitation methods*. They criticize that the experience of the common result processing is restricted to a limited number of screens and loses its presence in the room. Many facilitators use all walls in the room to hang up results achieved so far. This serves on the one hand as an overview and on the other acts as input for following exercises. This overview is lost in control concepts that offer just one big screen. The issue is strengthened in small group work. Assuming a large projection is available for the entire group, but not for every small group, the achieved results of each small group are not present in the room, but hidden in the IT tool. The presence of each individual contribution to a large and common visual workspace is very important for the facilitators, as it promotes interaction and involves participants. In addition, the physical action of the participants, which is desired by facilitators, is reduced when using digital devices to place a contribution. Moreover, facilitators fear that haptic perception, e.g. fixing and removing a post-it, is lost. As well, concerns are expressed regarding the structural requirements through digital letters. Within innovation workshops, especially in the early stages, contributions should emit no finality, but rather symbolize that they are not yet ready. Digital characters are perceived as mature compared to hand-written and are therefore only required in workshops that deal with concrete tasks at later stages of innovation processes.

5 Discussion

In this section we discuss our findings with respect to those in the literature and demonstrate open issues and implications for the design and development of solutions that favor the necessary value for practical use in interactive phases of innovation workshops.

---

7 "[...] we are often at the customer's office and can not install such a thing and first calibrate it and we are there one and a half days in advance to prepare that everything runs and [...] have to drill holes in the wall [...]."(I3)

8 "[...] you should watch out that it does not get out of hand, so let's say, that [...] it still retains the structure and that the facilitator [...] still has an overview of who does what and when [...]."(I17)

In the last years, research has made huge steps concerning the availability of new user interfaces, which provide workshop participants with much more than a desktop computer. Multiple users can edit shared artefacts on multiple devices in very natural ways, like touch or pen-based interactions. Furthermore, digital representations of real world artefacts (e.g. post-its) become more and more realistic. However, the comments of the facilitators indicate that some design principles of GSS (e.g. GroupSystem's) are still valid. The facilitators want to stay in control. Just sharing an artefact may work for small informal groups, but it does not work for facilitating larger groups. Facilitators fear that contributions stay unnoticed and participants fail in trying to cope with the complexity of the IT tool. They may spend too much time on choosing the right colour and size for their contribution. The facilitators also point to a new control challenge: while in prior times physical presence assured focus on a shared outcome, connected personal devices offer participant distraction any time during the workshops. As the bundling of attention of all participants is a central issue, there is still the need for a solution, which (1) fits unobtrusively into the workshop situation. It remains an interesting challenge how to provide computer based tools and at the same time (2) shut away distractions. Our results are in line with several studies showing, e.g. that the use of single-user systems negatively influences collaboration (Hilliges et al. 2007, Streitz et al. 1999). Therefore, the IT support should (3) encourage interaction on one or several common workspace(s) and allow the work on single-user systems only when needed, like consciously used parallel phases. Within parallel phases, the IT support should (4) provide the facilitator control options to prevent that contributions are not considered and avoid foreign activities.

If GSS had been a complete solution for the facilitators' needs, it would be widely adopted by now. Without directly pointing at GSS, the facilitators clearly indicate their preference for physical artefacts. They are widely available, have a different haptic quality and allow using the whole room as a collaboration arena. Taking into account Mark et al. (1997), who stated that IT support can limit facilitators, our results show that our interviewees also perceive this. The reason is that if the visualization of contributions is limited to one shared display, interim results lose their presence in the room and small group work is not supported by a large common workspace. The development of a technical solution, which (5) exploits the flexibility of the spatial conditions for visualization of the contributions as well as (6) supports each small group with a large common workspace, continues to be a challenge. This challenge is reinforced by the fact that in many cases workshops take place in unknown facilities. Therefore, we suggest that the IT support must (7) be portable and be independent from the technical infrastructure. Since the facilitators described the concern that usage complications might during the use and the initial setup of the system, it is inevitable that the IT tool (8) is reliable, does not require any prior knowledge and requires low setup time.

Similarly as approached by Haller et al. (2010) and Geyer et al. (2011) as well as advised by Scott et al. (2003) the facilitators wish their participants to experience haptic perception. Handwritten workshop contributions have personal touch and the appropriate level of "unfinishedness". Moreover, facilitators want their participants to be physically active during the workshops. While a digital participant is largely tied to the device and thus reduced to "eyes and hands", the analogue participant can freely roam around the room. This physical movement introduces a degree of serendipity into the analogue workshops that digital workshops lack. We suggest that (9) physical movements and haptic perception (including handwritten contributions) should be promoted by the IT support. For example, Streitz et al. (2001) presented a solution where participants can carry around digital information via physical representatives. It is an unintended contribution of research on the IT-support of collocated collaboration that its use has opened the eyes of researchers on qualities of physical artefacts. At this point, the question can be brought up if the real world should be integrated into the digital or vice versa. New studies present approaches that bring the digital world to the physical. Harboe et al. (2012) found out that despite the availability of digital solutions design teams still rely on post-its. Therefore, they suggest an augmented reality interface on a tablet computer to search through and identify paper notes immediately. In that way, they combine the benefits of a technical solution with the ones of physical notes. In our study, the facilitators stated that they appreciate the possibility of IT to (10) define contributions in different dimensions and planes as well as (11) integrate multimedia data to inspire participants. These benefits should be exploited since they constitute a significant advantage compared to the pure use of paper and pen. According to the benefits of IT support stated by Nunamaker et al. (1991) and Krcmar et al. (2001), the common work must (12) be documented and versioned automatically and (13) allow synchronous or asynchronous processing before and after the workshop.

6 Conclusion

Drawing from a series of interviews with 17 facilitators of innovation workshops we have presented a study of perceived benefits and barriers to the use of IT in interactive phases of innovation workshops. We discussed research that influences the design of new solutions. The results of our study show that currently the risks to disturb the workshops are perceived as too high by the facilitators. We identified that researchers in different fields already addressed several barriers of use, including control options for facilitators in GSS, the promotion of physical movements, as well as tangible user interfaces. Researchers are also starting to exploit benefits when designing IT-support, e.g. by the help of augmented reality interfaces. The combination of all these partial approaches to an integrated solution is tough. However, there is the chance to combine them step by step to finally provide solutions that favour the necessary value for practical use in interactive phases of innovation workshops.

Since we interviewed facilitators of innovation workshops, it requires caution when transferring our findings to other application areas. However, we believe that other types of workshops may have similar issues. A further limitation of our study is that we only highlight perceived benefits and barriers by facilitators of innovation workshops and most of them have not used a collaboration system within their workshops before. However, they represent key stakeholders in practice and decide on the use of IT. Since we do not aim to identify design principles within this paper, benefits and barriers we identified cannot exclusively act as a basis for the development of a solution. Our study aims to contribute to the understanding of concerns on the facilitator's side, influencing currently made usage decisions. Therefore, we reveal outstanding issues, show research opportunities and outline implications for the design and development of solutions.

In the aftermath, we derive design principles and concrete requirements on the basis of which we develop a prototype (Peffers et al. 2007), which addresses presented barriers and exploits benefits. Against this background, touch screens or projections in combination with voice input and tangible user interfaces will be investigated to see whether they can, e.g. maintain the level of attention. Additionally, augmented reality interfaces that blend the work with currently used tools, like approached by Harboe et al. (2012), will be taken into account. To ensure that the solution addresses the identified barriers, creates an added value and is accepted by users, the prototype will be evaluated in innovation workshops in practice.

References

Aiken, M., Hawley, D. & Zhang, W. (1994). *Increasing Meeting Efficiency with a GDSS. Industrial Management & Data Systems 94*(8), 13-16.

Alavi, M. (1993). An Assessment of Electronic Meeting Systems in a Corporate Setting. *Information & Management 25*(4), 175-182.

Bryman, A. & Bell, E. (2007). *Business Research Methods*. New York: Oxford University Press.

Corbin, J. & Strauss, A. (2008). *Basics of Qualitative Research: Techniques and Procedures for Developing Grounded Theory*. Sage.

Geyer, F., Pfeil, U., Höchtl, A., Budzinksi, J. & Reiterer, H. (2011). Designing Reality-Based Interfaces for Creative Group Work. In: *Proceedings of the 8th ACM Conference on Creativity & Cognition*. New York: ACM.

Gregor, S. & Hevner, A. (2013). Positioning and Presenting Design Science Research for Maximum Impact. *Management Information Systems Quarterly* 37 (2), 337-355.

Haller, M., Leitner, J., Seifried, T., Wallace, J., Scott, S.D., Richter C., Brandl, P., Gokcezade, A. & Hunter, S. (2010). The NiCE Discussion Room: Integrating Paper and Digital Media to Support Co-Located Group Meetings. In: *Proceedings of the SIGCHI Conference on Human Factors in Computing Systems*. Atlanta: ACM.

Harboe, G., Minke, J., Ilea, I., & Huang, E. M. (2012). Computer Support for Collaborative Data Analysis: Augmenting Paper Affinity Diagrams. In: *Proceedings of the ACM 2012 Conference on Computer Supported Cooperative Work*. New York: ACM.

Hauschildt, J., & Salomo, S. (2007). *Innovationsmanagement*. 4th edition. München: Vahlen.

Hennink, M., Hutter, I. & Bailey, A. (2011). *Qualitative Research Methods*. London: Sage.

Herrmann, T. & Nolte, A. (2010). The Integration of Collaborative Process Modeling and Electronic Brainstorming in Co-located Meetings. In: Kolfschoten, G., Herrmann, T. & Lukosch, S. (eds) *Collaboration and Technology*. Springer.

Hevner, A., March, S.T., Park, J. & Ram, S. (2004). Design Science in Information System Research. *MIS Quarterly 28*(1), 75-105.

Hilliges, O., Terrenghi, L., Boring, S., Kim, D., Richter, H. & Butz, A. (2007). Designing for collaborative creative problem solving. In: *Proceedings of the 6th ACM SIGCHI Conference on Creativity & Cognition*. Washington: ACM.

Jetter, H.C., Geyer, F., Reiterer, H., Dachselt, R., Fischer, G., Groh, R., Haller, M. & Herrmann, T. (2012). Designing Collaborative Interactive Spaces. In: *Proceedings of the International Working Conference on Advanced Visual Interfaces*. New York: ACM.

Katzenbach, J.R. & Smith, D.K. (2003). *Teams: Der Schlüssel zur Hochleistungsorganisation*. Frankfurt: Moderne Industrie.

Kolfschoten, G., & Vreede, G.-J. (2007). The Collaboration Engineering Approach for Designing. In: Haake, J., Ochoa, S. & Cechich, A. (eds) *Groupware: Design, Implementation, and Use*. Berlin: Springer.

Krcmar, H., Böhmann, T. & Klein, A. (2001). Sitzungsunterstützungssysteme. In: Schwabe, G., Streitz, N. & Unland, R. (eds) *CSCW-Kompendium*, Springer.

Mark, G., Haake, J.M. & Steritz, N.A. (1997). Hypermedia Use in Group Work: Changing the Product, Process, and Strategy. *Computer Supported Cooperative Work 6*(4), 327-368.

Nebe, K., Müller, T. & Klompmaker, F. (2011). An Investigation on Requirements for Co-located Group-Work Using Multitouch-, Pen-Based- and Tangible-Interaction. In: *Proceedings of the 14th International Conference on Human-Computer Interaction: Interaction Techniques and Environments - Volume Part II*. Springer.

Nielsen, M. F. (2012). Using Artifacts in Brainstorming Sessions to Secure Participation and Decouple Sequentiality. *Discourse Studies 14*(1), 87-109.

Nunamaker, J.F., Dennis, A.R., Valacich, J.S., Vogel, D. & George, J.F. (1991). Electronic Meeting Systems to Support Group Work. *Communications of the ACM 34*(7), 40-61.

Peffers, K., Tuunanen, T., Rothenberger, M.A. & Chatterjee, S. (2007). A Design Science Research Methodology for Information Systems Research. *Journal of Management Information Systems 24*(3), 45–77.

Schultze, U. & Avital, M. (2011). Designing Interviews to Generate Rich Data for Information Systems Research. *Information and Organization 21* (1), 1-16.

Schwabe, G. (1995). *Objekte der Gruppenarbeit: Ein Konzept für das Computer Aided Team*. Wiesbaden: Gabler.

Scott, S.D., Grant, K.D. & Mandryk, R.L. (2003). System Guidelines for Co-located, Collaborative Work on a Tabletop Display. In: *Proceedings of the Eighth Conference on European Conference on Computer Supported Cooperative Work*. Norwell: Kluwer Academic Publishers.

Stacey, K. & Vincent, J. (2011). Evaluation of an Electronic Interview with Multimedia Stimulus Materials for Gaining In-Depth Responses from Professionals. *Qualitative Research 11*(5), 605-624.

Streitz, N.A., Geißler, J., Holmer, T., Konomi, S., Müller-Thomfelde, C., Reischl, W., Rexroth, P., Seitz, P. & Steinmetz, R. (1999). i-LAND: an Interactive Landscape for Creativity and Innovation. In: *Proceedings of the SIGCHI Conference on Human Factors in Computing Systems*. New York: ACM.

Streitz, N.A., Tandler, P., Müller-Tomfelde, C., & Konomi, S. (2001). Roomware: Towards the Next Generation of Human-Computer Interaction Based on an Integrated Design of Real and Virtual Worlds. In: Carroll, J.M. (Ed) *Human-Computer Interaction in the New Millennium*. Addison-Wesley.

M. Koch, A. Butz & J. Schlichter (Hrsg.): Mensch und Computer 2014 Tagungsband,
München: Oldenbourg Wissenschaftsverlag, 2014, S. 65-74.

FabAR: Interaktive Fabrikation von 3D-Drucken durch Mashups

Christoph Beckmann, Mirko Fetter, Tom Gross

Lehrstuhl für Mensch-Computer-Interaktion, Otto-Friedrich-Universität Bamberg

Zusammenfassung

FabAR ist Interaktionskonzept und Werkzeug für die interaktive digitale Fabrikation von 3D-Modellen für den 3D-Druck durch Mashups. Benutzerinnen und Benutzer können durch das Zusammenspiel von Gestensteuerung und Augmented-Reality-Benutzungsschnittstelle 3D-Modelle direkt im 3D-Drucker bearbeiten, in Relation zu realen Objekten sehen und mehrfach miteinander kombinieren ohne auf komplexe CAD-Programme oder 3D-Modellierungswerkzeuge zurückzugreifen.

1 Einleitung und Hintergrund

Digital Fabrication (Gershenfeld 2005) verspricht Benutzerinnen und Benutzern die Herstellung von Gegenständen des täglichen Gebrauchs im eigenen Zuhause und findet immer raschere Verbreitung. Die Spannbreite der Anwendungsszenarien reicht von schnellen Reparaturen, wie einen Ersatzdeckel für den Wasserkocher bis hin zur Herstellung von selbstgestalteten Hüllen für ein Smartphone. Dabei sind neuartige Technologien wie 3D-Drucker und Lasercutter — die immer einfacher zugänglich und erschwinglicher werden — die treibende Kraft für die Umsetzung dieser Szenarien. Durch Entwicklungen wie FabLabs und Crowdfunding-Plattformen, propagieren einige den Beginn einer dritten industriellen Revolution: alle können eigene, physische Waren erzeugen, modifizieren und reparieren.

Während die zugrundeliegenden Technologien für die eigene, digitale Herstellung günstiger, verfügbarer und einfacher werden, ist die Gestaltung von 3D-Modellen als Eingabedaten, komplex, fehleranfällig und entkörpert. Aktuelle GUI-basierte CAD- und 3D-Modellierungswerkzeuge zum Entwerfen oder Modifizieren eigener Modelle erzeugen eine künstliche, digitale Barriere zwischen den Benutzerinnen und Benutzern (vornehmlich mit keiner oder wenig Erfahrung mit 3D-Modellierung) und den Werkstücken (Willis *et al.* 2011). Für sie ist die Lernkurve solcher GUI-basierter Werkzeuge oft sehr steil. Auch können sie etwa nur schwer die Relation zwischen virtuellen Modellen und vorhanden realen Objekten abschätzen, um diese nach dem 3D-Druck zu kombinieren. Somit fehlt ein Werkzeug, welches das Erstellen und Bearbeiten von Modellen für den 3D-Druck ermöglicht (Lau *et al.* 2012). Ansätze, wie *Interaktive Fabrikation* und *Situative Modellierung* wurden in der

Literatur als Lösungen vorgeschlagen. Interaktive Fabrikation überbrückt die digitalen Barriere durch alternative Benutzungsschnittstellen (Willis *et al.* 2011). Situative Modellierung führt Augmented Reality (AR) ein, um Objekte durch die überlagerte Darstellung von digitalen und realen Objekten einfacher miteinander zu kombinieren (Lau *et al.* 2012). Auch haben sich im Umfeld von 3D-Druckern Plattformen zum einfachen Austausch von 3D-Modellen für den Druck wie Thingiverse[1] und Bld3r[2] etabliert.

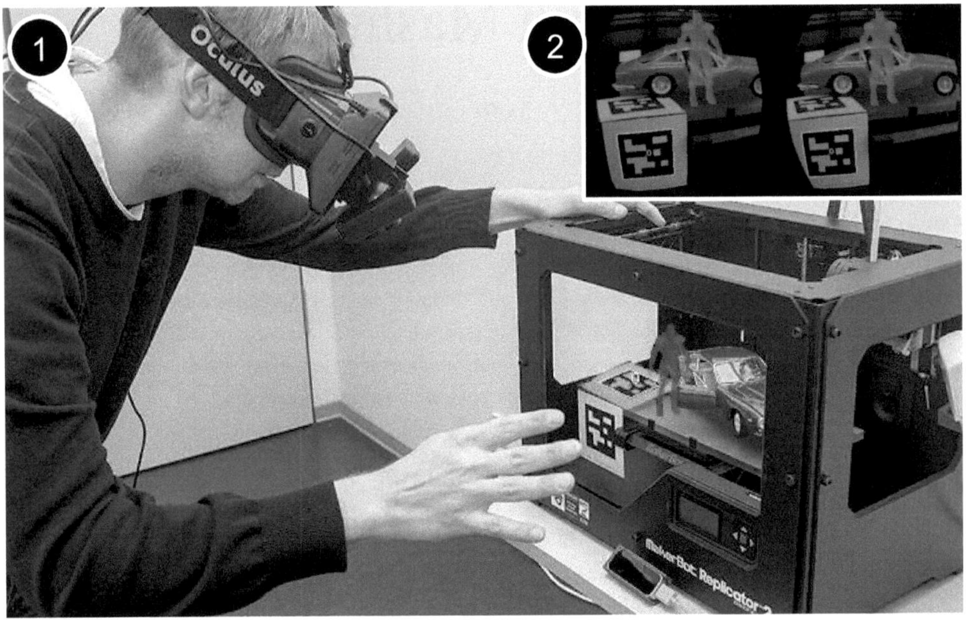

Abbildung 1. Das große Bild (1) zeigt FabAR während der Interaktion mit virtuellen und realen Objekten. Das kleine Bild (2) zeigt die stereoskopische Darstellung im AR-Headset.

Im vorliegenden Beitrag stellen wir mit FabAR ein Interaktionskonzept und ein System für die *Interaktive Fabrikation* von 3D-Drucken vor (siehe Abbildung 1). Es kombiniert die Stärken der oben beschriebenen Ansätze. Basierend auf dem Paradigma des Mashups (Hartmann *et al.* 2008) ermöglicht es Benutzerinnen und Benutzern direkt innerhalb eines 3D-Druckers und damit innerhalb des für die Fabrikation entscheidenden Referenzrahmens neue 3D-Modelle durch Bearbeiten und Kombinieren bestehender Modelle herzustellen. FabAR bietet durch das Zusammenspiel von AR und gestenbasierter Eingabe eine hohe Immersion. Nachfolgend stellen wir verwandte Arbeiten vor, beschreiben FabAR inklusive Benutzungsinteraktion, Anwendungsszenario, Implementierung, erstem Feedback und diskutieren unser Interaktionskonzept in Relation zum erhaltenen Feedback.

[1] http://www.thingiverse.com

[2] http://www.bld3r.com

2 Verwandte Arbeiten

Der Begriff *Interaktive Fabrikation* wurde basierend auf einigen Prototypen, die auf physischen Eingabemethoden setzen, um künstlerische, skulpturale Objekte zu erzeugen, geprägt (Willis *et al.* 2011). Andere, stärker technisch motivierte Ansätze im Bereich der *Interaktive Fabrikation,* sind einerseits FreeD V2 (Zoran *et al.* 2013), ein in der Hand haltbares Fräswerkzeug zum granularen Bearbeiten von bestehenden 3D-Modellen, und andererseits, das Constructable System (Mueller *et al.* 2012), welches Laser-Pointer als direktes Eingabewerkzeug für Schnitt- und Biegekanten eines Laser-Cutters einsetzt.

Der Begriff *Situative Modellierung* basiert auf zwei Systemen, die mittels AR eine explizite Referenz zu realen, physischen Objekten herstellen (Lau et al. 2012). Weitere Ansätze, wie CopyCAD (Follmer *et al.* 2010) und MixFab (Weichel *et al.* 2014) erlauben die Integration der Geometrie realer Objekten in 3D-Modelle. In diesem Zusammenhang wurde bereits gestenbasierte Eingabe zur Manipulation von 3D-Modellen erprobt. In MixFab können innerhalb einer durch Spezialhardware, dem Holodesk, definierten Mixed-Reality Umgebung reale Objekte gescannt und mit primitiven Formen durch Gesten zu neuen Objekten kombiniert werden. Spatial Sketch (Willis *et al.* 2011) und Sketch Funiture[3] ermöglichen es, durch Gesten im freien Raum, Design-Objekte und Möbel zu erstellen. Industrielle Kooperationen wie die zwischen Softkinetic und Makerbot adressieren in erster Linie das Einscannen von realen Objekten und gehen bezüglich der Kombination von virtuellen Modellen und realen Objekten momentan nicht über Produktankündigungen hinaus. Aktuelle AR- und gestenbasierte Systeme wie MetaPro[4] zeigen in diesem Zusammenhang die Realisierbarkeit von holographischen Benutzungsschnittstellen zur Erzeugung von 3D-Modellen ohne die Stärken der Überlagerung von realen Modellen und virtuellen Objekten zu nutzen. Darüberhinaus existieren jedoch weder Konzepte noch Systeme für die Interaktive Fabrikation innerhalb eines 3D-Drucker — der als für Benutzerinnen und Benutzern bekannte Referenz für die Interaktion von 3D-Modellen und realen Objekten dient.

Im Bereich der konventionellen CAD-Werkzeuge senken einfache und Web-basierte Programme die Einstiegsbarriere durch Reduktion des Funktionsumfangs (bspw. AutoDesk Tinkercad[5], AutoDesk 123D Design[6] und Thingiverse Customizer[7]). Jedoch erlauben es diese Werkzeuge nicht reale Objekte in Referenz zu 3D-Modellen zu setzen und bieten daher in Anwendungsszenarien nur wenig Unterstützung. Web-Dienste, wie Thingiverse bieten die Möglichkeit 3D-Modelle zu teilen und im bereits für den 3D-Druck optimierten Format runterzuladen. Jedoch scheitern Benutzerinnen und Benutzer häufig an der Anpassung der Modelle für ihr Anwendungsszenario ohne auf komplexe CAD-Werkzeuge für vergleichsweise triviale Anpassungen an reale Objekte zurückzugreifen.

---

[3] http://www.designfront.org/category.php?id=81&product=191

[4] http://www.spaceglasses.com/

[5] http://tinkercad.com/

[6] http://www.123dapp.com/design

[7] https://www.thingiverse.com/apps/customizer

3 FabAR

Für die *Interaktive Fabrikation* adressieren wir drei Herausforderungen mit FabAR: (1) bestehende Werkzeuge für die Modellierung von 3D-Drucken sind komplex. Benutzerinnen und Benutzer greifen häufig nur auf einen Bruchteil der Funktionen der Werkzeuge zurück und sind daher oft durch den großen Funktionsumfang überfordert. (2) Web-Dienste bieten zwar einen einfachen Zugang zu 3D-Modellen, jedoch benötigen Benutzerinnen und Benutzer einfache Werkzeuge um kleine und exakte Modifikationen der 3D-Modelle an ihren Anwendungskontext vorzunehmen. (3) Der Integrationsprozess (d.h. das Einpassen von 3D-Modellen in bestehende Gegenstände) ist häufig fehleranfällig und das bedeutet, dass Benutzerinnen und Benutzer mittels Ausprobierens 3D-Modelle mehrfach drucken und anpassen müssen (d.h. ein hoher Einsatz von Zeit bis zu mehreren Stunden und Druckmaterialien), bis sie mit dem Ergebnis zufrieden sind.

FabAR löst diese künstliche, digitale Barriere der klassischen und komplexen GUI-basierten Werkzeuge zugunsten einer einfachen Interaktion mit hoher Immersion. Nachfolgend beschreiben wir das Interaktionskonzept, ein Anwendungsszenario und die Implementierung.

3.1 Interaktionskonzept von FabAR

FabAR kombiniert Augmented Reality und gestenbasierte Eingaben, sodass Benutzerinnen und Benutzer interaktiv geladene 3D-Modelle direkt im 3D-Drucker auf dem Druckbett bearbeiten. Das Arbeiten im 3D-Drucker ist zentral, indem es den Kontext der Benutzung beachtet (vgl. Gross 2013) und infolgedessen den 3D-Druck bereits im Vorfeld abschätzen lässt. Zur besseren Einschätzung von Größenverhältnissen und einer späteren Passung können Benutzerinnen und Benutzer dem Paradigma des Mashups (Hartmann *et al.* 2008) folgen indem sie reale Objekte direkt neben virtuelle 3D-Modelle platzieren und sich so zeitaufwändige Anpassungen durch Ausprobieren ersparen (siehe Abbildung : reales rotes Auto und virtuelle grüne Figur). Durch Finger- und Handgesten vor dem 3D-Drucker können sie interaktiv 3D-Modelle direkt auf dem Druckbett positionieren und bewegen, sowie mit einem speziell auf ihre Bedürfnisse zugeschnittenen Funktionsumfang 3D-Modelle bearbeiten und miteinander kombinieren.

Für die Interaktion mit FabAR führen wir das Prinzip der *linearen schrittweisen Komposition* in Anlehnung an die Vorgehensweise der konstruktiven Festkörpergeometrie (Voelcker & Requicha 1977) ein: Benutzerinnen und Benutzer bauen iterativ ihr gewünschtes 3D-Modell für den Druck zusammen. Dazu kombinieren sie zwei bestehende Modelle in ein neues, welches dann weiter kombiniert werden kann; es können gleichzeitig maximal zwei Modelle bearbeitet werden. Wenn nur ein 3D-Modell geladen ist, so werden alle Bearbeitungen exklusiv darauf ausgeführt. Wird es zweites 3D-Modell geladen, so kann zwischen den Modellen zur Bearbeitung ausgewählt werden. In dem Moment, in dem ein drittes 3D-Modell geladen wird, werden die ersten beiden Modelle zu einem Modell kombiniert; sie können fortan nur als eine Einheit bearbeitet werden — ähnlich zur Gruppierungsfunktion in Grafikprogrammen. Diese Vorgehensweise führt zu einem linearen Prozess der iterativen Komposition (d.h. Kombination und Bearbeitung) bestehender 3D-Modelle.

Zur Komposition von 3D-Modellen bietet FabAR fünf grundlegende Bearbeitungsfunktionen an die durch Gesten ausgeführt und direkt angewendet werden (siehe Abbildung 2): Laden, Skalieren, Rotieren, Positionieren, und Auswählen von 3D-Modellen.

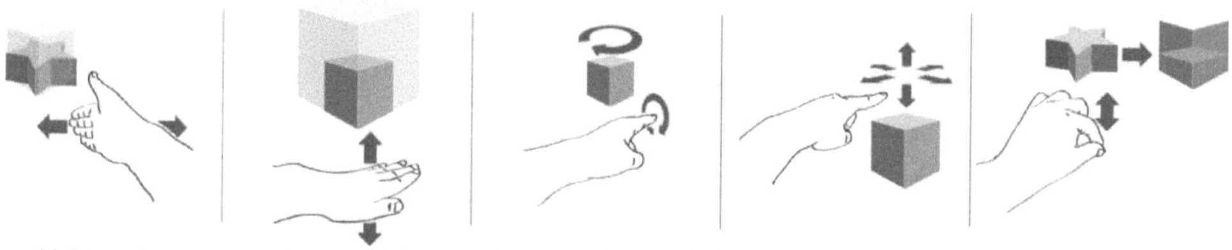

Abbildung 2. Die Bearbeitungsfunktionen und Gesten: Laden, Skalieren, Rotieren, Positionieren, und Auswählen.

Benutzerinnen und Benutzer können 3D-Modelle mittels einer horizontalen Wischgeste vor dem 3D-Drucker laden, indem sie durch einen Katalog an verfügbaren Modellen navigieren. Das Wischen von links nach rechts zeigt jeweils das nachfolgende und in die andere Richtung das vorherige Modell. Um ein Modell zu skalieren, führen sie eine vertikale Wischgeste auf dem aktuell geladenen Modell aus. Dabei wird jedes Wischen von unten nach oben in eine kontinuierliche Vergrößerung des ausgewählten Modells übersetzt. Das Wischen von oben nach unten verkleinert das Modell. Kreisförmiges Bewegen des Zeigefingers ist eine Rotation des 3D-Modells; die Rotationsrichtung des Modells ist mit der Bewegungsrichtung des Fingers synchronisiert. Die Rotationsgeschwindigkeit in Form einer nicht-isomorphen Übersetzung erlaubt eine feingranulare Rotation des 3D-Modells. Positionieren des 3D-Modells wird mit einer Zeigegeste realisiert. Dazu bewegen Benutzerinnen und Benutzer ihre Zeigefinger anhand der x-, y-, und z-Achse; das 3D-Modell folgt diesen Bewegungen. Das Auswählen von 3D-Modellen ist an die Zwickgeste gebunden, d.h. das Zusammenführen von Daumen- und Zeigefingerspitzen.

Ausgehend vom beschriebenen Paradigma des linearen iterativen Komponierens sind drei Zustände für eine Selektion möglich, durch die gewechselt werden kann: das erste Modell ist selektiert (d.h. alle Bearbeitungen erfolgen am ersten Modell), das zweite Model ist selektiert (d.h. alle Bearbeitungen erfolgen am zweiten Modell), beide Modelle sind selektiert (d.h. alle Bearbeitungen erfolgen an beiden Modellen als eine Einheit). Wird dann die Wischgeste zum Laden aktiviert, so werden die beiden selektierten Modelle in ein logisches Modell überführt.

3.2 Anwendungsszenario von FabAR

Zur Illustration der Benutzungsinteraktion von FabAR — dem Zusammenspiel der Gesten mit virtuellen 3D-Modellen und realen Objekten — zeigen wir nachfolgend die schrittweise Konstruktion eines 3D-Modells anhand eines Szenarios.

Eine Medienkünstlerin möchte mit einem *LEAP Motion Controller* Gesten von oben aufnehmen und anschließend für eine Installation verarbeiten. Zur einfachen Positionierung des Controllers für Ihren Prototypen entschließt sie sich diesen an eine Schreibtischlampe zu montieren — jedoch weiß sie nicht genau wie. Auf Thingiverse findet sie zahlreiche Gehäuse und Halterungen für den *LEAP Motion Controller*, aber keine passt an die

Schreibtischlampe. Sie sucht weiter nach einer Lösung zur Montage und entdeckt ein 3D-Modell eines E27-Schraubgewindes (dem Gewinde einer herkömmlichen Glühbirne). Sie lädt zwei Modelle runter, das E27-Schraubgewinde und eine Halterung für den Controller.

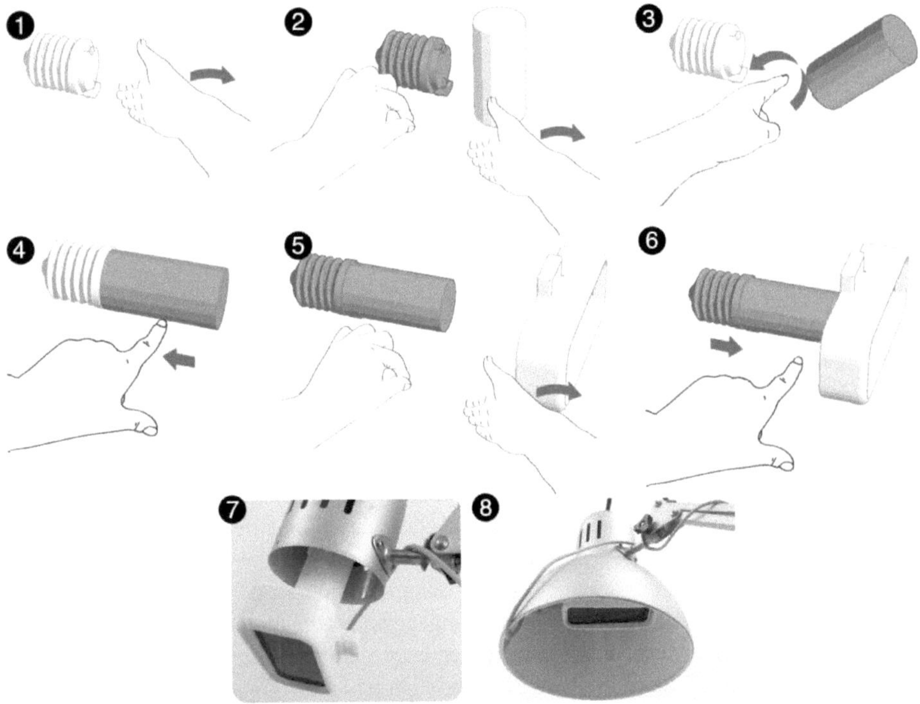

Abbildung 3. Die Benutzerin lädt das Schraubgewinde (1) und lädt den Zylinder (2) während Sie das Schraubgewinde mit der Zwickgeste festhält. Sie rotiert den Zylinder (3) und verschiebt diesen passgenau an das Schraubgewinde (4). Sie hält das kombinierte Objekt fest und lädt die Halterung dazu (5). Sie schiebt das neue Objekt an die Halterung (6). Nach dem Druck passt die Halterung in die Schraubfassung (7) und unter den Lampenschirm (8).

Mit FabAR kann sie die beiden Modelle laden und in ein neues, druckbares Modell kombinieren (siehe Abbildung 3). Sie legt die realen Objekte (d.h. Controller und Kopf der Schreibtischlampe) in den 3D-Drucker und sieht, dass die 3D-Modelle schon die richtige Größe haben. Entsprechend rotiert und transliert sie die Halterung des Controllers und positioniert diesen mit etwas Überlappung an das Schraubgewinde. Sie positioniert den Kopf der Schreibtischlampe so wie später die neue Halterung passen soll. Dabei stellt sie fest, dass der Lampenschirm zu eng ist um die breite Halterung des Controllers vollständig aufzunehmen: sie braucht eine Verlängerung zwischen Schraubgewinde und Halterung. Einen einfachen Zylinder (Mittelteil in Abbildung 3.6) findet sie ebenfalls bei Thingiverse und lädt diesen runter. Sie platziert die 3D-Modelle jeweils mit etwas Überlappung und druckt. Nach ca. 3 Stunden ist der Druck fertig; es passt perfekt (siehe Abbildung 3.7 und Abbildung 3.8).

3.3 Implementierung von FabAR

FabAR basiert auf Standardkomponenten: einem Makerbot Replicator 2 als 3D-Drucker, einem LEAP Motion Controller zur gestenbasierten Eingabe und einer Oculus Rift in Kombination mit zwei PS 3 Eye Kameras als günstiges AR-Headset. Unsere Software-Architektur folgt dem modularen Ansatz von openFrameworks[8] mit einer `FARController` Kontrollklasse und vier Subsystemen: `FARFrameGrabber`, `FARAR`, `FARDraw`, und `FARView`. Nachfolgend beschreiben wir die Bearbeitungsschritte.

Zur stereoskopischen Präsentation der Szene im AR-Headset benutzen wir zwei Kameras. Im `FARFrameGrabber` werden die Bilder beider via USB angeschlossenen Kameras abgerufen, rotiert und gespiegelt um die richtige Perspektive einzustellen. Vorbereitend für die AR-Markererkennung fertigen wir je eine S/W-Version der Einzelbilderpaare und eine Version mit reduziertem Tonwertumfang anhand eines Schwellwertes an. Letztere Version wird dann innerhalb des `FARAR` Subsystems zur AR-Markererkennung mittels des ARToolKit+ (Wagner & Schmalstieg 2007) weiterverarbeitet: für uns ist die Position des AR-Markers an dem Druckbett für die Platzierung von 3D-Modellen von Interesse. Die originalen Einzelbilderpaare werden im `FARDraw` Subsystem in einem OpenGL-Contexts nebeneinander und die aktivierten 3D-Modelle an die korrespondierenden Koordinaten gezeichnet. Um eine gewarpte stereoskopische Repräsentation zur Darstellung im AR-Headset zu erhalten wenden wir innerhalb des `FARView` Subsystems Vertex- und Fragmet-Shader an (siehe Abbildung .2). Die Darstellung läuft flüssig mit ca. 60 fps.

Zur Gestenerkennung greifen wir auf die vordefinierten Wisch-, Zeige- und Kreisgesten der LEAP C++ API[9] zurück und erkennen zusätzlich die Zwickgeste durch Auswertung der Positionen der Fingerspitzen. Der `FARController` verarbeitet alle Gesteneingaben und propagiert diese direkt an alle aktiven 3D-Modelle. Änderungen sind sofort sichtbar und persistent an den 3D-Modellen; diese können im STL-Format im- und exportiert werden.

4 Erstes Feedback zu FabAR

Für eine erste, informelle Benutzungsstudie zu FabAR rekrutierten wir 22 (zwei weibliche) Teilnehmerinnen und Teilnehmer zwischen 18 und 44 ($M = 25.93$; $SD = 5.97$) Jahren. Nach einer kurzen Erklärung von FabAR und dem Anpassen des AR-Headsets konnten die Teilnehmerinnen und Teilnehmer selbstständig FabAR für einige Minuten ausprobieren. In dieser ersten Studie waren wir in erster Linie an Rückmeldungen zur Robustheit von FabAR interessiert und haben daher die Teilnehmerinnen und Teilnehmer aufgefordert den Interaktionsrahmen sukzessive zu explorieren anstelle ihnen feste Aufgaben zuzuweisen und Bearbeitungszeiten zu messen; im 3D-Drucker waren das rote Auto wie in Abbildung zu sehen und Beispiel-3D-Modelle präpariert. Während des Tests haben wir die Interaktion der

[8] http://www.openframeworks.cc

[9] http://developer.leapmotion.com/ documentation/cpp/api/Leap.Frame.html

Teilnehmerinnen und Teilnehmer vor dem 3D-Drucker mit FabAR beobachtet und die stereoskopische Ansicht auf einem zweiten Bildschirm verfolgt. Wir konnten so die AR- und Gesten-Tracking-Genauigkeit analysieren sowie Eindrücke von der Interaktion an sich erhalten. Nach dem Test haben die Teilnehmerinnen und Teilnehmer den standardisierten INTUI Fragebogen (Ullrich & Diefenbach 2010) zu FabAR ausgefüllt (17 Fragen jeweils Likert-skaliert von 1-7) und so die Einfachheit der Interaktion mit FabAR bewertet.

Die Beobachtungen während der Studie zeigen vor allem zwei Dinge: (1) der Grad der Immersion, d.h. die stereoskopische Überlagerung von 3D-Modellen und realen Objekten war für viele Teilnehmerinnen und Teilnehmer ungewohnt, jedoch sehr hilfreich um Größen- und Passungsverhältnisse abschätzen zu können. Einige Teilnehmerinnen und Teilnehmer öffneten beispielsweise die Türen des roten Autos um 3D-Modelle von Figuren besser positionieren und skalieren zu können. Häufig haben wir beobachtet, dass sie ihre Perspektive auf die Szene im 3D-Drucker durch Veränderung von Körperhaltung, Abstand und Blickrichtung angepasst haben um Bearbeitungen genauer durchzuführen. (2) Auch wenn die Erkennung der AR-Marker zuverlässig war, kam es in den Grenzbereichen des AR-Headsets zu einer monoskopischen Überlagerung von 3D-Modellen und realen Objekten (d.h. wenn eine sehr steile Perspektive eingenommen wurde, so dass der Marker nur von einer Kamera erkannt wurde) — dies wurden von keinem Teilnehmenden expliziert.

Die Auswertung der INTUI-Fragebögen zeigt, dass die Teilnehmerinnen und Teilnehmer die Interaktion mit FabAR als überdurchschnittlich intuitiv beurteilen (Skala INT: $M = 5.14$, $SD = 1.08$). Besonders die Verbalisierungsfähigkeiten (Skala V: $M = 5.59$, $SD = 1.21$) und das magische Erleben (Skala X: $M = 5.47$, $SD = 1.00$) wurden positiv bewertet. Weiterhin bewerteten sie die Interaktion mit FabAR als eher mühelos (Skala M: $M = 4.27$, $SD = .90$), und beurteilten ihr Vorgehen als eher gefühlsgeleitet (Skala G: $M = 4.35$, $SD = 1.47$).

5 Diskussion

FabAR als Interaktionskonzept und System adressiert die Herausforderungen der *Interaktiven Fabrikation* aktiv und befähigt Benutzerinnen und Benutzer als Novizen im Bereich des 3D-Drucks ihr Ziel — im Sinne des Anwendungsszenarios — mühelos zu erreichen. Den Grundsätzen von Myers et al. (2000) folgend haben wir das Interaktionskonzept von FabAR bewusst minimal gestaltet: ein Interface soll sowohl einen einfachen Einstieg ermöglichen als auch genügend Reserven zur Bearbeitung komplexerer Aufgaben bereitstellen. Wie das erste Feedback von Benutzerinnen und Benutzern zeigt, unterstützt FabAR bereits den einfachen Einstieg. Komplexere Kompositionen mit einer Vielzahl an 3D-Modellen sind in FabAR möglich, jedoch haben wir vorerst komplexere Interaktionskonzepte zugunsten einer einfachen gestenbasierten Eingabe bewusst außen vor gelassen. Nachfolgend diskutieren wir die Möglichkeiten komplexerer Interaktions-möglichkeiten im Zusammenhang mit unseren ersten Beobachtungen.

Die Benutzerinnen und Benutzern sind von dem hohen Grad der Immersion in FabAR begeistert und zugleich mit einer für sie neuen Form der Interaktion konfrontiert. Einerseits konnten wir die Begeisterung direkt beobachten: die Benutzerinnen und Benutzer interagierten zugleich mit realen und virtuellen Objekten im 3D-Drucker und passten durch Gesten die 3D-Modelle den realen Gegenständen an. Auch bewerteten die Benutzerinnen und Benutzer die Skalen Verbalisierungsfähigkeit und magisches Erleben des Fragebogens hoch. Andererseits hat FabAR auf den Skalen Mühelosigkeit und Bauchgefühl nur knapp überdurchschnittlich gute Werte erhalten. Auch leitet sich aus dem Interaktionskonzept eine direkt strukturierte Arbeitsweise zum Erstellen von komplexeren Objekten ab. Der derzeitige Prozess ist strikt linear, d.h. zwei 3D-Modelle müssen vor dem Laden eines dritten Modells in ihrer nicht-abänderbaren Kombination sein. Prinzipiell sind auch große Kompositionen von 3D-Modellen möglich, sicher sind aber nur Kompositionen mit bis zu fünf 3D-Modellen praktikabel, da sich sonst die Zahl der nicht-abänderbaren Arbeitsschritte zu stark erhöht. Daher schlagen wir zwei einfache, aber unserer Auffassung nach wirkungsvolle Funktionen zur Integration vor: (1) *Rückgängig und Wiederholen* ermöglicht kurzfristige Korrekturen und (2) eine *Zwischenablage* gibt Freiraum um gute Modellkompositionen zu einem späteren Zeitpunkt einzusetzen. Beides sind klar Standardfunktionen interaktiver GUI-basierter System, jedoch ergeben sich in Kontext der Interaktiven Fabrikation neue Herausforderungen der Selektion und Gruppierung von 3D-Modellen. Das Zyklieren der Selektion, wie im aktuellen Prototypen möglich, ist bei mehr als drei Modellen unserer Ansicht nach anstrengend. Da bestehende Ansätze der Selektion im freien Raum durch einfach handhabbare Gesten nur wenig erforscht sind ergibt sich ein breites Feld für weitere Arbeiten (vgl. Vogel & Balakrishnan 2005).

Wir konnten beobachten, wie Benutzerinnen und Benutzer ihre Perspektive veränderten um Bearbeitungsschritte mit einer höheren Genauigkeit auszuführen, so sind sie bspw. zur Translation eines 3D-Modells näher an den 3D-Drucker herangetreten. Auch interpretieren wir die nur knapp überdurchschnittliche Bewertung auf der Skala Mühelosigkeit in Richtung der akkuraten Platzierung von 3D-Modellen auf dem Druckbett. In FabAR werden 3D-Modelle durch die Zeigegeste freihändig in der Luft durchgeführt. Die fehlende Genauigkeit dieser Freihandpositionen und mögliche Lösungen sind im Bereich der interaktiven Systeme bekannt — durch den Schnappmechanismus (Bier & Stone 1986) kann in FabAR eine höhere Präzision erreicht werden, ohne dass neue Gesten oder Steuerungsmöglichkeiten hinzugefügt werden müssen. Das Anbieten eines spezifischen Bearbeitungswerkzeugs zum Justieren und Ausrichten von 3D-Modellen als weitere Lösungsmöglichkeit erfordert hingegen wieder zusätzliche Gesten oder Steuerungsmöglichkeiten.

6 Resümee

Zusammenfassend haben wir mit FabAR sowohl ein Interaktionskonzept, als auch ein System vorgestellt, das es Benutzerinnen und Benutzern ermöglicht interaktiv 3D-Modelle für den 3D-Druck durch Mashups vorhandener Modelle herzustellen. FabAR zeigt die technische Umsetzbarkeit dieser Idee im Druckraum eines 3D-Druckers. Die informelle Benutzungsstudie zeigt, dass FabAR bereits intuitiv durch Benutzerinnen und Benutzer einzusetzen ist. In der Diskussion konnten wir zeigen, dass der Interaktionsraum 3D-Drucker viele Möglichkeiten der Integration nützlicher Funktionen etablierter 3D-Werkzeuge offen lässt und gleichzeitig die Herausforderungen einer handhabbaren Steuerung hoch sind.

Literaturverzeichnis

Bier, E.A. & Stone, M.C. Snap-Dragging. In *13th Annual Conference on Computer Graphics and Interactive Techniques - SIGGRAPH 1986* (18.-22. Aug., Dallas, TX). ACM Press, NY, 1986. pp. 233-240.

Follmer, S., Carr, D., Lovell, E. & Ishii, H. CopyCAD: Remixing Physical Objects With Copy and Paste From the Real World. In *23rd Annual ACM Symposium on User Interface Software and Technology - UIST 2010* (3.-6. Okt., New York NY). ACM Press, NY, 2010. pp. 381-382.

Gershenfeld, N. *Fab: The Coming Revolution on Your Desktop--from Personal Computers to Personal Fabrication.* Basic Books, Cambridge, MA, 2005.

Gross, T. Mensch-Computer-Interaktion in Wissenschaft und Praxis. *HMD - Praxis der Wirtschafts-informatik 50*, 294 (Dez. 2013). pp. 6-15.

Hartmann, B., Doorley, S. & Klemmer, S.R. Hacking, Mashing, Gluing: Understanding Opportunistic Design. *IEEE Pervasive Computing* 7, 3 (Juli 2008). pp. 46-54.

Mueller, S., Lopes, P. & Baudisch, P. Interactive Construction: Interactive Fabrication of Functional Mechanical Devices. In *25th Annual ACM Symposium on User Interface Software and Technology - UIST 2012* (7.-10. Okt., Cambridge, MA). ACM Press, NY, 2012. pp. 599-606.

Myers, B., Hudson, S.E. & Pausch, R. Past, Present and Future of User Interface Software Tools. *ACM Transactions on Computer-Human Interaction* 7, 1 (März 2000). pp. 3-28.

Ullrich, D. & Diefenbach, S. INTUI. Exploring the Facets of Intuitive Interaction. In *Mensch & Computer - M&C 2010* (12.-15. Sep., Duisburg). Oldenbourg, München, 2010. pp. 57-62.

Voelcker, H.B. & Requicha, A.A.G. Constructive Solid Geometry. *Reportnummer: TM-25, University of Rochester*. Production Automation Project, Rochester, N.Y., Nov. 1977.

Vogel, D. & Balakrishnan, R. Distant Freehand Pointing and Clicking on Very Large, High Resolution Displays. In *18th Annual ACM Symposium on User Interface Software and Technology - UIST 2005* (23.-26. Okt., Seattle, WA). ACM Press, NY, 2005. pp. 33-42.

Wagner, D. & Schmalstieg, D. ARToolKitPlus for Pose Tracking on Mobile Devices. In *12th Computer Vision Winter Workshop - CVWW 2007* (6.-8. Feb., Sankt Lambrecht, Österreich). 2007. pp. 1–8.

Weichel, C., Lau, M., Kim, D., Villar, N. & Gellersen, H. MixFab: A Mixed-Reality Environment for Personal Fabrication. In *Conference on Human Factors in Computing Systems - CHI 2014* (1. Apr.-1.Mai, Toronto, Ontario, Kanada). ACM Press, NY, 2014. pp. 3855-3864.

Willis, K.D.D., Xu, C., Wu, K.-J., Levin, G. & Gross, M.D. Interactive Fabrication: New Interfaces for Digital Fabrication. In *Fifth International Conference on Tangible Embedded Interaction - TEI 2011* (23.-26. Jan., Funchal, Portugal). ACM Press, NY, 2011. pp. 69-72.

Zoran, A., Shilkrot, R. & Paradiso, J. Human-Computer Interaction for Hybrid Carving. In *26th Annual ACM Symposium on User Interface Software and Technology - UIST 2013* (8.-11. Okt., St. Andrews, Schottland). ACM Press, NY, 2013. pp. 433-440.

Kontaktinformationen

Prof. Dr. Tom Gross, tom.gross(at)uni-bamberg.de, T. 0951-863-3940

M. Koch, A. Butz & J. Schlichter (Hrsg.): Mensch und Computer 2014 Tagungsband, München: Oldenbourg Wissenschaftsverlag, 2014, S. 75-84.

Entwurf und Evaluation eines Kommunikationskanals für Gesten in kollaborativen virtuellen 3D-Welten

Stefan Wittek[1], Niels Pinkwart[2]

Institut für Informatik, Technische Universität Clausthal[1]
Institut für Informatik, Humboldt-Universität zu Berlin[2]

Zusammenfassung

Diese Arbeit beschäftigt sich mit der Frage, wie sich ein direkter und kontinuierlicher Kommunikationskanal für Gesten in kollaborativen virtuellen 3D Welten auf die Benutzer dieser Welten auswirkt. Als Basis für die Untersuchung dieser Frage wird ein Prototyp vorgestellt, der Gesten mit Hilfe der Microsoft Kinect erfassen und übertragen kann. Weitere Interaktionen mit der 3D-Welt sind durch die Wii Remote möglich. Eine durchgeführte Studie zeigt, dass der Gestenkommunikationskanal für bestimmte Aufgaben intensiv genutzt wird und deutet zudem auf eine Steigerung der durch die Benutzer wahrgenommenen Präsenz in der virtuellen Welt hin.

1 Einleitung

Kollaborative virtuelle Welten sind synchrone, persistente Netzwerke von Menschen, die diese Menschen durch Avatare repräsentieren, ihnen gemeinsame, kollaborative Interaktionen erlauben und von Computernetzwerken bereitgestellt werden (in Anlehnung an (Bell, 2008, p. 2)). Beispiele für Einsatzgebiete dieser Welten im privaten Umfeld sind MMORPGs wie etwa World of Warcraft, dreidimensionale soziale Netzwerke wie beispielsweise Second Life und auf professionelle virtuelle Meetings ausgelegte Systeme wie etwa OpenWonderland. Kooperation basiert in allen drei Beispielen auf der Möglichkeit, innerhalb dieser Welten miteinander kommunizieren zu können. Für die unvermittelte zwischenmenschliche Kommunikation spielen nonverbale Elemente eine essenzielle Rolle. Da Avatare in virtuellen Welten die Nutzer nicht nur grafisch darstellen, sondern ihnen auch erlauben, durch sie mit der Welt und mit anderen Nutzern zu interagieren, ist es naheliegend, auch nonverbale Kommunikation auf Avatare abzubilden.

Der einfachste Ansatz hierzu besteht darin, Bewegungsabläufe der Avatare bereits vor einer konkreten Kommunikationssituation zu definieren und es dem Nutzer zu ermöglichen, diese vordefinierten Abläufe in einer konkreten Situation durch einen Trigger auf dem Avatar abzuspielen. Beispiele für solche Trigger sind Textkommandos (Salem and Earle, 2000), Elemente der GUI (Guye-Vuillème et al., 1999) oder dedizierte Eingabegeräte wie etwa der Beschleunigungssensor der Wii Remote (Sreedharan et al., 2007). Um die Bewegungsabläufe der Avatare besser an konkrete Situationen anpassen zu können, werden in einigen Ansätzen Trigger gewählt, aus denen sich bestimmte Parameter wie Geschwindigkeit und Dauer extrahieren lassen. Beispiele für derartige Trigger sind ein Grafiktablett (Barrientos and Canny, 2002) oder die Microsoft Kinect (Thai, 2011). Alle diese Ansätze haben gemeinsame Schwächen. So muss sich der Nutzer bewusst für das Senden eines nonverbalen Signals entscheiden, weshalb unbewusste nonverbale Signale nicht abgebildet werden können. Zudem muss er die Trigger kennen und während der Kommunikationssituation Aufmerksamkeit darauf verwenden, ein passendes Signal auszuwählen. Diese Probleme können umgangen werden, indem man dem Nutzer die direkte Kontrolle über die Bewegungsabläufe des Avatars gibt. Dies ist über verschiedene Eingabegeräte möglich. Allerdings sind diese Ansätze meist auf einzelne Körperteile beschränkt (Barrientos, 2000) oder verwenden am Nutzer angebrachte Sensoren (Chua et al., 2003; Duchowski et al., 2004; Steptoe et al., 2009), was die Gefahr birgt, den Nutzer abzulenken oder zu behindern. Zudem führt eine detailliertere Abbildung der Nutzerbewegungen auf seinen Avatar zu der Frage, wie es möglich ist, Akte der Kommunikation, wie etwa Gesten, von Bewegungen zu Steuerung in der Welt, beispielsweise über Maus und Tastatur, zu trennen.

Unser Ansatz besteht darin, die Bewegungsabläufe des Nutzers direkt, kontinuierlich und vollständig auf seinen Avatar abzubilden. Wir untersuchen in diesem Artikel die Fragestellung, ob die Möglichkeit zur direkten Gestenübertragung durch die Nutzer verwendet wird und ob sich für die Nutzer ein Mehrwert nachweisen lässt. Unser konkreter Untersuchungsgegenstand in diesem Artikel sind die Konzepte der Präsenz und der Kopräsenz. Mit dem Begriff der Präsenz wird dabei nach Witmer und Singer (1998) ein mentaler Zustand beschrieben, in dem sich ein Individuum geistig an einen anderen Ort versetzt fühlt. Analog hierzu bezeichnet Kopräsenz die subjektive Wahrnehmung, mit jemand anderem zusammen zu sein, selbst wenn man physikalisch voneinander entfernt ist (Mennecke et al., 2010; Slater et al., 2000). Es konnte bereits gezeigt werden, dass ein rudimentärer, triggerbasierter Ansatz die Kopräsenz der Nutzer einer virtuellen Welt steigern kann (Casanueva et al., 2001) und auch für die wahrgenommene Präsenz ist dieser Zusammenhang naheliegend. Deshalb formulieren wir die Hypothese, dass die Einführung der Gestenübertragung die von den Nutzern wahrgenommene Präsenz und Kopräsenz erhöht. Für die Überprüfung dieser Hypothese wurde ein auf der Microsoft Kinect basierender Prototyp entwickelt. Dieser verwendet zusätzlich die Wii Remote, um dem Nutzer die Navigation durch und Interaktion mit der virtuellen Welt zu ermöglichen, ohne den Kommunikationskanal für Gesten zu beeinflussen.

Abschnitt 2 dieses Artikels beschreibt den Aufbau des von uns erstellten Prototyps. In Abschnitt 3 wird die zur Untersuchung der aufgeworfenen Fragestellungen durchgeführte Studie dargestellt. Abschnitt 4 diskutiert die gewonnen Erkenntnisse.

2 Systembeschreibung

Als Grundlage für unseren Ansatz dient eine Server-Client Architektur, da diese auch bei vielen kollaborativen virtuellen Welten genutzt wird. Die Aufgabe des Servers liegt in der Simulation der 3D-Welt, während der Client die Welt darstellt und die Eingaben des Benutzers entgegennimmt. In unserem Ansatz werden zwei verschiedene Arten von Benutzereingaben unterschieden. Eine Eingabeart ist dabei die Körperhaltung des Nutzers, die mit der Kinect aufgenommen werden kann. Aus dieser wird ein sogenanntes Skelett extrahiert. Der Client überträgt diese Eingabe in ein Format, das auf Avatare angewendet werden kann und sendet dies über den Server an alle angeschlossen Clients. Hier wird sie auf die entfernte Instanz des Avatars angewendet. Somit werden alle mit der Kinect erfassten Bewegungen eines Benutzers für die anderen Benutzer (als Bewegungen des Avatars) sichtbar. Da die Beine des Avatars weiterhin genutzt werden sollen, um eine „laufen“ Animation darzustellen, wenn der Nutzer durch die Welt navigiert, konzentriert sich unser Ansatz auf die Übertragung von Bewegungen des Oberkörpers. Hierdurch wird der größte Teil möglicher Gesten abgedeckt. Die zweite Eingabeform, die der Client verarbeitet, sind Signale zur Navigation und Interaktion. Die naheliegende Lösung, auch hierfür die Kinect Eingabe zu verwenden, gestaltet sich aufgrund der möglichen wechselseitigen Überlagerung von Gesten zur Kommunikation und Bewegungssteuerung für Navigation und Interaktion schwierig. Auch die sonst übliche Verwendung von Maus und Tastatur für diese Aufgabe, ist nicht möglich, da der Nutzer für die Erfassung durch die Kinect frei im Raum stehen muss. Deshalb übernimmt in unserem Ansatz eine Wii Remote diese Aufgabe.

2.1 Technische Umsetzung

Der Prototyp verwendet den Second Life Viewer als Client und OpenSimulator als Server. Beide Systeme wurden für den Prototypen erweitert. Abbildung 1 zeigt die Architektur des Systems und die wesentlichen Informationsflüsse.

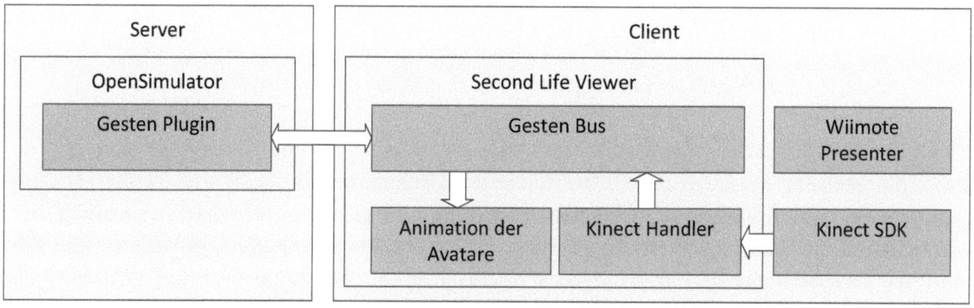

Abbildung 1: Architektur und Informationsfluss des Systems

Die Bereitstellung des Kommunikationskanals für Gesten zerfällt in zwei Aufgaben. Zunächst müssen die Daten der Kinect ausgelesen und umgewandelt werden. Danach müssen diese Daten auf die entfernten Kopien des betreffenden Avatares, welche die anderen Nutzer mit ihren Clients sehen, angewendet werden. Das Lesen und Umwandeln der Daten erfolgt im Client durch den Kinect Handler. Er ist in die Hauptschleife des Viewers integriert und liest durch das Kinect SDK generierte Kinect-Skelette (KS) aus.

Das KS unterscheidet sich in einigen Punkten von dem für den Viewer verwendbaren Viewer-Skelett (VS). Zunächst sind die Koordinatensysteme, die beiden Skeletten zugrunde liegen, nicht identisch. Dies kann durch eine einfache lineare Abbildung korrigiert werden.

Die Funktion $f\colon \begin{pmatrix} x \\ y \\ z \end{pmatrix} \rightarrow \begin{pmatrix} -z \\ -x \\ y \end{pmatrix}$ beschreibt diese Abbildung.

Zudem werden im KS lediglich die Positionen der Gelenke beschrieben. Um einen Avatar in die Pose eines Skelettes bringen zu können, ist allerding eine Beschreibung des Skeletts über die Drehungen der Gelenke in Form von Quaternionen notwendig. Um diese Beschreibung zu erhalten, werden pro Gelenkpunkt der zwischen den beiden zu einem Gelenk gehörigen Knochen eingeschlossene Winkel und die zugehörige Drehachse bestimmt. Seien $\overrightarrow{AB}$ und $\overrightarrow{BC}$ die beiden Knochen die das Gelenk B bilden. Dann sind $\alpha = \operatorname{acos}\left(\frac{\overrightarrow{AB} * \overrightarrow{BC}}{|\overrightarrow{AB}| * |\overrightarrow{BC}|}\right)$ und $\vec{V} = \overrightarrow{AB} \times \overrightarrow{BC}$ der Winkel und die Drehachse, aus denen sich ein entsprechendes Quaternion konstruieren lässt. Abbildung 2 illustriert diese Umwandung an einem Beispiel.

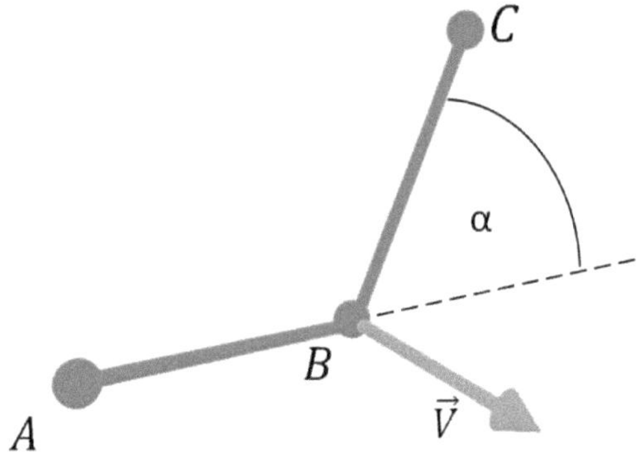

Abbildung 2: Beispiel für die Bestimmung eines Rotationsquaternions.

Wenn keinerlei Animation abgespielt wird, befindet sich ein Avatar in einer Grundstellung. Diese Grundstellung muss bei der Bestimmung der Drehungen berücksichtig werden. Hierzu lassen sich aus einem Skelett in dieser Grundstellung Korrekturquaternionen bestimmen, die als Konstanten gespeichert werden können. Diese Konstanten lassen sich dann auf die ermittelten Gelenkdrehungen anwenden. Schließlich ist zu beachten, dass die Struktur von KS und VS nicht identisch sind. Aus diesem Grund wurde ein Mapping definiert, das bestimmt, welche Gelenke des KS in welche Gelenke des VS umgewandelt werden.

Alle Avatare verfügen über eine eindeutige ID. Die ID des zum aktuellen Benutzer gehörenden Avatars wird mit dem ermittelten VS zusammen an den Gesten-Bus übergeben. Der Bus sendet diese Daten mit Hilfe eines entsprechend definierten Nachrichtentyps an den Server. Im Server läuft ein Plug-In, welches die Skelett-Nachrichten an alle Clients weiterleitet. Der Gesten-Bus der anderen Clients nimmt die Daten entgegen und speichert sie unter der ID des Avatars. Für jeden Avatar wurde bei dessen Erstellung eine Animation angelegt, welche über den Gesten-Bus angefragt werden kann. Das Animationsframework des Viewers wird schließlich verwendet, um Avatare in die beschriebene Pose zu bringen.

Um die Wii Remote für Navigation und Interaktion nutzen zu können, wird der sogenannte Wiimotepresenter (Smith and Kitzmann, 2008) verwendet. Die Software verfolgt das in (Yang and Li, 2011) beschriebene Konzept, um den Controller zur Emulation von Maus und Tastatur zu verwenden. Für den Viewer ist nicht zu erkennen, dass die Wiimote als Quelle der Eingaben dient. Die Hardware des Controllers ermöglicht es, die ungefähre Position auf der Leinwand zu ermitteln, auf die das Gerät zeigt. Diese Information nutzt der Präsenter, um den Mauszeiger an diese Stelle zu bewegen. Das erzeugte Verhalten ähnelt dem eines Laserpointers. Mit der „B"-Taste des Controllers kann der Nutzer einen Linksklick auslösen. Klickt er dabei auf ein 3D-Objekt im Viewer, verarbeitet dieser dies als eine „Berührung" des Objektes. Dies reicht als grundlegende Interaktionsmöglichkeit aus. Zur Navigation in der 3D-Welt werden die Tasten des Steuerkreuzes der Wii Remote auf die Pfeiltasten der Tastatur abgebildet. Dies ermöglicht es dem Nutzer, den Avatar nach rechts und links zu drehen sowie ihn vorwärts und rückwärts zu bewegen.

3 Evaluation

Die hier vorgestellte Studie soll zwei Fragen beantworten. Zum einen ist dies die Frage, ob der neuartige Kommunikationskanal für Gesten durch die Nutzer verwendet wird. Zum anderen soll überprüft werden, ob die Benutzer durch das System eine größere Präsenz und Kopräsenz wahrnehmen. Die Studie wurde mit 57 Teilnehmern durchgeführt. Unter ihnen waren 18 Frauen und 39 Männer.

3.2 Studiendesign

Für die Studie wurden die Teilnehmer in 19 Gruppen zu jeweils drei Personen zusammengefasst. Hierbei wurde auf eine gleichmäßige Verteilung der Geschlechter geachtet. Die Gruppen durchliefen nacheinander zwei Szenarien. Szenario 1 durchliefen 10 Gruppen mit aktivierter Gestenübertragung, bei 9 Gruppen war die Gestenübertragung nicht aktiv. In diesem Szenario wurden die wahrgenommene Präsenz und Kopräsenz der Teilnehmer vergleichend zwischen diesen beiden Bedingungen untersucht. Um die Steuerung mit der Wiimote als Störgröße auszuschließen, wurde diese in beiden Bedingungen deaktiviert (und war für die Aufgabe der Gruppen auch nicht nötig). In Szenario 2 waren die Gestenübertragung und die Wii Remote- Steuerung für alle Teilnehmer aktiv. Der Fokus dieses Szenarios lag auf der Eignung der Steuerung mit Hilfe der Wii Remote in Zusammenspiel mit dem Gestenkommunikationskanal. Es wurden neben der Usability des Gesamtsystems auch gezielte Fragen zu den beiden Eingabegeräten untersucht. Tabelle 3 gibt einen Überblick über das gewählte Studiendesign.

	19 Gruppen	
	10 Gruppen	9 Gruppen
Szenario 1	mit Gestenübertragung, keine Wii Remote	ohne Gestenübertragung, keine Wii Remote
Szenario 2	mit Gestenübertragung, mit Wii Remote	

Tabelle 3: Überblick über das Studiendesign

3.3 Aufbau

Die Teilnehmer einer Gruppe wurden für beide Szenarien in je einem von drei separaten Räumen untergebracht. Es wurde darauf geachtet, dass sie sich vor der Studie nicht begegneten. In den Räumen befand sich jeweils ein Laptop. An diesen war ein Beamer zur Ausgabe des Bildschirminhaltes auf einer Leinwand angeschlossen. Zudem waren eine Kinect, eine Wii Remote und ein Headset mit dem Gerät verbunden. Vor Beginn des Szenarios 1 wurden die Teilnehmer gebeten, sich an einen Punkt etwa 2,5 Meter vor der Leinwand aufzustellen und dort während der Szenarien zu verweilen. Die Kinect wurde unter der Leinwand positioniert und auf den Nutzer ausgerichtet. Zudem wurden die Teilnehmer gebeten, das Headset aufzusetzen. Mit dem Headset waren sie durch die Voice-over-IP Software Teamspeak miteinander verbunden. Zum Start der Szenarien wurde auf dem Laptop der Viewer gestartet und maximiert, so dass dieser die gesamte Leinwand einnahm. Die Teilnehmer erhielten eine Einweisung in die Gestenübertragung (falls diese aktiviert war) und zudem ein Handout, welches die jeweilige Aufgabe erläuterte.

Der Studienleiter befand sich während der Szenarien in einem vierten Raum und war von dort ebenfalls in die virtuelle Welt eingeloggt, hielt sich aber für den Verlauf der Szenarien im Hintergrund und beschränkte sich darauf, den Verlauf zu beobachten. Von seinem Client aus wurde der Studienverlauf in der Welt inklusive der Audiokommunikation aufgezeichnet.

3.4 Szenario 1

Für dieses Szenario befanden sich die drei Avatare in einem gemeinsamen virtuellen Raum. Sie standen in einem Kreis und die Kamera der Viewer war so ausgerichtet, dass jeder Teilnehmer die Avatare der beiden anderen Teilnehmer komplett sehen konnte. Die Navigation und Interaktion mit der 3D-Welt waren für alle Teilnehmer deaktiviert und die Wii Remote war versteckt.

Die Aufgabe der Teilnehmer bestand darin, eine Projektauswahlentscheidung innerhalb eines kommunalpolitischen Szenarios zu treffen. Jeder der Teilnehmer verfügte über Informationen zu einer von drei möglichen Projektenideen, die er den anderen vorstellen und die er innerhalb der folgenden Diskussion vertreten sollte. Obwohl jeder Teilnehmer die Anweisung hatte, seine Projektidee möglichst durchzusetzen, wurde allen Teilnehmern auch mitgeteilt, dass keine Entscheidung zu treffen der denkbar schlechteste Ausgang des Szenarios sei. Sie konnten also auch eine der anderen Projektideen wählen, falls sie für ihre eigene Idee keine Mehrheit finden konnten. Die Bearbeitungszeit für das Vorstellen und die Diskussion der Projektideen betrug 30 Minuten. Nach 25 Minuten wurden die Teilnehmer darauf hingewiesen, dass die Bearbeitungszeit bald endet. War nach 35 Minuten noch keine Entscheidung getroffen, wurde das Szenario beendet.

Nach dem Szenario füllten die Teilnehmer einen Fragebogen aus. Dieser enthielt 22 Aussagen, welche die Teilnehmer auf eine Likert-Skala mit sieben Abstufungen bewerten sollten. Hierin waren 10 Items des IGroup Presence Questionnaire aus (Schubert et al., 2001) enthalten. Diese wurden anschließend im Präsenzscore V_{IPQ} zusammengefasst. Dieser bewegt sich im Bereich von 0 und 60, wobei ein hoher Wert einer hohen Präsenz entspricht. Zudem enthielt der Fragebogen die 6 Aussagen des Fragebogens aus (Casanueva et al., 2001). Diese Fragen wurden ins Deutsche übersetzt und zu einem Kopräsenzscore V_{KP} zusammengefasst. Dieser bewegte sich im Bereich von 0 bis 36, wobei ein höherer Wert einer höheren Kopräsenz entspricht. Zudem enthielt der Fragebogen weitere Elemente bezüglich der Diskussion und der Sympathie, welche die Teilnehmer sich entgegenbrachten.

3.5 Szenario 2

In Szenario 2 waren Navigation und Interaktion über die Wii Remote aktiviert. Der eigentlichen Aufgabe wurde eine Eingewöhnung vorangestellt, in welcher die Teilnehmer in separaten Räumen der 3D-Welt mit der Steuerung experimentieren konnten. Nachdem alle Teilnehmer bestätigten, dass sie sich an die Steuerung gewöhnt hatten, wurden sie aufgefordert sich in einen vierten virtuellen Raum zu begeben.

In diesem Raum befand sich die eigentliche Aufgabe des Szenarios. Die Teilnehmer sollten ein kooperatives, dreidimensionales Memory-Spiel lösen. Das Spiel bestand aus 48 Karten auf die sich 24 Motive - jeweils in Paaren - verteilten. Die Karten waren zufällig auf die drei Seiten einer Pyramide aufgeteilt. Diese war so groß, dass jeder Teilnehmer nur eine Seite gleichzeitig erkennen konnte. Es wurde sichergestellt, dass sich Paare nie auf derselben Seite der Pyramide befanden. Die Karten waren zu Beginn alle verdeckt. Wenn ein Teilnehmer eine der Karten mit Hilfe der Wii Remote „berührte", wurde diese aufgedeckt. Danach konnte ein anderer Spieler eine weitere Karte aufdecken. Waren die Motive gleich, wurden die Karten entfernt. Das Ziel war es, alle Karten zu entfernen. Da ein einzelner Spieler immer nur eine Karte aufdecken und damit kein Paare entfernen konnte, war hierfür Zusammenarbeit notwendig. Die maximale Bearbeitungszeit betrug 20 Minuten, danach wurde das Spiel abgebrochen. Abbildung 3 zeigt einen Screenshot des Szenarios.

Nach dem Ende des Szenarios beantworteten alle Teilnehmer einen zweiten Fragebogen. Dieser enthielt 17 Aussagen, welche anhand eine Likert-Skala mit fünf Abstufungen bewertet werden sollten. Die Ankerpunkte der Skala waren „trifft gar nicht zu" und „trifft völlig zu". Der Fragebogen enthielt die 10 Elemente des System Usability Scale (SUS) Fragebogens (Brooke, 1996). Hieraus wurde der SUS Score V_{SUS} entsprechend der Vorschriften von Brooke berechnet. Zudem enthielt der Fragebogen Elemente zur Qualität der Gestenübertragung, zu Steuerung mit der Wii Remote und zur allgemeinen Bewertung der Aufgabe.

Abbildung 3: Szenario 2 (aus Vogelperspektive – die Teilnehmer hatten je nur Sicht auf eine Pyramidenseite)

3.6 Auswertung

Im Fragebogen zu Szenario 1 lag der Durchschnitt von V_{IPQ} für Teilnehmer mit Gestenübertragung mit 21,73 (SD=9,87) über dem der Teilnehmer ohne Gestenübertragung mit 16,26 (SD=11,41). Diese Ergebnisse weisen tendenziell in die erwartete Richtung, sind allerdings statistisch (knapp) nicht signifikant (p=0,0596). Der Durchschnitt der Variable V_{KP} liegt für Teilnehmer mit Gestenübertragung bei 26,87 (SD=4,97) und damit nur minimal über dem der Teilnehmer ohne Gestenübertragung mit 26,04 (SD=5,20). Dieser Unterschied ist nicht signifikant (p=0,5418). Im Fragebogen zu Szenario 2 lag der durchschnittliche durch die Teilnehmer vergebene SUS-Score bei 81,58. Dieser Wert ordnet sich in der Skala von Bangor (Bangor et al., 2009) zwischen „good" (71,4) und „excellent" (85,5) ein. Die Aussage „Mit der Steuerung durch den Controller bin ich gut zurechtgekommen." wurde im Durchschnitt mit 4,47 (SD=0,73) von 5 bewertet und damit deutlich bestätigt. Dies spricht dafür, dass die Steuerung mit der Wiimote durchaus für Navigation und Interaktion in virtuellen Welten geeignet ist. Die Aussage „Die Genauigkeit, mit der der Bewegungssensor meine Bewegungen übertragen hat, fand ich ausreichend" wurde im Durchschnitt mit 3,51 (SD=1,10) von möglichen 5 Punkten bewertet. Um die Nutzung von Gesten innerhalb beider Szenarien bewerten zu können, wurden die Aufzeichnungen des Studienverlaufes codiert und das Auftreten verschiedene Arten von Gesten untersucht. Es wurde dabei zwischen rhythmische Gesten zur Strukturierung und Betonung des Gesprochenen, Gesten zur Erläuterung des Gesprochenen (wie z.B. das Beschreiben einer Wendeltreppe durch eine spiralförmige Bewegung der Hand) und Zeigegesten unterschieden. Da diese Differenzierung keine weiterreichenden Erkenntnisse liefern konnte, soll hier nur auf die Gesamtzahl der Gesten eingegangen werden. Für Szenario 1 wurden nur Gruppen mit aktiver Gestenübertragung betrachtet, für Szenario 2 wurden alle Gruppen untersucht. Es wurde jeweils die Anzahl an Gesten aller drei Teilnehmer einer Gruppe summiert. Um die unterschiedlichen Bearbeitungsdauern zu berücksichtigen, wurden die Werte mit dieser Dauer in Bezug gesetzt. Die Angaben sind dementsprechend in Gesten pro Stunde. Der Durchschnitt dieses Wertes ist mit 123,9 (SD=66,7) für Szenario 1 signifikant (p=0,0003) größer als bei Szenario 2 mit 8,2 (SD=9,5).

4 Diskussion und Fazit

In diesem Artikel wurde ein neuartiger, auf der Kinect basierender Kommunikationskanal für Gesten in virtuellen 3D-Welten vorgestellt. Navigation und Interaktion mit der 3D-Welt erfolgen in diesem Ansatz getrennt hiervon mit Hilfe der Wii Remote. Die durchgeführte Studie hat gezeigt, dass Nutzer die Usability des Ansatzes sehr positiv bewerten. Auch einzeln werden Steuerung und Gestenübertragung positiv bewertet. Insbesondere erscheint die stark modifizierte Steuerung mit Hilfe der Wii Remote für 3D-Welten geeignet. Die ebenfalls mit dieser Studie untersuchte Hypothese, dass der Gestenkommunikationskanal die von den Benutzern wahrgenommene Präsenz und Kopräsenz steigert, konnte nicht bestätigt werden. Für die Präsenz liegt dies vermutlich an der doch recht geringen Stichprobengröße, da die vorliegenden Daten eine starke Tendenz in die vermutete Richtung aufweisen. Das Fehlen einer solchen Tendenz für die Kopräsenz der Teilnehmer steht im Wiederspruch zu den Ergebnissen von Casanueva (Casanueva et al., 2001). Möglicherweise ist der eingesetzte Fragebogen nicht sensibel genug, um eine eventuell dennoch vorhanden Unterschied zu detektieren. Zudem ist es möglich, dass die insgesamt gesteigerte Qualität der Darstellung der Avatare seit den Untersuchungen von Casanueva ein bereits sehr hohes Maß an Kopräsenz erzeugt und so den Unterschied, den die Gestenübertragung erzeugt, verdeckt.

Während Gesten in Szenario 1 durchaus rege genutzt wurden, gab es fast keinen Gesten-Gebrauch in Szenario 2. Eine Beeinflussung durch die nur in Szenario 2 aktive Wiimote erscheint aufgrund der hohen Usability und der guten direkten Bewertung der Steuerung unwahrscheinlich. Auch die Bewertung des Items „Der Controller in meiner Hand hat mich nicht daran gehindert, Gesten auszuführen." mit im Durchschnitt 3,18 (SD=1,31) von 5 spricht eher gegen eine solche Beeinflussung. Ähnlich wie bei unmittelbarer Kommunikation scheint es, dass die Nutzung des Gestenkanals stark von der jeweiligen Aufgabe abhängig ist. Dies wird auch durch die Bewertungen der Aussage „Ich glaube, die Gestenübertragung hat uns bei unserer Aufgabe geholfen" aus dem Fragebogen zum zweiten Szenario mit im Durchschnitt 1,73 (SD=0,82) von 5 gestützt. Zukünftige Untersuchungen im Bereich Gestensteuerung in 3D-Welten sollten sich daher stärker auf das Zusammenspiel zwischen Aufgabe und Gestennutzung fokussieren.

Literaturverzeichnis

Bier, E.A. & Stone, M.C. Snap-Dragging. In *13th Annual Conference on Computer Graphics and Interactive Techniques - SIGGRAPH 1986* (18.-22. Aug., Dallas, TX). ACM Press, NY, 1986. pp. 233-240.

Bangor, A., Kortum, P., Miller, J., 2009. Determining what individual SUS scores mean: Adding an adjective rating scale. J. Usability Stud. 4, 114–123.

Barrientos, F., 2000. Continuous control of avatar gesture, in: Proceedings of the 2000 ACM Workshops on Multimedia, MULTIMEDIA '00. ACM, New York and NY and USA, pp. 5–8.

Barrientos, F.A., Canny, J.F., 2002. Cursive: controlling expressive avatar gesture using pen gesture, in: Proceedings of the 4th International Conference on Collaborative Virtual Environments, CVE '02. ACM, New York and NY and USA, pp. 113–119.

Bell, M.., 2008. "Virtual Worlds Research: Past, Present & Future" July 2008: Toward a Definition of "Virtual Worlds". In: Journal of Virtual Worlds Research.

Brooke, J., 1996. SUS-A quick and dirty usability scale. Usability Eval. Ind. 189, 194.

Casanueva, J.., Blake, E.., others, 2001. The effects of avatars on co-presence in a collaborative virtual environment, in: Annual Conference of the South African Institute of Computer Scientists and Information Technologists (SAICSIT2001). Pretoria, South Africa.

Chua, P.T., Crivella, R., Daly, B., Hu, N., Schaaf, R., Ventura, D., Camill, T., Hodgins, J., Pausch, R., 2003. Training for Physical Tasks in Virtual Environments: Tai Chi, in: Proceedings of the IEEE Virtual Reality 2003, VR '03. IEEE Computer Society, Washington and DC and USA, p. 87.

Duchowski, A.T., Cournia, N., Cumming, B., McCallum, D., Gramopadhye, A., Greenstein, J., Sadasivan, S., Tyrrell, R.A., 2004. Visual deictic reference in a collaborative virtual environment, in: Proceedings of the 2004 Symposium on Eye Tracking Research & Applications, ETRA '04. ACM, New York and NY and USA, pp. 35–40.

Guye-Vuillème, A., Capin, T.., Pandzic, S., Thalmann, N.M., Thalmann, D., 1999. Nonverbal communication interface for collaborative virtual environments. Virtual Real. J. 4, 49–59.

Mennecke, B.E., Triplett, J.L., Hassall, L.M., Conde, Z.J., 2010. Embodied Social Presence Theory, in: Proceedings of the 2010 43rd Hawaii International Conference on System Sciences, HICSS '10. IEEE Computer Society, Washington and DC and USA, pp. 1–10.

Salem, B., Earle, N., 2000. Designing a non-verbal language for expressive avatars, in: Proceedings of the Third International Conference on Collaborative Virtual Environments, CVE '00. ACM, New York and NY and USA, pp. 93–101.

Schubert, T., Friedmann, F., Regenbrecht, H., 2001. The Experience of Presence: Factor Analytic Insights. Presence Teleoper Virtual Env. 10, 266–281.

Slater, M., Sadagic, A., Usoh, M., Schroeder, R., 2000. Small-Group Behavior in a Virtual and Real Environment: A Comparative Study. Presence Teleoperators Virtual Environ. 9, 37–51.

Smith, J., Kitzmann, I., 2008. Wiimotepresenter. Online verfügbar unter: https://sites.google.com/site/jasonlpsmith/wiimotepresenter

Sreedharan, S., Zurita, E.S., Plimmer, B., 2007. 3D input for 3D worlds, in: Proceedings of the 19th Australasian Conference on Computer-Human Interaction: Entertaining User Interfaces, OZCHI '07. ACM, New York and NY and USA, pp. 227–230.

Steptoe, W., Oyekoya, O., Murgia, A., Wolff, R., Rae, J., Guimaraes, E., Roberts, D., Steed, A., 2009. Eye Tracking for Avatar Eye Gaze Control During Object-Focused Multiparty Interaction in Immersive Collaborative Virtual Environments, in: Proceedings of the 2009 IEEE Virtual Reality Conference, VR '09. IEEE Computer Society, Washington and DC and USA, pp. 83–90.

Thai, P., 2011. Using Kinect and OpenNI to Embody an Avatar in Second Life. Online verfügbar unter: http://www.youtube.com/watch?v=ehTvtkybubM

Witmer, B.G., Singer, M.J., 1998. Measuring Presence in Virtual Environments: A Presence Questionnaire. Presence Teleoperators Virtual Environ. 7, 225–240.

Yang, Y., Li, L., 2011. Turn a Nintendo Wiimote into a Handheld Computer Mouse. IEEE Potentials 30, 12–16.

M. Koch, A. Butz & J. Schlichter (Hrsg.): Mensch und Computer 2014 Tagungsband,
München: Oldenbourg Wissenschaftsverlag, 2014, S. 85-94.

Intuitive Erzeugung von 3D-Modellen mit handgehaltenen Sensoren

Maximilian Sand, Dominik Henrich

Lehrstuhl für Robotik und Eingebettete Systeme, Universität Bayreuth

Zusammenfassung

Aufgrund der weit verbreiteten Verwendung von dreidimensionalen Computermodellen ist es wünschenswert, dass auch ungeübte Personen leicht ein digitales Modell eines realen Objektes oder einer Szene mit einem handgehaltenen Sensor erstellen können. Dazu wird eine Benutzerschnittstelle vorgestellt, die dem Anwender während der Aufnahme eine dreidimensionale Live-Rekonstruktion anzeigt, in die Hinweise zur Unterstützung des Aufnahmevorgangs eingeblendet werden. Unter Berücksichtigung von Verdeckungen wird der Nutzer auf noch nicht erfasste Bereiche hingewiesen. Dadurch kann der Aufnahmevorgang beschleunigt werden.

1 Einleitung und Motivation

Detaillierte dreidimensionale Computermodelle sind heutzutage allgegenwärtig. Mit den Ursprüngen in den Ingenieurswissenschaften zur Unterstützung der Konstruktion und Simulation, sind heute 3D-Modelle den meisten Personen durch Computerspiele oder Filme bekannt, in denen komplette virtuelle Welten erzeugt werden. Brillen für virtuelle Realität simulieren eine komplette Umgebung, in der die Nutzer zu unterschiedlichen Anwendungszwecken navigieren können. Die Erstellung eines dreidimensionalen Modells einer Umgebung oder einer realen Person ist hingegen meist nur mit Fachkenntnis zu bewerkstelligen. Durch die Entwicklung immer ausgereifterer Sensoren ist es möglich, 3D-Modelle mit einfacher Hardware zu erzeugen, indem ein Sensor um ein Objekt oder um eine Person oder durch eine Szene bewegt wird und dabei automatisch ein Computermodell erzeugt wird. Damit sind zukünftig viele Anwendungen vorstellbar: Die eigene Person könnte nach der Digitalisierung als dreidimensionaler Avatar in Spielen oder Kommunikationsplattformen verwendet werden. Planung und Einrichtung von Wohnungen könnte vereinfacht werden, indem ein reales Zimmer mit einem Smartphone aufgenommen wird und Möbel virtuell platziert werden.

Die Erzeugung von detailreichen, vollständigen Computermodellen von realen Objekten oder Umgebungen stellt den Anwender vor einige Herausforderungen: Es muss gewährleistet werden, dass jeder Teil eines Objekts mit der nötigen Auflösung erfasst wird. Zudem muss das Objekt vollständig erfasst werden, sodass das resultierende Modell kein Lücken aufweist.

Insbesondere wenn durch die Geometrie viele Verdeckungen auftreten, sind unter Umständen viele unterschiedliche Aufnahmepositionen nötig. Während automatisierte Systeme (beispielsweise unter Verwendung eines Roboterarms) dies berücksichtigen (Krainin et al. 2011), sind Rekonstruktionen durch handgehaltene Sensoren oft unvollständig, sodass erneute Aufnahmen oder eine Nachbearbeitung nötig sind.

In dieser Arbeit wird deshalb eine Schnittstelle zwischen Mensch und Computer vorgestellt und untersucht, die dem Anwender während eines Aufnahmeprozesses mit einer RGBD-Kamera Rückmeldungen über die Qualität und Vollständigkeit des bis dahin erzeugten Modells (kolorierte Punktwolke) liefert. Damit ist der Anwender in der Lage, direkt zu reagieren und weitere Aufnahmezyklen zu vermeiden. Diese Rückmeldungen des Systems werden in eine rekonstruierte 3D-Ansicht der Szene eingeblendet, sodass die Orientierung im Raum auch ungeübten Personen leicht fällt.

Dieser Beitrag gliedert sich wie folgt: Zuerst wird in Kapitel 2 der Stand der Forschung vorgestellt, in Kapitel 3 wird anschließend der eigene Ansatz zur Erzeugung der Rückmeldungen erläutert. In Kapitel 4 werden die durchgeführten Experimente mit Nutzern beschrieben.

2 Stand der Forschung

Der Großteil der Verfahren zur Rekonstruktion von realen Objekten sind vollautomatisierte Systeme, in denen der Sensor oder das aufzunehmende Objekt auf einem Gerät (beispielsweise auf einem Drehteller oder einem Roboterarm) montiert ist, und so die Aufnahmeposition angepasst werden kann. In einem ständigen Zyklus aus Planen, Aufnehmen, Registrieren und Integrieren (Scott et al. 2003) wird für jede Aufnahme die bestmögliche nächste Sensorposition ermittelt, sodass möglichst wenige Aufnahmen durchzuführen sind. Diese Problemstellung wird als *Next-Best-View*-Problem bezeichnet. Um auch bei einer hohen Anzahl an Freiheitsgraden einer Pose im Raum (drei für die Position plus drei für die Orientierung) brauchbare Laufzeiten zu erzielen, wird der Suchraum um das Objekt eingeschränkt, beispielsweise auf einen Zylinder (Pito 1999) oder eine Kugel (Banta et al. 2000). Keines dieser Verfahren kann mit mehreren Objekten und den daraus entstehenden Verdeckungen umgehen. Besser geeignet ist hier ein Verfahren auf Basis eines Voxelraumes (Potthast & Sukhatme 2013). Dabei wird der Raum in Voxel aufgeteilt, in denen jeweils ein Zustand (belegt, frei und unbekannt) gespeichert wird. Mit einem probabilistischen Ansatz wird anschließend eine Kamerapose hinsichtlich ihres Informationszugewinns bewertet.

Bestehende Systeme, in denen ein Mensch den Sensor bewegt, leisten zwar die Erstellung eines Computermodells, interagieren mit der Person aber wenig bis gar nicht. Systeme, die dem Anwender nur eine Live-Rekonstruktion in Form einer Punktwolke bieten (Izadi et al. 2011; Endres et al. 2012; Whelan et al. 2013; Stückler & Behnke 2014), haben den Nachteil, dass unnötige Wege zurückgelegt werden müssen, da fehlende oder schlechte erfasste Bereiche besonders in stark unstrukturierten Umgebungen mit vielen Verdeckungen nur schwer erkennbar sind. Nach einer Inspektion des Modells ist es dann nötig, erneut Szenenbilder aufzunehmen, um die Rekonstruktion zu verbessern.

Systeme, die eine Interaktion mit dem Nutzer unterstützen, teilen sich in zwei Gruppen auf: Bei der einen Gruppe unterstützen Benutzereingaben das Verfahren mit zusätzlichem Wissen, um ein besseres Ergebnis zu erhalten. Beispiele hierfür sind eine durch Handskizzen unterstützte Segmentierung (Sedlacek & Zara 2012) oder eine Korrektur von falschen Korrespondenzen (Schneider & Eisert 2012). Bei der anderen Gruppe werden die Nutzer direkt durch Rückmeldungen unterstützt. Das Verfahren in (Dellepiane et al. 2013) schlägt gute Aufnahmeposen vor, ist allerdings nur für einzelne Objekte anwendbar. Für unstrukturierte Umgebungen mit Verdeckungen zeigt die Arbeit von (Du et al. 2011) dem Nutzer eine Übersicht über noch nicht erfasste Bereiche als horizontaler 2D-Schnitt an. Damit kann der Nutzer jedoch nie die ganze Szene auf einmal überwachen und erhält keine Hinweise auf mögliche Aufnahmepositionen.

Insgesamt lässt sich feststellen, dass kein Verfahren in unstrukturierten Umgebungen anwendbar ist und gleichzeitig Rückmeldungen zu möglichen Aufnahmepositionen liefert, um so den Nutzer auf noch nicht erfasste Bereiche hinzuweisen.

3 Ansatz

In diesem Kapitel wird das entwickelte Verfahren zur Erzeugung von intuitiven Rückmeldungen an den Nutzer beschrieben. In Abschnitt 3.1 wird untersucht, welche Unterschiede zu automatisierten Systemen bestehen und welche Konsequenzen sich daraus ergeben. Abschnitt 3.2 beschreibt anschließend das Vorgehen zur Erzeugung von Rückmeldungen.

3.1 Problemanalyse

Eine mögliche Herangehensweise für ein interaktives System, das den Nutzer während der Aufnahme unterstützt, ist die Übertragung von Verfahren von vollautomatisierten Systemen. Die Anwendung von Next-Best-View-Algorithmen lassen sich jedoch nicht direkt übertragen, denn in automatisierten Systemen gelten folgende Eigenschaften: Erstens kann eine Sensorpose mit sehr hoher Genauigkeit sowie sehr schnell eingenommen werden, zweitens besitzt die ausführende Einheit kein Berechnungsvermögen oder Intelligenz. Für den Fall eines handgehaltenen Sensors gelten jedoch andere Voraussetzungen: Ein Mensch, der eine Kamera durch einen Raum bewegt, kennt weder das verwendete Koordinatensystem, noch könnte er im Raum eine vorgegebene Position ohne Markierungen oder andere Hilfssysteme zur Positionsbestimmung exakt einnehmen. Des Weiteren besitzt der Mensch ein räumliches Vorstellungsvermögen, sowie gute visuelle Wahrnehmung. Teilaufgaben, die für einen Computer aufwändig zu berechnen sind, aber für einen Menschen sofort ersichtlich sind, können dem Menschen überlassen werden. Daraus ergeben sich folgende Schlussfolgerungen für ein System mit handgehaltenen Sensoren: Das System muss unbekannte oder schlecht erfasste Bereiche feststellen und erkennen, aus welcher groben Richtung eine unverdeckte Erfassung möglich ist. Die Berechnung einer exakten Aufnahmepose ist nicht nötig, da der Nutzer diese nicht exakt einnehmen kann. Das Problem weist nun erheblich weniger Komplexität auf, da keine Pose mit sechs Freiheitsgraden gefunden werden muss. Es bleibt allerdings die Aufgabenstellung, eine passende Darstellung für diese Mensch-

Maschine-Interaktion zu finden, die eindeutig und klar wiedergibt, welche Bereiche im Raum gemeint sind, sodass der Nutzer leicht darauf reagieren kann.

3.2 Algorithmus

Dieses Kapitel stellt den entwickelten Algorithmus zum Erstellen von Nutzerhinweisen vor. Gegeben sei eine Sequenz von m Aufnahmen $I = (I_0, I_1, \dots, I_{m-1})$. Jede Aufnahme I_i besteht dabei aus der Position $p_i \epsilon \mathbb{R}^3$ der Kamera, der Orientierung $R_i \epsilon \mathbb{R}^{3\times 3}$ und den Sensorwerten als Punktwolke in Weltkoordinaten C_i, also $I_i = (p_i, R_i, C_i)$. Gesucht ist eine Menge von Nutzerhinweisen, die dem Benutzer schlecht erfasste Stellen aufzeigen soll. Ein Hinweis bestehe aus einer Position und einer Richtung mit folgender Bedeutung: Der Nutzer soll diese Position aus ungefähr dieser Richtung erfassen. Abbildung zeigt ein Beispiel in 2D.

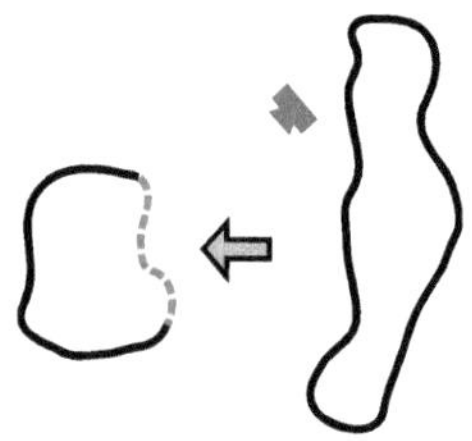

Abbildung 1: 2D-Illustration mit Objekten, von denen das linke noch nicht erfasste Bereiche enthält (gestrichelte Linie). Ein möglicher Nutzerhinweis (Pfeil) weist den Benutzer auf die Fehlstelle hin. Die fehlenden Stellen sollen dann durch den Benutzer von einer Position seiner Wahl (Kamerasymbol) aus aufgenommen werden.

Grundlegend kann man das Verfahren in sechs Schritte aufteilen: Zuerst wird ein Voxelgitter für den zu untersuchenden Bereich erstellt. Jedes Voxel enthält für jede seiner sechs Seitenflächen einen Zustand mit den möglichen Werten *unbekannt*, *belegt* und *frei*, sowie die Anzahl der Punkte im Voxel. Kommt eine neue Aufnahme hinzu, so werden die Zustände und der Punktzähler mittels eines Raycasting-Ansatzes aktualisiert. Anschließend werden sogenannte Fehlstrahlen aus dem Voxelraum extrahiert. Fehlstrahlen sind Kandidaten für spätere Nutzerhinweise und enthalten mehrere benachbarte Voxel mit unbekannten Seitenflächen in derselben Richtung. Alle Fehlstrahlen werden nun mithilfe eines Bewertungssystems hinsichtlich ihres Nutzens für den Anwender beurteilt. Fehlstrahlen mit hoher Bewertung werden anschließend in Nutzerhinweise umgewandelt, die als visuelle Repräsentation für den Nutzer dienen. Um die Zahl der Hinweise noch weiter zu reduzieren, können in einem letzten Schritt mehrere benachbarte Nutzerhinweise noch zusammengefasst werden. Im Folgenden werden nun die einzelnen Schritte näher erläutert.

3.2.1 Erstellung des Voxelraumes

Durch die Verwendung eines Voxelgitters wird der Raum in Raumwürfel unterteilt. Jedes Voxel $v \in V$ des Voxelraumes V mit $n = n_x \cdot n_y \cdot n_z$ Voxeln enthalte die Anzahl der Punkte im Voxel, sowie pro Seite einen Zustand $s(v, d) \in \{unbekannt, belegt, frei\}$. Die sechs Seiten eines Voxels seien mit $D = \{X^+, X^-, Y^+, Y^-, Z^+, Z^-\}$ bezeichnet. Diese Aufteilung in sechs Richtungen wird für die Hinweise genutzt, indem nur Hinweise generiert werden, die parallel zu den Normalen der sechs Voxelseiten orientiert sind. Wie in der Problemanalyse festgestellt, genügt diese Einschränkung, da der Nutzer die tatsächliche Aufnahmerichtung anschließend selbst bestimmt. Durch die Betrachtung von sechs Richtungen pro Voxel genügt ein verhältnismäßig grober Voxelraum für das Erstellen von Nutzerhinweisen. Dies beschleunigt auch das Raycasting und das Finden von Hinweisen. Die Größe einzelner Voxel sollte so gewählt werden, dass im Freiraum zwischen zwei realen Objekten mindestens ein komplettes Voxel liegt. Es empfiehlt sich daher eine Voxelseitengröße von $\frac{d_{min}}{2}$, wobei d_{min} der minimale Abstand zwischen zwei Objekten in der aufzunehmenden Szene ist.

3.2.2 Raycasting

Initial besitzen alle Seiten aller Voxel den Zustand *unbekannt*. Kommt eine neue Aufnahme $I_i = (p_i, R_i, C_i)$ hinzu, so müssen die Zustände aktualisiert werden. Dazu wird ein Raycasting-Ansatz für Punkte der Punktwolke C_i verwendet. Für einen Punkt $c \in C_i$ der Wolke müssen alle Voxel entlang des Strahls von p_i bis c auf *frei*, sowie das Voxel, das c enthält, auf *belegt* gesetzt werden. Zur Traversierung der Voxel wird das Verfahren von (Amanatides & Woo 1987) verwendet, das für jeden Punkt der Punktwolke parallel ausgeführt werden kann. Von jedem besuchten Voxel werden entsprechend der Komponenten des Richtungsvektors des Strahls die Zustände der drei zugehörigen Seiten auf *belegt* gesetzt. Beim Raycasting der Punkte einer Wolke ist es durch die grobe Auflösung des Voxelgitters möglich, dass mehrere Strahlen durch die gleiche Seite eines Voxel gehen, ein Teil davon im Voxel aufgrund von Punkten endet, ein anderer Teil davon allerdings durch das Voxel hindurch verläuft. In letzeren Fall wird der Zustand der betreffenden Voxelseite auf *belegt* gesetzt.

3.2.3 Finden von Fehlstrahlen

Im nächsten Schritt werden nun sogenannte Fehlstrahlen gefunden. Ein Fehlstrahl f sei definiert als das Tupel $f = (v_{start}, v_{ende}, d)$ mit $v_{start}, v_{ende} \in V$ und $d \in D$, und beschreibt eine Sequenz von hintereinanderliegenden Voxeln beginnend bei v_{start} und endend bei v_{ende}, die alle in der Richtung d den Zustand *unbekannt* besitzen. Der Grund, diese Voxel in einem Fehlstrahl zusammenzufassen, ist die Tatsache, dass diese unbekannten Seiten mit einer einzigen Aufnahme erfasst werden können, da sie hintereinanderliegen.

Die Position eines Voxels im Voxelraum V kann eindeutig durch seine Koordinate $(x, y, z) \in \mathbb{N}_0^3$ und $0 \leq x \leq n_x, 0 \leq y \leq n_y, 0 \leq z \leq n_z$ beschrieben werden. Im Folgenden werde nun eine einzelne Voxelsequenz betrachtet, die V in Richtung d durchläuft. Dadurch sind zwei der drei Koordinaten der Voxel fest, nur eine Koordinate ändert sich. Sei o.B.d.A. y und z fest und $0 \leq x \leq n_x$. Betrachtet man die Zustände der Voxel in d-Richtung, so entsteht eine Folge von Zuständen, die mit $s(x)$ bezeichnet werde (Abbildung 2).

Das Ziel ist es nun, innerhalb einer Voxelsequenz alle Fehlstrahlen, also eine Sequenz von aufeinanderfolgenden Voxeln mit Zustand *unbekannt*, zu finden. Die Positionen, an denen ein Fehlstrahl beginnt (v_{start}) und endet (v_{ende}), können dabei leicht ermittelt werden, indem eine Fallunterscheidung für zwei aufeinanderfolgende Zustände durchgeführt wird. Folgt beispielsweise auf einen *freien* Voxel ein *unbekannter* Voxel, so beginnt ein Fehlstrahl (z.B. bei $x = 1$ in Abbildung 2). Nach *belegten* Voxeln beginnt ein Fehlstrahl erst beim zweiten *unbekannten* Voxel ($x = 5$ in Abbildung 2). Dadurch wird verhindert, dass Fehlstrahlen Voxelseiten enthalten, die nie erfasst werden könnten, weil das in Richtung *d* vorhergehende Voxel *belegt* ist und somit diese Seite immer verdecken würde. Eine besondere Betrachtung verdienen Voxel, die aus Richtung *d unbekannt* sind, aber mehr als eine vorgegebene Anzahl an Punkten enthalten. Ein solches Voxel muss dann mindestens eine andere Seite besitzen, die *belegt* ist, und wird dann auch mit hoher Wahrscheinlichkeit aus Richtung *d belegt* sein. Das Verwenden einer Schwelle dient dazu, Fehlmessungen und Rauschen, die sich im Vorhandensein von einzelnen Punkten innerhalb eines Voxels widerspiegeln, zu ignorieren. Zusammenfassend ergibt sich also folgende Berechnungsvorschrift für eine Voxelsequenz: Durchlaufe die Voxelsequenz von Index $x = 0$ bis n_x und starte beziehungsweise beende einen Fehlstrahl anhand der Fälle in Tabelle 1. Falls ein Strahl noch aktiv ist, wenn das Ende der Sequenz erreicht ist, so beende diesen Strahl mit $v_{ende} = (n_x, y, z)$.

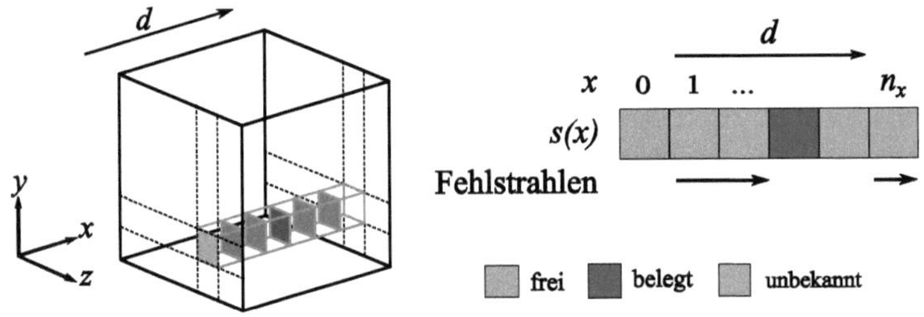

Abbildung 2: Eine Voxelsequenz in Richtung d innerhalb des Voxelraumes (links). Betrachtet man nur die Zustände in Richtung d, so entsteht eine Folge aus Zuständen s(x), die mit x parametrisiert ist (rechts). Daraus lassen sich Fehlstrahlen extrahieren.

Zustände $s(x-1)$,	$s(x)$	**Strahl ist nicht aktiv**	**Strahl ist aktiv**
frei, *unbekannt o.P.,*	*unbekannt o.P.* *unbekannt o.P.*	Neuer Strahl mit $v_{start} = (x, y, z)$	-
frei,	*unbekannt m.P.*	Strahl der Länge 1 mit $v_{start} = v_{ende} = (x, y, z)$	-
unbekannt o.P., *unbekannt o.P.,* *unbekannt m.P.,* *unbekannt m.P. ,*	*belegt* *frei* *belegt* *frei*	-	Beende Strahl bei $v_{ende} = (x-1, y, z)$
unbekannt o.P.,	*unbekannt m.P.*	Strahl der Länge 1 mit $v_{start} = v_{ende} = (x, y, z)$	Beende Strahl bei $v_{ende} = (x-1, y, z)$
sonst		-	-

Tabelle 1: Fallunterscheidung für den Durchlauf von Voxelsequenzen zur Erkennung von Fehlstrahlen in Richtung d. $0 < x < n_x$; *y, z fest. Beim Zustand* unbekannt *wird unterschieden zwischen* unbekannt ohne Punkte *(o.P.) und* unbekannt mit Punkten *(m.P.).*

Bisher wurden beim Durchlauf in Richtung d auch nur die Zustände in Richtung d betrachtet. Durch Anpassung der Fallunterscheidungen können auch Fehlstrahlen in die zu d entgegengesetzte Richtung erkannt werden. Insgesamt erfolgt also die Berechnung aller Fehlstrahlen folgendermaßen: Durchlaufe alle Voxel und überprüfe für alle sechs Richtungen, ob ein Fehlstrahl im aktuellen Voxel begonnen oder beendet werden muss, indem der Zustand dieses Voxels sowie die drei Zustände der benachbarten Vorgängervoxel ausgewertet werden.

3.2.4 Bewertung von Fehlstrahlen

Die Gesamtzahl der Fehlstrahlen im Voxelraum kann sehr groß werden und ist für eine sinnvolle Rückmeldung an den Benutzer noch weiter zu reduzieren. Dazu wird für jeden Fehlstrahl eine Bewertung errechnet, die dessen Relevanz beschreibt. Die Weiterverarbeitung der Fehlstrahlen kann dann beispielsweise nur für Fehlstrahlen mit einer Bewertung über einer bestimmten Schwelle erfolgen oder nur für die besten Fehlstrahlen.

Die Bewertung eines Fehlstrahls lässt sich nach folgenden Regeln berechnen: Enthält der letzte Voxel im Fehlstrahl oder der darauf folgende Voxel eine geringere Anzahl an Punkten, als eine Schwelle vorgibt, so ist die Bewertung Null. Dies bewirkt, dass nur Fehlstrahlen, die auf Voxeln mit Punkten, also mit bereits rekonstruierten Teilen der Szene, enden, eine hohe Bewertung bekommen und Punkte, die durch Sensorrauschen entstanden sind, ignoriert werden. Alle anderen Fehlstrahlen werden anhand ihrer Position im Voxelraum bewertet. Dies modelliert die Hypothese, dass Objekte im Inneren des Voxelraumes dem Nutzer wichtiger sind als Objekte direkt am Rand. Zur Berechnung wird für jeden Voxel im Fehlstrahl ein Wert errechnet, das Maximum davon ist die Bewertung des Fehlstrahls. Die Bewertung eines einzigen Voxel geschieht mittels einer Sigmoid-Funktion, die Voxel am Rand einen Wert von Null, und Voxel im Zentrum einen Wert von Eins zuweist.

3.2.5 Generierung von Nutzerhinweisen aus Fehlstrahlen

Um die Informationen der Fehlstrahlen an den Nutzer weiterzugeben, ist eine visuelle Darstellung, genannt Nutzerhinweis, nötig. Ein Nutzerhinweis besitzt eine Position und eine Richtung, die den Anwender anleiten soll, an dieser Position und aus ungefähr dieser Richtung eine weitere Erfassung der Szene durchzuführen. Eine einfache Visualisierung einer Position und einer Richtung ist ein Pfeil. Dieser kann innerhalb der 3D-Rekonstruktion eingeblendet werden, die Position im Raum sowie die Richtung sind damit leicht erkennbar. Für die Positionierung des Pfeils im Raum gibt es drei Möglichkeiten: Die visuelle Darstellung des Pfeil reicht von v_{start} bis v_{ende}, ein kurzer Pfeil wird bei v_{start} platziert, oder ein kurzer Pfeil wird bei v_{ende} platziert. Die erste Möglichkeit hat zwar den Vorteil, dass die Länge des zugrundeliegenden Fehlstrahls noch ersichtlich ist, doch die Visualisierung nimmt viel Platz in Anspruch. Ein Pfeil bei v_{start} besitzt den Vorteil, dass der komplette Fehlstrahl vor der Pfeilspitze liegt. Nimmt ein Nutzer die Position des Pfeils ein, so kann er vermutlich alle unbekannten Voxelseiten auf einmal erfassen. Platziert man den Pfeil bei v_{ende}, so deutet der Pfeil direkt auf einen Voxel, der Punkte und damit ein Objekt enthält. Dadurch ist klar, dass hier ein Objekt ist, das von dieser Seite aus noch nicht erfasst wurde.

3.2.6 Gruppierung von Nutzerhinweisen

Durch das Ignorieren von Fehlstrahlen mit einer niedrigen Bewertung kann man die Zahl der Nutzerhinweise einschränken. Nur die wichtigsten Stellen werden dadurch markiert. An flächigen Bereichen sind dennoch oftmals mehrere Nutzerhinweise direkt nebeneinander platziert. Diese können optional noch zu einem einzigen Nutzerhinweis zusammengefasst werden. Die Gruppierung ist dabei nur für Pfeile sinnvoll, die am Anfang oder am Ende des Fehlstrahls platziert sind. Alle Pfeile gleicher Richtung, die nebeneinander liegen, werden zusammengefasst. Es ist anzumerken, dass bei der Gruppierung von Pfeilen, die am Anfang eines Fehlstrahls platziert sind, ein anderes Ergebnis entsteht, als wenn Pfeile zusammengefasst werden, die am Ende eines Fehlstrahls platziert sind.

Um die Nutzerhinweise zu gruppieren, kann man wie folgt vorgehen: Alle Pfeile in Richtung d, die in Richtung d die gleiche Koordinate besitzen, liegen in einer Ebene und können potenziell zusammengefasst werden: Fasst man diese Ebene als Binärbild auf, in der entweder ein Pfeil vorhanden ist (Wert 1) oder nicht (Wert 0), so entspricht das Gruppierungsproblem einer Bildsegmentierung. Eine einfache Lösung liefert hier dann das *connected-components-labeling*, ein Standardverfahren aus der Bildverarbeitung (Stockman & Shapiro 2001).

4 Experimente

Die experimentelle Evaluation geschah mit folgendem Aufbau: Als Sensor wurde eine Microsoft Kinect XBox 360 verwendet, welche die erfassten Daten in Form einer kolorierten Punktwolke liefert. Die Bildrate wurde dabei auf 1 Hz festgelegt. Die Punktwolken wurden dann mittels Verfahren zur Berechnung der visuellen Odometrie auf Basis der Open-Source Software RTAB-Map (Labbè & Michaud 2013) registriert und fusioniert. Auf einem tragbaren Computer wird dem Anwender die Rekonstruktion als globale 3D-Punktwolke angezeigt. Die 3D-Ansicht kann dabei optional so eingestellt werden, dass die Szene stets aus der Perspektive der aktuellen Kameraposition angezeigt wird. Der Nutzer hat zudem die Möglichkeit, die Aufnahme zu starten, zu unterbrechen oder zu stoppen. In diese 3D-Ansicht werden während der Aufnahme die Nutzerhinweise als Pfeile eingeblendet, die mit jedem neuen Tiefenbild aktualisiert werden. Um die Menge der Pfeile zu reduzieren, werden nur Hinweise mit einer Bewertung von mindestens 0,9 angezeigt.

In einem ersten Versuch mit fünf Probanden wurde ermittelt, welche Art der Visualisierung (Position, Gruppierung und Anzahl der Nutzerhinweise) während der Aufnahme am intuitivsten für den Nutzer ist. Die Testpersonen rekonstruierten dabei mehrmals eine Roboterzelle und bewerteten anschließend die Rückmeldungen. In Abbildung 3 sind die Live-Rekonstruktionen mit unterschiedlichen Varianten der Visualisierung dargestellt. Durch Befragung ergab sich, dass die Probanden eine Positionierung am Fehlstrahlende klar bevorzugen: Es ergab sich eine Bewertung von +3,2 auf eines Skala von +4 (Strahlende) bis -4 (Strahlanfang). Ebenso ist eine Tendenz zu gruppierten Nutzerhinweisen zu erkennen (Bewertung von +1,8). Bei der Anzahl der Pfeile waren die meisten Probanden unentschieden, ob eine feste Anzahl oder eine feste Bewertungsschwelle verwendet wird (Bewertung von

-1.0). Da bei beiden Varianten der Unterschied in der Visualisierung nicht allzu groß ist, ist dieses Ergebnis nicht überraschend.

a) b) c) d) e)

Abbildung 3: Rekonstruktion eines Industrieroboters. Der Roboter wurde dabei noch nicht von hinten und von oben erfasst. Die generierten Nutzerhinweise (Pfeile) weisen den Anwender auf die fehlenden Bereiche hin. a) Aufnahmevorgang mit handgehaltenem Sensor. b) Ungruppierte Hinweise am Fehlstrahlende (rot = hohe Bewertung). c) Ungruppierte Hinweise am Fehlstrahlende mit Bewertung höher als 0,9. d) Ungruppierte Hinweisen am Fehlstrahlanfang mit Bewertung höher als 0,9. e) Gruppierte Hinweise am Fehlstrahlende mit Bewertung höher als 0,8.

In einem weiteren Versuch wurde das unterschiedliche Aufnahmeverhalten mit und ohne Rückmeldungen untersucht. Dazu sollten die Probanden eine Szene einmal mit und einmal ohne Hinweise aufnehmen, anschließend wurden die Rekonstruktionen verglichen. Bei der Aufnahme ohne Hilfen fällt auf, dass alle Nutzer zwar Verdeckungen berücksichtigen und auch bewusst Zwischenräume aufnehmen. Vier von fünf Probanden vergaßen jedoch, Aufnahmen von einer sehr niedrigen Position nahe dem Boden zu erstellen, um Flächen zu erfassen, die nur von dort aus sichtbar sind. Unter Zuhilfenahme der Nutzerhinweise wurden diese Bereiche nicht vergessen, da das System die Anwender darauf hingewiesen hatte. Allen Probanden fiel es leicht, die vorgeschlagenen Posen auch einzunehmen, da diese direkt in die Rekonstruktion eingeblendet sind und so eine Orientierung im Raum erleichtern.

5 Fazit

Diese Arbeit präsentiert eine Methode, mit der sich während einer Rekonstruktion mit einem handgehaltenen Sensor intuitive Nutzerhinweise generieren lassen. Im Vergleich zu bestehenden Ansätzen werden dabei unstrukturierte Umgebungen mit Verdeckungen unterstützt, sowie noch nicht erfasste Bereiche erkannt und eine Aufnahmeposition vorgeschlagen. Diese Hinweise können direkt in eine 3D-Live-Rekonstruktion eingeblendet werden und vereinfachen so nachweislich den Aufnahmeprozess. Weitere Schritte in Richtung einer intuitiven Schnittstelle könnten zukünftig die Verwendung einer Datenbrille (Einblendung der Nutzerhinweise in das reale Bild) oder von Smartphones mit integrierten Stereo- oder Tiefenkameras sein.

Literaturverzeichnis

Amanatides, J., & Woo, A. (1987). A Fast Voxel Traversal Algorithm for Ray Tracing. *Eurographics '87*, S. 3–10.

Banta, J.E., Wong, L.R., Dumont, C. & Abidi, M.A. (2000). A next-best-view system for autonomous 3-D object reconstruction. Systems. *IEEE Transactions on Man and Cybernetics, Part A: Systems and Humans*, S. 589–598.

Dellepiane, M., Cavarretta, E., Cignoni, P. & Scopigno, R. (2013). Assisted Multi-view Stereo Reconstruction. *International Conference on 3DV-Conference 2013*, S. 318–325.

Du, H., Henry, P., Ren, X., Cheng, M., Goldman, D.B., Seitz, S.M. & Fox, D. (2011). Interactive 3D modeling of indoor environments with a consumer depth camera. *Proceedings of the 13th International Conference on Ubiquitous Computing*, S. 75–84.

Endres, F., Hess, J., Engelhard, N., Sturm, J., Cremers, D. & Burgard, W. (2012). An Evaluation of the RGB-D SLAM System. *IEEE International Conference on Robotics and Automation (ICRA)*, S. 1691-1696.

Izadi, S., Kim, D., Hilliges, O., Molyneaux, D., Newcombe, R., Kohli, P., Shotton, J., Hodges, S., Freeman, D., Davison, A. & Fitzgibbon, A. (2011). KinectFusion: real-time 3D reconstruction and interaction using a moving depth camera. *Proceedings of the 24th Annual ACM Symposium on User Interface Software and Technology*, S. 559–568.

Krainin, M., Curless, B. & Fox, D. (2011). Autonomous generation of complete 3D object models using next best view manipulation planning, *IEEE International Conference on Robotics and Automation (ICRA)*, 2011. S. 5031–5037.

Labbé, M. & Michaud., F. (2013). Appearance-based loop closure detection in real-time for large-scale and long-term operation. *IEEE Transactions on Robotics*, 29(3), S. 734-745.

Pito, R. (1999). A solution to the next best view problem for automated surface acquisition. *IEEE Transactions on Pattern Analysis and Machine Intelligence*, 21(10), S. 1016–1030.

Potthast, C. & Sukhatme, G.S. (2013). A Probabilistic Framework for Next Best View Estimation in a Cluttered Environment. *Journal of Visual Communication and Image Representation.*

Schneider, D.C. & Eisert, P. (2012). On User-Interaction in 3D Reconstruction, *Eurographics 2012-Posters*, S. 13–14.

Scott, W.R., Roth, G., & Rivest, J.-F. (2003). View planning for automated three-dimensional object reconstruction and inspection. *ACM Computing Surveys*, 35(1), S. 64–96.

Sedlacek, D. & Zara, J. (2012). User Driven 3D Reconstruction Environment. In Bebis, G., Boyle, R., Parvin, B., Koracin, D., Fowlkes, C., Wang, S., Choi, M.-H., Mantler, S., Schulze, J., Acevedo, D., Mueller, K., Papka, M. (Hrsg.): *Advances in Visual Computing*. Berlin, Heidelberg: Springer. S. 104–114.

Stockman, G. & Shapiro, L.G. (2001). *Computer Vision.* Upper Saddle River, NJ, USA: Prentice Hall.

Stückler, J. & Behnke, S. (2014). Multi-Resolution Surfel Maps for Efficient Dense 3D Modeling and Tracking. *Journal of Visual Communication and Image Representation*, 25(1), S. 137-147.

Whelan, T., Kaess, M., Leonard, J.J. & McDonald, J.B. (2013). Deformation-based Loop Closure for Large Scale Dense RGB-D SLAM, *IEEE/RSJ International Conference on Intelligent Robots and Systems (IROS),* S. 548-555.

Kontaktinformationen

maximilian.sand@uni-bayreuth.de

M. Koch, A. Butz & J. Schlichter (Hrsg.): Mensch und Computer 2014 Tagungsband, München: Oldenbourg Wissenschaftsverlag, 2014, S. 95-104.

Using Web Analytics to Investigate the Navigational Behavior of Users

Marc Ahrens[1], Ralph Kölle[2], Katrin Werner[2], Thomas Mandl[2]

HIS Hochschul-Informations-System eG[1]
Institut für Informationswissenschaft und Sprachtechnologie, Universität Hildesheim[2]

Abstract

Today, web analytics and big data provide the basis for the evaluations of websites. However, the interpretation of this data in terms of Human Computer Interaction (HCI) can be challenging and there has been little progress in the systematic exploration of the potentials of web analytics within the usability evaluation domain. In this paper, we introduce a new approach to analyzing large amounts of usage data with the goal to detect usability problems in the use of a website. The underlying idea was that the analysis of patterns can support the HCI analysis of a website. To this end, we developed an extension for the open source web analytics package Piwik that allows investigating the navigational behavior of users through the abstraction of individual interaction paths. The developed system supports data mining on navigation logs and the discovery of interesting patterns.

1 Introduction

Today's relevance of the internet for private and commercial use can hardly be overestimated. Today, more than 50 million people in Germany use the Internet as integral part of their daily lives (Bundesverband Digitale Wirtschaft 2013). This includes all age groups, whereas 14-29 year old Germans have the highest online penetration rate. According to Bundesverband Digitale Wirtschaft (2013) almost all internet users (97.1 percent) have already searched for information on a product or service on the internet. However, offering a web page alone is not enough to guarantee commercial success. Along with design and content the navigation of the web page plays an important role. The best way to investigate the usability of a website is to conduct a dedicated user test in order to understand how potential users cope with the navigation. Unfortunately, running such tests is associated with high costs which in particular small and medium-sized enterprises are not able or willing to take. Log files are a comparatively cheap alternative to access large amounts of usage data. In this paper we introduce an approach for the investigation of the navigational behavior of users that combines web analytics with knowledge about the structure of the website. The main goal was to take the navigational behavior of real users and to determine patterns that signify usability problems (e.g. disorientation on a web page). We wanted to use the structural information about the web page to supplement the log file analysis. This means linking the information of the log files to the structure of the page. In order to allow for an easy integration into existing web pages we decided to implement the software component as a plugin for the widely used open source web analytics software Piwik.

Web analytics is the process of automatically tracking and analyzing the behavior of users interacting with a web page. The use of web analytics enables a company to discover new insights about their customers, to attract more visitors or to increase the sales per customer. In fact, the analysis of log file data is an important complement to usability tests. Whereas laboratory tests can only appraise the behavior of a small part of consumers (who are often not even real users), the usage of log data allows taking a closer look at the entire user population over a considerable period of time. However, both approaches have their own deficiencies and therefore it is important to understand their potentials and limitations.

Related work can be broadly divided into research concerned with finding practical ways to identify usability issues using web analytics and research aimed at analyzing navigational trails in order to relate frequent patterns of user behavior to usability issues.

1.1 Identification of Usability Issues Using Web Analytics

Claypool et al. (2001) examined which indicators best predict users' interest in the content of a website. In their study with 75 participants and 2267 analyzed web pages the authors used a browser specially developed for this investigation. Along with dwell time, mouse clicks and movements, information on scrolling results and the use of arrow keys, participants could communicate their interest in the web page content. Claypool et al. (2001) then examined correlations between the actions and the explicit statements of the participants. The results showed that both dwell time and the time that the participants used the scrolling function, were good indicators for the user's interest in a web page. With the help of these implicit indicators the researchers could predict interest with 70 percent likelihood.

Burton and Walther (2001) used server logs in order to investigate a usability guideline of Jakob Nielsen[1] that claims that it is not good usability to use frames in websites because frames tend to confuse users. Consequently, Burton and Walther (2001) conducted an online experiment that used log file data to compare user responses to three different versions of the same website. In each version the content was identical, but the structural layout varied. The versions compared included a pop-up version, a typical frame layout as well as a single long web page. The results indicated two main findings. First, frames do not affect the amount of time users spend on a website which was interpreted by Burton and Walther (2001) as an indication that frames are not as confusing to users as Nielsen assumes. And second, frames make a difference in the amount of content users consume.

Jürgens et al. (2010) used the web analytics software Piwik to investigate a website that contains information about mobile phones. The purpose of this study was to determine the

[1] http://www.nngroup.com/articles/original-top-ten-mistakes-in-web-design/

importance of standard web analytics metrics for usability evaluations of websites. The study analyzed data over a period of at least two months, focusing on how to relate this data with the three usability indicators effectiveness, efficiency and satisfaction. The structure of the evaluation was threefold: user properties and behavior, referrer and keywords, content use and navigational behavior. Overall, the study showed that in some instances it is possible to identify usability issues. With respect to the navigational behavior of users, Jürgens et al. (2010) observed that landing pages that only result in few user interactions may reflect a low acceptance rate.

In conclusion, we see that even though the study of Claypool et al. (2001) shows a connection between dwell time and user interest, according to Burton and Walther (2001) no direct inference about the information consumption can be drawn. Jürgens et al. (2010) on the other hand found that also in the case of content sites, web analytics data can be related to usability metrics if the navigational behavior is taken into account, as well.

1.2 Identification of Usability Issues Using Navigational Trails

Botafogo et al. (1992) analyzed websites in terms of the graph structure given by the links between subpages. In order to classify these hierarchical structures the authors introduced different measures such as *compactness* and *stratum*. Compactness specifies the connectedness of different subpages. For example, long click paths between different nodes decrease the compactness of the website. Stratum on the other hand measures the linearity of a webpage: the more options are available for the traversal of a web document, the lower its stratum value. Botafogo el al. (1992) do not recommend a desirable level of compactness or stratum, but understand these measures as a reference point to support the author by the design of a webpage.

There are also studies dealing with log file information in order to predict user behavior and interests. Pitkow and Pirolli (1999) studied the possibility to predict the next interaction of a user with a webserver conditioned on his previous interactions. In particular, they investigated how to reduce the model complexity of such a predictor without sacrificing the accuracy of the model. The key assumption in order to extract predictive information from the log files was to focus exclusively on the most frequent interaction patterns. In fact, their experiments show that compared to various Markov models the most frequent longest subsequences have the potential to achieve the same predictive power with a reduced computational complexity.

A study conducted by White and Drucker in 2007 tracked the interaction of 3291 participants with their browser for a period of five month and analyzed their search and browsing behavior. For the purpose of this study they represented the search trails of their participants as character strings and compared these with the help of the Levenshtein distance.The researchers were able to identify two different user types, which can be distinguished by their search and navigation behavior. While for example members of the first group tended to enter a search query, visit one result page and navigate through this page extensively before running another search, the behavior of members of the other group was less linear and showed a larger variety of interaction patterns which includes going back and forth between the results and in-between search queries.

The third study was part of the Logclef track of the Cross Language Evaluation Forum (CLEF) in 2009. Lamm et al. (2010) investigated the occurrence of interaction patterns within interaction logs from the European Library (TEL) website collected over a period of 18 month. The focus of this study lay on the evaluation of user sessions with respect to search success. Lamm et al. (2010) propose the use of a hyperbolic tree view to visualize interaction trails. This visualization provides a simple means of determining the behavior of users within an IR system such as TEL. The start node of the tree is the point of departure of all interaction trails covered in the tree view and each hierarchy level within the tree represents one interaction within TEL. Furthermore the size of the edges visualizes which percentage of the sessions contains these interactions. The working hypothesis here was that the analysis of log files may offer clues about success or failure of a user session. In this context, Lamm et al. (2010) assumed that certain user interactions as e.g. printing, saving or forwarding a search result are preferably made in successful sessions and the tree visualization allowed them to interactively explore those supposedly successful sessions.

Most recently, Han et al. (2013) used a process mining approach to analyze navigational patterns of users of a university website in order to increase its usability and efficiency. Using the open source process mining tool ProM, originally developed at Eindhoven University of Technology, the authors investigated the click behavior of 551 users. The proposed approach includes heuristic as well as fuzzy mining techniques and investigates the navigation patterns on a content level rather than regarding the hierarchical structure of the website. From their analysis Han et al. (2013) observed five major navigation patterns on the basis of which they were able to suggest possible improvements to the university website.

In summary, we have described four approaches to utilize navigational information in the context of usability. This allowed the authors either to identify typical user behavior (White & Drucker 2007; Lamm et al. 2010), typical information needs (Han et al. 2013) or to predict subsequent user behavior (Pitkow & Pirolli 1999). In constrast, Botafogo et al. (1992) investigated structural properties of websites without an explicit connection to usage data. In this work we want to combine these two approaches and relate the observed navigational patterns with structural properties of the website.

2 Piwik Plugin to Analyze Navigational Trails

With a focus towards privacy, Piwik is an open source alternative to Google Analytics. As other web analytics products Piwik provides the means to collect and analyze website usage data. Piwik is developed in PHP and stores data in a MySQL database. This facilitates the use on any web server configured accordingly. Piwik provides many statistical key figures, such as the referrer URL, visits over time, conversion rates and for us most importantly the subpages requested by a visitor.

The main goal of this research was to illustrate and provide some direction for dealing with the complexities of log file analysis in the context of usability evaluation. In the course of this, a new plugin for Piwik has been developed which visualizes the navigational behavior of website users in order to obtain additional usability data that can be used to identify root causes of usability problems. Drawing together the findings of section 1.1, we conclude that it is possible to identify implicit indicators of usability. Furthermore, the research described in section 1.2 implies that it is useful to look at the navigational trails of users in order to discover meaningful patterns and rules that regulate the behavior of users traversing a website. In comparison with tools like the Transitions Report in Piwik or the Visitors Flow in Google Analytics, which provide path analysis on the level of each single webpage, we want to abstract from this notion and focus on the navigational patterns with respect to the structural levels of a website. Figure 1 illustrates the hierarchical structure of a web page. This means that we ordered the subpages of a website into a tree according to their click distance from the start page. Here for example we see a web page with three clearly separated hierarchy levels.

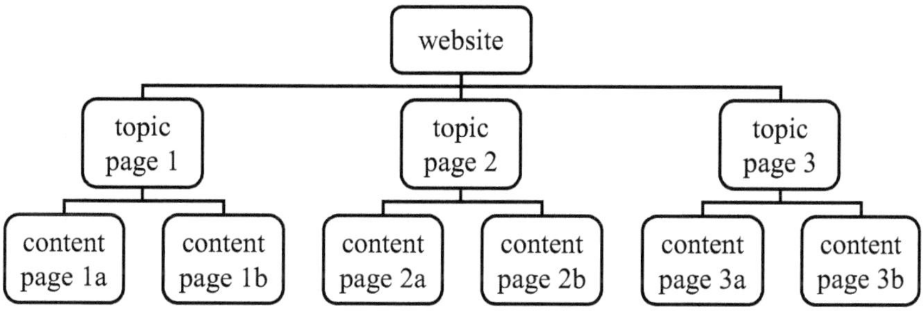

Figure 1: Diagram illustrating the hierarchy of a website

The developed software consists of two parts: *The Hierarchy Crawler* which constructs the hierarchy tree of a website and the new Piwik plugin which links this information with the available log file data. The two sections below describe how these two components work. The log for testing the software has been collected at the *usability-toolkit.de* website in the period from September 2010 until August 2012. All figures below are based on our test data.

2.1 The Hierarchy Crawler

The Hierarchy Crawler was developed to determine the hierarchical structure of a website on the basis of the address path of individual web pages. Static websites consist of actual HTML files stored in folders on a web server. In this case, the URL of a website contains its relative location on the server. However, if a website relies on a dynamical content management system (CMS), the web content is not stored in individual HTML files, but in a database. Hence, there is no folder path and the URL is created dynamically.

So far the Hierarchy Crawler requires static HTML files that are hierarchically stored in folders in order to determine the hierarchical structure of a website. The Hierarchy Crawler is written in Java. The only requirement for running the Hierarchy Crawler is the Java run time environment (JRE) in version 7. Figure 2 shows the Hierarchy Crawler after the crawling process is completed. The result set now contains a hierarchy tree for each sub-domain.

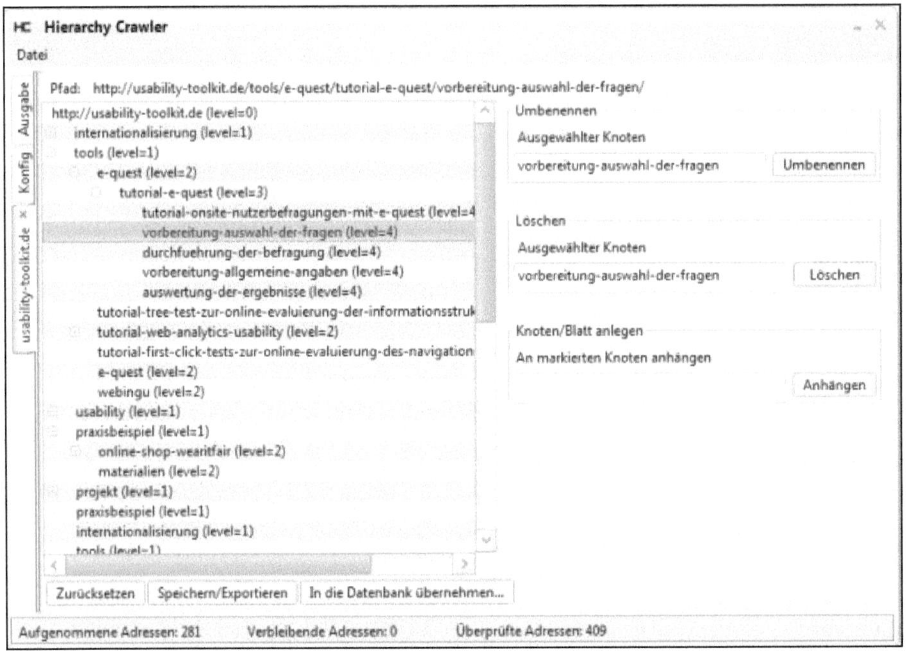

Figure 2: Result page of Hierarchy Crawler with hierarchy tree

2.2 The Hierarchy Plugin for Piwik

This new Piwik plugin links the usage data with the hierarchical topology provided by the Hierarchy Crawler. The Hierarchy Plugin extends the list of Piwik statistics by a new analysis option which is available in the Piwik dashboard as soon as the plugin has been activated and the import of the hierarchy data is completed. In the following, we briefly present how this new feature can be used.

Nr.	BesucherID	Anzahl der Links	Datum des Servers	Startzeit	Verweildauer	URL	Hierarchischer Klickpfad
1	24753	8	2012-08-08	12:28:38	4 Minuten 21s	• http://usability-toolkit.de/usability/navigation-auf-websites/navigationselemente/filterfunktion/ [4] • http://usability-toolkit.de/praxisbeispiel/ [1] • http://usability-toolkit.de/usability/ [1] • http://usability-toolkit.de/usability/filterfunktion/gestaltung-von-filterfunktionen/ [3] • http://usability-toolkit.de/usability/filterfunktion/wie-koennen-verschiedene-facettentypen-dargestellt-werden/ [3] • http://usability-toolkit.de/usability/filterfunktion/aktuelle-auswahl-hervorheben/ [3] • http://usability-toolkit.de/usability/filterfunktion/was-ist-bei-sehr-vielen-facetten-und-auspraegungen-zu-beachten/ [3] • http://usability-toolkit.de/usability/filterfunktion/empfehlungen-fuer-die-gestaltung/ [3]	→ [4] → [1] → [1] → [3] → [3] → [3] → [3] → [3]
2	24752	1	2012-08-08	12:06:18	0s	• http://usability-toolkit.de/usability/filterfunktion/gestaltung-von-filterfunktionen/ [3]	→ [3]
3	24751	1	2012-08-08	11:46:14	0s	• http://usability-toolkit.de/projekt/ueber-das-projekt/ [2]	→ [2]
4	24750	4	2012-08-08	10:44:51	14 Minuten 17s	• http://usability-toolkit.de/usability/usability-methoden/personas/ [3] • http://usability-toolkit.de/usability/usability-methoden/personas/ [3] • http://usability-toolkit.de/usability/usability-methoden/personas/ [3] • http://www.boxesandarrows.com/view/personas-and-the [→]	→ [3] → [3] → [3] → [→]
5	24749	1	2012-08-08	10:31:22	0s	• http://usability-toolkit.de/usability/usability-methoden/use-case-interaktionsszenario/ [3]	→ [3]

Figure 3: Table of evaluated datasets

Figure 3 shows the Hierarchy Plugin in action. This view provides access to all available log file records. In particular we can explore the click paths taken by different users supplemented with the hierarchical information. Aside from this table, the plugin offers further ways to visualize this data. In the left panel of figure 4 we see for example frequencies of different click path length.

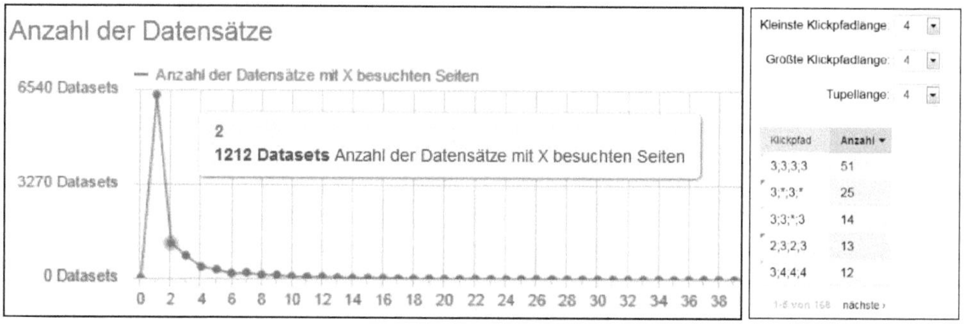

Figure 4:Left: Number of datasets with various click path length; Right: Most frequent subsequences with length 4

The table in figure 4 allows us to find the most frequently used sub-click path for a given minimum and maximum click path length. In this result table every click path is linked with the corresponding data set and allows for an easy identification of typical click paths. The integrated search function also allows searching for a specific click path. In addition, the click path data can be displayed as table, tag cloud, pie or bar chart.

3 Results from an Information Website

In this section we share some first experiences with our Piwik plugin. The log file from the usability-toolkit.de website mentioned previously provided the basis for this evaluation. First, we report some descriptive figures of our sample. We then focus on the analysis of the hierarchical information offered by the Piwik plugin. As already mentioned, the log file covers the period from September 2010 until August 2012. In this period 24793 visitors entered the website with an average length of stay of 2.67 minutes. The average click path length is 3; the average number of hierarchy level changes within a click path amounts to 1.

In order to investigate the navigational behavior of visitors to this website, we performed a sub-group analysis with respect to different click path lengths (CPL). In order to be able to make generalizable observations, we only took click paths (CP) into account which occurred with a relative frequency larger than 0.5 %. To this end, we only considered click paths with a CPL below 20. Table 1 shows the eight most frequent click path subsequences (CPS) of total length 2, 3 and 5. Note that in this case every occurrence of a pattern is counted regardless of its position in the overall click path. This means in particular that a single click path might contribute several times if it contains several instances of the same subsequence. We see that the most frequent behavior consists of a horizontal navigation within the third level of the hierarchy. It is also striking that hierarchy level zero (which refers to the start page of this website) is not contained within the eight most frequent subsequences.

min	*2*		*3*		*5*	
max	*20*		*20*		*20*	
CPL	*2*		*3*		*5*	
N	*35603*		*26410*		*15763*	
	CPS	**Freq**	**CPS**	**Freq**	**CPS**	**Freq**
1	3; 3	8044	3; 3; 3	3969	3; 3; 3; 3; 3	1482
2	2; 3	2559	4; 4; 4	1188	4; 4; 4; 4; 4	458
3	3; 2	2082	3; *; 3	1126	3; 2; 3; 2; 3	266
4	4; 4	2072	3; 2; 3	1103	3; *; 3; *; 3	251
5	3; *[2]	1907	2; 3; 2	829	3; 4; 3; 4; 3	247
6	2; 2	1742	3; 4; 2	761	2; 3; 2; 3; 2	217
7	1; 2	1647	2; 2; 2	661	2; 2; 2; 2; 2	210
8	3; 4	1496	2; 3; 3	623	2; 3; 3; 3; 3	208

Table 1: Most frequent click path subsequences of length 2, 3 and 5 (starting anywhere in the CP)

In addition, also the pages of the first hierarchy level are rarely accessed by the visitors. If we increase the CPL from 2 to 3, it becomes even more evident that visitors tend to stay within one hierarchy level rather than switching between hierarchy levels. If we interpret frequent changes of the hierarchy level as a search for the right information, one possible interpretation of this behavior would be that the web content of this website is logically structured so that frequent switches are not necessary to find what you seek. Qualitatively, this behavior remains stable if we further increase the CPL of the subsequences to 5.

min	*2*		*3*		*5*	
max	*20*		*20*		*20*	
CPL	*2*		*3*		*5*	
N	*9193*		*6241*		*3405*	
	CPS	**Freq**	**CPS**	**Freq**	**CPS**	**Freq**
1	3; 3	2510	3; 3; 3	877	3; 3 ;3 ;3; 3	240
2	3; *	1064	3; *; 3	593	3; *; 3; *; 3	133
3	3; 2	652	3; 2; 3	359	3; 2; 3; 2; 3	80
4	0; 1	645	0; 1; 2	254	4; 4; 4; 4; 4	66
5	2; 3	439	3; 3; 4	237	3; 3; 4; 3; 4	57
6	4; 4	405	0; 1; 1	203	3; 3; 4; 3; 3	55
7	3; 4	404	4; 4; 4	177	3; 4; 3; 4; 3	50
8	3; 1	391	3; 4; 3	159	3; 2; 3; 3; 3	49

Table 2: Most frequent click path subsequences of length 2, 3 and 5 (starting at the root of the CP)

[2] The * within a click path refers to a page view of an external website.

The picture does also not change if we restrict the selection to subsequences at the beginning of the click path. For starting sequences of length 2, we still find that the *3;3* click path is by far the most frequent hierarchy pattern (see table 2). Aside from the already mentioned horizontal navigational behavior observed within the overall click paths this tells us something about how people arrive at the pages of this website. Click paths, which have hierarchy, level 0 as their root element show up only with the fourth highest frequency, even though one might have it expected to be the most frequent pattern. Since with increasing hierarchy level the page URL becomes more complicated it is unlikely that users would type in these web addresses by hand. Hence, it seems plausible that external pages link directly to the desired hierarchy level and not to the start page of the website. Looking at the distribution of the referrer types agrees with this interpretation, but our Piwik plugin gives us the additional information that visitors are led directly to the third, the content containing, hierarchy level. From a usability perspective such user behavior implies for example that news and recent developments which are mentioned on the starting page won't usually be registered by the visitors and should therefore be directly accessible also from the third hierarchy level.

4 Discussion and Conclusions

This section contains an overview of what should be done in the next step. First of all, until now the Hierarchy Crawler cannot cope with arbitrary dynamical and static websites, hence there is room for improvement. One solution could be to define custom variables in Piwik that are assigned to the different hierarchy levels or page types. By integrating these variables into each subpage of a website, it should be possible to obtain the equivalent hierarchical statistics.

As already mentioned in the previous section, so far we did not have the resources to test the hierarchy approach as extensively as we would have liked. Thus, future studies will have to focus more closely on the evaluation of the developed Piwik plugin. One option would be to propose a framework to support and enhance log file analysis in the context of usability evaluation. Such a framework should specify metrics for comparing navigational trails, precise methodologies for interpreting these metrics as well as scenarios for integrating both log file analysis and user testing.

From a more empirical perspective it seems interesting to adopt the approach proposed by White and Drucker (2007) also for the analysis of navigational trails within the hierarchical structure of a website. On the one hand, it would be interesting to see if the two user types identified by White and Drucker (2007) are applicable to website usage. On the other hand, such an analysis could help to decide whether an unusual navigational behavior really points toward a usability problem or is only part of the typical behavior patterns of navigators or explorers. A similar starting point could be to further analyze the hierarchical structure of a website with respect to the interconnectedness. This would allow to access metrics such as compactness and stratum of Botafogo (1992) and open the possibility to connect these measures to the navigational behavior of the users.

Whereas log file data is sometimes hard to interpret, because the analysts do not know what users are thinking, laboratory user tests are often conducted with small sample sizes, which make it difficult to generalize the findings to the larger population of users. As a result of this research a new usability evaluation approach has been developed, which combines web analytics data with usability questions. In addition, two software applications were developed. A system to determine the hierarchical levels of a web page (The Hierarchy Crawler) as well as a plugin for Piwik (The Hierarchy Plugin), which allows to combine this hierarchical data with the data collected by Piwik and presenting the results in different display formats such as table, tag cloud, pie or bar chart. As a first application of these tools we analyzed log files of the website usability-toolkit.de. The most frequent click path subsequences showed a tendency for horizontal navigation behavior within the third hierarchy level. In addition, we could determine that the start page is seldomly visited, because external websites and search engines link directly to deeper pages.

References

Botafogo, R.; Rivlin, E. & Shneiderman, B. (1992): Structural Analysis of Hypertexts: Identifying Hierarchies and Useful Metrics. In: *ACM Transactions on Information Systems*, 10 (2), 142-180.

Burton, M. C. & Walther, J. B. (2001): The value of web log data in use-based design and testing. In: *Journal of Computer-Mediated Communication*, 6(3).

Bundesverband Digitale Wirtschaft (2013): *OVK Online-Report 2013/02* Available at: http://www.bvdw.org/mybvdw/media/download/ovk-report-2013-02.pdf?file=2951.

Claypool, M.; Le, P.; Wased, M. & Brown, D. (2001): Implicit Interest Indicators. In: *Proceedings of the 6th International Conference on Intelligent User Interfaces (IUI '01)*. New York: ACM, 33–40.

Han, K. H.; Hwang, B. & Jeon, J. (2013): A navigation pattern analysis of university department's websites using a processing mining approach. In: Innovations in Education and Teaching International, DOI: 10.1080/14703297.2013.832634.

Jürgens, J.; Mandl, T. & Womser-Hacker, C. (2010): Das Potenzial von Web Analytics für Usability-Evaluierungen. In: *Mensch & Computer 2010: Interaktive Kulturen.* Oldenbourg Verlag, 261-270.

Lamm, K.; Mandl, T. & Kölle, R. (2010): Search Path Visualization and Session Performance Evaluation with Log Files. In: *Multilingual Information Access Evaluation I: Proceedings of the 10th Workshop of the Cross-Language Evaluation Forum (CLEF '09)*. Berlin: Springer, 539–544.

Pitkow, J. & Pirolli, P. (1999): Mining Longest Repeating Subsequences to Predict World Wide Web Surfing. In: *Proc 2nd USENIX Symposium on Internet Technologies and Systems (USITS '99)*. Berkeley: USENIX Association, 139-150.

White, R. W. & Drucker, S. M. (2007): Investigating Behavioral Variability in Web Search. In: *Proc 16th International Conference on World Wide Web (WWW '07)*. New York: ACM, 21-30.

Kontaktinformationen

{koelle, katrin.werner, mandl}@uni-hildesheim.de

M. Koch, A. Butz & J. Schlichter (Hrsg.): Mensch und Computer 2014 Tagungsband,
München: Oldenbourg Wissenschaftsverlag, 2014, S. 105-114.

Vergleichende Evaluation zur Usability mobiler Web-Browser

Lukas Lamm, Manuel Burghardt, Christian Wolff

Lehrstuhl für Medieninformatik, Universität Regensburg

Zusammenfassung

Dieser Beitrag beschreibt eine vergleichende Usability-Evaluation der drei meistgenutzten Web-Browser für mobile Endgeräte. Dabei werden die zuvor identifizierten Hauptfunktionen der Browser durch entsprechend konstruierte Aufgaben mit sechs Studienteilnehmern ausführlich getestet. Die Ergebnisse werden in Form von *think aloud*-Protokollen sowie einer Abwandlung des *User Experience Questionnaire* (UEQ) dokumentiert und abschließend diskutiert.

1 Mobile Usability

Der in den letzten Jahren deutlich erkennbare Anstieg von internetfähigen Mobiltelefonen auf dem Markt bringt auch neue Anforderungen an die Benutzerfreundlichkeit von Webseiten auf mobilen Endgeräten mit sich. Dabei existieren zahlreiche Studien, welche die Relevanz mobiler Web-Browser als Zugangsmethode zum Internet belegen. Während einer Studie der Firma *Accenture* zufolge im Jahr 2011 bereits 28 % der Teilnehmer angaben, ihr Smartphone für den mobilen Internetzugang zu nutzen (Accenture, 2011), waren es im Folgejahr bereits 50 % der Befragten (Accenture, 2012). Eine weitere Studie der Unternehmen *Google* und *Nielsen* zeigt, dass 77 % der Suchanfragen auf mobilen Geräten in Situationen erfolgen, in denen gleichzeitig auch ein Desktop-PC zur Verfügung steht (Google & Nielsen, 2013). Dabei beeinflussen zwei wesentliche Faktoren die Usability von Webseiten auf mobilen Endgeräten: Einerseits müssen Inhalte, Navigations- und Interaktionskonzepte im Bereich des Webdesigns so angepasst werden, dass sie gut auf kleinen Bildschirmen dargestellt und ohne Eingabegeräte wie etwa Maus und Tastatur bedient werden können. Dazu haben sich in der Webdesign-Praxis Paradigmen wie etwa *mobile first* (Wroblewski, 2011) oder *responsive design* (Gardner 2011, Marcotte 2010) etabliert. Andererseits spielt als zweiter Usability-Faktor auch der Browser, in dem die mobile Webseite dargestellt wird, eine wichtige Rolle.

Bislang gibt es nur wenige Usability-Studien zu mobilen Web-Browsern: So untersuchen Roto & Kaikkonen (2003) den Web-Browser des Nokia 7650. Zum Zeitpunkt der Studie bestanden jedoch wesentliche Einschränkungen bezüglich der Hardware, wie etwa die geringe Bildschirmauflösung von 176 × 208 Pixeln und die Verfügbarkeit von nur 4096 Farben. In einer weiteren Studie wurde die Nutzungserfahrung von mobilen Browsern mit denen auf Desktop-PCs verglichen (Shrestha, 2007). Die Eingabemethode durch einen Joystick führte im Vergleich zur gewohnten Bedienung eines Browsers mit Tastatur und Maus zu Usability-Problemen. Voigts, Christmann & Hagenhoff (2011) führen verschiedene Ein- und Ausgabemethoden für die nutzerfreundliche Gestaltung von Web-Browsern auf; zudem werden mobile Web-Browser hinsichtlich technischer Aspekte der Seitendarstellung vorgestellt. Eine vergleichende Analyse der Interaktionsmöglichkeiten zeigt, dass sich die Usability zwischen den Endgeräten deutlich unterscheidet.

2 Ziel und Vorgehen

Ziel dieses Beitrags ist es, durch eine vergleichende Evaluation der Hauptfunktionen mobiler Web-Browser in Hinblick auf deren Usability wesentliche Aspekte benutzerfreundlicher Browser herauszuarbeiten, um so einerseits Entwicklern Anhaltspunkte für künftige Weiterentwicklungen zu geben, und andererseits Anwendern die Auswahl eines geeigneten mobilen Browsers zu erleichtern. In unserer Studie werden die drei am häufigsten verwendeten Smartphone-Browser mit Methoden des Usability Testing untersucht. Zur deren Ermittlung wurden unterschiedliche Statistik-Portale mit Nutzungsdaten zu mobilen Browsern ausgewertet (Kap. 3.1). Anschließend wurden die wesentlichen Funktionen mobiler Web-Browser mittels einer Explorationsstudie ermittelt (Kap. 3.2). Die Ergebnisse der Funktionsanalyse dienen der Formulierung von Tasks für die anschließenden Usability-Evaluation (Kap. 3.3 – 3.6). In der Evaluationsstudie wurde die Umsetzung der Funktionen in den einzelnen Browsern vergleichend mit sechs Nutzern analysiert. Dazu wurden neben qualitativen Daten in Form von Screenvideos und *think aloud*-Protokollen auch quantitative Daten mit einer für die Evaluation angepassten Version des *User Experience Questionnaires* (UEQ, vgl. Laugwitz et al. 2006) erhoben. Die Ergebnisse der Erhebung werden in Kap. 4 näher diskutiert; Kap. 5 fasst die Studie in einem kurzen Fazit zusammen.

3 Evaluationsdesign

Um die Usability mobiler Browser zu erfassen, wurde ein Experimentaldesign entwickelt, das im folgenden Abschnitt vorgestellt wird. Zunächst wird beschrieben, welche Browser als Testobjekte ausgewählt wurden. Im Anschluss daran werden wesentliche Funktionen mobiler Browser diskutiert, die als Grundlage für die Evaluations-Tasks dienen. Neben der Wahl der Testpersonen und dem Versuchsaufbau werden schließlich der Ablauf und die verwendeten Testmaterialien erläutert.

3.1 Browser für mobile Endgeräte

Die Internetseite *StatCounter*[1] bietet neben weiteren Statistiken zu verwandten Themen auch eine Übersicht über die am häufigsten verwendeten mobilen Web-Browser. Der Anbieter misst absolute Zugriffswerte auf über drei Millionen Partnerwebseiten. Eine weitere Datenquelle zur Browsernutzung ist die Webseite *NetMarketShare*[2]. Wie auch bei *StatCounter* werden die Nutzungsdaten über Partnerwebseiten ermittelt, allerdings liegen bei *NetMarketShare* mit 40.000 Webseiten weniger Daten zur Auswertung zugrunde. Zudem misst *NetMarketShare* nicht absolute Zugriffszahlen, sondern Aufrufe pro Person. Tabelle 1 liefert einen Überblick über die drei am häufigsten genutzten, mobilen Web-Browser laut der beiden beschriebenen Statistikportale. Eine Analyse der wichtigsten Merkmale und Funktionen mobiler Browser folgt im nächsten Abschnitt.

Browser	**Hersteller**	**Veröffentlichung**	**Engine**	**Betriebssystem-Kompatabilität**
Safari	Apple Inc.	Juni 2007	WebKit	iOS
Android Stock Browser	Google Inc.	September 2008	WebKit	Android
Opera Mini	Opera Software ASA	Herbst 2005	Small-Screen-Rendering über Proxy-Server	iOS, Android, Java-fähige Smartphones

Tabelle 1: Übersicht zu den drei am häufigsten genutzten, mobilen Web-Browsern.

3.2 Merkmale und Funktionen mobiler Browser

Um die Funktionen moderner Browser für das Experimentaldesign systematisch zu erfassen, wurde eine Exploration der drei meistverwendeten Browser durchgeführt. Dabei erfolgte die Erfassung in Form eines explorativen Walkthroughs der einzelnen Browser (Tabelle 2).

Generische Funktionsbeschreibung	**Apple Safari**	**Android Stock Browser**	**Opera Mini**
URL-Eingabe	Adressleiste	Omnibox	Adressleiste
Suchmaschinen-Suche	Suchleiste		Such- oder Adressleiste
Vorwärts-/Rückwärts-Navigation	Buttons in unterer Leiste	Im Optionsmenü, Android Zurück-Taste	Buttons in unterer Leiste
Tabs/Fenster	Button in unterer Leiste	Button neben Suchleiste	Button in unterer Leiste
Lesezeichen	Lesezeichenmanager	Im Optionsmenü	Button in der Adressleiste, Lesezeichenmanager

[1] StatCounter: Top 9 Mobile Browsers from Jan 2009 to Aug 2013, http://gs.statcounter.com/#mobile_browser-ww-monthly-200901-201308, letzter Zugriff am 18.6.2014

[2] NetMarketShare: Mobile browser market share, http://www.netmarketshare.com (Timeframe: 2008 – 2013), letzter Zugriff am 19.3.2014

Verlauf	Im Lesezeichen-Menü	Im Lesezeichenmanager	Im Optionsmenü
Seite durchsuchen	Über Suchleiste	Im Optionsmenü	Im Optionsmenü
Teilen	Teilen-Menü (beschränkt)	Im Optionsmenü (Apps können Eintrag hinzufügen)	Im Optionsmenü (beschränkt)
Offline-Zugriff	Leseliste	Im Optionsmenü	Im Optionsmenü
Desktop-Version	Nicht verfügbar	Im Optionsmenü	Nicht verfügbar

Tabelle 2: Hauptfunktionen der drei meistgenutzten, mobilen Browser.

3.3 Testpersonen

Um den Ablauf der Usability-Evaluation und die Verständlichkeit der Tasks zu überprüfen, wurde ein Pretest mit einer Testperson durchgeführt. Da sich keine Probleme bei der Durchführung ergaben, wurden die Daten des Pretests ebenfalls für die Auswertung verwendet. Für die Tests wurden weitere fünf Testpersonen herangezogen. Laut Nielsen (1998) ist diese Anzahl an Testpersonen ausreichend, um etwa 80 % der vorhandenen Usability-Probleme aufzudecken (*guerilla usability approach*). Bei den Testpersonen handelt es sich durchweg um Studenten der Universität Regensburg im Alter von 22 bis 26 Jahren. Alle Testpersonen wiesen bereits Erfahrung im Umgang mit Smartphones auf; somit konnte der Einfluss des „mobilen Endgeräts“ als Störvariable für den Usability-Test minimiert werden.

3.4 Versuchsaufbau

Die Evaluation wurde in einem ruhigen Raum mit wenig Ablenkung durchgeführt („Wohnzimmer-Setting“). Das gewählte Umfeld erleichterte zudem die Datenerhebung in Form von Screenvideos und *think aloud*-Protokollen, da Störquellen weitestgehend vermieden werden konnten. Eine Sitzung dauerte jeweils ca. eine Stunde, wobei jeder der Probanden alle drei Browser randomisiert mit sechs Testszenarien zu acht Hauptfunktionen mobiler Browser testete. Als Testgeräte kamen dabei ein *iPhone 4* (Betriebssystem: *iOS 6*) von *Apple* für die Browser *Safari* und *Opera Mini* zum Einsatz, während für *Androids Stock Browser* ein *HTC Sensation* (Betriebssystem: *JellyBean*, Ver. 4.1.2) verwendet wurde.

3.5 Testablauf

Zu Beginn jeder Testsitzung wurden den Studienteilnehmern die wesentlichen Ziele der Evaluation kurz erläutert (*briefing*). Dabei wurden neben der allgemeinen Vorgehensweise auch die Methoden der Datenerhebung erklärt: Einerseits erfolgte die Datenerfassung durch die Aufzeichnung des Bildschirms sowie der Äußerungen während der Evaluation. Andererseits wurden vom Testleiter Schlüsselereignisse und Aussagen der Testpersonen in *think aloud*-Protokollen schriftlich dokumentiert. Danach füllten die Studienteilnehmern eine Einverständniserklärung zur Nutzung der Daten und einen Fragebogen zur Erhebung demografischer Daten und Informationen zur Smartphone- und Interneterfahrung aus. Anschließend wurden die drei Browser in randomisierter Reihenfolge getestet. Dazu mussten die

Testpersonen mit jedem Web-Browser die gleichen sechs Testszenarien absolvieren. Im Anschluss an den Test eines Browsers wurde jeweils eine Teilmenge der Fragen des UEQ beantwortet. Nachdem alle drei Browser getestet wurden erfolgte ein *debriefing* der Teilnehmer, in dem mögliche Fragen zum Testablauf oder zu speziellen Handlungsschritten gemeinsam diskutiert wurden. Somit wurde sichergestellt, dass Unklarheiten für die Auswertung aufgelöst wurden.

3.6 Testmaterialien

Der zu Beginn jeder Testsitzung gestellte Fragebogen umfasste Fragen zu demografischen Daten wie etwa Alter, Geschlecht, Beruf und Schulbildung. Ferner wurden Informationen zu Vorkenntnissen der Nutzer im Umgang mit Internet und Web-Browsern sowie die allgemeine Erfahrung mit Smartphones erfasst. Zudem erhielten alle Studienteilnehmern sechs Aufgaben in gedruckter Form, die sicherstellen, dass die zuvor ermittelten Hauptfunktionen, die alle drei Browser gemeinsam haben, während der Evaluation von den Nutzern exploriert werden.

> *Beispiel*: Aufgabe (1) Sie sind auf der Suche nach neuen Kleidungsstücken und möchten dazu auf Zalando etwas Passendes finden. Besuchen Sie www.zalando.de und wählen ein beliebiges Kleidungsstück für die nähere Betrachtung aus. Da Ihnen das Kleidungsstück gefällt, möchten Sie die Detailseite als Lesezeichen speichern.

Im Anschluss an den Test jedes Browsers erhielten die Probanden einen Fragebogen zur Erfassung der Usability der Testobjekte. Dazu wurde aus dem UEQ die Dimension der *Benutzungsqualität* isoliert. Die beiden anderen Dimensionen (*Attraktivität* und *Designqualität*) sind für die Erhebung der Usability nicht relevant, und wurden deshalb zur Minimierung der Belastung für die Testpersonen aus dem Fragebogen entfernt.

4 Diskussion der Ergebnisse

Bei der Auswertung der Evaluationsergebnisse wurden die Daten des UEQ mit den Usability-Problemen aus den *think aloud*-Protokollen abgeglichen. Zur Vorbereitung wurden die Probleme nach Schweregrad und Auftretenswahrscheinlichkeit sortiert (vgl. Rubin & Chisnell, 2008). Die Mittelwerte für die drei Skalen „Durchschaubarkeit“, „Effizienz“ und „Steuerbarkeit“ der Dimension der Benutzungsqualität des UEQ liegen zwischen +3 und -3. Dabei entsprechen Werte zwischen +1 und -1 einer neutralen Beurteilung. Niedrigere Werte als -1 entsprechen einer negativen, und Werte höher als +1 einer positiven Bewertung. Da Extremwerte bei Likert-Skalen vermieden werden sollten, ergibt sich ein Wertebereich zwischen +2 und -2. Werte an der oberen oder unteren Grenze dieses Felds können als signifikant positiv bzw. negativ interpretiert werden (Rauschenberger, Schrepp, Perez-Cota, Olschner & Thomaschewski, 2013). Tabelle 3 fasst die quantitativen Ergebnisse zusammen:

Funktion	Browser	Durchschau-barkeit	Effizienz	Steuer-barkeit	Usability-Probleme	Durchschnitt. Severity Rank
Aufrufen einer URL	Android	2,125	1,500	2,083	1	3
	Safari	1,917	0,792	1,792	1	3
	Opera	2,000	1,333	1,875	2	3
Suche in einer Suchmaschine	Android	2,542	2,125	2,292	1	3
	Safari	1,625	1,458	1,292	1	3
	Opera	2,000	1,708	1,583	1	4
Vorwärts- / Rückwärts-navigation	Android	1,750	1,542	1,708	1	3
	Safari	1,958	1,708	1,958	1	3
	Opera	1,417	1,500	1,167	3	3
Surfen mit Tabs / Fenstern	Android	1,917	1,375	1,708	1	6
	Safari	1,917	1,000	1,833	0	0
	Opera	1,458	1,333	1,667	0	0
Verwalten von Lesezeichen	Android	1,875	1,792	1,958	2	3
	Safari	-0,208	0,000	-0,167	5	3,8
	Opera	0,917	0,958	0,750	4	3,5
Anwendung des Surfverlaufs	Android	1,792	1,083	2,000	2	5
	Safari	1,167	0,958	0,792	0	0
	Opera	1,875	1,125	1,625	0	0
Speichern für Offline-Zugriff	Android	1,625	1,542	1,708	0	0
	Safari	0,167	0,667	0,417	3	5
	Opera	0,542	0,583	0,667	3	5
Durchsuchen einer Seite	Android	1,958	1,708	1,958	0	0
	Safari	-1,000	0,750	-0,417	4	6
	Opera	1,458	1,625	1,875	1	3

Tabelle 3: Mittelwerte des UEQ.

Im Folgenden werden die wesentlichen Ergebnisse für jede der Browser-Hauptfunktionen diskutiert, und als Fazit für die Entwickler künftiger Browser zusammengefasst.

Funktion: Aufrufen einer URL

Im ersten der sechs gestellten Tasks bestand die Aufgabe darin, eine vorgegebene URL aufzurufen. In allen drei Browsern findet sich dazu eine Eingabeleiste am oberen Rand der Anwendung. Am besten wird bei dieser Funktion *Googles Android Stock Browser* bewertet, vermutlich da durch den Verzicht auf eine separate Suchleiste (statt dessen: *Omnibox*) eine bessere Übersichtlichkeit entsteht. Einige Testpersonen bemängelten, dass bei *Safari* während des Ladens einer Seite keine weitere Interaktion möglich ist.

Fazit: Kombination von URL-Adressleiste und Suchleiste wird am besten bewertet.

Funktion: Suche in einer Suchmaschine

Zur Untersuchung der Integration von Suchmaschinen in den drei Browsern sollten die Probanden über die Suchmaschine *Google* einen Artikel in der *Wikipedia* aufrufen. Auch bei dieser Funktion wird der *Android Stock Browser* durch die einzelne, multifunktionale Eingabeleiste (*Omnibox*) besser als seine Konkurrenten bewertet. Die beiden Browser *Safari* und *Opera* nutzen für die Formulierung einer Anfrage an die eingestellte Suchmaschine ein eigenes Eingabefeld, das allerdings von einigen Probanden übersehen wird. Alle drei Browser werden für diese Hauptaufgabe eines mobilen Browsers durchweg positiv beurteilt, was sich auch in der geringen Anzahl der Usability-Probleme niederschlägt.

Fazit: Kombination von URL-Adressleiste und Suchleiste wird am besten bewertet.

Funktion: Vorwärts- / Rückwärtsnavigation

In der Funktion zur Vorwärts- und Rückwärtsnavigation innerhalb des Browsers liegen die Bewertungen für die drei Browser in allen Skalen der Benutzungsqualität des UEQ im positiven Bereich. In den Browsern *Safari* und *Opera* ist die Funktion über zwei Pfeile am unteren Rand des Anwendungsbereichs realisiert, bei *Android Stock Browser* erfolgt die Rückwärtsnavigation über den standardmäßigen Hardware-Button und die Vorwärtsnavigation über das Optionsmenü.

Fazit: Im Falle des Android-Browsers liegt es nahe, die auf dieser Plattform etablierte Funktion (Hardware-Button für „ein Schritt zurück“) für die Rückwärtsnavigation im Browser zu verwenden; ansonsten sollten sich mobile Browser an Navigationselementen orientieren, die für den Desktop-Bereich bereits etabliert sind.

Funktion: Surfen mit Tabs / Fenstern

In zwei der sechs Tasks wurde die Funktion zum Surfen mit Fenstern überprüft. Bei den Browsern *Safari* und *Opera* kam es dabei zu keinerlei Usability-Problemen. Einige Nutzer merkten zur Schaltfläche des *Android Stock Browser* zur Auslösung des Features an, dass diese nicht die Funktion zum Wechseln von Fenstern suggeriert. Des Weiteren verbirgt sich hinter der genannten Schaltfläche nicht nur die benötigte Funktion, sondern darüber hinaus auch noch Buttons zum Browserverlauf und den Lesezeichen. Da im *Android Stock Browser* viele Funktionen in das Optionsmenü verlagert wurden, vermuteten einige Nutzer die Schaltfläche zur Fensterverwaltung zunächst ebenfalls darin.

Fazit: Safari und Opera verwenden ein weitgehend konventionalisiertes Icon für das Öffnen von Tabs, das sich zudem an der gleichen Position, am unteren Bildschirmrand befindet. Das Surfen mit mehreren Tabs / Fenstern ist eine essenzielle Funktion mobiler Browser und sollte direkt mit einem Klick erreichbar sein und nicht mit anderen Funktionen (Bookmarks, Verlauf, etc.) in einem Menü vermischt werden.

Funktion: Verwalten von Lesezeichen

Bei der Lesezeichenverwaltung wurde der *Android Stock Browser* durchweg besser bewertet als die beiden anderen Browser. Dies ist vor allem durch die spezifischen Usability-Probleme von Safari und Opera zu erklären. Bei Safari vermissten manche Probanden die Möglichkeit zum Öffnen von Kontextmenüs mit einem langen Klick. Weitere Probleme bei *Safari* hängen mit der Gestaltung der Lesezeichenliste und dem häufig nicht gefundenen Button zum Hinzufügen eines Lesezeichens über das „Teilen“-Menü zusammen. Bei *Operas* Browser trat mehrfach das Problem auf, dass die Nutzer den Button zum Hinzufügen von Lesezeichen in Form eines Plus-Icons, mit dem Favicon der Webseite verwechselten. Des Weiteren wurde mangelndes Feedback und die Sortierung der Lesezeichenliste bemängelt.

Fazit: Während bei Opera und Safari das Erstellen neuer Lesezeichen über die jeweiligen Icons nicht intuitiv ist, kann die Funktion beim Android-Browser direkt über den Hardware-Button „Kontext-Menü" erreicht werden, wo sie als gut verständliche Wortmarke („Lesezeichen hinzufügen") aufgeführt ist.

Funktion: Anwendung des Surfverlaufs

In einem weiteren Task sollte eine bereits aufgerufene Seite über den Surfverlauf der Browser erneut besucht werden. Bei den beiden Browsern *Opera* und *Safari* traten dabei keinerlei Schwierigkeiten auf. Trotz der positiven Beurteilungen für den *Android Stock Browser* wurden bei dieser Funktion einige Usability-Probleme entdeckt: Durch die Auslagerung zentraler Funktionen in das *Android*-spezifische Optionsmenü vermuteten einige Nutzer auch den Surfverlauf dort. Durch die Platzierung dieser Funktion im gleichen Menü, in dem auch Fenster und Lesezeichen verwaltet werden können, und das ungünstig gewählte Icon zu diesem Menü, traten bei einigen Probanden ebenfalls Probleme auf.

Fazit: Bei *Safari* und *Opera* kam es zu keinerlei Problemen. Bei *Opera* ist die Funktion des Surfverlaufs im Menü des Browsers untergebracht. *Safari* platziert den Verlauf im Lesezeichenmenü oberhalb der eigentlichen Lesezeichen. Ein Problem im *Android Stock Browser* ist die stark erschwerte Erreichbarkeit des Surfverlaufs.

Funktion: Speichern einer Seite für den Offline-Zugriff

Die Möglichkeit zur Speicherung von Webseiten für den Offline-Zugriff ist hauptsächlich bei mobilen Browsern zu finden und ermöglicht das Lesen von zuvor gespeicherten Seiten auch in Situationen, in denen kein Internetzugang möglich ist. Bei dieser Funktion wird der *Android Stock Browser* am besten bewertet. In *Safari* wird die Funktion als *Leseliste* bezeichnet, was bei einigen Nutzern zu Verwirrung führte. Das bereits bei der Funktion zum Hinzufügen von Lesezeichen erwähnte Icon in Form eines Plus-Zeichens kommt bei *Operas* Browser auch bei der Speicherung von Seiten für den Offline-Zugriff zum Einsatz, und wird hier ebenfalls mit dem Favicon der Seite verwechselt. Auch bei dieser Funktion wurde von einigen Nutzern die Sortierung der bereits gespeicherten Seiten bemängelt. Ein weiteres Manko bei *Opera* stellt die Schaltfläche für den Offline-Zugriff im Menü dar. Das Icon in Form einer Kamera und das Label führte bei einigen Nutzern zu Verwirrung.

Fazit: Der *Android Stock Browser* platziert die Funktion zum Speichern von Seiten im bereits erwähnten, betriebssystem-spezifischen Kontextmenü. Ein Problem stellt – wie bei der Funktion des Surfverlaufs – die schwere Erreichbarkeit der gespeicherten Seiten dar. Allerdings führte dies bei den Nutzern zu keinen großen Schwierigkeiten, da die Navigationsschritte bereits aus vorangehenden Tasks bekannt waren; dies lässt wiederum auf ein leicht zu erlernendes Interaktionskonzept schließen.

Funktion: Durchsuchen einer Webseite

Auch bei der Funktion zum Durchsuchen von Webseiten treten beim *Android Stock Browser* keinerlei Probleme auf. Bei *Opera* wurde die ungenügende Hervorhebung, falls die Suche keine Treffer ergibt, bemängelt. In *Safari* traten bei der Evaluation dieser Funktion erhebliche Mängel auf: Fünf der sechs Testpersonen mussten die Aufgabe frühzeitig abbrechen, da sie die Funktion im Browser nicht fanden. Lediglich ein Proband erkannte die Suchleiste am rechten, oberen Rand des Browsers, die gewöhnlich zur Suche in Suchmaschinen verwendet wird, als Möglichkeit zur Suche auf der Seite. Allerdings führte das fehlende Feedback, wenn keine Treffer gefunden wurden, zu dem Problem, dass durch das Drücken der Bestätigen-Taste in der Tastatur die Google-Suche ausgelöst wurde.

Fazit: Suchfenster im rechten, oberen Bildschirmbereich (direkt neben der URL-Eingabe) werden als Möglichkeit der Web-Suche erkannt (gelerntes Verhalten aus dem Desktop-Bereich). Aus diesem Grund sollte die eher selten verwendete Funktion der seiteninternen Suche nicht an dieser Stelle platziert werden, sondern in ein Kontextmenü ausgelagert werden.

5 Zusammenfassung

Dieser Beitrag beschreibt eine vergleichende Usability-Evaluation von drei häufig genutzten Web-Browsern für mobile Endgeräte. Dabei wurden zunächst wesentliche Funktionen mobiler Browser mithilfe eines explorativen Walkthroughs ermittelt. Diese Funktionen wurden dann in einer Benutzerstudie in Form spezifischer Tasks evaluiert. Es zeigt sich, dass typische Funktionen teilweise sehr unterschiedlich von den unterschiedlichen Browsern umgesetzt werden, und die verschiedenen Browser dementsprechend unterschiedliche Usability-Probleme aufweisen. Die Ergebnisse mögen als Anhaltspunkt für Browser-Entwickler dienen, um die erkannten Schwächen der jeweiligen Browser zu optimieren, oder Anwender bei der Auswahl eines benutzerfreundlichen, mobilen Browsers unterstützen. Zudem können die identifizierten Hauptfunktionen mobiler Browser als Grundlage für weitere Evaluationsstudien (andere Browser / mehr Testpersonen / etc.) herangezogen werden, und mit kleineren Anpassungen auch auf den Desktop-Bereich übertragen werden.

Literaturverzeichnis

Accenture. (2011). Mobile Web Watch 2011. < http://www.accenture.com/SiteCollectionDocuments/Local_Germany/PDF/Accenture-Studie-Mobile-Web-Watch-2011.pdf>, letzter Zugriff am 19.3.2014

Accenture. (2012). Mobile Web Watch 2012. <http://www.accenture.com/SiteCollectionDocuments/PDF/Accenture-Study-Mobile-Web-Watch-Germany-Austria-Switzerland-EN.pdf>, letzter Zugriff am 19.3.2014

Gardner, B. S. (2011). Responsive Web Design: Enriching the User Experience. In: Sigma (Noblis Technical Journal) 11(1), 13–19.

Google, & Nielsen. (2013). Mobile Search Moments Study: Understanding how mobile drives conversions. <http://www.google.com/think/research-studies/creating-moments-that-matter.html>, letzter Zugriff am 19.3.2014

Laugwitz, B., Schrepp, M., & Held, T. (2006). Konstruktion eines Fragebogens zur Messung der User Experience von Softwareprodukten. In: Heinicke, A. (Hg.) Mensch und Computer im Strukturwandel. Proc. Mensch & Computer 2006, Gelsenkirchen, September 2006, München / Wien: Oldenbourg Verlag, 125–134.

Marcotte, E. (2010). Responsive Web Design. A List Apart. <http://alistapart.com/article/responsive-web-design>, letzter Zugriff am 19.3.2014

Nielsen, J. (1998). Cost of User Testing a Website. <http://www.nngroup.com/articles/cost-of-user-testing-a-website/>, letzter Zugriff am 19.3.2014

Rauschenberger, M., Schrepp, M., Perez-Cota, M., Olschner, S., & Thomaschewski, J. (2013). Efficient Measurement of the User Experience of Interactive Products. How to use the User Experience Questionnaire (UEQ).Example: Spanish Language Version. International Journal of Interactive Multimedia and Artificial Intelligence, 2(1), 39–45.

Roto, V., & Kaikkonen, A. (2003). Perception of Narrow Web Pages on a Mobile Phone. In Proc. 19th International Symposium on Human Factors in Telecommunications 2003 (HFT 2003), Berlin, December 2003. Boston: Information Gatekeepers, 187-194.

Rubin, J., & Chisnell, D. (2008). Handbook of usability testing (2nd ed.). Indianapolis: Wiley.

Shrestha, S. (2007). Mobile web browsing. In Chong, P. H. J.; Cheok, A. D. (Hrsg.) Proc. 4th International Conference on Mobile Technology, Applications, and Systems (Mobility 2007), Singapur, September 2007. New York: ACM Press, 187-194.

Voigts, R., Christmann, S., & Hagenhoff, S. (2011). Mobile Web Browsers (Working Paper No. 01). <http://www2.as.wiwi.uni-goettingen.de/getfile?DateiID=713>, letzter Zugriff am 19.3.2014

Wroblewski, L. (2011). Mobile First. New York: A Book Apart.

Kontaktinformationen

Manuel Burghardt
Lehrstuhl für Medieninformatik
Universität Regensburg
93040 Regensburg

E-Mail: manuel.burghardt@ur.de
Webseite: www.mi.ur.de

M. Koch, A. Butz & J. Schlichter (Hrsg.): Mensch und Computer 2014 Tagungsband,
München: Oldenbourg Wissenschaftsverlag, 2014, S. 115-124.

Adaptierbare Qualitätsbewertung bürgergenerierter Inhalte aus sozialen Medien

Christian Reuter, Michael Ritzkatis

Institut für Wirtschaftsinformatik, Universität Siegen

Zusammenfassung

Zwei Drittel aller Internetnutzer in Deutschland nutzen soziale Medien. Neben der Kommunikation mit eigenen Kontakten werden dort auch vermehrt Fotos, Filme und Inhalte ganz bewusst öffentlich geteilt. Vergangene Ereignisse, wie das Hochwasser in Mitteleuropa im Juni 2013, haben gezeigt, dass diese alltäglichen Verhaltensweisen ebenso in Ausnahmesituationen fortgeführt werden und bürgergenierte Inhalte auch dann beispielsweise über Facebook und Twitter verbreitet werden. Diese werden in Teilen von Behörden und Organisationen mit Sicherheitsaufgaben (BOS), wie der Polizei und Feuerwehr, ausgewertet und für die Lagebeurteilung genutzt. Dieser Beitrag stellt, basierend auf einer Analyse verwandter Arbeiten, die Ergebnisse einer empirischen Untersuchung zur Nutzung bürgergenerierter Inhalte und die Bedingungen für deren Integration in die Lagebeurteilung durch BOS dar. Die hieraus gewonnenen Erkenntnisse münden in Anforderungen an einen adaptierbaren Bewertungsmechanismus für bürgergenerierte Inhalte aus sozialen Medien.

1 Einleitung

Gemäß einer repräsentativen Studie des Bundesverbands Informationswirtschaft, Telekommunikation und neue Medien (BITKOM, 2013) sind mehr als drei Viertel der Internetnutzer in mindestens einem sozialen Netzwerk angemeldet, zwei Drittel sind aktive Nutzer. Auch wenn das Versenden privater Nachrichten die am häufigsten genutzte Funktionalität ist (85%), kommen das Hochladen eigener Fotos und Filme (65%) sowie das Teilen von Fotos, Videos, Texten oder Links (65%) auf beachtliche Nutzungszahlen. Auch in Ausnahmesituationen, wie dem Love-Parade Unglück 2010 (Reuter et al., 2011), der Nuklearkatastrophe von Fukushima (Thomson et al., 2012) oder zuletzt dem mitteleuropäischen Hochwasser 2013 (Kaufhold & Reuter, 2014), wurden soziale Medien von Betroffenen und Helfern genutzt, um Informationen bereitzustellen und auszutauschen. Doch (wie) werden diese Inhalte in der Gefahrenabwehr durch BOS genutzt? Und welche Anforderungen ergeben sich für die Gestaltung interaktiver Systeme zur Bewertung und Selektion dieser Inhalte? Basierend auf einer Darstellung relevanter Vorarbeiten (Kapitel 2) stellt dieser Beitrag die Ergebnisse einer empirischen Untersuchung zur Nutzung bürgergenerierter Inhalte durch BOS vor (Kapitel 3) und leitet Anforderungen für einen adaptierbaren Bewertungsmechanismus her (Kapitel 4).

2 Lagebeurteilung mit sozialen Medien

Informationen sind für die Beurteilung einer Schadenslage unerlässlich. Sie müssen zur richtigen Zeit, am richtigen Ort und in der richtigen Form vorhanden sein (Ley et al., 2012). Da Schadenslagen nicht nur zeitkritisch sondern auch einzigartig sind, bestehen ganz spezielle Informationsbedürfnisse, die im Vorfeld nicht bekannt sein können, und es fällt schwer, alle möglicherweise benötigten Informationen vorzuhalten (Turoff et al., 2004). Die Verfügbarkeit möglichst vieler Quellen, auf die ohne Verzögerung zugegriffen werden kann, erscheint notwendig. Gleichzeitig muss eine mögliche Informationsüberflutung verhindert werden, um die Entscheidungsfindung nicht zu beeinträchtigen (Hiltz & Plotnick, 2013).

Neben automatisiert bereitgestellten Informationen (Wetterdaten, Pegelstände, etc.) können zwei verschiedene Klassen menschlicher Informationsquellen unterschieden werden: Einsatzkräfte vor Ort, welche angefragt werden können (Ludwig et al., 2013; Reuter & Ritzkatis, 2013), sowie Personen oder Organisationen, die nicht aktiv an der Schadensbewältigung beteiligt sind. Bei einem Hausbrand kann die Anzahl der Bewohner über das Einwohnermeldeamt erfragt werden, wohingegen die Beurteilung der Größe des Feuers und möglicher Anwesender nur vor Ort begutachtet werden kann. Bei einem Stromausfall kann der Stromnetzbetreiber den Einsatzkräften schneller und besser Informationen über die betroffenen Gebiete zukommen lassen, als wenn diese vor Ort ermittelt werden würden (Ley et al., 2012). Die Bilder mancher Schäden finden sich jedoch in sozialen Medien. Durch diese Beispiele wird deutlich, dass extern beschaffte Informationen einerseits den Ablauf beschleunigen können und andererseits zum Teil vor Ort gar nicht ermittelt werden können. Nicht immer berichten Bürger dabei in Form von sachlichen Informationen. In einigen Fällen kommt es bei diesen subjektiven Informationsmeldungen dazu, dass eine gewisse Art von Selbstjustiz entsteht (Rizza et al., 2013). Daneben kann es zu Fehlinformationen kommen, wenn Situationen bewusst oder unbewusst fehlerhaft geschildert werden; sei es, weil sie einigen Aspekten nicht genügend Bedeutung widmen oder aber weil sie die Situation falsch wiedergeben (Thomson et al., 2012). Es gibt jedoch auch Informationen, die nicht auf alternative Weise beschafft werden können (Zagel, 2012). Zur Selektion und Nutzung bürgergenerierte Informationen existieren bereits einige Ansätze, die allerdings keine umfassende Qualitätsbewertung unterstützen:

- *Twitcident* (Terpstra et al., 2012) dient der Selektion von Tweets auf Basis von Schlagwörtern, der Art der Nachricht oder eines Nutzers mit anschließender Darstellung auf einer Karte. Derzeit bietet es leider keine Qualitätsbewertung anhand von Metainformationen wie bspw. dem Zeitpunkt der Erstellung – weiterhin bezieht es keine Informationen aus anderen sozialen Medien.
- *SensePlace2* (Robinson et al., 2013) demonstriert ebenfalls eine Möglichkeit, georeferenzierte Informationen aus Tweets zu extrahieren und diese in einer Lagekarte

darzustellen. Es handelt sich jedoch um eine umfängliche Erfassung ohne Qualitätsbewertung, die die Problematik der Informationsflut nicht adressiert.

- *Tweet4act* (Chowdhury et al. 2013) ermöglicht die Ermittlung und Klassifizierung von Informationen, die über Twitter verbreitet wurden. Dabei wird jede Nachricht mit einem schadenslagenspezifischen Wörterbuch in eine Schadensperiode klassifiziert. Hierfür wird sich spezieller Methoden des Maschinellen Lernens auf Basis von Wörterbüchern oder Sprachklassifizierungen.
- Mit *TwitInfo* (Marcus et al., 2011) können viele Informationen eines speziellen Ereignisses gesammelt, klassifiziert und visualisiert werden. Neben einer graphischen Visualisierung werden viele Informationen über die eigentliche Qualität der Informationen präsentiert. Eine persönliche Gewichtung der Qualitätsansprüche des Benutzers findet keine Anwendung.
- Mit *Ushahidi* (Mcclendon & Robinson, 2012) können sich Bürger gegenseitig Informationen zukommen lassen. Darüber hinaus ist es prinzipiell möglich, die Daten auch Einsatzkräften zur Verfügung zu stellen. Die direkte Kommunikation und ungefilterte Informationsbereitstellung birgt jedoch die Gefahr einer Informationsflut und fordert den Empfänger zu einer manuellen Qualitätsbewertung auf.
- Mit *Tweak the Tweet* (Starbird & Stamberger, 2010) wird die Auswertung und Klassifizierung der Informationen unterstützt. Obwohl diese Syntax verschiedene Qualitätsbewertungen ermöglicht, verhindert die Auswertung von Informationen nur eines bestimmten Formats auch eine übersichtliche Lagedarstellung.

Zusammengefasst lässt sich feststellen, dass bereits viele Studien und Ansätze den Umgang mit bürgergenerierten Inhalten thematisieren, jedoch die Thematik der Qualitätsbewertung, wenn überhaupt, nur rudimentär behandeln. Um die tatsächliche Nutzung bürgergenerierter Inhalte und die Bedingungen für deren Integration in die Lagebeurteilung von BOS zu erarbeiten, erscheint eine empirische Studie sinnvoll.

3 Empirische Studie: Nutzung bürgergenerierter Inhalte

Die dieser Arbeit zugrunde liegende empirische Studie der Informations- und Kommunikationsaktivitäten von BOS (hier insbesondere der Feuerwehr und Polizei) sowie Infrastrukturbetreiber (Stromnetz) wurde 2010 bis 2012 in zwei geographisch und strukturell verschiedenen Kreisen Nordrhein-Westfalens durchgeführt. Es wurden verschiedene qualitative Methoden wie Dokumentenanalysen, Beobachtungen, teilstrukturierte Interviews und Gruppendiskussionen durchgeführt und ausgewertet. Neben einer Fokussierung auf Improvisationspraktiken (Ley et al., 2012), der Zusammenarbeit örtlich verteilter Kräfte (Reuter & Ritzkatis, 2013) und der Reporting-Praktiken (Ludwig et al., 2013) wurde die Kooperation mit Bürgern und die Nutzung bürgergenerierter Inhalte thematisiert.

Ziel der *Dokumentenanalyse* war die Untersuchung offizieller Arbeitsabläufe mit Hilfe von Gesetzen und Richtlinien. Die *Beobachtungen* dienten dazu, Erkenntnisse über die tatsächliche praktische Arbeit zu erhalten. Diese wurden in der Leitstelle während eines normalen Arbeitstages (neun Stunden), im Krisenstab und der Einsatzleitung einer Krisenübung (vier Stunden) und eines Großereignisses (sechs Stunden) durchgeführt. Die 22 semi-strukturierten *Interviews* (je 90 Minuten; nummeriert als I01-22) dienten der Reflexion der Arbeitspraxis, der Identifikation möglicher IT-Unterstützung und interorganisationaler Informationsbedarfe und wurden mit Einsatzkräften verschiedener Ebenen durchgeführt. Sie fokussierten im ersten Teil die Arbeitstätigkeiten in normalen Lagen, im zweiten Teil potentielle Aufgaben im vorgelegten Szenario und im dritten Teil genutzte Informations- und Kommunikationstechnologien. Fünf ergänzende Interviews (je 60 Minuten; nummeriert als IM01-05) fokussierten mobile Kollaborationspraktiken. Die vier *Gruppendiskussionen* (je vier Stunden, nummeriert als W1-4) dienten der Erfassung kommunikativer Arbeitspraxen. Bei der Auswertung des vorliegenden Datenmaterials wurde sich an der Grounded Theory (Strauss, 2004) orientiert. Dazu wurden die Transskripte offen kodiert und die Aussagen in Textbausteine und spätere Kategorien aufgeteilt.

3.1 Nutzung sozialer Medien zur Lagebeurteilung

Generell kann eine Lagebeurteilung nicht nur auf Basis der organisationsinternen Informationen stattfinden. Externe Informationen können einen Informationsgewinn darstellen (W3). Insbesondere werden neben textuellen Informationen gerne von Bürgern veröffentlichte Bilder verwendet, mit denen der Schadenshergang bzw. der aktuelle Zustand besser beurteilt werden kann: *„Twitter ist ja häufig schneller mit Informationen als das bei uns über Polizeifunk oder Handy gelaufen ist. Wenn ich das bei Demogeschehen oder sonstiges sehe. [...] Auch diese sind häufig mit Bildern oder Videos hinterlegt im Internet zu finden bei aktuellen Ereignissen. Also da werden wir in Zukunft deutlich mehr mit zu tun haben, da bin ich mir ganz sicher"* (I2). Ein Beispiel ist die Nachbetrachtung eines Ereignisses: *„Unsere Ermittler, die nutzen diese Brandbilder ganz gerne, weil unsere Kripo ist natürlich in den Entstehungsphasen eines Brandes oder so sind die ja nicht vor Ort. Die sind natürlich dann sehr oft angewiesen [auf diese] [...] um diesen Brandverlauf dann noch einmal zu sehen"* (I02).

Informationen müssen aber nicht immer hilfreich sein: *„Informationen bringen immer dann was, wenn sie mein Verhalten beeinflussen. Immer dann, wenn Informationen da sind, die keinen Einfluss auf mein Verhalten haben, ist es eine Reizüberflutung"* (I06). Daher wird versucht, vor allem relevante Informationen zu sammeln: *„Wir versuchen ja von jedem Anrufer Informationen zu bekommen"* (I15). Auch im Einsatzgeschehen selbst werden Personen vor Ort aktiv und unterstützen die Einsatzkräfte: *„Es sind viele spezielle Sachen, wo man Grundkenntnisse oder Vorwissen haben sollte, aber es gibt auch viele Sachen, wo man auf Wissen und Fähigkeiten der Bürger zurückgreifen kann"* (I11). Abgesehen davon haben die Einsatzkräfte auch ganz besondere Anforderungen an alle Informationen, denn *„eine Information in einer Einsatzleitung z. B. zu haben, heißt nicht, dass man mit der Information auch irgendetwas machen kann"* (I06). Ungeachtet der Informationsmasse übt der Zeitfaktor erheblichen Druck auf die Einsatzkräfte aus. Daher ist es immens wichtig, dass jegliche Operation zeitnah durchgeführt wird. Daher besteht *„keine Zeit mich mit Fremden noch zu beschäftigen"* (I02). Die Fehlerhaftigkeit bürgergenerierter Informationen bleibt jedoch bestehen und macht deshalb eine Bewertung notwendig.

3.2 Selektion, Verarbeitung und Qualitätsbewertung

Im Einsatzgeschehen stellt sich die Frage: *„Wer bewertet das nun [...] und bringt uns das überhaupt in der Lagebeurteilung vorwärts?“* (I03). Vor allem die Masse der bürgergenierten Inhalte macht deren Nutzung problematisch: *„Und vor allen Dingen ist von den 300 ja 290 Müll. Da kannste aus zehn Informationen was für die raus ziehen“* (I02). Bei der Masse entsteht schnell das Problem, diese geeignet zu verarbeiten *„Du musst die halt alle lesen. Wenn da eine Vorgliederung da wäre, wäre das natürlich sehr hilfreich“* (I02). Aus diesem Grund ist eine automatische Filterung empfehlenswert: *„Es wäre schön, wenn man einen Filter drin hätte, der die wichtigen von den unwichtigen trennt“* (I03). Jedoch ist eine gewisse quantitative Häufigkeit einer Information notwendig, damit diese von den Einsatzkräften als glaubwürdig erachtet werden kann: *„Wenn ich eine Quelle habe, ist das ein Problem. Wenn ich fünf Quellen habe, ist das sicherlich seriöser als eine“* (I15). Insbesondere sind externe Quellen für Fehlinformationen anfällig (I14, I15) und müssen deshalb überprüft werden (I15): Man *„muss vorsichtig sein mit dem was drin steht, weil es nicht immer so ist, wie es wirklich ist“* (I14) - *„Da zeigt sich natürlich immer wieder, dass wir da aufs Glatteis geführt werden sollen [...] und wir müssen die Informationen bewerten für uns“* (I02). Dabei handelt es sich nicht immer um bewusste Fehlinformationen, sondern um die Art der subjektiven Wahrnehmung einer Situation, die für einen neutralen Betrachter ein anderes Bild ergeben kann. Insgesamt scheitert der Einsatz von Bürgerinformationen aus sozialen Medien an der Bewertung der Informationen durch Einsatzkräfte, denn *„da ist einfach irgend so ein Flaschenhals, über den wir nicht drüber kommen“* (I02).

Insgesamt ist erkennbar, dass *„je präziser die Informationen sind, desto besser sind die [Informationen]“* (I02). Diese Präzision der Informationen kann durch eine Bewertung sichergestellt werden. Insbesondere muss sichergestellt sein, dass die gefilterten Informationen einen Mehrwert für die Einsatzkräfte darstellen (I02, I03). Eine globale Filterung erweist sich auch als schwierig, *„weil was für den Abschnittsführer wichtig ist, das kann man, glaube ich, im Vorfeld nicht unbedingt filtern. Das kann sein, dass er die gleichen Informationen benötigt wie die Einsatzleitung“* (IM01). Daher muss eine Flexibilität der Bewertungskriterien gegeben sein (I19). Die persönliche Auswahl der Informationen muss aufgrund des zeitkritischen Aspekts von Schadenslagen unterstützt werden, denn jede Einsatzkraft muss *„relativ schnell das Wichtige vom Unwichtigen“* (I19) trennen.

Das erstellte Bild muss auf jeden Fall eine gewisse Aussagekraft widerspiegeln und hilfreich bei der Beurteilung der Situation sein: *„Wenn der jetzt ein Foto von einem Fenster macht, weiß ich, der hat da gestanden. Aber wo befindet sich das Fenster?“* (I16). Also benötigen die Bilder genau wie normale Textinformationen weitere Metainformationen. Bilder können gerade im Szenario der Beurteilung von Menschenmassen bei Großveranstaltungen sehr hilfreich sein: *„Hätte man festgestellt, dass sich an bestimmten Bereichen ein Personenstau ergeben hätte, hätte im oberen Bereich, also im Zulauf, sofort durch die Security der Zulauf gesperrt werden können“* (I06). Obwohl sich daraus motiviert, dass viele Informationen gesammelt werden sollten, wissen *„die meisten Leute [...] ja gar nicht, worauf es ankommt und was für Informationen wir haben müssten“* (I02). Somit besteht die Gefahr, dass Informationen keinen Mehrwert bieten und auch im Einsatzgeschehen nicht genutzt werden können: *„Ich glaube kaum, dass jemand, der nicht aus dem polizeilichen oder aus dem Feuer-*

wehrbereich kommt, in der Lage ist, in so einer Stresssituation notwendige Informationen zu liefern" (I02). Ein unausgebildeter Bürger kann dieses Wissen in den seltensten Fällen besitzen. *„Von daher muss man mit solchen Informationen sehr vorsichtig umgehen"* (I14).

Letztlich muss die Einsatzkraft die Verantwortung über die Handlungen übernehmen und entscheiden, ob eine Information verwendet wird oder nicht (I15). Fehlbewertungen sind sowohl durch Menschenhand als auch durch Computerunterstützung möglich. Egal wie gut durchdacht der Bewertungsmechanismus ist, es wird *„ein Restrisiko [geben] und das muss der Verantwortliche tragen, so einfach ist das"* (I15). Aus diesem Grund sind die Einsatzkräfte auch sehr vorsichtig in der Benutzung von externen Informationen. Abschließend lässt sich festhalten, dass *„Informationen zu bewerten, richtig zu bewerten und damit umzugehen [...] eine sehr anspruchsvolle Aufgabe ist"* (I15). Jede einzelne Information ist dabei wie ein Baustein zur Erstellung des gesamten Lagebildes zu betrachten: *„Also immer mehr an dieses Skelett, was man zunächst hat, Fleisch dran zu bringen, damit man nachher ein Bild hat, nicht nur eine Silhouette, sondern eine Gestalt und dass diese Gestalt dann maßgeblich ist für irgendwelche polizeiliche Maßnahmen"* (I16). Die Lagebeurteilung beeinflusst also die Maßnahmen, die die Lage wiederum verändern können. Jedoch ist eine Erhöhung der Masse an Informationen nicht sinnvoll, denn Informationen sind nicht immer brauchbar.

4 Adaptierbare Bewertung bürgergenerierter Inhalte

4.1 Synopse der Anforderungen

Die Literatur sowie die empirische Studie haben gezeigt, dass die Bewertung der Masseninformationen und die Extraktion der relevanten Informationen die größte Herausforderung darstellen. Auf dieser Basis wurde ein Bewertungsmechanismus für soziale Medien erstellt.

- *Plattformübergreifende Suche*: Durch eine offene Konzeptionierung können prinzipiell verschiedene Quellen für die Informationssuche einbezogen werden. So ergibt sich eine große Zeitersparnis, da die verschiedenen Quellen nicht separat durchsucht werden müssen. Die ebenfalls daraus resultierende größere Bandbreite kann eine bessere Verifizierung der vorhandenen Informationen auf Richtigkeit ermöglichen. So können einerseits verschiedene Informationstypen sowie andererseits ein umfassenderes Lagebild entstehen.
- *Automatisierte Verarbeitung*: Die Masse von bürgergenerierten Informationen macht eine manuelle Verarbeitung in zeitkritischen Schadenslagen schwierig. Daher werden die Informationen automatisiert nach den Vorgaben des Benutzers verarbeitet. Im Idealfall muss er nur wenige und insbesondere für ihn relevante Informationen betrachten.
- *Flexible und adaptierbare Bewertung*: Unsere empirische Studie hat gezeigt, dass unterschiedliche Schadenslagen unterschiedliche Informationen in verschiedenen Verdichtungen erfordern. Zusätzlich sind Qualitätsanforderungen immer abhängig vom Nutzer. Daher wird die Wahl und Gewichtung der Bewertungsmethoden allein in das Ermessen des Benutzers gelegt.

- *Nachvollziehbarkeit der Ergebnisse*: Um das Vertrauen der Benutzer in den Automatismus der Qualitätsbewertung zu erhöhen, wird dieser Vorgang so transparent wie möglich gestaltet. Es soll für den Benutzer nachvollziehbar sein, warum eine Information wie bewertet wurde. Dadurch begibt er sich nicht in eine Abhängigkeit eines geschlossenen Bewertungssystems, denn letztendlich muss die Einsatzkraft die Verwendung der Information verantworten.

4.2 Realisierung eines adaptierbaren Bewertungsservices

Zur Realisierung eines adaptierbaren Bewertungsservices wurden verschiedene Technologien verwendet. Spezielle APIs dienen dem Zugriff auf die Inhalte aus sozialen Medien – derzeit die Twitter Streaming API (https://dev.twitter.com/docs/api/streaming), Twitter REST API (https://dev.twitter.com/docs/api) sowie Facebook Graph API (https://developers.facebook.com/docs/graph-api). Die Inhalte werden anschließend in das OpenSocial Format (http://opensocial.org/) konvertiert. Das eigentliche Bewertungstool ist mit einer serviceorientierten Architektur (SOA) unter Zuhilfenahme des Apache Tomcat, zur Zentralisierung der Bewertung, realisiert. Eine Bereitstellung der bewerteten Daten in einem allgemeinem Format (hier: JavaScript Object Notation - JSON) ermöglicht eine Einbindung in verschiedene Architekturen.

Alle übermittelten Inhalte werden hinsichtlich jedes selektierten Bewertungskriteriums mit einem Maß des relativen Erfüllungsgrades, gemessen an der schlechtesten und besten Information in der Datensammlung, bewertet. Diese Bewertung kann sowohl auf Basis von Metadaten als auch mit Hilfe von Text-Mining-Methoden stattfinden. Insgesamt stellt das Bewertungstool 15 Bewertungsmethoden bereit, die sich in folgende vier Kategorien unterteilen lassen:

1. *Metadaten:* Autorenhäufigkeit, zeitliche Nähe, örtliche Nähe, Anzahl Follower/Likes, Metadaten
2. *Inhalt* (syntaktischer und semantischer Aufbau der Information sowie das Vorkommen gewisser Wortsequenzen)*:* Suchbegriffhäufigkeit, Stopwords
3. *Klassifikation* (semantische Bedeutung): Sentiment Analyse, Fear Factor, Happiness Factor
4. *Wissenschaftliche Methoden* (statistische Verfahren)*:* Shannonscher Informationsgehalt, Term Frequency – Inverse Document Frequency

Von diesen Bewertungsmethoden kann die Anwendung wählen, welche sie mit welchem Gewicht verwenden möchte. Durch diese Auswahl und die verschiedenen Kategorien wird ein Einsatz des Bewertungstools in einer Vielzahl von unterschiedlichen Einsatzszenarien möglich. Die Ergebnisse inklusive der Originaldaten werden in JSON bereitgestellt und können weiterverarbeitet werden.

4.3 Prototypische Integration in eine Facebook-Applikation

Zur Illustration der Funktionalität wurde dieses prototypisch in eine Facebook-Anwendung, die ungebundene Helfer in ihrer Arbeit der Schadensbewältigung durch die medienübergreifende Informationssuche und die Informationsgenerierung unterstützen soll, integriert

(Kaufhold & Reuter, 2014). Innerhalb dieser Anwendung werden dem Benutzer die 15 Bewertungsmethoden durch vereinfachte sprachliche Beschreibungen statt durch formale Definitionen erläutert. Bei jedem gibt der Benutzer die persönliche Wichtigkeit über einen stufenweise einstellbaren Schieberegler an (Abbildung 1). Dazu werden bereitgestellte Schnittstellen des Bewertungsservices verwendet, sodass eine zentrale, serverseitige Qualitätsbewertung möglich ist.

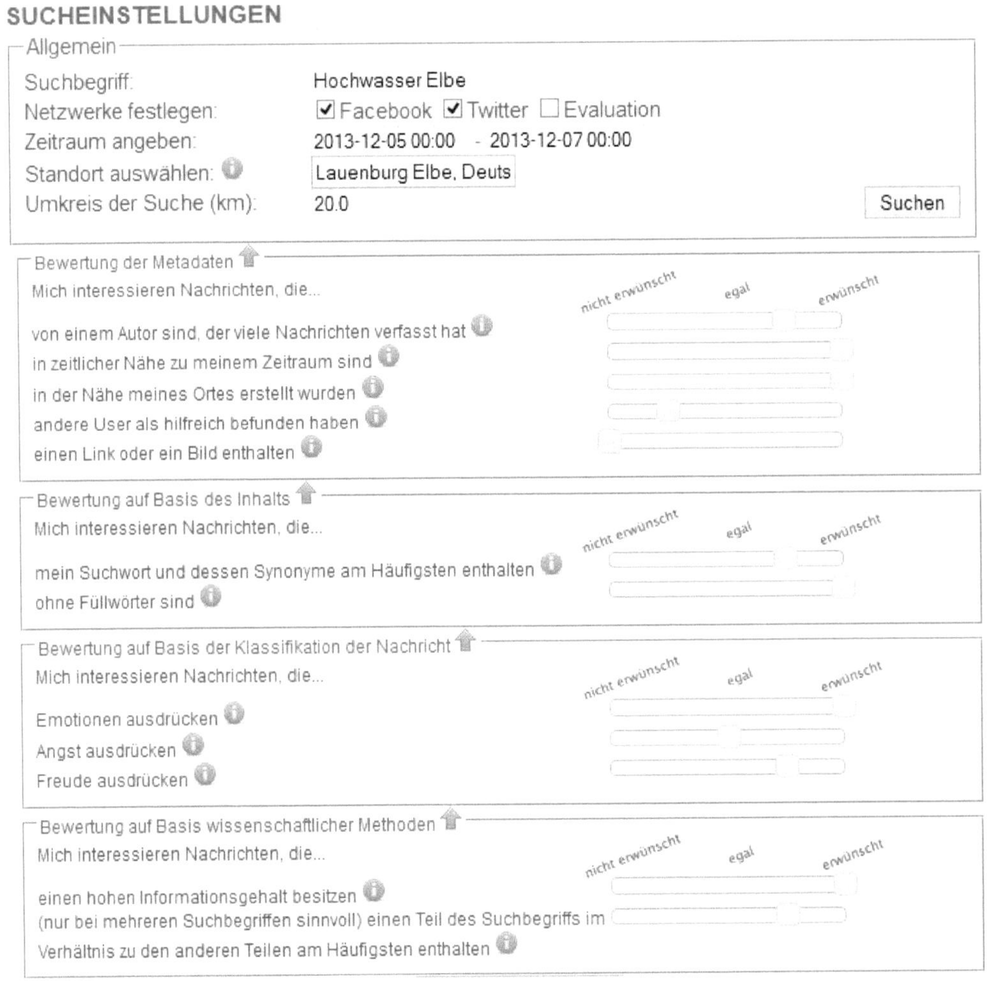

Abbildung 1: Adaptierbare Informationssuche und Qualitätsbewertung mithilfe von Schiebereglern

Die Ergebnisse dieser Informationssuche und Bewertung werden sowohl tabellarisch mit verschiedenen Metainformationen, die als MouseOver-Text angezeigt werden, als auch visuell auf einer Lagekarte zur direkten Bestimmung der Nähe der Information zum Suchstandort dargestellt. Bei jeder Information wird die Bewertung jedes einzelnen Bewertungskriteriums dem Benutzer in Form eines Ampelsystems zur Verfügung gestellt. (Abbildung 2).

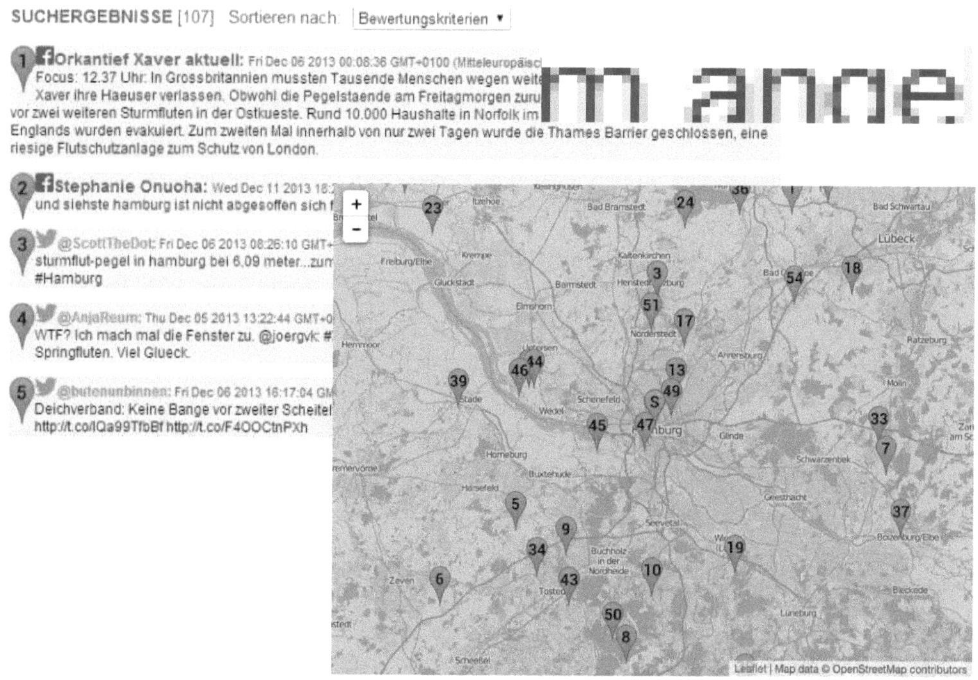

Abbildung 2: Suchergebnisse (links) inkl. Ampelsystem (oben rechts) und Darstellung auf der Karte (rechts)

5 Fazit

Dieser Artikel betrachtet die adaptierbare Qualitätsbewertung bürgergenerierter Inhalte aus sozialen Medien. Der Kernbeitrag stellt eine empirische Studie zum Umgang mit bürgergenerierten Inhalten in Schadenslagen dar. Hierdurch wurden die derzeitigen Hindernisse sowie Anforderungen an eine adaptierbare Qualitätsbewertung deutlich. Diese münden in ein Konzept eines adaptierbaren Bewertungsservices, der flexibel in verschiedene Anwendungen integriert werden kann. Gegenüber den im Beitrag vorgestellten Ansätzen (*Twitcident*, *SensePlace2*, *Tweet4act*, *TwitInfo*) werden nicht nur Daten aus genau einem Netzwerk, insbesondere Twitter, verwendet, sondern unterschiedliche Informationsquellen unterstützt. Im Unterschied zu *Tweak the Tweet* werden aus den Informationsquellen sämtliche Informationen und nicht nur eines gewissen Formats betrachtet. Eine Evaluation, die nicht Bestandteil dieses Beitrags ist, soll den praktischen Nutzen adaptierbarer Qualitätsbewertung ergründen und die Möglichkeiten der Artikulation von Qualitätsanforderungen erforschen.

Gefördert im Rahmen des EU-FP7-Projekts „EmerGent" (Fördernummer 608352).

Literatur

BITKOM. (2013). Soziale Netzwerke 2013 - Eine repräsentative Untersuchung zur Nutzung sozialer Netzwerke im Internet. Berlin, Germany.

Chowdhury, S., Amer-Yahia, S., Castillo, C., Imran, M., & Asghar, M. R. (2013). Tweet4act: Using Incident-Specific Profiles for Classifying Crisis-Related Messages. In Proc. ISCRAM (pp. 834–839). Baden-Baden, Germany.

Hiltz, S., & Plotnick, L. (2013). Dealing with Information Overload When Using Social Media for Emergency Management: Emerging Solutions. In Proc. ISCRAM (pp. 823–827). Baden-Baden.

Kaufhold, M.-A., & Reuter, C. (2014). Vernetzte Selbsthilfe in Sozialen Medien beim Hochwasser 2013 in Deutschland. I-Com - Zeitschrift Für Interaktive und Kooperative Medien, 13(1), 20–28.

Ley, B., Pipek, V., Reuter, C., & Wiedenhoefer, T. (2012). Supporting Improvisation Work in Inter-Organizational Crisis Management. In Proc. CHI (pp. 1529–1538). Austin, USA: ACM Press.

Ludwig, T., Reuter, C., & Pipek, V. (2013). What You See Is What I Need: Mobile Reporting Practices in Emergencies. In Proc. ECSCW (pp. 181–206). Paphos, Cyrus: Springer.

Marcus, A., Bernstein, M., & Badar, O. (2011). Twitinfo: aggregating and visualizing microblogs for event exploration. Proc. CHI, Vancouver, Canada.

Marino, T., Nascimento, B. do, & Borges, M. (2012). GIS Supporting Data Gathering and Fast Decision Making in Emergencies Situations. Proc. ISCRAM - Vancouver, Canada, 1–6.

McClendon, S., & Robinson, A. C. (2012). Leveraging Geospatially-Oriented Social Media Communications in Disaster Response. In Proc. ISCRAM. Vancouver, Canada.

Reuter, C., Marx, A., & Pipek, V. (2011). Desaster 2.0: Einbeziehung von Bürgern in das Krisenmanagement. In Mensch & Computer 2011 (pp. 141–150). München: Oldenbourg-Verlag.

Reuter, C., & Ritzkatis, M. (2013). Unterstützung mobiler Geo-Kollaboration zur Lageeinschätzung von Feuerwehr und Polizei. In Proc. WI (pp. 1877–1891). Leipzig, Germany.

Rizza, C., Pereira, Â., & Curvelo, P. (2013). Do-it-yourself Justice-Considerations of Social Media use in a Crisis Situation: The Case of the 2011 Vancouver Riots. Proc. ISCRAM, Baden-Baden, Germany, 411–415.

Robinson, A., Savelyev, A., Pezanowski, S., & MacEachren, A. M. (2013). Understanding the Utility of Geospatial Information in Social Media. Proc. ISCRAM. Baden-Baden, Germany, 918–922.

Starbird, K., & Stamberger, J. (2010). Tweak the Tweet: Leveraging Microblogging Proliferation with a Prescriptive Syntax to Support Citizen Reporting. In Proc. ISCRAM. Seattle, USA.

Strauss, A. L. (2004). Methodologische Grundlagen der Grounded Theory. In J. Strübing & B. Schnettler (Eds.), Methodologie interpretativer Sozialforschung: Klassische Grundlagentexte (pp. 427–453). Konstanz, Germany: UVK.

Terpstra, T., Vries, A. de, Stronkman, R., & Paradies, G. L. (2012). Towards a realtime Twitter analysis during crises for operational crisis management. In Proc. ISCRAM. Vancouver, Canada.

Thomson, R., Ito, N., Suda, H., & Lin, F. (2012). Trusting Tweets: The Fukushima Disaster and Information Source Credibility on Twitter. In Proc. ISCRAM (pp. 1–10). Vancouver, Canada.

Turoff, M., Chumer, M., van de Walle, B., & Yao, X. (2004). The design of a dynamic emergency response management information system (DERMIS). JITTA, 5(4), 1–35.

Zagel, B. (2012). Soziale Netzwerke als Impulsgeber für das Verkehrs-und Sicherheitsmanagement bei Großveranstaltungen. In A. Koch, T. Kutzner, & T. Eder (Eds.), Geoinformationssysteme (pp. 223–232). Berlin/Offenbach: VDE Verlag.

M. Koch, A. Butz & J. Schlichter (Hrsg.): Mensch und Computer 2014 Tagungsband,
München: Oldenbourg Wissenschaftsverlag, 2014, S. 125-134.

The Awareness-/Coordination-Support-System Paradox

Christoph Oemig, Tom Gross

Human-Computer Interaction Group, University of Bamberg, Germany

Abstract

Coordination and awareness have been topics in the area of Computer-Supported Cooperative Work (CSCW) starting from day one. Effortless coordination has been a major goal ever since. However, while awareness research became quite popular, coordination got increasingly out of focus. Its concepts stayed rather theoretical lacking concrete steps towards the original goal due to the absence of appropriate measurement techniques and tools. There is even an on-going general dispute if discount usability techniques deliver valid results as compared to real-world field studies. This paper supports their validity and demonstrates how the Standardized Coordination Task Assessment (SCTA) technique is used to extend the mechanics of collaboration, a framework for discount usability evaluations, allowing awareness and coordination effort assessments. The results appeared not only to be reasonable but the experiment revealed an effect we named the awareness-/coordination-support system paradox.

1 Introduction

Coordination and awareness have been topics in the area of Computer-Supported Cooperative Work (CSCW) starting from day one. Since 1992 it is known that mutual awareness is a fundamental concept that facilitates coordination (Beaudouin-Lafon & Karsenty 1992). The latter was originally conceived as part of the 3C Model constituting the three main areas of CSCW (Ellis et al. 1991): communication, coordination, and cooperation. "Effortless coordination" (Gross 2013) or at least reducing coordination efforts to a minimum has been a major goal ever since. However, trying to achieve this goal revealed three major problems: First, in the past decades coordination and coordination support got increasingly out of focus (though being the higher goal). Focussing on awareness only was more popular but produced rather problematic results over time (Schmidt 2002). Second, coordination and direct coordination support stayed rather theoretical besides a few exceptions, e.g., the Coordinator (Flores et al. 1988). Most efforts delivered mainly concepts like the well-known *coordination theory* (Malone & Crowstone 1990) or the empirically based *coordination mechanisms* (Schmidt & Simone 1996). Yet, the positive effects of mutual awareness and coordination based upon that remained hard to measure. This leads to the final third problem: the measurement techniques and tools. There is still an ongoing dispute on whether the evaluation of cooperative systems using discount techniques delivers valid results (Steves et al. 2001). As one of these the *mechanics of collaboration* (Gutwin & Greenberg 2000) are a framework providing the necessary constructs but lacking a concrete measurement approach in the area of coordination and awareness. However, with the advent of the *Standardized Coordination Task Assessment (SCTA)* (Oemig & Gross 2011) appeared a new discount technique especially facilitating distinct awareness support and coordination support efficiency measurements.

This paper demonstrates how we use the SCTA to fill these gaps by extending the mechanics of collaboration adding the concepts and means for awareness and coordination support assessments. This especially facilitates the incremental development of effective support systems. After taking a brief look at related work we introduce the necessary background concepts, assumptions, and the measurement approach. We describe how they were applied in an experiment which also revealed an effect we named the *awareness-/coordination-support-system paradox*. After presenting and discussing the results this paper concludes with possible future work.

2 Related Work

Our work was inspired by mainly two research areas: Human Factors and CSCW. The former provides assessment methods like the *Situation Awareness Global Assessment Technique (SAGAT)* (Endsley et al. 1998), which is one of the most famous in this area. It was developed to assess situation awareness (SA) of air traffic controllers. SAGAT uses freeze probes to query participants concerning their perception of the current situation. The system's displays are blanked and the simulation is suspended while subjects quickly answer questions about their current perceptions of the situation. The method uses a predefined awareness model that includes Level 1 (perception of data), Level 2 (comprehension of meaning) and Level 3 (projection of the near future).

In CSCW there is still an ongoing discussion about whether discount usability evaluation techniques deliver valid results. Steves et al. (2001) proved their effective role in the evaluation of cooperative systems. Their study showed that discount techniques (heuristics, checklists, etc.) discovered many issues also found by real users in real work situations—but at tremendously lower cost (effort and time). Gutwin & Greenberg (2000) even suggest a conceptual framework that describes the *mechanics of collaboration*, i.e., "the low level actions and interactions that must be carried out to complete a task in a shared manner. These include communication, coordination, planning, monitoring, assistance, and protection" (p.116). Their hypothesis: some usability problems in cooperative systems are not inherently tied to the social context in which the system is used. They are rather a result of poor support for these mechanics. Their framework suggests three general measures: effectiveness, efficiency, and satisfaction.

3 The Measurement Extension Concept

Our concept picks up where the mechanics of collaboration left off: coordination is part of the mechanics while efficiency is part of the measures. Yet, **there is no defined way in the framework that combines the two in a concrete measurement approach**. This paper demonstrates how this gap can be closed using the SCTA approach. This section provides the overall rationale explaining the necessary background concepts, assumptions and measurement approach.

3.1 Background

When talking about efforts concerning awareness and coordination we especially focus on efforts imposed on the human being. Figure depicts effort areas, key concepts and support systems.

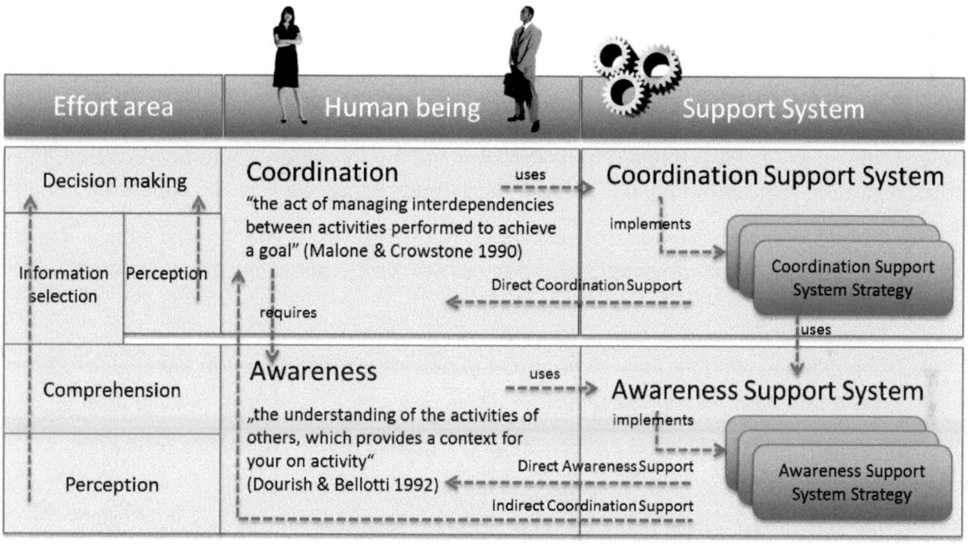

Figure 1: Overview of the key concepts, terms and their relationships.

We identified areas of effort resembling the above-mentioned three level model of situation awareness (Endsley 1995):

- **Perception**: continuous perception of relevant information from the environment
- **Comprehension**: processing information about the present and the past to arrange them in a common context
- **Information selection**: choosing the relevant information from the common context needed for decision making
- **Decision-making**: choosing a future options

Having these areas in mind, decreasing the effort can be achieved only in a few ways: either by increasing efficiency of each single process or by moving efforts to substitute systems, i.e., by introducing specialized support systems. Examples are to reduce the information being perceived, formatting it for eased comprehension, or rule-based preparations of options for decision-making. Thus it becomes rather a question of splitting the overall effort between humans and support systems.

The parts of the system that take over these activities are the *awareness support system* and the *coordination support system*. Awareness support systems typically address the processes of perception (relevant to awareness) and comprehension. They let the user know who is around and what is going on. Awareness support can be realized in many different ways, one way of realization is called awareness support system strategy or short *awareness strategy*. Coordination support systems typically address the processes of perception (relevant to decision making), information selection and decision-making. Coordination support can be realized in different ways starting from providing all information that is needed up to nearly making the decision. The way it is realized is called coordination support system strategy or short *coordination strategy*.

3.2 Assumptions

Knowing the areas of effort it needs to be determined how this effort could be measured. For efforts regarding awareness on the side of the human being we use the following set of assumptions:

1. *If I am aware about something, I can answer probe questions about it quickly and correctly.*
2. *The longer the answer takes, the more effort is involved.*
3. *The effort needed to answer the probe question is proportional to the regular effort during the task without a probe.*

For efforts regarding coordination on the side of the human being, we use the following:

1. *If I know my options, I can make correct and quick probe decisions.*
2. *The longer a decision takes, the more effort is involved.*
3. *The effort needed to make the probe decision is proportional to the regular effort during the task without a probe.*

From these assumptions we are able to conclude the following: If options needed for my decision can be derived from that something I am aware of then awareness information facilitates coordination decisions (i.e., awareness facilitates coordination). Further we see that these options also can be derived from sources other than awareness information (e.g., from a coordination strategy). Using awareness support as a source thus becomes only one out of many other possibilities (cf. Figure 1). This finally leads to the following question: if there is a coordination strategy that actually does not involve awareness information, what happens to the awareness processes or the awareness support system? The next section describes the experiment used for verification.

3.3 Measurement Approach

The Standardized Coordination Task Assessment (SCTA) (see Oemig & Gross 2011 for details) is a measurement approach that applies a standard primary task (the counting of letters) to generate a certain awareness and coordination workload for a group of people. The group's goal is to count as many letters as possible. This allows the observation and assessment of awareness and coordination support strategies by measuring the efforts that remain imposed on the human being. The SCTA uses freeze probes to query participants about aspects of their awareness and their decision-making. Its basic assumptions are those described in the previous section. The tool *SCTA Tracer* (Oemig & Gross 2012) uses questions concerning people and artefacts: Who counted a's? Were b's counted? Who may count c's next? What may count user A next? The application measures response times and whether the answer was correct or not. This corresponds to the efficiency measure of the mechanics of collaboration: quick and correct answers indicate smaller efforts and thus reasonable awareness or coordination support. The questions asked during the freeze probes are generated from the counting data the participants create during their task. Further advantages of the SCTA are its quantitative approach (number of correct answers, answering speed, performance (i.e. the number of counted letters)) and its simple reproduction of equivalent primary tasks, allowing large-scale measurements at very low cost.

4 Experiment

In order to demonstrate the extension of the mechanics of collaboration and to answer the open questions we designed an experiment contrasting a simple awareness support strategy and a simple coordination support strategy. Additionally, we used a control group with no support at all. In a first step the overall setup is described, a second step offers some of the experiment's results.

4.1 Setup

We defined three types of settings we wanted to measure. In a first setting we introduce a simple awareness support system. It implements a simple awareness strategy that notifies the user about what letter another user is about to count and about actual counting results (shown as "awareness display" in Figure 2). The second setting utilizes a simple coordination support strategy, we learned from earlier user feedback: the total number of letters is divided by the number of participants. Each user is assigned a respective fraction thereof. Once a letter is counted it is marked in the coordination support window (shown as "coordination display" in Figure 2). Thus the user does not need to know what the others are counting. The system basically coordinates the counting effort. Therefore, the coordination effort is expected to be at a minimum in this case. A third setting, the control group received no treatment at all. In order to avoid or minimize cofounding influences the experiment setting is selected by random for a single experiment run (i.e., the counting task). In the next step, the participants are assigned to the run by random as well.

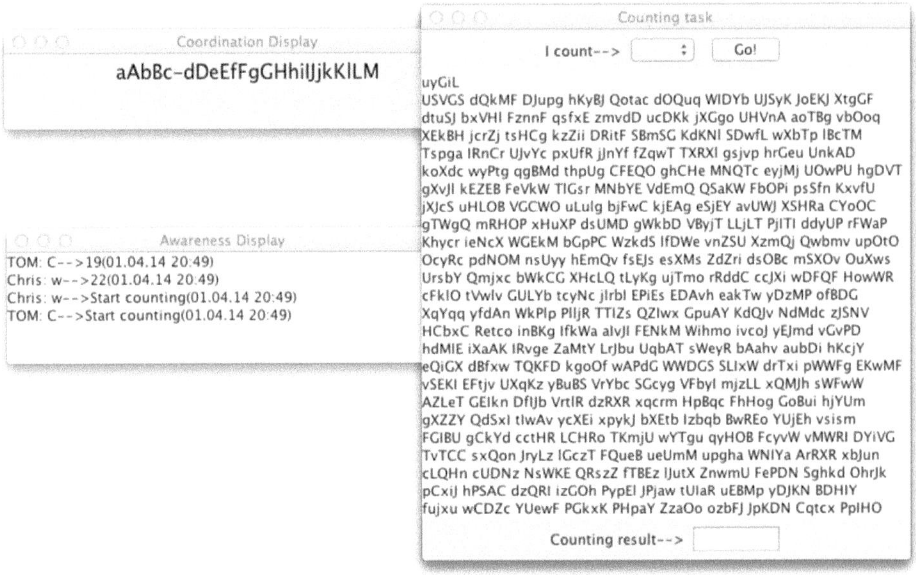

Figure 2: The SCTA counting task with awareness support and coordination support. This setup was not used in the experiment but it is to show all support options in one image. The experiment used either a simple awareness support, coordination support or no support at all.

There was a total number of 24 participants, 34% female and 66% male in a range of 17 to 40 years with the majority drawn from a computer science class (including the teacher) of a German High School. We only focused on dyads, i.e. from the total number of participants we always arranged groups with two members. They used individual computers separated by blinds so they could not see each other. They were not allowed to talk or to communicate by other means outside the provided tools. Since multiple counting tasks took place concurrently, participants did not even know with whom they were actually working (no real names were used). A counting task lasted 10 minutes interrupted by three freeze probes. These asked the participant two questions concerning group awareness, two questions concerning self awareness and two questions regarding coordination. Thus a total of 18 questions had to be answered by a participant during a run. Besides the performance (total number of counted letters) the coordination error rate (duplicate letters) was measured and recorded.

4.2 Results

This section briefly describes some of the most important results of this experiment. These are derived from the response time diagram (cf. Figure 3) and the success rates, performances and coordination errors shown in Table 1.

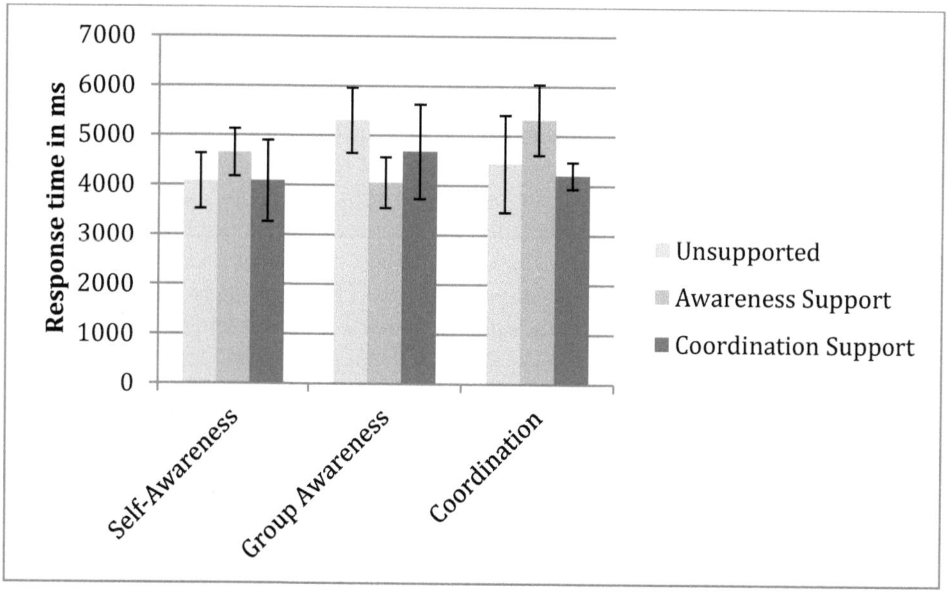

Figure 3: Mean response times per question area for each experiment type including standard error.

At first we looked for the most successful and fastest support for the SCTA categories self awareness, group awareness, and coordination. The experiment without any support type was the winner in the self awareness category (4s, 95%) since participants probably had nothing else to really focus on. Not surprisingly the awareness support experiment type was the most successful and fastest (4s, 75%) in the category of group awareness. Last but not least the coordination support type experiment performed best (4.2s, 95%) in the coordination category. But the most interesting lies beyond the expected, which rather proves that the approach generally appears to work. Concerning our assumptions we could verify that awareness support facilitates coordination.

	Success Rate (%)			**Performance (Avg)**	**Coordination Errors (Avg)**
	Self Aw.	Group Aw.	Coordination		
Unsupported	**95%,**	38%,	25%	6	1
Awareness Support	88%,	**75%,**	70%	6	0
Coordination Support	75%,	63%,	**95%**	7	0

Table 1: Success rates (percentage of correct answers), performance (total number of letters counted), and coordination errors (number of letters counted multiple times).

However, it was not the fastest (5.2s) and created some errors (success rate 70%), which might be due to its indirect nature in supporting coordination as mentioned in the concept.

Only the direct coordination support performed better (4.2s, 95%), while the results for coordination of the unsupported type suggest that the participants were guessing (4.5s, 25%).

Furthermore, the data suggests that the coordination support does not require the user to have superior levels of self- and group awareness. Participants answered slower and increasingly wrong but overall performed best indicating that they do not really need this knowledge. We named this effect the *awareness-/coordination-support system paradox*: while awareness support facilitates coordination support the latter has not necessarily a need for the former. As expected the third setting (no support) shows the highest number of coordination errors. Yet, all types showed nearly the same overall performance. This is probably due to the large number of different countable letters (whole alphabet, small and capital letters) and the large quantity of each single letter. Therefore also the coordination errors are low requiring the reduction of the number of different letters to allow more coordination errors to occur.

4.3 Discussion & Consequences

The experiment revealed some new insights and new problems regarding the goal of effortless coordination:

- **The awareness-/coordination-support system paradox**: this effect described above has the consequence that when developing a coordination support system it needs to be carefully reviewed which awareness information is still needed by the user. This adds another possibility to create more efficiency but, as the next insight shows, one needs to be careful.
- **Effortless coordination's anti-social tendency**: driving efficiency to the extreme may sacrifice social subtleties for its own purpose. Though performing best some participants mentioned that they did not like the coordination support experiment type. They could not see what their partner was doing or if he needed assistance. Reducing efforts to the minimum also contradicts general design principles of human-work. The consequence is not only to measure response times and errors but also include means to measure satisfaction. This is also mentioned as part of the mechanics of collaboration.
- **Self awareness obviously needs no support**: the unsupported experiment type actually removed all efforts concerning perception and comprehension from the user without offering a substitute. However, according to the measurement, participants performed even better in the category of self awareness suggesting that it is agnostic of any support system used. As a consequence self awareness does not need to be supported releasing screen estate and other resources for other information. Yet, it needs to be verified if this remains true for more complex settings.

The experiment further created insights regarding the used approach:

- **The twofold letter problem**: there were too many letters in too high quantities making it easy for the participants to avoid coordination errors. Further, this fact reduced the total number of letters counted since the participants spent longer times counting a single letter. This in turn reduced the effort needed to coordinate the situation. As a consequence future experiments will dramatically decrease the number of letters and their quantities.

- **Don't know/don't care answer options**: Another point mentioned by participants was that for some questions they would prefer an "I don't know" answer option instead of being forced to some other answer. This can also be derived from the results: the "I don't know" answers are those where there is a quick wrong or deliberate answer while producing an overall high performance. However, it needs to be discussed if an "I don't know" answer is sufficient or if an "I don't care" needs to be introduced as well since some of the knowledge is really not needed as the found paradox implies.
- **Freeze probes killing counting results**: Another aspect mentioned by participants is that the freeze probes prevented them sometimes from finishing their counting. Since there were only a few letters counted but those at high quantities this might have a large impact which can be avoided by smaller quantities for each letter and again reducing the number of letters overall.

5 Conclusion

In this paper we introduced a practical step towards the goal of effortless coordination. Extending on the mechanics of collaboration we used the SCTA technique to actually measure the performance, response times and success rates of different approaches trying to reduce the coordination efforts by introducing more efficiency or by moving them to support systems. In doing so we showed the effect we named the awareness-/coordination-support system paradox: while awareness support facilitates coordination support the latter has not necessarily a need for the former. It also turned out that there is a another yet disregarded constraint in the context of awareness and coordination support: the goal of effortless coordination must not sacrifice social subtleties for its own purpose.

However, this was actually just the beginning. Among many other possibilities a whole range of similar experiments can be done with group sizes beyond the dyad in one run adding more complexity, or with a longer duration beyond 10 minutes. There are many ways to refine the support systems and to repeat the measuring in an iterative approach including a comparison of results—a procedure actually intended by the authors of the mechanics of collaboration and of the SCTA.

References

Beaudouin-Lafon, M. and Karsenty (1992). *A. Transparency and Awareness in a Real-time Groupware System.* In Proceedings of The ACM Symposium on User Interface Software andTechnology - UIST'92 (Nov. 15-18, Monterey, CA). ACM, N.Y., 1992. pp. 171-180.

Endsley, M.R. (1995). *Toward a theory of situation awareness in dynamic systems.* Human Factors 37(1), 32–64.

Endsley, M.R., Selcon, S.J., Hardiman, T.D., Croft, D.G. (1998). *A comparative evaluation of SAGAT and SART for evaluations of situation awareness.* In Proceedings of the Human Factors and Ergonomics Society Annual Meeting, 1998, pp. 82.-86. Santa Monica, CA: Human Factors and Ergonomics Society

Ellis, C. A.; Gibbs, S. J. & Rein, G. (1991). *Groupware: Some Issues and Experiences.* Commun. ACM, ACM, 1991, 34, 39-58

Flores, F.; Graves, M.; Hartfield, B. & Winograd, T. (1988). *Computer Systems and the Design of Organizational Interaction.* ACM Trans. Inf. Syst., ACM, 1988, 6, 153-172

Gross, T. (2013). *Supporting Effortless Coordination: 25 Years of Awareness Research.* Computer Supported Cooperative Work: The Journal of Collaborative Computing, Springer-Verlag 22, 4-6 (Aug.-Dec. 2013). pp. 425-474. (SpringerLink, DOI:10.1007/s10606-013-9190-x).

Gutwin, C., Greenberg, S. (2000) *The mechanics of collaboration developing low cost usability evaluation methods for shared workspaces.* Proceedings of IEEE Workshop on Enabling Technologies – Infrastructure for Collaborative Enterprises, 116-121.

Malone, T. W. & Crowston, K. (1990). *What is Coordination Theory and How Can It Help Design Cooperative Work Systems?* Proceedings of the 1990 ACM Conference on Computer-supported Cooperative Work, ACM, 1990, 357-370

Oemig, C. & Gross, T. (2011). *Illusive, Ineffective, Inefficient, Ideal: Standardized Coordination Task Assessments of Awareness Support.* Mensch & Computer 2011: überMEDIEN|ÜBERmorgen, Oldenbourg Verlag, 2011, 353-356

Oemig, C. & Gross, T. (2012). *SCTA Tracer: A Distributed Environment for Standardized Awareness Support Assessments.* In Proceedings of the Twentieth Euromicro Conference on Parallel, Distributed, and Network-Based Processing - PDP 2012 (Feb. 15-17, Garching, Germany). IEEE Computer Society Press, Los Alamitos, 2012. pp. 52-56.

Schmidt, K. (2002). *The Problem with 'Awareness': Introductory Remarks on 'Awareness in CSCW'.* Comput. Supported Coop. Work, Kluwer Academic Publishers, 2002, 11, 285-298

Schmidt, K. & Simone, C. (1996). *Coordination Mechanisms: Towards a Conceptual Foundation of CSCW Systems Design.* Comput. Supported Coop. Work, Kluwer Academic Publishers, 1996, 5, 155-200

Steves, M. P., Morse, E., Gutwin, C., und Greenberg, S. (2001). *A comparison of usage evaluation and inspection methods for assessing groupware usability.* In GROUP '01: Proceedings of the 2001 International ACM SIGGROUP Conference on Supporting Group Work, Seiten 125–134, New York, NY, USA. ACM Press

Acknowledgements

We like to thank all people participating in the initial setup of the assessment, especially our beta testers Michel Greiner and Nils Hottes, the participants of our experiment, and all reviewers for their valuable comments and suggestions on earlier versions of this work.

Contact Information

Prof. Dr. Tom Gross, E. tom.gross(at)uni-bamberg.de, T.(+49-951)863-3940

Christoph Oemig, MSc., coemig(at)acm.org

M. Koch, A. Butz & J. Schlichter (Hrsg.): Mensch und Computer 2014 Tagungsband,
München: Oldenbourg Wissenschaftsverlag, 2014, S. 135-144.

Trail Building During Complex Search Tasks

Sebastian Franken[1], Ulrich Norbisrath[2]

Fraunhofer FIT, Sankt Augustin, Germany[1]
ulno.net, Gillette, WY, USA[2]

Abstract

Users frequently perform searches that do not only have simple fact retrieval in mind, but aim for more comprehensive results. These complex search tasks need to be distinguished from simple search tasks, where an information need can be fulfilled by simple fact finding. While search engine support for simple search tasks is satisfactory, it lacks in support for complex search tasks, leading to an increasing discontent about the interaction with the search engine of choice. In this paper we address the question, how to give tool support for complex search tasks. We present the logging framework 'SearchTrails', which captures the course of user actions of any search task and presents a corresponding graph visualization. We conducted a qualitative user study of SearchTrails and present first promising results.

1 Introduction

Literature review indicates discontent with popular search engines to fulfill some particular information needs. It turns out that this discontent is mainly visible in search tasks which are classified as exploratory or complex (Marchionini 2006; Aula & Russell 2009; Singer et al. 2012). In this paper we address the research question of how it is possible to give tool support for complex search tasks. We present a logging framework which is able to capture the course of any exploratory or complex search and allows presenting a graph visualization of it. We carried out an initial qualitative study using this new framework involving seven participants. The results indicate interest and acceptance of our chosen support method and outline benefits, shortcomings, and possible future improvements.

Users frequently perform searches that aim for more than simple fact retrieval. These searches aim for more comprehensive results, stretch over a certain amount of time, and are not completed within one session. Examples for search tasks like these could be: booking a holiday trip, building some technical device on your own, or staying informed about the market situation for one specific appliance over a period of time. Personal experience shows that we stumble upon interesting web sites during the course of such searches, but quickly move on from preliminary results to other web sites that seem more promising. Even if addresses of the visited pages can still be retrieved from the browser cache, the important pages are usually lost. Some days later, searchers might be interested again in the information on the intermediate sites, but are not able to get back to them. Our study participants also reported these situations. This is where an idea of (Bush 1945) comes into place: He suggests that navigating through the hypertext is stored in so-called 'trails' that could later be recalled and extended. This idea gets picked up by (Bates 1989), who already suggests that the search for information is comparable to the process of 'Berrypicking', in which many highly qualitative information bits get picked during a search. She opposes this to classic information retrieval, in which a query should be answered by only one perfectly matching document. Today's search engines get better and better in helping users to find fact-based information, but they lack support for gathering many pieces of information on a specific topic (e.g. Booking a holiday trip, which includes comparing different ways of traveling, different hotels, and related activities) (Singer et al. 2012). The well-supported fact searches are often part of connected complex search tasks. These sets of connected searches need to be supported. The approach presented here does exactly this: it visually logs the users' paths when traversing the web, offering possibilities to capture specific information and providing a way back to information alternatives seen in earlier stages of the search process.

Arguably, bookmarking the valuable pages might solve the mentioned problems. However, this does not work in the aforementioned cases, where users retroactively start appreciating the value of a visited website after they have already left it. We monitored that people hesitate to bookmark sites to avoid bookmarking too many sites. They also often end up being stored unsorted in the bookmark folder or a browser toolbar. Managing bookmarks as a part of the follow-up process of search is time consuming, especially with the help of the built-in browser bookmark managing tools. Social bookmarking services like Delicious[1], Tumblr[2], or Pinterest[3] also do not help in our cases, as they do not store the context in which a bookmark was created and require similar follow-up work as browser bookmarks. Recovering sites via the back button or the browser history is also tedious; especially when a user has visited many pages on a topic. If the visit lies back in time, relocating the page gets even harder.

(Singer et al. 2012a) show that the aforementioned discontent is based in the character of the search task, which is not supported well by todays' search engines. Current search engines perform well on lookup or fact finding tasks (Jansen 2006) and therefore yield positive user satisfaction in this discipline (Singer et al. 2012a). They are trained on fact retrieval and on delivering exactly matching documents to the searcher (Marchionini 2006). This type of search could also be described as a kind of one-shot-search, i.e. a 'search and forget' mode, in which for a given query the search results are returned, but then forgotten by the search engine. (Broder 2002) and (Rose & Levinson 2004) both analyzed and classified search tasks in the types of their underlying motivation. They showed that in 50-60% of search tasks, users are looking for more than simple fact retrieval or lookup of sources, but are rather looking for information that they assume not to find on one specific site, but a collection of pages, where every page adds to the overall result. Complex or exploratory search deals exactly

[1] https://delicious.com/, Accessed 2014/03/17

[2] https://www.tumblr.com/, Accessed 2014/03/04

[3] https://www.pinterest.com/, Accessed 2014/03/04

with these types of search, and in this contribution, we combine Bush's idea of logging and building visual trails through the Internet with the added benefit of metadata and the added possibility of storing selected parts of websites to support these types of search.

Consider as an example a search task about crypto currencies: 'What are they, what is their current status, how do you obtain them?' During a web search, people discover pretty early the page about crypto currencies from Wikipedia[4] and learn about bitcoins, bitcoin clients, and some of their properties, like being limited and community supported. In our set of test users, they often also discover some properties about currencies in general (fiat money, trading of currencies). Usually, test users study a lot about bitcoins and their inner workings and find some sites where one can purchase them. They usually also forget things they discovered in the beginning, like how a proof-of-work works or where they could find a simple introduction to the cryptography related to bitcoins. Also, the idea of mining becomes more interesting the longer one studies the topic of crypto currencies, which makes people want to go back to the sites they previously visited and gather relevant information from these pages.

In the following sections, we will look at the underlying theoretical concepts, as well as existing search loggers, then describe the architecture and implementation of our search support tool, present a small user study and its qualitative results. We will conclude with a discussion of the results and an outlook on the work to be done in the future.

2 Theoretical background and related work

First approaches to identify different natures of search tasks start with (Broder 2002), who identifies navigational, transactional, and informational search tasks by the query entered into the search engine. When performing navigational queries, users have in mind reaching a particular site, expecting to find information on that site. With transactional queries, users try to find a page where some action should be performed, e.g. accessing a database or downloading data. With informational queries, users try to find information that should be processed by reading and either satisfies the information need, or triggers a new query to refine the information. An interesting observation is that "in almost 15% of all searches the desired target is a good collection of links on the subject, rather than a good document" (Broder 2002). Broders' work got independently refined later by (Rose & Levinson 2004); their results match in their core with Broders' results. They also developed a trichotomy of user goals, consisting of navigational, informational, and resource-oriented (instead of transacttional) goals. Additionally, the authors added a sub-classification of goals. While Broder states that 39-50% of all queries are informational, Rose and Levinson show that up to 60% of all queries are informational. (Lewandowski 2006) shows that almost 50% of all queries sent to search engines are informational, while navigational queries account for a much larger share of queries than transactional ones. Considering that informational search tasks tend to be time consuming and span over multiple sessions, these search tasks count for a large

[4] www.wikipedia.com, Accessed 2014/03/24

share of time consumed when searching (Singer 2012). This shows the importance of exploratory or complex search tasks.

Early research of structuring user goals in web search laid the foundations for more formal definitions of search tasks. Search activities were grouped by (Marchionini 2006) into the three overlapping categories of 'Lookup', 'Learn', and 'Investigate' (gray part in Fig. 1). 'Lookup' comes close to navigational and transactional search tasks, as it consists of e.g. fact retrieval, navigation, transaction, or verification. 'Learn' consists of more complex activities, such as e.g. knowledge acquisition, comparison, or aggregation, while 'Investigate' consists of analysis, synthesis, or evaluation. Exploratory search, as framed by Marchionini, can be seen as a combination of the search activities of Learn and Investigate. He states that 'investigative searching is more concerned with recall [...] than precision [...] and thus not well supported by today's Web search engines.' A definition of exploratory search is given in (White et al. 2008), stating that 'Exploratory search can be used to describe an information-seeking problem context that is open-ended, persistent, and multi-faceted; and to describe information-seeking processes that are opportunistic, iterative, and multi-tactical. In the first sense, exploratory search is commonly used in scientific discovery, learning, and decision-making contexts. In the second sense, exploratory tactics are used in all manner of information seeking and reflect seeker preferences and experience as much as the goal'.

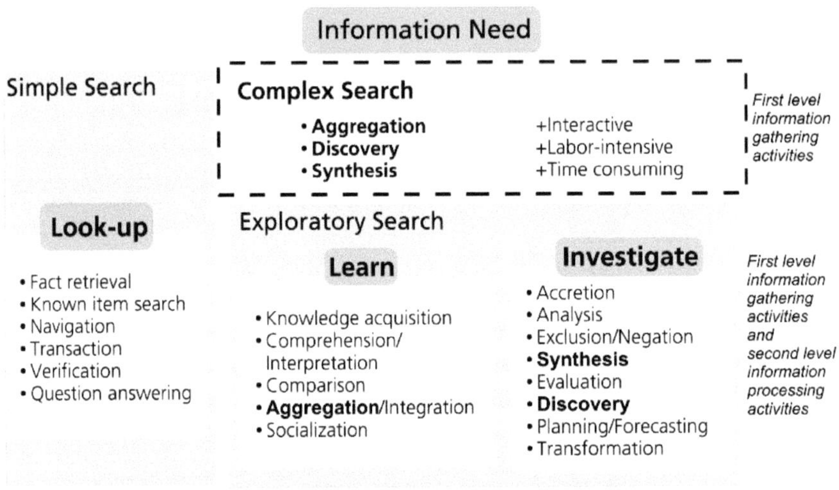

Figure 1: Complex and exploratory search (from (Singer 2012)).

Figure 1 shows that the core components of exploratory search are 'Learn' and 'Investigate', each of them again containing different subtasks. These subtasks imply relatively high cognitive effort, especially when it comes to subtasks like analysis, evaluation, or planning. The necessary cognitive effort is hard to measure by purely implemented solutions, like we are presenting here. Therefore, we stick to the definition of complex search, as presented in (Singer 2012), who defines complex search as "tasks where users are required to follow a multi-step and time consuming process that is not answerable with one query, requiring synthesized information from more than one retrieved web page or document to be solved. The process to work to complex search tasks usually comprises at least one of the process steps aggregation, discovery, and synthesis." This avoids the cognitively high loaded aspects of Marchionini's definition. It has the added benefit of covering complex search activities with limited cognitive loads into the definition, which would not be covered by Marchionini, e.g. checking the availability and prices of certain products in a number of web portals. However, complex search tasks often require synthesis of the information found or even yield discoveries which extend or alter the initial search task goal.

To find out how users cope with the challenges of complex search tasks, some systems have been developed which try to register the user interactions during the search process. In most cases, these search logging systems were constructed as browser plug-ins, storing information about the visited pages and sometimes posing questions to the users while performing certain tasks. An early approach was an Internet Explorer plug-in with built-in questionnaires (Fox et al. 2005) that was used to compare explicit and implicit measures of user satisfaction. Another approach was the Wrapper system (Jansen et al. 2006) which was installed to the user's system and logged the interaction with the browser and the browser's interaction with the system. It could be shown that users 'may seek information over an extended period [of time] and on multiple information systems'. The SearchLogger system was built by (Singer et al. 2011). It consists of a Firefox plug-in allowing configuring a list of search-tasks and selecting one of them, recording all user interactions with the browser, and storing this information centrally on a logging server to be evaluated. It comes with some guidelines how to evaluate the logged data. However, logged information is not visible to the user searching. Therefore, there is no direct feedback to the user, which could facilitate the search task. SearchLogger was mainly used to proof the existence of complex search and to allow its classification. Based on the observations derived from the user studies carried out with SearchLogger, a user centric model for increasing user satisfaction was developed.

Early approaches on collaborative search, such as the co-browsing idea in (Gross 1998) or collaborative bookmarking in the Social Web Cockpit (Prinz & Graether 2000) supported remotely controlled browsers for synchronous browsing or creation of community bookmarks, but no cooperative, context-preserving, or asynchronous exploration of information spaces. Faceted search can alleviate information complexity in very specific cases, e.g. when databases are preprocessed with large effort, or by relying on object-unspecific metadata (Franken & Prinz 2009). These approaches can only offer very little support if it comes to complex search cases, as these span over time and a multitude of resources.

The search logging systems presented here mainly focus on gathering data from the users via browser logging, system logging, and questionnaires. Our tool goes beyond that, as it uses the information gathered to actively support the users in their tasks. In the next section, we will present an overview over the newly developed system and outline key characteristics of our user study.

3 The SearchTrails tool

With our tool, we address the missing support during complex search. In contrast to the search loggers described before, our goal is not only to monitor the user's search behavior but also to provide immediate feedback and support to address discovery, aggregation, and synthesis needs while users carry out their search tasks.

To achieve this, we decided to build a plug-in for the chrome browser[5], which logs the users' interactions with the browser (Figure 2). This approach has several advantages: While providing full access to the Internet and its resources, the plug-in monitors all interactions with the browser (and the Internet) and stores the relevant actions unobtrusively. Therefore, we are not relying on any preprocessed data bases (like in faceted solutions) and allow free-form, open-ended search processes. We can omit intermediate and interrupting questions, and have very minor installation effort. The internal structure consists of three parts: The logging engine logs the events and builds a logical representation of the search process. The storage engine stores the log as a JSON-object and reports about the changes, which are visualized by the rendering engine. The storage engine also stores the log on a remote server.

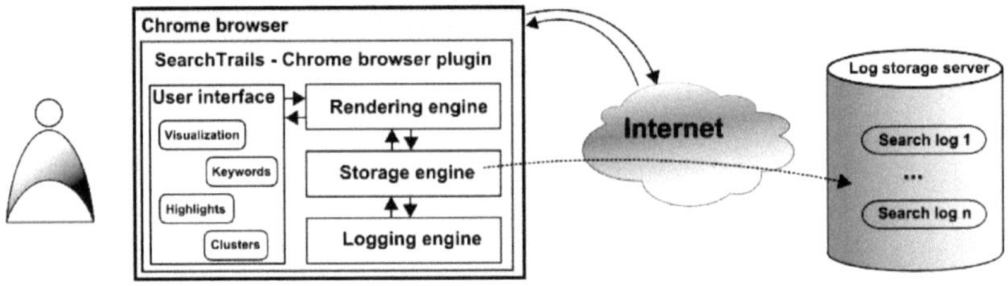

Figure 2: Schematic view of the SearchTrails architecture.

SearchTrails itself works as follows: It monitors the opening, closing, and switching between tabs and the change of URLs with the help of a logging engine that logs, filters, and interprets the user interactions and generates the metadata for the visited URLs. The visited URLs get transformed into nodes in the graph visualization. The visualization is done by the rendering engine and is shown in a separate tab, which is excluded from the logging itself. It is based on a bidirectional graph in a forced-directed layout (see Figure 3). For each visited URL, important keywords get stored and displayed in a table next to the visualization, if a keyword appears on two or more pages the user visited. This metadata gets also stored in the search logs. To ease the synthesis of information (as one of the key points of complex search), selected text can be stored on a key press and gets displayed with its original URL in a highlights table. Nodes belonging to the same host are clustered by a colored hull and can be reduced on click to reduce complexity of the visualization, but still being sensible to user interactions, even if not being visible. The storage engine stores the search logs remotely on a server, without requiring user interaction. As our tool does not judge the correctness of search results, it also stores irrelevant search results. This can be valuable in terms of showing that desired information was not present at certain pages. Fig. 3 shows an example visualization for the 'Beethoven' task, with the search trail visualized (1) (which shows a rather linear approach of searching, while trails for more complex search tasks may show more cyclic approaches), a colored node (2), symbolizing that there are highlights appended to it,

[5] https://www.google.de/intl/de/chrome/browser/, Accessed 2014/03/05

the highlights-overview being turned on (3), a list of keywords to the right (4), and a cluster with 3 nodes from the same host (5) (all nodes from Youtube).

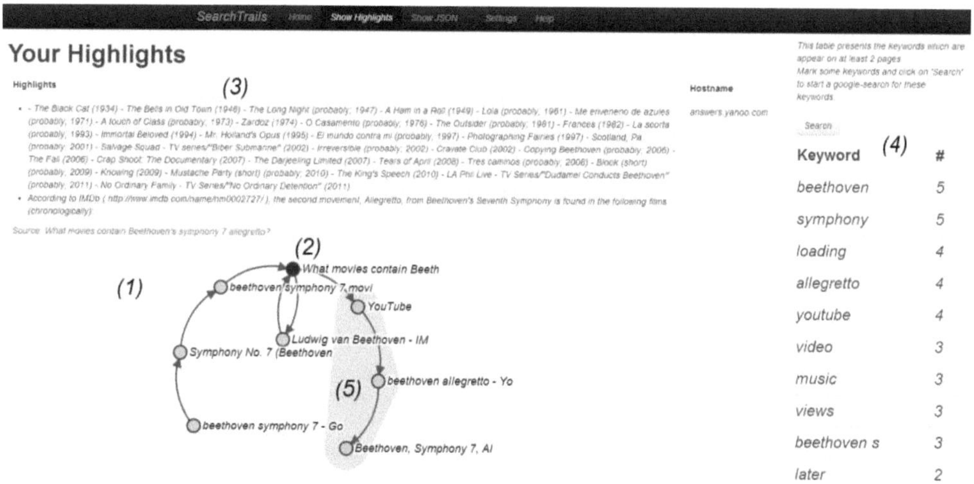

Figure 3: An example Search Trail and highlights for the 'Beethoven' search task.

4 User study

The evaluated version of SearchTrails evolved from a domain survey of related work and personal interviews with potential users of the system. A user study was needed to verify the design decisions made and to reveal advantages and flaws of the system. We did a study with seven participants with academic background, performing complex search tasks with and without the help of SearchTrails. The authors were not taking part in this study.

We generated a set of 4 search tasks. One is a simple search task (finding films using Beethoven's 7th symphony as a score), and three tasks are examples for complex search ('Building Your Own Video Glasses', 'Checking the Availability and Transport Possibilities for a Product', and the aforementioned 'Crypto Currency' search task). We asked the participants to dismiss one uninteresting task for the evaluation to ensure that there is a personal engagement in the selected search tasks. As the creation of complex search tasks is sensible, we checked our search tasks against the four criteria given by (Kules & Capra 2009). First, the tasks should indicate uncertainty and ambiguity in the information need. We ensured this by posing open-ended questions that could be tackled from various starting points. Second, the tasks should suggest knowledge acquisition, comparison or discovery. As our tasks are from domains that our test users were unfamiliar with, we could ensure to fulfill this criterion. Third, the tasks should provide a low level of specifity about the information necessary and how to find the information. We ensure this by leaving open how and which information should be gathered. Fourth, the task should provide enough imaginative context in order for the users to relate and apply the situation. We generated tasks with a practical focus, to ensure our participants could easily engage in them.

The user study starts with the installation of SearchTrails and a practical introduction to make sure the users understand its features and know how to handle them. Of the three tasks the participants had to perform without supervision, we selected the simple search task for the start. This allows our participants to get acquainted with the system and to have a negative probe in terms of looking at complex tasks. Of the following two complex search tasks, one is carried out with the help of SearchTrails. This means that the users have the system on a second screen, while actually searching on the first screen. Another task is done without SearchTrails being visible; it is running in the background without the participants being able to look at it. Participants fill out a small questionnaire with 5-point Likert and open-ended questions after each search task. In addition, we analyzed the remotely stored search logs.

5 Evaluation

Doing an evaluation of a complex search support system with visualization is a difficult task: 'the evaluation of visualization systems that can support exploratory search tasks is not well understood' (Koshman 2006). Koshman also mentions testing metrics affecting the evaluation of exploratory search visualization systems, which helped us to make the results comparable with later evaluations. Among her metrics are: Training length, in our case long enough to make the user know how to handle the system; Task type, timing and purpose, in our case complex tasks for non-domain-expert users, with no time limit; Number of visualization system features, here an operational prototype with the aforementioned features; Type of visualization, here a force-directed graph layout; User types, here information professionals, but no domain experts considering the tasks; Response type, in our case a combination of 5-point Likert and open ended questionnaire items; and the speed of the system, which was asked in the questionnaire, and turned out to be sufficient.

In this initial, qualitative user study we already got some very interesting results. Task 1 is a simple search, as it could be fulfilled with the following search query *'wiki beethoven 7th symphony'* and visiting the first Wikipedia entry. Participants liked the highlighting function of our tool in that search task. We suppose that the highlighting stores important results and therefore enables the user to continue a search, although the core results are already found (User quote: '*pro: Saving results for later reuse*'). It might offer a feeling of security to the user to be able to go back to earlier findings ('*visualize the path especially when stepping back*').

As we expected, the search tasks were new to our participants ('*new topic for me, a lot of information*'), and they were motivated to explore the new topics ('*exploring a topic I've been wondering about for a while*'); therefore our example tasks matched the criteria by Kules & Capra mentioned above. Considering the second task, where participants should search without the help of SearchTrails, they reported that the task '*was quite tedious, [as] it required exploration of dozens of web sites, changing search queries several times, and subdividing queries.*' Comments to our third task (searching with the help of SearchTrails) were also very encouraging: Participants liked the '*Visualization of visited pages*', the possibility to store '*text snippets from the web pages*', and '*modifying search queries (→ keywords)*'. Participants also appreciated the clustering of nodes: '*Pro: Clustering nodes*'.

In general, the synthesis feature in SearchTrails yielded very positive comments. Five of our seven participants mentioned that the synthesis feature allows easy selection and compilation of relevant phrases. Highlighting was extremely helpful and alone justified the use of our tool ('*I will now miss the highlighter*'). Concerning keywords, the results were mixed. While one user mentioned that there are too many irrelevant keywords ('*keyword list was helpful, but contained irrelevant entries*'), two other users used the feature and found it interesting to be pointed to other relevant search terms ('*"Finding" new search queries based on keywords*' and '*It helped to identify the keyword related to the subject of crypto*'). The overall positive reactions of our study participants are encouraging to extend and improve SearchTrails.

6 Discussion and outlook

Information synthesis comprises the steps of information ordering, automatic editing, information fusion, and information compression (Singer et al. 2012). When it comes to synthesis, our literature survey showed that this aspect of complex search is not supported at all in the present search systems. With our system, we can offer fast and easy synthesis of diverse web-snippets and still capture their context. The responses of our participants show that this is the most important feature in the case of individual use. With respect to our research question, the results indicate that building a search trail is a means to support complex search tasks. The keyword suggestions and the clustering mechanism provide additional benefit to users. Nevertheless, some flaws were revealed in our study: Highlighting parts from pdf-files does not always work, there were irrelevant stopwords, manual adding and removing of highlights is missing, and the possibility of removing nodes from the graph is not yet provided. We will implement the support for recreating search trails, allowing extending a search and handing over a search trail in order to search collaboratively. Overall, the evaluation results are very promising and will positively influence the future work on SearchTrails.

Acknowledgements

Thanks to our study participants, notably Kamila and Zarina from Nazarbayev University, Astana, and Constantin, Nils, Wolfgang, Maren, and Urs from Fraunhofer FIT.

References

Aula, A., Russell, D.M. (2009). Complex and Exploratory Web Search. In: Marchionini, G. et al., Information Seeking Support Systems: An Invitational Workshop (06/2008, Chapel Hill), pp. 23-24.

Bush, V. (1945). As we may think. In: The Atlantic Monthly 176, July 1945.

Bates, M.J. (1989). The Design of Browsing and Berrypicking Techniques for the Online Search Interface. Online Information Reviews, Vol. 13, Issue 5, pp. 407-424.

Broder, A. (2002). A taxonomy of web search. In: SIGIR Forum, Fall 2002, Vol. 36, No. 2, pp. 3-10.

Fox, S., Karnawat, K., Mydland, M., Dumais, S., White, T. (2005). Evaluating Implicit Measures to Improve Web Search. In: ACM Transactions on Inf. Syst. Vol.23, No.2, Apr. 2005, pp. 147-168.

Franken, S., Prinz, W. (2009). FacetBrowse: Facettenbasiertes Browsen im Groupware Kontext. In: Wandke, H., Kain, S., Struve, D. Mensch & Computer 2009, Oldenbourg, pp. 123-132.

Gross, T. (1998). CSCW3: Transparenz- und Kollaborationsunterstützung für das WWW. In: Herrmann, T., Just-Hahn, K.: Proc. of D-CSCW'98, pp. 37-50.

Jansen, B.J. (2006). Using Temporal Patterns of Interactions to Design Effective Automated Searching Assistance. In: Communications of the ACM, April 2006/Vol. 49, No. 4, pp. 72-74.

Jansen, B.J., Ramadoss, R., Zhang, M., Zang, N., (2006). Wrapper: An Application for Evaluating Exploratory Search Systems Outside of the Lab. In: Proceedings of SIGR 2006, Aug. 6-11, Seattle.

Koshman, S., (2006). Exploratory Search Visualization: Identifying Factors Affecting Evaluation. In: Proc. of the ACM SIGIR 2006 Workshop on "Evaluating Exploratory Search Systems", pp. 20-23.

Kules, B., Capra, R., (2009). Designing Exploratory Search Tasks for User Studies of Information Seeking Support Systems. JCDL '09, June 15-19, Austin, Texas, p. 419.

Lewandowski, D. (2006). Query types and search topics of German Web search engine users, In: Information Services and Use, Vol. 26, Jan. 2006, pp. 261-269.

Marchionini, G. (2006). Exploratory Search: From Finding to Understanding. In: Communications of the ACM, April 2006/Vol. 49, No. 4, pp. 41-46.

Prinz, W., Graether, W. (2000). Das Social Web Cockpit: Ein Assistent für virtuelle Gemeinschaften. In: Reichwald, R., Schlichter, J.: Proceedings of D-CSCW 2000, pp. 127-138.

Rose, D.E., Levinson, D. (2004). Understanding User Goals in Web Search. In: Proceedings of WWW 2004, May 17-22, New York, pp. 13-19.

Singer, G. (2012). Web search engines and complex information needs. Dissertationes Mathematicae Universitatis Tartuensis, Order No. 446, ISSN: 1024-4212.

Singer, G., Danilov, D., Norbisrath, U. (2012). Complex search: aggregation, discovery, and synthesis. In: Proceedings of the Estonian Academy of Sciences, 2012, **61,** 2, pp. 89-106.

Singer, G., Norbisrath, U., Lewandowski, D. (2012a). Ordinary Search Engine Users assessing Difficulty, Effort, and Outcome for Simple and Complex Search Tasks. In: Proc.IiiX'12, Nijmegen.

Singer, G., Norbisrath, U., Vainikko, E., Kikkas, H., Lewandowski, D. (2011). Search-Logger - Analyzing Exploratory Search Tasks. In: SAC'11, March 21-25, Taichung. Taiwan, pp. 751-756.

White, R.W., Marchionini, G., Muresan, G. (2008). Evaluating Exploratory Search Systems. In: Information Processing and Management: An Int. Journal, Vol. 44/2, March 2008, pp. 433-436.

Contact information

Sebastian Franken, Fraunhofer FIT, sebastian.franken@fit.fraunhofer.de
Dr. Ulrich Norbisrath, ulno.net, research@ulno.net

M. Koch, A. Butz & J. Schlichter (Hrsg.): Mensch und Computer 2014 Tagungsband, München: Oldenbourg Wissenschaftsverlag, 2014, S. 145-154.

Participatory Sensing im Rahmen empirischer Forschung

Thomas Ludwig, Simon Scholl

Institut für Wirtschaftsinformatik, Universität Siegen

Zusammenfassung

Die Erfassung der Mensch-Maschine-Interaktion in dynamischen alltäglichen Gegebenheiten beschäftigt die HCI Domäne bereits seit nunmehr einigen Jahren. Obwohl die technischen Möglichkeiten mobiler Systeme ausgiebig erforscht sind, fehlt es vor allem an großflächigen kontext- und nutzerbasierten Studien zu Fragen des Umgangs dieser Systeme in realen Gegebenheiten. Da Smartphones ihre Besitzer auf dem Weg durch den Alltag ständig begleiten, kann das Konzept des Participatory Sensing bei der Erfassung in den Fokus rücken. In diesem Beitrag wird auf Basis einer qualitativen empirischen Studie die Android Applikation PartS, welche anhand des Participatory Sensing Konzeptes die empirische Forschung in mobilen Kontexten unterstützen soll, entwickelt und mit potenziellen Endnutzern evaluiert. Unser Beitrag illustriert, wie eine aktive Teilhabe von Nutzern an dem gesamten Forschungsprozess die Erfassung mobiler Nutzungsdaten verbessern kann.

1 Einleitung

Mobile Geräte wie Smartphones sind aus unserer heutigen Gesellschaft nicht mehr wegzudenken. Während diese in vielen Regionen mit geringer Festnetz-Infrastruktur – etwa in ländlichen Regionen Südamerikas oder Afrikas – häufig die Stelle von Festnetztelefonen einnehmen und kollektiv von einem festen Standort aus genutzt werden, haben sie sich in den westlichen und asiatischen Industrienationen zu personalisierten Medien einzelner Nutzer entwickelt. Durch diese Personalisierung ergibt sich der Standort des mobilen Geräts nunmehr implizit durch den seines Besitzers. Der dabei ständig variierende Kontext des Individuums konfrontiert somit auch das mobile Gerät mit dynamischen Situationen. Die Applikationen der mobilen Geräte greifen dabei auf die integrierte Sensorik (z.B. GPS) zurück, um den Besitzer in der jeweiligen Situation (in situ) zu unterstützen. Wie diese Interaktion zwischen Mensch und Gerät vor allem innerhalb dynamischer alltäglicher Kontexte stattfindet, beschäftigt Forscher der HCI Domäne bereits seit nunmehr einigen Jahren. Und obwohl die technischen Möglichkeiten mobiler Systeme mittlerweile ausgiebig erforscht sind, fehlt es noch immer vor allem an großflächigen kontext- (d.h. in situ) und nutzerbasierten (mit Blick auf das interagierende Individuum) Studien zu Fragen der

Akzeptanz, Aneignung und des Umgangs mit solchen Systemen in realen Gegebenheiten. Kontext- und nutzerbasierte Studien werden dabei als die Untersuchung des Verhaltens des Nutzers in seinem natürlichen Umfeld, sowie dessen tatsächlichen Interaktionen in Bezug zum eigenen Kontext verstanden. Um solche Studien zu ermöglichen wurden bereits Ansätze entwickelt die weit über die klassischen empirischen Methoden hinausgehen und durch moderne mobile Geräte ist es mittlerweile möglich, zuverlässige Daten über den Kontext eines Nutzers zu erfassen. Doch nach wie vor existieren bislang keine umfassenden Ansätze das Nutzerverhalten im Rahmen großflächiger und langfristiger Studien, aber dennoch in realen und alltäglichen Situationen zu erforschen. Mit diesem Beitrag zeigen wir wie das Konzept des Participatory Sensings in die empirische Forschung integriert werden kann, um dadurch die Umsetzung solcher Studien zu forcieren. Dazu zeigen wir zu Beginn aktuelle Ansätze zur Erfassung des in situ Nutzerverhaltens auf (Kap. 2). Um die Erfassung von Nutzerdaten aus Nutzersicht zu verstehen präsentieren wir im Anschluss unsere empirische Studie (Kap. 3). Auf deren Basis entwickelten wir die mobile Android App PartS, welche die Umsetzung großflächiger, langfristiger Studien in realen Gegebenheiten unterstützten soll (Kap. 4) und evaluierten diese anhand ihrer Usability mit einer kleinen Nutzerzahl (Kap. 5).

2 Methoden zur in situ Erfassung des Nutzerverhaltens

Um auf die dynamischen Gegebenheiten eines mobilen Kontextes und das Verhalten eines Nutzers erfassen zu können, wurden die klassischen ethnographischen Methoden um solche der Diary Studies, Experience Sampling Method, Day Reconstruction Method oder Data-Logging ergänzt (Wei 2007). Bei Diary Studies führt ein Nutzer eigenständig Tagebuch über erlebte Ereignisse und durchgeführte Handlungen. Sie lassen sich in zeit- und eventbasierte Formen unterscheiden (Bolger et al. 2003), wobei die Hauptproblematik darin liegt, dass die Teilnehmer *selbst* aktiv werden müssen, was einen hohen Aufwand für die Teilnehmer impliziert. Um diesen Aufwand zu begrenzen entwickelten Brandt et al. (2007) die Snippet-Technik. Damit können in einer Situation schnell Rumpf-Berichte angefertigt werden, welche durch den Nutzer retroperspektivisch weiter ausgeführt werden. Daneben existiert die Experience Sampling Methode, welche einen signalbasierten Mechanismus verwendet und den Nutzer auffordert seine momentane Situation zu schildern (Consolvo & Walker 2003). Möller et al. (2013) zeigten dabei allerdings, dass durch reines Self-Reporting nur 40-70% des tatsächlichen Verhaltens berichtet wird. Um solche negativen Einflüsse zu vermeiden, verlagert die Day Reconstruction Methode das eigentliche Reporting auf einen späteren Zeitpunkt und erfasst in situ nur diverse Kontextdaten (Kahneman et al. 2004). Diese werden dem Nutzer zu einem späteren Zeitpunkt mit samt Verständnisfragen vorgelegt und kombinieren Vorteile der offline Methoden wie Diary Studies mit der Genauigkeit introspektiver Ansätze (Brandt et al. 2007).

Da mobile Geräte mittlerweile stark personalisierte Medien geworden sind, repräsentiert das *Mobile Data Logging* einen wichtigen Teil bei einer der Erfassung des Nutzerverhaltens. Dabei werden Sensordaten automatisiert im Hintergrund erfasst, um Schlüsse auf ein mögliches Verhalten ziehen zu können. Eine solche automatisierte Erfassung wirft spezielle Fragen im Hinblick auf die Privatsphäre auf. Khovanskaya et al. (2013) zeigten, dass aus

Nutzersicht aktuelle Ansätze zur Erfassung von Nutzungsdaten *„do a poor job of communicating the scope of data collected [...] or explicitly acknowledging the values embedded in decisions about which data are collected and how they are reflected back to the user"*. Böhmer et al. (2011) wiesen auf den Einfluss des sozialen Kontext auf die Nutzung von Smartphones hin und Kujala & Miron-Shatz (2013) zeigten die Relevanz von der Intention eines Nutzers sowie dessen Motivation zur Nutzung eines mobilen Gerätes, wodurch ein reines Logging von Daten ungeeignet zur Erfassung des Nutzerverhaltens ist. Um solchen Limitationen entgegenzuwirken, existieren Ansätze zur Verknüpfung des automatischen Data Logging und des Self Reporting. Froehlich et al. (2007) kombinieren das Logging von Smartphone Daten mit gezielten Fragebögen, wobei Liu et al. (2010) für zusätzliche tiefgründige Interviews plädierten, da ansonsten das Nutzerverhalten nicht geeignet abgebildet werden könne. Andere kombinieren Data Logging mit detaillierten visuellen Aufnahmen durch Sensecams (Brown et al. 2013; Gouveia & Karapanos 2013). Durch den Kameraeinsatz ist es zwar möglich verschiedene Sichtweisen auf den Kontext der Teilnehmer einzunehmen (Brown et al. 2013), die visuellen Aufnahmen hielten jedoch Nutzer von Besuchen öffentlicher Plätze sowie des Arbeitsplatzes ab und erlauben aufgrund des hohen Kamerapreises lediglich Studien mit kurzer Laufzeit und kleinem Teilnehmerfeld.

Da sich die Aneignung mobiler Endgeräte aber erst über eine lange Laufzeit entwickelt (Karapanos et al. 2009), sind langfristige Studien notwendig, die durch aktuelle Methoden nicht gewährleistet werden können. Aktuelle großflächige Studien werden stets zu sehr konkreten Fragestellungen durchgeführt, wie zum Beispiel die Nutzung des Akkus (Athukorala et al. 2014; Ferreira et al. 2011) oder die Nutzung des Webbrowsers (Shirazi et al. 2013). Eine Möglichkeit auf diese Problematik angemessen zu reagieren, kann das Konzept des Participatory Sensing bieten. *„Beim Participatory Sensing sammelt eine Menge von Personen in einer Datensammelkampagne mithilfe weitverbreiteter mobiler Endgeräte orts- oder raumbezogene, häufig auch zeitbezogene, Messwerte, Daten oder Informationen, welche mit den eingebauten Mechanismen des mobilen Endgeräts erfasst werden können"* (Abecker et al. 2012). Dabei wird der Nutzer nicht nur als „beforschtes Objekt", sondern als Partizipierender zur langfristigen aktiven Wissensgenerierung betrachtet (De Cristofaro & Soriente 2012). Soziale Netzwerke oder Wikis zeigen schon lange, dass Teilhabe ein enormes Potenzial bieten kann (Beckmann et al. 2012). Diese Teilhabe in der Forschung zu nutzen kann Synergien für eine einzigartige Datenerfassung generieren. Im Fokus des Participatory Sensing steht die Beteiligung möglichst vieler Nutzer in einer vernetzten Umgebung, um möglichst genaue und umfangreiche Informationen zu erheben (Burke et al. 2006). Wichtige Herausforderungen ergeben sich dabei in Bezug auf die Privatsphäre um Nutzungsbarrieren auf Seiten des potenziellen Nutzers abzubauen (De Cristofaro & Soriente 2012). Darüber hinaus müssen Participatory Sensing Systeme dem Nutzer Motivations- und Anreizmechanismen bieten, sodass die Partizipation durch diese aktiv ausgeführt wird (Wang et al 2013). Bisherige Ansätze (z.B. AWARE oder das Funf Framework) präparieren die mobilen Geräte der Nutzer im Vorfeld, was großflächige Studien verhindert oder bieten nicht genügend Anreize, was langfristige Studien verhindert und stellen somit keine Grundlage für eine umfassende empirische Forschung dar. Es Bedarf also Studien, um zu verstehen *ob und wie Participatory Sensing in die Forschung integriert werden kann*.

3 Empirische Studie

Um die aktuelle allgemeine Nutzung und Rahmenbedingungen mobiler Applikationen aus Nutzersicht, sowie Anforderungen an eine aktive Einbindung in langfristige empirische Forschungsprozesse zu verstehen, wurden neun teilstrukturierte Interviews (I01-09, sieben männlich, zwei weiblich) mit Studenten (20-25 Jahre), wissenschaftlichen Mitarbeitern (28 Jahre), sowie Mitarbeitern der Verwaltung (28 Jahre) geführt. Wir erfassten Herausforderungen, die bei der langfristigen Erfassung von in situ Informationen, sowie der Interaktion zwischen Forschern und Teilnehmern adressiert werden sollten. Die Interviews dauerten im Durschnitt 45 Minuten und wurden transkribiert. Um die Genauigkeit zu erhöhen, wurden im Rahmen der qualitativer Methodentriangulation (Olsen 2004) zentrale Aussagen der qualitativen Analyse in Form eines quantitativen Onlinefragebogens verifiziert. Dieser umfasste 27 Fragen und war über einen Zeitraum von zwei Wochen aktiv. Die Teilnehmer der Onlinebefragung wurden durch die Verbreitung des Umfragelinks auf Facebook akquiriert, wobei insgesamt über 190 Teilnehmer an dem Fragebogen teilnahmen. Die Ergebnisse der quantitativen Studie sind als Prozentsätze im Fließtext mit angegeben.

Bei einem Großteil der Teilnehmer herrscht aktuell ein Bewusstsein darüber, dass mobile Applikationen Rechte von Dateneinsicht und -zugriff einfordern. *„Das kann ja bis zum Komplettzugriff auf mein Handy führen und deswegen achte ich da schon sehr drauf“* (I05). Dabei ist die klare Darstellung der Zugriffsrechte eine der wichtigsten Säulen bei der Nutzung. Gerade weil die Tendenz besteht, dass eine übermäßige Datenerfassung bei Applikationen zu Nutzungsbarrieren führt, ist es nötig entsprechende kommunikative Werkzeuge einzusetzen, um über die Intention benötigter Rechte zu informieren. Andernfalls ist die Gefahr groß, dass Anwender die Partizipation nicht beginnen oder frühzeitig beenden. Die Onlinebefragung zeigte ebenfalls, dass 84% der Smartphone Nutzer sich über Sensorzugriffe von Apps bewusst sind. *„Ich versuche das im Auge zu behalten, wenn sie zu viele Daten wollen, versuche ich das zu umgehen. Ich schaue dann nach Alternativen“* (I03).

Unter Berücksichtigung einer transparenten Darstellung erhöht sich die Bereitschaft persönliche Daten preiszugeben. *„Es sollte natürlich transparent sein, worauf wirklich Zugriff genommen wird, was mit den Daten passiert.“* (I08). Die derzeitige Auskunft über benötigte Datenerfassungen wird kritisch gesehen: *„[...] aus den Texten geht ja nicht hervor, was dies im Endeffekt wirklich bedeutet“* (I03). 88% der Online-Befragten teilen diese Meinung. Wie Transparenz für den einzelnen Anwender gestaltet sein soll, ist hingegen sehr individuell: Ist es für die einen ausreichend wenn *vor* dem Download einer App klar ist wofür die Zugriffe benötigt werden (I09), ist es für die anderen wichtig *während* der Nutzung einzusehen, wann welche Daten übermittelt werden (I04). 71% der Onlinebefragten möchten dabei selbst entscheiden, welche Daten sie wann preisgeben.

In Bezug auf Anonymität und wie sich die Bereitstellung von Nutzungsdaten im Zusammenhang von Forschungsstudien gestalten gaben die Teilnehmer an *„anonymisierte Daten sind generell für mich kein Problem und wenn sie einem Forschungszweck dienen, kann ich diese auch preisgeben“* (I01). Dabei scheint eine Anonymisierung zur Glaubwürdigkeit eines Systems beizutragen und für manche Teilnehmer gehörte es zu den Grundanforderungen, *„dass die Daten nicht missbraucht werden, anonymisiert und nur in* *diesem Kontext verwendet werden"* (I04). Befragte die generell keine Barrieren in der Datenerfassung sehen, äußerten keine Bedenken bezüglich der Anonymisierung (I07, I08).

Um Aufschluss darüber zu erhalten, inwieweit die Befragten dazu bereit sind aktiv Berichte abzugeben, wurden sie nach ihren aktuellen Gewohnheiten hinsichtlich Feedbacks in diesem Bereich gefragt. Eine Erkenntnis war, dass sie bei der Abgabe von Feedback erwarteten, dass eine Reaktion eintritt. *„Ich habe nichts davon, wenn ich anderen Leuten sage, ob eine App gut ist oder nicht"* (I06). Die Onlinebefragung ergab, dass 57% aktuell noch nie Feedback gegeben hat. Die Gründe lagen mit 53% hauptsächlich darin, dass entweder der Prozess zu komplex gestaltet ist oder Befragte keinen Nutzen solcher Feedbacks sahen. Daraus lässt sich ableiten, dass Partizipations- und Motivationsaspekte für den Nutzer klar ersichtlich sein müssen. Dabei bestimmen die Rahmenbedingungen in welchen Situationen ein Nutzer dazu in der Lage und gewillt ist, Feedback zu erstellen oder abzugeben. *„[...] Motivation ein Feedback zu geben eher in einer ruhigen Minute"* (I01). Auch hier kommt der Zweckverbund zum tragen, wobei ersichtlich sein muss wofür Feedback benötigt wird: *„Man geht so etwas wahrscheinlich eher an, wenn man weiß, wofür solche Daten erhoben werden. Man weiß, dann es hat eine gewisse Relevanz"* (I01). Im wissenschaftlichen Kontext würden 42% aller Onlinebefragten sehr gerne *aktiv* Feedback geben, woraus folgt, dass ein wissenschaftliches System den Forschungskontext klar kommunizieren sollte. Gleichzeitig muss eine Anwendung, welche die Nutzer zum aktiven Reporting motivieren möchte den Nutzerkontext berücksichtigen um nur in geeigneten Situationen den Nutzer aufzufordern: *„[...] wenn jetzt ständig Popups auftauchen würden, ohne dass ich die Applikation gestartet habe, dann würde das für mich schon einen technischen Schaden bedeuten, weil es mich bei der Nutzung des Gerätes beeinträchtigen würde"* (I02). Die Teilnehmer sagten, sie können sich nicht nur vorstellen aktiv Feedback zu geben, sondern weiter in den gesamten Forschungsprozess, beispielsweise in Form der Ergebniseinsicht teilgenommener Studien, mit einbezogen zu werden (I01). Dies erfordert ein hohes Maß an Flexibilität in den Nutzungsmöglichkeiten. 38% möchten wissen, wer ihre Daten einsehen kann, 36% gaben an, dass sie selbst die Kontrolle über ihre Daten behalten und explizit eine Studie auswählen möchten, für die sie Daten preisgeben.

Im Hinblick auf die Bereitschaft zur Partizipation stellt sich die Herausforderung eine langfristige Motivation zu schaffen. *„[...] wenn das eine App wäre die ich mir installiere, wo der Herausgeber klar zu sehen ist, und für eine bestimmte Studie eine Anfrage käme, mit Beschreibung was diese umfasst, da kann ich mir vorstellen dran teilzunehmen"* (I03). Die Nutzer sind nicht nur daran interessiert Daten im Nachhinein einzusehen, sondern vor allem *während* des Forschungsprozesses. Ein Teilnehmer meinte sogar man solle aus der ganzen Erfassung ein *„Community-Ding"* (I04) machen *„[...], dass man einzelne Projekte finden und diese konkret unterstützen kann, weil man es interessant findet. Das ist dann wesentlich zielgerichteter, man hat Kontrolle darüber und es ist nicht wahllos"* (I04). Die Möglichkeit zur Auswahl von Studien in Verbindung mit Informationen über die Forschenden wurde als stark fördernd für die eigene Teilhabebereitschaft empfunden: *„Oder man hat so einen News-Stream in dem sich die einzelnen Gruppen vorstellen, wo sie erklären können was sie gerade erforschen oder Anbindung an soziale Netzwerke, du kannst dir ja quasi vorstellen wie Kickstarter nur auf Daten bezogen"* (I04).

4 Participatory Sensing in der empirischen Forschung: Die mobile Android Applikation PartS

Unsere empirische Studie zeigte, dass die langfristige Erfassung von Nutzerdaten inklusive des Kontextes Methoden benötigt, die als *„Community-Ding"* konzipiert sind und die Nutzer aktiv als Partizipierende und nicht nur passiv als Datenproduzenten betrachtet. Participatory Sensing bietet ein Konzept, mit welchem eine bestimmte Personenmenge über einen gewissen Zeitraum Daten mit den eingebauten Mechanismen des mobilen Gerätes erfasst und übermittelt. Diese erfassten Sensorinformationen (z.B. Standort) können im Rahmen empirischer Studien den Forschern Aufschlüsse über den Kontext eines Teilnehmers geben. In dem Kontext empirischer Forschung sollten allerdings zusätzlich die typischen Kommunikationsformen zwischen Nutzer und Forscher, wie bidirektionale Gespräche oder Umfragen möglich sein. Da Nutzer bei der Nutzung von Applikationen einen ständigen Vergleich zwischen Datenzugriff und Nutzen vollziehen, müssen Anreize geschaffen werden. Dazu reicht oftmals der wissenschaftliche Kontext und die Möglichkeit aus, nur jene Projekte auszuwählen, deren Thematik spannend ist und die Nutzer aus Eigeninteresse teilnehmen möchten. Dabei muss klar erkennbar sein, wer der Ersteller eines Projektes ist und auf welche Sensoren und mobilen Daten wann und vor allem warum zugegriffen wird. Gleichzeitig muss dem Teilnehmer zu jederzeit transparent sein, welche Daten übermittelt werden, wobei die Sensor- und Nutzerdaten anonymisiert werden müssen. Um den Community-Gedanken weiter voranzutreiben, ist es wichtig dem Nutzer stets aktuelle Projektergebnisse und -fortschritte zu präsentieren und ggf. gemeinsam zu diskutieren.

Um das Konzept zu überprüfen entwickelten wir die mobile Android Applikation ‚PartS' als Teil einer service-orientierten Client-Server-Architektur. Das Server-Backend der Gesamtapplikation bietet Forschern eine Plattform zur Verwaltung von Studien, der Dateneinsicht und Kommunikation mit Nutzern der mobilen Applikation. Im Folgenden wird nur die mobile App PartS beschrieben, wodurch allerdings die Funktionalitäten des Backend ersichtlich werden. Aufgrund der Anonymisierung wird bei dem Start-up der App nur nach Geschlecht und Geburtsjahr gefragt, da diese Daten laut Teilnehmer als unbedenklich gelten, uns aber eine demographische Einordnung und kontextuelle Bezüge ermöglichen. Über die Navigation (Abb. 1, links) können alle Funktionsbereiche der App angesteuert werden. Die App unterteilt sich in *Home*, *Projekte*, *Fragebögen*, *Nutzungsdaten* und *Einstellungen*.

Der Home-Bereich umfasst – ähnlich der Facebook-Wall – alle Meldungen jener Projekte, an denen ein Nutzer partizipiert (Abb. 1, rechts). Hier können die Forscher über das Backend den Teilnehmern Meldungen und Ergebnisse aus den Studien zukommen lassen. Der Projektbereich beinhaltet eine Übersicht aller zur Verfügung stehenden Projekte und jene an denen ein Nutzer bereits teilnimmt. Der Nutzer hat dabei freie Auswahl. Hier existieren zwei Projekte (Abb. 2). Zu einem einzelnen Projekt gibt es die Möglichkeit inhaltliche Details und gewünschte Zugriffsrechte einzusehen, sowie eine direkte Kommunikation mit den Forschenden aufzubauen. Die Detailsicht (Abb. 3) bietet alle wichtigen Details eines Projektes, damit der Nutzer sich im Vorfeld über Ziel und Metadaten geeignet informieren kann. Über die Sicht der Zugriffsrechte kann die Art der durch ein Projekt benötigten Sensordaten eingesehen werden. So ist es möglich, dass Forscher eine Studie zu Bewegungsmuster erstellen, bei denen beispielsweise nur Standortinformationen von Relevanz sind. Beim Anlegen eines Projektes hat der Forscher die Auswahl über *alle* gewünschten Sensor- und Nutzungsdaten. Falls einem Nutzer die Zugriffsrechte oder Informationen nicht zusagen, muss er die Teilnahme dieses Projektes gar nicht erst antreten.

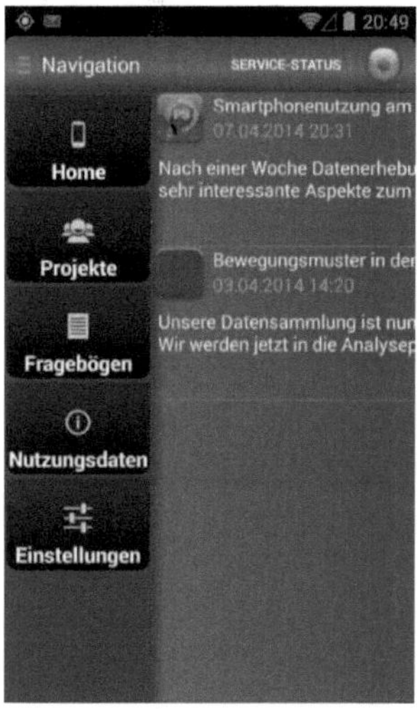

Abbildung 1: Navigationsleiste

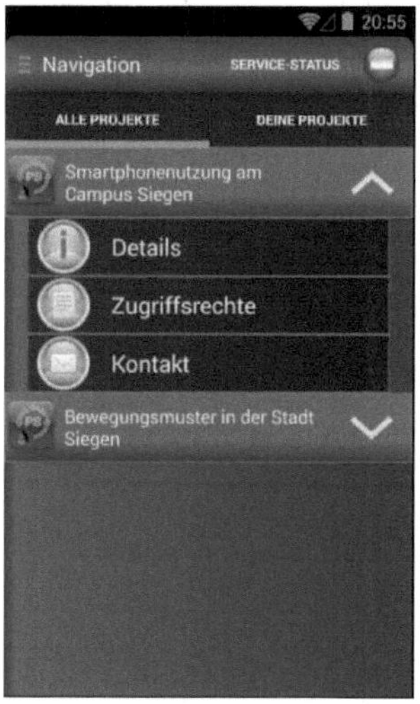

Abbildung 2: Projektübersicht

Abbildung 3: Projektdetails

Die Nachrichtensicht umfasst einen Chat zum direkten Austausch zwischen Nutzern und Forschenden (Abb. 4). Nachdem ein Teilnehmer einem Projekt beigetreten ist erscheint es unter „Deine Projekte". Ab diesem Zeitpunkt startet ein Service im Hintergrund, welcher die projektspezifischen benötigten Sensordaten mit Hilfe des modifizierten Funf Frameworks (http://www.funf.org/) erfasst und den Forschern gemäß den transparent gestalteten Zugriffswünschen zur Verfügung gestellt. Während der Teilnahme erhält der Partizipierende Neuigkeiten und Ergebnisse des Projektes. Dabei wird er über eingehende Nachrichten via Push benachrichtigt, wodurch individuelle Informationen entsprechend seiner jeweiligen Projektteilhaben geliefert werden. Ist die Teilnahme nicht mehr erwünscht, kann diese jederzeit beendet werden. Da die automatisch erfassten Daten, wie in der Literatur bereits gezeigt, nicht ausreichen, hat der Forscher zusätzlich die Möglichkeit gezielte Fragebögen zu erstellen. In dem Bereich ‚Fragebögen' erhält der Nutzer eine Liste aller zur Verfügung stehenden Fragebögen (Abb. 5). Diese Fragebögen können dabei eventbasiert auf Basis der erfassten Daten gestartet werden, beispielsweise wenn sich ein Nutzer in dem Radius von 50 Metern um die Universität befindet. Für die Fragebögen stehen eine Vielzahl von Elementen zur Verfügung die im Backend konfiguriert werden können. In dem Bereich der Nutzungsdaten, können die Teilnehmer jederzeit den Umfang der erfassten und übermittelten Daten einsehen (Abb. 6). Diese finden sich nach ihrer Art kategorisiert und werden dem Nutzer mitsamt einem beschreibenden Text visualisiert dargestellt. So wird als Nebeneffekt der Teilnahme an Forschungsprojekten dem Nutzer ein Self Reporting Tool an die Hand gegeben, mit dem das eigene Nutzungsverhalten eingesehen werden kann.

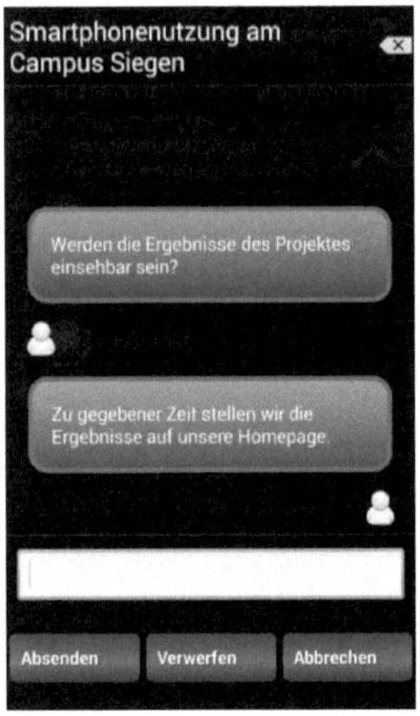

Abbildung 4: Nachrichtensicht

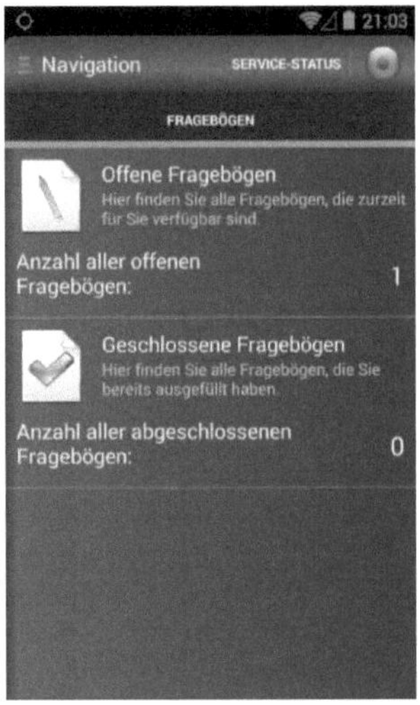

Abbildung 5: Fragebögen

Abbildung 6: Nutzungsdaten

5 Evaluation

Um PartS hinsichtlich Funktionalität, Usability und auf das partizipativem Potential zu testen, wurde eine Evaluation mit möglichen Endnutzern durchgeführt. Diese fand entlang eines Szenarios statt, in dem die Teilnehmer durch eine konkrete Nutzungssituation geführt wurden. Das Szenario bestand aus einer Studie zur Analyse des Verhaltens von Studenten aus Siegen. Die insgesamt sechs Teilnehmer bestanden aus Befragten der Empirie und aus Erstnutzern, um Referenzwerte und gleichzeitig Ersteinschätzungen zu erhalten. Währenddessen fand eine Befragung anhand eines Leitfadens statt, der vor allem Fragen der Gesamtfunktionalität, des Designs sowie Nutzerführung fokussierte. Zusätzlich wurde die „Thinking Aloud"-Methode (Nielsen 1993) eingesetzt, um Intentionen erfassen zu können.

Hinsichtlich der Bedienung entsprach die App den Erwartungen der Probanden aus der Empirie. Besonders da man sich bei der Menüführung an Facebook orientierte, konnten sich die Teilnehmer schnell zurechtfinden: *„Ich habe oben eine Leiste, oben links ein Navigationsmenü, welches sich aufklappt, was auch einem gängigen Aufbau entspricht. Von daher lässt sich das Ganze einfach bedienen"* (E06). Bei der Projektverwaltung wurde eine dynamische Verwaltung der Zugriffsrechte einzelner Projekte gewünscht. *„Es kann ja sein, dass ich an verschiedenen Projekten teilnehme und ich möchte gerade nicht, dass ein bestimmtes Projekt meinen Bewegungsablauf verfolgt, dann wäre es schon sinnvoll, dass ich das darüber individuell steuern könnte"* (E04). Hier wurde die Privatsphäre in den Fokus gestellt, um situativ bestimmte Dienste von der Datenerfassung auszuschließen, beispielsweise während des Surfens im Internet. Die Neuigkeiten und Ergebnisse aus den Projekten heraus werden durchweg positiv betrachtet: *„Ich finde das ganz gut mit der Benachrichtigung, dass ich stets auf dem Laufenden gehalten werde"* (E06). Vor allem der transparente Informationsprozess über aktuelle Projekte und die Möglichkeit des direkten Kontaktes zu den Forschern bildeten wichtige Vertrauensmechanismen.

Bei der Einsicht erfasster und übermittelten Nutzungs- und Sensordaten wollten die Teilnehmer vor allem ihre Daten im Vergleich zum Teilnehmerkollektiv betrachten (E02). Es sei ein Anreiz sichtbar über die Ergebnisse aus den Fragebögen informiert zu werden: *„Es würden mich Ergebnisse von den Fragebögen interessieren, wenn es erlaubt ist, dass der Nutzer die einsehen kann"* (E05). Zum Abschluss sollten die Nutzer noch einmal ihre Erfahrung reflektieren, wobei neue Aspekte zur Schaffung erweiterter Anreize angesprochen wurden: *„dass man irgendwie eine Möglichkeit hat auch Vorschläge für Projekte zu machen. Das man angeben kann was mich interessiert und dies an den Forschenden gesendet wird. Das würde natürlich die Involvierung des Nutzers in die App noch stärken"* (E02). Weitergehend bestand ein Interesse eigene Projektideen einzubringen, um selbst mit anderen Teilnehmern neue Erkenntnisse zu schaffen. Auch im Bezug zur Privatsphäre wurden Vorschläge der freiwilligen und partiellen Aufhebung der Anonymisierung vorgeschlagen. *„Vielleicht zum Thema Anonymisierung, dass man einen Dialog hat, wo man seine Daten eintragen kann und wenn man sie leer lässt keine Informationen gespeichert werden"* (E04).

6 Fazit

Aktuelle Methoden zur in situ Erfassung des Nutzerverhaltens sind aufgrund finanzieller, technischer oder organisatorischer Restriktionen überwiegend für kleine und kurzfristige Studien oder für konkrete Anwendungsszenarien konzipiert. Dabei sind langfristige großflächige Studien notwendig, um die Aneignung und den Umgang mittels mobiler Systeme zu verstehen. Basierend auf der Literaturstudie scheint das Konzept des Participatory Sensing ein geeigneter Ansatz zu sein, da es die Nutzer aktiv mit in den Prozess der Datenerfassung und Wissensgenerierung einbezieht. Mit dem Paper haben wir Rahmenbedingungen und Restriktionen für die Konzeption und das Design einer auf Participatory Sensing basierten Applikation untersucht. In unserer empirischen Studie des aktuellen Nutzungsverhaltens hinsichtlich Datenschutz, Privatsphäre und Potenzialen haben wir Anforderungen an eine Applikation herausgearbeitet. Diese waren neben der Transparenz vor und während der Nutzung, insbesondere die freie Wahl zur Partizipation an interessanten Projekten, das Interesse an Ergebnissen und dem Gefühl Teil etwas Ganzen zu sein. Darauf aufbauend wurde mit der mobilen Android App PartS ein Interaktionskonzept konzipiert, welches Forschern und potenziellen Partizipierenden eine Plattform zur Kooperation und Austausch bietet. Die App PartS ermöglicht auf Basis von Projekte Nutzer aktiv in den Forschungsprozess einzubinden, sowie zu motivieren und somit zur automatisierten Datenübermittlung zu stimulieren. Die Evaluation zeigte, dass ein solches Interaktionskonzept bei der Erfassung von Nutzerdaten und Intentionen im dynamischen alltäglichen Kontext unterstützen kann. Gleichzeitig zeigen die Ergebnisse allerdings auch, dass eine noch stärkere Einbindung der Teilnehmer in den gesamten Prozess, wie durch das Erstellen eigener Studien erwünscht ist. Eine Limitation des Beitrages ist vor allem das universitäre Teilnehmerfeld, da dieses der Regel nach offener für Forschungskonzepte ist. Eine Ausweitung auf weitere Anwendungsfelder gilt es zukünftig großflächig zu evaluieren.

Literaturverzeichnis

Abecker, A., Kazakos, W., Melo Borges, J. de, & Zacharias, V. (2012). Beiträge zu einer Technologie für Anwendungen des Participatory Sensing. In *AGIT 2012*. Salzburg.

Athukorala, K., et al. (2014). How Carat Affects User Behavior: Implications for Mobile Battery Awareness Applications. In *Proc. CHI '14* (pp. 1029–1038).

Beckmann, C., Herr, S., & Gross, T. (2012). Gemeinsam einig: Partizipation in Gruppenempfehlungs-systemen. *Mensch & Computer* (pp. 113–122). München: Oldenbourg Verlag.

Böhmer, M., Hecht, B., Johannes, S., Krüger, A., & Bauer, G. (2011). Falling Asleep with Angry Birds, Facebook and Kindle – A Large Scale Study on Mobile Application Usage. In *Proc. 13th MobileHCI* (pp. 47–56). Stockholm, Sweden:

Bolger, N., Davis, A., & Rafaeli, E. (2003). Diary methods: capturing life as it is lived. *Annual Review of Psychology*, *54*(1), 579–616.

Brandt, J., Weiss, N., & Klemmer, S. R. (2007). txt 4 l8r : Lowering the Burden for Diary Studies Under Mobile Conditions. In ACM (Ed.), *EA CHI '07* (pp. 2303–2308). ACM New York.

Brown, B., McGregor, M., & Laurier, E. (2013). iPhone in vivo : Video Analysis of Mobile Device Use. In *Proc. CHI '13* (pp. 1031–1040). Paris, France: ACM.

Burke, J., Estrin, D., Hansen, M., Parker, A., Ramanathan, N., Reddy, S., & Srivastava, M. B. (2006). Participatory Sensing. *IEEE Internet Computing*, *14*, (pp. 12–42).

Consolvo, S., & Walker, M. (2003). Using the experience sampling method to evaluate ubicomp applications. *IEEE Pervasive Computing*, *2* (2), (pp. 24–31).

De Cristofaro, E., & Soriente, C. (2012). Participatory Privacy: Enabling Privacy in Participatory Sensing. *Network Security*, (January, pp. 1–11).

Ferreira, D., Dey, A. K., & Kostakos, V. (2011). Understanding human-smartphone concerns: A study of battery life. In *Lecture Notes in Computer Science* Vol. 6696 LNCS, (pp. 19–33).

Froehlich, J., Chen, M. , Consolvo, S., Harrison, B., & Landay, J. (2007). MyExperience: a system for in situ tracing and capturing of user feedback on mobile phones. In *Proc. 5th MobiSys* (pp. 57–70).

Gouveia, R., & Karapanos, E. (2013). Footprint Tracker: Supporting Diary Studies with Lifelogging. In *Proc. CHI '13* (pp. 2921–2930). ACM.

Kahneman, D., Krueger, A. B., Schkade, D. A., Schwarz, N., & Stone, A. (2004). A survey method for characterizing daily life experience: the day reconstruction method *Science*, *306* (5702), 1776–80.

Karapanos, E., Zimmerman, J., Forlizzi, J., & Martens, J.-B. (2009). User Experience Over Time: An Initial Framework. In *Proc. CHI '09* (pp. 729–738). ACM.

Khovanskaya, V., Baumer, E., P. S., Cosley, D., Voida, S., & Gay, G. (2013). "Everybody Knows What You're Doing". In *Proc. CHI '13* (pp. 3403–3412). Paris, France: ACM.

Kujala, S., & Miron-Shatz, T. (2013). Emotions , Experiences and Usability in Real-Life Mobile Phone Use. In *Proc. CHI '13* (pp. 1061–1070). Paris, France: ACM.

Liu, N., Liu, Y., & Wang, X. (2010). Data logging plus e-diary: towards an online evaluation approach of mobile service field trial. In *Proc. 12th MobileHCI* (pp. 287–290). ACM.

Möller, A., Kranz, M., Schmid, B., Roalter, L., & Diewald, S. (2013). Investigating self-reporting behavior in long-term studies. In *Proc. CHI '13* (p. 2931). New York, New York, USA: ACM.

Nielsen, J. (1993). *Usability Engineering*. (J. Nielsen, Ed.) *Usability Engineering* (Vol. 44, p. 362).

Olsen, W. (2004). Triangulation in Social Research: Qualitative and Quantitative Methods Can Really Be Mixed. In M. Holborn & Haralambos (Eds.), *Developments in Sociology* (pp. 1–30). Causeway.

Shirazi, A. S., Henze, N., Dingler, T., Schmidt, A., & Kunze, K. (2013). Upright or Sideways? Analysis of Smartphone Postures in the Wild. In *Proc. 15th MobileHCI* (pp. 362–371).

Wang, H., et al. (2013). An Optimized Directional Distribution Strategy of the Incentive Mechanism in SenseUtil-Based Participatory Sensing Environment. In Proc. *9th MSN* (pp. 67–71).

Wei, C. Y. (2007). Capturing Mobile Phone Usage: Research Methods for Mobile Studies. In *2007 IEEE IPCC* (pp. 1–6). Seattle, WA.

M. Koch, A. Butz & J. Schlichter (Hrsg.): Mensch und Computer 2014 Tagungsband,
München: Oldenbourg Wissenschaftsverlag, 2014, S. 155-164.

Abstrakte virtuelle Umgebung für die Schlaganfalltherapie

Thomas Schüler

Institut für Informatik, Universität Osnabrück

Zusammenfassung

Virtuelle Umgebungen können Schlaganfallpatienten den Eindruck vermitteln, Bewegungen mit ihrer betroffenen Körperseite durchzuführen. Dadurch werden die geschädigten Hirnzentren stimuliert und das motorische Lernen wird begünstigt. Abstrakte Umgebungen binden dabei die Aufmerksamkeit des Nutzers und regen zu explorierendem Verhalten an. Sie bieten das Potential zur Entwicklung völlig neuer Therapieverfahren, die ohne die Technologie nicht möglich sind. Dieser Artikel erläutert die Hintergründe für einen entsprechenden, technisch gestützten therapeutischen Ansatz. Das Therapiesystem AVUS (Abstrakte virtuelle Umgebung für Schlaganfalltherapie) wird vorgestellt, welches in enger Rückkopplung mit Patienten und Therapeuten entwickelt wurde. In einer Pilotstudie wurde das System erstmals in der klinischen Anwendung überprüft. Die Ergebnisse der Studie unterstützen die Plausibilität des Ansatzes und weisen auf positive Effekte des Trainings bzgl. der Motivation der Patienten und deren subjektiven Einschätzung des Therapieerfolgs hin.

1 Einleitung

Der Schlaganfall ist weltweit eine der häufigsten Ursachen für Behinderungen im Erwachsenenalter. In Deutschland ereignen sich derzeit jährlich ca. 196.000 erstmalige Schlaganfälle und weitere ca. 66.000 wiederholte Schlaganfälle (Heuschmann et al. 2010). Durch die zu erwartende Alterung der Bevölkerung ist mit einer steigenden absoluten Zahl an Schlaganfallpatienten zu rechnen. Eine systematische Versorgung durch therapeutische Interventionen beeinflusst den Erfolg der Rehabilitation positiv (Langhorne et al. 2011). Vor diesem Hintergrund gewinnt die (Weiter-)Entwicklung effektiver Therapieverfahren an Dringlichkeit.

Ein wesentliches Ziel der Rehabilitation ist die Wiederherstellung motorischer Fähigkeiten. Neben einer guten klinischen Versorgung spielt hierfür die Motivation und die Einstellung der Patienten eine wichtige Rolle (Langhorne et al. 2011). Seit einigen Jahren wird der Einsatz von Virtueller Realität (VR) und Computerspielen zur Unterstützung von Physio- und Ergotherapie unter dem Stichwort „VR Rehabilitation“ (manchmal auch Cybertherapy, Telerehabilitation oder Exergaming) untersucht (Burdea 2003). Die positiven Effekte der Technologie für die Patientenmotivation sind gut dokumentiert und weitere Vorteile werden herausgestellt (Lange et al. 2009). Für die motorische Rehabilitation nach einem Schlaganfall wurden verschiedene Systeme entwickelt und erfolgreich getestet (Laver et al. 2012).

Neben den motivationalen Aspekten und der Unterstützung herkömmlicher Therapie bietet der Einsatz von VR auch das Potential zur Entwicklung völlig neuer Therapieverfahren, die ohne die Technologie nicht möglich sind. Durch algorithmische Transformationen können bspw. visuelle Reize als Reaktion auf Bewegungen gezielt erzeugt werden. Seit einigen Jahren ist bekannt, dass visuelle Eindrücke in Verbindung mit motorischer Aktivität eine wesentliche Rolle für das motorische Lernen spielen (Wulf et al. 2011). Bei der Beobachtung von Bewegungen werden weitgehend dieselben Hirnregionen aktiviert, wie bei der tatsächlichen Durchführung derselben Bewegungen (Small et al. 2010). Mit Hilfe von VR und sensorbasierten Interaktionsgeräten können Bewegungsvisualisierungen beliebig gestaltet werden. So können variantenreiche Darstellungsformen zur Förderung des motorischen Lernens nach einem Schlaganfall angeboten und untersucht werden.

Dieser Artikel beschreibt die Hintergründe, die Umsetzung und die empirische Überprüfung eines entsprechenden technisch gestützten, therapeutischen Ansatzes. Ein Therapiesystem, welches Bewegungsvisualisierungen mit unterschiedlichen Abstraktionsgraden anbietet, wird vorgestellt und erste Ergebnisse aus einer Pilotstudie werden diskutiert. Der nächste Abschnitt erläutert hierfür relevante Grundlagen des motorischen Lernens.

2 Motorisches Lernen durch visuelle Illusionen

Die kognitiven Prozesse, die an motorischen Aktionen beteiligt sind, können als ein „observation-execution-matching"-System beschrieben werden (Small et al. 2010). Ein Subjekt löst ein motorisches Kommando aus, mit dem Ziel, eine bestimmte Aktion durchzuführen. Dieses Kommando wird dann einerseits verwendet, um die entsprechenden Muskeln zu (de-)aktivieren und andererseits, um das Ergebnis der Aktion vorherzusagen. Die Vorhersage wird anschließend mit den tatsächlich resultierenden Sinneseindrücken abgeglichen und eventuelle Abweichungen werden in den folgenden motorischen Kommandos berücksichtigt. Diese Prozesse des Durchführens und Abgleichens von Bewegungen laufen weitgehend unbewusst und kleinschrittig in schneller Wiederholung ab.

Interessanterweise dominiert das visuelle System diese Prozesse. Zielgerichtete motorische Aktionen sind häufig visuell kontrolliert und die Sinneseindrücke des Auges werden für die subjektive Körperwahrnehmung stärker gewichtet, als Empfindungen, die über andere Sinne vermittelt werden (Lenggenhager et al. 2007). Eine wichtige Rolle spielen die sogenannten Spiegelneurone (Small et al. 2010). Diese sind vor allem in motorischen Hirnarealen zu finden und das Besondere an ihnen ist, dass sie sowohl bei der Durchführung als auch bei der Beobachtung und sogar bei der reinen Vorstellung von Bewegungen aktiv sind. Wenn visuelle Informationen den Eindruck einer Bewegungsausführung vermitteln, wird daher weitgehend dieselbe neurologische Aktivität ausgelöst, die auch bei der tatsächlichen Durchführung derselben Bewegung ausgelöst wird.

Die beschriebenen Eigenschaften des Gehirns werden für die motorische Rehabilitation nach einem Schlaganfall ausgenutzt. Durch visuelle Illusionen von Bewegungen können Fähigkeiten trainiert werden, zu denen die Patienten tatsächlich nicht in der Lage sind. Die Spiegeltherapie (Ramachandran & Altschuler 2009) ist ein Beispiel für diesen Ansatz. Hierbei wird ein Spiegel so auf der sagittalen Körperachse vor einem Patienten positioniert, dass das Spiegelbild der gesunden Körperseite die betroffene Extremität „überlagert". Der Patient wird dann aufgefordert, die gesunde Extremität zu bewegen und dabei in den Spiegel zu schauen. Die Instruktionen sind weiterhin derart, dass synchrone Bewegungen mit beiden Extremitäten vorgestellt werden und die Patienten sich auf die Illusion einlassen. Gelingt diese Konzentrationsleistung bestätigt die visuelle Wahrnehmung die korrekte Ausführung einer motorischen Aktion und die entsprechende Bewegung wird trainiert. Die positiven Effekte der Spiegeltherapie für die motorische Rehabilitation nach einem Schlaganfall sind inzwischen belegt (Thieme et al. 2012).

Vergleichbare Illusionen von Bewegungen können auch durch VR hervorgerufen werden. Mit einem Therapiesystem für Schlaganfallpatienten wurde dies umgesetzt und überprüft (Eng et al. 2007). Das System zeigt virtuelle Arme aus einer Ego-Perspektive, die von den Patienten mit Hilfe eines eigens entwickelten Motion-Tracking-Geräts durch natürliche Bewegungen gesteuert werden. In der VR können die Aktionen der gesunden Seite dann für den betroffenen Arm gespiegelt werden, so dass beide Arme symmetrische Bewegungen zeigen. Die Patienten führen verschiedene Aufgaben aus, bspw. das Fangen von heranfliegenden Bällen. Andere Studien untersuchten die neurologische Reaktion bei der Interaktion mit solchen virtuellen Spiegelillusionen (Saleh et al. 2013; Dohle et al. 2011). Sie zeigten, dass hierbei tatsächlich Aktivität in motorischen Hirnzentren der betroffenen Seite ausgelöst wird.

3 Abstrakte Illusionen von Bewegungen

Die eben genannten VR-Systeme demonstrieren, dass mit virtuellen Abbildern von Armen Bewegungsillusionen hervorgerufen werden können, die mit solchen in einem Spiegel vergleichbar sind. Der vorliegende Artikel stellt darüber hinaus die Frage, ob durch den Einsatz der Technologie auch andere visuelle Effekte den Eindruck von Bewegung erzeugen und die Rehabilitation sogar zusätzlich fördern können. Algorithmische Transformationen können abstrakte Visualisierungen generieren, die motorische Aktionen der Patienten darstellen. Solche Darstellungsformen weisen einige Potentiale auf:

- Die zunächst unbekannten abstrakten Bewegungseffekte müssen von den Patienten durch selbstgesteuertes, explorierendes Verhalten gelernt werden, was für die motorische Rehabilitation als förderlich beschrieben wird (Wulf et al. 2011).
- Erzeugen die abstrakten Visualisierungen bei unterschiedlichen motorischen Fähigkeitsniveaus interessante, ästhetisch ansprechende Darstellungen, kann dies den Patienten ein Gefühl von Kompetenz und Autonomie vermitteln. Dies unterstützt die Motivation beim Training und kann die Rehabilitation positiv beeinflussen (Wulf et al. 2011).

- Als wesentliche Voraussetzung für die therapeutische Effektivität der Spiegelillusionen gilt ein Gefühl von Kontrolle über die visuellen Effekte (Dohle et al. 2011). Wird eine virtuelle Umgebung verwendet, muss diese auf die Bewegungen der Patienten erwartungsgemäß reagieren. Bei realistischen Darstellungsformen kann dies nur schwer umgesetzt werden, da es prinzipiell nicht möglich ist für alle Bewegungsintentionen, die Patienten in realistischen Welten entwickeln können, entsprechende Reaktionen des technischen Systems vorzusehen. Abstrakte Umgebungen machen demgegenüber einen eingeschränkten Handlungsraum von vornherein deutlich und die Erwartungen der Patienten sind auf die Erfahrungen mit dem System beschränkt. Ein Gefühl von Kontrolle wird sich in diesen Umgebungen daher leichter einstellen.
- Abstrakte Bewegungsvisualisierungen binden auf besondere Weise die Aufmerksamkeit der Patienten. Durch die ungewohnte und reduzierte Darstellung der motorischen Informationen wird die Konzentration auf die Illusion erleichtert. Die Möglichkeiten solcher außergewöhnlichen sensomotorischen Erfahrungen waren die ursprüngliche Triebfeder der VR-Forschung (Biocca et al. 1995).

Bislang ist jedoch unklar, ob abstrakte Bewegungsvisualisierungen im Rahmen des in Abschnitt 2 erläuterten „observation-execution-matching"-Systems gleichermaßen die Ausführung eines motorischen Kommandos bestätigen können. Erkenntnisse über die kognitiven Prozesse bei der Bewegungsvorstellung deuten auf die grundsätzliche Möglichkeit hin. Die neurologische Aktivität bei der mentalen Drehung von abstrakten geometrischen Objekten ist vergleichbar mit jener bei der Vorstellung einer entsprechenden Drehbewegung der eigenen Körperteile (Kosslyn et al. 2001). In beiden Fällen sind motorische Areale aktiv und dies wird auf die oben beschriebene Funktionsweise der Spiegelneurone zurückgeführt. Es wird angenommen, dass die Spiegelneurone auf ähnliche Weise auch bei der Beobachtung abstrakter Bewegungsvisualisierungen angesprochen werden.

Weitere Hinweise gibt die Forschung zum Präsenzgefühl in virtuellen Umgebungen. Dieses zeichnet sich dadurch aus, dass eine Person medienvermittelte Sinnesreize als real empfindet und die Rolle der technischen Geräte als Ursache der Reize übersieht (Lombard & Ditton 1997). Personen können dieses Gefühl auch in abstrakten virtuellen Umgebungen empfinden und die Exploration interessanter, ästhetisch ansprechender Darstellungsformen hat sogar eine präsenzfördernde Wirkung. Das Gefühl stellt sich jedoch nur ein, wenn die Person in der virtuellen Umgebung handeln und alle Intentionen in Aktionen übersetzen kann (Riva et al. 2010). Die virtuellen Effekte müssen als unmittelbare Folgen der eigenen Handlungen wahrgenommen werden. Dass dies in abstrakten Umgebungen möglich ist, deutet darauf hin, dass damit auch im therapeutischen Kontext Bewegungsillusionen erzeugt werden können.

4 Entwicklung des AVUS Therapiesystems

Ausgehend von den vorstehend beschriebenen theoretischen Überlegungen wurde eine Software für die Therapie mit Schlaganfallpatienten entwickelt. Die „Abstrakte virtuelle Umgebung für Schlaganfalltherapie" (AVUS) verwendet abstrakte Visualisierungen, deren Formen durch die Bewegungen des Oberkörpers kontinuierlich beeinflusst werden. Jede Bewegung resultiert in einem direkten visuellen Effekt. Zusätzlich wird atmosphärische Musik mit einem eindeutigen Rhythmus abgespielt, die über diesen und die Lautstärke ebenfalls in die Visualisierungen rückwirkt. Durch diese Integration von Sinnesreizen auf mehreren Kanälen kann das Präsenzgefühl der Patienten gestärkt werden (Lombard & Ditton 1997). Es wird eine Atmosphäre erzeugt, die zu explorierendem Verhalten und zu Bewegung anregt und die gleichzeitig die Konzentration auf die visuellen Effekte erleichtert.

Die Bewegungen der Patienten werden mit einem MS Kinect Sensor aufgezeichnet und mit dem OpenNI-SDK in eine Skelettstruktur überführt. Für die Verwendung im therapeutischen Rahmen werden zusätzliche Berechnungen (z.B. Spiegelung von Körperteilen, Winkelberechnungen, statistische Auswertung) in einer eigenen Bibliothek vorgenommen. Die Bewegungsinformationen werden unter Verwendung des Processing-Frameworks visualisiert.

Abbildung 1: Visualisierungstypen im AVUS System: Waveform, Generative Tree und Ellipsoidal Visualisation (Aufnahmen des Autors)

Derzeit sind drei verschiedene Visualisierungstypen implementiert (siehe Abbildung 1). Diese stellen die Bewegungen der Patienten in einer abstrakten und reduzierten Weise dar. Die Waveform Visualisierung (WF) überträgt die mit Bezug zu den Schultern relative Position der Ellbogen und Handgelenke auf eine Wellenform, mit der gleichzeitig Samples der begleitenden Musik dargestellt werden. Die Generative Tree Visualisierung (GT) verwendet einen mathematischen Baumgraphen, in dessen rekursiven Algorithmus abwechselnd die Flexionswinkel des Schultergelenks bzw. des Ellbogengelenks für die Darstellung einfließen. Die Musik wirkt sich hier auf die Strichstärke der Äste und die relative Orientierung der Blätter des Baumes aus. Die Ellipsoidal Visualisierung (EL) stellt säulenförmige Strukturen dar, deren Position durch die Position der Hände bestimmt ist und deren Durchmesser und Orientierung im Raum mit den Flexionswinkeln der Gelenke variiert. Das Spektrogramm der Musik bestimmt die Strichstärke der verschiedenfarbigen Orbitlinien.

Die Visualisierungen weisen steigenden Abstraktionsgrad vom menschlichen Oberkörper auf. Dies ermöglicht einerseits eine weitergehende Untersuchung des Ansatzes hinsichtlich eines vertretbaren Abstraktionsniveaus und bietet darüber hinaus die Möglichkeit steigender kognitiver Anforderungen während der Therapie. Alle Varianten werden mit ca. 30fps berechnet und vermitteln den Eindruck kontinuierlicher Interaktion. Für jede Therapiesitzung können Einstellungen vorgenommen werden. Wesentlich ist die Möglichkeit des Wechsels zwischen zwei Modi, dem *veritablen Modus*, in dem die tatsächlichen Bewegungsdaten beider Körperseiten verwendet werden und dem *Spiegeltherapie Modus*, in dem die Bewegungsdaten der gesunden Seite für die betroffene Seite gespiegelt werden.

Die Softwareentwicklung erfolgte benutzerzentriert und es wurden Rückmeldungen von Patienten und Therapeuten zu frühen Prototypen in die aktuelle Version integriert. Diese Rückmeldungen bestätigten die Plausibilität des Ansatzes und deuteten positive Auswirkungen auf die Rehabilitation an. Es ergab sich ein vielversprechender Ablauf der Intervention, bei dem die Patienten die Reaktionen des Systems eigenständig explorieren und auf selbstbestimmte Weise aktive Bewegungen mit den oberen Extremitäten üben. Bzgl. der Visualisierungen wurde eine reduzierte Darstellung vor einem schwarzen Hintergrund angeraten, um die kognitive Verarbeitung für die Patienten zu erleichtern. In diesen frühen Tests wurde auf die Möglichkeit zur körperlichen Identifikation mit den Visualisierungen hingewiesen.

5 Empirische Überprüfung

Das vorgestellte Therapiesystem wurde im Rahmen einer Pilotstudie mit acht Schlaganfallpatienten in einem neurologischen Rehabilitationszentrum getestet. Das Ziel der Studie war es, erste Informationen über die klinische Anwendung der AVUS zu erheben.

5.1 Protokoll der klinischen Pilotstudie

Die Studie war als kontrollierte Fallserie angelegt und richtete sich an hemiparetische Patienten, die wenigstens minimale proximale Armfunktion auf der betroffenen Seite zeigten. Ausschlusskriterien grenzten die Gruppe zusätzlich ein (visuelle oder starke kognitive Einschränkungen, Demenz, Aphasie, Epilepsie). Die Teilnehmer wurden in zwei Gruppen randomisiert. Die Experimentalgruppe (EG, fünf Patienten) trainierte eine Woche lang täglich ca. 30 Minuten unter therapeutischer Aufsicht mit dem AVUS-System. Die Kontrollgruppe (KG, drei Patienten) führte für dieselbe Dauer unspezifische Bewegungsübungen zu Musik unter therapeutischer Aufsicht durch. Beide Interventionen wurden zusätzlich zum üblichen Therapieprogramm angeboten. Das Studienprotokoll entsprach den ethischen Konventionen der Helsinki-Deklaration der World-Medical Association (www.wma.net).

Die EG durchlief in den 30 Minuten der Intervention drei Phasen mit Entspannungspausen. Zu Beginn wurden zuvor aufgezeichnete Bewegungen abgespielt und visualisiert. Die Patienten betrachteten die Visualisierungen und sollten sich dabei mental vorstellen, die entsprechenden Bewegungen durchzuführen. Dies geschah zur Einstimmung auf die Therapie. Anschließend interagierten die Patienten für etwa fünf Minuten im veritablen Modus mit den Visualisierungen. Sie wurden instruiert, so gut wie möglich gleichmäßige Bewegungen mit beiden Armen zu versuchen und ihre Aufmerksamkeit ganz auf die virtuelle Umgebung zu lenken. In diesem Durchgang wurde der Zusammenhang zwischen Bewegungen und den visuellen Effekten erfahren. Bei gleichbleibenden Instruktionen interagierten die Patienten in der letzten Phase erneut etwa fünf Minuten im Spiegeltherapie Modus. Hierbei erzeugten sie symmetrische Effekte, wodurch ein Eindruck von gleichmäßiger Bewegung auf beiden Körperseiten entstand. Für die EG wurde motorisches Lernen funktionaler Bewegungen auf der betroffenen Seite, sowie gesteigerte Motivation zur Durchführung der Therapie erwartet.

Vor und nach der Studie wurden motorische Funktionstests durchgeführt (Fugl-Meyer-Test FMT-OE, (Duncan et al. 1983)). Außerdem schätzten der Patienten nach Abschluss der Studie ihren subjektiven Eindruck der Funktionsverbesserung auf einer farbigen Analogskala (FAS) ein. Innerhalb der EG wurde nach jeder Intervention das subjektiv erfahrene Präsenzgefühl mit dem iGroup Presence Questionaire (IPQ, (Schubert et al. 2001)) erhoben. Im Rahmen von etwa 30-minütigen Leitfadeninterviews äußerten die Teilnehmer der EG außerdem ihre Erfahrungen mit dem Therapiesystem.

5.2 Ergebnisse

Die Studie wurde im Frühjahr 2013 durchgeführt. Die organisatorischen Abläufe waren erfolgreich und die technologische Installation erfolgte problemlos. Das AVUS Therapiesystem war im klinischen Kontext anwendbar. Alle Teilnehmer absolvierten das Programm vollständig. Die Daten einer Patientin aus der KG wurden jedoch von der Analyse ausgeschlossen, da diese Person im Laufe der Studienwoche stürzte und ihre Ergebnisse dadurch stark beeinflusst wurden. Abbildung 2 zeigt Eindrücke aus der Intervention mit der EG.

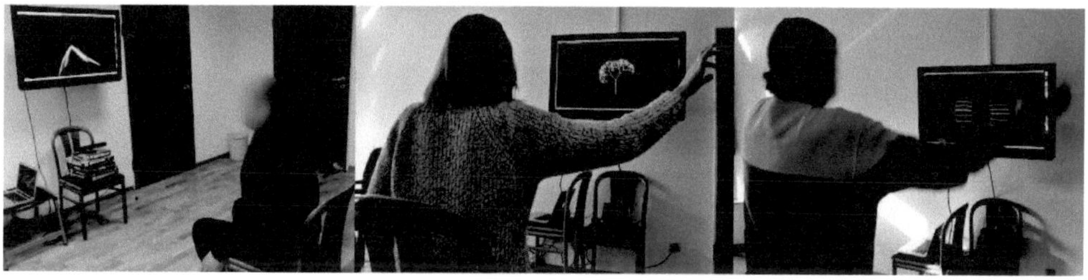

Abbildung 2: Eindrücke aus der Experimentalgruppen-Intervention mit dem AVUS Therapiesystem (Aufnahmen des Autors)

	Experimentalgruppe					**Kontrollgruppe**	
Instrument	**SC**	**RI**	**RE**	**HG**	**NE**	**KE**	**WE**
Alter/Geschl.	51/w	72/m	50/m	75/m	68/m	55/m	85/m
Betr. Seite/onset	L/6Mo	R/3Mo	L/1Mo	R/3Mo	L/1Mo	R/7Mo	L/1Mo
FMT-OE	*max: 66*						
pre	13	10	15	49	29	42	17
Verbesserung	5(38%)	1(10%)	3(20%)	2(4%)	4(13%)	6(14%)	4(23%)
FAS	*max: 10,0*						
post	8,1	1,0	9,5	7,6	7,4	8,3	6,3
IPQ	*max: 6,0*						
Präsenz (Mittel)	5,5	0,6	5,5	4,5	1,6		
Interviews	*AVUS Argumente gesamt: 141*						
AVUS Argu.	38	13	25	41	24		
pos/neg/neutral	12/1/25	1/4/8	14/0/11	22/0/19	4/3/17		
Bevorzugte Vis	WF	WF/GT	WF/GT	GT	WF		

Tabelle 1: Quantitative Ergebnisse der Pilotstudie

Die Tabelle 1 gibt einen Überblick über die erhobenen Daten und demographische Informationen der verbliebenen sieben Teilnehmer. Die Altersspanne der Patienten war breit (50-85 Jahre) und nur ein Patient war weiblich. Die Seite der Hemiparese war ausgeglichen und der Zeitpunkt des Schlaganfalls lag zum Studienzeitpunkt zwischen einem und sieben Monaten zurück.

Vor Studienbeginn unterschieden sich die Patienten in der motorischen Funktion deutlich (10-49 im FMT-OE). Alle Patienten verbesserten ihre Funktion moderat (+1 bis +6), wobei die relativen Veränderungen sich deutlich unterschieden (+4% bis +38%). Die Patienten in der KG verbesserten sich tendenziell mehr als die Patienten der EG, wobei die höchste relative Verbesserung jedoch von einer Patientin der EG erzielt wurde.

Die Selbsteinschätzung der Funktionsverbesserung wurde durch eine metrische Messung der Markierung auf der Analogskala ermittelt, deren Länge 10cm betrug. Die meisten Einschätzungen erfolgten deutlich positiv (>6,3) mit Ausnahme der eines Patienten aus der EG (1,0).

Die Ergebnisse der Präsenzfragebögen werden durch die Mittelwerte der fünf Messungen je Patient der EG angezeigt. Drei Patienten erlebten im Mittel ein starkes Präsenzgefühls (>4,5) und zwei Patienten erlebten ein schwaches Präsenzgefühls (<1,6).

Die im Rahmen der Interviews von den Patienten gelieferten Argumente wurden bei der qualitativen Auswertung von zwei Personen unabhängig voneinander kategorisiert und ausgezählt. Die Tabelle 1 zeigt die Anzahl der Argumente, welche das AVUS Therapiesystem betrafen (insgesamt 141 Argumente), sowie deren Aufschlüsselung nach eindeutig enthaltenen Konnotationen. Neben der überwiegenden Nennung nicht oder unklar konnotierter Argumente (insgesamt 80) fällt der hohe Anteil an positiv konnotierten Argumenten auf (53). Lediglich ein Patient äußerte sich überwiegend neutral oder negativ, während solche Argumente ansonsten selten vorkamen (8).

6 Diskussion

Eine statistische Auswertung der vorliegenden Daten war aufgrund der geringen Teilnehmerzahl an der Pilotstudie nicht möglich. Das Ziel war jedoch die erstmalige Untersuchung der AVUS in einem klinischen Kontext und das Sammeln von Informationen als Grundlage für weitere Untersuchungen. Es können einige Tendenzen erkannt werden.

Die motorischen Verbesserungen der Patienten in der EG und der KG fielen vergleichbar aus, so dass negative Effekte der AVUS unwahrscheinlich sind. Solche konnten bei der Studiendurchführung auch nicht erkannt werden. Über die zusätzliche körperliche Betätigung hinaus konnte ein Trainingseffekt der AVUS aber noch nicht festgestellt werden.

Die visuelle Gestaltung und die musikalische Komponente der AVUS hoben alle Patienten als motivierend und stimmig hervor. Die Interaktion mit der abstrakten Umgebung wurde in den Interviews als wohltuend und animierend bezeichnet. Einige Patienten berichteten, dass sie durch die Therapie mehr Aktivität bei anderen Trainingssitzungen und im Alltag zeigten. Bzgl. der bevorzugten Visualisierungsform ist eine Tendenz hin zu den weniger abstrakten

Varianten der WF und der GT zu erkennen. Dies deutet auf das Bedürfnis hin, in den Visualisierungen noch entfernt anthropomorphe Züge erkennen zu können.

Auffällig ist der enge Zusammenhang zwischen dem erlebten Präsenzgefühl und der subjektiven Bewertung der Therapie mit der FAS und in den Interviews. Patienten die ein starkes Präsenzempfinden hatten, bewerteten die Intervention positiver, als solche mit einem geringen Präsenzempfinden. Diese Ergebnisse spiegeln auch das beobachtete Verhalten und die Motivation bei der Durchführung der Übungen wider. Offenbar konnten sich einige Patienten besonders gut in die abstrakten Visualisierungen hineinversetzen und bewerteten die Therapie dann besser.

Darüber hinaus wiesen Aussagen auf die Effektivität der visuellen Illusion im Spiegeltherapiemodus hin. Mehrere Patienten berichteten von einem positiven Gefühl der Bewegungsfreiheit beim Wechsel vom veritablen in den Spiegeltherapiemodus. Der Patient RE hatte zudem Erfahrungen mit der herkömmlichen Therapieform. Er bezeichnete die Interaktion mit der AVUS als kognitiv einfacher gegenüber der Beobachtung von Bewegung in einem Spiegel und ihm fiel die Konzentration dabei leichter.

Der Patient NE, dessen Präsenzergebnis niedrig war, deutete an, dass eine bessere technische Ausrüstung zu einer stärkeren Immersion in die virtuelle Umgebung führen könnte und seine Beurteilung der Therapie sich dadurch verbessern würde. Im Rahmen der Studie mussten die Ausgabegeräte aufgrund klinischer Rahmenbedingungen einfach gehalten werden (siehe Abbildung 2). Offenbar können jedoch bspw. eine raumgreifende Projektion und die Verwendung von Raumklangsystemen die Konzentration auf die AVUS verbessern.

Anhand dieser Ergebnisse kann angenommen werden, dass die Therapieform nicht für alle Patienten gleichermaßen geeignet ist, dass aber diejenigen, die sich darauf einlassen können, sowohl motorisch als auch persönlich von der Interaktion mit der AVUS profitieren. Insbesondere die von den Patienten geäußerten, positiven Auswirkungen auf die Motivation und die Animation zu Bewegungen im Alltag sind für die Rehabilitation nach einem Schlaganfall vor dem Hintergrund eines häufig verringerten Selbstbewusstseins der Patienten besonders hervorzuheben. Für eindeutige Aussagen bzgl. der therapeutischen Wirksamkeit der AVUS sind allerdings umfangreichere klinische Studien erforderlich.

7 Fazit

In diesem Artikel wurde das Potential abstrakter virtueller Umgebungen für die neurologische Therapie mit visuellen Illusionen erörtert und es wurde ein Therapiesystem vorgestellt, welches auf diesen theoretischen Überlegungen aufbaut. Im Rahmen einer Pilotstudie wurde das entwickelte System in der klinischen Anwendung überprüft. Die Ergebnisse der Studie können lediglich tendenzielle Informationen liefern, sie unterstützen jedoch die Plausibilität des therapeutischen Ansatzes, demonstrieren die klinische Anwendbarkeit des Systems und weisen auf positive Effekte des Trainings bzgl. der Motivation der Patienten sowie der subjektiven Einschätzung des Therapieerfolgs hin. Zudem zeigte sich, dass Patienten auch in abstrakten virtuellen Umgebungen ein starkes Präsenzgefühl entwickeln können. Hierdurch wird die Konzentration auf die Bewegungsillusionen erleichtert, was für das motorische Lernen von hoher Bedeutung ist.

Zukünftige Entwicklungen werden das Therapiesystem erweitern. Besonders die musikalische Komponente soll umfassender integriert werden. Ausgehend von den Ergebnissen der Pilotstudie soll außerdem eine größere klinische Evaluation durchgeführt werden, um die therapeutische Wirkung abstrakter Bewegungsillusionen zu klären. Zudem wird die Bedeutung des Präsenzgefühls für die VR Rehabilitation weiter untersucht.

Literaturverzeichnis

Burdea, G.C., 2003. Virtual rehabilitation-benefits and challenges. *Methods of information in medicine*, 42(5), 519–523.

Dohle, C. et al., 2011. Representation of virtual arm movements in precuneus. *Experimental brain research*, 208(4), 543–555.

Duncan, P.W., Propst, M. & Nelson, S.G., 1983. Reliability of the Fugl-Meyer assessment of sensorimotor recovery following cerebrovascular accident. *Physical Therapy*, 63(10).

Eng, K. et al., 2007. Interactive visuo-motor therapy system for stroke rehabilitation. *Medical and biological engineering and computing*, 45(9), 901–907.

Heuschmann, P. et al., 2010. Schlaganfallhäufigkeit und Versorgung von Schlaganfallpatienten in Deutschland. *Aktuelle Neurologie*, 37(07), 333–340.

Kosslyn, S.M., Ganis, G. & Thompson, W.L., 2001. Neural foundations of imagery. *Nature Reviews Neuroscience*, 2(9), 635–642.

Lange, B., Flynn, S. & Rizzo, A., 2009. Game-based telerehabilitation. *European journal of physical and rehabilitation medicine*, 45(1), 143–151.

Langhorne, P., Bernhardt, J. & Kwakkel, G., 2011. Stroke rehabilitation. *Lancet*, 377(9778).

Laver, K. et al., 2012. Cochrane review: virtual reality for stroke rehabilitation. *European journal of physical and rehabilitation medicine*, 48(3), 523–530.

Lenggenhager, B. et al., 2007. Video ergo sum: manipulating bodily self-consciousness. *Science*, 317 (1096).

Lombard, M. et al., 1997. At the heart of it all: The concept of presence. *Journal of computer-mediated communication*, 3(2).

Ramachandran, V.S. & Altschuler, E.L., 2009. The use of visual feedback, in particular mirror visual feedback, in restoring brain function. *Brain*, 132(Pt 7), 1693–1710.

Riva, G. et al., 2010. From intention to action: The role of presence. *New Ideas in Psychology*, 29(1), 24–37.

Saleh, S., Adamovich, S.V. & Tunik, E., 2013. Mirrored Feedback in Chronic Stroke. *Neurorehabilitation and Neural Repair*. Published online first.

Schubert, T., Friedmann, F. & Regenbrecht, H., 2001. The experience of presence: Factor analytic insights. *Presence: Teleoperators and Virtual Environments*, 10(3).

Small, S.L., Buccino, G. & Solodkin, A., 2010. The mirror neuron system and treatment of stroke. *Developmental Psychobiology*, 54(3), 293–310.

Thieme, H. et al., 2012. Mirror therapy for improving motor function after stroke. *The Cochrane Library*, (3).

Wulf, G., Lewthwaite, R. & Winstein, C., 2011. Motorisches Lernen und grundlegende psychologische Bedürfnisse. *Neuroreha nach Schlaganfall*. Stuttgart: Thieme.

M. Koch, A. Butz & J. Schlichter (Hrsg.): Mensch und Computer 2014 Tagungsband,
München: Oldenbourg Wissenschaftsverlag, 2014, S. 165-174.

Evaluation der Interaktion mit einer AR-basierten Smartphone-App

Michael Domhardt, Radomir Dinic, Thomas Stütz, Simon Ginzinger

Studiengang MultiMediaTechnology, Fachhochschule Salzburg

Zusammenfassung

Menschen wie Diabetiker oder Herzpatienten mit verordneter Ernährungstherapie sind auf die exakte Portionsgrößenbestimmung ihrer Mahlzeiten angewiesen. Bisherige Ansätze, dies mittels digitaler Bildverarbeitung zu vereinfachen, erwiesen sich als wenig benutzbar. In diesem Beitrag wird die Interaktion mit einer AR-basierten Smartphone-App untersucht. Dazu wurden zwei touchbasierte AR-Interaktionskonzepte (3-Punkt und Mesh) implementiert und im Rahmen eines Nutzertests (n = 28) verglichen. Interaktionsprobleme verhinderten in 3 % der AR-Messungen ein Ergebnis. Eine Analyse dieser Probleme ermöglichte das Ableiten von Verbesserungsvorschlägen für die Benutzungsschnittstelle der Smartphone-App.

1 Einleitung

Mobile Anwendungen können zu einem gesunden Lebensstil der Nutzer beitragen. Eine Vielzahl an Fitness- und Gesundheitsanwendungen ist in den App-Stores von Apple[1], Google[2] und Microsoft[3] erhältlich. Eine Herausforderung bei der Entwicklung dieser Anwendungen war bisher die Erfassung und Analyse des Ernährungsverhaltens sowie die Bestimmung konkreter Nährwerte, wie sie von Diabetikern oder anderen Patienten mit ärztlich verordneter Ernährungstherapie benötigt werden. Etablierte Anwendungen setzen dabei oft auf die manuelle Abschätzung des Volumens der einzelnen Bestandteile einer Mahlzeit und die aufwändige Suche nach dem entsprechenden Lebensmittel in langen Tabellen durch den Nutzer. Die meisten Menschen haben allerdings Probleme beim manuellen Schätzen der Portionsgröße einer Mahlzeit (Schap et al. 2011). Durch Nutzung des Smartphones als technisches Hilfsmittel bei der Portionsgrößenbestimmung lässt sich dieses Problem umgehen (Six et al. 2010).

---

[1] https://itunes.apple.com/us/genre/ios-health-fitness/id6013

[2] https://play.google.com/store/apps/category/HEALTH_AND_FITNESS

[3] http://www.windowsphone.com/en-us/store/top-rated-apps/health-fitness/healthandfitness

Aktuelle Ansätze nutzen die Kamera des Smartphones, um das Essen zu fotografieren (z. B. Daugherty et al. 2012, Kitamura et al. 2010). Einige Anwendungen versuchen zudem einzelne Schritte des Prozesses der Nährwertermittlung zu automatisieren. So erleichtert das System „FoodLog[4]" von Kitamura et al. (2010) und Aizawa et al. (2013) die Auswahl des korrekten Lebensmittels, indem es basierend auf einem aufgenommenen Foto optisch ähnliche Lebensmittel vorschlägt. Die Abschätzung des Volumens bleibt bei FoodLog Aufgabe des Nutzers. Die Identifikation des Lebensmittels auf Basis digitaler Bildverarbeitung ist auch Bestandteil der Arbeiten von Joutou und Yanai (2009) sowie Matsuda und Yanai (2012). Das im Rahmen des TADA-Projekts[5] (technology assisted dietary assessment) entwickelte System benötigt ein einzelnes Foto der Mahlzeit und einen Referenzmarker als Größenreferenz, um die Nährwertangaben zu ermitteln (Chae et al. 2011, Woo et al. 2010, Zhu et al. 2010). Der Ansatz von Daugherty et al. (2012), Chen et al. (2012) und Jia et al. (2012) basiert ebenfalls auf einem einzelnen Foto und nutzt den Teller als Referenzmarker sowie ein vordefiniertes 3D-Modell der Lebensmittel zur Volumenbestimmung. Dieses System setzt einen Teller mit bekannten Abmessungen voraus und ist dadurch in seiner Benutzbarkeit beschränkt. Das Projekt „GoCarb" adressiert die Bedürfnisse von Diabetikern (Anthimopoulos et al. 2013, Dehais et al. 2013) und verwendet zwei Bilder und einen Referenzmarker für eine größenkorrekte 3D-Rekonstruktion des Volumens der Mahlzeit. Der Ansatz nutzt ausschließlich Methoden der digitalen Bildverarbeitung zur Aufteilung einer Mahlzeit in einzelne Lebensmittel, zur Erkennung der Lebensmittel (Anthimopoulos et al. 2013) und zur 3D-Rekonstruktion des Volumens (Dehais et al. 2013). Der Ansatz von Kong und Tan (2012) benötigt drei Fotos vom Lebensmittel, die aus verschiedenen Winkeln aufgenommen wurden, um mittels digitaler Bildverarbeitung das Volumen zu bestimmen. Zur Verringerung der Fehlerrate wurden von Xu et al. (2013) zusätzliche Kontextinformationen verwendet, wie z. B. Daten aus einer vorangestellten Aufteilung und Klassifikation der Lebensmittel einer Mahlzeit.

Die meisten vorgestellten Ansätze zur Volumenabschätzung von Lebensmitteln nutzen anspruchsvolle Bildverarbeitungsverfahren. Während in einigen Studien vielversprechende Teilergebnisse bei der digitalen Bildverarbeitung erzielt wurden (Dehais et al. 2013, Xu et al. 2013), verhindern mehrere Probleme den erfolgreichen Einsatz in alltäglichen Anwendungsfällen. Ein Problem sind die benötigten Zeiten für die digitale Bildverarbeitung. Dehais et al. (2013) berichten von einer Verarbeitungsdauer von 15 Sekunden auf einem Desktop-Computer. Zur automatisierten Verarbeitung der aufgenommenen Bilder müssen neben einem Marker als Größenreferenz zusätzlich oft Umgebungsbedingungen wie Beleuchtung oder Kontrast berücksichtigt werden, was sich im Alltag als sehr schwierig erweisen dürfte.

Zur Lösung der Schwierigkeiten der bisherigen Studien wurde eine Smartphone-App zur Unterstützung von Patienten entwickelt, welche den Ansatz der erweiterten Realität (AR, Augmented Reality) zur Bestimmung des Volumens von Lebensmitteln nutzt. Die hier vorgestellte Studie umfasst die Untersuchung der Interaktion mit dieser AR-basierten Smartphone-App bei der Volumenbestimmung von Lebensmitteln.

---

[4] https://play.google.com/store/apps/details?id=jp.co.foolog.cal

[5] http://www.tadaproject.com

2 Die mobile AR-App zur Volumenbestimmung

Die eingesetzte Smartphone-App wurde mit dem Unity-Framework[6] (Interface inkl. 3D-Objekte und Interaktionskonzept) und der Vuforia-Plattform von Qualcomm[7] (digitale Bildverarbeitung) entwickelt. Zur Durchführung der Studie wurde eine angepasste Version der App erstellt, die zwei unterschiedliche AR-Verfahren enthält, mit deren Hilfe die dreidimensionale Form des Lebensmittels auf dem Teller und damit auch das Volumen bestimmt wird. Dazu positioniert der Nutzer bei beiden AR-Verfahren das Smartphone so, dass der Teller mit dem Lebensmittel von der Kamera erfasst wird. Ein im Kamerabild befindlicher Marker ermöglicht eine automatische Kalibrierung des Bildes, so dass unabhängig von den Kameraeigenschaften des verwendeten Mobiltelefons die Maßstabstreue gewährleistet ist. Das Kamerabild wird in Echtzeit dargestellt und fungiert als grafische Benutzungsschnittstelle. Mittels Toucheingaben kann der Benutzer das entsprechende Lebensmittel auswählen und am Livebild dessen Form nachbilden.

Zum Erstellen der dreidimensionalen Form stehen den beiden implementierten AR-Verfahren entsprechend zwei unterschiedliche Interaktionsmöglichkeiten zur Verfügung: das Erstellen einer Kuppel mittels 3-Punkt-Eingabe (3-Punkt, Abbildung 1 links) und das Erzeugen eines beliebigen Volumens mittels Nachbildens (Mesh, Abbildung 1 rechts).

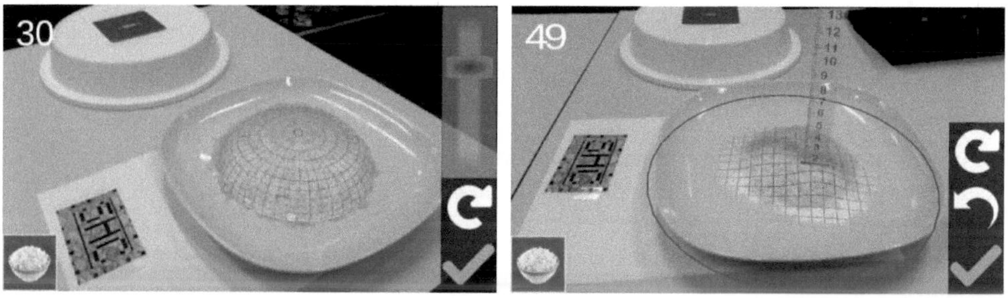

Abbildung 1: Screenshot der AR-Anwendung mit 3-Punkt-Eingabe (links) und Mesh-Eingabe (rechts)

Bei der 3-Punkt-Eingabe wird das Volumen durch das Festlegen von drei Punkten einer Kuppel bestimmt. Der Nutzer tippt im Kamerabild auf die Außenränder der Portion, um den Durchmesser und die Höhe der Kuppel festzulegen (grüne Kreise in Abbildung 1 links). Auch nach dem Festlegen der Punkte ist die Form über die grünen Buttons veränderbar. Die Konvexität der Kuppel wird über den grünen Schieberegler am rechten Rand eingestellt. Das auf diese Weise erstelle Volumenobjekt lässt sich per Drag-and-drop verschieben. In der unteren rechten Ecke der grafischen Benutzungsschnittstelle befinden sich zwei Schaltflächen zum vollständigen Zurücksetzen und zum Bestätigen einer Messung.

---

[6] http://unity3D.com

[7] http://www.qualcomm.com/solutions/augmented-reality

Das zweite AR-Interaktionskonzept besteht im Nachbilden des Essens mit dem Finger. Dabei hebt sich ein Gitter (Mesh) aus der Tellerfläche und grenzt mit dieser ein Volumen ab. Je länger der Finger auf dem Display bleibt, desto höher hebt sich das Mesh über den Teller. Das Lineal markiert maßstabsgetreu den höchsten Punkt des gezeichneten Volumens (blaue Skala in Abbildung 1 rechts). Die untere rechte Ecke des Interfaces enthält Schaltflächen für das komplette und schrittweise Zurücksetzen sowie zum Bestätigen der Eingabe.

Bei beiden Interaktionsmöglichkeiten war zu Evaluationszwecken ein Countdown in der linken oberen Ecke vorhanden, der die restliche Zeit für die Interaktion in Sekunden anzeigte. Die zulässige maximale Interaktionsdauer wurde für die Evaluation auf eine Minute festgelegt. Nach Ablauf dieser Zeit oder bei Bestätigung einer Messung durch den Nutzer wurde automatisch ein Screenshot erzeugt und ein Eintrag im Logfile angelegt. Eine auffällige visuelle Rückmeldung wurde automatisch aktiviert, sobald der Referenzmarker durch Bewegungen des Smartphones aus dem Kamerabild verschwand. In der linken unteren Ecke wurde das entsprechende Lebensmittel angezeigt. Die Lebensmittelauswahl wurde für die Studie auf Reis beschränkt.

3 Methodisches Vorgehen

Um die Interaktion mit den verschiedenen AR-Verfahren zu untersuchen, wurde eine empirische Laborstudie geplant und durchgeführt. Der Begriff der Benutzbarkeit wurde durch quantitative Maße zur Effektivität und Effizienz sowie eine qualitative Einschätzung zur Nutzerinteraktion operationalisiert. Anhand der Effektivität wurden die beiden AR-Verfahren mit zwei etablierten Methoden zur Volumenbestimmung verglichen.

Der Versuch wurde als Within-Subject-Design konzipiert (Coolican 2009), wobei jeder Versuchsteilnehmer das Volumen von drei unterschiedlichen Portionen Reis mit den beiden AR- und zwei Referenzverfahren bestimmen musste. Die drei Portionen wurden anstatt mit Zahlen farblich markiert (rot, grün, blau), um das Implizieren einer Reihenfolge zu vermeiden und dennoch eine Unterscheidbarkeit zu ermöglichen. Eine zusätzliche vierte Portion (grau markiert) wurde für Trainingszwecke mit der AR-Anwendung vorbereitet. Die Portionen wurden bei jeder Schätzung abgedeckt, so dass jeweils nur eine einzelne Portion sichtbar war. Auf diese Weise wurde ein direkter Vergleich der Portionen verhindert.

In einer Vorstudie wurde mit identischer Softwareumgebung (Unity-Framework und Vuforia-Plattform, vgl. Abschnitt 2) die Genauigkeit einer AR-basierten Längenmessung untersucht (Stütz et al. 2014b). Den beiden AR-Verfahren wurde die freie Schätzung des Volumens und die Schätzung mit Hilfe eines Referenzobjektes (eigene Faust) als etablierte Verfahren zur Volumenbestimmung gegenübergestellt, denn Byrd-Bredbenner und Schwartz (2004) hatten gezeigt, dass sich die Genauigkeit beim Abschätzen von Portionsgrößen verbessert, wenn die Portion mental mit Objekten bekannter Größe verglichen wird. Die Genauigkeit der AR-Verfahren wurde in Stütz et al. (2014a) untersucht. Dabei wurde eine signifikant bessere Genauigkeit der 3-Punkt-Messung als bestes AR-Verfahren gegenüber dem freien Schätzen als bestes manuelles Verfahren nachgewiesen.

Die Versuchsteilnehmer wurden unter den Studierenden der Institution angeworben. Die Teilnahme erfolgte auf freiwilliger Basis ohne Versuchspersonenvergütung.

Ein Versuchsdurchgang mit einem Probanden war in zwei Schritte unterteilt, in denen ein Smartphone[8] mit der in Abschnitt 2 beschriebenen App zur Volumenbestimmung zum Einsatz kam. Der Proband durfte mit jedem der beiden implementierten AR-Verfahren eine Übungsmessung der grau markierten Portion vornehmen, um sich mit dem jeweiligen Interaktionskonzept vertraut zu machen. Anschließend war mit Hilfe des Smartphones das Volumen der einzelnen Portion zu bestimmen. Die Abfolge der Portionen und der AR-Verfahren entsprach einem ausgeglichenen Versuchsplan, wodurch der Einfluss von Reihenfolgeeffekten minimiert wurde (Sauro und Lewis 2012). Das Volumen der Faust des Probanden wurde am Ende des Versuchs über die Verdrängung von Wasser in einem Messbecher ermittelt.

Die Versuchsergebnisse umfassten den Grad der Aufgabenerfüllung zur Operationalisierung der Effektivität. Die Effizienz wurde anhand der Interaktionsdauer bestimmt. Die qualitativen Daten zur Benutzbarkeit beinhalteten neben der Auswertung der Screenshots Antworten auf zwei Fragen zur Interaktion mit der Anwendung. Eine offene Frage umfasste hierbei das Verbesserungspotenzial der App; eine geschlossene Frage beschäftigte sich mit dem Störpotenzial des notwendigen Referenzmarkers.

Die Antworten auf diese Fragen wurden vom Versuchsleiter protokolliert. Die Protokollierung der Messungen mit der AR-Anwendung erfolgte automatisch. Bei der Bestätigung jeder AR-Messung wurde automatisch ein Screenshots gespeichert.

Als Versuchsumgebung (Abbildung 2) diente ein automatisch temperierter Raum mit geschlossenen Jalousien sowie künstliche Beleuchtung, um konstante Versuchsbedingungen zu garantieren. Die Portionen wurden auf einem langen Tisch in einer Reihe aufgebaut. Um zwischen den Portionen zu wechseln, saßen Proband und Versuchsleiter jeweils auf einem Bürostuhl mit Rollen. Auf diese Weise mussten die Portionen nicht bewegt werden, wodurch die Form des Volumens unverändert blieb.

Abbildung 2: Versuchsaufbau mit farblich markierten Portionen und Bürostühlen für den Probanden (schwarz) und den Versuchsleiter (grau)

Die Studie wurde innerhalb eines Tages durchgeführt. Im Rahmen der Analyse der qualitativen Daten nach Mayring (2010) wurden die Antworten der Probanden inhaltlich kategorisiert

[8] Samsung Galaxy S III mit Android 4.3

und gezählt. Die Screenshots der AR-Messungen wurden auf Interaktionsprobleme analysiert. Dazu zählt zum Beispiel, ob überhaupt ein Volumen per Touchinteraktion erzeugt wurde oder ob der Marker nicht erfasst wurde. Auf Basis dieser Analyse wurden Vorschläge zur Verbesserung der App abgeleitet.

4 Ergebnisse

Vier Frauen und 24 Männer im Durchschnittsalter von 24,6 ± 2,9 Jahren nahmen an der Studie teil (s. Abbildung 3 links). Durch die Volumenermittlung von 28 Probanden bei drei verschiedenen Portionen waren maximal 84 Messungen je Verfahren möglich. Durch Fehleingaben von fünf Probanden wurden beim Einsatz der AR-Anwendung keine Volumen ermittelt. Die verbliebenen Messungen der betroffenen Probanden wurden daraufhin ebenfalls aus dem Datensatz entfernt ($n_{frei} = 84$, $n_{Faust} = 84$, $n_{3\text{-}Punkt} = 69$, $n_{Mesh} = 69$). Der höheren Genauigkeit der beiden AR-Verfahren (vgl. Abschnitt 2) steht ein Datenausfall von 3,0 % gegenüber (5 von 168 Messungen). Der Vergleich der Interaktionsdauer der beiden AR-Verfahren (s. Abbildung 3 rechts) ergab keinen signifikanten Unterschied (Wilcoxon-Vorzeichen-Rangsummentest: $p = 0.28$, $Z = -1.09$).

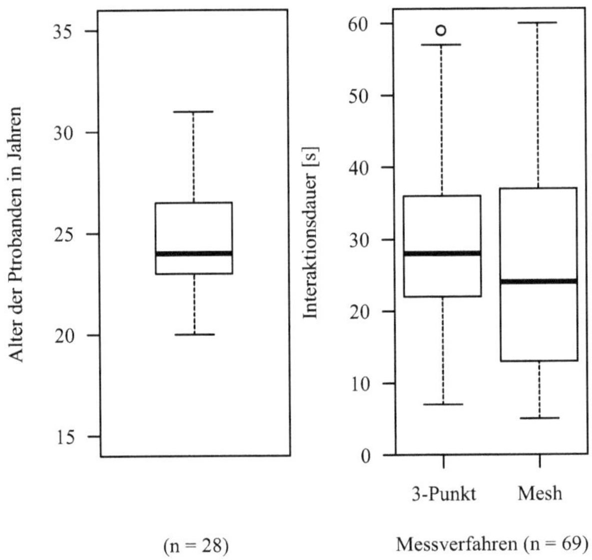

Abbildung 3: Altersverteilung der Stichprobe und Interaktionsdauer

Die Analyse der qualitativen Daten resultierte in 56 Einzelnennungen zur AR-Benutzungsschnittstelle, welche anhand der Inhaltsanalyse 13 Kategorien zugeordnet werden konnten. Davon betrafen drei Kategorien allgemeine Probleme beider AR-Verfahren. Es wurde angemerkt, dass der interagierende Finger das Display verdeckte und die Buttons nicht intuitiv verständlich waren. Zudem fehlten den Probanden auditive Rückmeldungen für kritische Systemzustände (z. B. nicht erfasster Referenzmarker).

Das 3-Punkt-Verfahren wurde in zehn von elf Nennungen vor dem Mesh-Verfahren bevorzugt. Kritik gab es zur Beschränkung auf Lebensmittel, die sich kuppelförmig portionieren lassen. Der Button zum Verschieben der Kuppel wurde als zu klein kritisiert.

Das Mesh-Verfahren stuften 16 Probanden als zu empfindlich ein. Eine kurze Berührung führte zu einer großen Volumenzunahme, wodurch kleine Portionen schwer zu messen waren. Ebenso wurde das schrittweise Zurücksetzen der Eingaben per Schaltfläche als ungenügend beurteilt.

Anhand der Screenshots konnten Interaktionsprobleme identifiziert werden. Beim Versuch einen Button zu betätigen, wurde bei 23 von 84 Messungen mit dem Mesh-Verfahren das Volumen versehentlich vergrößert (Abbildung 4 A). Bei 5 von insgesamt 168 AR-Messungen kam es zur versehentlichen Bestätigung der Messung, ohne ein Volumen zu erstellen (Abbildung 4 B). In zwei Fällen wurde nach Ablauf der vorgegebenen Interaktionszeit kein Volumen verzeichnet (Abbildung 4 C). In sieben Fällen wurde die Messung ohne erfassten Marker bestätigt, obwohl ein Volumen erstellt wurde (Abbildung 4 D).

Abbildung 4: Interaktionsprobleme mit den unterschiedlichen Interaktionskonzepten der beiden AR-Verfahren

Die aus der Analyse resultierenden Verbesserungsvorschläge umfassen die Überarbeitung der Buttons und die Implementierung multimodaler Rückmeldungen. In leisen Umgebungen ist z. B. die Nutzung des Vibrationsalarms des Smartphones zur Signalisierung kritischer Systemzustände denkbar. Anstelle des dargestellten Countdowns wird in der finalen Version das ermittelte Volumen bzw. der errechnete Nährwert der Portion dargestellt. Das Verschieben der Kuppel wird beim 3-Punkt-Verfahren so realisiert, dass die gesamte Kuppel als Schaltfläche fungiert. Das Mesh-Verfahren lässt sich durch eine Softwareanpassung unempfindlicher gestalten. Durch ein konsistentes Interaktionskonzept zur Vergrößerung und Verkleinerung des Volumens kann beim Mesh-Verfahren auf beide Buttons zum Zurücksetzen verzichtet werden. Im Umfeld des Buttons zum Bestätigen einer Messung ist ein nicht interaktiver Bereich vorzusehen.

5 Fazit und Ausblick

Anhand der durchgeführten Studie konnte gezeigt werden, dass die AR-basierte Smartphone-App zur Volumenbestimmung von Reis verwendbar ist. Lediglich drei Prozent der Messungen haben nicht funktioniert. Dies war auf Interaktionsprobleme mit der Benutzungsschnittstelle zurückzuführen, deren Ursachen anhand einer Analyse identifiziert werden konnten.

Die Implementierung der AR-Verfahren erwies sich im Gegensatz zu vielen der vorgestellten Ansätze als benutzbar. Ein herkömmliches Android-Smartphone reicht aus, um direkt nach der Bestätigung der Eingabe das Ergebnis zu erhalten. Die Interaktion war bei 75 % der Probanden in weniger als 40 Sekunden erfolgreich abgeschlossen. Der notwendige Marker zur Größenreferenz kann in Zukunft durch einen Alltagsgegenstand (z. B. eine Kreditkarte oder Geldschein) ersetzt werden. Besondere Anforderungen an die Umgebungsbedingungen (z. B. Farbe des Lebensmittels oder des Tisches) werden nicht gestellt. Die beobachtete Ausfallrate sollte sich durch eine überarbeitete Benutzungsschnittstelle reduzieren lassen, da konkrete Hinweise für die Verbesserung bereits ermittelt werden konnten.

Die Ergebnisse zeigen, dass die Interaktionskonzepte einer AR-basierten Smartphone-App einen hohen Einfluss auf die Benutzbarkeit haben. Technische Leistungsparameter wie Genauigkeit und Rechenzeit der digitalen Bildverarbeitung sind lediglich grundlegende Funktionsvoraussetzungen, die sich mit dem heutigen Stand der Technik auf herkömmlichen Smartphones realisieren lassen. Diese Technologie hat ein großes Potenzial, durch die teilautomatisierte Erfassung und Analyse der Nährwerte von Lebensmitteln ein gesundes und bewusstes Ernährungsverhalten des Nutzes zu fördern.

Nachdem die technische Realisierung von AR-basierten Smartphone-Apps keine Hürde mehr darstellt, sollten sich zukünftige Studien stärker auf den Alltagseinsatz dieser Technologie konzentrieren. Eine entsprechend konzipierte Folgestudie ermöglicht den Vergleich der Gebrauchstauglichkeit zwischen den vorgestellten AR-Verfahren und den in der Einleitung beschriebenen Ansätzen. Mit einer repräsentativen Stichprobe können dabei neben der zielgruppenspezifischen Anpassung des Interaktionskonzeptes auch Fragen zum Einfluss der Technikaffinität auf die Gebrauchstauglichkeit und Akzeptanz beantwortet werden.

Literatur

Aizawa, K., Maruyama, Y., Li, H., Morikawa, C. (2013). Food Balance Estimation by Using Personal Dietary Tendencies in a Multimedia Food Log. Transactions on Multimedia, 15(8), 2176-2185.

Anthimopoulos, M., Dehais, J., Diem, P., Mougiakakou, S. (2013). Segmentation and recognition of multi-food meal images for carbohydrate counting. In: Nikita, K.S. und Fotiadis, D.I. (Hrsg.). 13th International Conference on Bioinformatics and Bioengineering. Piscataway: IEEE, S. 1-4.

Byrd-Bredbenner, C., Schwartz, J. (2004). The effect of practical portion size measurement aids on the accuracy of portion size estimates made by young adults. Journal of human nutrition and dietetics, 17(4), 351-357.

Chae, J., Woo, I., Kim, S., Maciejewski, R., Zhu, F., Delp, E.J., Boushey, C.J., Ebert, D.S. (2011). Volume Estimation Using Food Specific Shape Templates in Mobile Image-Based Dietary Assessment. Proceedings of SPIE, (7873).

Chen, H.-C., Jia, W., Li, Z., Sun, Y.-N., Sun, M. (2012). 3D/2D model-to-image registration for quantitative dietary assessment. In: Obeid, I. und Silage, D. (Hrsg.). 38th Annual Northeast Bioengineering Conference, S. 95-96.

Coolican, H. (2009). Research Methods and Statistics in Psychology. 5. Auflage. London: Hodder Education.

Daugherty, L.B., Schap, E.T., Ettienne-Gittens, R., Zhu, M.F., Bosch, M., Delp, J.E., Ebert, S.D., Kerr, A.D., Boushey, J.C. (2012). Novel Technologies for Assessing Dietary Intake: Evaluating the Usability of a Mobile Telephone Food Record Among Adults and Adolescents. Journal of Medical Internet Research, 14(2), e58.

Dehais, J., Shevchik, S., Diem, P., Mougiakakou, S.G. (2013). Food volume computation for self dietary assessment applications. In: Nikita, K.S. und Fotiadis, D.I. (Hrsg.). 13th International Conference on Bioinformatics and Bioengineering. Piscataway: IEEE, S. 1-4.

Jia, W., Yue, Y., Fernstrom, J.D., Zhang, Z., Yang, Y., Sun, M. (2012). 3D localization of circular feature in 2D image and application to food volume estimation. In: Khoo, M.C.K., Cauwenberghs, G., Weiland, J.D. und Chien, S. (Hrsg.). Annual International Conference of Engineering in Medicine and Biology Society. Piscataway: IEEE, S. 4545-4548.

Joutou, T., Yanai, K. (2009). A food image recognition system with Multiple Kernel Learning. In: Bayoumi, M., Farag, A. und Eldesouki, A. (Hrsg.). 16th International Conference on Image Processing. Piscataway: IEEE, S. 285-288.

Kitamura, K., Silva, C. de, Yamasaki, T., Aizawa, K. (2010). Image processing based approach to food balance analysis for personal food logging. In: International Conference on Multimedia and Expo. Piscataway: IEEE, S. 625-630.

Kong, F., Tan, J. (2012). DietCam: Automatic dietary assessment with mobile camera phones. Pervasive and Mobile Computing, 8(1), 147-163.

Matsuda, Y., Yanai, K. (2012). Multiple-food recognition considering co-occurrence employing manifold ranking. In: Eklundh, J.-O., Ohta, Y. und Tanimoto, S. (Hrsg.). 21st International Conference on Pattern Recognition. Piscataway: IEEE, S. 2017-2020.

Mayring, P. (2010). Qualitative Inhaltsanalyse – Grundlagen und Techniken. 11. Auflage. Weinheim: Beltz.

Sauro, J., Lewis, J.R. (2012). Quantifying the User Experience: Practical Statistics for User Research. Amsterdam: Morgan Kaufmann.

Schap, T.E., Six, B.L., Delp, E.J., Ebert, D.S., Kerr, D.A., Boushey, C.J. (2011). Adolescents in the United States can identify familiar foods at the time of consumption and when prompted with an image 14 h postprandial, but poorly estimate portions. Public Health Nutrition, 14(7), 1184-1191.

Six, B.L., Schap, T.E., Zhu, F.M., Mariappan, A., Bosch, M., Delp, E.J., Ebert, D.S., Kerr, D.A., Boushey, C.J. (2010). Evidence-based development of a mobile telephone food record. Journal of the American Dietetic Association, 110(1), 74-79.

Stütz, T., Dinic, R., Domhardt, M., Ginzinger, S. (2014a). Can mobile augmented reality systems assist in portion estimation? A User Study. (eingereicht). In: Klinker, G. und Navab, N. (Hrsg.). International Symposium on Mixed and Augmented Reality. Piscataway: IEEE.

Stütz, T., Dinic, R., Oostingh, G.J., Ginzinger, S. (2014b). EatAR: Mobile Augmented Reality Assisted Nutrition Assessment. 8. Forschungsforum der Österreichischen Fachhochschulen.

Woo, I., Otsmo, K., Kim, S., Ebert, D.S., Delp, E.J., Boushey, C.J. (2010). Automatic portion estimation and visual refinement in mobile dietary assessment. Proceedings of SPIE, 7533.

Xu, C., He, Y., Khannan, N., Parra, A., Boushey, C., Delp, E. (2013). Image-based Food Volume Estimation. In: Aizawa, K., Funatomi, T. und Yamakata, Y. (Hrsg.). 5th International Workshop on Multimedia for Cooking & Eating Activities. New York: ACM, S. 75-80.

Zhu, F., Bosch, M., Woo, I., Kim, S.Y., Boushey, C.J., Ebert, D.S., Delp, E.J. (2010). The Use of Mobile Devices in Aiding Dietary Assessment and Evaluation. Selected Topics in Signal Processing, 4(4), 756-766.

Kontaktinformationen

Simon Ginzinger, Fachhochschule Salzburg GmbH, MMT MultiMediaTechnology, Urstein Sued 1, 5412 Puch/Salzburg, Austria, Simon.Ginzinger@fh-salzburg.ac.at

Danksagung

Die Autoren bedanken sich bei den StudentInnen, die an der Studie teilgenommen haben. Diese Arbeit wurde von der Österreichischen Forschungsförderungsgesellschaft, Projektnummer 839076 (SmartHealthCheck), gefördert.

M. Koch, A. Butz & J. Schlichter (Hrsg.): Mensch und Computer 2014 Tagungsband,
München: Oldenbourg Wissenschaftsverlag, 2014, S. 175-184.

Nutzerintegration in Softwareprojekte durch Multi-Channel Feedback

Sebastian Draxler[1], Oliver Stickel[1], Dominique Winter[2], Gunnar Stevens[1]

Human Computer Interaction, Universität Siegen[1]
Buhl Data Service GmbH[2]

Zusammenfassung

In diesem Beitrag stellen wir die Ergebnisse einer empirischen Feldstudie bei einem bekannten deutschen Softwareunternehmen vor. Das Ziel war es, den dort durchgeführten Entwicklungsprozess unter Einbeziehung der Nutzer besser zu verstehen, um von einem erfolgreichen Beispiel zu lernen. Innerhalb dieser Arbeit betrachten wir Benutzerbeteiligung als ein Hilfsmittel um gute Usability und User Experience zu erzeugen. Wir ergründen, welche Rollen im Unternehmen dazu beitragen, mit welchen Mitteln und auf welchen Ebenen Nutzer und Hersteller miteinander kommunizieren, sowie welche Kanäle, Tools und Praktiken eingebunden sind. Die Arbeit mit diesem Multi-Channel Nutzerfeedback ist ein Beispiel, wie der Aspekt der iterativen und evaluierenden Weiterentwicklung der eher abstrakten DIN 9241-210 für konkret umgesetzt werden kann.

1 Einleitung

Computer sind im betrieblichen Ablauf von Unternehmen sowie dem privaten Sektor nicht mehr wegzudenken. Gebrauchstaugliche, eine positive User Experience (UX) hervorrufende und an den realen Bedürfnissen der Endanwender entwickelte Software ist dementsprechend zu einem entscheidenden Wettbewerbsfaktor geworden. Einer der wichtigsten Faktoren für die Erreichung dieses Ziels ist die systematische Einbeziehung der Nutzer-Communities in den Entwicklungs- und Innovationsprozess (Pipek & Wulf 2009; Hansson et al. 2004). Dies gilt in der frühen Phase der Ideenfindung (Chesbrough 2003), beim Entwurf konkreter Gestaltungslösungen (Schuler & Namioka 1993), als auch bei abschließenden Qualitätskontrollen durch den Nutzer (Nielsen 1994). Deshalb sollten das Wissen, die Meinungen und die Ideen der Nutzer idealerweise in allen Phasen der Produktentwicklung in einen geeigneten Diskurs mit weiteren relevanten Akteuren (z.B. Entwicklern oder Unternehmensvertretern) überführt werden, welcher wiederum in eine geordnete Umsetzung von Innovationen mündet. Es ist jedoch zu konstatieren, dass etablierte Vorgehensmodelle und Usability- / UX-Methoden aufgrund von zeitlichen, logistischen sowie finanziellen Voraussetzungen bisher oft nicht oder unvollständig von softwareentwickelnden KMU angewendet werden (Hering et al. 2013). Von der anfänglichen Ideenfindung bis zur späteren Evaluation der Umsetzung finden sich akute Defizite in der Einbeziehung des Nutzers.

Der bekannte DIN EN ISO 9241-210:2011-01 (ISO 2010) Standard soll genau dazu als Anleitung dienen. An verschiedenen Stellen fordert er die Integration von Nutzern und weiteren Stakeholdern in den Entwicklungsprozess. Gleichzeitig lässt die Beschreibung jedoch Lücken was die konkrete Umsetzung angeht, die es in der alltäglichen Situation entwickelnder Organisationen zu füllen gilt. Vor allem Beispiele für geeignete Rollen und Mechanismen, werden gerade nicht genannt (ISO 2010, Abschnitt 5.3). Uns interessierte daher die Forschungsfrage: *Wie binden erfolgreiche KMU ihre Nutzer in Ideenfindung, Design und (Wieter-)entwicklung ihrer Softwareprodukte ein, um eine positive Usability und UX zu erzeugen?*

Ausgehend von dieser Fragestellung präsentiert diese Arbeit eine Studie, die den Nutzereinbezug bei einem bekannten deutschen Softwarehersteller untersucht, der hinsichtlich dieses Einbezuges eine Vorreiterrolle einnimmt. Insbesondere fokussieren wir auf beteiligte Rollen, Kommunikationskanäle und verwendete, unterstützende Technik – alle Bereiche zusammen ergeben die „Nutzerintegration durch Multi-Channel Feedback".

2 Nutzerzentrierung und Community-Zentrierung

Participatory Design (PD) in der Softwareentwicklung geht davon aus, dass Entwickler in der Regel nicht über ein ausreichendes Wissen der tatsächlichen Praxis von Endnutzern verfügen. Konkrete Dimensionen dieses Problems zeigen Greenbaum und Kyng (1991) auf. Sie benennen als Herausforderungen für Entwickler die Berücksichtigung von Arbeitspraxen, die Zusammenarbeit mit echten Nutzern, das Begreifen von Aufgaben als situierte Handlungen sowie das Verstehen von Arbeit als soziale Handlung. Es existieren weiterhin verschiedene nutzerzentrierte Vorgehensmodelle wie z.B. STEPS (Floyd et al. 1989) mit seinem Fokus auf zyklische Entwicklungsphasen unter Nutzerbeteiligung. Eine Übersicht über weitere Arbeiten mit Verfahrensvorschlägen für Nutzereinbezug findet sich bei Muller et al. (1997).

Als heute verbreiteter Standard im Bereich der nutzerzentrierten Entwicklung ist die ISO-Norm 9241 (*Ergonomics of Human-System Interaction)* zu nennen, insbesondere der Teil 210 (ISO 2010). Primär Großunternehmen setzen diese und assoziierte, etablierte Testverfahren zunehmend ein. Für KMU finden diese Modelle und Methoden aus finanziellen, organisatorischen und zeitlichen Gründen jedoch immer noch kaum Anwendung (Hering et al. 2013). Das nutzerzentrierte Vorgehen, beschrieben in Teil 210 (Abschnitt 5.3, (c) und (d)) empfiehlt bzw. fordert das *„Identifizieren der Personen und Organisation(en), die für die menschzentrierten Gestaltungsaktivitäten verantwortlich sind."* und das *„Entwickeln von effektiven Verfahren zum Einrichten von Rückmeldungen und zum Informationsaustausch über menschzentrierte Gestaltungsaktivitäten, soweit sie weitere Gestaltungsaktivitäten und Kompromisse beeinflussen, und von Verfahren zur Dokumentation der Ergebnisse dieser Aktivitäten"* (ISO 210). Dabei werden allerdings keinerlei Ratschläge bei der Besetzung dieser Rollen oder Auswahl von Rückkanälen gegeben.

Agile Methoden, wie beispielsweise Scrum, fordern ebenfalls die Integration von Nutzern und anderen Stakeholdern in den Entwicklungsprozess. Dabei bleiben die Empfehlungen allerdings auf der Ebene, einzelne Nutzer des Kunden kontinuierlich mit dem Entwicklungsteam zusammenarbeiten zu lassen. In den letzten Jahren wurde vermehrt versucht Scrum mit UCD Ansätzen zu integrieren, indem Sprints von Design- und Entwicklungsabteilungen synchronisiert wurden, etc. Diese Mechanismen gehen allerdings schon davon aus, dass geeignete Rollen und Kanäle für Kundenfeedback existieren.

Hansson et al. (2004) folgen dem Grundgedanken der Open Innovation Chesbrough (2003) und machten deutlich, wie wichtig die Einbeziehung von Feedback aus Nutzer-Communities in einem Softwareprojekt ist. Die Interaktionspraxis solcher Prozesse wurden z.B. von Barcellini et al. (2008) beschrieben. Vor allem die Kernteilnehmerrollen, wie z.B. Administratoren und Entwickler, aber auch sog. „boundary spanners", die zwischen Entwicklern und Nutzern vernetzen wurden untersucht.

Weitere Arbeiten fokussieren eher auf die Werkzeuge, die zum Nutzereinbezug verwendet wurden. So fanden beispielsweise Farshcian und Divitini (1999) eine starke Verwendung von E-Mail zur asynchronen Zusammenarbeit. Yetim et al. (2012) zeigten, wie Mechanismen zur Erfassung nutzungsrelevanter Information direkt in Anwendungen integriert werden können. Erfolgreiche kommerzielle Systeme im Bereich Community Driven Development sind z.B. Web 2.0 Plattformen wie UserVoice und GetSatisfaction.

3 Methodik und Setting der Studie

Zur Beantwortung der Forschungsfrage suchten wir ein erfolgreiches mittelständisches Unternehmen, welches Wert auf den Einbezug von Nutzern in die Entwicklung legt und entsprechende Maßnahmen bereits umsetzt. Mit der Buhl Data Services GmbH konnte ein solches Unternehmen gefunden werden. Mit über 650 Mitarbeitern, einem Umsatz von ca. 70 Millionen Euro und einer breiten Produktpalette, steht Buhl stellvertretend für deutsche Mittelständler im Bereich der Softwareentwicklung. Das Unternehmen entwickelt und vertreibt Produkte, welche direkt den Endbenutzer adressieren.

Wir betrachten hier das Produktentwicklungsteam der Finanzverwaltungs-Software finanzblick, die kostenlos im Web, sowie auf den mobilen Plattformen iOS und Android verfügbar ist. Neben Teilen des Produktentwicklungsteams untersuchten wir die verschiedenen Abteilungen mit Nutzerkontakt, die quer zur Produktentwicklung liegen. Dies sind die Supportabteilung und das sogenannte Customer Lab, welches Usability-Studien und ähnliche Aufgaben übernimmt. Beide Abteilungen sind vor Ort im Unternehmen integriert.

Die Ergebnisse dieser Studie basieren auf jeweils etwa einstündigen, semi-strukturierten Interviews mit PO1, SMM, Leiter Support, Mitarbeiter Support, Entwickler und Customer Lab. Jedes Interview dauerte etwa eine Stunde und fokussierte auf Kontakte mit den Nutzern, deren Integration in den Entwicklungsprozess, sowie Mechanismen, wie entstehende Informationen (z.B. Anforderungen) im Prozess weiter verarbeitet werden. Zusätzlich führten wir teilnehmende Beobachtungen bei einer Usability-Studie mit Nutzern (ca. 3 Stunden) und bei einem Scrum Sprint Planungsmeeting (ca. 4 Stunden) durch. Es wurden Audioaufzeichnungen der Interviews und Beobachtungen angefertigt, ergänzt durch Feldnotizen. Zusätzlich wurden verschiedene Artefakte gesammelt, beispielsweise User Stories, Usability-Berichte. Audiomaterial wurde für die Analyse transkribiert. Die Daten wurden nach Grounded Theory (Strauss & Corbin 1996) und unter Fokussierung auf die zuvor genannte Fragestellung codiert. Im Verlauf wurden telefonisch drei Kurzinterviews geführt (jeweils 15min mit PO, SMM und Support), um Fragen die sich in der Analyse ergeben hatten zu klären. Im Folgenden präsentieren wir die wichtigsten drei Kategorien der Analyse.

4 Analyse des Multi-Channel Feedback Prozesses

Die Entwicklung von finanzblick ist im Unternehmen als agiles Projekt nach Scrum[1] strukturiert. Dabei folgt man dem Ansatz kontinuierlicher Releases, d.h. das Produkt wird seit mehr als zwei Jahren kontinuierlich weiterentwickelt und in kleinen, schnellzyklischen Releases veröffentlicht. Scrum unterstützt das Entwicklungsteam dabei, da es die Entwicklung in Teilschritte (Sprints) gliedert. Hier sind dies etwa vier Wochen lange Weiterentwicklungsphasen mit Planungsmeetings zwischen den Sprints. Jeder Sprint wird mit einer veröffentlichungsfähigen Version beendet, was sich gut mit dem Releaseverhalten vereinbaren lässt.

4.1 Rollen mit Nutzerkontakt im Unternehmen

Die zentrale koordinierende Rolle der Produktentwicklung ist die des **Product Owner (PO)**. Sie stellt innerhalb des Entwicklungsteams den Vertreter sämtlicher Stakeholder dar. Der Product Owner soll die Vision des Produkts kommunizieren und die Stoßrichtung im Sinne der Nutzer vorgeben. Anders als bei Scrum üblich, besitzt finanzblick ein Product Owner-Team aus zwei Personen. PO1 setzt dabei die strategische Vision um. PO2 zeigt sich für die Details der täglichen Entwicklung verantwortlich.

Im untersuchten Fall erstellt das PO-Team so genannte User Stories. Diese sind Anforderungen in Form kurzer textueller Beschreibungen aus der Sicht einer Nutzerrolle (z.B. „Als Anwender möchte ich meinen Kontostand einsehen können, damit ich weiß wieviel Geld mir zur Verfügung steht.“). Sie werden durch Diskussion innerhalb des Produktteams konkretisiert und durch Akzeptanzkriterien vervollständigt, die definieren wann die Anforderung als erfüllt zu betrachten ist (Cohn 2004). Auch für die Auswahl und Priorisierung der User Stories hinsichtlich Abarbeitung zeigen sich die PO verantwortlich. Das PO-Team bespricht User Stories gemeinsam hinsichtlich Vereinbarkeit mit der Produktvision, Kundenutzen, Usability u.ä. Aspekten. Falls notwendig werden andere Mitglieder des Entwicklungsteams bei der Entscheidungsfindung je nach Problemlage hinzugezogen, z.B. CTO oder Designer. Diese User Story-Planung wird vor der Sprint-Planung durchgeführt (bei der dann auch die Entwickler anwesend sind). Product Owner versuchen vor allem lernen wie der Benutzer denkt. Feedback der Nutzer kann ihnen direkt Ideen geben, aber auch das Bild des Nutzers

[1] Eine detaillierte Übersicht über Scrum findet sich hier: https://www.scrum.org/Scrum-Guide

verbessern. Dazu erhalten sie Informationen von Support, Social Media Management und Customer Lab.

Das Unternehmen arbeitet mit einem festen Stamm aus erfahrenen **Support**mitarbeitern, die sich vor Ort im Unternehmen befinden. Ihre Aufgabe ist einerseits, Ansprechpartner bei technischen und Nutzungsproblemen zu sein, gleichzeitig treffen hier aber auch Wünsche über neue Funktionen von Kundenseite ein.

Mit dem **Social Media Management (SMM)** wird außerdem eine besondere Rolle unterhalten, die ausschließlich an den Social Media-Präsenzen des Unternehmens und der Produkte arbeitet. Sie pflegt aktuelle Information zu neuen Funktionen oder Problemen in Blogs, Twitter und Facebook. Zusätzlich aber überwacht sie auch aktiv den Austausch der Nutzer, greift ein wo es nötig ist und reagiert auf direkte Anfragen, ähnlich wie der Support.

Die dritte Rolle ergibt sich aus dem **Customer Lab (CL)**. Hier werden Benutzungstests von Produkten mit Nutzern durchgeführt. Tests werden auf Anfrage der Produktentwicklungsteams z.B. während der Entwicklung neuer Funktionen angestoßen. Auch in früheren Phasen bietet das Customer Lab Möglichkeiten, Nutzer in die Entwicklung einzubeziehen.

Das PO-Team, SMM, sowie gegebenenfalls auch Support und das Customer Lab treffen zur User Story-Planung zusammen. So tragen Support und SMM aktuelle Probleme oder Wünsche aus Supportanfragen bzw. Facebook- und Twitter-Einträgen zusammen und bringen diese in die Diskussion neuer User Stories ein. Das Customer Lab wirkt hier vor allem durch das Einbringen von Feedback, welches während Benutzertests aufgenommen wurde.

Die Entwickler in diesem Produktentwicklugnsteam haben keinen direkten Kontakt mit Nutzern. Sie erhalten Feedback von Nutzern ausschließlich in modifizierter Form als User Stories.

4.2 Kanäle und Medien zum Austausch mit Nutzern

Das Produktentwicklungsteam, also die PO, CTO, Entwickler und der Scrum Master, nutzen ein gemeinsames Softwaresystem zur Planung der Sprints, hier Microsofts **Team Foundation Server (TFS)**. Das System ist als Bug Tracker und Projektplanungswerkzeug ausgelegt. Es wurde im Unternehmen erweitert, damit zusätzliche Aufgabenarten abgebildet werden können. Neben Incident Klassen wie Fehler oder Aufgabe wurde das System explizit um die Klasse *Kundenwunsch* erweitert. Das PO-Team nutzt das System um User Stories abzulegen, die später von CTO und Entwicklern in kleinere Aufgaben aufgebrochen werden. Diese werden ebenfalls im TFS erstellt und zeitlich eingeschätzt. TFS ist damit die wichtigste Verbindung zwischen PO-Team als Visionsträger und Vertreter des Nutzers sowie den Entwicklern. Die festgehaltenen Informationen, werden jedoch im Gespräch weiter Kontextualisiert.

TFS stellt dabei das Ziel der Daten aus verschiedenen Kommunikationskanälen dar. Diese schließen E-Mail, Telefon und durch die kurzen Wege innerhalb der Organisation vor allem auch das persönliche Gespräch ein. Auch wenn die PO nicht täglich im Kontakt mit Nutzern sind, werden ihnen Mails, die über spezielle produktspezifische **E-Mailadressen** ankommen, zugestellt. Diese E-Mailadressen sind innerhalb des Produkts vermerkt und erlauben Nutzern damit den direkten Kontakt. Hier besteht insbesondere Kontakt mit eher engagierten Langzeitnutzern, die immer wieder Verbesserungen oder Probleme melden. Außerdem überwachen die PO **Bewertungen und Kommentare** in den App Stores der mobilen Plattformen.

Das Supportteam bietet Unterstützung per **E-Mail, Telefon, Brief und Fax** an. Außerdem unterhält es produktspezifische **Foren**. Anrufe und schriftlicher Verkehr werden festgehalten. Kontakte, die klar technische Fehler, Nutzungsprobleme oder Verbesserungsvorschläge betreffen, werden allerdings entsprechend vermerkt und in TFS übertragen. Das Forum wird zwar vom Supportteam überwacht, die Leitlinie ist allerdings, dass sich Nutzer gegenseitig helfen sollen. Erst wenn eine Anfrage zu lange unbeantwortet bleibt, schreitet das Supportteam ein und hilft weiter. Werden hier Diskussionen entdeckt, die als Fehler oder Verbesserungsvorschlag eingeordnet werden können, wird dies ebenfalls in TFS übertragen.

Die wichtigsten Kommunikationskanäle des SMM stellen **Facebook** und **Twitter** dar. Auf beiden Plattformen unterhält das Unternehmen eine Präsenz für das Unternehmen, sowie weitere für die meisten Produkte. Zusätzlich pflegt das SMM die **Blog**s, auch hier einmal für das Unternehmen und die jeweiligen Produkte. Einerseits ist das SMM verantwortlich dafür, dass Neuigkeiten wie z.B. die Veröffentlichung von neuen Versionen den Nutzern kommuniziert werden, aber auch bei gemeldeten Fehlern transparent und schnell zu kommunizieren, dass diese bekannt sind und wie und wann sie behoben werden. Gleichzeitig setzt man einen guten Teil der Arbeitszeit dafür ein, diese Medien zu überwachen und die verschiedenen Stimmungen auf den Plattformen einzufangen. Hier werden Feature-Wünsche und Bugs schnell zu einer Diskussion innerhalb der großen Community mit mehreren hundert Personen. Das SMM gibt Wünsche, die ein gewisses Gewicht erlangen, an das PO-Team weiter und hat durch die Argumentationslinien der Nutzer auf den Plattformen auch oft die notwendigen Begründungen um die Entscheidungsträger von guten Ideen zu überzeugen. Bei Routinefällen (Bspw. Unterstützung einer neuen Bank), kommuniziert es ebenfalls direkt mit dem Entwicklungsteam. Dies geschieht per E-Mail oder im direkten Gespräch.

Das Customer Lab führt **vor Ort** regelmäßig **Sitzungen mit Benutzern** durch. Im Laufe jedes Tests werden 5-20 Probanden eingeladen. Die Probanden nutzen Software und artikulieren mittels der Thinking Aloud-Methode (Nielsen 1994) ihre Gedanken. Probanden, sowie Bildschirme werden auf Video aufgezeichnet. Die Daten werden je nach Bedarf durch heuristische Evaluationen und Cognitive Walkthroughs ergänzt. Aktuell weitet das Customer Lab seine Aufgaben aus, indem nun auch im Rahmen des User Research Benutzer zu Hause besucht werden. So kann Nutzern bei der Arbeit mit der Software über die Schulter geschaut werden, statt sie vorgefertigte Testaufgaben abarbeiten zu lassen. Probanden werden über die Website oder Zeitungsannoncen rekrutiert. Nach jedem Test wird ein Bericht erstellt, der direkt an das PO-Team geleitet und in Teilen in den TFS eingepflegt wird.

Als Befragungsmöglichkeit vom Unternehmen in Richtung der Anwender hat sich der Net Promoter Score Fragebogen (NPS) als nützlich erwiesen. Hier wird dem Nutzer nur eine einzige Frage gestellt: „Würden Sie das Produkt einem Bekannten weiter empfehlen?“. Je nach Antwort (1 gar nicht – 10 ja, uneingeschränkt). Bei der Einblendung des NPS gibt das Unternehmen dem Nutzer zugleich die Möglichkeit, Kontaktdaten für Rückfragen anzugeben. Üblicherweise wird im Anschluß ein Teil der Probanden, wenn gewünscht, telefonisch oder per Mail kontaktiert oder in das Customer Lab eingeladen. Dies betrifft vor allem diejenigem Nutzer mit Bewertungen zwischen 7-8 und 4-5 da hier eine unzufriedenheit vermutet wird, die der Nutzer reflektieren kann. Dabei wird darauf geachtet, dass Nutzer nicht durch zu häufige Einblendung belästigt werden. Umfragen mit einem Teil der Nutzer werden weniger als 1x pro Monat durchgeführt.

4.3 Feedback im Produktentwicklungsprozess

Mit einer sechsstelligen Anzahl aktiver Nutzer ist die Menge an eingehendem Nutzerfeedback enorm. An verschiedenen Stellen des Arbeitsprozesses findet daher eine Filterung, Aggregation und Bewertung statt. Die übergeordnete Idee stammt aus früheren Erfahrungen des Unternehmens mit Nutzerintegration, die eher im Stile der Participatory Design-Tradition (Greenbaum & Kyng 1991) durchgeführt wurde. Dabei wurde das Feedback von besonders engagierten Nutzern sehr direkt umgesetzt. Diese sehr tief gehende Beteiligung einer Nutzergruppe mit hoher Expertise war allerdings nicht repräsentativ für die breite Zielgruppe. Entsprechend steht heute im Vordergrund, ob sich Vorschläge mit der Produktvision in Einklang bringen lassen und welche Zielgruppe angesprochen werden könnte.

Die wichtigste Rolle im Filterprozess ist die des PO. Schlussendlich entscheidet sie, ob und inwiefern aus Vorschlägen User Stories werden. Dabei bleibt die Möglichkeit, die Grundidee aufzugreifen, sie aber so zu modifizieren, dass sie mit der Produktvision kompatibel bleibt. In einigen Fällen wurden Vorschläge explizit nicht umgesetzt, da diese die Produktvision unterwandert oder relevante Zielgruppen aus Sicht der PO nicht angesprochen hätten.

Das Customer Lab nimmt keine Auswahl oder Filterung vor, aggregiert Nutzerfeedback aber zu konsistenten Berichten für das PO-Team. Das SMM filtert solche Anfragen, von denen es aufgrund früherer Entscheidungen des PO-Teams genau weiß, dass sie nicht umgesetzt werden. Findet es in den sozialen Medien allerdings neue Vorschläge, oder bekommen existierende Ideen ein neues, quantitatives oder qualitatives Gewicht, wird das PO-Team informiert (unter Einbezug von möglichst viel Kontext aus den sozialen Medien).

Bemerkenswert sind die Filterstrukturen des Supports. Feedback wird nicht nur aufgenommen, sondern auch innerhalb einer Gruppe, die für ein bestimmtes Produkt zuständig ist bewertet. Beiträge, die nicht der Produktvision entsprechen, werden u.U. nicht an den PO weiter gegeben. Andere Beiträge werden aggregiert, wenn sie die gleiche Idee betreffen.

Die verschiedenen Teilprozesse der Aggregation und Bewertung können qualitative und quantitative Filterung unterschieden werden. Quantitatives Filtern betrifft die Frequenz mit der ein bestimmter Vorschlag auftritt. Insbesondere das Supportteam macht von dieser Technik Gebrauch, nicht zuletzt dank einer Datenbank mit Kundeninteraktionen, die quantitative Abfragen vereinfacht. Für das SMM sind „likes“, „retweets“ oder Anzahl der Beteiligten an der Diskussion Teil der Bewertungsgrundlage. Quantitative Aspekte sind jedoch keine Garantie, dass eine Idee umgesetzt wird, so wird z.B. ein bestimmtes Feature in finanzblick, das schon lange von vielen Nutzern gefordert wird, nicht umgesetzt, da es einem mittelfristig geplanten anderen Feature zuwiderlaufen würde. Qualitatives Filtern folgt stärker der Erfahrung der Beteiligten. Es bedeutet, die Vorschläge genau zu durchdenken und Umsetzungen und deren Bedeutung für das Produkt zu visualisieren um dann darüber zu entscheiden. Das SMM, sowie die PO verlassen sich stärker auf diese Möglichkeit. Dabei ist allerdings zu betonen, dass sich beide Filterprozesse ergänzen.

5 Diskussion

Das Unternehmen hat für die kontinuierliche und nutzerzentrierte Entwicklung von finanzblick ein gut aufeinander abgestimmtes Team etabliert. Die Wünsche der Nutzer werden dabei sehr ernst genommen und gelangen über verschiedene Rückkanäle in den Entwicklungsprozess (siehe Tabelle 1). Dieses Verfahren haben *Nutzerintegration durch Multi-Channel Feedback* genannt. Es dient als Beispiel dafür wie Unternehmen die ISO 9241-210, insbesondere die Abschnitte 5.3 c) und d) zur Planung von Rollen und Rückkanälen für den Prozess, umsetzen können. Im Folgenden möchten wir die Besonderheiten des Prozesses diskutieren.

Feedback Kanal	**Einsatz**	**Bedeutung für den Prozess**
E-Mail Product Owner	Nutzer kontaktieren Verantwortlichen f. das Produkt (Wünsche)	Detailliertes Feedback; Nutzergetrieben
Telefon, Brief, Fax, Forum Support	Nutzer wenden sich Hilfesuchend an den Support	Feedback Einzelner; Bugs und Wünsche; aggregierbar; Nutzergetrieben
App Stores Product Owner	Nutzer Bewerten und Kommentieren Produkt	Feedback vieler; Aktive Suche nötig; Nutzergetrieben
Facebook, Twitter Social Media Management (SMM)	Nutzer erbitten Hilfe, äußern Wünsche. Unternehmen kündigt behobene Bugs und neue Versionen an.	Feedback vieler; Aggregation auf Plattform; Nutzergetrieben und Unternehmensgetrieben
Blog SMM	Unternehmen kündigt Neuigkeiten zum Produkt und neue Versionen an.	Information der Nutzer; kein Rückkanal; Unt.-getrieben
Benutzertests Customer Lab	Usability Tests, Workshops, Befragungen	Unternehmensgetrieben; sehr detaillierte Einzelberichte
NPS Automatisiert/PO	Kontaktherstellung	Unternehmensgetrieben; nur Kontaktanbahnung

Tabelle 1: Übersicht über Feedbackkanäle und Medien.

Wir haben dargelegt, dass die Entwickler im finanzblick Team anders als beispielsweise vom Participatory Design gefordert (Floyd et al. 1989), keinen direkten Kontakt mit den Nutzern haben. Sie arbeiten auf Basis von User Stories, welche die Wünsche und Sichtweisen der Nutzer widerspiegeln sollen. Dies erlaubt eine Entlastung der Entwickler und Fokussierung auf ihre Kernaufgaben. In Unternehmen mit weniger Personal gehen wir allerdings davon aus, dass Entwickler in der einen oder anderen Form stärkeren Kontakt mit Nutzern haben.

Rückkanäle wie Social Media, Anfragen beim Support oder E-Mail bieten auch Nutzern die dem Unternehmen bisher unbekannt sind verschiedene Möglichkeiten, sich im Prozess zu beteiligen. Dies ist in den meisten Participatory Design Methoden ebenfalls nicht vorgesehen und kann eher als Ansatz der Open Innovation (Chesbrough 2003) klassifiziert werden, was gerade die möglichen Innovationen durch im Prozess bisher unbekannte Personen hervorhebt. Wir betrachten diese Rückkanäle als Möglichkeiten des Nutzers, aus eigenem Antrieb, Feedback in den Entwicklungsprozess einzubringen und eine Weiterentwicklung anzustoßen.

Gleichzeitig existiert im Unternehmen der Bedarf bestimmte Stellen des Produktes gezielt zu verbessern, die vielleicht nicht von Nutzern erkannt werden. Dafür wurden ebenfalls Rückkanäle zum Nutzer eingerichtet. Beispiele sind Aufrufe zur Bewertung neuer Features über Social Media Kanäle oder die Kontaktanbahnung mit Endnutzern über den NPS Fragebogen, gefolgt von der Einladung in das Customer Lab. Dort können gemeinsam mit Nutzern Mockups diskutiert und prototypisch umgesetzte Features in Form von Benutzertests (Nielsen 1994) mit anschließenden Interviews evaluiert werden. Diese Mechanismen dienen stärker dem klassischen Requirements Engineering und Usability Testing um Unsicherheiten im Entwicklungsprozess zu reduzieren.

Mechanismen wie die Filterung und Aggregation von Meinungen und Wünschen wurden an verschiedenen Stellen des Prozesses ausgemacht. Diese Methoden wurden eingesetzt, um sich nicht in Sonderfällen einzelner Nutzer die nicht zur Zielgruppe gehören, zu verlieren. Dabei zeigte sich, dass diese vor allem in Gruppen aus mehreren Personen diskutiert wurden; vor allem im Sprint Planning Meeting in welchem User Stories erstellt werden. Ähnliches wird in Verfahren der Open Innovation vorgesehen (Chesbrough 2003). Hier verbleibt die Hoheit über Bewertung von Vorschlägen allerdings beim Unternehmen. Abstimmungsverfahren im Rahmen von Open Innovation Maßnahmen implizieren dagegen einen größeren Einfluss der Nutzer auf Entscheidungen.

Der in den letzten Jahren etablierte Prozess hinter finanzblick, kann mit einer kontinuierlich steigenden Zahl aktiver Nutzer und sehr positiven Bewertungen in den App Stores durchaus als Erfolg gewertet werden. Diese iterative, nutzerzentrierte Form der Weiterentwicklung des Produktes ist vor allem durch den hier vorgestellten Multi-Channel User-Feedback Ansatz in Kombination mit dem agilen Scrum Vorgehen möglich. Scrum gibt dabei mit den hier auf vier Wochen fest gelegten Sprint Zyklen den Rhythmus für die Entwicklung vor. Die Ergebnisse der verschiedenen Feedback-Mechanismen werden in diesen integriert.

Literatur

ISO, 2010. ISO 9241-210: Ergonomie der Mensch-System-Interaktion: Teil 210: Prozess zur Gestaltung gebrauchstauglicher interaktiver Systeme, Berlin: DIN Deutsches Institut für Normung.

Barcellini, F., Détienne, F. & Burkhardt, J.-M., 2008. User and developer mediation in an Open Source Software community: Boundary spanning through cross participation in online discussions. International Journal of Human-Computer Studies, 66(7), p.558–570.

Chesbrough, H.W., 2003. Open Innovation: The New Imperative for Creating and Profiting from Technology, Harvard Business Press.

Cohn, M., 2004. User stories applied: for agile software development, Boston: Addison-Wesley.

Farshchian, B.A. & Divitini, M., 1999. Using Email and WWW in a Distributed Participatory Design Project. SIGGROUP Bull., 20(1), p.10–15.

Floyd, C., Reisin, F.-M. & Schmidt, G., 1989. STEPS to Software Development with Users. In ESEC '89: Proc. 2nd European Software Engineering Conference. London, UK: Springer, p. 48—64.

Greenbaum, J. & Kyng, M., 1991. Design at Work: Cooperative Design of Computer Systems 1st ed., CRC.

Hering, D. et al., 2013. Usability-Hindernisse bei Software entwickelnden KMU. In S. Boll, S. Maaß, & R. Malaka, eds. M&C2013 - Workshopband. München: Oldenbourg Verlag, pp. 9–18.

Muller, M.J., Haslwanter, J.H. & Dayton, T., 1997. Participatory Practices in the Software Lifecycle. In M. G. Helander, T. K. Landauer, & P. V. Prabhu, eds. Elsevier, pp. 256–297.

Nielsen, J., 1994. Usability engineering, Cambridge, Mass.: AP Professional.

Pipek, V. & Wulf, V., 2009. Infrastructuring: Towards an Integrated Perspetive on the Design and Use of Information Technology. Journal of the Association of Information System (JAIS).

Schuler, D. & Namioka, A., 1993. Participatory Design Principles and Practices, Lawrence Erlbaum Associates.

Strauss, A. & Corbin, J., 1996. Grounded Theory: Grundlagen Qualitativer Sozialforschung, BeltzPVU.

Yetim, F. et al., 2012. Fostering Continuous User Participation by Embedding a Communication Support Tool in User Interfaces. AIS Transactions on Human-Computer Interaction, 4(2), p.153–168.

Kontaktinformationen

Sebastian Draxler, Oliver Stickel, Gunnar Stevens (name.vorname@uni-siegen.de)
Universität Siegen, Hölderlinstrasse 3, 57068 Siegen

Dominique Winter (dwinter@buhl-data.com)
Buhl Data Service GmbH, Am Siebertsweiher 3/5, 57290 Neunkirchen

M. Koch, A. Butz & J. Schlichter (Hrsg.): Mensch und Computer 2014 Tagungsband,
München: Oldenbourg Wissenschaftsverlag, 2014, S. 185-194.

Usability Readiness of German Software SMEs – Three Segments and their Characteristics

Karl Werder[2], Phillip Haake[2], Alexander Maedche[1,2]

Chair of Information Systems IV, University of Mannheim, http://eris.bwl.uni-mannheim.de[1]
Institute for Enterprise Systems, University of Mannheim, http://ines.uni-mannheim.de[2]

Abstract

German small-and-medium sized software companies are facing an increasing pressure by their users with regards to usability expectations. While some software companies still heavily emphasize functional aspects of their products, others have identified the potential of usability to differentiate themselves. The study has an exploratory nature and employs cluster analysis to investigate responses of German SME software companies with a specific focus on usability. We identify three segments of companies, i.e. Usability Sleeper, Usability Executers and Usability Performers. While the first perform worst, the Usability Executers show high usability readiness with regard to software development (SD) processes. Usability Performers further separate themselves through higher employees' expertise. Subsequent analysis of these sub-segments reveals that business sector and management support are key differentiators amongst them. For practitioners the results presented in this paper describe the characteristics of SME software companies in Germany with mature usability.

1 Introduction

Small and medium-sized enterprises (SMEs) in Germany are often highly specialized firms and known to be the drivers for innovation in the German economy (Simon 2009). The same holds true for the German software industry. In addition, software companies are facing multiple challenges, e.g. cost pressures, increasing global competition and growing expectations of users (Woywode et al. 2012). More recently, software firms are facing end-users that are surrounded by easy-to-use software-based solutions in their private life. Thus, they begin to expect a comparable usability of the software solutions at their workplace. This demand for usability should not only be considered a threat, but as an opportunity to seek competitive advantage (Gemser et al.2006). Especially, software firms in the US have been able to develop software products with superior usability and leverage their usability know-how for achieving such advantages (Scheiber et al. 2012). As a result, the German federal ministry for economics and technology initiated the execution of a comprehensive empirical study in 2011 (UIG study) to explore the status quo of usability methods in German SMEs (Woywode et al. 2012). The study was designed to capture the status quo of German SMEs in the software industry and user organizations with regard to the knowledge and actual use of usability concepts. In part, it was concluded that there is still a large gap between US and German software firms in the adoption of usability practices and knowledge. Usability is an important factor that influences the success of SD efforts and is therefore often used to measure software product quality (Madan & Dubey 2012). Hence, this paper specifically investigates possible segments focusing on the usability readiness of German SMEs. A segmentation of the responses to the software company questionnaire of the UIG study is presented. Such an approach allows to answer the following two research questions: Do different segments with regard to usability readiness in German software SMEs exist? What are the characteristics of these segments?

The remainder of this paper will first present related work to the study. In section 3, the research approach including data collection and analysis will be presented. Section 4, includes a description of the results focusing on the identified dimensions and segments. The discussion in section 5 is used to explain the results of the research and to put them into context. The paper ends with a conclusion, the limitations of the study.

2 Related Work

The German software business environment can be separated in a primary and a secondary sector, which have been described by Friedewald et al. (2001). Most firms in the primary sector (e.g. data processing firms) specialize in SD and sales. They usually have less than ten employees. This sector of the German software industry is dominated by SAP (Brault et al. 2013). However, many smaller players thrive in the largest European software market (Brault et al. 2013). The secondary sector is dominated by larger firms that develop software, which is included in their products or accompanies them (Friedewald et al. 2001). Since this is study is based on the UIG-study (Woywode et al. 2012) we use the same EU - definition to categorize primary sector software SMEs. Accordingly, companies with an annual turnover below 50 million Euros and less than 250 employees are defined as SMEs (European Union Commission 2003).

Usability is a socio-material concept (Riemer & Vehring 2010) and a very important characteristics of software products. They need to be developed with stringent methods (Madan & Dubey 2012). Prior research already indicated the need for training and education of developments team to achieve significant improvements with regard to usability (Seffah & Metzker 2004). Nonetheless, various definitions for usability exist (cf. Madan & Dubey 2012). For the purpose of this research we adopt the ISO standard (International Organization for Standardization 1998).There is little research on the aspect of usability methods for small and medium sized SD organizations (Woywode et al. 2012). We add to this research by exploring the influencing factors for the incorporation of usability methods in such firms.

3 Research Method

3.1 Data Collection

Specific emphasis was set to collect a representative sample of SMEs in Germany to allow for generalization. We collected data from software companies with 6-10 employees on average. The sample representing software companies covered 1.756 companies with 208 respondents, i.e. a response rate of 11.85 %. The data collection was conducted from January to November 2011. Initially, the software companies were approached via postal mail with an option to complete the questionnaire electronically. A unique identifier assured that each response was given by companies from the defined sample. Three days after postal delivery, the companies were approached via phone to increase the response rate. The questionnaire covered various aspects of usability affecting the company on an organizational and product level. On the organizational level questions related to the performance and environment of the company, employee selection and expertise, usability self-assessment, knowledge sources and knowledge exchange with environment, customers and users, and general information about the company. On the product level information about the SD process with a specific focus on usability aspects were gathered. The questionnaire contained 54 mandatory questions and 83 items. All items used and described below were measured on a 7-point Likert scale[1]. Moreover, the questionnaire gathered further optional information on the individual and company level.

In the following we present only the parts of the survey that are relevant to answering our research question. With regard to the SD process we focused on the following categories on the product level: the usage of usability methods, the actual UI development process and the inclusion of users into the development process. Furthermore, we first looked at employee expertise, which includes the different roles that are trained on the subject of usability, whether an employee willing to speak at a convention about usability methods could be identified, and the self-assessment along the two categories, i.e. the usability rating of the own software products and the general attitude of management towards usability. The questionnaire also assessed the contribution of individual customer segments to overall turnover and the importance of trends within the next 5 years. Companies' development in the last 3 years was assessed along key performance indicators, i.e. turnover, number of employees, customer satisfaction and profit.

[1] The entire questionnaire is publicly accessible in Woywode et al. (2012)

3.2 Data Analysis

For the statistical analysis we employed SPSS v22. We started analyzing the dataset of software companies using exploratory factor analysis. However, SPSS was unsuccessful in calculating the correlation matrix for all items, as it was not found to be positive definite. When reducing the included items to focus on a subsection of the questionnaire, it became possible to calculate the correlation matrix, but we were not able to find a combination that leads to a determinant that is high enough to rule out any multicollinearity issues. Therefore, we opted for an alternative approach, identifying dimensions of thematically related questions in the questionnaire. Therefore, for the remaining 49 items we calculated the Cronbach's alpha for those items contributing to a dimension. Cronbach's alpha α is a reliability measure, whereas N refers to the number of items used to build the dimensions.

Following the successful identification of dimensions we used this angle to determine possible segments in a two-step process. Through the exploratory nature of this research, we first investigated the identification of possible segments via the use of hierarchical cluster analysis (Kachigan 1986). As input for clustering we selected the dimension related to the user-centered software development process (UCSDP) readiness, whereas we define readiness as the adoption level of usability methods, techniques and practices. We ground this decision in the fact that the development process readiness is a key factor influencing the product quality (Harter et al. 2000). Using between groups linkage, i.e. the mean distance of all pairs across two segments, lead to the creation of two segments. Once we identified the existence of the two segments, we created new items segmenting the two using the K-means algorithm (Mackay 2003). Subsequently, we employed crosstabs and independent sample t-test to better understand the characteristics of the identified segments and possible contrasts within the segments. Preliminary results were discussed with four IS experts indicating further differentiating factors.

4 Results

4.1 Descriptive Results – Key Dimensions

User-Centered Software Development Process (UCSDP): The first dimension looks at the SD process with a specific focus on usability, overall using 11 items. Five items referring to usability methods measured the insensitivity of use of 1) methods for user analysis (e.g. contextual interviewing, scenarios, user profiles), 2) design methods (e.g. wireframes, prototyping), 3) usability evaluation methods (e.g. user testing, heuristics / guidelines), 4) specialized usability software (e.g. Balsamiq), and 5) whether such methods are already applied for a long time. Two items measured the development process for the user interface, i.e. the design of the UI before the development activities and the use of style guides for the development activities. Furthermore, four items measured the inclusion of users in the SD process. The items asked whether the users are interviewed 1) about typical tasks that the software is going to be used for (e.g. use cases, scenarios), 2) to generate user profiles, and 3) to assess first mock-ups of the user interface. Furthermore, it was assessed whether 4) the software is always tested on usability aspects before releasing the product into the market. We can summarize all items related to the development process to a reliable dimension looking at the entire UCSDP (Cronbach's alpha (α) = 0.864; Number of items (N) =11).

Management Assessment. To better understand the management perspective of usability subjects, we also asked questions related to their support and understanding of such topics. Items included whether management a) sees the need to support usability on an ongoing basis, b) is enthusiastic about opportunities offered through usability, c) invests time required to understand how the companies can profit from usability, d) decided to prioritize usability aspects over functional aspects, e) defined clear usability goals, and f) supports the achievement of usability goals. The aforementioned items lead to a reliable dimension of perceived management support (α = 0.928; N=6). Besides questions related to specific characteristics of the organization, we also asked firms to self-assess the evolution of their company throughout the past 3 years. The items included the development of the turnover, number of employees, customer satisfaction, and profit. Moreover, we asked to self-evaluate the development of their turnover, number of employees and profit related to their industry's average, and their overall impression of the companies development over the last 3 years. We can summarize these items into a reliable dimension measuring the companies development over the last 3 years (α = 0.891; N=8).

Human Resources. We relied on different items about employee skills relevant for the recruitment of new hires to construct the employee recruitment dimension (α = 0.763; N=6). All items are measured from unimportant to very important. Six skills or knowledge areas had to be assessed, i.e. programming, design and presentation, usability, psychology, economics, and business informatics. Measuring the training efforts of the firms lead to a highly reliable dimension (α = 0.861; N=5). The dimension assessed the degree of decision authority of employees with usability responsibility, whether developers, usability employees, or employee affected by the SD process are trained on usability subjects, and whether employees are trained for a long time on usability subjects. All items were measured from strong disagreement to strong agreement on a seven-point Likert scale. Likewise the expertise of employees was measured and resulted in a reliable dimension (α = 0.894; N=3). The subjects were confronted with a hypothetical questions, assuming that a large convention invites the company to talk about usability. The questions assessed whether or not the firm has an employee who could be send to the convention, being an expert on method of user research, methods to design an application and usability evaluation methods.

Business Environment. The dimension competitive environment was measured as the development of the firm's environment over the last 3 years and was found to be reliable (α=0.796; N=5). The growth opportunity in the current competitive environment and the rate of innovation in the industry were both measured from dramatically decreasing to dramatically increasing. Furthermore, the change in production and service technologies, and the change of customer needs were both measured from no change to strong change. The research and development activities in the industry were measured from strong decreasing to strong increasing. The contribution of product offerings to the company's turnover was found to be reliable after removing one item, that asked rather openly for the contribution of other services (α = 0.622; N=5). Assessing the relative importance of the sale of standard software licenses, the implementation of standard software, the development of custom made software, the execution of maintenance and support, and the execution of trainings and instructions was measured from not important to very important.

4.2 Segments

Resulting from the cluster analysis we identify segments in our dataset and describe these in further detail. It is noteworthy, that our list of dimensions is not exhaustive. However, based on the insights of the discussions and our understanding of the underlying data we deem the following dimensions as highly relevant for the context of our investigation. Moreover, further characteristics of such segments are identified and presented below (see also Figure 1).

Usability Sleepers vs Usability Executors

We found the user-centered development process dimension to be a leading criteria for distinguishing the responses. This higher level dimension is constructed from the dimensions of usability methods, development process and inclusion of user (see Appendix). Using this higher level dimension to build segments, we find a low readiness segment (M=2.71; SD=0.84 N=79) that is substantially different from the high readiness segment (M=4.78; SD=0.73; N=88). Besides the chosen dimension related to the development process, we identified differences in employee related measurement. Using an independent samples t-test to compare the groups along the expertise of employees dimension, finding a highly significant difference (t=-8.460; p=.000). This means that companies with high UCSDP readiness also feel confident to talk about their expertise in methods of user research, methods to design an application and usability evaluation methods.

A closer look at the Usability Performers segment

Having gathered knowledge on the differences of the original segments, we turned our interest to those companies that seem to be at the forefront already. Therefore, we had another look at the high readiness segment in particular, trying to find further distinguishing characteristics within this segment of companies. We analyzed the data within the high readiness segment again using an exploratory approach. We started to identify possible sub-segments within the high readiness segment along the expertise dimension. Once we confirmed the existence of two sub-segments we used the k-means clustering algorithm to establish a new variable assigning each dataset to one of the sub-segments. Therefore, establishing a sub-segment with low employee expertise (M=2.53; SD=1.38; N=40) and a second sub-segment with high employee expertise (M=5.14; SD=1.27; N=44).

For those companies that have higher employee expertise, we also find a significant difference in the contribution of customers from the retail industry (t=-2.302; p=.024). This reflects a higher contribution to the overall turnover from the customer-oriented industry. Also, we find a significant difference in the responses of perceived usability of competitor's products (t=-2.259; p=.027). Moreover, the perceived importance of usability as a trend over the next 5 years shows a significant difference for companies with higher employee expertise (t=-2.526; p=.014). These differences indicate that firms with higher employee expertise on usability also perceive more competitive pressure. We performed independent samples t-test's to analyze the two groups, identifying significant differences in the dimension perceived management support (t=-2.0375; p=.041). Management support is an important influencing factor for the direction and priorities of organizations. We find that firms with higher employee expertise with regard to usability also have a management that is more enthusiastic about usability. Besides, management also invests more time to understand the benefits of usability to the company as a whole. Moreover, the management in such companies clearly defines usability goals and it assigns higher value to usability than functional aspects of the product. In addition, we find that firms with more expertise on usability also seem to have more customers from the retail industry. Furthermore, these companies perceive more competitive pressure and in turn exhibit more management support on usability matters.

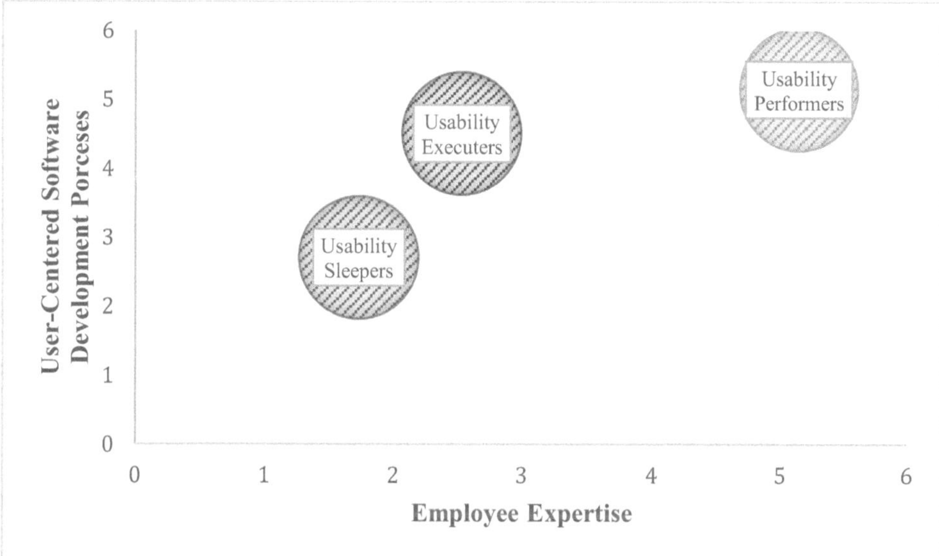

Figure 1 – Visualization of the three identified segments

5 Discussion

The thorough analysis of the questionnaire and our exploratory approach allowed us to identify two important differentiators among the high usability readiness firms. First, we will discuss the influence of business sector under consideration of usability in the SD process. Second, the outmost importance of management support for the success of efforts for increased usability will be stressed.

The influence of the business sector on usability readiness

The business sector seems to have an important moderating role as those software companies which have a high share of revenue from the retail sector also have more usability expertise in their company. This development might be induced by the general development of e-commerce. Usability expertise and even user experience management have progressed much faster in e-commerce as in the traditional enterprise systems realm. Retail firms have to think about the new threats to their business model through the new multi-channel business environment. The retail industry is adapting to new challenges through fierce international competition. Such companies (e.g. Amazon) have analyzed usability and user experience of their online presences in great detail. Furthermore, user organizations in the retail industry are close to B2C customers and generally have less specialized staff. These two factors may lead to additional pressure towards usability of enterprise systems in the retail sector. All in all, there are strong indicators that the user organization and their demands act as accelerators for usability developments in the German software industry. SMEs that have a profound knowledge of usability methods also seem to have a significantly different view on the perceived usability of competitors' products. They perceive the products of competitors as to be significantly better in terms of usability than those in the segment with a lower readiness. This shows the great value of usability knowledge as enabler for observing and understanding competitive threats. However, this can also be interpreted as being due to the business sector that the firms are in, since user organizations' expectations seem to fuel the usability efforts of the software SMEs. What is more, the perceived importance of usability as a trend over the next five years also varies significantly between high and low segment firms. Greater knowledge is connected with a higher perceived importance of the usability trend.

The influence of management support on usability readiness

Management support has long been known to be important for the overall success of information systems projects (Doll 1985). Our exploratory analysis leads to the finding of significantly higher management support for usability initiatives for the sub-segment of firms with a high usability expertise. The enthusiasm of the management about usability seems to be an important driver for gathering usability knowledge in an organization. This finding is further supported by the fact that there is also a significant difference in the reported time that is invested by the management to understand the benefits of usability to the company between the two segments. The prioritization of usability over functional aspects and the definition of clear usability goals was significantly higher for firms in the segment with a very high usability expertise. In turn this means further knowledge with regard to user research, application design, and methods for usability evaluation. Thus, it can be said that management support is crucial for the success of usability initiatives and the general depth of the implementation of usability methods in German software SMEs.

Today, German software SMEs face the growing pressure of end-user expectations in terms of the growing demand for the consumerization of their products (Degarmo et al. 2011; Scheiber et al. 2012). It seems necessary that firms react to this trend or even shape it proactively (e.g. Degarmo et al. 2011). To develop a holistic strategy for implementing usability methods in their SD organizations can be a key mechanism for German Software SME's to deal with competitive pressure arising from the trend of consumerization for end-users. Already, some firms are responding to the growing market pressure by developing a deeper understanding about usability design methods and how they can enable themselves to meet the clients' demands. However, the results of the study indicate that many German software

SMEs are still in strategic straightjackets. They are mainly focused on the design and inclusion of new functions into their products (Scheiber et al. 2012) instead of the overall value creation for the end-user and subsequently customer organization. This is a potential impediment to future growth as more and more customer organizations in Germany seem to focus on usability (Scheiber et al. 2012).

6 Conclusion

German software SMEs can be divided into segments of firms that either have a high usability readiness and those that have a significantly lower one. In addition, the segment of high readiness firms can be differentiated even more alongside other characteristics, such as managements' attitude towards usability and the general perception of the business sector. We were able to show that environmental factors seem to influence the absorption of usability methods in the German software industry, which mainly provides highly specialized solutions for specific applications markets. Furthermore, it has been shown that the management's perception is of particular importance for determining the intensity of a firm's usability initiatives. Implications for practitioners are that clear responsibilities for the usability matters in development organizations have to be assigned. In addition, managers should be aware that people-oriented management is necessary to foster the awareness for usability in the organization. These insights complement earlier findings such as e.g. the need for a usability budget (Woywode et al. 2012).

Finally, some limitations of our research have to be mentioned. The explored data set was obtained in 2011. Hence, the knowledge of usability methods can be much more widespread today. Moreover, the responses to the questionnaire are dominated by managing directors of the software firms with a size of 6-10 employees. Hence, we have to acknowledge that the sample has an impact on the responses to the questions related to management support. Thus, related questions can only be interpreted as a self-reported measure of the status quo.

Our future research focuses on the diagnosing the status quo of usability methods in SD organizations along principles for user-centered and agile SD. Such a diagnosis is required in order to develop actionable recommendations for practitioners based on the already determined principles. For instance, we want to devise management instructions for implementing usability methods in SD teams. The perspective of the user organization on factors influencing the usability of enterprise systems should also be addressed.

References

Brault, C., Lykkegaard, B., & Roques, B.-L. (2013). Ranking of the Top 100 European Software Vendor (pp. 1–7). Paris, FR.

Degarmo, T., Garland, P., & Stuckey, D. A. (2011). The consumerization of IT: The next-generation CIO (pp. 1–26). Delaware, USA.

Doll, W. J. (1985). Avenues for Top Management Involvement in Successful MIS Development. MIS Quarterly, 9(1), 17–35.

European Union Commission. (2003). COMMISSION RECOMMENDATION - of 6 May 2003 concerning the definition of micro, small and medium-sized enterprises. Official Journal of the European Union, L 124, 36–41.

Friedewald, M., Rombach, H. D., Stahl, P., Broy, M., Hartkopf, S., Kimpeler, S., ... Zoche, P. (2001). Softwareentwicklung in Deutschland - Eine Bestandsaufnahme. Informatik-Spektrum, 24(2), 81–90.

Gemser, G., Jacobs, D., & Ten Cate, R. (2006). Design and Competitive Advantage in Technology-Driven Sectors: The Role of Usability and Aesthetics in Dutch IT Companies. Technology Analysis & Strategic Management, 18(5), 561–580.

Harter, D. E., Krishnan, M. S., & Slaughter, S. A. (2000). Effects of process maturity on quality, cycle time, and effort in software product development. Management Science, 46(4), 451–466.

International Organization for Standardization. (1998). ISO 9241-11: Ergonomic Requirements for Office Work with Visual Display Terminals (VDTs): Part 11: Guidance on Usability. Geneva, CH: International Organization for Standardization.

Kachigan, S. K. (1986). Statistical Analysis: An Interdisciplinary Introduction to Univariate and Multivariate Methods (p. 589). New York, NY, USA: Radius Press.

Mackay, D. J. C. (2003). Information Theory , Inference , and Learning Algorithms (p. 640). Cambridge, UK: Cambridge University Press.

Madan, A., & Dubey, S. K. (2012). Usability Evalution Methods: A Literature Review. International Journal of Engineering Science & ..., 4(2), 590–599.

Riemer, K., & Vehring, N. (2010). IT'S NOT A PROPERTY! EXPLORING THE SOCIO-MATERIALITY OF SOFTWARE USABILITY. In International Conference on Information Systems (p. Paper 215). St. Louis, MI, USA: AIS.

Scheiber, F., Wruk, D., Oberg, A., Britsch, J., Woywode, M., Maedche, A., ... Plach, M. (2012). Software Usability in Small and Medium Sized Enterprises in Germany: An Empirical Study. In A. Maedche, A. Botzenhardt, & L. Neer (Eds.), Software for People (pp. 39–52). Berlin, DE: Springer.

Seffah, B. A., & Metzker, E. (2004). The Obstacles and Myths of Usability and Software Engineering - Avoiding the usability pitfalls involved in managing the software development life cycle. Communications of the ACM, 47(12), 71–76.

Simon, H. (2009). Hidden Champions of the Twenty-First Century: The Success Strategies of Unknown World Market Leaders (p. 402). Dordrecht, NL: Springer.

Woywode, M., Mädche, A., Wallach, D., & Plach, M. (2012). Gebrauchstauglichkeit von Anwendungssoftware als Wettbewerbsfaktor für kleine und mittlere Unternehmen (KMU) : Abschlussbericht (p. 357). Mannheim, DE.

M. Koch, A. Butz & J. Schlichter (Hrsg.): Mensch und Computer 2014 Tagungsband,
München: Oldenbourg Wissenschaftsverlag, 2014, S. 195-204.

CONTEX(T)PLORER: A Mobile Inspector for Ubiquitous Environments

Maximilian Schirmer[1], Sven Bertel[1], Ronja Lars Wilkening[2]

Usability Research Group, Bauhaus-Universität Weimar[1]
plazz entertainment AG[2]

Abstract

The complex invisible interactions between components of ubiquitous environments present a challenge for end-users and thereby raise concerns of privacy and nontransparency. In this paper, we will introduce CONTEX(T)PLORER, a mobile inspector system that aims at lowering the acceptance barrier of ubiquitous computing environments. The inspector actively involves end-users in an in-situ investigation process: users select, explore, and inspect components in a ubiquitous environment while interacting with them. Individual components are used as entry points to the process. We will present a brief overview of the system's concept and implementation, and will discuss related work.

1 Introduction and Motivation

Due to the continuous technological and conceptual advances in the fields of mobile devices, cloud computing, and context awareness, the visions of ambient intelligence and ubiquitous computing are turning into an everyday reality. For example, smartphones can act as ambient sensor nodes (Schirmer & Höpfner 2011) thanks to their increased processing power and capabilities. Furthermore, active research in the field of context awareness provides interesting concepts for automatically adapting user environments based on detected contexts (Brown, et al. 1997, Rittenbruch 2002, Schilit, et al. 1994, Schmohl & Baumgarten 2008).

In this paper, we will repeatedly refer to the following ambient intelligence *scenario*: A group of co-workers whose workplaces are scattered throughout a large office building like to spend their coffee breaks together. Inviting everyone or making appointments is not practical for this group and has proven ineffective in the past, for instance as suitable times for breaks are likely to vary depending on employees' activities and schedules. Instead, smart ubiquitous technology installed in the coffee break room detects the number of people present and their current activities. When pre-defined people count and activity levels are reached, all interested "coffee breakers" are automatically notified. Also, the fully-automated coffee machine is triggered to prepare additional coffee for all participants that are expected to join. All ubiquitous environment components are tagged with QR codes for identification. One day, Jane, a new employee, joins the group and is baffled by the electronic components installed in the coffee kitchen. She is concerned by the components' potential to monitor activities of employees and has strong privacy concerns.

This scenario illustrates that, due to the experimental and advanced nature of the smart, interconnected components, and even with only a small number of components, the data flow in a ubiquitous environment can quickly become complex and overwhelming for the end-user. Such complexity can easily make it difficult to understand and oversee the results of their actions within the environment, to the effect that, for end-users, the embedded system and its functioning become nontransparent. Privacy concerns may arise, for example, due to embedded systems tracking the whereabouts of users or disclosing this information. Concerns resulting from such nontransparency (Weiser, et al. 1999) constitute a high acceptance barrier for ambient intelligence and ubiquitous computing. Lowering this barrier marks the first necessary step towards more widespread acceptance of such concepts and technologies.

In this paper, we will present the concept and a first prototype for CONTEX(T)PLORER, a mobile system that allows users to learn about the current state of a ubiquitous environment through component-based in-situ investigation. We favour this in-situ approach because it lowers the level of knowledge required to understanding which components are relevant when users interact with a ubiquitous environment. The system's investigation process aims at increasing the transparency in ubiquitous environments for their users by revealing the environment's components and interactions between them. It is built to support an interaction process with three steps: (1) *selection* of components of interest to a user, (2) *exploration* of the selected components' composition with respect to the structure of the environment, and (3) detailed *inspection* and manipulation of specific components.

The paper is structured as follows: Section 2 will present the main conceptual aspects of CONTEX(T)PLORER. Section 3 will introduce the prototype implementation and discusses aspects of user interaction with the system. Section 4 will give an overview of related work. Section 5 will summarise the paper and provide an outlook on future work.

2 Interaction Concept

CONTEX(T)PLORER is a mobile system that allows in-situ configuration and exploration of ubiquitous environment components at the same time at which users are interacting with them. It focuses on short-term, target-oriented configuration tasks that are conducted with on-site access to the components. Our main motivation for designing this system was to alleviate privacy concerns by allowing users in a ubiquitous environment to transparently learn about available components and their interconnections. We believe that in order to incorporate privacy aspects into ubiquitous computing, a seamless interplay of social norms, legal protection, and technology is required. An early concept in ubiquitous computing, feedback and control (Bellotti & Sellen 1993), is often stated as the happy medium towards privacy-aware ubiquitous computing. For us, feedback in this context means to inform users about information flows, to inform them which information is currently being disclosed, and to whom. Control on the other hand is supposed to put users into the position to define which information they want to disclose, and to whom.

In the scope of this paper, we will use the following types of ubiquitous environment component types: (1) sensors, (2) processors, and (3) actuators. Sensors gather data about users and their environments; processors evaluate sensor data and generate output based on aggregation or filtering; and actuators initiate reactions in the environment. Typically, these components are managed by sensor platforms or event-notification infrastructures (e.g., (Carzaniga, et al. 2001, Fitzpatrick, et al. 1999, Funk, et al. 2011, Gross, et al. 2006)).

From a technological point of view, the scenario introduced in the previous section may likely be realised based on movement and noise sensors in the coffee break room, and based on calendar sensors on the participants' computers. Processors in the form of threshold comparators (for movement and/or noise) and a calendar event parser aggregate and analyse incoming sensor data in order to determine activity in the room, as well as degrees of availability of individual participants. Based on the processors' results, email notifications and a control unit for the coffee machine are then triggered as actuators.

The new employee Jane uses CONTEX(T)PLORER to identify the ominous components in the coffee kitchen, and to learn about their interconnections as well as about the data flow between them. Because the system runs directly on her smartphone, she can experiment and interact with the components in-situ, and directly see the effects of her actions in the graphical user interface of CONTEX(T)PLORER.

2.1 Building Blocks

CONTEX(T)PLORER consists of three main conceptual building blocks. Based on our informal observations of typical interactions with sensor platforms and ubiquitous environments, we structured them into the three steps *selection*, *exploration*, and *inspection*. The steps occur in the sequence that we describe here, and each step's results influence the following steps. We understand this sequence as a form of applying a drill-down navigation paradigm from traditional graphical user interfaces to an interaction process that starts in the real world and ends with fine-grained insight and control of the inner workings of smart components in a ubiquitous environment.

Selection is a natural starting point for the interaction with environment components. It enables users to detect all available components in the environment and to define their personal components of interest by communicating their interest to the inspector system. The selection process is realised by scanning and interpreting component identifiers, enabling users to actively define their entry points to the subsequent exploration process. In our *scenario*, Jane selects one of the sensor components in the coffee kitchen by scanning their QR code. That way, she does not require any knowledge about the component, other than where its location is marked in the environment.

The process of selecting components is shown in Figure 1(a) and employs one of a wide range of possible component identification methods. Often this is realised as browsing a list of available components, entering an identification number, or using a scanning method. Setting filters to confine the search space simplifies the selection process. Such filters can restrict the set of components by type, location, function, or by other relevant parameters.

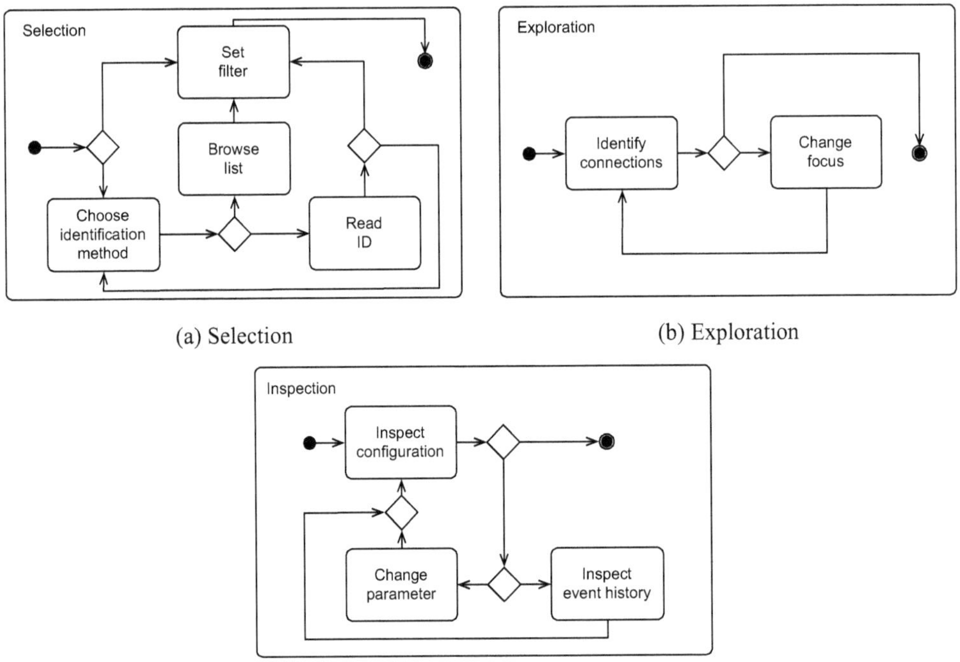

(a) Selection (b) Exploration

(c) Inspection

Figure 1: Activity diagrams of the interaction steps.

Exploration helps users to learn about the environment's structure and the transitive interconnections between components by visualising all relevant components. Components can also be clustered in order to abstract from their complexity. In the exploration process, users are able to analyse the composition of these logical clusters of components. During the process, users incrementally shift the visualisation's focus until they reach a desired component for closer inspection (cf. Figure 1(b)). Reflecting back on our *scenario*, Jane has selected a noise sensor in the coffee kitchen in the first step. She is now able to see all outgoing connections from this sensor. By setting the focus to one of the connected threshold processors, she ultimately explores the complete data flow from her sensor up to an actuator at the end of the processing chain. In essence, exploration employs selection to give users the opportunity to shift focus between several components of interest.

Inspection allows users to view the current component values as well as the history of events associated with this component. Furthermore, configuration parameters are checked and configured in order to change the environment's behaviour (cf. Figure 1(c)).

In our *scenario*, Jane has reached a desktop notification actuator that sends messages to the computers of co-workers who subscribed to be notified when the conditions seem appropriate for the initiation of a coffee break. Of course, the actuator does not expose the identities of the subscribers. From the history log of events, she learns that the default setting of the actuators sends out repeated notifications until users either accept or decline the invitation. She finds this setting too annoying and configures her actuator to show only a small notification window that disappears after a few seconds.

2.2 Graph Visualisation and Animation

CONTEX(T)PLORER provides a rich graph visualisation of components and their interconnections. In the visualisation, we distinguish two types of graph nodes: cluster nodes and regular nodes. Cluster nodes encapsulate a number of other nodes and thereby provide abstraction or grouping of environment components (cf. Figure 2).

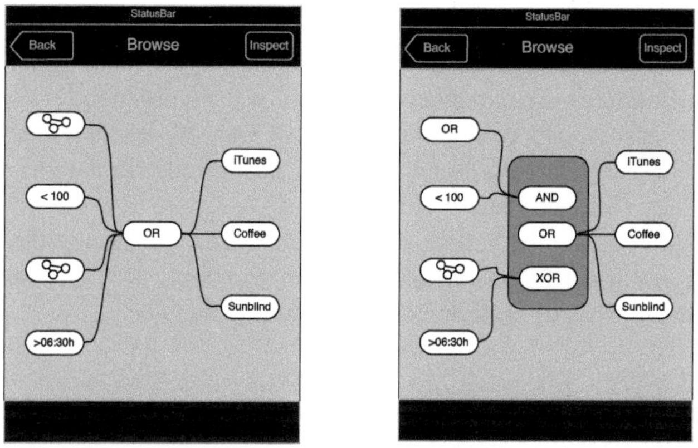

(a) Regular nodes (b) Cluster node

Figure 2: Node types in the graph visualisation.

At any time, the visualisation provides a single logical viewing frame, consisting of a focus node in the centre, and neighbouring nodes positioned to the left and right of it. If the focus node is a cluster node, all other nodes that have connections to nodes outside of the cluster are displayed inside of the focus node. This helps to visualise the data flow between this cluster and other clusters. Users then change focus by pressing on any one of the displayed nodes, the inspector then displays this node's logical viewing frame. As we have previously introduced, changing focus is an essential part in our interaction process. That is why we have used animations to provide users with a clear understanding of the transitions that occur from one focus to another. Foremost, this means that users should be able to see which nodes are identical in two consecutive logical viewing frames. Figure 3 outlines the animation steps during a change of focus. Shaded nodes are visible in the start view, but not in the finish view. Dotted nodes are spawned and white nodes remain visible throughout the sequence.

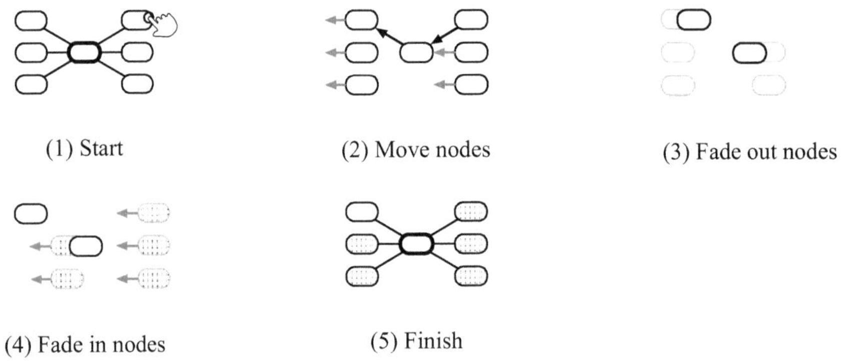

Figure 3: Sequence of animation steps during focus change.

During the animation, an already visible node is moved to the centre. This node may be positioned to the left/right of, or inside (cluster) the old focus node. Figure 3(1) points out that a user selects a neighbouring node to the right of the current focus node. The position of the selected node determines the movement direction of the animation (cf. Figure 3(2)). The previous focus node assumes its position at the left or right border, while all nodes that are not part of the new logical viewing frame move out horizontally in the animation direction. At the same time, they fade out visually (cf. Figure 3(3)). Figure 3(4) shows how new nodes fade in while they move along the animation direction to their position in the logical viewing frame. Finally, the result of the animation is shown in Figure 3(5) and provides the final arrangement with the new focus node and all neighbouring nodes.

3 Prototype and Walkthrough

The CONTEX(T)PLORER prototype is realised as a mobile application on the Apple iPhone platform. We have deployed and successfully tested the application on iPhone 3GS, iPhone 4 and iPhone 5 devices. CONTEX(T)PLORER possesses a modular architecture with modules for *selection*, *exploration*, and *inspection*, and an adapter module responsible for the connection between the graphical user interface and the data model. The sequence of these modules follows a task model derived from our informal observations of typical interactions with sensor platforms and ubiquitous environments. Currently, we can either use an SQLite database that simulates structural information (i.e., components with parameters and values, interconnections, and clusters) about environments, or our lightweight smartphone sensor data distribution platform. The platform collects sensor data from smartphones and provides a socket-based interface for accessing the gathered sensor data. Due to the modular nature of the adapter pattern that we employed in the implementation of CONTEX(T)PLORER's data model, we can connect to existing sensor platforms with manageable effort. It is also possible to combine collections of components from different platforms as a single data model.

As shown in Figure 4(a), users initiate the *selection process* from a structured list of components. Typically, this list is already populated with previously discovered components. Users add nearby components by scanning their QR codes. Each environment component is associated with a QR code as visual identifier. Users can also add components by browsing the complete list of all available sensors, processors, and actuators (provided by the corresponding sensor platform). After users have assembled their individual list of components, they can mark particular components of interest. These components are then highlighted to indicate that they are included in the exploration process. Users can also choose to ignore such highlighting and include all components in the list by toggling a switch button. In our *scenario*, Jane wonders what kind of equipment all the strange components in the kitchen are. She scans the QR code of a noise sensor and begins to explore.

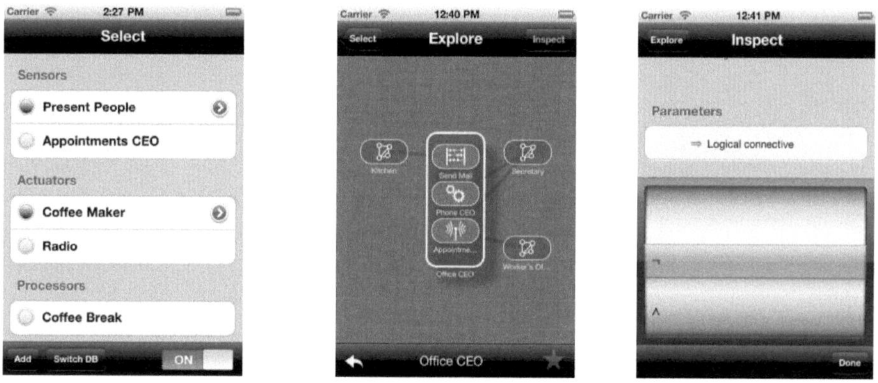

(a) (b) (c)

Figure 4: Graphical user interface of CONTEX(T)PLORER.

The *exploration process* as shown in Figure 4(b) provides a dynamic graph visualisation with animations. Animations help users to keep track of components and connections while navigating through the graph structure. Each node in the graph represents an environment component or an aggregated cluster of components. Nodes are labelled with identifiers and provide icons according to their type. When users tap a node in the graph, the view centres on this node and its connected neighbours. Additionally, the centred node is highlighted by a white border and shadow. If the centred node is a cluster, the enclosed components with connections to nodes outside of the cluster are revealed. At any time, users can navigate backwards along their exploration path with the help of a "back button". Furthermore, a star-shaped button allows users to mark components they have discovered in the exploration process to be included in their own component list. Following our previous *scenario*, the coffee kitchen is a cluster of components (movement/noise sensors, coffee machine actuator), with connections to other clusters for participants' offices (calendar sensors, email notification actuator), and to a cluster of processors (activity, availability).

Users start the *inspection process* (cf. Figure 4(c)) by navigating to a component node and tapping the "Inspect" button. The application presents an inspection view with meta information about the selected component (i.e., name, description, and icon), a list of parameters, and a list of inputs and outputs with their current values. Tapping on one of the list items reveals additional details. For parameters, a configuration interface with text fields and drop-down lists of possible configuration values is presented. For inputs and outputs, the application shows a list of received or sent values with timestamps. In our *scenario*, Jane inspects the notification actuator and sets her personal notification preferences. The user interface elements in the inspection view correspond to the complexity of the inspected components. For example, simple processor components may only require sliders or drop-down menus, while more complex ones may require the user to make changes to a script using a text field.

4 Related Work

CONTEX(T)PLORER is closely related to the field of end-user configuration of ubiquitous environments. Within this active field of research, several interactive editor applications exist that allow users to learn about the components in their environment, and to actively change the configuration of these components. The *Speakeasy Browser* (Newman, et al. 2002) is a text-based editor that allows the configuration of various environment components by forming connections between available modules, which are visualised in a tree structure. The editor follows the paradigm of a file browser and is realised as a website, so that it can also be accessed by mobile devices. In contrast to CONTEX(T)PLORER, the editor does not provide any graphical abstractions. The *Jigsaw Editor* (Humble, et al. 2003) puts great emphasis on an easy-to-use, abstract graphical user interface. Available environment components are visualised as jigsaw pieces. However, this simplified user interface also limits its capabilities. In contrast to CONTEX(T)PLORER, the editor does not allow users to filter available components, and it cannot be used in-situ on a mobile device. The *CollaborationBus: Aqua Editor* (Schirmer & Gross 2011) is a graphical editor for ubiquitous environments that uses a graph-based visualisation of the interconnections between components. It finds similarities between environment configurations. In contrast to CONTEX(T)PLORER, the editor cannot be used in-situ on a mobile device, does not cluster components and does not provide component filtering. CONTEX(T)PLORER is also related to the concept of the inspector window in graphical user interfaces: a special palette window found in a wide range of desktop applications. Mostly used in productivity tools, the inspector provides information and manipulation of an entity's properties. The content of the inspector changes adaptively with the currently selected entity. Users typically select an entity in their productivity environment (e.g., a shape in a vector drawing application, a sound clip in an audio editor, or a piece of text in a text editor), the inspector window reacts to this selection and displays information and settings for this entity. Users then explore their options and learn about their selection, before they finally interact with the settings to manipulate their selected entity. This behaviour served as a model for the interaction process of CONTEX(T)PLORER, and we aimed to translate it to a mobile platform. Our goals behind introducing a dedicated *inspection* building block that helps rendering ubiquitous technical components and their interrelations less opaque for the user are comparable to goals behind rendering automatically generated user models and user profiles less opaque for the modelled/profiled user (e.g., (Ahn, et al. 2007, Carmichael, et al. 2005)). The goal of *scrutability* (Kay 2006) is comparable to our goal of *transparency*.

5 Discussion and Outlook

In this paper, we introduced CONTEX(T)PLORER, a mobile inspector for ubiquitous environments. The inspector is based on a concept for a three-fold investigation process that allows users to explore an environment *in-situ*, while interacting with its components. We presented our first implementation of the concept and described its user interaction. The implementation provides a modular architecture with an adapter interface for connecting sensor platforms. CONTEX(T)PLORER goes beyond other currently existing approaches in that it combines graphical, user-explorable abstractions of components' interconnections with display filtering options (e.g., based on an end-user's preferences) and a tiered investigation process. This functionality is realised on a mobile platform for in-situ use.

The current QR-code-based identification mechanism in our prototype system clearly collides with the intended invisibility of ubiquitous computing devices; it has been chosen purely for our proof of concept. We will explore additional identification methods, for example indoor positioning or beacon-based methods (using Wifi or Bluetooth LE), as these methods involve far less explicit interactions. We are currently implementing and improving a sensor platform for using smartphone sensor data in ubiquitous environments that will soon become the primary data source for CONTEX(T)PLORER. Furthermore, we plan to pay closer attention to the interaction steps described in this paper. Specifically, one can question whether an *exploration* step always needs to follow a *selection* step, or whether both may not also occur in reversed or repeatedly alternating orders. We will conduct further user studies to test the hypotheses derived from our informal observations of the structure of the inspection process and to learn about usability issues our design might have.

For future work, we believe that it would be interesting to explore the possibility of using the gathered context data of the sensor platform in order to improve the selection phase. In the most simple use case, this could help to adapt the search space in a different way for novice users and expert users. Other options could be highlighting the most frequently used components or dynamically adapting the level of detail in clusters (e.g., based on different profiles of interest, contexts, or on different roles of end-users). Last, it seems useful to examine what kind of inspections best serve to alleviate (or substantiate) end-users' privacy concerns. For example, when nontransparency of the ubiquitous system's structure is at the root of privacy concerns, does it suffice to present some (selected) uses of the collected data (such as was the case for Jane, in our scenario above)? Or, would alleviating privacy concerns usually necessitate communicating all uses of the collected data? If the latter is the case, the inspection process presented here may be easily extended to include information on the user's progress of inspecting all the relevant components and their interconnections, guiding the inspection process by marking up those components and interconnections which the user has not yet inspected.

References

Ahn, J. W., et al. (2007). Open user profiles for adaptive news systems: help or harm? *Proc. of 16th international conference on World Wide Web*, ACM, 11-20.

Bellotti, V., Sellen, A. (1993). Design for privacy in ubiquitous computing environments. *Proc. of ECSCW'93*, ACM, 77-92.

Brown, P. J., et al. (1997) Context-aware Applications: from the Laboratory to the Marketplace. *IEEE Personal Communications*, 4, 58-64.

Carmichael, D. J., et al. (2005) Consistent modelling of users, devices and sensors in a ubiquitous computing environment. *User Modelling and User-Adapted Interaction*, 15, 197-234.

Carzaniga, A., et al. (2001) Design and Evaluation of a Wide-Area Event Notification Service. *ACM Transactions on Computer Systems*, 19, 332-383.

Fitzpatrick, G., et al. (1999). Augmenting the workaday world with Elvin. *Proc. of Sixth European Conference on Computer Supported Cooperative Work - ECSCW'99*, 431-450.

Funk, A., et al. (2011). Open Sensor Platforms: The Sensor Web Enablement Framework and Beyond. *Proc. of 6. Konferenz Mobile und ubiquitäre Informationssysteme - MMS'11*, 39-52.

Gross, T., et al. (2006) Sens-ation: A Service-Oriented Platform for Developing Sensor-Based Infrastructures. *IJIPT*, 1, 159-167.

Humble, J., et al. (2003). "Playing with the Bits": User-configuration of Ubiquitous Domestic Environments. *Proc. of UbiComp'03*, 256-263.

Kay, J. (2006). Scrutable adaptation: because we can and must. *Proc. of Adaptive hypermedia and adaptive web-based systems, 4th international conference*, Springer, 11-19.

Newman, M. W., et al. (2002). Designing for Serendipity: Supporting End-user Configuration of Ubiquitous Computing Environments. *Proc. of DIS'02*, 147-156.

Rittenbruch, M. (2002) Atmosphere: A Framework for Contextual Awareness. *Int. Journal of Human-Computer Interaction*, 14, 159-180.

Schilit, B. N., et al. (1994). Context-Aware Computing Applications. *Proc. of First Workshop on Mobile Computing Systems and Applications - WMCSA'94*, 85-90.

Schirmer, M., Gross, T. (2011) Lightweight Editing of Distributed Ubiquitous Environments - The CollaborationBus Aqua Editor. *CollTech 2010 Proc.*, 2.

Schirmer, M., Höpfner, H. (2011). SenST: Approaches for Reducing the Energy Consumption of Smartphone-Based Context Recognition. *Proc. of CONTEXT'11*, 250-263.

Schmohl, R., Baumgarten, U. (2008). Context-aware Computing: a Survey Preparing a Generalized Approach. *Proc. of IMECS 2008*, 744-750.

Weiser, M., et al. (1999) The Origins of Ubiquitous Computing Research at PARC in the late 1980s. *IBM Systems Journal*, 38, 693-696.

M. Koch, A. Butz & J. Schlichter (Hrsg.): Mensch und Computer 2014 Tagungsband,
München: Oldenbourg Wissenschaftsverlag, 2014, S. 205-214.

Visualizing Locations for a Search Engine for the Physical World

Markus Funk, Robin Boldt, Marcus Eisele, Taha Yalcin, Niels Henze, Albrecht Schmidt

Institute for Visualization and Interactive Systems, University of Stuttgart

Abstract

Today, search engines on the Internet allow us to instantly find almost any kind of information or media. Unfortunately, the same capabilities are not available in the physical world, except for in industrial settings such as automated warehouses. Therefore, we implemented a stationary prototype that supports finding objects in everyday environments. The location is represented using a web-based search interface. In a user study, we compared four different representations for our stationary object finding system. Results favor a last seen image representation and a 2d map and show that more complex representations are not suitable for representing results of a search engine for the physical world. The participants were throughout positive about using a system like this in their daily lives, although there were concerns for privacy. Based on these results, we argue that scalable physical search engines can be built for everyday environments; that searching for physical objects can be made understandable to users; and that there are many practical and commercial cases where such systems would be beneficial.

1 Introduction

In the digital world, we are used to being able to easily find information through a variety of search engines and information retrieval tools. Almost any piece of information or media created by man can now be located through a simple keyword search. In the physical world, on the other hand, we do not have similar abilities to search and locate items.

In this paper, we ask the question if it would be possible to apply the same principles that currently power digital search engines to the physical world? If so, what happens when it becomes possible to find literally everything? Imagine if the location of any physical object would be instantly available for searching, in the same way that popular Internet search engines allow us to find information on the World Wide Web today. This would mean that you could ask a system where you left your keys, or what place a book was last seen.

This could have long-ranging effects on human behavior. In the virtual domain, desktop search engines have already changed the behavior of users. For many users carefully organized hierarchical structures of folders, as well as specific Internet addresses, have become irrelevant. If the vision of a physical search engine becomes reality, it would facilitate not just the solution of trivial problems, such as finding a missing item. It could potentially change the way we interact with the world. Currently, humans use many strategies to manage and arrange the objects around us (Kirsh, 1995). If that was not necessary, we could instead organize objects according to practical or aesthetic criteria. We could even stop caring exactly where an object is, as long is it is findable – such as all those books lent to friends, which are currently to be considered lost. Furthermore, knowing about the things we use and their locations would allow completely new systems for personalization and context-aware services, as well as facilitate fundamentally new business models. We could potentially apply all the algorithms currently in use to recommend and target content on the Internet to the physical world.

For those kinds of search engines for the physical world, the representation of search results is important. In this paper, we want to find out which representation of locations is most suitable for a room-level environment like a living room or an office room. Traditionally, location is represented through 2D, 3D or textual representations, which need knowledge about the environment. Recently it has been proposed to represent indoor location through a last seen image representation. In this paper, we compare these four representations by conducting a user study inside a room-level test scenario. We show that an image-based representation of search results that does not require a model of the environment and no exact location of objects results in the same performance as more complex representations. Consequently, scalable and model-independent real-world search engines become feasible. In the following, we give an overview about related work, describe the four representations and present the results of the study.

2 Related Work

Search engines for the Internet are today a well established part of the Information Retrieval field, and have become the foundation of successful companies such as Google and Yahoo!. The vision of search in the real world has initially been tightly linked to wearable cameras and the search and indexing of personal first-person view recordings (Mann, 1998). An example of the use of video retrieval techniques in this context can be found in (Tancharoen et al., 2005). More general concepts for search engines for the physical world are a much newer concept and have emerged over the last few years with advances in camera technologies, sensors, and computer vision algorithms. On a conceptual level, they can be considered a part of the Internet of Things (IoT) vision, where real-world physical objects get connected and equipped with processing and sensing capabilities (Mattern & Floerkemeier, 2010). Typically, this has been achieved by attaching electronics or tags directly to the objects that are to be monitored. Early examples of systems that use tags to connect physical objects to digital information include Webstickers (Ljungstrand et al., 2000), where a printed barcode sticker could be attached to any object to associate it with an online URL; and the collection of systems that demonstrate how electronic tags can bridge physical and virtual worlds as seen in (Want et al. 1999) However, neither of these systems kept track of the location of tagged objects, but rather used the objects to access information or initiate actions, hence providing physical objects as links or pointers to information (Holmquist et al., 1999). This means that a coarse location of an object is known only at the time when its tag is read and the whereabouts of the reader is (Song et al., 2007).

Going beyond simple proximity information, a location technology has to be included. There are basically two options: either that tags can locate where they are, or the elements that read the tags can provide location information. Are variety of solutions are possible here. The combined use of the commercial Ubisense asset tracking system and visual markers is explored in (Song et al., 2007). Changes in the location and position of objects can be measured using passive RFID tags, which is experimentally assessed in (Fishkin et al., 2004) A reverse approach for locating objects is suggested in (Bohn, 2008), where the infrastructure (e.g. the floor) contains a dense grid of RFID tags and the object includes a reader. By reading the tags and consulting a map in which the tag locations are noted, an object can determine its location. Recently, the idea of using tags and other means to locate and search for entities in the real world has been explored in several projects. A comprehensive survey of such tag-based real-world search engines can be found in (Roemer et al., 2010).

For smart environments, a number of systems for indexing and searching objects have been explored. SearchLight presents a search function for pervasive environments using a ceiling-mounted camera/projector system (Butz et al., 2004). A system with a similar objective, but using ultrasound and RFID is presented in (Nakada et al., 2005). Another search engine for everyday objects that are tagged with RFID is presented in (Nickels et al., 2013). The paper describes a hierarchical approach to the search process and requires the instrumentation of furniture with readers. All of these approaches typically require a significant infrastructure and an augmentation of all objects with RFID or visual tags. One example that does not require tagging is Distributed Image Search (DIS) (Yan et al., 2008), which allows for searching of visual features using a submitted image. However, DIS does not build a database of known objects but acts purely by identifying visual features in the image stream. The Antonius system (Funk et al., 2013) equips the user with a wearable camera, which is constantly recognizing previously registered objects.

Location can be represented *physically*, *symbolically*, *absolutely*, or *relatively* (Hightower & Borriello, 2001). A taxonomy for visualizing location-based information is introduced by (Suomela & Lehikoinen, 2004). They distinguish between the dimensions (3D, 2D, 1D, and none) and the view: first person view and third person view - where first person is the representation of location from a user-centric view and third person is the representation of location combined with the user's current position. The taxonomy is denoted as MV (m, v), where m is the dimension and v is the view.

Different techniques to visualize an object's indoor location would require different technical implementations. Presenting the location of an object in a 3D representation, for example, requires a localization technique and a model of the environment. In contrast, presenting the location by providing an image of the surrounding of the object's current location (Funk et al., 2014) requires a camera system. Thus, it is important to learn about the differences between representation techniques for object's indoor locations to guide the technical development of object localization systems.

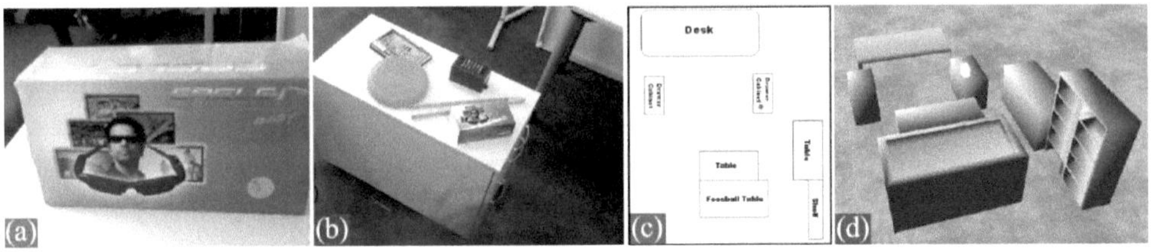

Figure 1: Representations used in our prototype: (a) Reference image that is displayed to the user to find an object and to initialize the image search. (b)–(d) Representations displayed in our prototype to find an object: (b) Last seen image representation, (c) 2D map representation with the object as red dot, and (d) full 3D representation of the demo scenario (sought object is represented as a white box).

3 Representation of Location

In our prototypical implementation, we compare four different representations (see Figure 1) of search results in context of a real-world search engine. It is designed to present the search result using one of the four representations. To describe the four representations, we use the taxonomy by (Suomela & Lehikoinen, 2004) and the categories of representing location after (Hightower & Borriello, 2001).

Textual representation

For the textual representation, we defined logical zones within the demo scenario (Kirsh, 1995). The zones are located on furniture placed in the room and named accordingly. Also, there is a huge zone, which reaches over the whole room. When zones are included in a larger zone, including zones are written after the parent zone. E.g. a shelf, which is in the lab will be represented as "lab–>shelf". This symbolic representation is in the category MV(0,0).

2D representation

The 2D representation uses a 2D map of the demo scenario (see Figure 2). The map is aligned north-up (up on the map corresponds to north in the environment). The location of the sought object is denoted as a red dot. The user's position is not displayed, as we use a MV(2,1) first person view with absolute representation.

3D representation

For the 3D representation, we created a 3D model of the demo scenario using Google SketchUp 8. The 3D representation is not part of the web-application as we used the OGRE engine to display the 3D model. Sought objects are displayed as a white box at the exact 3D location as in the real world. The user is able to move freely through the 3D space of this absolute representation viewing from a MV(3,1) first person view.

Last seen image

As an alternative representation, we use the last seen image. It displays the last picture, in which the sought object was recognized. The image also shows surrounding objects or furniture and gives the user contextual information about the location of the object (see Figure 2). This relative representation can be categorized as MV(3,1).

Figure 2 – A participant is trying to find an object in the demo scenario.

4 Evaluation

We conducted a controlled lab study to compare the 4 location representations in the context of a real-world search engine. In the study, the participants had to locate objects using a real-world search engine with each of the representations.

Method

We conducted the study using a repeated measures design with the 4 search layouts as independent variable. The order of the conditions was counterbalanced using Balanced Latin Square. We used objective and subjective measures as dependent variables. As objective measures, we used the time a participant needs to understand where an object is located (understanding time) and the time a participant needs to find and touch the object (task completion time). To determine the understanding time, we measured the time the participant spent in front of the PC using the search interface with the current location representation. The task completion time was measured from the moment the participant left the PC until the sought object was touched. In addition, we collected qualitative subjective feedback from the participants using the NASA TLX (Hart & Staveland, 1988) and the SUS (Bangor et al., 2008) questionnaire after each condition.

First, participants were given time to make themselves familiar with the demo scenario (see Figure 2). The scenario contained about 50 objects, which were placed onto furniture in order to make the search task harder. In addition, we used 12 searchable objects, which were not part of the scenario that was shown to the participant at the beginning. Each of the searchable objects belongs to one of the categories: small, medium or large. To prevent the participant from memorizing an object's location, a searchable object was placed into the scenario secretly after the participant was familiar with the scenario. The order of the searchable objects' sizes was also counterbalanced in each condition. For each of the four representations, the participant had to search for three objects - one belonging to each category. Therefore, the participant used our application, which displayed a reference image and one of the four location representations. After an object was found, it was removed from the scenario and a new object was placed without the participant seeing the new location. When the participants found three objects using one representation, they were asked to fill the SUS and TLX questionnaires.

We recruited 28 participants (9 female, 19 male). The participants were between 11 and 44 years old (M=26.1, SD=6,55). Most of the participants were students with various majors, e.g. computer science, international business administration or mechanics. In an initial questionnaire, 26 participants stated to be searching for something at least once per week. In fact, 17 participants stated to search for an object daily.

Results

Including welcoming the participant, a short introduction to the topic and the demo scenario and all questionnaires, the study took around 30 minutes per participant. We used an analysis of variance (ANOVA) to compare the conditions with paired t-tests as follow-up post-hoc tests. Bonferroni correction is used to prevent inflation of type I errors.

Detailed descriptive statistical results are shown in Table 1. For all conditions participants reported a low task load between 23.53 and 28.28 on the NASA TLX scale (between 0=no task load and 120=high task load). An ANOVA revealed no significant differences between the conditions for the NASA TLX ($F(3, 81)=1.277$, $p=0.288$). With scores between 74.82 and 80.71 participants rated all search layouts similarly high on the SUS (between 1=not usable and 100=highly usable) and an ANOVA revealed no significant differences ($F(3, 81)=1.304$, $p=0.279$). The average task completion time is between 5.45s and 6.00s. Again, an ANOVA did not reveal a significant difference between the conditions ($F(3, 81)=0.934$, $p=0.428$).

On average, participants needed 9.94s to understand the textual description, 10.66s to understand the image, 9.41s to understand the 2D-map, and 12.63s to understand the 3D-map. An ANOVA revealed a significant difference for the time participants needed to understand the search layouts ($F(3, 81)=8.740$, $p<0.001$). Follow-up post-hoc test revealed that participants needed significantly more time to understand the 3D scene compared to the textual description ($p=0.006$) and the 2D-map ($p<0.001$).

Representation	**TLX-Score**	**SUS-Score**	**Task Completion Time**	**Understanding Time**
Textual Description	28.28 (SD=19.16)	74.82 (SD=17.11)	5.68s (SD=1.38)	9.94s (SD=3.74)
Last Seen Image	27.67 (SD=16.59)	79.19 (SD=12.24)	5.45s (SD=1.05)	10.66s (SD=4.45)
2D-Map	23.53 (SD=14.22)	80.71 (SD=14.65)	6.00s (SD=2.49)	9.41s (SD=4.12)
3D-Scene	24.50 (SD=14.88)	78.39 (SD=14.06)	5.61s (SD=2.40)	12.63s (SD=5.65)

Table 1: Results of the user study. All scores and times are the arithmetic mean over all participants.

5 Discussion

The results of the user study reveal, that all four representations have no significant differences in task load, usability and task completion time. Only the understanding time of the 3D-scene representation proved to be significantly worse than the other representation's understanding time. The results are so far independent from the technology that is used to implement a real-world search engine. According to the results, a real-world search engine does not need to implement a 3D scene or an accurate floor plan of the area to display search results as they are needed by the 3D, 2D and textual representation. It can be argued that if a wearable camera is used to recognize an object within a room a last seen image representation would be the easiest representation to implement. It might be sufficient to provide a room-level location information combined with a last seen image representation rather than implementing a model of the environment.

Figure 3 – An overview of all used objects in our contextual follow-up study. In the images there is enough contextual information that detailed location information might not be needed.

6 Contextual Follow-up Study

We conducted a follow-up study to further investigate how accurate the simpler image-based representation is. Therefore, we took pictures of 20 objects in an office environment. The office consists of 12 rooms. We recruited 10 participants (1 female, 9 male, average age 33.7, SD=6.37), who are familiar with the office environment, and showed them the pictures. The participants had to name the room, in which the object is located. Overall the participants could name 18,6 (SD=1.07) of the 20 rooms in the pictures correctly, which is a success rate of 93%. The most common error, which was made by 6 participants, was a picture taken in front of a shelf, where just the content of the shelf was visible. The results of the study show that participants, who are familiar with the scenario, can identify an object's position if the location information is vague, e.g. "in this building" by using the contextual information provided in a last seen image.

7 System Recommendation

Based on the results of both of our studies, we recommend a camera-based search engine which can be installed firmly in an environment, e.g. a living room or running on a wearable computer e.g. on smart glasses. By combining a last seen image representation of search results and a room-level indoor location information e.g. WiFi-based, a wearable search engine for the real world can function in new environments without having a model of the scene and without using a precise indoor-location system.

8 Conclusion

In this paper, we compared four representations for search results of a real-world search engine. In our study participants were able to locate physical objects based on an image-based representation. In two studies we found that an image-based representation is as suitable for presenting real-world search results as 2D, 3D or textual representation. Furthermore, an image-based representation does not need any model of the environment and does not need precise location information. We believe that by using an image-based representation of search results, a scalable and model-independent real-world search engine can be built.

Acknowledgements

This project is sponsored by the German Research Foundation (DFG) in the Cluster of Excellence in Simulation Technology (EXC 310/1) at the University of Stuttgart.

References

Bangor, A., Kortum, P. T., and Miller, J. T. (2008) An empirical evaluation of the system usability scale. Intl. Journal of Human–Computer Interaction 24.

Bohn, J. (2008) Prototypical implementation of location-aware services based on a middleware architecture for super-distributed RFID tag infrastructures. *Personal and Ubiquitous Computing*, 12(2), 155-166.

Butz, A., Schneider, M., and Spassova, M. Searchlight–a lightweight search function for pervasive environments. In *Pervasive Computing*. 2004.

Fishkin, K., Jiang, B., Philipose, M., & Roy, S. (2004) I sense a disturbance in the force: Unobtrusive detection of interactions with RFID-tagged objects. *UbiComp 2004: Ubiquitous Computing*, 268-282.

Funk, M., Schmidt, A., and Holmquist, L. E. (2013) Antonius: A mobile search engine for the physical world. In *Adj. Proc. of Ubicomp*.

Funk, M., Boldt, R., Pfleging, B., Pfeiffer, M., Henze, N., & Schmidt, A. (2014) Representing indoor location of objects on wearable computers with head-mounted displays. *In Proc. of the 5th Augmented Human International Conference*, 18-22.

Hart, S. G., and Staveland, L. E. (1988) Development of nasa-tlx: Results of empirical and theoretical research. *Human mental workload* 1.

Hightower, J., and Borriello, G. (2001) Location systems for ubiquitous computing. *Computer 34.*

Holmquist, L.E., Redström, J. and Ljungstrand, P. (1999) Token-Based Access to Digital Information. Proc. *Handheld and Ubiquitous Computing 1999,* Springer-Verlag.

Kirsh, D. (1995). The intelligent use of space. *Artificial intelligence*, *73*(1), 31-68.

Leutenegger, S., Chli, M., & Siegwart, R. Y. (2011, November). BRISK: Binary robust invariant scalable keypoints. In *Computer Vision (ICCV), 2011 IEEE International Conference on* (pp. 2548-2555). IEEE.

Ljungstrand, P., Redström, J. and Holmquist, L.E. (2000) WebStickers: using physical tokens to access, manage and share bookmarks to the Web. In *Proceedings of DARE – Designing Augmented Reality Environments,* ACM Press.

Mann, S. (1998) 'WearCam' (The wearable camera): personal imaging systems for long-term use in wearable tetherless computer-mediated reality and personal photo/videographic memory prosthesis. In *Wearable Computers, 1998. Digest of Papers. Second International Symposium on (pp. 124-131).* IEEE.

Mattern, F., Floerkemeier, C. (2010) From the Internet of Computers to the Internet of Things. In: Kai Sachs, Ilia Petrov, Pablo Guerrero (Eds.): *From Active Data Management to Event-Based Systems and More.* LNCS, Vol. 6462, Springer, pp. 242-259.

Nakada, T., Kanai, H., & Kunifuji, S. (2005) A support system for finding lost objects using spotlight. In *Proceedings of the 7th international conference on Human computer interaction with mobile devices & services* (pp. 321-322). ACM.

Nickels, J., Knierim, P., Könings, B., Schaub, F., Wiedersheim, B., Musiol, S., & Weber, M. (2013). Find my stuff: supporting physical objects search with relative positioning. In *Proceedings of the 2013 ACM international joint conference on Pervasive and ubiquitous computing* (pp. 325-334). ACM.

Roemer, K., Ostermaier, B., Mattern, F., Fahrmair, M., Kellerer, W. (2010) Real-Time Search for Real-World Entities: A Survey. *Proceedings of The IEEE* , vol. 98, no. 11, pp. 1887-1902.

Song, J., Haas, C. T., & Caldas, C. H. (2007). A proximity-based method for locating RFID tagged objects. *Advanced Engineering Informatics*, *21*(4), 367-376.

Suomela, R., and Lehikoinen, J. (2004) Taxonomy for visualizing location-based information. *Virtual Reality 8.*

Tancharoen, D., Yamasaki, T., & Aizawa, K. (2005). Practical experience recording and indexing of Life Log video. In *Proceedings of the 2nd ACM workshop on Continuous archival and retrieval of personal experiences* (pp. 61-66). ACM.

Want, R., Fishkin, K.P., Gujar, A. and. Harrison, B.L. (1999) Bridging physical and virtual worlds with electronic tags. In *Proceedings of the ACM Conference on Human Factors in Computing Systems (CHI'99),* ACM Press.

Yan, T., Ganesan, D., & Manmatha, R. (2008). Distributed image search in camera sensor networks. In *Proceedings of the 6th ACM conference on Embedded network sensor systems* (pp. 155-168). ACM.

Contact information

VIS, University of Stuttgart, Pfaffenwaldring 5a, 70569, Stuttgart Germany

{markus.funk, niels.henze, albrecht.schmidt}@vis.uni-stuttgart.de

{boldtrn, eiselems, yalcinta}@studi.informatik.uni-stuttgart.de

M. Koch, A. Butz & J. Schlichter (Hrsg.): Mensch und Computer 2014 Tagungsband,
München: Oldenbourg Wissenschaftsverlag, 2014, S. 215-224.

Haltungserfassung zur Anpassung mobiler Nutzungsschnittstellen

Timo Henrich, Christian Plegge, Martin Westhoven, Thomas Alexander

Human Factors, Fraunhofer FKIE

Zusammenfassung

Die Kenntnis und Berücksichtigung des Fokus der visuellen Aufmerksamkeit ermöglicht die Adaption von Nutzungsschnittstellen. Während dieser in stationären Systemen z. B. durch Blickbewegungsmessungen relativ präzise bestimmt werden kann, ist dies auf Mobilgeräten, bedingt durch die Dynamik der Körperbewegungen des Nutzers, nicht immer möglich. Es wird ein Verfahren zur Abschätzung des Fokus der visuellen Aufmerksamkeit aus Informationen zur Körperhaltung in einem Verbundsystem aus Smartglasses und am Unterarm getragenem Smartphone vorgestellt. Das Verfahren zielt auf eine schnelle und robuste Erkennung im Gehen und im Stehen ab, ohne die Verwendung zusätzlicher Hardware. Das Ziel einer ergonomischen, praktikablen Lösung wird durch Kombination von Lageinformationen der genutzten Geräte mit bekannten, anatomischen Bewegungslimitationen des Menschen erreicht. In Abhängigkeit zur gewählten Parametrisierung beträgt die durchschnittliche Erkennungsrate des Verfahrens rund 98%.

1 Einleitung

Mobile Applikationen sind längst im privaten als auch beruflichen Alltag vieler Menschen verankert. Bei der Nutzung konkurrieren sie mit parallel ausgeführten Tätigkeiten um die Aufmerksamkeit des Nutzers (Oulasvirta et al., 2005). Hierdurch kann der Nutzer überlastet und seine Leistungsfähigkeit beeinträchtigt werden.

Durch eine auf die jeweils ausgeübte Tätigkeit abgestimmte Nutzungsschnittstelle kann dieser Gefahr entgegen gewirkt werden. Eine wesentliche Rolle spielen hierbei die verwendeten Mobilgeräte, häufig auch Smart Devices genannt. Neben Smartphones gewinnen auch neue Geräteklassen wie Smartglasses[1] oder Smartwatches[2] an Bedeutung.

Smartphones ermöglichen die Ein- und Ausgabe komplexer Daten, binden dabei aber die visuelle Aufmerksamkeit des Nutzers. Smartwatches verfügen über ähnliche, aber auf Grund

[1] http://www.bitkom.org/de/markt_statistik/64026_76148.aspx

[2] http://www.bitkom.org/de/markt_statistik/64050_77281.aspx

Smartglasses ermöglichen eine in das Sichtfeld des Nutzers eingebettete Informationsdarstellung, während er parallel einen Teil seiner Aufmerksamkeit der Umgebung widmen kann. Daher können die letzten beiden Ziele zusammengefasst werden. Liegt die Aufmerksamkeit des Nutzers in der Umgebung, sind die von den Smartglasses zur Verfügung gestellte Informationen trotzdem sichtbar und Überlagerungen mit der Umgebung potenziell erwünscht. Folglich ist es für eine adaptive Anpassung der Nutzungsschnittstelle der beiden Geräte ausreichend zu wissen, ob in einer Situation das Smartphone betrachtet wird oder nicht.

Die Nutzung unterschiedlicher Smart Devices erfordert je nach Geräteklasse spezifische Körperhaltungen zur Interaktion mit dem jeweiligen Gerät. Die Kombination aus Smartglasses und am Unterarm getragenem Smartphone erlaubt die Einteilung der möglichen Körperhaltungen in vier Kategorien. So ist es möglich, dass der Nutzer den Arm durch Innenrotation im Schulter- und Beugung im Ellenbogengelenk zur Interaktion mit dem Smartphone vor dem Körper hält (Abbildung 1, a & c). Darüber hinaus muss unterschieden werden, ob er seinen Blick auf das Smartphone gerichtet hat (Abbildung 1, c) oder der Kopf in eine andere Richtung rotiert ist (Abbildung 1, a & b). Ebenso müssen Körperhaltungen erkannt werden, in denen die Kopfhaltung jener bei der Interaktion mit dem Smartphone ähneln, diese jedoch aufgrund der Ausrichtung des Smartphones nicht stattfinden kann (Abbildung 1, d).

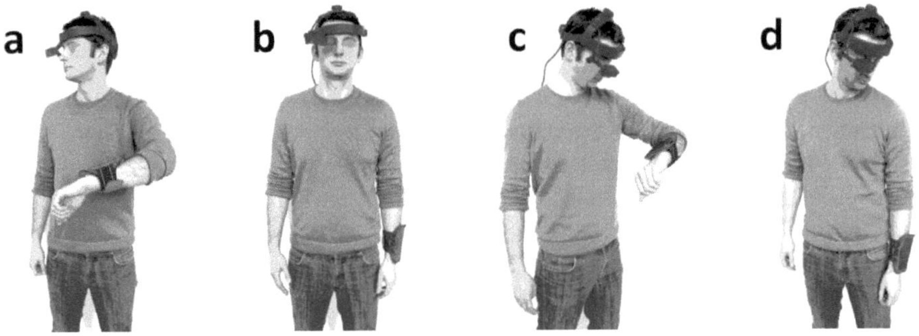

Abbildung 1 Mögliche Körperhaltungen bei Nutzung von Smart Devices

3.2 Erfassung der Körperhaltung durch Geräteorientierung

Körperhaltungen können auf verschiedene Weisen erfasst werden. Der Einsatz markerbasierter, hoch präziser und in den Bewegungswissenschaften etablierter Systeme (z.B. VICON) ist für den mobilen Einsatz i.d.R. nicht zu realisieren. Mobile Systeme verwenden jedoch meist Messverfahren, die ohnehin in Smart Devices integriert sind. Aufgrund der dadurch vereinfachten Überführung des Verfahrens in die Praxis können die Daten direkt durch Smart Devices erhoben werden. Durch die Trageweise der Smart Devices sind Unterarm, respektive Kopf, bereits mit den gerätespezifischen Inertialsensoren versehen. Abbildung 2 veranschaulicht dies für die betrachteten Smart Devices. Die Rohdaten, bestehend aus Akzelerometer-, Gyroskop- und Magnetometerdaten, werden z. B. mittels Kalman-Filtern (Kalman, 1960) zu Rotationsdaten vorverarbeitet. Folglich kann die Rotation der Geräte als Abbild der Rotation der repräsentierten Körperteile betrachtet werden.

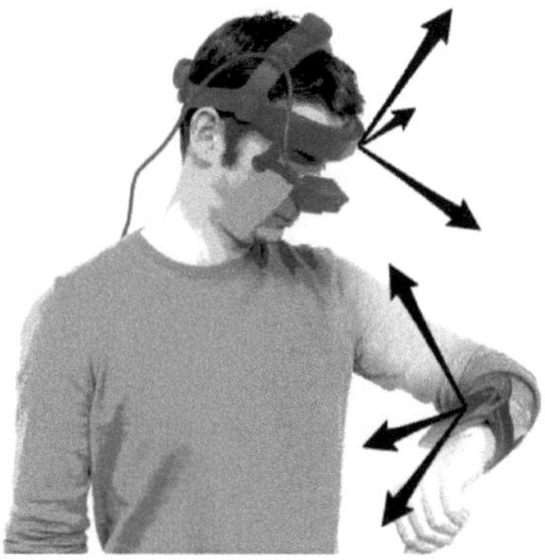

Abbildung 2 Trageweise der betrachteten Smart Devices und deren Orientierung

3.3 Erkennung einer spezifischen Körperhaltung

Die Orientierung im Raum wird in der Regel als Rotation um eine oder mehrere Achsen ausgedrückt. Typische Notationen zur Angabe von Rotationen sind Eulerwinkel oder Quaternionen. Letztere werden verwendet, da Eulerwinkel das Problem des „Gimbal Lock" hervorrufen können, dem Verlust eines Freiheitsgrads bei Annäherung des Nickwinkels an 90°.

Die Orientierung eines einzelnen Gerätes ist definiert durch die Rotationsquaternion $q_{device} = (x, y, z, w)^T$. Der Rotationsunterschied zwischen Geräten kann durch die Transformationsquaternion $q_{\delta_{1,2}} = q_{device_1}{}^{-1} * q_{device_2}$ beschrieben werden. Sie gibt die nötige Rotation an, um von der Rotation des ersten zu der des zweiten Gerätes zu gelangen.

q_{Ref} gebe nun eine Rotation zwischen zwei Geräten an, von der bekannt ist, dass wenn sie eingenommen wird der VFOA auf einem bestimmten Gerät des Geräteverbundes liegt. Dann kann für die aktuelle Rotation zwischen den Geräten $q_{aktuell}$ mit einer Metrik der Abstand zur Referenz bestimmt werden. Als Metrik wird hierbei $\phi(q_1, q_2) = 1 - |q_1 \cdot q_2|$ verwendet, wobei „·" das Skalarprodukt darstellt. Sie wurde ursprünglich eingesetzt um die Differenz zwischen euklidischen Transformationen zu beschreiben (Kuffner, 2004). Sie weist eine vergleichsweise niedrige Berechnungskomplexität auf (Huynh, 2009).

Für den Fall, dass zwei Geräte eingesetzt werden, gilt eine Rotation genau dann als erkannt, wenn $\phi(q_{Ref}, q_{aktuell}) < \varepsilon$, mit $\varepsilon \in [0,1]$ einem festzulegenden Schwellwert. Prinzipiell ist eine Erweiterung des Ansatzes auf mehr als zwei Geräte möglich, allerdings steigt der Berechnungsaufwand quadratisch mit der Anzahl der Geräte, wenn naiv die Rotationsdifferenzen zwischen allen Geräten untereinander betrachtet werden. Der Berechnungsaufwand für eine feste Anzahl von Geräten ist konstant. Auf einem gängigen Smartphone (Galaxy S3 GT-I9300, Samsung) ist die Berechnung in Echtzeit möglich (Durchschnitt <1ms).

4 Messreihe zur Parametrisierung

Durch eine Messreihe wurden Referenzrotationen sowie Schwellwerte für typische Einsatzbedingungen mobiler Applikationen erhoben.

4.1 Apparatus

Für die Messreihe wurde ein gängiges Smartphone (Galaxy S3 GT-I9300, Samsung) verwendet, das mittels einer speziellen Halterung am vorderen Unterarm befestigt wurde. Das untere, distale Drittel des Armes besitzt ein relativ homogenes Rotationsverhalten. Daher ist diese Anbringung ähnlich der einer Armbanduhr respektive Smartwatch. Zudem wurde ein Head Mounted Display (Lite-Eye LE-750 A, Lite-Eye Systems) mit angebrachtem Inertialsensor (InertiaCube3, Intersense) verwendet. Deren Steuerung erfolgte über einen Laptop.

Während der Messreihe wurde die Orientierung von Unterarm und Kopf, ausgedrückt durch die jeweiligen Inertialsensordaten, alle 25ms und zusätzlich bei der Eingabe über das Smartphone erfasst. Um die Sensordaten ggf. nachvollziehen zu können, wurden die Durchgänge als Video und mit einem VICON-System (VICON Bonita, Oxford Metrics), dem Goldstandard markerbasierter Bewegungsanalysesysteme (Kugler et al., 2012), aufgezeichnet.

4.2 Aufgabe & Design

Die Aufgabe wurde bewusst einfach gehalten und zielt primär darauf ab, den Nutzer bei Eingabe auf dem am Arm getragenen Smartphone eine entsprechende Körperhaltung einnehmen und das Display fixieren zu lassen. In zufällig permutierten Abständen von 5-7s wurde einer von vier verschiedenen Buchstaben auf einer Leinwand dargestellt. Dieser sollte über eine Softwaretastatur auf dem Smartphone eingegeben werden. Die Anordnung der Tasten wurde vor jeder Eingabe geändert, da so unmittelbar vor der Eingabe das Gerät betrachtet werden musste. Es kann daher davon ausgegangen werden, dass der VFOA zu diesem Zeitpunkt auf dem Smartphone liegt.

Charakteristisch für mobile Anwendungen ist die Nutzung sowohl im Stehen als auch im Gehen. Es wurden drei verschiedene Geschwindigkeiten untersucht: Stehen (S, 0 km/h), langsames Gehen (L, 2,5 km/h) und Gehen (G, 5 km/h). Alle Teilnehmer absolvierten die Aufgabe unter diesen drei Bedingungen. Durch Verwendung eines Laufbands konnte eine konstante Gehgeschwindigkeit gewährleistet, sowie das VICON-System eingesetzt werden. Beim Gehen wurden die Versuchsteilnehmer gegen Stürze mittels eines Brustgurts gesichert.

4.3 Ablauf

An der Messreihe nahmen 12 Mitarbeiter des Institutes im Alter von 26 bis 39 Jahren teil. 7 davon waren männlich. Die Reihenfolge der durchlaufenen Geschwindigkeiten wurde vollständig permutiert und von jeweils zwei Versuchsteilnehmern durchlaufen. Die Zuordnung zu einer Reihenfolge erfolgte zufällig. Da eine möglichst große Bandbreite an Körperhaltungen erfasst werden sollte, wurden die Teilnehmer aufgefordert zwischen zwei Eingaben den Arm wieder in die Ruheposition zu bewegen, d. h. hängen zu lassen.

4.4 Ergebnisse

Der Vergleich der Geräteorientierung, gemessen durch die Inertialsensorik, mit der durch das VICON-System gemessenen, ergab keine nennenswerten Unterschiede, weshalb im Weiteren aus Gründen der Anwendungsnähe mit den Daten der Inertialsensoren verfahren wird.

Pro Teilnehmer und Versuchsbedingung wurde zunächst eine Referenzrotation bestimmt. Hierfür wurde jeweils zum Zeitpunkt der ersten drei Eingaben, die Transformationsquaternion zwischen Smartglasses und –phone ermittelt und eine mittlere Rotation bestimmt (Markley et al., 2007). Anhand der so ermittelten Referenzrotation wurden anschließend alle Eingaben, respektive Transformationsquaternionen, bewertet. Die Daten eines Teilnehmers unter der Bedingung G konnten nicht verwendet werden, da die Aufgabenstellung nicht durchgängig befolgt wurde.

Abbildung 3 zeigt exemplarisch die Abstände der Transformationsquaternionen zur ermittelten Referenz für zwei Teilnehmer unter der Bedingung „Gehen“.

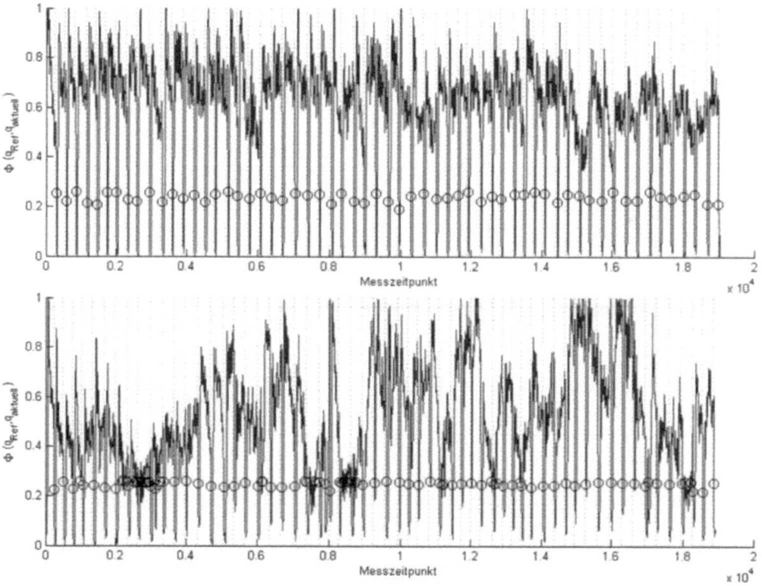

Abbildung 3 Abstand aktuelle Geräteorientierung zur Referenz für zwei Teilnehmer: oben normal, unten verrauscht

Die Qualität der erhobenen Daten hängt von den übrigen Bewegungen des Teilnehmers während des Versuchs ab. Abbildung 3 (unten) zeigt die Daten eines Teilnehmers, der zwischen den Eingaben die Arme stark schwingen ließ. Die Daten sind entsprechend verrauscht. In beiden Fällen ist jedoch zu erkennen, dass sich zum Zeitpunkt der Eingabe (gestrichelte Linie) der Abstand zwischen Transformationsrotation und Referenz deutlich verringert.

Tabelle 1 zeigt die Erkennungsraten und Fehlerzahlen. Die Erkennungsrate gibt an, wie viele der Eingabesituationen mit der ermittelten Referenzrotation detektiert worden wären. Die Fehlerzahl gibt die Anzahl der falsch positiven Detektionen außerhalb dieser Situationen an. Erwartungsgemäß steigt die Anzahl letzterer mit einem größeren Schwellwert an. Es werden nur Schwellwerte berichtet, deren Erkennungsrate in allen Bedingungen größer 80% sind und bei denen im Mittel weniger als 15 Fehlerkennungen auftraten. Bedingt durch die Aufgabe ist die Anzahl der möglichen, negativen Erkennungen unbekannt. Zur Ermittlung eines Schwellwerts, der eine gute Erkennungsrate bei geringer Fehleranzahl besitzt, wurde daher die Anzahl der falsch negativen in Relation zur Anzahl der falsch positiven Erkennungen gesetzt. Für die Bedingung S, ist der Quotient für $\varepsilon = 0{,}17$ am Geringsten. Für die Bedingungen L und G erzielt $\varepsilon = 0{,}24$ die besten Ergebnisse.

		Erkennungsraten [%]			**Fehlerzahlen [abs]**		
ε		**S**	**L**	**G**	**S**	**L**	**G**
0,16	Ø	98,45	99,01	97,69	5,17	1,42	1,09
	SD	1,97	2,45	5,64	8,97	2,54	9,71
0,17	Ø	98,73	99,01	97,69	5,67	1,67	7,45
	SD	2,41	2,45	5,63	10,14	3,17	10,64
0,18	Ø	98,59	99,01	98	6,25	1,75	7,45
	SD	2,38	2,45	4,66	11,3	3,31	12,2
0,19	Ø	98,16	99,15	98,15	6,92	1,92	7,91
	SD	2,93	1,98	4,18	13,06	3,78	12,53
0,20	Ø	98,02	99,29	98,46	7,83	3,17	8
	SD	2,97	1,53	3,26	15,13	6,34	16,64
0,21	Ø	98,02	99,29	98,46	8,83	4,17	9,64
	SD	2,88	1,53	3,26	17,08	8,27	16,4
0,22	Ø	97,6	99,44	98,46	9,08	4,92	10,55
	SD	3,66	1,5	2,88	18,08	9,12	18,13
0,23	Ø	97,6	99,58	98,77	9,08	5,67	11,91
	SD	3,65	1,05	2,16	18,64	10,64	21,2
0,24	Ø	97,03	99,72	99,08	8,67	6,75	19,09
	SD	4,69	0,66	1,76	18,83	12,73	22,98
0,25	Ø	96,47	99,58	99,23	9,08	7,5	14,45
	SD	6,44	1,05	1,58	19,56	14,16	25,47

Tabelle 1 Erkennungsraten und Fehlerzahlen bei Anwendung des Algorithmus für verschiedene Schwellwerte

Mögliche Ursachen für die Notwendigkeit eines strengeren Schwellwertes für die Bedingung S können zum einen in der Versuchsaufgabe selbst, aber auch im Unterschied zum durch das Gehen induzierten Bewegungsablauf liegen. So konnte durch die Videoaufzeichnungen für S im Vergleich zu L und G ein größeres Repertoire von Bewegungen festgestellt werden.

Die angegebene Fehleranzahl beinhaltet auch potenziell korrekte Erkennungen außerhalb der eigentlichen Aufgabe. Vereinzelt blickten die Nutzer bspw. zwischen den Eingaben auf die das Smartphone, um die Justierung der Armhalterung zu überprüfen. Die Anzahl falsch positiver Erkennungen ist folglich als „Worst Case" zu interpretieren.

Die ermittelten Schwellwerte zeigen, dass die Abweichungen zur jeweiligen Referenzrotation für alle Teilnehmer auf einem ähnlichen Niveau liegen. In einem nächsten Schritt soll untersucht werden, ob dies auch auf die individuell ermittelten Referenzrotationen zutrifft.

5 Zusammenfassung & Ausblick

Die Kenntnis des visuellen Fokus der Aufmerksamkeit (VFOA) ist wesentlich, um effiziente Nutzungsschnittstellen zu gestalten, die dem Nutzer die parallele Nutzung einer Anwendung über mehrere Smart Devices erlaubt. Es wurde ein Verfahren vorgestellt, welches die Rotationsdaten der ohnehin genutzten Geräte in Kombination mit Informationen über den anatomischen Bewegungsspielraum zur Vorhersage des VFOA und insbesondere des zurzeit betrachteten Zieles (Smart Device bzw. Umgebung) nutzt.

Durch eine Versuchsreihe wurde eine Parametrisierung für das Verfahren sowohl für die Nutzung im Stehen, langsamen und normalen Gehen ermittelt. Auf den erhobenen Daten kann der visuelle Fokus der Aufmerksamkeit mit ca. 98% Genauigkeit bestimmt werden.

Künftig soll das Verfahren validiert und generalisiert werden. Das Verfahren und die ermittelte Parametrisierung sollen zur Gestaltung einer geräteübergreifenden, konsistenten Nutzungsschnittstelle für eine mobile Applikation verwendet werden. Neben der Informationsausgabe sollen auch Eingabemethoden in Abhängigkeit des VFOA adaptiert werden. So kann z. B. die Toucheingabe von Smartphones optimiert werden, um die Steuerung von via Smartglasses dargestellten Nutzungsschnittstellen zu ermöglichen.

Literaturverzeichnis

Bulling, A., Blanke, U., & Schiele, B. (2014). A Tutorial on Human Activity Recognition Using Body-worn Inertial Sensors. *ACM Comput. Surv.*, *46*(3), 33:1–33:33.

Hacke, W., & Poeck, K. (2010). *Neurologie: mit... 83 Tabellen*. Springer.

Holmqvist, K., Nyström, M., Andersson, R., Dewhurst, R., Jarodzka, H., & Van de Weijer, J. (2011). *Eye tracking: A comprehensive guide to methods and measures*. Oxford University Press.

Huynh, D. Q. (2009). Metrics for 3D rotations: Comparison and analysis. *Journal of Mathematical Imaging and Vision*, *35*(2), 155–164.

Kalman, R. E. (1960). A new approach to linear filtering and prediction problems. *Journal of basic Engineering*, *82*(1), 35–45.

Kuffner, J. J. (2004). Effective sampling and distance metrics for 3D rigid body path planning. In *Robotics and Automation, 2004. Proceedings. ICRA'04. 2004 IEEE International Conference on* (Vol. 4, pp. 3993–3998). IEEE.

Kugler, P., Schlarb, H., Blinn, J., Picard, A., & Eskofier, B. (2012). A wireless trigger for synchronization of wearable sensors to external systems during recording of human gait. In *Engineer-*

ing in Medicine and Biology Society (EMBC), 2012 Annual International Conference of the IEEE (pp. 4537–4540). IEEE.

Markley, F. L., Cheng, Y., Crassidis, J. L., & Oshman, Y. (2007). Averaging quaternions. *Journal of Guidance, Control, and Dynamics*, *30*(4), 1193–1197.

Mayr, E., Knipfer, K., & Wessel, D. (2009). In-sights into mobile learning: An exploration of mobile eye tracking methodology for learning in museums. In *G. Vavoula, N. Pachler, & A. Kukulska-Hulme (Eds.), Researching mobile learning: Frameworks, tools and research designs* (pp. 189–204). Oxford, England: Peter Lang.

Oulasvirta, A., Tamminen, S., Roto, V., & Kuorelahti, J. (2005). Interaction in 4-second bursts: the fragmented nature of attentional resources in mobile HCI. In *Proceedings of the SIGCHI Conference on Human Factors in Computing Systems* (pp. 919–928). New York, NY, USA: ACM.

Santosa, S., & Wigdor, D. (2013). A field study of multi-device workflows in distributed workspaces. In *Proceedings of the 2013 ACM international joint conference on Pervasive and ubiquitous computing* (pp. 63–72). New York, NY, USA: ACM.

Seel, T., Schauer, T., & Raisch, J. (2012). Joint axis and position estimation from inertial measurement data by exploiting kinematic constraints. In *2012 IEEE International Conference on Control Applications (CCA)* (pp. 45–49).

Smith, K., Ba, S. O., Odobez, J.-M., & Gatica-Perez, D. (2008). Tracking the visual focus of attention for a varying number of wandering people. *Pattern Analysis and Machine Intelligence, IEEE Transactions on*, *30*(7), 1212–1229.

Winter, D. A. (2009). *Biomechanics and Motor Control of Human Movement* (4th ed.). Hoboken, New Jersey: John Wiley & Sons, Inc.

Kontaktinformationen

Timo Henrich, Christian Plegge, Martin Westhoven, Thomas Alexander
timo.henrich|christian.plegge|martin.westhoven|thomas.alexander@fkie.fraunhofer.de
Fraunhofer-Institut für Kommunikation, Informationsverarbeitung und Ergonomie FKIE
Fraunhoferstraße Str. 20
53343 Wachtberg

M. Koch, A. Butz & J. Schlichter (Hrsg.): Mensch und Computer 2014 Tagungsband,
München: Oldenbourg Wissenschaftsverlag, 2014, S. 225-234.

Entwicklung semantischer Produktdatenmodelle durch Domänenexperten: Fehleranalyse und Werkzeugunterstützung

Werner Gaulke, Jürgen Ziegler

Universität Duisburg-Essen

Zusammenfassung

Semantisch modellierte Daten in Form von Ontologien bilden eine Grundlage für unterschiedlichste intelligente Funktionen, insbesondere ermöglichen sie eine verbesserte Unterstützung bei der Suche und Filterung von Information. Dies gilt auch im Bereich des Electronic Commerce, wo semantische Produktdatenmodelle eine zunehmende Rolle spielen. Typischerweise werden diese Modelle aber von Domänenexperten erstellt, die mit semantischen Modellierungstechniken nicht oder nur wenig vertraut sind. Dieser Beitrag stellt einen auf die E-Commerce-Domäne zugeschnittenen Editor vor, der nicht-technische Benutzer dabei unterstützt, formal und fachlich korrekte Modelle zu erstellen. Auf Grundlage einer erstellten Fehlerklassifizierung wird dieser Editor empirisch mit einer generischen Modellierungsmethode verglichen. Die Ergebnisse zeigen einerseits einen Vorteil des domänenspezifischen Werkzeugs, andererseits werden aus einer Fehleranalyse Gestaltungsvorschläge zur weiteren Optimierung domänenspezifischer Modellierungswerkzeuge abgeleitet.

1 Einleitung

Die Verfügbarkeit von Datenmodellen, welche die Anwendungsdomäne in fachlich angemessener und korrekter Weise reflektiert, bildet eine der grundlegenden Voraussetzungen nicht nur für die Entwicklung der Funktionalität eines Systems sondern auch für die Gestaltung gebrauchstauglicher Nutzerschnittstellen (Akscyn, Yoder, & McCracken, 1988). Dies gilt in besonderem Maß auch für den Bereich des Electronic Commerce, wo sinnvoll strukturierte Produktdaten leistungsfähige Mechanismen für das Durchsuchen, Filtern, Empfehlen und Präsentieren von Produkten z. B. im Online-Shop ermöglichen (s. z. B. Hearst, 2008; Jannach et. al. 2011). In den letzten Jahren werden im E-Commerce zunehmend formale Datenmodelle und –repräsentationen auf Basis semantischer Techniken herangezogen, um eindeutige, anbieterübergreifende und vernetzbare Produktbeschreibungen zu erhalten (s. z.B. Barbau et al. 2012). Meta-Modelle wie Good Relations (Hepp, 2008) sollen die einheitliche Modellierung semantischer Produktdaten unterstützen.

Ein zentrales Problem für einen breiteren Einsatz semantischer Techniken ist in den Kenntnissen und Fähigkeiten der Zielgruppe zu sehen, die in der Praxis üblicherweise für das Erstellen von Produktdaten zuständig ist. Hierbei handelt es sich meist um Produkt-verantwortliche bei Herstellern, Shop-Betreibern oder Vergleichsportalen. Diese Personen besitzen zwar fundiertes Domänenwissen, haben aber in der Regel keinen (informations-) technischen Hintergrund oder Vorbildung in semantischen Techniken. Bisherige Werkzeuge zur Modellierung semantischer Daten wie z.B. Protégé[1] richten sich jedoch primär an Experten mit ausgeprägtem Wissen über verwendete Modellierungssprachen, wie das Resource Description Framework (RDF) oder die Web Ontology Language (OWL)[2]. Eine höhere Verbreitung semantischer Technologien erfordert deshalb zielgruppengerechte Werkzeuge.

Ein wesentlicher Ansatzpunkt, um ein handhabbares Werkzeug zur Produktdatenmodellierung für Fachexperten zu erreichen, kann in einer domänenspezifischen Reduktion der Komplexität gesehen werden. Hierbei sind mehrere kritische Abwägungen zu treffen. Zunächst stellt sich die Frage, welche Modellierungsaspekte überhaupt unterstützt werden. Im allgemeinen Ontology Engineering wird stark auf das Erstellen korrekter Klassifikationen und das Erzeugen von Relationen zwischen Ressourcen abgehoben. Aus durchgeführten informellen Analysen mit Anwendern im E-Commerce-Bereich zeigte sich jedoch, dass Produktmanager meist nur für einen engen Ausschnitt eines Sortiments zuständig sind und sich häufig vorgegebener Klassifikationsstrukturen oder –Standards wie eCl@ass, UNSPC[3] oder händlereigenen Sortierung bedienen (müssen). Hingegen bildet die korrekte Modellierung der typischerweise umfangreichen Produkteigenschaften (‚Properties' in der Diktion onto-logischer Modellierung) oft den Kern der Aufgabenstellung und bildet gleichzeitig - aufgrund vieler möglicher Fehlerquellen - ein zentrales Problem. Auch stellt sich die Frage, welche Vorgaben von Properties, Typen oder Wertebereichen die Aufgabe unterstützen können.

Im vorliegenden Beitrag stehen zur Beantwortung dieser Fragen zwei Beiträge im Fokus. Zum einen wird ein von den Autoren entwickeltes domänenangepasstes Werkzeug zur semantischen Produktmodellierung vorgestellt. Zum zweiten wird auf Grundlage verwandter Arbeiten sowie den Erfahrungen aus einem Forschungsprojekt zu diesem Thema eine Klassifikation von Fehlern bei der Erstellung ontologischer Datenmodelle aufgestellt. Diese Fehlerklassifikation wird herangezogen, um in einer empirischen Studie die Erstellung von Produktontologien in zwei unterschiedlichen Konditionen (Modellierung mittels Ontologie-beschreibungssprache vs. Modellierung mit domänenspezifischen Werkzeug) zu bewerten. Hieraus werden Hinweise für die Gestaltung fachspezifischer Ontologiewerkzeuge abgeleitet.

---

[1] http://protege.stanford.edu/

[2] http://www.w3.org/RDF/ bzw. http://www.w3.org/TR/owl2-overview/

[3] www.eclass.de bzw. http://www.unspsc.org/ (United Nations standard for products and services code)

2 Verwandte Arbeiten

Modellierung von Ontologien ist ein aktives Forschungsfeld, welches auf Grundlage semantischer Modellierungssprachen zahlreiche Werkzeuge und Entwicklungsprozesse hervorgebracht hat. Grundsätzlich kann die Modellierung semantischer Modelle unter Zuhilfenahme eines einfachen Texteditors direkt in der Notation der entsprechenden Sprache wie OWL oder RDF erfolgen. Demgegenüber stehen dedizierte Ontologieeditoren, die durch eine Abstraktion der zugrunde liegenden formalen Methode dem Anwender einen alternativen Zugang ermöglichen sollen. Vergleichsweise niedrige Abstrahierung erfolgt durch Editoren wie Protégé (Knublauch, Fergerson, Noy, & Musen, 2004) oder dem NeOn Toolkit (Haase et al., 2008), welche durch hierarchische Auflistungen die enthaltenen Konzepte verdeutlichen. Ein höherer Abstraktionsgrad wird in Wiki-basierten Ansätzen verfolgt. In (Bry, Schaffert, Vrandečić, & Weiand, 2012) wird ein Überblick über kollaborative Editoren auf Basis eines Wiki-Systems gegeben. Diese Editoren bilden Verknüpfungen zwischen Einträgen semantisch ab und erlauben die Angabe formaler Konzepte für beschriebene Inhalte.

Ungeachtet des eingesetzten Werkzeugs gestalten sich die Prozesse zur Modellierung einer Domäne inkrementell. Der Begriff des Ontology Maturing (Braun, Kunzmann, & Schmidt, 2012) bezeichnet den Entwicklungsprozess der schrittweisen Formalisierung abzubildender Konzepte. Während der Entwicklung kann dabei auf bewährte Entwurfsmuster zurückgegriffen werden, die sich aus Erfahrungen von Modellierungsexperten ableiten (Roussey, Corcho, & Vilches-Blázquez, 2009). Ferner ist eine Unterstützung durch das eingesetzte Werkzeug denkbar. Die Wahl sinnvoller Standardwerte und Hilfemechanismen (Rector et al., 2004) sowie die Integration automatisierter Prüfmechanismen zur Identifikation von Inkonsistenzen und Widersprüchen (Kalyanpur, Parsia, Sirin, & Cuenca-grau, 2006) sind denkbar.

Die Bewertung der Qualität erstellter Modelle erfolgt in der Regel durch Experten der formalisierten Domäne mit entsprechenden technischen Kenntnissen. Zur Unterstützung dieser Reviewprozesse stellen (Poveda-Villalón, Suárez-Figueroa, & Gómez-Pérez, 2010) eine Sammlung und Klassifizierung von typischen Fehlern in der Ontologieentwicklung vor. Die Autoren unterscheiden insgesamt 24 mögliche Fehler, die sie in zwei mögliche Kategorisierungen einsortieren. Zum einen sind die Fehler in Struktur, Funktion und Usability unterscheidbar und zum anderen wird eine Aufteilung in Konsistenz, Vollständigkeit und Prägnanz vorgeschlagen. Eine Benutzerstudie ermittelt die Verteilung der Fehler. Es häufen sich unkritische Fehler wie vergessene Annotationen. Semantische Konzepte werden meist korrekt angewendet, was der technischen Vorbildung der Teilnehmer zuzuschreiben ist.

Anhand der betrachteten Literatur lässt sich erkennen, dass sowohl Entwicklungsprozesse als auch Strategien zur Fehlervermeidung und Erkennung bis dato primär auf den technisch versierten Anwender abzielen. Vorgestellte Sammlungen von Entwurfsmustern und Fehlerarten erfüllen im jeweils angewendeten Kontext ihre Funktion, sind aber teilweise zu unspezifisch bzw. zu feingranular um allgemeiner angewendet werden zu können. Die Autoren des vorliegenden Artikels stellen im Folgenden eine generische Fehlerklassifizierung vor, die in der nachfolgenden Studie Anwendung findet.

3 Fehlerklassifizierung

An dieser Stelle wird eine Klassifizierung möglicher Fehler vorgestellt, die bei der Modellierung semantischer Daten auftreten können. Die Klassifizierung soll generell eine systematischere Untersuchung von Modellierungsfehlern ermöglichen, speziell wird sie im Weiteren für einen empirischen Vergleich zweier Modellierungsansätze herangezogen. Definierte Fehlerarten leiten sich teilweise aus den vorgestellten Arbeiten ab und wurden für eine vollständigere Abdeckung um zusätzliche Typen ergänzt. Um eine Balance zwischen Handhabung und Detailgrad zu erreichen, werden einige Fehlertypen zusammengefasst.

Auf der obersten Ebene wird zwischen formalen, semantischen und Usability-bezogenen Fehlern unterschieden. Letztere treten bei Verwendung eines Modellierungswerkzeugs auf.

Formale Fehler

Formale Fehler entstehen bei der fehlerhaften Anwendung der Konstrukte der verwendeten Modellierungssprache. Beispiele hierfür sind Syntaxfehler oder falsch eingesetzte Schlüsselwörter. Ein fehlendes oder falsches Verständnis semantischer Grundkonzepte fällt ebenfalls in diese Kategorie. Damit sind formale Fehler abhängig von der verwendeten Modellierungssprache sowie der Kenntnis des Anwenders über deren Aufbau und Konzepte.

Zur weiteren Unterteilung werden folgende Fehlertypen unterschieden:

- *[F1] Syntaxfehler*: Ausdrücke die, durch falsch eingesetzte/fehlende Symbole, nicht dem schematischen Aufbau der verwendeten Modellierungssprache entsprechen.
- *[F2] Formalsemantische Fehler*: Semantische Grundkonzepte der verwendeten Modellierungssprache sind nicht bekannt oder werden falsch eingesetzt.

Semantikfehler

In der Kategorie der Semantikfehler werden Fehler eingeordnet, die einen Sachverhalt zwar formal korrekt modellieren, aber in Hinblick auf die modellierte Domäne oder den Verwendungszweck des Modells unvollständig, falsch oder widersprüchlich sind. Darunter fallen zum Beispiel unpassende Datentypen oder zyklische Definitionen. Semantikfehler sind in der Regel nur mit fachlicher Kenntnis der jeweiligen Domäne zu identifizieren.

Es werden folgende Fehlertypen unterschieden:

- *[S1] Fachterminologische Fehler*: Es werden fachlich nicht korrekte Begriffe als Bezeichner für Klassen / Ressourcen bzw. angegebene Synonyme verwendet.
- *[S2] Eigenschaftsfehler*: Definition von nicht klassenzugehörigen Eigenschaften.
- *[S3] Typfehler*: Falsche Verwendung von Datentypen, insbesondere zu breite oder unspezifische Typen / Wertebereiche für modellierte Eigenschaften.
- *[S4] Klasse-Instanz-Verwechslung*: Entitäten werden fälschlicherweise als Klasse statt als Instanz (oder umgekehrt) definiert.
- *[S5] Kategorisierungsfehler*: Falsche Einordnung von Klassen in Hierarchien.
- *[S6] Relationsfehler:* Modellierte Beziehungen zwischen Ressourcen sind widersprüchlich, zyklisch oder führen zu falschen Beschränkungen des Wertebereichs.

Usability-bezogene Fehler

Unter Usability-bezogenen Fehlern verstehen wir Probleme, die auf eine Fehlbedienung des verwendeten Editors zurückzuführen sind, ohne dass das Modellieren selbst als problematisch einzustufen wäre. Usability-Fehler können in ihrer Konsequenz entweder zu formalen oder semantischen Fehlern führen. Die Einordnung von Problemen als Usability-Fehler kann in der Regel nur auf Basis des beobachteten Nutzerverhaltens erfolgen. Der somit erfasste Einfluss der Gebrauchstauglichkeit auf das erstellte Modell verhindert eine Irrtümliche Anlastung der Fehler an die Modellierungssprache oder das zugrundeliegende Meta-Modell.

Es werden folgende Fehlertypen unterschieden:

- *[U1] Aufwandserhöhende Fehler*: Die Zielerreichung erfordert durch ineffiziente Pfade / inkonsistente Gestaltung zusätzlichen Korrekturaufwand durch den Anwender.
- *[U2] Ergebnisverfälschende Fehler*: Die Zielerreichung wird z.B. durch falsche Bezeichner und nicht eindeutige Wahlmöglichkeiten durch das Werkzeug verhindert.

4 Ein Editor für Produktontologien

Im Rahmen eines Projektes zu ontologie-basiertem Produktdatenmanagement[4] wurde ein speziell auf den E-Commerce-Bereich zugeschnittener Produkt-Ontologieeditor (PONTE Editor) entwickelt. Mit der Domänenfokussierung geht eine Spezialisierung auf zielgruppen-abgestimmte Funktionalitäten des Editors einher. Im Gegensatz zu den in Abschnitt 2 vorgestellten Ansätzen stehen hier Anwender mit ausgeprägtem Domänenwissen ohne spezielle technische Schulung im Vordergrund. Im Mittelpunkt der Tätigkeiten befindet sich die Erfassung von Produkteigenschaften für die Weiterverarbeitung bzw. Einsatz in E-Commerce Systemen. Die exakte Definition der Eigenschaften, bestehend aus Datentyp, Wertebereich, Einheit und ggf. Aufzählungen, ist für diesen Anwendungsfall entscheidend.

Den Anforderungen der Zielgruppe entsprechend verbirgt der Editor zugrunde liegende semantische Formate und nutzt die Metapher und Terminologien eines Datenblattes zur Visualisierung der modellierten Produkte. Der Editor ermöglicht die Einordnung von Produktklassen in standardisierte Kategorisierungen, welche im E-Commerce üblich sind, sowie die Definition von Produkteigenschaften. Technische Basis bildet dabei das auf E-Commerce zugeschnittene Good-Relations Meta-Modell (Hepp, 2008). Die mit dem PONTE-Editor erstellte Modelle entsprechen diesem Modell und sind im- und exportierbar.

Abbildung 1 zeigt im linken Bereich die Hauptansicht des Editors welche einen Ausschnitt einer Produktontologie für Fahrräder darstellt. Das Datenblatt unterteilt sich in grundlegende Attribute (Name, Synonyme und die verknüpfte Kategorie) sowie Produkteigenschaften. Diese unterteilen sich ferner in Standardeigenschaften (*standard product features*) wie z.B. Gewicht und Größe sowie produktspezifische Eigenschaften (*custom product features*).

[4] http://opdm-project.org

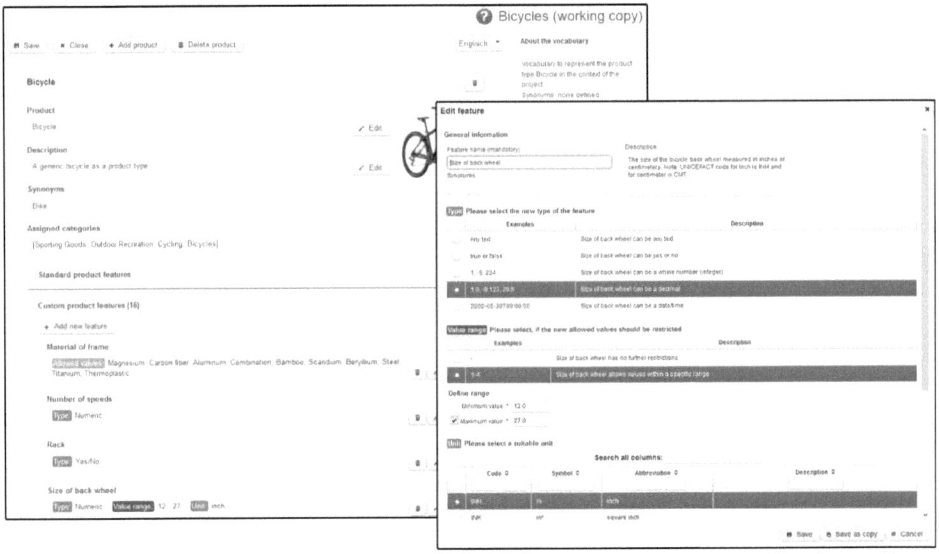

Abbildung 1 (Links) Hauptansicht des PONTE Editors. Produktklassen werden als Datenblatt dargestellt mit Auflistung aller Eigenschaften. (Rechts) Dialog zur Erstellung/Bearbeitung von Produkteigenschaften.

Produktspezifische Eigenschaften werden in einem Dialog (Abbildung 1, rechte Hälfte) bearbeitet. Die Konfiguration besteht aus mehreren Schritten. Zunächst wird der Datentyp („type“) gewählt, der den Wert String, Boolean, Ganzzahl, Fließzahl sowie Datumswert annehmen kann. Obwohl diese Auswahl einschränkend erscheint, hat die Analyse existierender Produktblätter gezeigt, dass diese Typen gängige Produktbeschreibungen lückenlos erfassen können, wenn sie zusätzlich durch Wertebereiche und die Angabe von Einheiten ergänzt wird. Diese Angabe erfolgt in Schritt zwei und drei. Für numerische Typen können hier obere und untere Grenzen angegeben, sowie passende Einheiten aus dem UN/CEFACT[5] Standard gewählt werden. Ferner besteht die Möglichkeit, Aufzählungen von konkret vorgegebenen Werten für String-Datentypen anzugeben. Im Editor vorgenommene Änderungen werden sofort übernommen und sorgen so für direktes Feedback.

5 Studie zur Onlogieerstellung

In einer empirischen Studie wurde untersucht, wie sich der Einsatz eines maßgeschneiderten Editors gegenüber einem generischen, textuellen Modellierungsansatz auf die Fehlerquote auswirkt. Im Rahmen der Studie lösen die Probanden Modellierungsaufgaben. Die Lösung erfolgt entweder mit Hilfe des in Abschnitt 4 vorgestellten PONTE Editors oder durch Formulierung von N3 Ausdrücken in einem Texteditor. Die N3 Notation[6] wurde gewählt, da diese gegenüber RDF/XML Notation einfacher nachzuvollziehen und zu formulieren ist.

[5] United Nations Centre for Trade Facilitation and E-business (http://www.unece.org/cefact.html)

[6] http://www.w3.org/TeamSubmission/n3/

5.1 Studienaufbau und Durchführung

Insgesamt 18 Probanden nahmen an der Studie teil, davon 12 weibliche und 6 männliche Teilnehmer, mit einem durchschnittlichen Alter von 22,17 (SD=3,365) Jahren. Die Teilnehmer waren Studierende eines medieninformatischen Studiengangs ohne Vorerfahrung in semantischen Techniken. Teilnahme wurde durch Vergabe von Versuchspersonenstunden motiviert. In einem Within-Subjects-Design lösten die Probanden drei Modellierungsaufgaben von ansteigender Komplexität jeweils mit beiden Editoren.

In Aufgabe 1 wurde eine Ontologie (TabletPC) bearbeitet. Teilaufgaben waren die Ergänzung von Synonymen, Entfernung/Bearbeitung von Eigenschaften sowie Einfügen eines Attributes. Inhalt von Aufgabe 2 war die Umformung einer existierenden Ontologie (Bücher) in eine verwandte Domäne (Comics). Dies umfasste Änderungen an der Produktklasse, Anpassen der Klassifizierung sowie Ergänzung von drei vorgegebenen Eigenschaften. Aufgabe 3 forderte die selbständige Definition einer neuen Ontologie (Smartphones). Anhand exemplarischer Produktbeschreibungen sollten folgende Ziele erfüllt werden: Definition der Produktklasse, Auswahl der Kategorie sowie Erstellung von mindestens drei Eigenschaften.

Testumgebung und Instruktionen

Zu Beginn wurde den Probanden Sinn und Funktion strukturierter Produktbeschreibungen erläutert. Aufgaben wurden in schriftlicher Form ausgehändigt. Vor Beginn der Arbeiten am Texteditor wurden Grundlagen des N3 Formates erläutert und ein Referenzblatt ausgehändigt. Die Reihenfolge der Editoren wurde mit jedem Teilnehmer gewechselt. Die Studie wurde an einem PC mit Windows 7 und Firefox 22 für den PONTE Editor, sowie Eclipse 4.3 als Texteditor durchgeführt. Interaktionen wurden mit der Software Morae 3.3 aufgezeichnet.

5.2 Versuchsergebnisse

Von den Probanden erstellte Modelle wurden in einem Expertenreview bewertet. Die Ergebnisse wurden in die Kategorien „gelöst“ für fehlerfreie Lösungen, „mit Fehlern“ für Modelle die einen oder mehrere Fehler enthielten, welche die Lösung nicht invalidierten, sowie „nicht gelöst“ für abgebrochene oder komplett falsche Lösungen.

Abbildung 2 zeigt die prozentuale Verteilung des Lösungsgrades der einzelnen Aufgaben nach Editor. Der zusammengefasste Lösungsgrad für den Editor beträgt 41%, für PONTE 84%. Werden mit Fehlern gelöste Teilaufgaben hinzugefügt erhöht sich der Lösungsgrad auf 65% für den Editor und 99% für PONTE.

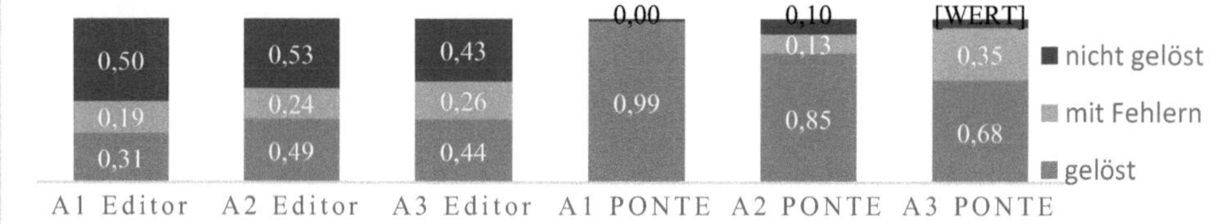

Abbildung 2: Prozentuale Verteilung des Aufgabenlösungsgrades

5.2.1 Fehlerzahlen

In den Lösungen wurden insgesamt 199 Fehler aus der in Abschnitt 3 vorgestellten Kategorisierung identifiziert. Zu beachten ist, dass der Aufgabenlösungsgrad beider Editoren unterschiedlich ausfällt. Aus diesem Grund wurde eine gewichtete Fehlerzahl errechnet, welche die rund 35% nicht erfolgreich gelösten Aufgaben mit dem Texteditor berücksichtigt. Dazu wurde die Anzahl absoluter Fehler pro Fehlertyp durch den durchschnittlichen Lösungsgrad geteilt. Abbildung 3 stellt die absoluten und gewichteten Fehlerzahlen dar.

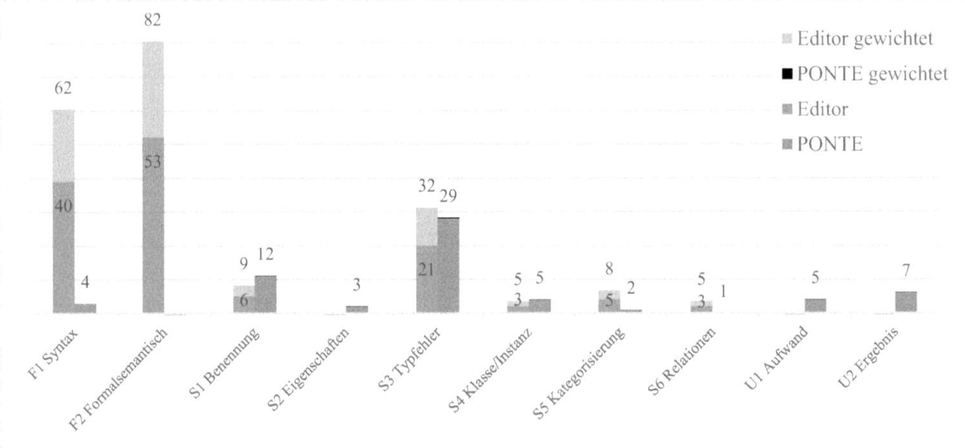

Abbildung 3: Häufigkeit der absoluten und gewichteten Fehlerarten nach Typ. Formale Fehler häufen sich im Texteditor. Semantikfehler sind in beiden Werkzeugen zu finden und konzentrieren sich auf die Benennungs- (S1) und Typfehler (S3). Für eine bessere Übersicht wird beim PONTE Editor nur der gewichtete Wert abgebildet.

Die Verteilung zeigt, dass sich im Texteditor formale Fehler häufen. Dies umfasst zum einen Syntaxfehler (F1), z.B. durch nicht abgeschlossene Statements, zum anderen aber ebenfalls die falsche Anwendung vorhandener Sprachmittel (F2). In PONTE beobachtete Syntaxfehler beziehen sich auf die Eingabe von Synonymen mit nicht korrektem Trennzeichen. Semantikfehler häufen sich im Bereich Typfehler (S3). Dieser entsteht bei falscher oder fehlender Angabe von Datentypen für Produkteigenschaften. Usability-Fehler wurden im PONTE-Editor bei der Wahl der Kategorisierung für die Produktklasse identifiziert. Einigen Anwendern gelang nicht auf Anhieb die Auswahl der gewünschten Kategorie. Als Resultat wurden entweder zusätzliche Schritte benötigt (U1) oder die Auswahl blieb fehlerhaft (U2).

6 Diskussion und abgeleitete Gestaltungsempfehlungen

Die im vorherigen Abschnitt vorgestellte Studie verdeutlicht, dass eine Beschränkung der Ausdrucksmächtigkeit auf die Erfordernisse des Anwendungsbereichs sowie das Verbergen der Formalismen den Nutzern hilft, formale Fehler bei der Ontologie-Erstellung zu reduzieren. Zwar könnten Syntaxfehler (F1) durch eine Validierung bei der freien Eingabe vermieden werden, ausgeprägtes Fachwissen semantischer Grundkonzepte ist aber weiterhin erforderlich. Die Abstraktionen eines domänenspezifischen Editors helfen hingegen Fehler, insbesondere formale Fehler, zu verhindern. Unter Verwendung eines hinreichend spezifizierten Meta-Modells, können zudem Eingaben bis zu einem gewissen Grad überprüft werden.

Die Verteilung semantischer Fehler zeigt bei beiden Editoren gewisse Ähnlichkeiten. Insbesondere die Modellierung von Produktattributen erwies sich oft aufgrund fehlender Datentypen (Texteditor) und Einheiten (PONTE) als nicht detailreich genug. Im Falle des PONTE Editors wird zwar meist der richtige Datentyp gewählt, die Angabe einer Maßeinheit wurde aber oft vergessen oder war nicht korrekt. Andere aufgetretene Fehlertypen lassen sich hauptsächlich auf ein falsches Verständnis der modellierten Domäne zurückführen. Diese Aspekte verdeutlichen, dass eine gebrauchstaugliche Oberfläche zwar einen wichtigen Schritt zur Fehlerreduzierung darstellt, aber darüber hinaus zusätzliche Unterstützung für den Anwender nötig ist. Zum Beispiel könnte der Editor durch Beispiele motivieren Produkteigenschaften möglichst vollständig zu definieren. Auch die Integration einer Kooperationsunterstützung oder von Peer-Review-Verfahren wären zur Fehlervermeidung hilfreich.

Aus der vorliegenden Untersuchung und den gewonnenen Erfahrungen lassen sich einige Leitlinien für domänenspezifische Editoren ableiten. (1) Die Wahl einer strukturell geeigneten und *zielgruppengerechten Metapher* (im vorliegenden Fall ein Datenblatt) für die entsprechende Domäne unterstützt das Verstehen des Modellierungsziels und des erforderlichen Vorgehens. (2) Neben einer geeigneten Visualisierung ist die Wahl einer *passenden Terminologie* von hoher Relevanz. (3) Die *Verwendung eines geeigneten Meta-Modells* ist wesentlich sowohl für den Entwurf eines domänenspezifischen Editors als auch für die Vermeidung von Fehlern bei der Nutzung. Auch wird der Austausch mit externen Systemen erleichtert. (4) Zusätzlich hilft eine *Restriktion der Sprachmittel* auf eine sinnvolle Untermenge die Komplexität des Editors zu reduzieren. Die Teilmenge semantischer Konzepte ist so zu wählen, dass für die jeweilige Domäne die fachlichen Anforderungen in (fast) allen Fällen erfüllt werden können. (5) Der Editor selbst sollte gängigen Empfehlungen benutzerfreundlicher Gestaltung folgen und durch *Verdeutlichung von Aktionen* dem Benutzer die Auswirkungen von Aktionen unmittelbar darstellen. (6) Durch die *Veranschaulichung gängiger Modellierungsmuster und -beispiele* aus der entsprechenden Domäne können Anwender in ihrer Modellierungsaktivität unterstützt werden. Eine Empfehlungsfunktion könnte dem Benutzer Beispiele für den Modellierungsfall präsentieren. Im Fall von PONTE könnte z.B. die Darstellung möglicher Instanzdaten die Wahl korrekter Einheiten erleichtern.

Abschließend kann festgestellt werden, dass die Einstiegshürde der Modellierung semantischer Daten für Domänenexperten mit Hilfe eines maßgeschneiderten Werkzeuges gesenkt werden konnte. Die mit Hilfe der aufgestellten Fehlerklassifizierung durchgeführte Analyse zeigt, dass neben einer Abbildung der technischen Konzepte auf eine verständliche Metapher zusätzliche, ggf. aktive Unterstützungsfunktionen geboten werden sollten. Die vorgestellten Empfehlungen sollen helfen, schon in der Entwurfsphase maßgeschneiderter Werkzeuge relevante Fragestellungen zu beachten. Eine weitere Vertiefung dieser Gestaltungsempfehlungen wird im Rahmen von Folgearbeiten angestrebt.

Danksagung

Die vorliegende Entwicklung wurde gemeinsam mit Partnern des von der EU geförderten Projekts OPDM durchgeführt, denen an dieser Stelle herzlich gedankt sei.

Literaturverzeichnis

Akscyn, R., Yoder, E., & McCracken, D. (1988). The data model is the heart of interface design. In *Proceedings of the SIGCHI conference on Human factors in computing systems - CHI '88* (pp. 115–120). New York, New York, USA: ACM Press.

Barbau, R., Krima, S., Rachuri, S., Narayanan, A., Fiorentini, X., Foufou, S., & Sriram, R. D. (2012). OntoSTEP: Enriching product model data using ontologies. *Computer-Aided Design*, *44*(6), 575–590.

Braun, S., Kunzmann, C., & Schmidt, A. P. (2012). Semantic people tagging and ontology maturing: an enterprise social media approach to competence management. *International Journal of Knowledge and Learning*, *8*(1/2), 86.

Bry, F., Schaffert, S., Vrandečić, D., & Weiand, K. (2012). Semantic wikis: Approaches, applications, and perspectives. *Reasoning Web. Semantic Technologies for Advanced Query Answering*, *7487*, 329–369.

Gangemi, A. (2005). Ontology design patterns for semantic web content. *The Semantic Web–ISWC 2005*, *3729*, 262–276.

Haase, P., Lewen, H., Studer, R., Tran, T. D., Erdmann, M., D'Aquin, M., & Motta, E. (2008). The NeOn Ontology Engineering Toolkit. In *WWW 2008 Developers Track*.

Hearst, M. A. (2008). UIs for Faceted Navigation Recent Advances and Remaining Open Problems. In *Workshop on Computer Interaction and Information Retrieval, HCIR 2008*.

Hepp, M. (2008). Goodrelations: An ontology for describing products and services offers on the web. *Knowledge Engineering: Practice and Patterns*, 329–346.

Jannach, D., Zanker, M., Felfernig, A., & Friedrich, G. (2011). *Recommender Systems: An Introduction*. Cambridge University Press.

Kalyanpur, A., Parsia, B., Sirin, E., & Cuenca-grau, B. (2006). Repairing Unsatisfiable Concepts in OWL. *Lecture Notes in Computer Science*, *4011*, 170–184.

Knublauch, H., Fergerson, R. W., Noy, N. F., & Musen, M. A. (2004). The Protégé OWL Plugin: An Open Development Environment for Semantic Web Applications. In S. McIlraith, D. Plexousakis, & F. van Harmelen (Eds.), *The Semantic Web – ISWC 2004* (pp. 229–243). Hiroshima: Springer Berlin Heidelberg.

Poveda-Villalón, M., Suárez-Figueroa, M. C., & Gómez-Pérez, A. (2010). A double classification of common pitfalls in ontologies. In *Proceedings of the Workshop on Ontology Quality - OntoQual 2010* (pp. 1–12).

Rector, A. L., Drummond, N., Horridge, M., Rogers, J., Knublauch, H., Stevens, R., … Wroe, C. (2004). Designing user interfaces to minimise common errors in ontology development: the CO-ODE and HyOntUse projects. In *Proceedings of the UK e-Science All Hands Meeting*.

Roussey, C., Corcho, O., & Vilches-Blázquez, L. M. (2009). A catalogue of OWL ontology antipatterns. In *Proceedings of the fifth international conference on Knowledge capture - K-CAP '09* (p. 205). New York, New York, USA: ACM Press.

M. Koch, A. Butz & J. Schlichter (Hrsg.): Mensch und Computer 2014 Tagungsband,
München: Oldenbourg Wissenschaftsverlag, 2014, S. 235-244.

OsiriX in Motion – Ein Prototyp zur berührungslosen Interaktion im OP

Marcel Reich[1], Christian Hetterich[1], Gerald Weisser[2], Gerrit Meixner[1]

[1]UniTyLab, Hochschule Heilbronn, Max-Planck-Str. 39, 74081 Heilbronn

[2]Institut für klinische Radiologie und Nuklearmedizin, Universitätsklinikum Mannheim, Theodor-Kutzer-Ufer 1-3, 68167 Mannheim

Zusammenfassung

Zur Behandlung eines Patienten müssen Chirurgen heutzutage mit einer zunehmenden Zahl an computerbasierten medizinischen Systemen intraoperativ arbeiten. Dabei besteht die größte Herausforderung vor allem darin, dass viele Peripheriegeräte nur schwer sterilisierbar sind. Im Rahmen des Projektes *OsiriX in Motion* wurde ein Plug-In zur berührungslosen Interaktion im Operationssaal entwickelt. Das Plug-In ermöglicht eine 1-Hand-Interaktion zur Steuerung von OsiriX, einer Software zur Darstellung und Verarbeitung radiologischer DICOM-Bilddaten. Das Gestenvokabular des Plug-Ins folgt einem einheitlichen Konzept und ermöglicht somit das schnelle Erlernen der Bedienung.

1 Einleitung

Zur Behandlung eines Patienten müssen Chirurgen heutzutage mit einer zunehmenden Zahl an computerbasierten medizinischen Systemen arbeiten. Diese Entwicklung ist nicht nur auf die Betrachtung von Aufnahmen vor einer Operation beschränkt, häufig müssen auch intraoperativ erstellte Bilder begutachtet werden. Dabei besteht die größte Herausforderung vor allem darin, mit nur schwer sterilisierbaren Peripheriegeräten zu arbeiten (Graetzel et al., 2004) und gleichzeitig die Grenze zwischen sterilem und nicht-sterilem OP-Bereich beizubehalten (Johnson et al., 2011). Dieses Problem soll mit Hilfe berührungsloser Interaktionssysteme auf Basis von Sprachbefehlen oder Körpergesten gelöst werden. Sprachbasierte Interaktionssysteme sind jedoch anfällig gegen Umgebungsgeräusche im OP und arbeiten daher nicht zuverlässig (Jalaliniya et al., 2013). Aus diesem Grund beschäftigt sich dieser Beitrag mit der Entwicklung und der Evaluation eines berührungslosen, gestengesteuerten Interaktionssystems: OsiriX in Motion (OiM). OiM ist als Plug-In zur Steuerung von

OsiriX[1], einer MAC OS X basierten Software zur Darstellung und Verarbeitung radiologischer DICOM-Bilddaten (u.a. CT, MRT und Röntgen), entwickelt worden.

Der Rest des Beitrages ist wie folgt gegliedert: Kapitel 2 beschreibt den aktuellen Stand der Wissenschaft, bevor in Kapitel 3 näher auf die verwendete Hard- und Software eingegangen wird. Kapitel 4 beschreibt die Entwicklung von OiM und Kapitel 5 gibt einen Überblick über die Evaluationsergebnisse. Kapitel 6 schließt diesen Beitrag mit einer Diskussion und einem Ausblick ab.

2 Stand der Wissenschaft

Bisherige Ansätze zur Steuerung während einer Operation umfassen folgende vier Arten:

1. Wechsel des Operateurs zwischen sterilem und nicht-sterilem Bereich,
2. Steuerung durch Sprachbefehle,
3. Delegation von Aufgaben an einen Assistenten und
4. Nutzung von Fußpedalen.

Diese vier Arten werden im Folgenden genauer betrachtet.

2.1 Wechsel von sterilem in nicht-sterilen Bereich

Bei dieser Vorgehensweise unterbricht der Chirurg die Operation des Patienten und wechselt in den nicht-sterilen Bereich, um die gewünschte Aktion auszuführen. Nach der Aktion muss der Operateur allerdings erneut die Hände reinigen und die Handschuhe wechseln, was unvermeidlich zu längeren OP-Zeiten führen kann und mit einem höheren Patientenrisiko einhergeht (Ebert et al., 2012).

2.2 Sprachbefehle

Bei dieser Art der Steuerung trägt der Chirurg ein Headset und interagiert mittels Sprachbefehlen mit dem System. Auf diese Weise wird dem Chirurg das berührungslose Arbeiten mit dem System ermöglicht und er kann beide Hände wie gewohnt zum Operieren nutzen. Doch die Nachteile überwiegen: Zum einen erschweren laute Umgebungsgeräusche im OP (z.B. Pumpen, EKG) das Erkennen der Sprachbefehle (Johnson et al., 2011), zum anderen kann das System nur schwer zwischen Anweisungen und der Konversation zwischen zwei Ärzten differenzieren. Aus diesem Grund hat sich der Gebrauch bestimmter Startsequenzen (vgl. Google Glass: „OK Glass, …“) etabliert, was jedoch die Gebrauchs-tauglichkeit des Systems herabsetzt.

[1] http://www.osirix-viewer.com

2.3 Delegation an einen Assistenten

Die Delegation von Sprachefehlen an einen Assistenten bietet ebenfalls den Vorteil, dass der Chirurg den Patienten mit beiden Händen operieren kann. Der Assistent übernimmt auf diese Weise z.B. die Translation oder Rotation einer radiologischen Aufnahme. Allerdings birgt diese Art der Steuerung einen entscheidenden Nachteil: Durch Missverständnisse in der Kommunikation zwischen Operateur und Assistent kann es zu Fehlern in der Interaktion mit dem System kommen, was zu Verzögerungen im OP-Ablauf führen kann. In einer Untersuchung von (Graetzel et al., 2004) benötigte ein OP-Team mit dieser Methode sieben Minuten, um einen einzelnen Mausklick auszuführen. Aus diesem Grund sollte die Delegation nur in gut eingespielten OP-Teams eingesetzt werden.

2.4 Fußpedal

Eine weitere Interaktionsmöglichkeit ist der Einsatz von Fußpedalen, welche in der interventionellen Radiologie und der Chirurgie häufig zum Einsatz kommen. Sie werden beispielsweise verwendet, um die Helligkeit im OP oder die Höhe des OP-Tisches zu verändern. Auch bei diesem Ansatz kann der Chirurg beide Hände für die Operation nutzen. Aufgrund der zu geringen Präzision sind diese Geräte für die Interaktion im OP aber ungeeignet.

Nachdem die bisher vorgestellten Ansätze intra-operativer Steuerung skizziert wurden, werden nun die Vor- und Nachteile der berührungslosen Interaktion durch Gesten dargestellt. Tan et al. entwickelten 2013 eine berührungslose Benutzungsschnittstelle für die intra-operative Steuerung eines DICOM-Viewers mit Hilfe der Microsoft Kinect (Tan et al., 2013). Eine daran angeschlossene Umfrage unter 29 Radiologen ergab, dass 69% der Befragten einen Nutzen in der berührungslosen Interaktion sehen. Darüber hinaus sind sie der Überzeugung, dass diese Art der Interaktion die Sterilität im OP aufrechterhalten kann. Als nachteilig sehen die Radiologen jedoch, dass für Gesten beide Hände eingesetzt werden müssen. Darüber hinaus beansprucht die Erkennung der Gesten durch die Kinect zu viel Platz, welcher im OP in den seltensten Fällen zur Verfügung steht. Ferner können bei längerer Interaktion mit dem System Ermüdungserscheinungen des Arms („gorilla arm") auftreten (O'Hara et. al, 2014).

Bisher publizierte Implementierungen zur Gestensteuerung des DICOM-Viewers OsiriX nutzen zur Erkennung von Gesten stereokamerabasierte Verfahren (Kipshagen et al., 2009) oder Infrarot-Laserprojektoren wie die Kinect von Microsoft (Ebert et al., 2012). Die hier vorgestellte Lösung mit dem LMC erkennt Gesten mit Hilfe von Infrarot-Technologie, durch die eine deutlich höhere Präzision erreicht werden kann. Allerdings ist der Interaktionsbereich im Vergleich zu stereo- bzw. time-of-flight-kamerabasierten Verfahren um ein Vielfaches geringer. Aus diesem Grund unterscheidet sich die Interaktion mit dem LMC wesentlich von der Arbeitsweise bislang entwickelter Systeme.

3 Material und Methoden

Zunächst wird die dem Projekt zugrundeliegende Hardware und anschließend die verwendete Software sowie die zur Implementierung notwendigen Tools beschrieben.

3.1 Hardware

Für die Implementierung des Prototyps wurde ein 15" MacBook Pro mit einem 2 GHz Intel Core i7 Prozessor und 8GB Arbeitsspeicher verwendet. Zur Erfassung der Gesten wurde der Leap Motion Controller eingesetzt. Der Controller ist 8 x 3 x 1,27 cm groß und wiegt 45 Gramm. Die Oberseite des Geräts besteht aus Plastik und ist für infrarotes Licht durchlässig. Dies erlaubt den drei im Gerät befindlichen LEDs infrarotes Licht zu emittieren und ermöglicht auf diese Weise die Aufnahme der Tiefenkamera. Nachdem der LMC mit dem Computer verbunden wurde, können Fingerbewegungen mit einer Rate von ca. 200 Frames pro Sekunde und einer Präzision von 0,01 mm übertragen werden. Die Auswertung der Daten wird dabei von dem angeschlossenen PC übernommen. Die Erkennung von Bewegungen erfolgt innerhalb der Interaktionsbox, die in Form einer um 180° rotierten Pyramide im Bereich von 2,5 – 60 cm vom Controller aufgespannt wird (vgl. Abbildung 1).

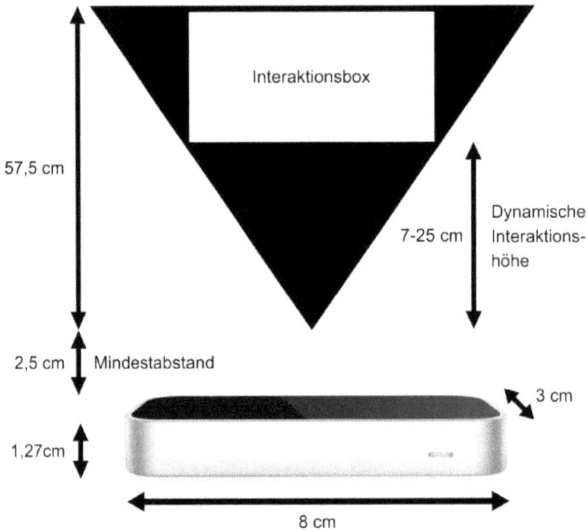

Abbildung 1: Abmessungen und Darstellung der Interaktionsbox des Leap Motion Controllers

3.2 Software

Zur Entwicklung wurde das LMC-SDK in v.1.0.9 und die Entwicklungsumgebung Xcode in v.5.0.1 eingesetzt. Das Plugin wurde unter Mac OS X 10.9.1 Mavericks für die 32-bit Variante von OsiriX (v.5.8.5) in der Programmiersprache Objective-C++ entwickelt.

4 Entwicklung

Der Prototyp beschränkt sich auf den Anwendungsfall der intra-operativen Interaktion mit radiologischen 3D-Bild-Datensätzen. Das Hauptziel besteht darin, dem Anwender einen möglichst großen Umfang an Funktionen zur Verfügung stellen zu können und gleichzeitig den Aufwand zum Erlernen der Bedienung des Systems gering zu halten. Zudem sollte darauf geachtet werden, dass die Software mit einer Hand gesteuert werden kann, da dem Chirurg während einer Operation häufig nicht beide Hände für die Interaktion zur Verfügung stehen (Graetzel et al., 2004). Bisher veröffentlichte Ansätze (Ebert et al., 2012; Tan et al., 2013; Bizzotto et. al, 2014) haben diesen wichtigen Aspekt nicht beachtet. Des Weiteren ist OsiriX in Motion über die Plugin-Schnittstelle in OsiriX integriert und hat somit Zugriff auf alle Funktionen der OsiriX-API. Dies unterscheidet OiM von bisherigen Lösungen wie beispielsweise (Bizzotto et. al, 2014), welche die Applikation GameWave[2] aus dem Leap Motion Online-Store verwenden und ausschließlich Tastenkürzel für den Aufruf bestimmter Funktionen an OsiriX weiterleiten.

4.1 Design

Für die prototypische Integration in den klinischen Workflow wurden zunächst Funktionen zur Schichtselektion, Fensterung, Translation, Rotation und den Vergrößerungsfaktor implementiert. Die Funktionen wurden in einem kreisrunden Menü angeordnet, welches sich in der Mitte des Bildschirms öffnet (vgl. Abbildung 2).

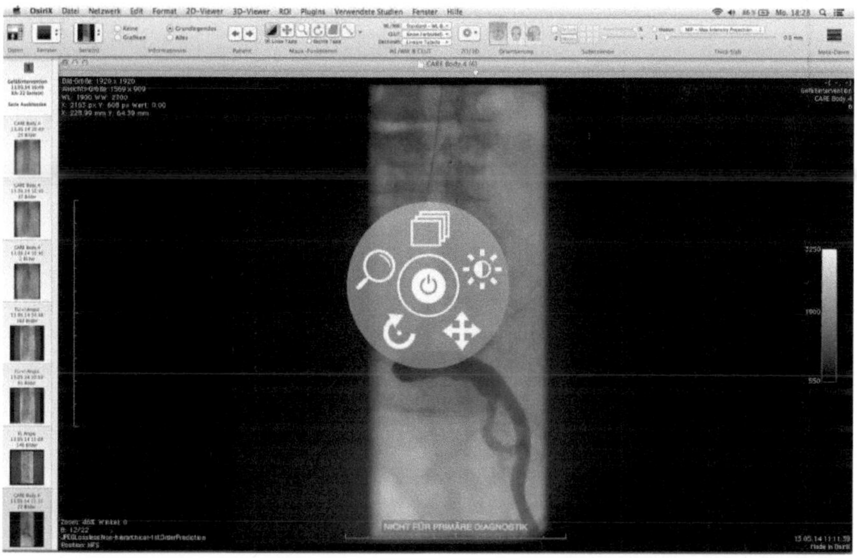

Abbildung 2: Im OsiriX-Viewer geöffneter Angiographie Datensatz mit gestartetem OiM Plugin

[2] www.uwyn.com

Die Gestaltung des Icons der jeweiligen Funktion erfolgte nach den Empfehlungen des Integrating the Healthcare Enterprise (IHE)-Profils „Basic Image Review“[3].

Ziel bei OiM war, ein möglichst geringes Gestenvokabular bereitzustellen, wodurch das Erlernen erleichtert wird. Aus diesem Grund basieren alle Interaktionen auf einem einheitlichen Konzept. Die Auswahl eines Menüpunktes erfolgt in Abhängigkeit der Richtung des ausgestreckten Zeigefingers. Wird die Position des Fingers circa 1,5 Sekunden nicht verändert, startet der selektierte Interaktionsmodus. Diese Art der Funktionswahl wurde aufgrund der höheren Zielgenauigkeit von „wait to click“ im Gegensatz zu einem Tap verwendet (Graetzel et al., 2004). Nach Start des Interaktionsmodus verkleinert sich das Menü und bewegt sich an den Rand des OsiriX-Fensters (vgl. Abbildung 3).

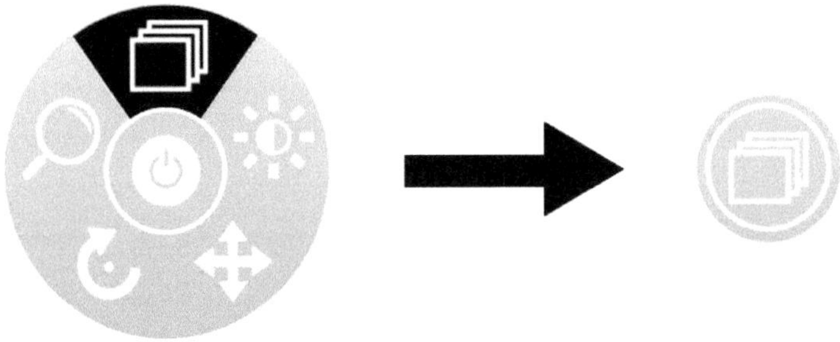

*Abbildung 3: **(links)** Hauptmenü mit ausgewählter Schichtselektion, **(rechts)** Verkleinerung und Verschiebung des Menüs an den Rand des OsiriX-Fensters*

Nach Auswahl des gewünschten Modus kann nun durch Spreizen der Finger der flachen Hand die Interaktion begonnen und durch Zusammenführen der Finger wieder beendet werden (vgl. Abbildung 4). Dieses Konzept wurde gewählt, da der Einsatz einer weiteren Geste dazu geführt hat, dass die Interaktion beim Wechsel der Gesten ungewollt fortgeführt wurde.

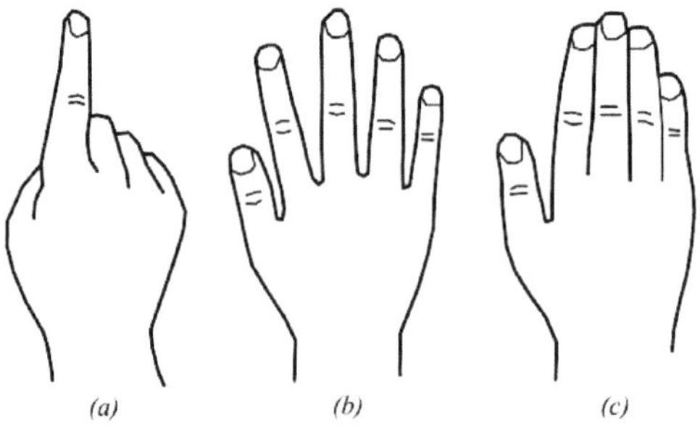

*Abbildung 4: Die Interaktionsarten von OsiriX in Motion: **(a)** Auswahl der Funktion durch Zeigen und Halten, **(b)** Beginn der Interaktion durch Spreizen der Finger, **(c)** Beenden der Interaktion durch Anlegen der Finger*

[3] http://www.ihe.net/Technical_Framework/upload/IHE_RAD_Suppl_BIR.pdf, S. 42-52

4.2 Funktionen

Es folgt eine Beschreibung, wie die Interaktion mit der jeweiligen Funktion realisiert wurde.

4.2.1 Schichtselektion

Die Schichtselektion ermöglicht den Wechsel zur nächsten bzw. vorherigen Schicht in einer Bildserie. Um zur nächsten Schicht zu gelangen, wird die Hand im rechten Bereich der Interaktionsbox positioniert, die vorherige Schicht wird durch das Halten der Hand im linken Bereich erreicht. Je weiter sich die Hand vom Zentrum der Interaktionsbox entfernt, desto schneller werden die Schichten durchlaufen (vgl. Abbildung 5a). Auf diese Weise ist es möglich, selbst in großen Datensätzen gezielt Schichten auszuwählen.

4.2.2 Kontrastanpassung

Die Kontrastanpassung vereint die Einstellung des Kontrasts (Window Level) und der Intensität (Window Width) in einer Funktion. Der Kontrast kann durch vertikales Bewegen der Hand erhöht bzw. verringert werden. Die Anpassung der Intensität erfolgt durch horizontale Bewegung der Hand (vgl. Abbildung 5b).

4.2.3 Translation

Die Translationsfunktion ermöglicht das Verschieben des Bildes gemäß der Bewegung der Hand nach links, rechts, oben oder unten (vgl. Abbildung 5a). Auch hier erfolgt die Aktion langsamer, wenn die Hand im inneren Bereich der Interaktionsbox gehalten wird, oder schneller, wenn sie sich im äußeren Bereich befindet.

4.2.4 Rotation

Das Bild wird analog zum Neigungswinkel der Hand im bzw. gegen den Uhrzeigersinn rotiert. Die Stärke der Neigung bestimmt dabei die Rotationsgeschwindigkeit: Ein Winkel größer als 45 Grad lässt das Bild kontinuierlich rotieren, mit kleinerem Winkel ist es möglich, das Bild schrittweise um ein Grad zu drehen (vgl. Abbildung 5c).

4.2.5 Vergrößerung

Diese Funktion ändert den Vergrößerungsfaktor des Bildes: Durch Heranziehen der Hand zum Anwender wird das Bild vergrößert und durch Wegschieben entsprechend verkleinert (vgl. Abbildung 5d).

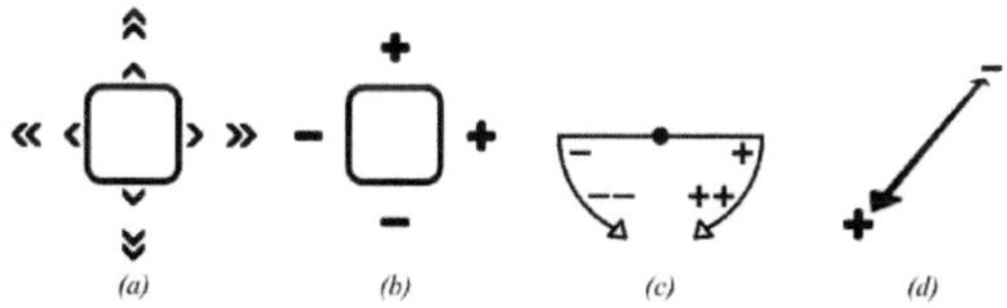

*Abbildung 5: Interaktionsmöglichkeiten der flachen Hand bei gespreizten Fingern: **(a)** Schichtauswahl durch Bewegung nach links und rechts, Translation des Bildes nach links, rechts, oben und unten, **(b)** Anpassung des Kontrastes oben/unten und der Intensität links/rechts, **(c)** Rotation gegen und mit dem Uhrzeigersinn links/rechts, **(d)** Veränderung des Vergrößerungsfaktors vor/zurück*

5 Evaluation

Um OiM zu evaluieren, wurde eine Kooperation mit der Abteilung Interventionelle Radiologie des Universitätsklinikums Mannheim initiiert. Schwerpunkt dieser Abteilung ist die Durchführung von Angiographien, d.h. der Darstellung von Blutgefäßen mittels bildgebender Verfahren wie beispielsweise der kontrastmittelgestützten Computer-tomographie. Ein Eingriff dauert in der Regel zwei Stunden, von denen der Operateur etwa drei bis vier Minuten mit OsiriX interagiert. Um dies durchzuführen, muss der Arzt momentan den Eingriff unterbrechen, die OP-Handschuhe ausziehen und in den Nebenraum wechseln. Erst nach erneuter Sterilisation kann die Intervention fortgeführt werden.

5.1 Vorbereitung

Für den Spezialfall der Angiographie musste die ursprüngliche Funktionalität von OiM angepasst werden. Die Option Aufnahmen zu rotieren wird hier nicht benötigt, stattdessen muss es möglich sein, den in OsiriX integrierten digitalen Subtraktionsangiographie Modus (DSA) an- und auszuschalten. Als weitere Anpassung wurde der Wunsch seitens des Universitätsklinikums Mannheim geäußert, zwischen den einzelnen Serien der DICOM-Studie des Patienten zu wechseln. Diese Funktionalität wird benötigt, da während einer Intervention häufig neue Aufnahmen akquiriert werden und man mit den neuen Bildern auch gestengestützt interagieren möchte. Für die Evaluation von OiM wurde vorerst nur die Aktivierung des DSA-Modus übernommen und die Rotations-Funktionalität aus dem Menü entfernt. Die Integration des Serienwechsels ist in einer zukünftigen Version geplant.

5.2 Durchführung

Um den möglichen Einsatz von OiM während einer Angiographie beurteilen zu können, testeten zwei Angiographie-Ärzte und ein Oberarzt OiM außerhalb des sterilen Bereichs. Alle drei Personen kennen OsiriX und arbeiten täglich damit. Nur ein Arzt kannte den Leap Motion Controller bereits vor der Evaluation, das Gerät wurde bisher allerdings von keinem der Probanden verwendet. Schon nach einer kurzen, etwa fünf-minütigen Einführung in den LMC und das Interaktionskonzept von OiM waren die Ärzte in der Lage, das Plug-In selbständig zu bedienen und konnten sich einen Eindruck der berührungslosen Interaktion verschaffen. Im Anschluss daran wurden ihnen analog zu (Tan et al., 2013) folgende fünf Fragen gestellt: **1.** Könnte es bei der Nutzung des Systems Probleme mit der Aufrechterhaltung des sterilen Umfelds geben? **2.** Was könnten Vorteile des Systems sein? **3.** Welche Nachteile bzw. Einschränkungen hat das System? **4.** Haben Sie das Gefühl, dass der Einsatz des Systems in der Angiographie von Nutzen sein kann?

5.3 Ergebnisse

Die Befragung der drei Angiographie-Ärzte resultierte in einem homogenen Meinungsbild. Als großer Vorteil, der sich durch den Einsatz von OiM in der Angiographie ergeben würde, nannten die Probanden das schnellere Arbeiten. Dies wurde mit der Vermeidung des

Wechsels in den nicht-sterilen Raum und somit auch des Austauschs der OP-Handschuhe begründet. Der schnellere Wechsel ermöglicht somit zum einen das Einsparen kostenintensiver OP-Minuten, zum anderen werden Patienten einem geringeren Risiko ausgesetzt.

Als negativer Punkt wurde die Montageposition des LMC im Angiographie-Saal diskutiert. Eine mögliche Stelle wäre die Befestigung des Controllers an der OP-Ampel, einem an der Decke befestigten Block aus sechs Monitoren. Dies hätte jedoch zur Folge, dass sich der Operateur, um mit OiM zu interagieren, über den Patienten lehnen müsste. Zudem besteht hier die Gefahr, dass die OP-Ampel berührt wird und der Arzt dadurch nicht mehr steril ist. Als alternative Position wurde ebenfalls ein Feld neben den Joysticks am Angiographie-Tisch in Erwägung gezogen. An dieser Stelle könnte der LMC jedoch fälschlicherweise Bewegungen des Arztes als Interaktion verstehen. Um dies zu vermeiden, müsste eine zusätzliche, eindeutige Start- bzw. Stop-Geste implementiert werden.

Zusammenfassend waren die drei Ärzte von den Möglichkeiten von OiM überzeugt und sehen einen wertvollen Mehrwert in der Angiographie. Da bisher jedoch nur eine Beta-Version vorliegt, ist ein Einsatz im produktiven Umfeld noch nicht denkbar.

6 Diskussion und Ausblick

In dieser Arbeit wurde ein Prototyp zur berührungslosen Steuerung des DICOM-Viewers OsiriX vorgestellt. Dazu wurden zunächst die bisher veröffentlichen Lösungen verglichen und daraus Anforderungen abgeleitet. Dabei hat sich gezeigt, dass die Kinect-basierten Systeme bisher hauptsächlich 2-Hand-Interaktionen unterstützen (Ebert et al., 2012; Tan et al., 2013), der Chirurg jedoch möglichst beide Hände zum Operieren benötigt. Aus diesem Grund wurde OiM ausschließlich für die Bedienung mit 1-Hand-Gesten konzipiert. Der Funktionsumfang bei bisher veröffentlichten Lösungen ist begrenzt. Nichtsdestoweniger nutzen diese Systeme eine Vielzahl an unterschiedlichen Gesten, wodurch deren Lernphase sehr zeitaufwendig ist. Bei OiM ist das Gestenvokabular verhältnismäßig gering, da die eingesetzten Gesten einem einheitlichen Konzept folgen und somit das Erlernen erleichtern (Gallo et al., 2011). Durch den geringeren Interaktionsradius erfolgt die Ausführung und Erkennung der Gesten auf engem Raum, was sowohl dem Platzproblem im OP-Saal entgegenwirkt, als auch den Ermüdungserscheinungen des Arms („gorilla arm"). Die Ergebnisse der Evaluation zeigen, dass der Einsatz von OiM einen Mehrwert bieten kann. Durch das direkte Arbeiten am OP-Tisch werden wertvolle OP-Zeit eingespart.

Darüber hinaus zeigte sich, dass die Integration des LMC über die OsiriX-Plugin Schnittstelle auch im kommerziellen Bereich aktuell große Beachtung findet. Die Firma aycan verfolgt mit dem Plugin ayGesture einen gleichartigen Ansatz. Aycan entwickelt auf Basis der Open Source-Variante von OsiriX eine nach deutschem Medizinproduktegesetz zertifizierte Version (OsiriX Pro) zum Einsatz im klinischen Bereich. Eine erste Version zur Demonstration der Plugin-Funktionalität wurde auf dem 95. Deutschen Röntgenkongress in Hamburg vorgestellt. Der offizielle Termin für den Verkaufsstart ist nach aktuellem Stand noch offen. OiM befindet sich ebenfalls noch in einem Beta-Stadium, sodass die notwendige Robustheit und Fehlerfreiheit für den produktiven Einsatz aktuell noch nicht gewährleistet werden kann. Zudem bietet der Prototyp nicht die gewünschte Konfigurierbarkeit, um ihn für unterschiedliche Bereiche und individuelle Wünsche anpassen zu können. Aus diesem Grund soll in den nachfolgenden Versionen ein Konfigurationsprogramm entwickelt werden, das per Drag & Drop das individuelle Zusammenstellen von Funktionen ermöglicht. Für die Weiterentwicklung wird der Programmcode auf der Plattform OpossUMM[4] zur freien Verfügung veröffentlicht.

Literaturverzeichnis

Bizzotto, N., Costanzo, A., Bizzotto, L., Regis, D., Sandri, A., & Magnan, B. (2014). Leap Motion Gesture Control With OsiriX in the Operating Room to Control Imaging First Experiences During Live Surgery. *Surgical innovation*, 1553350614528384.

Ebert, L. C., Hatch, G., Ampanozi, G., Thali, M. J., & Ross, S. (2012). You can't touch this touch-free navigation through radiological images. *Surgical Innovation* 19(3), 301–307.

Gallo, L., Placitelli, A. P., & Ciampi, M. (2011). Controller-free exploration of medical image data: Experiencing the kinect. In *Computer-Based Medical Systems (CBMS), 2011 24th International Symposium on* (pp. 1–6). IEEE.

Graetzel, C., Fong, T., Grange, S., & Baur, C. (2004). A non-contact mouse for surgeon-computer interaction. *Technology and Health Care* 12(3), 245–257.

Jalaliniya, S., Smith, J., Sousa, M., Büthe, L., & Pederson, T. (2013). Touch-less interaction with medical images using hand & foot gestures. *In Proceedings of the 2013 ACM conference on Pervasive and ubiquitous computing adjunct publication* (pp. 1265–1274). ACM.

Johnson, R., O'Hara, K., Sellen, A., Cousins, C., & Criminisi, A. (2011). Exploring the potential for touchless interaction in image-guided interventional radiology. *In Proceedings of the SIGCHI Conference on Human Factors in Computing Systems* (pp. 3323–3332).

Kipshagen, T., Graw, M., Tronnier, V., Bonsanto, M., & Hofmann, U. G. (2009). Touch-and marker-free interaction with medical software. *In World Congress on Medical Physics and Biomedical Engineering*, September 7-12, 2009, Munich, Germany (pp. 75-78). Springer Berlin Heidelberg.

O'Hara, K., Gonzalez, G., Sellen, A., Penney, G., Varnavas, A., Mentis, H., ... & Carrell, T. (2014). Touchless interaction in surgery. *Communications of the ACM*, 57(1), 70-77.

Schwarz, L. A., Bigdelou, A., & Navab, N. (2011). Learning gestures for customizable human-computer interaction in the operating room. In *Medical Image Computing and Computer-Assisted Intervention–MICCAI 2011* (pp. 129-136). Springer Berlin Heidelberg.

Tan, J. H., Chao, C., Zawaideh, M., Roberts, A. C., & Kinney, T. B. (2013). Informatics in radiology: Developing a touchless user interface for intraoperative image control during interventional radiology procedures. *Radiographics* 33(2), E61–E70.

[4] http://www.opossumm.de

M. Koch, A. Butz & J. Schlichter (Hrsg.): Mensch und Computer 2014 Tagungsband,
München: Oldenbourg Wissenschaftsverlag, 2014, S. 245-254.

Empfehlungen für die Gestaltung von Erratbarkeitsstudien zur Ermittlung von benutzerdefinierten Gesten

Mirko Fetter, Tom Gross

Lehrstuhl für Mensch-Computer-Interaktion, Otto-Friedrich-Universität Bamberg

Zusammenfassung

Dieser Beitrag gibt Empfehlungen, die es bei der Gestaltung von Erratbarkeitsstudien (Guessability Studies) zur Ermittlung von durch Benutzerinnen und Benutzer definierten Gesten zu beachten gilt. Basierend auf einer Analyse verwandter Arbeiten und einer eigenen Studie identifizieren wir kritische Aspekte und geben Hinweise für die Gestaltung und Durchführung von Erratbarkeitsstudien.

1 Einführung

Während die Eingabe durch Freihandgesten seit deren Präsentation in frühen Systemen wie Put-That-There [Bolt 1980] in den achtziger Jahren eine lange Tradition in der Mensch-Computer-Interaktionsforschung hat, werden seit kurzem entsprechende Eingabesysteme auch einem breiteren Personenkreis zugänglich gemacht. Vorangetrieben durch die Spiele-industrie mit neuen Eingabekonzepten für Videospielkonsolen wie z.B. der Playstation EyeToy, der Nintendo Wii, und der Microsoft Kinect wurden Systeme mit Gesteneingabe in den letzten Jahren allgegenwärtiger. Mit neuen Eingabegeräten wie der LEAP Motion oder der Myo[1] tritt diese Technologie ihren Weg von der Nische im Wohnzimmer in unser tägliches Leben an. Die dahinterstehende Idee ist, durch die Gesteneingabe die Tür zu natürlicheren Benutzungsschnittstellen aufzustoßen [Wigdor & Wixon 2011], um so die intuitive Nutzung von Computertechnologie zu erlauben.

Jedoch sind zahlreiche auf Gesten basierende Eingabesysteme häufig noch wenig intuitiv und eher als künstlich anzusehen [Malizia & Bellucci 2012]. So müssen eine Menge von neuen, synthetischen Gesten erlernt und erinnert werden, die ähnlich wie Kommandos dann eine symbolische Eingabe von Befehlen ermöglichen. Aus diesem Grund müssen Gesten natürlich und konsistent gestaltet werden [Baudel & Beaudouin-Lafon 2012]. Wie Gesten

[1] http://www.leapmotion.com/ sowie http://www.thalmic.com/en/myo/

derartig gestaltet werden können, ist allerdings noch wenig erforscht. Generell lassen sich zwei Herangehensweisen unterscheiden [Cafaro *et al.* 2014]: Top-Down und Bottom-Up. Beim Top-Down Ansatz entwerfen die Designer eines Systems die Gesten, mit denen das System zu kontrollieren ist. Beim Bottom-Up Ansatz wird eine Gruppe von Benutzerinnen und Benutzern aufgefordert, geeignete Gesten für die Interaktion mit einem System in so genannten Erratbarkeitsstudien vorzuschlagen [Wobbrock *et al.* 2005; Wobbrock *et al.* 2009] — ein Ansatz, der sich zunehmender Beliebtheit erfreut, allerdings im Detail in der Umsetzung einige herausfordernde Aspekte birgt. Wir fanden in eigenen und verwandten Arbeiten Anzeichnen dafür, dass diese Aspekte einen großen Einfluss auf das zu erwartende Ergebnis der Studie haben. Eine systematische Aufarbeitung, die diese Aspekte adressiert und diskutiert, gibt es allerdings bisher nicht. Um genauere Erkenntnis darüber zu erlangen, wie unterschiedliche Entscheidungen bei der Gestaltung von Erratbarkeitsstudien deren Resultat beeinflussen, haben wir eine eigene Studie durchgeführt, die gezielt bestimmte Aspekte davon beleuchtet. Im Folgenden motivieren wir ausgehend von der Analyse verwandter Arbeiten und vor dem Hintergrund unserer eigenen Studie eine Sammlung von Gestaltungshinweisen für die Planung und Durchführung von Erratbarkeitsstudien.

2 Hintergrund und Verwandte Arbeiten

Im Folgenden erläutern wir Top-Down und Bottom-Up Ansätze für den Entwurf von Gestensets und diskutieren Vor- und Nachteile. Ferner geben wir eine kurze Einführung in die Methodik der Erratbarkeitsstudien und diskutieren Arbeiten, die diese Methode einsetzen.

Beim Top-Down Ansatz entwerfen Interaktionsdesignerinnen und -designer die Gesten, die es erlauben, ein System zu kontrollieren, selbst. Sie sind dabei geleitet von domänenspezifischen Rahmenwerken und Richtlinien (z.B. [Lao *et al.* 2009]), Wissen über den Designspace (z.B. [Marquardt *et al.* 2011]), sowie dem generellen Verständnis menschlichen Verhaltens und menschlicher Kommunikation (z.B. [McNeil 1992]). Folglich bietet dieser Ansatz einige Vorteile. Erstens besteht eine große Chance, dass ein gut gestaltetes Gestenset eine Gestensprache formt, bei der die Gesten, die zu kohärenten Interaktionsmöglichkeiten gehören, auch selbst kohärente Gruppen bilden, und somit einfacher zu merken sind. Zudem können bei der Gestaltung technische Gesichtspunkte Berücksichtigung finden und die Gesten so gestaltet werden, dass sie für das unterliegende Erkennungssystem gut unterscheidbar sind, um so die Fehlertoleranz des Systems zu erhöhen [Pavlovic *et al.* 1997]. Schließlich können zur Vorbeugung von Ermüdungserscheinungen [Yee 2009] ergonomische Erwägungen bei der Gestaltung berücksichtigt werden [Nielsen *et al.* 2004].

Bottom-Up Ansätze basieren auf der Idee des partizipativen Gestaltens [Schuler & Namioka 1993], und haben folglich zum Ziel, Endbenutzerinnen und -benutzern aktiv in den Entwurfsprozess mit einzubeziehen. Für die Gestaltung von benutzerdefinierten Gesten erfreut sich die Methode der Erratbarkeitsstudie (Guessability Study) [Wobbrock *et al.* 2005; Wobbrock *et al.* 2009] zunehmender Beliebtheit. Das Besondere dieser Methode ist, dass sie als Vorgehen des partizipativen Designs dennoch auf eine strikte statistische Auswertung setzt. Das Ziel der Methode ist, Gestensets zu entwickeln, die von möglichst vielen Personen intuitiv benutzt werden können. Die Methode ist darauf ausgelegt, Gestensets zu kreieren für welche die Wahrscheinlichkeit die richtigen Gesten zu erraten, maximiert ist. Die Erratbarkeit ist dabei ein Kriterium für die Erlernbarkeit von Systemen [Dix *et al.* 1993, pp. 261-274]. Das Vorgehen ist wie folgt: In einer Studie werden Personen nacheinander eine Reihe von Interaktionsmöglichkeiten in Form einer Systemreaktion präsentiert—der *Effekt* oder die *Referenz*. Für jede dieser Interaktionen soll vom Teilnehmenden eine geeignete Geste—die *Ursache* oder das *Symbol*—vorschlagen werden. In [Wobbrock *et al.* 2009] wurden beispielsweise Teilnehmenden einer Studie die Reaktionen des Systems auf die Auswahl sowie das Verschieben von Objekten auf einem Multitouchtisch präsentiert. Die Teilnehmenden demonstrierten zu einem großen Teil entsprechend eine *Tap-Geste bzw. eine Drag-Geste als Vorschlag. Zu Beurteilung der Erratbarkeit eines Gestensets, wird die Übereinstimmung Ü als Maß herangezogen, die sich auf folgende Weise berechnen lässt:*

$$Ü=\frac{\sum_{e\in E}\sum_{V_i\subseteq V_e}\left(\frac{|V_i|}{|V_e|}\right)^2}{|E|}$$

Dabei ist *e* ein spezifischer Effekt (d.h. eine Systemreaktion) aus der Liste aller untersuchten Effekte *E*; V_e ist die Menge aller vorgeschlagenen Ursachen (d.h. die Gesten) für einen Effekt *e*; und V_i die Untermenge von identischen Ursachen (d.h. gleiche Gesten). Angenommen in einer Studie mit 8 Teilnehmenden wurde für den Effekt *Licht einschalten* sechsmal ein Klatschen und zweimal ein Schnipsen als Geste vorgeschlagen, so ergibt sich für diesen Effekt eine Übereistimmung $Ü=(6/8)^2+(2/8)^2=0{,}63$. Wäre Klatschen nur fünfmal vorgeschlagen worden und stattdessen eine weitere, dritte Geste einmal, verringert sich die Übereinstimmung auf $Ü=(5/8)^2+(2/8)^2+(1/8)^2=0{,}47$. Der Durchschnitt über alle Übereinstimmungen für alle Effekte gibt demnach dic Übereinstimmung für das Gestenset. Je mehr sich dieser Wert der eins annähert, desto konsensualer das resultierende Gestenset.

Dieser Ansatz wurde in einer Reihe von verwandten Arbeiten verwendet und diskutiert. Frisch et al. [2009] nutzen die Methode zur Ermittlung von Multitouch- und Stift-Gesten. In der Diskussion reflektieren sie die Doppeldeutigkeiten, welche durch diese Methoden entstehen können, wenn eine Geste für zwei Aktionen vorgeschlagen wird oder zwei Gesten durch die Erkennungsverfahren nicht voneinander unterscheidbar sind. Ruiz et al. [Ruiz *et al.* 2011] nutzten Erratbarkeitsstudien für die Entwicklung von Gesten für die mobile Interaktion. Die Autoren machen darauf aufmerksam, dass viele der resultierenden Gesten nur eine geringe kinetische Energie aufweisen; ein Umstand, der es den Entwicklern schwer macht, diese von normalen Bewegungen im täglichen Gebrauch zu differenzieren. Piumsomboon et al. [2013] nutzten die Methode, um ein Gestenset für den Bereich der Erweiterten Realität zu erstellen. In ihrer Analyse machen sie darauf aufmerksam, dass abstraktere Interaktionen zu einer niedrigeren Übereinstimmung führen und bemerken ebenfalls das Problem von Doppeldeutigkeiten. In ihrem Ansatz, Gesten für die Eingabe von Sonderzeichen auf Touchscreen-Tastaturen zu verwenden, verzichten Findlater et al. [2012] auf Grund der geringen Übereinstimmungswerte auf einige Kommandos, die sie dann als Widgets umsetzten. Die Problematik des Interpretationsspielraums bei der Beurteilung der Ähnlichkeit von Gesten wird z.B. bei einer Studie von Fußgesten erörtert [Alexander *et al.*

2012]. Sowohl [Wobbrock *et al.* 2009], [Morris 2012], als auch [Micire *et al.* 2009] finden Hinweise in ihren Studienresultaten das häufig bekannte Konzepte und mentale Modelle (z.B. WIMP-Paradigma) von den Teilnehmenden kopiert oder imitiert werden.

3 Studiendesign, Durchführung und Auswertung

Um aufzuzeigen inwieweit Entscheidungen im Studiendesign das Resultat von Erratbarkeitsstudien beeinflussen, führten wir eine eigene Studie durch. Im Folgenden erläutern wir Studiendesign, Durchführung, und Auswertung.

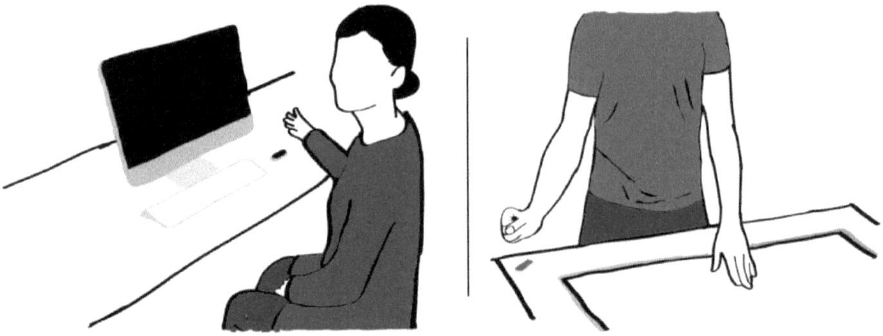

Abbildung 1. Skizzen zur Illustration der Szenarien periphere Interaktion (links) und interaktiver Tisch (rechts).

3.1 Zugrundeliegenden Szenarien

Als Rahmen für die Studie entwickelten wir zwei Szenarien (vgl. Abbildung 1)—*periphere Interaktion* (PI) und *interaktiver Tisch* (IT)—die den Teilnehmenden als Hintergrund für die Studie präsentiert wurden. In beiden Szenarien wurde die Eingabemodalität auf Freihand-Gesten [Wigdor & Wixon 2011] beschränkt die Mittels eines geeigneten Gerätes erkannt werden können (d.h. LEAP Motion Kontroller[2]). Um unser Untersuchungsziel zur verfolgen, war der erste Schritt, zwei Szenarien zu entwerfen, die auf unterschiedlichen Abstraktionsebenen angesiedelt sind. Für jedes der beiden Szenarien wurden die in Tabelle 1 aufgelisteten sieben Systemreaktionen (Effekte) entwickelt für die Gesten gefunden werden sollten. Während die Interaktionsmöglichkeiten im PI-Szenario als eher komplex, abstrakt, und außergewöhnlich einzustufen sind, setzen wir im IT-Szenario auf Systemreaktionen die im Vergleich eher simpel, ikonisch, und alltäglich sind. Weiterhin wurden für beide Szenarien die Effekte gezielt so gestaltet, dass sie teilweise als Paarungen, Gegensätze oder Abfolgen (z.B.: Kopieren, Ausschneiden, Einfügen) interpretiert werden können.

No.	Periphere Interaktion	Interaktiver Tisch
1	Musik Pausieren	Kopieren

[2] http://www.leapmotion.com/

2	Video Pausieren	Ausschneiden
3	Computer Stummschalten	Einfügen
4	Alle Instant Messenger auf ‚Nicht stören'	Löschen
5	Aktuelles Fenster Minimieren	Widerrufen (Undo)
6	Alle Fenster Minimieren (Desktop zeigen)	Wiederholen (Redo)
7	Bildschirm Ausschalten	Alles Markieren

Tabelle 1. Übersicht und Abfolge aller Systeminteraktionen für beide Szenarien.

Das Szenario *periphere Interaktion* zielt auf Büroarbeiterinnen und -arbeiter von ab, die einige Funktionen ihres Arbeitsplatzrechners mittels Gesten im Randbereich der eigenen Aufmerksamkeit steuern wollen [Bakker *et al.* 2012]. Das Szenario enthält Systemreaktionen, die eine Person dann steuern möchte, wenn eine weitere Person das Büro betritt (z.B. Computer stummschalten oder Instant Messenger-Status ändern). Der Einsatz von Gesten soll dabei eine subtile Nutzung unterstützen die es erlaubt die Aufmerksamkeit auf den Besucher, nicht auf die Aufgabe, zu richten. Wenn jemand das Büro betritt kann die Geste mit einer Hand über der Tastatur erfolgen, während sich der Körper — und somit die Aufmerksamkeit — seitwärts zur Tür richtet (vgl. Abbildung 1 links).

Das Szenario *interaktiver Tisch* zielt auf den schnellen und direkten Zugang zu grundlegenden Funktionen mittels Gesten in der Luft bei der Bedienung von interaktiven Multitouch-Tischen wie beispielsweise Kopieren, Ausschneiden und Einfügen. Die Person kann die Gesten mit einer Hand oberhalb der Tischkante ausführen, während mit der anderen Hand auf dem Tisch das Artefakt, auf dem die Aktion ausgeführt werden soll, durch Berührung selektiert wird (vgl. Abbildung 1 rechts).

3.2 Durchführung der Studie

Die Studie wurde in unserem Usability Labor durchgeführt und mittels zwei (PI) bzw. drei (IT) Kameras aus mehreren Perspektiven aufgezeichnet (vgl. Abbildung 2).

Abbildung 2. Standbild der Aufzeichnung aus drei Kameraperspektiven beim IT-Szenario.

Für die Studie rekrutierten wir 20 Teilnehmende (6 weiblich, alle Rechtshänder) mittels Convenience Sampling aus Studierenden verschiedener Fachbereiche. Jeder Teilnehmende erhielt zu Beginn der Studie eine kurze Einführung in den Ablauf. Die beiden Szenarien wurden jeweils nacheinander durchgeführt, wobei davor das jeweilige Szenario im Detail erläutert wurde und die Möglichkeit bestand, sich kurz durch Ausprobieren mit den Prozedere vertraut zu machen. Daraufhin wurden in beiden Szenarien die jeweils sieben Effekte der Reihe nach durchgegangen. Die Teilnehmenden hatten pro Effekt maximal eine Minute Zeit, sich eine Geste zu überlegen, um diese dann in drei Wiederholungen zu demonstrieren. Dabei war lautes Denken erlaubt. Nach der dritten Demonstration wurde mit dem nächsten Effekt fortgefahren. Nachdem alle Effekte eines Szenarios durchgegangen waren, wurde das Vorgehen für das andere Szenario wiederholt. Sowohl die Reihenfolge der Szenarien als auch die Reihenfolge der Effekte wurden zur Verminderung von Reihenstellungseffekten jeweils paarweise invertiert. Für das PI-Szenario nahmen die Teilnehmenden auf einem Schreibtischstuhl vor einem Desktoprechner Platz. Die Leap Motion wurde dabei rechts neben der Tastatur platziert; links befand sich eine Tür, auf welche die Teilnehmenden ihre Aufmerksamkeit durch eine Kopfdrehung richten sollten, während sie die Geste mit der rechten Hand blind demonstrierten. Zwischen jeder Demonstration wurden die Teilnehmenden gebeten, beide Hände auf die Tastatur als neutrale Position zu legen. Für das IT-Szenario wurden die Teilnehmenden gebeten sich an der Längsseite eines Multitouch-Tisches zu positionieren. Die Leap Motion wurde rechts auf der Einfassung des Tisches platziert. Auf den ausgeschalteten Tisch wurde mittels Klebstreifen eine Markierung angebracht, die das zu selektierende Artefakt darstellte. Eine weitere Markierung auf der Hälfte der Längsseite kennzeichnet die neutrale Position, zu der die Teilnehmenden zwischen jeder Demonstration mit beiden Händen zurückkehren sollten. Für eine Demonstration sollten die Teilnehmenden jeweils mit der linken Hand das Artefakt selektieren und mit der rechten Hand die Geste über der Leap Motion ausführen.

3.3 Auswertung und Ergebnisse

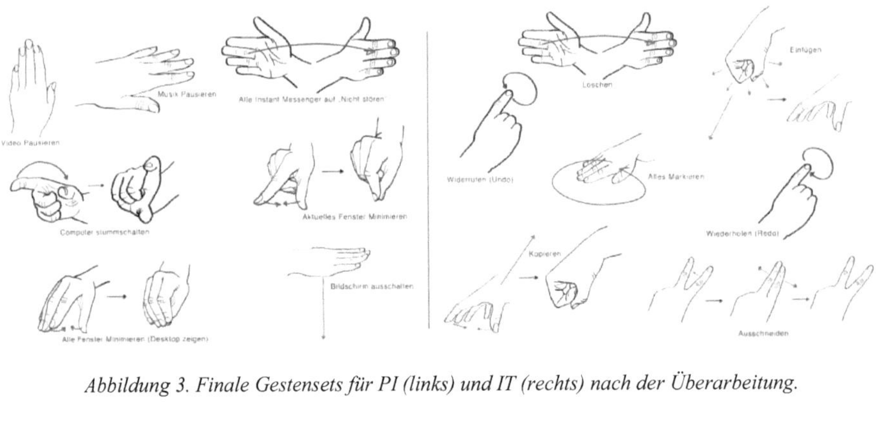

Abbildung 3. Finale Gestensets für PI (links) und IT (rechts) nach der Überarbeitung.

Insgesamt wurden von uns 280 Videos mit jeweils drei Demonstrationen einer Geste aufgezeichnet. Die Gesten wurden von drei verschiedenen Personen analysiert, um einen Effekt bei der Kodierung (d.h. Coder Bias) zu vermindern. Dabei wurden jeweils die 20 Videos für jeden Effekt durchgeschaut, die Gesten als kurze freitextliche Beschreibungen transkribiert, und die Häufigkeit für alle unterschiedlichen Gesten für einen Effekt gezählt. Nach der individuellen Transkription, wurden in einer Sitzung die Ergebnisse miteinander verglichen und durch Diskussion unter Einbezug der Videos finale Häufigkeiten und

Übereinstimmungen ermittelt. Für die beiden resultierende Gestensets wie sie in Abbildung 3 zu sehen sind, waren allerdings noch weitere Anpassungsschritte nötig, um Konflikte aufzulösen, und ein kohärentes und von der Technologie erkennbares Gestenset zu gestalten, auf die wir im nächsten Abschnitt eingehen.

4 Gestaltungsempfehlungen für Erratbarkeitsstudien

Basierend auf unserer Studie können wir nun komprimiert aufzeigen, welche Aspekte bei der Durchführung von Erratbarkeitsstudien von Bedeutung sind. Im Folgenden explizieren wir diese Aspekte und geben Hinweise und Empfehlungen für die Gestaltung von Studien.

Wie in anderen Arbeiten erwähnt hat die *konzeptuelle Komplexität* der untersuchten Interaktionen einen deutlichen Einfluss auf das Resultat von Erratbarkeitsstudien. So ist die Übereinstimmung im abstrakteren PI-Szenario insgesamt niedriger als im konkreteren IT-Szenario. Während im IT-Szenario der Effekt *Kopieren* die größte Übereinstimmung mit 15 von 20 Demonstrationen der gleichen Geste erreicht, sind es im PI-Szenario für den Effekt *Computer stummschalten* nur 6 von 20 Demonstrationen der identische Geste. Insgesamt verzeichnete die Gewinnergeste — d.h. die am häufigsten demonstrierte Geste — für einen Effekt im IT-Szenario im Durchschnitt 8 von 20 Demonstrationen (SD=3,6), während im PI-Szenario im Durchschnitt schon 4,3 von 20 (SD=0,8) gleiche Demonstrationen ausreichten. Die zu erwartende Erratbarkeit einer Geste liegt folglich im PI-Szenario unter 25 Prozent und ist somit als eher gering einzuschätzen. Dieser Unterschied zwischen den beiden Szenarien äußerte sich auch im eher zögerlichen Verhalten und den Äußerungen der Teilnehmenden im PI-Szenario. Unser Ergebnis legt nahe, dass die Methode für abstraktere Domänen deswegen nur bedingt geeignet ist. Auf der anderen Seite war mit 10 von 20 Demonstrationen die ‚Schere'-Geste für den Effekt *Ausschneiden* die Geste mit der zweithöchsten Übereinstimmung. Da die Schere häufig als Icon für den Ausschneide-Befehl verwendet wird, legt dieses Ergebnis nahe, das bei konzeptionell gewöhnlicheren Interaktionen, oft auf mentale Modelle aus dem Desktopbereich zurückgegriffen wird. Weitere, ähnliche Ergebnisse in unserer Studie und oben beschriebene Aussagen in verwandten Arbeiten lassen die Schlussfolgerung zu, dass die entstehenden Gestensets in ihrem Innovationscharakter dadurch deutlich beschränkt sind. Folglich ergibt sich für den sinnvollen Einsatz der Methode ein schmaler Korridor von Einsatzgebieten.

Ein weiterer Aspekt, dem Beachtung geschenkt werden sollte, ist die besondere Auswirkung einer *Randomisierung*. Natürlich existiert zunächst — wie bei anderen Experimenten auch — die Gefahr der systemischen Beeinflussung des Ergebnisses durch *Reihenstellungseffekte* (z.B. *Lerneffekte, Ermüdung,* oder Motivationsverlust). Folglich empfiehlt es sich, durch die Randomisierung in der Versuchsabfolge — beispielsweise durch Item-Rotation — Abhilfe zu schaffen. Gegen eine Randomisierung spricht jedoch die Tatsache, dass Interaktionen mit einem System häufig sinnbildende Paarungen, Gegensätze, oder Abfolgen darstellen, die durch kohärente Gesten repräsentiert werden sollten. In unserer Studie konnten wir anhand der einfachen Umkehrung der Effekt-Reihenfolge Auswirkungen erkennen. So verwirrte beispielsweise die umgekehrte Reihenfolge die Teilnehmenden (z.B. beim Effekt *Wieder-*

holen vor *Widerrufen*) oder die Gesten wurden in unterschiedlicher Reihenfolge vorgeschlagen (z.B. bei den Effekten *Aktuelles Fenster Minimieren* und *Alle Fenster Minimieren*) und reduzierten so die Gesamtübereinstimmung. Eine ähnliche Überlegung für die Reihenfolge der Präsentation unterschiedlicher Effekte, betrifft die unterschiedliche Bedeutsamkeit einer Interaktion für das System. Dieser Aspekt leitet über zu der Frage, wie mit identischen Gesten umgegangen werden soll. Für die Studie brauchen die Teilnehmenden klare Anweisungen, ob eine identische Geste für einen späteren Effekt erneut demonstriert werden darf, wenn sie dort als passender empfunden wird. Letztlich ist noch die Überlegung zu treffen ob statt einer festgelegten Reihenfolge oder einer Zufallsreihenfolge die Möglichkeit gegeben werden sollte, die Reihenfolge durch den Teilnehmenden festlegen zu lassen, der zu Beginn der Studie eine Übersicht über alle Effekte gezeigt bekommt. Während sich dies positiv auf die Entwicklung eines in sich konziseren Gestensets auswirken kann, hat das niedrigere Momentum an Spontanität evtl. negative Auswirkung auf die Erratbarkeit. Als guter Kompromiss für ein Vorgehen erscheint dabei der Ansatz von Piumsomboon et al. [2013] die statt einer vollständigen Durchmischung aller Effekte, die Abfolge von zusammengehörigen Gruppen von Effekten randomisieren.

Schließlich gilt es auch in der *Auswertung, Analyse, und Interpretation* der Ergebnisse Einiges zu beachten. In unserer Auswertung durch drei Personen zeigten sich deutliche Unterschiede. So wurde die Ähnlichkeit von Gesten teilweise verschieden interpretiert. Gesten die von der Lage (z.B. horizontale oder vertikale ‚Schere'-Geste), der Richtung (z.B. von links nach rechts oder umgekehrt) oder der Anzahl der benutzen Finger (z.B. ‚Greif'-Geste mit der ganzen Hand oder mit zwei Finger) unterschiedlich ausgeführt wurden, wurden auch abweichend als übereinstimmend interpretiert. Die Entscheidung, ob zwei Gesten als identisch zu beurteilen sind, beinhaltet oft schon ein gestalterisches Element und sollte somit durch Personen mit Domänenwissen erfolgen. Im nächsten Schritt, bei der Zuweisung der Gesten zu einem Effekt auf Basis der Häufigkeit, stellt die Auflösung von Konflikten bei gleichhäufigen Gesten für unterschiedliche Effekte eine weiter Herausforderung dar. Gerade im PI-Szenario war der Unterschied zwischen der häufigsten und den nachfolgenden Gesten statistisch oft marginal. Hier ist es oft sinnvoll, den Effekt der Erratbarkeit nicht zu hoch zu bewerten, und im Zweifelsfall jene Geste zu wählen, die sich in die gesamten Gestensprache am besten einfügt. So wurde in unserem Fall für den Effekt *Wiederholen* die ‚Kreisbewegungs'-Geste im Uhrzeigersinn ausgewählt, obwohl sie nicht die am häufigsten vorgeschlagene Geste war, aber auf ein logisches Paar mit der Geste gegen den Uhrzeigersinn für den Effekt *Widerrufen* bildet. In einem letzten Überarbeitungsschritt müssen sowohl die einzelnen Gesten sowie das Gestenset als Ganzes hinsichtlich technischer und ergonomischer Aspekte beurteilt werden. Aus der Sicht der technischen Machbarkeit ist beispielsweise zu beachten, ob: die demonstrierten Gesten von der eingesetzten Technologie erfasst werden können; unterschiedliche Gesten hinreichend voneinander, und von sonstigen Bewegungen, unterschieden werden können; sowie einfachere Gesten nicht in Komplexeren enthalten sind. In unserem Fall waren einige vorgeschlagene Gesten technisch von der Leap Motion nicht erfassbar (z.B. vertikale Überdeckung der Finger) und wurden deshalb abgeändert (z.B. gedreht auf der Z-Achse) oder getauscht. Ebenso gilt es, die vorgeschlagenen Gesten hinsichtlich ihrer Ergonomie zu bewerten und individuell ergonomische Gesten vorzuziehen. Insgesamt bleibt zu sagen, das Designerinnen und Designer für ein in sich schlüssiges, funktionierendes und ergonomisches Gestenset manuelle Optimierungen vornehmen sollten.

5 Zusammenfassung

Unser Beitrag ist eine komprimierte Hinweissammlung, die es bei der Gestaltung von Erratbarkeitsstudien zu beachten gilt, auf Basis unser eigenen Studie und der Analyse von verwandten Arbeiten. Abschließend ist zu sagen, dass der Hauptzweck der Methode — die Erhöhung der Erratbarkeit — für die in der Literatur häufig anzutreffenden Studiengrößen mit um die 20 Teilnehmenden auf Grund der limitierten Generalisierbarkeit stark eingeschränkt ist. Eine Nachbearbeitung der Gestensets ist daher immer empfehlenswert und oft von Nöten. Eine Alternative bieten solche Ansätze, die Bottom-Up und Top-Down Ansätze vereinen und ein weniger striktes Vorgehen vorschreiben [Nielsen et al. 2004].

Literaturverzeichnis

Alexander, J., Han, T., Judd, W., Irani, P. and Subramanian, S. Putting Your Best Foot Forward: Investigating Real-world Mappings for Foot-based Gestures. In Proc. of CHI 2012 (5.-10. Mai, Austin, USA). ACM, NY, USA, 2012. pp. 1229-1238.

Bakker, S., Van Den Hoven, E. and Eggen, B. Acting by Hand: Informing Interaction Design for the Periphery of People's Attention. Interacting with Computers 34, 3 (2012). pp. 119-130.

Baudel, T. and Beaudouin-Lafon, M. Charade: Remote Control of Objects Using Free-hand Gestures. Communications of the ACM 36, 7 (März 2012). pp. 28-35

Bolt, R.A. "Put-That-There": Voice and Gesture at the Graphics Interface. In Proc. of SIGGRAPH 1980 (Jul. 14-18, Seattle, USA). ACM, NY, USA, 1980. pp. 262-270.

Cafaro, F., Lyons, L., Kang, R., Radinsky, J., Roberts, J. and Vogt, K. Framed Guessability: Using Embodied Allegories to Increase User Agreement on Gesture Sets. In Proc. of TEI 2014 (16.-18. Feb., München). ACM, NY, USA, 2014. pp. 197-204.

Dix, A.J., Finlay, J., Abowd, G.D. and Beale, R. Human-Computer Interaction. Prentice Hall International Ltd, Hertfordshire, UK, 1993.

Findlater, L., Lee, B. and Wobbrock, J.O. Beyond QWERTY: Augmenting Touch Screen Keyboards with Multi-Touch Gestures for Non-Alphanumeric Input. In Proc. of CHI 2012 (5.1-. Mai, Austin, USA). ACM, NY, USA, 2012. pp. 2679-2682.

Frisch, M., Heydekorn, J. and Dachselt, R. Investigating Multi-Touch and Pen Gestures for Diagram Editing on Interactive Surfaces. In Proc. of ITS 2009 (23.-25. Nov., Banff). ACM, NY, USA, 2009. pp. 149-156.

Lao, S., Heng, X., Zhang, G., Ling, Y. and Wang, P. A Gestural Interaction Design Model for Multi-touch Displays. In Proc. of BCS-HCI 2009 (1.-5. Sep., Cambridge, UK). *BCS*, Swinton, UK, 2009. pp. 440-446.

Malizia, A. and Bellucci, A. The Artificiality of Natural User Interfaces. Communications of the ACM 55, 3 (März 2012). pp. 36-38.

Marquardt, N., Jota, R., Greenberg, S. and Jorge, J.A. The Continuous Interaction Space. In Proc. of INTERACT 2011 (5.-9. Sept., Lisabon, Portugal). Springer, Heidelberg, 2011. pp. 461-476.

McNeil, D. Hand and Mind: What Gestures Reveal about Thought. University of Chicago Press, Chicago, IL, USA, 1992.

Micire, M., Desai, M., Courtemanche, A., Tsui, K.M. and Yanco, H.A. Analysis of Natural Gestures for Controlling Robot Teams on Multi-touch Tabletop Surfaces. In Proc. of ITS 2009 (23.-25. Nov., Banff, Kanada). ACM, NY, USA, 2009. pp. 41-48.

Morris, M.R. Web on the Wall: Insights from a Multimodal Interaction Elicitation Study In Proc. of ITS 2012 (11.-14. Nov., Cambridge,, USA). ACM, NY, USA, 2012. pp. 95-104.

Nielsen, M., Störring, M., Moeslund, T.B. and Granum, E. A Procedure for Developing Intuitive and Ergonomic Gesture Interfaces for HCI. In Camurri, A. and Volpe, G., eds. Gesture-Based Communication in HCI. Springer, Heidelberg, 2004. pp. 409-420.

Pavlovic, V.I., Sharma, R. and Huang, T.S. Visual Interpretation of Hand Gestures for Human-Computer Interaction: A Review. IEEE TPAMI 19, 7 (Juli 1997). pp. 677-695.

Piumsomboon, T., Clark, A., Billinghurst, M. and Cockburn, A. User-Defined Gestures for Augmented Reality. In Ext. Abs. of CHI 2013 (27. Apr. 27 - 2. Mai, Paris). ACM, NY, USA, 2013. pp. 955-960.

Ruiz, J., Li, Y. and Lank, E. User-defined Motion Gestures for Mobile Interaction. In Proc. of CHI 2011 (7.-12. Mai, Vancouver, Kanada). ACM, NY, USA, 2011. pp. 197-206.

Schuler, D. and Namioka, A. Participatory Design: Principles and Practices. Lawrence Erlbaum Associates, Hillsdale, NJ, USA, 1993.

Wigdor, D. and Wixon, D. Brave NUI World: Designing Natural User Interfaces for Touch and Gesture. Morgan Kaufman, San Francisco, USA, 2011.

Wobbrock, J.O., Aung, H.H., Rothrock, B. and Myers, B.A. Maximizing the Guessability of Symbolic Input. In Ext. Abs. of CHI 2005 (2.-7. Apr., Portland, USA). ACM, NY, USA, 2005. pp. 1869-1872.

Wobbrock, J.O., Morris, M.R. and Wilson, A.D. User-Defined Gestures for Surface Computing. In Proc. of CHI 2009 (4.-9. Apr., Boston, USA). ACM, NY, USA, 2009. pp. 1083-1092.

Yee, W. Potential Limitations of Multi-touch GestureVocabulary: Differentiation, Adoption, Fatigue In Proc. of HCII 2009 (19.-214. Jul., San Diego, USA). Springer, Heidelberg, 2009. pp. 291-300.

Danksagung

Wir danken den Mitgliedern des Cooperative Media Lab, im speziellen Lisa Homuth, Mike Imhof, Yasir Isitan, Verena Pinkwart, Alexander Schreiner, und Tobias Weith.

Kontaktinformationen

Prof. Dr. Tom Gross, tom.gross(at)uni-bamberg.de, T. 0951/863-3940

M. Koch, A. Butz & J. Schlichter (Hrsg.): Mensch und Computer 2014 Tagungsband,
München: Oldenbourg Wissenschaftsverlag, 2014, S. 255-264.

Zwischen Design und Flexibilität – Zur Ergonomie des Flat Design

Felix Winkelnkemper, Reinhard Keil

Heinz Nixdorf Institut, Universität Paderborn

Zusammenfassung

Damit eine Software erfolgreich ist, muss sie nicht nur schnell und fehlerfrei funktionieren, sondern auch hedonischen und designerischen Ansprüchen genügen. Die Herangehens- und Sichtweisen von Softwareentwicklern und Designern liegen jedoch traditionell weit auseinander. Während Designer typischerweise Gestaltung und Funktionalität integriert zur Perfektion bringen, ist ein Softwareentwickler meist gezwungen, seine Produkte so zu gestalten, dass sie für eine Vielzahl von Zwecken eingesetzt und angepasst werden können. Um dennoch Programme gestalten zu können, die den designerischen Ansprüchen zumindest nahe kommen, greifen Softwareentwickler auf Entwicklungs-Frameworks und Design-Ressourcen zurück. Der Beitrag zeigt am Beispiel des Flat Design, dass durch den Einsatz beliebter Ressourcen nicht automatisch gut nutzbare Software entsteht, und ist somit ein Plädoyer dafür, dass Softwareentwickler grundlegende ergonomische Erkenntnisse benötigen.

1 Einleitung

Software muss einer Vielzahl von Anforderungen genügen. Neben der korrekten Funktion sind dies vor allem die Gebrauchstauglichkeit und immer mehr auch Anforderungen an eine ästhetische Oberflächengestaltung (siehe Hassenzahl 2001; Thielsch & Hassenzahl 2008). Die technische Disziplin der Softwareentwicklung muss sich mehr und mehr mit Fragen aus der Sphäre des Designs beschäftigen. Die Zusammenarbeit von Designern und Informatikern gestaltet sich jedoch in vielfacher Hinsicht schwierig. Zwei grundverschiedene Denk- und Sichtweisen prallen hier aufeinander. Das wird auch an dem Themenschwerpunkt „Usability und Ästhetik“ (Burmester et al. 2008) der Zeitschrift i-com deutlich.

Designer beschäftigen sich mit ästhetischen Qualitäten. Ästhetik wird in der Regel dem künstlerischen Bereich zugeordnet, indem kreatives Vorgehen, Schönheit und emotionales Ansprechen im Vordergrund stehen. Designer betrachten das Produkt als Ganzes. Funktion und Gestaltung gehen Hand in Hand und sind nicht voneinander getrennt zu betrachten. Um diese Verschmelzung von Aussehen und Funktion zu erreichen, legen sie ein hohes Maß an Perfektionismus an den Tag. Folgende Bemerkung über die Entwicklung des Fußes des aktuellen iMac von Apple durch Jonathan Ive ist hierfür ein gutes Beispiel:

> [Ive] spent "months and months and months" working out the exact shape of the stand of the desktop iMac computer because "it's very hard to design something that you almost do not see because it just seems so obvious, natural and inevitable". (Arlidge 2014)

Ein gutes Design sticht immer heraus und bedeutet immer einen sehr hohen Aufwand. Charakteristisch für Softwareentwickler ist jedoch, dass sie nicht ein einzelnes Produkt entwerfen, sondern in der Regel Software herstellen, die sich durch kleinere Anpassungen für eine Vielzahl von Einsatzzwecken eignen muss. Dabei ist es das Ziel, möglichst viel zu formalisieren und zugleich Spielraum und Flexibilität für die jeweils individuelle Ausgestaltung zu erreichen. Gute Software muss anpassbar sein, sie steht nie für sich, sondern muss sich einfügen in ein Betriebssystem oder in eine Unternehmenskultur. Ein Softwareentwickler betrachtet also selten ein einzelnes Produkt für einen einzelnen Zweck, sondern meist die Vielfältigkeit der konkreten Ausprägungen seines Produkts. Eine komplett integrierte Betrachtung von Funktion, Nutzung und Gestaltung ist ihm nicht möglich. Damit die durch Informatiker erstellte Software dennoch gestalterischen Ansprüchen genügen kann, greifen Entwickler auf Entwicklungs-Frameworks und Design-Ressourcen zurück, um die Gestaltungsbereiche und damit die Kompetenzfelder zu entkoppeln.

Mit Hilfe von Entwicklungs-Frameworks soll erreicht werden, dass der funktionale Kern eines Produkts möglichst stark von der Benutzeroberfläche abgekoppelt wird.[1] Dies erlaubt es, diese Bereiche getrennt voneinander zu entwickeln, und entlastet den Verantwortlichen für den einen Bereich jeweils von den Kompetenzen für den anderen Bereich. Bei der Ausgestaltung der Oberflächen kann der Softwareentwickler heute auf vielfältige Design-Ressourcen zurückgreifen. Das sind z. B. Schriften, Icons oder Farbkombinationen, die nicht jedesmal aufs Neue gestaltet, sondern aus einschlägigen Quellen (zum Beispiel aus dem Fundus des Betriebssystems) übernommen werden. Diese Entkopplung der Kompetenzfelder ermöglicht es Softwareentwicklern erst, Programmoberflächen zu erzeugen, die den ästhetischen Ansprüchen der Nutzer gerecht werden können, indem die Gestaltungsaufgabe generalisiert und ins Vorfeld verlagert wird. Entwicklungs-Frameworks und Design-Ressourcen sind jedoch leider kein Garant dafür, dass die gestalteten Programmoberflächen schön oder gar ergonomisch sind. So schränkt die Verwendung von Frameworks Gestaltungsspielräume ein, wenn das, was sich nicht mit Hilfe der im jeweiligen Framework enthaltenen Werkzeuge und Generatoren umsetzen lässt, dem obligatorischen Zeit- und Kostendruck geopfert wird. Eine häufige Folge des Einsatzes von Frameworks sind sehr schematische Benutzungsoberflächen, wenn die Trennung der Gestaltungsbereiche dazu führt, dass die Nutzungsoberfläche nachlaufend, wie als nötiges Übel, entwickelt wird.

Die Menge von Design-Ressourcen ist unübersichtlich. Gerade durch den Innovationsdruck des Webdesigns emergieren in der letzten Zeit immer wieder Design-Richtlinien und dazugehörige Ressourcen, die stark Stilen oder Moden unterworfen sind, die den jeweiligen Zeitgeist widerspiegeln (siehe Platz 2008) und dann in die Design-Guidelines der Hersteller

[1] Paradigmatische Grundlage hierfür ist das Seeheim-Modell, das schon 1983 begründet worden ist und die Schnittstelle in die drei Bereiche Dialogeinheit, Präsentation und Anwendungsschnittstelle unterteilt (siehe Pfaff 1983).

Eingang finden. Am Beispiel des populären Flat Design soll im Folgenden genauer dargelegt werden, dass weit verbreitete und umfassend angewandte Design-Trends dem Stand der ergonomischen Erkenntnis teilweise kolossal widersprechen.

2 Flat Design

Flat Design ist ein Beispiel für einen modernen Design-Trend, der nicht etwa von einer eindeutig benennbaren Design-bildenden Instanz propagiert wurde, sondern im Diskurs vor allem in Blogs und Web-Magazinen zu emergieren schien. Großen Einfluss wird dem von Microsoft zunächst mit Windows Phone, dann Ende 2012 mit Windows 8 im Computerbereich eingeführten kachelbasierten Design zugeschrieben (zum Beispiel in Bilton 2013 oder Greif 2013). Microsoft selbst verwandte den Begriff „Flat Design" jedoch nicht. Abbildung 1 zeigt an Hand der Suchhäufigkeit bei Google, dass der Begriff 2013 große Popularität erlangte (rote Kurve oben). Ein Großteil der im Jahre 2013 zu diesem Thema erschienenen Beiträge setzt Flat Design in Gegensatz zum so genannten Skeuomorphismus. Wie in Abbildung 1 (blaue Kurve unten) zu sehen, war dieser Begriff vor Ende 2012 nicht im öffentlichen Interesse. Der deutsche Wikipedia-Artikel „Skeuomorphismus" besteht gar erst seit Mai 2013.

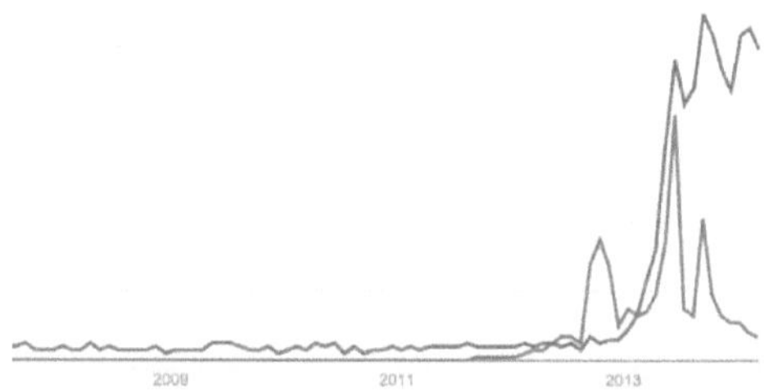

Abbildung 1: Die Begriffe „flat design" (oben) und „skeuomorphism" (unten) bei Google Trends

Eben dieser Wikipedia-Artikel beschreibt Skeuomorphismus als „eine Stilrichtung hauptsächlich im Design, bei der Objekte in ihrer Gestaltung ein anderes Material oder eine Form eines älteren, vertrauten Gegenstands nachahmen, ohne dass diese durch ihre Funktion begründet ist." Die Kritik an einem solchen Stil ist nicht neu. Schon (Platz 2008) wunderte sich über den Trend, in der Bildschirmgestaltung Plastizität, Glanzeffekte und Spiegelungen zu mimen, während man gleichzeitig im Hardwaredesign darum bemüht ist, all dies zu vermeiden. Gerade durch das – seinerzeit noch sehr neue – iPhone halte ein Design Einzug, das sich „so sehr in den Vordergrund der Betrachtung [drängt], dass man bezweifeln kann, ob dies noch der Verständlichkeit und Bedienbarkeit zuträglich ist." Er kritisiert das mit der Nachahmung physikalischer Gegenstände einhergehende, an der physikalischen Welt ausgerichtete Verständnis.[2] Das was auf dem Bildschirm zu sehen ist, seien daher eher Scheinbilder denn Sinnbilder. Die Möglichkeit, „der Verdichtung und Anreicherung von Informationen und das Potential von Formen und Farben, eine eigene Sprachebene zu etablieren [...]", bliebe übersehen und ungenutzt.

In der Tat scheint der aktuelle Flat-Design-Trend den Beobachtungen Platz' genau zu entsprechen, verspricht er doch ein Ende der überkandidelten Schnörkel in den Nutzeroberflächen, all der Zierrahmen und Abrundungen, der Papier- und Ledertexturen, der Glas-Buttons und virtuellen Eselsohren (siehe z. B. Mayer 2013 oder Musngi 2013). Doch nicht nur die Texturen und unsinnigen Metaphern verschwinden mit dem Flat Design. Ein Button verfügt nicht mehr über die bis vor Kurzem noch allgegenwärtigen abgerundeten Ecken, über keinen Farbverlauf, keine Schattenkanten und schon gar keinen Schlagschatten. Im Flat Design tritt an seine Stelle eine rechteckige farbige Fläche mit einem einfach gehaltenen Piktogramm und einem prägnanten Text in einer klaren Schrift.

Versucht man die Beiträge in Blogs und Magazinen zusammenzufassen, sind dies die Charakteristika des Flat Design:

- keine naturähnlichen Texturen wie Holz oder Glasoberflächen,
- keine Schlagschatten, Schattenkanten oder Farbverläufe,
- keine Abrundungen oder Verzierungen,
- eine starke Betonung der Typographie,
- Verwendung von fünf bis acht freundlichen, hellen Farben,
- Verwendung einfach gestalteter, großer Piktogramme.

Für dieses neue Design, das in manchen Beiträgen gar als Revolution betitelt wird, werden allerlei vernünftelnde Begründungen angegeben. Das neue Design sei ein „rationaler und funktionaler" Schritt in die Zukunft (Mayer 2013). Funktionalität und Ästhetik seien durch Flat Design „in complete harmony" (Clum 2013). Neben diesen eher den Geschmack betreffenden Aussagen werden teils auch technische Begründungen angeführt. Mit Flat Design sei es leichter, eine Vielzahl von Plattformen zu bedienen (Mayer 2013). Speziell sei Flat Design eine geradezu logische Folge des geringen Bildschirmplatzes auf Mobiltelefonen (Bilton 2013), was insofern zweifelhaft ist, als es ja gerade das Design des iPhones war, mit dem eine übertrieben realistische Darstellung in die Welt kam. Der Aufruf „Avoid too many bells and whistles" (Clum 2013) weist auf den vermeintlichen Hauptvorteil des Flat Design hin. All das, was über Flat Design hinausginge, also neben Texturen auch jede Darstellung von Tiefe durch Schatten oder Farbverlauf, sei reine Ablenkung von der eigentlichen Funktionalität und behindere daher mehr, als sie nutze. Schlussendlich wird behauptet, Flat Design sei per se nutzerfreundlich und lege den Fokus auf Usability (Clum 2013-2). Ein Web-Beitrag

[2] (Greif 2013) beschreibt ein schönes Beispiel dafür, was passiert, wenn man sich beim grafischen Design eines digitalen Kalenders zu sehr an physikalischen Kalendern orientiert. Unreflektiert wird dann zum Beispiel auch die strikte Einteilung des Kalenders in Monate und Wochen übernommen, obwohl es in einem digitalen Kalender keine Notwendigkeit für einen solchen Zwang gibt.

geht gar so weit zu behaupten, dass ein normaler Benutzer bei einer Anwendung im Flat Design keinerlei Notwendigkeit mehr habe, eine Bedienungsanleitung zu nutzen, da ja alles selbsterklärend sei (Musngi 2013). Ohne auf alle Argumente und Behauptungen im Einzelnen eingehen zu wollen, wird klar, dass auf Grundlage dieser Argumente nur schwerlich eine Bewertung abgegeben werden kann.

3 Flat Design und Tiefenwahrnehmung

Bei jeder Gestaltung einer Nutzungsoberfläche gilt es, grafische Objekte auf dem Bildschirm anzuzeigen und diese möglichst so zu gestalten, dass sie vom menschlichen Wahrnehmungsapparat effektiv und effizient aufgenommen werden können. Hierfür ist es notwendig, sich über einige Eigenarten der menschlichen Wahrnehmung klar zu werden.

Abbildung 2: So in etwa kann man sich das Gesichtsfeld eines Menschen vorstellen.

Die Wahrnehmung des Menschen ist angepasst an seine Umwelt (siehe z. B. Hoffman 2001, Seite 40 oder Zimbardo 1995, Seite 188). Im Laufe der Jahrtausende der Menschheitsgeschichte waren die Menschen klar im Vorteil, deren Wahrnehmung schnell und effektiv war. Es galt, in der Masse der sie umgebenden Reize schnell auf diejenigen Reize reagieren zu können, die für das schiere Überleben oder das Jagen wichtig waren. Anderes konnte dabei ruhig hintenüber fallen. Der Schnelligkeitsgewinn wird durch einen Informationsverlust erkauft. Die menschliche Wahrnehmung ist also immer selektiv. Diese Selektivität fängt dabei schon in der Anatomie des Auges an. Es kann nur in einem sehr kleinen Bereich in der Mitte des Wahrnehmungsfelds überhaupt scharf sehen (siehe Falk et al. 1990, Seite 157), drum herum ist alles unscharf und farblos, dafür aber sehr bewegungsempfindlich (siehe Abbildung 2). Der Verlust an Genauigkeit wird erkauft durch eine hohe Aufmerksamkeitsleitung, die zum Beispiel bei herannahenden Raubtieren die wichtigere Qualität darstellte.

Dass das wahrgenommene Bild dennoch vollständig erscheint, ist der Leistung des Gehirns zu verdanken. Das Gehirn „rät“ gewissermaßen, wie das Bild zu vervollständigen ist. An Hand dieser Hypothese wird dann gegebenenfalls das Auge bewegt. Unsere Gehirne sind an die Umwelt, also an Landschaften auf der Erde, so gut angepasst, dass die Hypothesen meist stimmen. Beim Umherschauen in einer Landschaft kann beispielsweise davon ausgegangen werden, dass Objekte, sobald sie aus dem Wahrnehmungsfeld geraten, nicht auf einmal verschwinden oder ausgetauscht werden. Tun sie dies, wie in einem Trick, doch, fällt es schwer oder dauert es sehr lange, dies zu bemerken, denn das menschliche Gehirn ist für solche Situationen nicht ausgelegt. Um sich in der Umgebung zurechtzufinden, ist es notwendig, die wahrgenommenen Objekte schnell voneinander unterscheiden zu können. Unser Wahrnehmungsapparat ist dabei in der Erkennung der Übergänge zwischen Vordergrund und Hintergrund besonders effektiv und kann in üblichen Situationen den Vordergrund vom Hintergrund trennen, ohne die Szenerie komplett mit dem Auge „erwandern“ zu müssen. Lokale Hinweise im relativ kleinen scharfen Sichtfeld reichen dafür aus.

Folgende vereinfachte Konstruktion hilft, solche Hinweise herauszuarbeiten: Gegeben ist die Fotografie einer Landschaft, über die ein weißes Blatt Papier gelegt ist, in das ein relativ kleines Loch geschnitten wurde. Es ist also immer nur ein kleiner Teil des Bildes sichtbar. Nur an Hand dieses Ausschnitts soll nun bestimmt werden, ob ein Objekt ein anderes verdeckt und, falls dies der Fall ist, welches Objekt vorne und welches hinten liegt. Schnell lassen sich eine Reihe von Hypothesen aufstellen, die sich in der Fachliteratur bestätigt finden. Sie basieren auf üblichen Wahrnehmungssituationen. Bei der Betrachtung weiter entfernter Objekte in einer Landschaft liegt mehr Luft zwischen dem Betrachter und dem Objekt als bei nahen Objekten. Da diese Luft oft schmutzig oder dunstig ist, sich Licht also zerstreut oder gedämpft wird, lassen sich folgende Hypothesen formulieren (siehe zum Beispiel Falk et al. 1990, Seite 243).

1. Eine Vordergrund-Hintergrund-Verdeckung liegt dann vor, wenn man im Bildausschnitt eine Kante, also einen abrupten Farb-, Sättigungs- oder Helligkeitsunterschied ausmachen kann.
2. Auf Grund der Luft-Streuung liegt die ungesättigtere Farbe im Hintergrund, die gesättigtere im Vordergrund.
3. Geht man davon aus, dass man nicht gegen die Sonne blickt, liegt das hellere Objekt tendenziell im Vordergrund, denn das Licht entfernterer Objekte wird durch die Luft abgedunkelt.

Weitere Hypothesen beziehen sich auf Licht und Schatten und gehen von der üblichen Situation aus, dass das Licht vom Himmel her scheint (siehe hierzu Hoffman 2001, Seite 153).

4. Erkennt man einen Schlagschatten, liegt die Fläche, auf die der Schatten fällt, im Hintergrund, die andere im Vordergrund.
5. Erkennt man eine dunkle Objektbegrenzung, handelt es sich offenbar um eine lichtabgewandte Kante eines Objekts. Die Kante begrenzt also das oben liegende Vordergrundobjekt.
6. Erkennt man eine helle Objektbegrenzung, handelt es sich um eine lichtzugewandte Kante; das Vordergrundobjekt liegt also offenbar unten.

Letztlich kann bei einer kontinuierlichen Helligkeitsveränderung von einem Beleuchtungsverlauf ausgegangen werden (Hoffman 2001, Seite 150).

7. Erkennt man einen Helligkeitsverlauf, kann geschlossen werden, von welcher Seite das Licht kommt. Die Regeln 5 und 6 können dann auch auf linke und rechte Objektbegrenzungen angewandt werden.

Jedes natürliche Objekt, das über einem anderen liegt, wirft in der Regel einen Schatten oder hebt sich durch Unterschiede in Helligkeit oder Sättigung ab. Genau diese Informationen nutzt das Auge zur Erschließung des Wahrnehmungsfelds. Diese Erkenntnisse lassen sich auf User-Interfaces übertragen, da es auch hier gilt, den Nutzer beim Erkennen und Trennen dieser Vordergrund- und Hintergrundobjekte visuell zu unterstützen. Auf dem Bildschirm eine flache Welt zu gestalten nimmt dem Nutzer eine der natürlichsten Möglichkeiten, Strukturen zu erkennen, denn in der natürlichen Umwelt gibt es kein Flat Design. Buttons, als aktive Objekte, müssen sich irgendwie hervorheben; Hinweismeldungen liegen vor dem Anwendungsfenster und verdecken es teilweise; auch Fenster verdecken einander teilweise. Die in der natürlichen Umwelt bewährten Wahrnehmungsmuster zu übertragen bedeutet, auch hier lokale Hinweisreize zu geben:

1. Vordergrund vom Hintergrund durch eine klare Kante, also einen hohen Kontrast, voneinander abgrenzen.
2. Den Hintergrund mit einer weniger gesättigten Farbe versehen als den Vordergrund.
3. Den Vordergrund heller gestalten als den Hintergrund.
4. Vordergrundobjekte mit einem leichten Schlagschatten versehen.
5. Unter der Annahme, dass sich die Lichtquelle oben links befindet, die Vordergrundobjekte oben und links mit einer hellen Kante, unten und rechts mit einer dunklen Kante abgrenzen.
6. Durch einen leichten Helligkeitsverlauf andeuten, wo sich die Lichtquelle befindet.

Abbildung 3 zeigt Variationen dieser Hinweise. Natürlich bietet es sich nicht immer an, all diese lokalen Hinweise auf einmal anzuwenden. Jeder dieser kleinen Tricks in Maßen angewandt hilft den Nutzern einer Oberfläche jedoch, die Elemente abzugrenzen und in ihrer Anordnung zu erkennen. Sie sind keine überflüssigen visuellen Ornamente, nicht einfach nur Ablenkung oder Zierwerk.

Abbildung 3: Beispiele für die Unterstützung der Tiefenwahrnehmung durch Sättigungsabstufung oben und Helligkeitsabstufung unten, jeweils unterstützt durch Schlagschatten, Schlagschatten und Helligkeitsverlauf, Konturlinien, Konturlinien und Helligkeitsverlauf

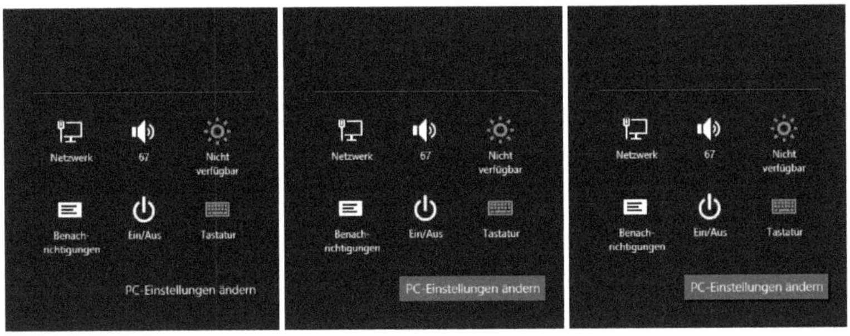

Abbildung 4: Die Windows 8-Seitenleiste im Original, mit einer Helligkeitsabstufung, zusätzlich mit Schattenwurf

Abbildung 4 zeigt ein Beispiel, bei dem durch zu starke Vereinfachung jeder Hinweisreiz fehlt. Der Schriftzug „PC-Einstellungen ändern“ wirkt daher eher wie eine Beschriftung für die darüber befindlichen Funktions-Icons denn als Schaltfläche. Schon ein Abheben des Buttons durch einen helleren Hintergrund reicht aus, um die Tiefenwahrnehmung zu unterstützen und die Oberfläche somit verständlicher und ergonomischer zu gestalten.

4 Flat Design und Farbe

Während sich das Flat Design im Allgemeinen sehr zurückhaltend gibt, was auffällige Elemente und Effekte angeht, wird bei Farben das genaue Gegenteil propagiert. Fünf bis acht kräftige Farben dürfen es gerne sein, um dem Design ein freundliches Aussehen zu geben. Farbe ist ein schwieriges Gestaltungsmittel im Bereich der Gestaltung von Nutzungsoberflächen, vor allem, wenn stark gesättigte Farben verwendet werden. Sie eignen sich hervorragend, um Elemente auszuzeichnen, sodass sie aus der Menge von Objekten herausfallen. Einer der Kreise in Abbildung 5 fällt aufgrund seiner Farbe sofort ins Auge, er lenkt die Aufmerksamkeit. Diese Aufmerksamkeitsleitung geschieht vorbewusst, das heißt, noch bevor ein Betrachter die Chance hat darüber nachzudenken, sorgt sein Wahrnehmungssystem für die Lenkung der Aufmerksamkeit (siehe Zimbardo 1995, Seite 231). In der Gestaltung grafischer Nutzungsoberflächen wird das ausgenutzt, wenn zum Beispiel ein fehlerhaft ausgefülltes Formularfeld mit einer Signalfarbe hervorgehoben wird. Die Aufmerksamkeitsleitung ist dann gewünscht.

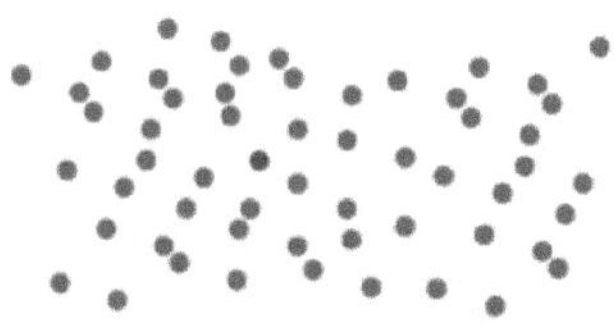

Abbildung 5: Farben sind dazu geeignet, einzelne Objekte unter anderen hervorzuheben.

Umgekehrt heißt das, dass große Anstrengungen erforderlich sind, die Aufmerksamkeit wieder auf etwas anderes zu richten, wenn das farbige Element die ganze Zeit „Hierhin gucken!" ruft. Ein Farbschema mit fünf leuchtenden Farben, wie im Flat Design üblich, führt zwangsläufig zu Problemen: Es ist schwer, die Farben so auszubalancieren, dass sich nicht eine Farbe in den Vordergrund spielt und ablenkt. Gibt es mehrere auffällige Farben im Ensemble, ist der Benutzer hin- und hergerissen, wird von jeder Seite her angeschrien. Jetzt noch mit Farbe etwas herauszustellen ist nicht mehr möglich. Mit Farbe bewusst Objekte hervorheben geht nur, wenn die übrigen Objekte farblich zurückhaltend, also idealerweise Ton in Ton gestaltet sind. Hinzu kommen noch optische Probleme wie chromatische Aberration (siehe Falk et al. 1995, Seite 97). Licht verschiedener Wellenlängen wird im Auge unterschiedlich gebrochen, was dazu führt, dass zum Beispiel gesättigtes Blau anders fokussiert werden muss als gesättigtes Rot. Stehen die Farben in all ihrer Pracht nebeneinander oder aufeinander, ist immer eine von ihnen unscharf, das Auge muss laufend neu fokussieren, Augen- und Kopfschmerzen sind unvermeidlich.

5 Abschlussbemerkungen und Fazit

Natürlich gibt es auch positive ergonomische Aspekte des Flat Design. Im Vergleich mit weit überladenen Oberflächen der jüngeren Vergangenheit wirkt Flat Design erfreulich simpel und aufgeräumt. Ergonomisch geradezu vorbildlich ist die Befreiung des Icon-Designs von vielem Ballast. Hier waren über Jahre komplexeste, unruhige und teilweise nur schwer unterscheidbare Piktogramme im Einsatz. Mit dem Aufkommen des Flat Design sehen wir zunehmend einfache und dennoch gut unterscheidbare, wiedererkennbare Piktogramme.[3] Die Begründungen, die für diese Piktogramme angegeben werden, verwundern allerdings ebenso, wie die anfangs kommentierten Begründungen für flache Oberflächen: Die neuen

[3] Siehe hierzu das Konzept der globalen Icons bei (Wandmacher 1993).

Piktogramme seien selbsterklärend und würden ihre Geschichte auf einfachere Art und Weise erzählen. Natürlich ist aber kein Piktogramm dieser Welt selbsterklärend und Geschichten erzählen Piktogramme auch nicht.

Als Fazit des Exkurses ins Flat Design lässt sich festhalten, dass der Einsatz von Ressourcen dem Softwareentwickler zwar helfen kann, Produkte zu gestalten, die Design-Anforderungen genügen. Damit diese auch verantwortungsvoll für die Gestaltung anspruchsvoller, gebrauchstauglicher Oberflächen genutzt werden können, sind Grundkenntnisse der Ergonomie unabdingbar.

Literaturverzeichnis

Arlidge, J. (2014): Jonathan Ive Designs Tomorrow. New York: Time. http://time.com/jonathan-ive-apple-interview. Aufruf: 15.3.2014

Bilton, N. (2013): The Flattening of Design. New York Times. http://bits.blogs.nytimes.com/2013/04/23/the-flattening-of-design. Aufruf: 15.3.2014

Brill, D., Falk, D., Stork, D. (1990): Ein Blick ins Licht. Heidelberg, Berlin: Springer

Burmester , M., Hassenzahl, M., Kaiser, K., Koller, F. (Hrsg.) (2008): Themenschwerpunkt: Usability und Ästhetik. i-com, Heft 3/2008. München: Oldenbourg

Clum, L. (2013): A look at Flat Design and Why It's Significant. UX Magazine. https://uxmag.com/articles/a-look-at-flat-design-and-why-its-significant. Aufruf 15.3.2014

Clum, L. (2013-2): What is Flat Design?. Creative Bloq. http://www.creativebloq.com/graphic-design/what-flat-design-3132112. Aufruf 15.3.2014

Greif, S. (2013): Flat Pixels. Sachagreif.com. http://sachagreif.com/flat-pixels. Aufruf 15.3.2014

Hassenzahl, M. (2001): The Effect of Perceived Hedonic Quality on Product Appealingness. In: Int. Journal of Human-Computer Interaction 13 (2001) 4, S. 481-499

Hoffman, D. (2001): Visuelle Intelligenz – Wie die Welt im Kopf entsteht. 3. Auflage. Stuttgart: Klett-Cotta

Mayer, M. (2013): Flat Design – Was es ist, warum es bleibt. Manx. http://www.manx.de/flat-design-was-es-ist-warum-es-bleibt. Aufruf: 15.3.2014

Musngi, R. (2013): Basic Principles of Flat Design – And Resources to Get You Started! 1st. Web Designer. http://www.1stwebdesigner.com/design/flat-design-principles. Aufruf 15.3.2014

Pfaff, G. E. (Hrsg.) (1983): User Interface Management Systems: Proceedings of the Seeheim Workshop. Berlin: Springer

Platz, A. (2008): Von der Immaterialisation des Materiellen zur Materialisation des Immateriellen. In: i-com, Heft 3/2008, S. 46-49. München: Oldenbourg

Thielsch, M. T. & Hassenzahl, M. (2008): Achtmal Schönheit. In: i-com, Heft 3/2008, S. 50-55. München: Oldenbourg

Wandmacher, J. (1993): Softwareergonomie. Berlin: Walter de Crayter & Co.

Zimbardo, P. (1995): Psychologie, 6. Auflage. Heidelberg: Springer

M. Koch, A. Butz & J. Schlichter (Hrsg.): Mensch und Computer 2014 Tagungsband,
München: Oldenbourg Wissenschaftsverlag, 2014, S. 265-274.

Hypothesengeleitete Gestaltung von Benutzungsoberflächen

Reinhard Keil, Christian Schild

Heinz Nixdorf Institut, Universität Paderborn

Zusammenfassung

Die Gestaltung von Benutzungsoberflächen wird gemeinhin als kreativer Prozess verstanden, der sich im Dialog mit den Nutzern vollziehen sollte. Die entscheidende Frage dabei ist, inwieweit ein solch kreativer Gestaltungsprozess einer wissenschaftlichen Herangehensweise zugänglich ist. Eine solche Herangehensweise hätte das Ziel, nicht nur Methoden zur Überprüfung der Gebrauchstauglichkeit zu entwickeln, sondern validierbares Gestaltungswissen, das im Entwicklungsprozess prospektiv nutzbar ist. Der Beitrag stellt einen Ansatz für eine hypothesengeleitete Technikgestaltung vor, bei dem Entwurfsmuster (patterns) und die damit verbundenen Kräfte (forces) genutzt werden, um Gestaltungshypothesen abzuleiten, zu validieren und mit entsprechenden theoretischen Annahmen in einer Mustersprache zu systematisieren und festzuhalten. Eine Mustersprache wäre dann nicht in erster Linie eine Sammlung von „Muster"-Lösungen oder Lösungsschemata, sondern ein Vehikel für eine hypothesengeleitete Technikgestaltung und Theoriebildung aus dem Blickwinkel der Informatik.

1 Einleitung

Die Gestaltung von Benutzungsoberflächen stellt Informatiker vor vielfältige Herausforderungen. Gestaltungsprozesse entziehen sich grundsätzlich einem streng regelgeleiteten Vorgehen, doch ist es notwendig, angesichts der Komplexität des Problems, handlungsleitendes Wissen zur Unterstützung heranzuziehen. Dabei stehen den Entwicklern Heuristiken, Style Guides und eine Fülle von Einzelbeispielen zur Verfügung. Erstere eignen sich vorwiegend zur schnellen Bewertung fertiger Benutzungsoberflächen, Style Guides zum Nachbilden von Standards und Beispiele zur Vermeidung der häufigsten Fehler. Eine Systematisierung von Gestaltungswissen ist damit kaum möglich. Das gilt – wie noch zu zeigen ist – auch für die Gestaltgesetze, die nur hilfreich sind, je deutlicher sie verletzt werden.. Für eine wissenschaftliche Fundierung des Gestaltungsprozesses reicht das aber nicht aus. Wie Rauterberg bereits 2000 bewusst provokant konstatierte, liefere das Gebiet der Software-Ergonomie bislang nur „usability engineering methods" statt „validated design relevant knowledge" (Rauterberg 2000, S. 78). Ein neuer theoretischer Fokus zur Erforschung des Interaktionsraums sei erforderlich, denn tradierte theoriegetriebene positivistische Wissenschaftsansätze würden die Realität der Gestaltung nicht erreichen (siehe auch Rauterberg 2003).

Aus der Sicht der Informatik ist hierbei wichtig, dass der Gegenstandsbereich der Theoriebildung ein anderer ist als z. B. für Psychologen. Das bedeutet, nicht-mentale Modelle (Dutke 1994), kognitive Schemata oder andere Modelle, die für die psychologische Forschung im Zentrum stehen, können hier nicht die entscheidende Rolle spielen, sondern Eigenschaften und Merkmale des zu gestaltenden Produkts müssen im Vordergrund der Betrachtung stehen. Bislang aber fehlen für eine Theoriebildung aus der Sicht der Informatik geeignete Ansätze, um den von Rauterberg als „Interaktionsraum" bezeichneten Gegenstandsbereich der Software-Ergonomie konzeptualisieren zu können, ohne dabei zum Amateur-Psychologen mutieren zu müssen.

Unser Ansatz ist es, Entwurfsmuster (Alexander 1964) als Grundlage für eine hypothesengeleitete Technikgestaltung zu nutzen und über den Prozess der Validierung solche Muster zugleich weiterzuentwickeln. Entwurfsmuster könnten dann nicht nur tradierte „Muster"-Lösungen repräsentieren, sondern als Entwurfssprache zugleich validiertes Designwissen verkörpern, das für eine prospektive Gestaltung nutzbar wäre. Dazu ist allerdings erforderlich, das Konzept der Kräfte systematisch zu berücksichtigen und in einen theoretischen Rahmen einzubetten. Die entscheidende Idee, die hier vorgestellt wird, besteht darin, Entwurfsmuster als ein Vehikel für eine hypothesengeleitete Technikgestaltung zu nutzen.

Dieses aus der Sicht der Informatik angelegte Forschungsparadigma im Bereich der Mensch-Rechner-Interaktion ist zunächst als Forschungshypothese zu werten. Das damit verbundene Gestaltungspotenzial soll an einem Kernbeispiel der Ergonomie verdeutlicht werden. Um aber validiertes Designwissen in Form einer Mustersprache (Borchers 2001, S. 360) durchgehend zu entwickeln, bedarf es weiterer Beispiele und Fundierungen.

2 Hypothesengeleitete Gestaltung

Die angemessene Gestaltung von Benutzungsoberflächen sollte ein wesentliches Moment der Informatikkompetenz verkörpern. Ein benutzerzentriertes Vorgehen ist zwar notwendig, aber nicht hinreichend, da die Nutzer in der Regel nicht in der Lage sind, alle für eine angemessene Systemgestaltung erforderlichen Qualitätsmerkmale und Anforderungen explizit zu formulieren und auch neue innovative Elemente hinsichtlich ihres Lösungsbeitrags zu kennen und zu bewerten. Dies ist für die Nutzer auch nicht erforderlich, wohl aber für die Entwickler solcher Systeme. Dazu aber sind interdisziplinäres Wissen und die Zusammenarbeit mit anderen Disziplinen notwendig. Dies erfordert jedoch eine theoretische Fundierung, die es gestattet, prospektives Gestaltungswissen unabhängig von den Forschungsparadigmen der jeweils anderen Disziplin zu fundieren und weiterzuentwickeln. In diesem Sinne sehen wir eine hypothesengeleitete Technikgestaltung als ein wirksames Mittel an, um

- Theorieansätze und Methoden anderer Disziplinen hinsichtlich ihrer Eignung zu bewerten und zu selektieren,

- Erkenntnisse und Einsichten aus verschiedenen Bereichen so zu integrieren, dass sie zu einer Gestaltungsorientierung verdichtet werden können,
- auf der Basis theoretischer Überlegungen überprüfbare Hypothesen aufstellen zu können, um so auch aus der Informatik heraus Gestaltungswissen weiterentwickeln und damit den interdisziplinären Diskurs bereichern zu können,
- Grenzen und Probleme zu identifizieren, die mit dem jeweiligen Ansatz verbunden sind, um so eine kontinuierliche selbstkritische Justierung und Positionierung im Wissenschaftsgefüge vornehmen zu können (Keil 2011, S. 166).

Zusammengefasst geht es also darum, den Gegenstandsbereich der Forschung aus der Sicht der Informatik zu konzeptualisieren und einen theoretischen Rahmen zu entwickeln, der zu Wissen aus anderen Disziplinen anschlussfähig ist, jedoch Informatiker nicht zugleich zwingt, Gestaltungskonzepte den dortigen Modellvorstellungen unterzuordnen oder alle Aspekte auszublenden, die in diesen Modellen keinen Platz haben, für die Gestaltung jedoch relevant sind.

Entwurfsmuster können hier einen adäquaten Ausgangspunkt für die Konzeptualisierung bieten. Ihre Vorteile sind in der Informatik seit längerem bekannt (Gamma et al. 1994) und inzwischen auch auf die Entwicklung von Benutzungsoberflächen übertragen (Tidwell 2005). Jedoch weisen diese Sammlungen von Entwurfsmustern das Problem auf, dass sie noch nicht zu einer wirklichen Mustersprache (pattern language) verbunden worden sind. Ein entscheidendes Manko ist, dass das Konzept der Kräfte (forces), die für Alexander eine zentrale Rolle für die Formierung einer Mustersprache bilden, bislang nicht adäquat berücksichtigt worden sind.

Die grundlegende Idee besteht nun darin, Entwurfsmuster nicht nur zur Beschreibung feststehender Lösungen zu nutzen, sondern über die Kräfte (forces) diese in einen Rahmen zur hypothesengeleiteten Technikgestaltung einzubetten (vgl. Abb. 3). Dabei geht es darum, gesichertes oder besser validierbares Gestaltungswissen in Form von Entwurfsmustern niederzulegen. Zusätzlich wird ein theoretischer Rahmen benötigt, der es gestattet, Hypothesen abzuleiten (Abb. 1, Punkt 1), in Verbindung mit innovativen Entwicklungen ein System zu gestalten (Abb. 1, Punkt 2), das System bzw. einzelne Bereiche oder Features zu evaluieren (Abb. 1, Punkt 3), die Befunde für eine Revision der Gestaltungsmuster zu nutzen (Abb. 1, Punkt 4) und die einzelnen Muster systematisch zueinander in Beziehung zu setzen. Die Verknüpfung mit dem theoretischen Rahmen erfolgt dabei über das Konzept der Kräfte (forces), denn die Begründung und Analyse der auftretenden Kräfte erlauben es, einerseits gewonnenes und als gesichert angesehenes Wissen gestaltungsgerecht zu formulieren und andererseits durch die Ableitung neuer Hypothesen diesen Wissensschatz anzupassen und zu erweitern. Der Vorteil ist, dass man sich mit diesen Mustern weitgehend im Kompetenzbereich der Informatik bewegen kann. Zugleich bieten die Kräfte eine wirksame Schnittstelle zu anderen Disziplinen, die es ermöglicht, dort gewonnene Erkenntnisse zu übernehmen bzw. an deren jeweiligen Methoden und Modellansätzen anzuknüpfen.

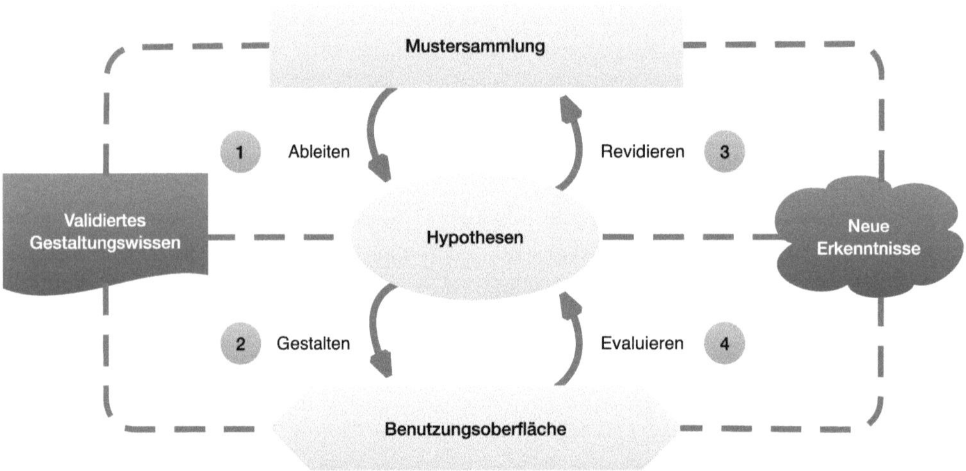

Abbildung 1: Prozess der hypothesengeleiteten Technikgestaltung

Bezüglich des Vorgehens ist anzumerken, dass die vier Punkte in Abb. 1 natürlich nicht einer prozessualen Reihenfolge oder Vorgehensweise entsprechen. Vielmehr handelt es sich hier um ein vielfältiges Jojo-Vorgehen (top down – bottom up bzw. induktiv – deduktiv) auf unterschiedlichen Abstraktionsebenen und Gestaltungsniveaus. Welchen Vorteil die Bestimmung der Kräfte (forces) hat, soll an zwei bekannten Beispielen verdeutlicht werden, die in vielen Publikationen zu finden sind: Konsistenz und Strukturiertheit.

3 Prospektive Gestaltung

Heuristiken und Gestaltungskriterien sind wichtige und nützliche Hilfsmittel zur Gestaltung, doch fehlt ihnen das Potenzial für systematische Fundierung. Die Gründe hierfür sind vielfältig, lassen sich aber im Kern auf zwei wesentliche Punkte zurückführen: Ihnen fehlt a) ein gemeinsamer theoretischer Hintergrund und b) die Thematisierung von Gestaltungskonflikten, die sich aus widersprüchlichen Kräftekonstellationen ergeben (sieh Keil, Schild (2913). Genau diese Austarierung widersprüchlicher Kräfte ist aber für Alexanders Mustersprachen konstituiv. Punkt a) soll kurz am Beispiel Konsistenz und Punkt b) am Beispiel Strukturiertheit illustriert werden.

3.1 Konsistenz

Bei Shneiderman wird diese Anforderung in der ersten goldenen Regel für den Entwurf von Benutzungsschnittstellen *Strive for consistency* (Shneiderman 2009, S. 88) formuliert: »Consistent sequences of actions should be required in similar situations; identical terminology should be used in prompts, menus, and help screens and consistent color, layout, capitalization, fonts and so on should be employed throughout.« In den Grundsätzen der Dialoggestaltung (DIN EN ISO 9241, Teil 110) wird die Forderung innerhalb der Erwartungskonformität erhoben. Auch Nielsen weist Konsistenz als eine seiner 10 Heuristik-Regeln für die Gestaltung aus,[1] beschreibt sie aber nur salopp: „Users should not have to wonder whether different words, situations, or actions mean the same thing. Follow platform conventions." Gewiss ist es ein Leichtes, schlechte Gestaltungsbeispiele aufzuführen, bei denen das Kriterium der Konsistenz verletzt ist, doch so „selbst"-verständlich das klingt, muss doch konstatiert werden, dass weder klar ist, wann Nutzer sich über Unterschiede wundern und wann nicht, noch wie man in Konfliktfällen mit dem Kriterium umgeht. So stellte Grudin schon 1989 fest, dass Konsistenz den Nutzern das Erlernen von Systemen erleichtere, dies jedoch häufig im Konflikt zu einer guten Usability stehe (Grudin 1989, S. 1166) und es generell nicht möglich sei, ein System vollständig konsistent zu gestalten (a.a.O., S. 1171). In einigen Fällen könne es notwendig sein, Inkonsistenzen in Kauf zu nehmen, um die Aufmerksamkeit von Benutzern gezielt zu lenken (Benyon 2010, S. 91). Schließlich konnten Carroll und Mazur zeigen, dass selbst inkonsistente Metaphern einen positiven Effekt für die Nutzer haben (Caroll & Mazur 1986, S. 43 u. 48). Und auch die Inkonsistenz beim Drag und Drop, wo die gleiche Verschiebehandlung je nach Zielpunkt unterschiedliche Effekte hat, fällt Nutzern in der Regel nicht auf. Noch fataler aber ist, dass die Konsistenzregel, Meldungen immer an der gleichen Stelle auf dem Bildschirm zu platzieren (Erwartungskonformität nach DIN 9241, Teil 110), der Forderung widerspricht, Rückmeldung stets am Ort der Handlung unterzubringen, weil dort auch die Aufmerksamkeit ruht (Keil-Slawik 1990, S. 174 ff.).

Alle diese Beispiele liefern nützliche Einsichten für die Gestaltung, entziehen sich jedoch aufgrund eines fehlenden gemeinsamen theoretischen Hintergrundes dem Versuch, im Sinne Rauterbergs validierbares Gestaltungswissen aufzubauen und zu systematisieren. Nielsen selbst nutzt für seinen Versuch, die erklärende Kraft seiner Heuristikregeln zu verbessern, das statistische Instrument der Faktorenanalyse, bei der aber auch wieder nur bestehende Fehler erkannt und (ex post) den Heuristiken zugeordnet werden (Nielsen 1994). In der Konsequenz gewinnt man so Kategorien, die statistisch unabhängig voneinander sind, bei denen damit zugleich Abhängigkeiten und Widersprüche systematisch ausgeblendet werden.[2]

Hier setzt das Konzept der Kräfte an, denn genau dieser Zusammenhang soll über das Konzept der Kräfte erschlossen werden. Bei Alexander werden diese durch Anforderungen verkörpert, die sich aus dem Gestaltungskontext ergeben wie z.B. Schutz vor Sonneneinstrahlung und Bedarf nach Licht. Ein gutes Muster verkörpert eine gelungene Austarierung solcher Kräfte, das aber je nach aktuellem Gestaltungskontext angepasst werden muss. In unserem Fall sind Kräfte z.B. die Verringerung des Wahrnehmungsaufwandes durch Einfachheit oder die Unterstützung der Gestaltwahrnehmung durch lokale Zusatzinformationen am Fixationsunkten von Sakkadensequenzen. Am nachfolgenden Bespiel soll die Rolle solcher Kräfte verdeutlicht werden.

[1] Für die aktuellste Fassung und das Zitat siehe: http://www.nngroup.com/articles/ten-usability-heuristics/.

[2] Auf den gleichen Ansatz geht auch die ursprüngliche Fassung der fünf „Grundsätze zur Dialoggestaltung" zurück. Dazu betonte Dzida selbst, dass lediglich die Ausdifferenzierung der Prinzipien empirisch belegt ist, nicht jedoch die damit verbundenen Gestaltungsanforderungen (1989, S. 40).

3.2 Strukturiertheit

Ähnlich wie mit der Konsistenz verhält es sich mit der Strukturierung der Bildschirminhalte. Dabei geht es darum, wie Bildschirmobjekte so angeordnet werden, dass sich die Nutzer möglichst gut und schnell darin zurechtfinden. In der Ergonomie-Literatur finden sich dazu fast ausschließlich Hinweise auf die Gestaltgesetze nach Wertheimer (1923) in einer stark reduzierten Form. Jedoch ist es kaum möglich, mithilfe der Gestaltgesetze alleine zu guten Ergebnissen zu kommen. Probleme sind auch hier Mehrdeutigkeiten bei der Figur-Grund-Unterscheidung, stark unterschiedliche Kataloge von Gestaltgesetzen und die Tatsache, dass sich einzelne Gesetze widersprechen oder es unklar ist, welches in einer bestimmten Konstellation zum Zuge kommt. Konsequenterweise kommen Stadler, Seeger, Raeithel (1977, S. 169) zu dem Schluss, dass die Gestaltgesetze nicht zur prospektiven Beschreibung der Wahrnehmung geeignet sind, sondern nur ex post Einordnungen ermöglichen. D. h. wenn man weiß, welche Gestalt von einer Person wahrgenommen wird, kann man das Gestaltgesetz angeben, das zum Zuge gekommen ist – und selbst das geht schon nicht, sobald man sich von sehr elementaren Strichzeichnungen entfernt.

Abgesehen von lehrbuchartigen Kurzdarstellungen der Gestaltgesetze ist es auch hier nicht möglich, sie wirklich konstruktiv zur Gestaltung zu verwenden, wenn man nicht über umfangreiches Wissen verfügt, um sich in der Fülle der gestalt- und kognitionspsychologischen Literatur zurechtzufinden.

Es fehlt also den Entwicklern ein gestaltungsrelevanter Begründungszusammenhang, der es ermöglicht festzustellen, welche Erkenntnisse der Psychologie wann und in welcher Konstellation tatsächlich gestaltungsleitend sein könnten. Genau diese Lücke soll nachfolgend geschlossen werden.

3.3 Lokalität versus Geschlossenheit

Das Gestaltgesetz der Geschlossenheit besagt, dass unser Wahrnehmungssystem geschlossene Figuren als Ganzheit erkennt. Als Konsequenz findet man bis heute durchgängig Anwendungsbeispiele, bei denen zusammengehörige Bildschirmobjekte durch eine Umrandung als Gruppe oder Einheit gekennzeichnet werden. Diese Einheiten werden zudem noch geschachtelt, um damit Untereinheiten zu schaffen, die in Verbindung mit der Leseflussrichtung eine Kombination von Zeilen und Spalten ergeben.

Es wird aber keine Kraft angegeben, warum oder unter welchen Umständen diese Art der Geschlossenheit entscheidend für die Wahrnehmung ist. Tatsächlich stellen – vor allem bei großen Bildschirmen – solche geschachtelten Umrandungen für das Auge ein Problem: „Nur in der Fovea ist ein scharfes Bildsehen mit hohem Auflösungsvermögen möglich." (Ronacher & Hemminger, S. 102) Um also eine Gestalt zu erkennen, erfolgt die visuelle Wahrnehmung in einer Sequenz von Sakkaden, die jeweils durch Fixationspunkte unterbrochen werden. An diesen Punkten erfolgt die eigentliche Informationsaufnahme, bevor das Auge zum nächsten, potenziell relevanten Punkt springt. Die in Abb. 2 eingezeichneten Kreise entsprechen solchen Fixationspunkten. Um also für den mittleren Bereich zu entscheiden, wo sich die jeweils zu einer Linie gehörende Form schließt, muss das Auge gewissermaßen mehrere Möglichkeiten explorieren, denn am Fixationspunkt ist nicht erkennbar, auf welcher Seite eine Linie oder Ecke bzw. Hintergrund ist. Generell kann man die Wahrnehmung als hypothesengeleiteten Prozess betrachten, der aus einzelnen Details der Wahrnehmung unter Zuhilfenahme von Hypothesen Annahmen über die tatsächliche Form der Figuren trifft (Gregory 2001). Um einen solchen Prozess zu Unterstützen, muss also die Hypothesenbildung (Orientierung) durch Zusatzinforationen an den Fixationspunkten geeignet unterstützt werden.

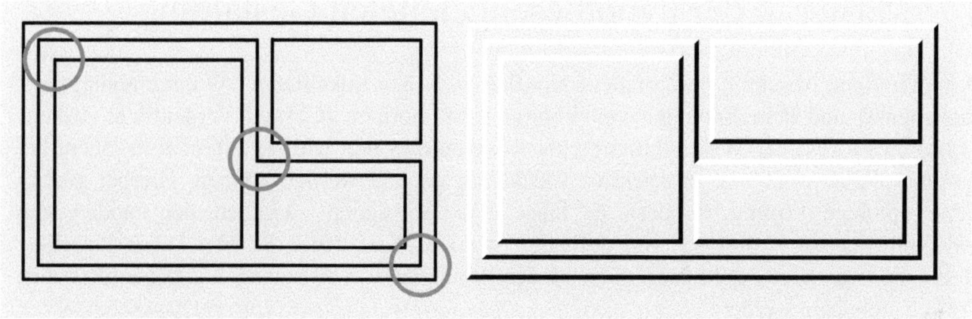

Abbildung 2: Gerahmte Figuren mit Fixationspunkten und gestapelte Figuren

Vor diesem Hintergrund kann man jetzt auch überlegen, wie man eine Oberfläche gestalten muss, um einen solchen Prozess möglichst gut zu unterstützen bzw. ihm nicht im Wege zu stehen. Der rechte Teil von Abb. 2 zeigt den Lösungsansatz bzw. das Entwurfsmuster, das wir als „Stapeln statt Umrahmen" bezeichnen. Zeichnet man die Fixationspunkte an derselben Stelle ein wie im linken Teil der Abbildung, fällt sofort ins Auge, dass an jedem Fixationspunkt eine zusätzliche Information vorhanden ist, die es gestattet zu entscheiden, auf welcher Seite der Kante jeweils der Hintergrund bzw. der Vordergrund zu erwarten ist. Das menschliche Wahrnehmungssystem geht davon aus, dass Licht von oben kommt (genauer: „über Kopf", Hoffmann 2001, S. 153), somit interpretiert das Wahrnehmungssystem eine dunkle Kante als Schatten und damit als untere Begrenzung einer Figur und umgekehrt. Zugleich erhält man an den Eckpunkten jeweils eine eindeutige Farbkombination. Damit ist unmittelbar klar, in welcher Richtung die Schließung der Figur zu erwarten ist. Der Aufwand zum Explorieren des Wahrnehmungsfelds wird deutlich reduziert. Das zeigte sich darin, dass Nutzer, denen beide Alternativen vorgelegt wurden, in Bezug auf die rechte Abbildung kommentierten: „Jetzt sehe ich ja sofort, wo der TAB-Sprung lang läuft."

Das Entwurfsmuster Stapeln statt Umrahmen ist einerseits anschlussfähig zu kognitionspsychologischen Modellen der Wahrnehmung und ermöglicht andererseits durch die Orientierung an der Anforderung (force) „Zusatzinformation für die Verbesserung der Orientierung an Fixationspunkten bereitzustellen" die Formulierung von validierbaren Gestaltungshinweisen (Mustern), die sich direkt auf den Gestaltungsgegenstand beziehen und ohne komplexe Kenntnisse aus der Kognitionspsychologie umgesetzt werden können.

Entscheidend für die weiteren Überlegungen ist nun, dass das Konzept der Kräfte bei Entwurfsmustern besonders geeignet ist, um die hier vorgestellten theoretischen Überlegungen angemessen abzubilden. Denn Wissen für eine prospektive Gestaltung kann nicht das Ergebnis vorhersagen, sondern gibt Anhaltspunkte, wie man zu einer angemessenen Lösung kommt und welche Aspekte in der jeweiligen Situation zu beachten sind. Die Wirksamkeit der einzelnen Kräfte und ihr Zusammenspiel mit andern Kräften muss für den jeweiligen jeweiligen Gestaltungskontext validiert werden.

4 Muster in der hypothesengeleiteten Gestaltung

Der im vorigen Abschnitt beschriebene Konflikt zwischen Lokalität der Wahrnehmung (Fixationspunkt) und dem Erkennen von Figuren bzw. Formen (Gestalt) verdeutlicht, welche Kräfte im Prozess der Wahrnehmung eine Rolle spielen und wie sie zugleich in einem bestimmten Kontext für die prospektive Gestaltung genutzt werden können. Hierbei gibt es keine optimale Lösung, sondern es muss eine Abwägung zwischen den beiden sich widersprechenden Anforderungen gefunden werden (Keil 2013, S. 74). Diese Konflikte bilden die Grundlage der Muster, die nach den Prinzipien von Alexander aus gegensätzlichen Kräften aufgebaut werden:

»The idea of a diagram, or pattern, is very simple. It is an abstract pattern of physical relationships which resolves a small system of interacting and conflicting forces, and is indepent of all other forces, and of all other possible diagrams.« (Alexander 1964, Vorwort)

Durch die Einbettung in einen entsprechenden theoretischen Rahmen ist es möglich, die Kräfte über grundlegende Erkenntnisse z. B. aus anderen Disziplinen zu verbinden oder auch mit eigenen Erfahrungen und empirischen Befunden. Dadurch können sie als Hypothese genutzt werden und es ist möglich zu validieren, an welchen Stellen sich z. B. neue Konflikte ergeben oder Erwartungen nicht bestätigt werden. Ein Beispiel hierfür ist die Gestaltung von Schriften, bei denen neben der lokalen Wahrnehmung auch die Gleichförmigkeit der Gestaltung eine Rolle spielt. Das Wortbild (Umrandung eines Worts mit Ober- und Unterlängen) spielt hier eine andere Rolle als eine Fläche zur Strukturierung des Bildschirmaufbaus; und beide sind wiederum zu unterscheiden von der Strukturierung von Texten durch Absätze, Einrückungen und Aufzählungen. Die Kraft, „Unterstützung an Fixationspunkten" gilt zwar in allen diesen Beispielen, muss aber jeweils gegenüber anderen konkurrierenden Kräften abgewogen werden. Mal kommt die prä-attemptive Wahrnehmung hinzu, mal geht es um explorierende Suchprozesse auf Webseiten. Die jeweilig identifizierten Kräfte liefern dabei im jeweiligen Kontext Gestaltungshypothesen, die sich unmittelbar auf den Gestaltungsgegenstand beziehen (z. B. Hervorheben in einem Fall, Gleichförmigkeit in einem anderen).

Der Vorteil des Konzepts der Kräfte ist, dass sie einerseits nicht ein Ergebnis beschreiben wie z. B. das Gesetz der Geschlossenheit, sondern Entwickler darauf aufmerksam machen, welche Aspekte sie beim Finden einer Lösung berücksichtigen müssen. Andererseits ermöglicht die Validierung des jeweiligen Ergebnisses auch die Formulierung einer Musterlösung, die so lange übertragen werden kann, solange keine Veränderung der Kräfte bzw. ihrer Wirkungen anliegt. Der Prozess ist rückbezüglich kondensiert, liefert aber gleichwohl übertragbare Lösungsansätze in Form von Entwurfsmustern, die zudem – und das ist die entscheidende Forschungshypothese hier – letztlich auch systematisiert bzw. (hierarchisch) strukturiert, d. h. zu einer Entwurfssprache verdichtet werden können.

5 Zusammenfassung und Ausblick

Der vorliegende Ansatz verfolgt das Ziel, ein Forschungsparadigma aufzustellen, das es aus Sicht der Informatik ermöglicht, validierbares Gestaltungswissen zu entwickeln, zu tradieren und fortzuschreiben, und das zugleich die Anschlussfähigkeit zu anderen wissenschaftlichen Disziplinen sichert. Im vorliegenden Fall wurde dies exemplarisch an einem sehr grundlegenden Beispiel der Software-Ergonomie verdeutlicht. Die Autoren gehen davon aus, das sich z. B. die Probleme mit dem Kriterium der Konsistenz auf ähnliche Art und Weise angehen lassen. Hier wäre zu schauen, ob die Gestaltung eines statischen Bildschirmaufbaus anderen Kräften unterliegt als die Gestaltung eines Wahrnehmungsraums, der sich über mehrere Bildschirmaufbauten hinweg erstreckt. Dabei müsste zugleich festgestellt werden, in welcher Form sich jeweils Präferenzen für die Orts- oder Bildcodierung ergeben. Auch hier gibt es bereits vielfältige Ansätze und Untersuchungen, die bislang aber noch nicht systematisch in einen prospektiven Gestaltungsansatz überführt worden sind. Weitere Beispiele für Gestaltungskonflikte und ihre unterschiedlichen Ausprägungen wurden in (Keil & Schild 2013) beschrieben.

Auch wenn sich manche der hier formulierten Erwartungen nicht erfüllen lassen sollten, wäre es dennoch hilfreich zu erkunden, inwieweit es tatsächlich möglich ist, aus der Sicht der Informatik und zur Unterstützung einer prospektiven Systemgestaltung ein solches Forschungsparadigma zu verfolgen. Es würde der Informatik etwas mehr Unabhängigkeit gegenüber Konzepten und Modellen aus anderen Disziplinen geben und würde es erlauben, spezifische Erfordernisse des Gestaltungsprozesses angemessener zu berücksichtigen.

Literaturverzeichnis

Alexander, C. (1964). Notes on the synthesis of form. Harvard University Press.

Benyon, D. (2010). Designing interactive systems: A comprehensive guide to HCI and Interaction Design (2nd edition). Pearson Education Canada.

Borchers, J. (2001). A pattern approach to interaction design. AI & SOCIETY **15**: 359-376.

Carroll, J. M. & Mazur, S. A. (1986). Lisa learning. IEEE Computer, November, S. 35-49.

Dutke, S. (1994). Mentale Modelle: Konstrukte des Wissens und Verstehens. Kognitionspsychologische Grundlagen für die Software-Ergonomie (Reihe Arbeit und Technik, Bd. 4). Göttingen: Verlag für Angewandte Psychologie.

Gamma, E., Helm, R., Johnson, R. & Vlissides, J. (1994). Design patterns: Elements of reusable object-oriented software. Addison-Wesley Professional.

Gregory, R. L. (2001). Auge und Gehirn – Psychologie des Sehens. Hamburg: Rohwolt.

Grudin, J. (1989). The case against user interface consistency. Communications of the ACM, 32(10): 1164-1173.

Dzida, W. (1989). The development of ergonomic standards. SIGCHI Bulletin 20(3): 35-43.

Hoffmann, D. (2001). Visuelle Intelligenz – Wie die Welt im Kopf entsteht. 3. Auflage. Stuttgart: Klett-Cotta.

Keil, R. (2011). Hypothesengeleitete Technikgestaltung als Grundlage einer kontextuellen Informatik. In Informationstechnik und ihre Organisationslücken. Sozial, politische und rechtliche Dimensionen aus der Sicht von Wissenschaft und Praxis. S. 165-184. Andreas Breiter, Martin Wind.

Keil, R. & Schild, C. (2013). Gestaltungskonflikte in der Softwareergonomie. In S. Boll, S. Maaß & R. Malaka (Hrsg.). Mensch & Computer 2013 – Tagungsband, S. 67-76. Gesellschaft für Informatik. München: Oldenbourg.

Nielsen, J. (1994). Enhancing the explanatory power of usability heuristics. In: CHI '94: „Celebrating Independance". Proceedings of the SIGCHI Conference on Human Factors in Computing Systems. New York: ACM, S. 52-58.

Rauterberg, G. W. M. (2003). Human-Computer Interaction research: a paradigm clash? In: A. Kameas & N. Streitz (Hrsg.). Tales of the Disappearing Computer. Proceedings of the Disappearing Computer Conference, 1-4 June, Santorini, Greece. Patras, Griechenland: CTI Press, S. 157-164.

Rauterberg, G. W. M. (2001). How to characterize a research line for user-system interaction. IPO Annual Progress Report, 35, S. 66-86.

Ronacher B. & Hemminger, H. (1978). Einführung in die Nerven- und Sinnesphysiologie. Quelle & Meyer.

Shneiderman, B., Plaisant, C., Cohen, M. & Jacobs, S. (2009). Designing the user interface: Strategies for effective Human-Computer Interaction (5th edition). Prentice Hall.

Stadler, M., Seeger, F. & Raeitel, A. (1977). Psychologie der Wahrnehmung. München: Juventa.

Tidwell, J. (2005). Designing interfaces – patterns for effective interaction Design: O'Reilly Media, Inc.

Wertheimer, M. (1923). Untersuchungen zur Lehre von der Gestalt. II. Psychologische Forschung 4, S. 301-350. München: Springer.

Winograd, T. (1990). What can we teach about human-computer interaction? In: Proceedings SIGCHI Conference on Human Factors in Computing Systems: Empowering People. Seattle (WA), S. 443-449.

Kontaktinformationen

Prof. Dr.-Ing. Reinhard Keil
Heinz Nixdorf Institut
Universität Paderborn
Kontextuelle Informatik
Fürstenallee 11
33102 Paderborn

+49 5251 60-6411
reinhard.keil@hni.uni-paderborn.de

Christian Schild
Heinz Nixdorf Institut
Universität Paderborn
Kontextuelle Informatik
Fürstenallee 11
33102 Paderborn

+49 5251 60-6416
christian.schild@uni-paderborn.de

M. Koch, A. Butz & J. Schlichter (Hrsg.): Mensch und Computer 2014 Tagungsband,
München: Oldenbourg Wissenschaftsverlag, 2014, S. 275-284.

Heuristiken für Information Appliances

Patricia Böhm, Tim Schneidermeier, Christian Wolff

Lehrstuhl für Medieninformatik, Universität Regensburg

Zusammenfassung

Dieser Beitrag stellt Usability-Heuristiken für Information Appliances und deren Entwicklung vor. Information Appliances bezeichnen elektronische Geräte, die für eine spezielle Funktion (z. B. Fotografieren bei einer Digitalkamera) gestaltet werden, und deren Bedienung ohne bzw. mit minimalem Lernaufwand möglich sein soll. Heuristiken aus dem Softwarebereich sind nicht ausreichend zur Beurteilung der Usability dieser Geräte, da sie sich in Aufgabenorientierung, Interaktionselementen und Nutzungskontext unterscheiden. Daher wurden angepasste Heuristiken aus etablierten Usability-Heuristiken und unter Einbezug von Richtlinien für Produktdesign, für die Gestaltung mobiler Geräte sowie für kleine Displays abgeleitet. Das resultierende Heuristikenset wurde zur Evaluation zweier Geräte herangezogen und mit den Ergebnissen von Nutzertests verglichen. Die hohe Übereinstimmung der Befunde deutet auf eine ausreichende Validität der Heuristiken als Evaluationsmethode hin.

1 Einleitung und Motivation

Viele Alltagsgeräte – hier als *Information Appliances* bezeichnet – weisen mittlerweile interaktive Benutzerschnittstellen auf. Die stetige Zunahme des Funktionsumfangs scheint auch zu einer (unerwünschten) Zunahme der Bedienkomplexität zu führen: Alan Cooper vergleicht die Bedienkomplexität eines Radioweckers mit der eines Personal Computers (Cooper 2004). Waschmaschine, Herd, Mikrowelle, Heiz- und Kühleinheiten zählen in den USA zu den Produkten mit den meisten Kundenreklamationen (Barnett 2012), wobei nicht defekte Geräte, sondern eine Überforderung der Benutzer bei der Bedienung der Geräte zu den Beschwerden führt (den Ouden 2006). Die Gründe für die mangelhafte Usability sind vielschichtig: Zum einen führen immer leistungsfähigere Mikroprozessoren in den Geräten zu mehr Funktionalität und Komplexität, die nachweislich von Verbrauchern präferiert wird (Thompson, Hamilton & Rust 2005, 435), zum anderen fehlt häufig aufgrund eingeschränkter Ressourcen das systematische Einbeziehen von Usabilityaspekten in den Entwicklungsprozess (Baumann & Thomas 2001, 7).

Heuristiken und die heuristische Evaluation bieten sich durch den geringen erforderlichen Ressourcenaufwand für das Usability Engineering von *Information Appliances* an. Die Heuristiken aus dem Software-Bereich sind nicht ausreichend, um die besonderen Anforderungen der Interaktion mit *Alltagsgeräten* zu beurteilen. Beispielsweise fordert Nielsens Usability-Heuristik „Consistency and standards", dass zur Vorbeugung von Verwirrung beim Benutzer Plattform-Konventionen hinsichtlich Wording, Aktionen und Situationen eingehalten werden sollen (Nielsen 1994). Dieses Prinzip beinhaltet nicht die besonderen Aspekte für die konsistente Gestaltung von *Alltagsgeräten*. Neben Handlungsabläufen und Terminologie müssen de facto-Standards des jeweiligen Gerätetyps analysiert und interpretiert werden (Mauney & Masterton 2008, 349).

Um den Einsatzbereich der Gestaltungsprinzipien abzustecken, geben wir in Abschnitt 2 eine Begriffsdefinition von *Information Appliance*. Anschließend wird die recherchebasierte Ableitung der Heuristiken näher erläutert. Die resultierenden Usability-Prinzipien werden exemplarisch in Abschnitt 4 aufgezeigt. Abschließend wird in Abschnitt 5 die Validierung der Heuristiken im Rahmen einer Usability-Evaluation zweier *Information Appliances* beschrieben.

2 Definition des Gegenstandsbereichs

In der Literatur finden sich zahlreiche Begrifflichkeiten für den Bereich interaktiver *Alltagsgeräte*. Je nach thematischen Fokus werden unterschiedliche Bezeichnungen verwendet: *Small Screen Interfaces* (Mauney & Masterton 2008), *Nontraditional Interfaces* (Kortum 2008), *Consumer Electronic Devices* (Han et al. 2001), *Useware* (Zühlke 2004), *Electronic Appliances* (Baumann & Thomas 2001) und *Information Appliances* (Norman 1999; Mohageg & Wagner 2000).

Die in diesem Beitrag vorgestellten Heuristiken zielen auf Produkte mit einem spezifischen bzw. eingeschränkten Funktionsumfang, zum Beispiel Digitalkameras, Stereoanlagen, Mikrowellenherde, Radiowecker, Kopiergeräte etc. Vor diesem Hintergrund bietet sich der Begriff der *Information Appliances* an. Der Begriff wurde von Jeff Raskin geprägt (Raskin 1979 / 1982) und in der Literatur von Donald Norman (1999) verbreitet und bezeichnet Geräte, die im Gegensatz zu einem Personal Computer für eine spezifische Aufgabe gestaltet wurden, auch für Laien und Erstnutzer einfach zu bedienen sind und Informationen mit anderen *Information Appliances* austauschen können. Mohageg & Wagner (2000) erweitern das Verständnis: „It [an information appliance] is a device that performs only a few tasks but does them well, efficiently, and with little conscious effort from the user" (Mohageg & Wagner 2000, 28).

Aus der Definition ergeben sich zwei Usability-Anforderungen für *Information Appliances*:

1. *Spezifischer Funktionsumfang*: Das Interface muss an die spezielle Aufgabe angepasst sein.
2. *Selbsterklärungsfähigkeit*: Die Interaktion muss mit geringem Lernaufwand möglich sein.

Neben den genannten Usability-Zielen ist die Interaktion der Information Appliances durch weitere Charakteristika gekennzeichnet, die sie von dem Desktop-Setting der Softwarenutzung unterscheiden. Nutzungskontext, Anzeigegeräte und Eingabemöglichkeiten sind grundlegende Faktoren, die bei der Entwicklung der Heuristiken berücksichtigt werden müssen. Für die Erstellung der angepassten Bewertungskriterien wurden exemplarisch folgende Charakteristika berücksichtigt, da sie für viele – wenngleich nicht alle – Information Appliances zutreffend sind[1]:

- Kleines Display als Anzeigegerät
- Kombination aus Hard- und Software-Bedienelementen für die Eingabe
- Mobiler Nutzungskontext

3 Entwicklung der Heuristiken

3.1 Heuristiken und Guidelines

Für die Ableitung der angepassten Heuristiken wurden abstrakte Prinzipien anhand konkreter Gestaltungsempfehlungen, sogenannter „Guidelines", überprüft und mit diesen kombiniert. Warum dieses Vorgehen sinnvoll ist, um Nachteile bzw. Unschärfe von abstrakten Heuristiken auszugleichen, soll kurz erläutert werden: Allgemein dienen Designregeln dazu, Erkenntnisse aus Theorien, empirischen Untersuchungen oder praktischen Erfahrungen so festzuhalten, dass sie den Designprozess für weitere Produkte unterstützen können (Burmester & Machate 2003, 43). Die Dokumentation von Gestaltungserkenntnissen kann in unterschiedlichen Formen erfolgen: Prinzipien, Heuristiken oder Guidelines besitzen durch ihren variierenden Aufbau und Abstraktionsgrad jeweils bestimmte Vor- und Nachteile. Prinzipien und Heuristiken wie etwa Shneidermans (2010) *Eight Golden Rules of Interface Design* oder Nielsens (1994) *Ten Usability Heuristics* stellen allgemeine und knapp formulierte Gestaltungsregeln dar (Shneiderman & Pleasant 2010; Nielsen 1994). Sie beinhalten allgemeingültiges bzw. elementares Wissen über menschliche Wahrnehmung und Informationsverarbeitung und besitzen deshalb eine breite Gültigkeit (Ohnemus 1997, 190). Der Nachteil von Heuristiken bzw. Prinzipien besteht in ihrer hohen Abstraktion. Die sehr allgemeinen, knappen Regeln müssen richtig interpretiert werden. Um die Unschärfe der Heuristiken auszugleichen, können Guidelines herangezogen werden. Sie enthalten konkrete Designempfehlungen in Form von Beispielen und konkreten Gestaltungsanweisungen (Shneiderman & Pleasant 2010, 75) und können somit den Kontext der Heuristiken vereindeutigen.

[1] Es existieren andere Ausprägungen der Charakteristika wie zum Beispiel ein großes Display bei einem Fernsehgerät. Für andere Ausprägungen müssen die Heuristiken gemäß dem Vorgehen in Abschnitt 3.2 ergänzt und für die Evaluation verwendet werden.

3.2 Recherchebasierte Ableitung

Neue bzw. domänenspezifische Heuristiken können entweder durch einen problembasierten oder einen recherchebasierten Ansatz abgeleitet werden (Ling & Salvendy 2005, 187). Die problembasierte Herangehensweise dokumentiert Beobachtungen, Anforderungen und Probleme aus Usability-Evaluationen. Der recherchebasierte Ansatz identifiziert Anforderungen und Schlüsselfaktoren einer Domäne aus einer geeigneten Literaturgrundlage. Die problembasierte Ableitung von Heuristiken geht zwar von empirischen Beobachtungen aus, erscheint aber für eine Ableitung von generischen Heuristiken für *Information Appliances* zu abhängig von den untersuchten Objekten. Das neue Heuristikenset wurde daher recherchebasiert auf der Basis einer breiten Literaturgrundlage abgeleitet.

Die Ableitung neuer Heurisiken erfolgt im recherchebasierten Ansätzen in einem dreistufigen Verfahren: Zunächst wird ein geeignetes Set, häufig Nielsens *Ten Usability Heuristics* (Nielsen 1994) als Ausgangspunkt ausgewählt. Die darin enthaltenen Heuristiken werden auf ihre Gültigkeit mit den spezifischen Usabilityzielen der neuen Domäne abgeglichen und unter Umständen gestrichen oder modifiziert. In einem weiteren Schritt werden neue domänenspezifische Heuristiken ergänzt (Ling & Salvendy 2005, 183-187).

Zunächst wurden etablierte Heuristikensets aus den Bereichen Web- und Software-Ergonomie als Grundlage verwendet. Die Regeln aus den Standardwerken von Nielsen (1994), Shneiderman (2010), Norman (1990) und die Grundsätze der Dialoggestaltung nach DIN EN ISO 9241-110 (2006) wurden in einer Excel-Tabelle erfasst. Damit ein inhaltlicher Abgleich mit den domänenspezifischen Regeln erfolgen konnte, wurden die Prinzipien verschlagwortet. Die Schlagworte wurden nach den Kriterien der Aussagekraft und Trennschärfe gewählt und iterativ verfeinert. Die resultierenden Schlagworte waren „Konsistenz“, „Feedback“, „Steuerbarkeit“, „Fehlerbehandlung“, „Aufgabenangemessenheit“, „Hilfe und Dokumentation“ und „Gedächtnisentlastung“.

In einem nächsten Schritt wurden Quellen aus den Bereichen Produkt- und Gerätedesign (Kortum 2008, Baumann & Lanz 1998; Baumann 2001; Martel & Mavromatti 2001, Rams 1995, Lidwell et al. 2004) auf darin enthaltene Gestaltungsempfehlungen geprüft.

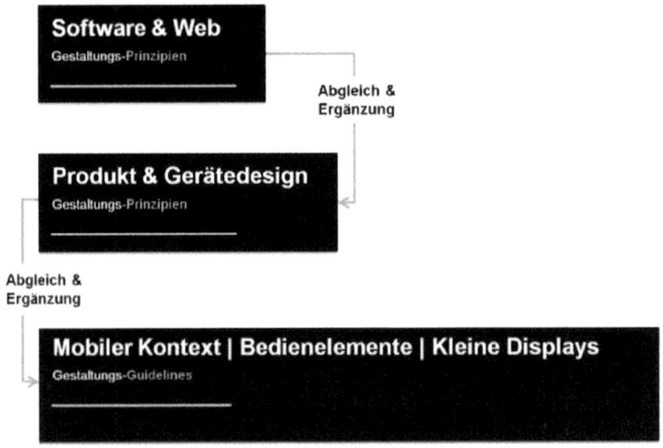

Abbildung 1 Verfahren der Ableitung der Heuristiken

Auch Konzepte des *joy of use*-Modells nach Hassenzahl wurden aufgenommen (Hassenzahl 2003). Die Empfehlungen wurden zusammengefasst, in die Tabelle aufgenommen und ebenfalls verschlagwortet. Es ergaben sich neue Schlagworte wie „Selbsterklärungsfähigkeit", "Universelles und flexibles Design", sowie „Hedonische Qualität". Mithilfe der vergebenen Schlagworte wurden die Heuristiken systematisch verglichen, modifiziert und ergänzt.

In einem letzten Schritt wurden die identifizierten Heuristiken um konkrete Design Guidelines basierend auf den grundlegenden Charakteristika von Information Appliances (vgl. oben Abschnitt 2) wie mobiler Kontext (Tarasewich & Gong 2004; Longoria 2004; Häkkila 2006), Hardware-Bedienelemente (Baumann 2001; Ahlstrom & Kudrick 2004; O'Hara et al. 2002) und Guidelines für kleine Displays (Mauney & Masterton 2008; Kärkkäinen & Laarni 2002) ergänzt. Das Kriterium zur Auswahl relevanter Guidelines war die Konkretisierung der Heuristik, dass heißt, die Empfehlungen sollten den allgemeinen Grundsatz konkretisieren und überprüfbarer machen.

4 Heuristikenset

4.1 Heuristiken erster Ebene

Das entstandene Set umfasst neun Heuristiken und ist in Gestaltungsregeln erster Ebene und zweiter Ebene gegliedert. Die Regeln der ersten Ebene folgen dem typischen Aufbau bei Nielsen (1994) oder Shneiderman (Shneiderman & Plaisant 2010). Sie bestehen aus einem Titel und einer prägnanten Formulierung des Prinzips in einem Satz.

1. Konsistenz: Das Gerät ist einheitlich gestaltet und entspricht anwendbaren Standards.
2. Feedback: Jeder Bedienvorgang, auch Tastenduck, besitzt unmittelbare, angemessene und wahrnehmbare Rückmeldung.
3. Einfache Handhabung: Die Bedienung sollte möglichst effizient und einfach sein und dem Benutzer trotzdem das Gefühl der Kontrolle geben.
4. Fehlervermeidung: Bedienfehler in Form von nicht-unterstützen Bedienhandlungen, versehentlicher Betätigung oder Verwechslung von Funktionen sollte vorgebeugt werden.
5. Aufgabenangemessenheit: Das Gerät sollte die vom Benutzer erwarteten und benötigten Funktionen enthalten und das UI an seine Aufgaben angepasst sein.
6. Hilfe und Dokumentation: Bei Bedienproblemen und zur Unterstützung des Erlernens neuer Funktionen sollte das Gerät passende Informationen bereitstellen.
7. Selbsterklärungsfähigkeit: Die Grundfunktionen sollten ohne Instruktionen oder Handbuch auf Anhieb bedienbar sein.

8. Flexible Nutzung: Das Gerät kann von Menschen mit unterschiedlichen Fähigkeiten und Vorlieben und unter verschiedenen Bedingungen in alltäglichen Situationen genutzt werden.

9. Hedonische Qualität: Das Gerät besitzt ästhetische Eigenschaften, die Bedürfnisse der Benutzer wie Stimulation und Identität erfüllen.

4.2 Regeln zweiter Ebene am Beispiel der Heuristik „Aufgabenangemessenheit"

Um die Heuristiken erster Ebene zu konkretisieren, wurden Gestaltungsempfehlungen zweiter Ebene formuliert. Diese Regeln besitzen verschiedene Bezugsbereiche, die in der Tabelle in der rechten Spalte eingetragen sind. „A" steht für den Bezugsbereich allgemein und ist gültig für alle *Information Appliances*. Die restlichen Markierungen stehen für Charakteristika, die für viele Geräte zutreffen: „H" steht für „hardwarebasierte" Interaktion, „D" für kleine Displays, „M" für mobiler Kontext.

	Aufgabenangemessenheit	**Bezugs-bereich**
1.	Die Funktionalität ist ausreichend für Benutzeraufgaben und enthält relevante Kontrollmöglichkeiten (Isonorm 9241 110 2008-2009, 9; Martel & Mavromatti 2001, 79 ff.)	A
2.	Wichtige bzw. häufig genutzte sowie kritische Funktionen müssen leicht bzw. direkt zugänglich sein (Mohageg, Wagner 2000, 39ff.; Martel & Mavromatti 2001, 81)	A
3.	Die Tasten und Menüoptionen sollten nach Aufgaben benannt sein (Baumann 1998, 10)	A
4.	Bedienschritte und Dialogablauf sollten sich Aufgaben entsprechen und nicht interner Logik (Baumann 1998, 10)	H
5.	Bedienelemente sind passend für die jeweilige Aufgabe (stabil, ausreichende Präzision und Wertebereich; angemessene Exaktheit; Schnelligkeit) (Martel & Mavromatti 2001, 81 f.; O'Hara et al. 2002, 217f.)	H
6.	Wichtige Informationen sind aus maximaler Betrachtungsdistanz erkennbar und lesbar (ausgenommen bildliche Darstellungen) (O'Hara et al. 2002, 15; Martel, Mavromatti 2001, 83f.)	D
7.	Die Displayfläche ist ausreichend groß, um alle benötigten Informationen auf einmal anzuzeigen (O'Hara et al. 2002, 17; Longoria 2004, 119ff.)	D
8.	Das Display ermöglicht eine angemessene Hervorhebung von kritischen Informationen, Statusveränderungen, kritische Daten oder besondere Bedingungen durch Farbe, Fettdruck, Rahmen). (O'Hara et al. 2002, 15; Mauney & Masterton 2008, 347; Bertini 2006,121.)	D

9. Größe und Form ermöglichen eine leichte Transportierbarkeit (Bertini 2006, 121.)	M

Tabelle 1: Heuristiken zweiter Ebene am Beispiel Aufgabenangemessenheit

5 Evaluation der Heuristiken

Die neuen Heuristiken wurden abschließend hinsichtlich ihrer Eignung zur Evaluation von *Information Appliances* evaluiert. Zur Bewertung von Evaluationsmethoden können drei Maße herangezogen werden: Vollständigkeit, Validität und Reliabilität (Hartson, Andre & Williges 2003). Vollständigkeit gibt an, wie viele der vorhandenen Probleme eines Systems tatsächlich durch eine Methode gefunden werden (Sears 197, 215; Hartson, Andre & Williges 2003, 161). Validität ist ein Maß, das bestimmt, inwieweit die identifizierten Usability-Probleme „echte" Befunde und keine *false positives* darstellen (Sears 1997, 214f.; Hartson, Andre & Williges 2003, 163). Reliabilität ist ein Qualitätsmaß, das die Konsistenz der Ergebnisse unterschiedlicher Evaluatoren anzeigt (Hartson, Andres & Williges 2003, 167).

Grundlage für die Berechnung der Performanzmaße sind Konzepte der Signal-Detektions-Theorie: Treffer sind „echte" Usability-Befunde, die durch die Methode identifiziert wurden. Auslassungen sind Befunde, die mit der Methode nicht erfasst wurden. Bei falschen Alarmen handelt es sich um Probleme, die durch die Methode angenommen, aber nicht „echt" sind. (Hartson, Andre & Williges 2003, 166). Zur Bestimmung der Performanzmaße wird ein Set an Usability-Problemen benötigt, das dem Echtheitskriterium genügt und als vollständig angenommen werden kann. Ein Standardverfahren, um dieses Set zu generieren, ist ein laborbasierter Nutzertest (Hartson, Andre & Williges 2003, 156)

Um die Heuristiken zu prüfen, wurden zwei Beispielgeräte mithilfe der Prinzipien evaluiert und die Befunde durch die Ergebnisse einer zweiten nutzerbasierten Evaluation validiert. Die Heuristische Evaluation erfolgte in einer aufgabenorientierten Weise, als sogenannter *Heuristic Walkthrough* (Sears 1997). Dabei wurden die Interfaces zunächst anhand vorher festgelegter Aufgaben und mithilfe der Leitfragen aus dem *Cognitive Walkthrough* (Wharton, Rieman & Lewis 1994, 111) exploriert und in einem zweiten Durchgang systematisch die Einhaltung der Heuristiken geprüft und Verstöße als Usability-Probleme vermerkt. Als Untersuchungsgegenstand dienten eine Bridgekamera (*Nikon P100*) und ein Kopiergerät (*Sharp MX-M450U*). Beide Geräte stellen aufgrund ihrer Charakteristika (kleine Displays, Kombination aus Hard- und Software-Bedienelementen) und verschiedene Nutzungskontexte (mobil, stationär) geeignete *Information Appliances* für die Validierung der neuen Bewertungskriterien dar.

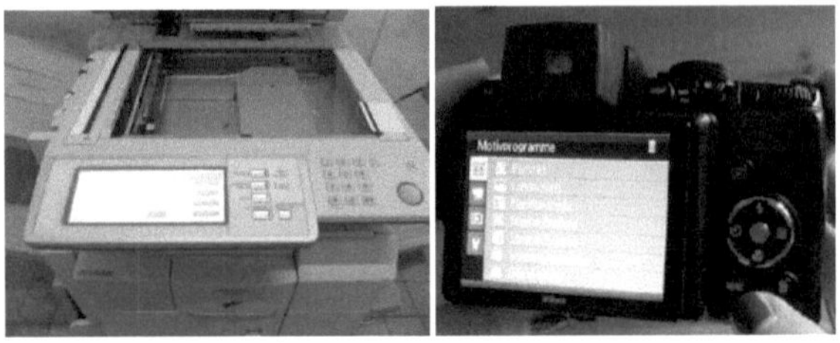

Abbildung 2 Untersuchungsobjekte Kopierer und Bridgekamera (eigene Bilder)

Um Vollständigkeit und Validität dieser Usability-Evaluation bestimmen zu können, wurde eine zweite Evaluation mit Nutzern durchgeführt. 20 Probanden führten in einer Laborumgebung typische Aufgaben mit den Geräten durch. Die Nutzungsszenarien umfassten Aufgaben, die neben den automatischen oder Standardfunktionen auch manuelle Einstellungen in realistischem Umfang erforderten. Bei der Digitalkamera wurde beispielsweise neben dem Schnappschussmodus und Zoom als Standardfunktionen auch die Auswahl eines passenden Motivprogramms getestet. Fortgeschrittene manuelle Einstellungen von Blende und Belichtungszeit wurden nicht getestet, da sie für den gewählten Kameratyp eher selten genutzte Funktionen darstellen.

Durch einen Vergleich der Usability-Befunde aus beiden Evaluationen können Vollständigkeit und Validität der heuristischen Evaluation berechnet werden. Für die Vollständigkeit wird die Anzahl der in der heuristischen Evaluation gefundenen, realen Usability-Probleme in Bezug zu allen realen (im Nutzertest aufgetretenen) Problemen gesetzt (Sears 1997, 215; Hartson, Andre &Williges 2003, 161). Bei der heuristischen Evaluation der Kamera wurden 10 von 13 Usability-Problemen gefunden und bei dem Kopiergerät 11 von 14. Für die Beurteilung der Validität werden die realen, identifizierten Usability-Probleme aus der heuristischen Evaluation zu der Anzahl aller gefundenen Probleme in der heuristischen Evaluation gesetzt (Sears 1997, 214f.; Hartson, Andre & Williges 2003, 163f.). Bei der Heuristischen Evaluation der Kamera sind 10 von 11 Problemen reale Befunde. Bei dem Kopiergerät sind 11 von 14 Problemen reale Befunde. Insgesamt deuten diese Ergebnisse auf eine gute Vollständigkeit und Validität der Evaluationsmethode hin.

6 Diskussion und Ausblick

Um die Usability von *Information Appliances* einfach und ressourcenschoned evaluieren zu können, wurden angepasste Heuristiken mit einem recherchebasierten Verfahren abgeleitet. Dabei wurden exemplarische Charakteristika der Geräte wie kleine Displays, hard-und softwarebasierte Interaktion und mobiler Kontext bei der Einbeziehung konkreter Gestaltungsempfehlungen berücksichtigt. Die neun Heuristiken wurden zur Evaluation zweier beispielhafter Geräte, einer Digitalkamera und einem Kopiergerät, herangezogen. Ein Vergleich der Befunde mit den Ergebnissen aus einem Nutzertest deutet auf ein eine relativ hohe Vollständigkeit und Validität der Ergebnisse der Evaluationsmethode an. Die Reliabilität der heuristischen Evaluation konnte im Rahmen der ersten Überprüfung nicht erhoben werden, da hierfür die Ergebnisse mehrerer Evaluatoren gegenübergestellt werden müssen. Für eine weitere Überprüfung der Heuristiken sind zusätzlich Evaluationen mit anderen Geräten und mit mehreren Evaluatoren nötig.

Auch die inhaltliche Ebene der Heuristiken ist noch nicht erschöpft. Es existieren Designbereiche, die noch nicht in der Literatur beleuchtet wurden und in einem recherchebasierten Ansatz deshalb offen blieben: Zum Beispiel die sinnvolle Kombination von Hardware-Elementen mit Touchscreens oder die Gestaltung von Hilfeformen, mit denen auch komplexe Interaktionen bewältigt werden können. Diese Fragen können nur durch problemorientierte Ansätze, also Usability-Untersuchungen von geeigneten Lösungen, beantwortet werden.

Literaturverzeichnis

Ahlstrom, V. & Kudrick, B. (2004). *Human Factors Criteria for the Design and Acquisition of Non-keyboard Interaction.* A Revision to Chapter 9 of the Human Factors Design Standard. National Technical Information Service: Springfield.

Baumann, K., & Lanz, H. (1998). *Mensch-Maschine-Schnittstellen elektronischer Geräte: Leitfaden für Design und Schaltungstechnik.* Berlin: Springer.

Baumann, K., & Thomas, B. (Hrsg.) (2001). *User Interface Design for Electronic Appliances.* London: Taylor & Francis.

Barnett, J. (2012, March 8). The top 10 categories: What consumers complain about most. *CNN edition international.* http://edition.cnn.com/2012/03/08/us/top-10-consumer-complaints. [Zugriff 6/2014].

Burmester, M. & Machate, J. (2003). Creative design of interactive products and use of usability guidelines - a contradiction? In J. Jack, C. Stephanidis, & D. & Harris (Hrsg.): *Human-computer interaction: theory and practice.* Mahwah, NJ, United States: Lawrence Erlbaum Associates Inc., S.43-46.

Cooper, A. (2004). *The inmates are running the asylum* ([Nachdr.]). Indianapolis: SAMS.

den Ouden, E., Yuan, L., Sonnemans, P. J. M., & Brombacher, A. C. (2006). Quality and Reliability Problems from a Consumer's Perspective: an Increasing Problem Overlooked by Businesses? *Quality and Reliability Engineering International*, 22(7), S. 821-838. John Wiley & Sons, Ltd.

DIN EN ISO 9241-110 (2006). *Ergonomie der Mensch-System-Interaktion - Teil 110: Grundsätze der Dialoggestaltung.* Beuth, Berlin.

Han, S. H., Yun, M. H., Kwahk, J. & Hong, S. W. (2001). Usability of consumer electronic products. *5th Pan-Pacific Conference on Occupational Ergonomics*, 28(3–4), S. 143–151.

Hartson, H., Andre, T., &. Williges, R. (2003). Criteria for evaluating usability evaluation methods. *International Journal of Human-Computer Interaction*, 15(1), S. 373-410.

Hassenzahl, M. 2003. "The thing and I: Understanding the relationship between user and product." In *Funology: From usability to enjoyment*, 31–42. Dordrecht ; Boston: Kluwer Academic Publishers.

Häkkila, J. (2006). *Usability with context-aware mobile applications: Case studies and design guidelines.* Oulu: University of Oulu.

Kärkkäinen, L., & Laarni, J. (2002). Designing for small display screens. *Proceedings of the second Nordic conference on Human-computer interaction.* New York, USA: ACM, S. 227-230.

Kortum, P. (2008). *HCI beyond the GUI: design for haptic, speech, olfactory and other nontraditional interfaces.* Amsterdam; Boston: Elsevier/Morgan Kaufmann.

Lidwell, W., Holden, K., & Butler, J. (2004). *Design: Die 100 Prinzipien für erfolgreiche Gestaltung.* München: Stiebner.

Ling, C., & Salvendy, G. (2005). Extension of heuristic evaluation method: a review and reappraisal. *Ergonomia An International Journal of Ergonomics and Human Factors*, 27(3), S. 179-197.

Mohageg, M., & Wagner, A. (2000). Design Considerations for Information Appliances. In E. Bergman (Hrsg.): *Information appliances and beyond* (S. 27-52). San Francisco, Calif: Kaufmann.

Nielsen, J., & Molich, R. (1990). Heuristic evaluation of user interfaces. *Proceedings of the SIGCHI conference on Human factors in computing systems Empowering people - CHI '90.* New York, USA: ACM Press, S. 249-256.

Nielsen, J. (1994). Heuristic Evaluation. In J. Nielsen & R. L. Mack (Hrsg.): *Usability inspection methods.* New York: Wiley, S. 25-62.

Norman, D. (1990). *The design of everyday things.* New York: Doubleday.

Norman, D. (1999). *The Invisible Computer: Why good products can fail the personal computer is so complex and information appliances are the solution.* London: MIT Press.

O'Hara, J.M., Brown, W.S., Lewis, P.M., & Persensky, J.J. (2002). *Human-System Interface Design Review Guidelines (NUREG-0700).* Washington, DC: U.S. Nuclear Regulatory Commission.

Ohnemus, K. R. (1997). Web style guides: who, what, where. In: *SIGDOC '97, Proceedings of the 15th annual international conference on Computer documentation.* New York, USA: ACM, S. 189-197.

Rams, D. (1995). *Weniger aber besser.* Hamburg: Klatt.

Sears, & A. (1997). Heuristic Walkthroughs: Finding the problems without the noise. International *Journal of Human-Computer Interaction*, (3), S. 213-234.

Thompson, D.V., Hamilton, R.W. & Rust, R.T. (2005). Feature Fatigue: When Product Capabilities Become Too Much of a Good Thing. *Journal of Marketing Research*, Vol. XLII, S. 431-442.

Wharton, C., Rieman, J. & Lewis, C. P. P. (1994). The Cognitive Walkthrough Method: A Practitioner's Guide. In J. Nielsen & R. L. Mack (Hg.), *Usability inspection methods* (S. 105-140). New York: Wiley.

Kurzbeiträge

M. Koch, A. Butz & J. Schlichter (Hrsg.): Mensch und Computer 2014 Tagungsband,
München: Oldenbourg Wissenschaftsverlag, 2014, S. 287-290.

Adaptive eLearning based on individual learning styles – Performance and emotional factors

Jennifer Beckmann[1], Sven Bertel[2], Steffi Zander[2]

Fachhochschule Südwestfalen[1]
Bauhaus Universität Weimar[2]

Abstract

Adaptive eLearning systems are able to adjust to a user's learning needs, usually by user modeling or tracking progress. Such learner-adaptive behavior has rapidly become a hot topic for eLearning. This contribution presents original research on using differences in individual learning styles. Factors related to performance, motivation, satisfaction, and previous knowledge were targeted and used to assess the effectiveness of the approach.

1 Introduction

Compared to traditional, classroom-based learning, eLearning is e.g. characterized by a dramatically decreased instructor/student ratio and an increased variation in the student population and in contexts and patterns of use. In brief, there exists less option for the instructor to adapt and mediate a course's content to the individual student, and more need to do so. This is a gap that eLearning systems need to increasingly fill. We believe that a promising approach to filling the gap lies in tailoring or mediating the standard content of online courses such that it will adequately fit and adapt to students' individual backgrounds and learning styles. The goal is to maintain efficiency and effectiveness of the individual learning experience. A number of important learner variables to which a system can adapt address cognitive factors. Mayer and Massa (2003) differentiate between *cognitive abilities* (what people are capable of doing), *cognitive styles* (ways in which people process and represent information), and *learning preferences* (ways in which people like information to be presented to them). We will employ this categorization, while referring to Mayer and Massa's *learning preferences* as *learning styles*.

This paper presents original research on whether an adaptation of eLearning material to inter-individual differences in learning styles can increase learning effectiveness and efficiency, learner motivation, and learner satisfaction. We will present a behavioral study and analyze and discuss resulting data. The paper will conclude with a discussion and future work.

2 Methodology and Method

For modeling learning styles on an individual basis, we chose to employ the *Felder-Silverman Learning Style Model* (*FSLSM;* Felder & Silverman 1988). On the *visual/verbal* dimension of the *FSLSM* a predominantly visual learner remembers best what she sees e.g. as pictures whereas a predominantly verbal learner prefers words in written or spoken form to learn. Within this study, we chose to focus on adapting eLearning material along this style, because the dimension is well-investigated, also in cognitive style research, and because an adaptation of the presentation format of our learning material could be achieved with limited resources. Few previous studies have employed the *visual/verbal* dimension in the context of adaptive eLearning (e.g. Brown et al. 2006). While these usually focused on measuring performance-related outcomes, we chose to take a step further and also focused on emotional factors related to learner satisfaction and motivation. We deem learner's motivation to be essential for learning outcome, and believe high motivation levels to be an important precondition for sustained engagement in learning. Our main research questions were as follows: (Q1) Is there a positive influence of a good fit between the format of the learning material and the learning style on learning performance? (Q2) Does a good fit increase learner motivation and satisfaction?

To answer these questions, we designed a study. 53 participants (26♀, 27♂), with a mean age of 25.3 years [20-34 years], participated voluntarily. There was no reward in terms of money or credits. The study was conducted under laboratory conditions at Bauhaus-Universität Weimar to control and minimize effects of distraction and disruption. Participants were mostly students of *Computer Science and Media* degree programs. They learned at PCs with our *Moodle* system and were told that they would be given a quiz about the learning material. Participants were also provided with a questionnaire on their intrinsic motivation and satisfaction. The learning material was taken from an established eLearning course intended for future civil engineers on the theory of oscillations. The chosen chapters were comprehensible with secondary school knowledge. And the material was reproduced in two versions: one centered mostly on using illustrative diagrams, the other on using textual descripttions. The lecturer of the original course acted as an expert evaluator and ensured that both versions contained the same information and that expected learning times were each at 20 minutes.

The study was of mixed design. As between-subject component, two groups (A & B) were formed, which received the same learning units, however in different display formats (*visual* or *verbal*). One half of all units were presented according to the individual learning style, the other half were presented in the opposite format. The within-subject component contained the questions of the quiz, and all participants were given the same set of questions. Based on the research questions, the independent variable was the display format. As dependent variables, study time, test performance as well as learner motivation, and satisfaction with the learning material were used. In addition, participants' previous relevant knowledge were established.

3 Results

As it turns out, ¾ of our participants had a visual learning style. This corresponds with findings of other studies that about 74% of natural science study program students (*N>2800*) have visual learning styles (Felder & Spurlin 2005). A correlation analysis and a set of ANCOVAs showed that previous knowledge had no influence on learning outcomes, nor did it influence motivation, satisfaction, or study times. The main focus of the analysis lies on the group of moderate to strong visual learners, as they constituted the largest learning style group of our subjects. The two key findings of the study are that (1) there was no significant influence of a good or bad fit between the material format and individual learning style on study time and learning outcomes, but that (2) there was an influence on learner satisfaction and motivation.

Visual participants who received pictorial material in lesson 1 were significantly more motivated than visual participants who started with the text material. Interestingly, such high motivation levels did not decline after the second lesson, which was presented as a mismatch (i.e., in text form). In group B, participants started with text; for the visual participants, motivation increased significantly after lesson 2 in which material was presented as pictures. One interpretation of our data is that high motivation levels caused by style-matched material declines slowly during a mismatch, and that it rises more quickly when mismatched material is followed by matched material. Visual learners were thus highly significantly more pleased with pictorial material. They did not like to learn with text only. For detailed results see Table 1, interestingly, none of these tests remain significant when aggregating data from all visual learners (including balanced visual learners). This shows that the effects reported here are really related to an expressed visual learning style, and that learners' individual strengths of style expressions may be just as important for designing effective adaptive behavior in eLearning systems as a sorting into dichotomous visual/verbal categories.

subject of investigation	**group A** *N=13* l1: pictures l2: text	**group B** *N=10* l1: text l2: pictures	**test results** (Mann-Whitney-U, due to the non-normal distribution of data)
study time			
lesson 1	*M=13.63 min*	*M=10.52 min*	*U=40.00, Z=1,550, ns, r=−.32*
lesson 2	*M=10.10 min*	*M=9.23 min*	*U=56.00, Z=−0.558, ns, r=−.12*
learning outcome			
lesson 1	*M=79.86%*	*M=75%*	*U=43.50, Z=−1,340, ns, r=−.28*
lesson 2	*M=71.87%*	*M=72.29%*	*U=64.50, Z=−.031, ns, r=−.01*
intrinsic motivation			
lesson 1	*M=12.54*	*M=8.70*	*U=26.50, Z=−2.409, p<.05, r=−.50*
lesson 2	*M=12.23*	*M=10.60*	*U=51.00, Z=−0,873, ns, r=−.18*
satisfaction			
lesson 1	*M=9.23*	*M=6.0*	*U=23.00, Z=−2.654, p<.01, r=−.55*
lesson 2	*M=3.54*	*M=10.00*	*U=2.00, Z=−4.002, p<.001, r=−.83*

Table 1: Overview over the test results

4 Conclusion, Discussion and Future Work

The aim of this contribution was to see how adaptive behavior can be infused into an existing eLearning platform by categorizing learners into subpopulations according to their individual learning styles, and by then presenting learning material in different matched and mismatched versions for each subpopulation. In our study we found no significant influences of a style-matched presentation of learning material on study time and learning outcome. This finding is in line with former research on this topic. However, we equally focused learner motivation and satisfaction. For scores of these factors, a presentation of learning material that is well matched to the individual's style of learning turned out to be highly important.

Emotional factors should not be underestimated for eLearning, as they play a substantial role for self-regulated learning. As Schiefele and Schreyer (1994) demonstrated, intrinsic learning motivation is significantly positively correlated with measures of learning success. In addition, Levy (2007) identified learner satisfaction as a major factor drop out quotes of eLearning courses. Even though the study on which we reported here did not show a direct influence of style-matched material onto learning success, one could argue that via the discovered strong influence of style-matched learning material on intrinsic motivation, as well as via the influence of intrinsic motivation on learning success widely established elsewhere, an indirect effect of learning style on learning success likely exists. This point clearly requires further and more systematic research. Further work is also needed to investigate the long-term impacts of style-matched courses on the performance-related factors, either directly, or indirectly via emotional factors. We thus suggest to conduct a long-term study, and to employ a suitable test-retest procedure that would have to be developed. Moreover, there is a need to conduct such study with a larger sample to verify the results obtained here also for the verbal learners.

References

Brown, E., Brailsford, T., Fisher, T., Moore, A. & Ashman, H. (2006). Reappraising cognitive styles in adaptive web applications. In: *WWW '06* (pp. 327–335). New York, NY, USA: ACM.

Felder, R. M. & Silverman, L. K. (1988). Learning and teaching styles in engineering education. *Engineering education*, *78*(7), 674–681.

Felder, R. M. & Spurlin, J. (2005). Applications, reliability and validity of the index of learning styles. *International Journal of Engineering Education*, *21*(1), 103–112.

Levy, Y. (2007). Comparing dropouts and persistence in e-learning courses. *Computers & Education*, *48*(2), 185–204.

Mayer, R. E. & Massa, L. J. (2003). Three Facets of Visual and Verbal Learners: Cognitive Ability, Cognitive Style, and Learning Preference. *Journal of Educational Psychology*, *95*(4), 833–841.

Schiefele, U. & Schreyer, I. (1994). Intrinische Lernmotivation und Lernen: ein Überblick zu Ergebnissen der Forschung; 1994. *Zeitschrift für Pädagogische Psychologie*, (8), 1–13.

M. Koch, A. Butz & J. Schlichter (Hrsg.): Mensch und Computer 2014 Tagungsband,
München: Oldenbourg Wissenschaftsverlag, 2014, S. 291-294.

Anforderungserhebung für ein peripheres Benachrichtigungssystem

Laura Ackermann

DE|RE|SA (Design Research Salzburg), Fachhochschule Salzburg GmbH

Zusammenfassung

Zur Unterstützung von Beschäftigten am Computerarbeitsplatz wurde ein Assistenzsystem mit peripheren Benachrichtigungen entwickelt. Da für die Anforderungserhebung dieses neuartigen Systems keine etablierten Methoden der Nutzereinbindung zur Verfügung standen, wurde ein eigener Fragebogen konzipiert, der auf der Activity Theory und dem IRC-Modell basiert. Auf diese Weise konnten der Kontext des Assistenzsystems berücksichtigt und konkrete Gestaltungshinweise für die peripheren Benachrichtigungen gewonnen werden. Die Ergebnisse zeigen, dass sich das gewählte Vorgehen zur Anforderungserhebung bei Benachrichtigungssystemen grundsätzlich eignet.

1 Hintergrund und Problemstellung

In Deutschland leisten 17 Millionen Menschen Büroarbeit; 90 % von ihnen nutzen hierfür Computer (BAuA 2010). Dabei begegnen sie verschiedenen Herausforderungen, wie beispielsweise Termin- und Leistungsdruck, zahlreichen Unterbrechungen und häufigen Wechseln zwischen unterschiedlichen Aufgaben (Brenscheidt et al. 2008). Zudem werden Beschäftigte am Computerarbeitsplatz mit einer großen Menge an Informationen konfrontiert. Viele dieser Informationen werden dabei als störend empfunden, da sie entweder nicht hilfreich sind oder zu ungünstigen Zeitpunkten wahrgenommen werden (Kniewel et al. 2013). Ein Ansatz zur Unterstützung der Beschäftigten können Assistenzsysteme mit peripheren Benachrichtigungen sein. Diese können Informationen enthalten, die nicht für die aktuell bearbeitete Aufgabe benötigt werden, aber dennoch vom Nutzer erwünscht sind (Maglio & Campbell 2000). Die primäre Aufmerksamkeit wird nicht zwangsweise auf das Assistenzsystem gelenkt (Stasko et al. 2004), indem dieses in der Peripherie des Nutzers platziert wird – beispielsweise am Rand des Computermonitors oder als eigenständiges Gerät auf dem Schreibtisch. Da es sich bei peripheren Benachrichtigungen um ein neuartiges Interaktionskonzept handelt, für das keine etablierten Methoden zur Nutzereinbindung vorhanden waren, musste ein geeignetes Vorgehen für die Anforderungserhebung gefunden werden.

2 Methode

Der Fokus der Anforderungserhebung lag auf den Fragestellungen, *welche* Informationen der Nutzer durch das Assistenzsystem erhalten möchte und *wie* die Informationen dargeboten werden sollen. Zur Ermittlung der inhaltlichen Anforderungen sowie der Anforderungen an die Gestaltung der Benachrichtigungen diente eine Befragung mit potentiellen Nutzern des Assistenzsystems. Hierzu wurden mit der *Activity Theory* und dem *IRC-Modell* geeignete theoretische Ansätze identifiziert und in einen Online-Fragebogen integriert.

2.1 Inhaltliche Anforderungen: Activity Theory

Da vergleichbare Assistenzsysteme in der Praxis nicht etabliert sind und die Befragung nicht während der eigentlichen Bürotätigkeit durchgeführt wurde, sollte den Probanden innerhalb des Fragebogens der Arbeitskontext ins Bewusstsein gerufen werden. Hierzu wurde die *Activity Theory* nach Leontiev (1977) herangezogen. Nach Kaptelinin et al. (1999) eignet sie sich dazu, den Kontext von Computertechnologien bereits frühzeitig in der Systementwicklung zu berücksichtigen.

Bei der *Activity Theory* handelt es sich um ein Rahmenwerk, das verschiedene Formen menschlicher Tätigkeiten beschreibt (Kuutti 1996). Die Basiseinheit stellt dabei die Aktivität (*activity*) dar. Eine Aktivität (Abb. 1) ist eine Form des Handelns, die auf ein Objekt gerichtet ist (Kuuti 1996). Ziel einer Aktivität ist es, ein Objekt in ein Ergebnis zu transformieren. Ein Ergebnis kann dabei etwas Greifbares, wie z.B. ein Produkt, aber auch etwas Abstraktes, wie z.B. eine Idee, sein. Als vermittelndes Element zwischen dem Subjekt (Nutzer) und dem Objekt einer Aktivität dient das Werkzeug. Es ermöglicht dem Subjekt einerseits den Transformationsprozess des Objektes, andererseits beschränkt es die Sicht auf das Objekt, d.h. weitere Eigenschaften des Objekts bleiben möglicherweise unsichtbar. Um die Beziehungen zwischen einem Individuum und weiteren Beteiligten in einer Aktivität verstehen zu können, wird diese Struktur um die Gemeinschaft als weitere Komponente ergänzt. Regeln bestimmen den Umgang von Menschen in einer Gruppe und treten daher als Vermittler zwischen Subjekt und Gemeinschaft auf. Die Beziehung zwischen Objekt und Gemeinschaft ist durch Arbeitsteilung geprägt, da hierbei mehrere Menschen gemeinsam an Objekten arbeiten können.

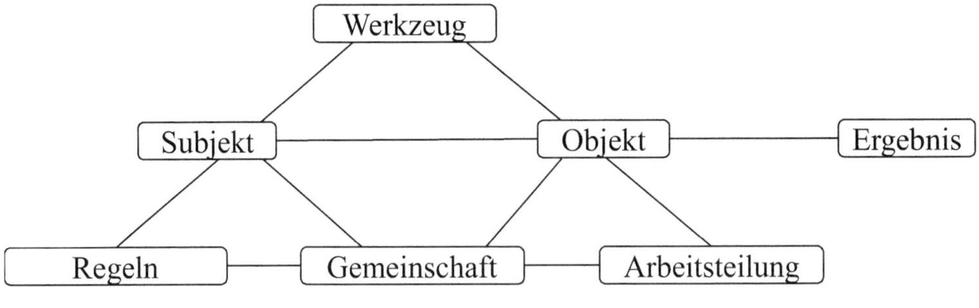

Abbildung 1: Modell der Aktivität entsprechend der Activity Theory nach Kuutti (1996)

2.2 Gestaltung der Benachrichtigungen: IRC-Modell

Um die Aufteilung der Aufmerksamkeitsressourcen des Nutzers (Goldstein 2008) zwischen der aktuellen Tätigkeit einerseits und dem Assistenzsystem andererseits angemessen zu berücksichtigen, müssen die Benachrichtigungsparameter Unterbrechung, Reaktion und Verständnis an die Ziele des Nutzers angepasst werden (Berry 2003). Diese drei Parameter sind im Fokus des *IRC-Modells* nach McCrickard et al. (2003).

Die *Unterbrechung (interruption, I)* resultiert aus einem Ereignis, das zum Wechsel von der (Primär-) Aufgabe zur Benachrichtigung und somit zur Neuzuteilung der Aufmerksamkeit auffordert. Insbesondere für dringende Informationen oder synchrone Kommunikation ist eine absichtliche Ablenkung von anderen Aufgaben notwendig. Die *Reaktion (reaction, R)* bezeichnet eine schnelle und genaue Antwort auf Reize von Benachrichtigungssystemen und wird realisiert, indem man ein schnelles Verarbeiten und Verstehen der Information durch den Einsatz von Farben, Formen und Bewegung erlaubt. Das *Verständnis (comprehension, C)* beschreibt ein tieferes und einprägsames Verstehen der Information mit dem Ziel, die Information zu verarbeiten und für einen späteren Zeitpunkt Sinn daraus zu ziehen. Aus den jeweils unterschiedlichen Ausprägungen dieser drei Parameter ergeben sich die Gestaltungsmöglichkeiten für das Assistenzsystem: Eine Anzeige, die lediglich ein Indikator für einen bestimmten Wert beinhaltet (z.B. aktuelle Erreichbarkeit einer Kollegin), unterbricht beispielsweise den Nutzer nicht, bietet jedoch auch nur einen geringen Beitrag zu einem tieferen Verständnis.

2.3 Integration in einen Fragebogen

Aus den sechs verschiedenen Kategorien der *Activity Theory* entstanden fünf Bereiche im Fragebogen, da *Objekt* und *Ergebnis* beim vorliegenden Anwendungsfall zusammengefasst werden konnten. Zum besseren Verständnis wurden die Kategorien durch weniger abstrakte Formulierungen beschrieben und jeweils anhand eines Beispiels aus dem Arbeitsalltag erläutert. Jeder dieser fünf Bereiche enthielt offene Antwortmöglichkeiten, in denen die Befragten frei angeben konnten, über welche Zustände oder Veränderungen sie benachrichtigt werden möchten. Zusätzlich zu der Angabe der gewünschten Informationen waren sie aufgefordert, ihre Anforderungen bezüglich der Benachrichtigungsparameter *Unterbrechung*, *Reaktion* und *Verständnis* anzugeben. Hierfür standen entsprechend McCrickard et al. (2003) jeweils zwei Ausprägungen zur Auswahl. Um die Anforderungen priorisieren zu können, wurde die Wichtigkeit der gewünschten Informationen über eine fünfstufige Likert-Skala abgefragt.

3 Anwendung und Ausblick

Die Anwendung des Fragebogens erfolgte in einer Online-Befragung (n = 20). Da das System Menschen in Büroarbeit unterstützen soll, wurden hierzu Angestellte mit überwiegender Tätigkeit am Computerarbeitsplatz als Probanden gewählt. Die Antworten wurden durch eine qualitative Inhaltsanalyse (Mayring 2010) sowie quantitativ ausgewertet. Auf diese Weise konnten 60 inhaltliche Anforderungen sowie deren gewünschte Ausprägungen hinsichtlich der Benachrichtigungsparameter *Unterbrechung, Reaktion* und *Verständnis* ermittelt werden. Probleme zeigten sich bei dem Verständnis der Probanden für das grundlegende Konzept des Assistenzsystems. Dies führte dazu, dass teilweise Antworten gegeben wurden, die für ein Benachrichtigungssystem eher unbedeutend sind, z.B. das eigene Körpergewicht. Die Anwendbarkeit des Fragebogens für weitere, beispielsweise mobile, Benachrichtigungssysteme soll in zukünftigen Studien überprüft werden.

Literaturverzeichnis

Berry, B. (2003). Adapting Heuristics for Notification Systems. *Proceedings of 41st Annual ACM Southeast Conference.* Savannah: ACM. S. 144-149.

Brenscheidt, F., Lüther, S. & Siefer, A. (2008). *Arbeitswelt im Wandel: Zahlen, Daten, Fakten.* Dortmund: Bundesanstalt für Arbeitsschutz und Arbeitsmedizin (BAuA). http://www.baua.de/de/Publikationen/Broschueren/A59.html. Überprüft am 29.4.2014.

BAuA (Bundesanstalt für Arbeitsschutz und Arbeitsmedizin) (Hrsg.) (2010). *Wohlbefinden im Büro: Arbeits- und Gesundheitsschutz bei der Büroarbeit.* http://www.baua.de/de/Publikationen/Broschueren/A11.html. Überprüft am 29.4.2014.

Goldstein, E. B. (2008): *Wahrnehmungspsychologie: Der Grundkurs.* Heidelberg: Spektrum.

Kaptelinin, V., Nardi, B. A. & Macaulay, C. (1999). The Activity Checklist: A Tool for Representing the "Space" of Context. *Interactions 6* 4, 27-39.

Kniewel, R., Gerhold, M., Parusel, M., Ackermann, L. & Schmidt, L. (2013). Assistenzsystem für den Computerarbeitsplatz zur Vermeidung von Überbeanspruchung. In Verband der Elektrotechnik Elektronik Informationstechnik e. V. (Hrsg.): *Lebensqualität im Wandel von Demografie und Technik.* Berlin: VDE-Verlag. S. 438-442.

Kuutti, K. (1996). Activity Theory as a Potential Framework for Human-Computer Interaction Research. In Nardi, B. A. (Hrsg.): *Context and Consciousness: Activity Theory and Human-Computer Interaction.* Cambridge: MIT Press. S. 17-44.

Leontiev, A. N. (1977). Activity and Consciousness. *Philosophy in the U.S.S.R.: Problems of Dialectical Materialism.* Moskau: Progress Publishers. 180-202.

Maglio, P. & Campbell, C. (2000): Tradeoffs in Displaying Peripheral Information. *CHI Letters 2* 1, 241-248.

Mayring, P. (2010). *Qualitative Inhaltsanalyse: Grundlagen und Techniken.* Weinheim: Beltz Verlag.

McCrickard, D. S., Chewar, C., Somervell, J. P. & Ndiwalana, A. (2003): A Model for Notification Systems Evaluation – Assessing User Goals for Multitasking Activity. *ACM Transactions on Computer-Human Interaction 10* 4, 312–338.

Stasko, J., Miller, T., Pousman, Z., Plaue, C. & Ullah, O. (2004): Personalized Peripheral Information Awareness through Information Art. In Davies, N., Mynatt, E. & Siio, I.: *UbiComp 2004: Proceedings of the 6th International Conference on Ubiquitous Computing.* Nottingham: Springer. S. 18-35.

M. Koch, A. Butz & J. Schlichter (Hrsg.): Mensch und Computer 2014 Tagungsband,
München: Oldenbourg Wissenschaftsverlag, 2014, S. 295-298.

Auswertung von Reverse Card Sorting Experimenten

Daniel Brumberg, Gerd Szwillus

Institut für Informatik, Universität Paderborn

Zusammenfassung

In Reverse Card Sorting (RCS) Experimenten wird untersucht, inwieweit die Benennung und Strukturierung der Begriffe der Informationsarchitektur eines Webauftritts für die Besucher plausibel und nachvollziehbar definiert wurde. Im Gegensatz zum Usability-Test an den fertig gestalteten Webseiten orientiert sich das RCS-Experiment ausschließlich an den verwendeten Linkankertexten und blendet damit einen möglichen positiven oder negativen Einfluss durch die visuelle Gestaltung aus. In diesem Paper wird eine softwareunterstützte Methode zur Auswertung derartiger Experimente beschrieben und an einem realistischen Beispiel demonstriert. Die Methode erlaubt darüber hinaus eine Kategorisierung typischen Fehlverhaltens des Besuchers während der Navigation.

1 Reverse Card Sorting

Es passiert nicht selten, dass man während der Navigation innerhalb eines Webauftritts plötzlich vor der Frage steht: „Wie geht es denn hier weiter?“ Man hat ein bestimmtes Ziel, möchte eine konkrete Fragestellung klären, ist sich auch sicher, dass die Information in dem Webauftritt vorhanden ist, findet aber im sichtbaren Angebot an Links keinen, der richtig oder auch nur einigermaßen passend erscheint. Um solche Situationen im Vorfeld zu erkennen, kann der Entwickler des Auftritts Usability-Tests durchführen – allerdings muss dafür der Webauftritt bereits existieren. Eine Alternative stellt Reverse Card Sorting (RCS) dar.

Um RCS-Experimente durchzuführen, wird nicht der fertige Webauftritt benötigt, sondern lediglich eine Spezifikation der geplanten Informationsarchitektur (IA). Diese wird als Navigationsstruktur in das Verfahren eingebracht, die die Namen der Links und die Verlinkungsstruktur beinhaltet. Die gemeinhin als Hierarchie bezeichnete Navigationsstruktur ist bei realen Webauftritten in den seltensten Fällen eine "echte" Hierarchie, sondern typischerweise eine zusätzlich nicht-hierarchisch vernetzte Hypertextstruktur, allerdings mit einer unterliegenden Hierarchie; sie wird daher vom Besucher trotzdem als primär hierarchisch empfunden. Für die hier behandelten RCS-Experimente wurde die Webapplikation WeCaSo (Vdovkin 2009; Barbula 2011) verwendet; die Abbildung auf der nächsten Seite zeigt einen Ausschnitt der Spezifikation der Navigationsstruktur der Website der DLRG, die als Fallstudie untersucht wurde. Die unterliegende Hierarchie wird darin deutlich, allerdings sind auch

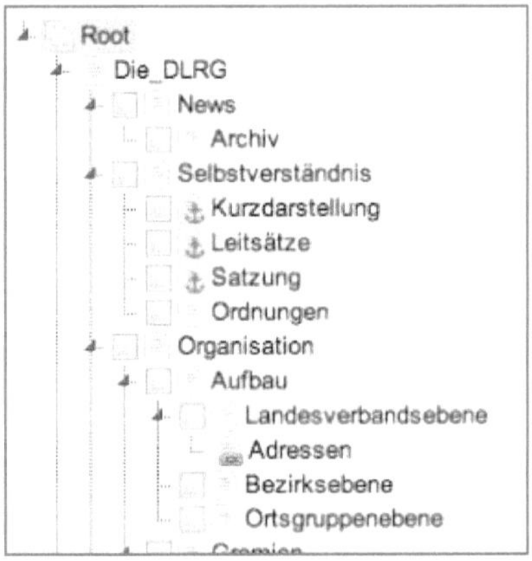

viele Verbindungen „quer" zur Hierarchie eingefügt worden (erkennbar am „Link"-Symbol, etwa bei „Adressen").

Basierend auf der Spezifikation der Navigationsstruktur werden in RCS-Experimenten den Versuchspersonen Navigationsaufgaben gestellt, die sie in der spezifizierten Informationsarchitektur durch Auffinden der „richtigen" Zielseite bewältigen müssen. Eine Beispielaufgabe aus dem DLRG-Experiment etwa war die Suche nach Informationen zur Frage „Was tun bei Eisunfällen?" Die folgende Abbildung zeigt die Sicht der Versuchspersonen im Laufe des Experimentes bei Bearbeiten dieser Aufgabe.

Aus der Literatur sind mehrere RCS-Systeme bekannt, wie etwa TreeJack (Optimal Workshop 2012) oder als Komponente von MindCanvas (Uzanto Consulting) bzw. der C-Inspector (Schilb). Allerdings ist allen Varianten gemeinsam, dass sie von echten Hierarchien ausgehen, was eine unrealistische Voraussetzung ist. Gerade das Zulassen nicht-hierarchischer „Querverbindungen" gestaltet die Analyse schwierig.

2 Auswertung

Während des Experiments zeichnet WeCaSo die durchlaufenen Knoten, gewählten Links, und auch die zugehörigen Wartezeiten auf; auch ein eventueller Abbruch wird dokumentiert. Als Ergebnis eines WeCaSo-Experimentes entsteht daher pro Aufgabe ein Pfad der durchlaufenen Knoten mit zugeordneten Zeitangaben. Da der Webauftritt nicht streng hierarchisch ist, kann es durchaus mehrere, verschiedene Pfade geben, die zum Ziel führen.

Um systematisch an die Auswertung heranzugehen, wird aufbauend auf einem Grundgerüst an Definitionen festgelegt, wie „weit" zwei Seiten in der IA voneinander entfernt sind (Distanzbegriff). Diese Definition erlaubt es, Problemstellen in einem Pfad zu erkennen, indem wir untersuchen, ob der Besucher sich in einem Navigationsschritt vom Zielknoten entfernt, statt sich ihm zu nähern, oder auch ob er zwar den richtigen Weg geht, darüber aber sehr lange nachdenkt. Um einen gesamten Pfad in seiner „Falschheit" zu bewerten, muss berücksichtigt werden, dass der Pfad mehrere solcher Problemstellen enthalten kann, und dass „frühe" Fehler bei der Navigation als stärker zu bewerten sind, da sie den Besucher in völlig falsche Bereiche der IA führen. Hierzu werden die Knoten in der Navigationsstruktur mit einem sogenannten Rang bewertet, der den Abstand zum Startpunkt repräsentiert. Zusätzlich wird die Wartezeit vor der nächsten Entscheidung einbezogen, wobei wir davon ausgegangen sind, dass lange Wartezeiten gleichzusetzen sind mit einer schwierigen Entscheidungssituation für die Versuchsperson. Insgesamt entstand so ein Kalkül, mit dem durch Analyse aller gesammelten Pfade der Versuchspersonen eine Bewertung der einzelnen Seiten des Webauftritts als mehr oder weniger problematisch berechnet werden kann (Brumberg 2013).

Bei der Betrachtung der Experimentergebnisse aus der DLRG-Fallstudie kristallisierten sich typische Verhaltensstrukturen der Versuchspersonen heraus. Wir haben diese Fehlverhaltensmuster gezielt untersucht, um sicherzustellen, dass der oben skizzierte Analysealgorithmus die Muster zuverlässig erkennt. Für die folgenden vier Muster war das der Fall: Durchlaufen eines direkten (ohne Kreise), aber unnötig langen Pfades zum Ziel, Durchlaufen eines Kreises, Wiederholen einer bereits als Fehler erkannten Entscheidung und Abbruch oder Umkehren, obwohl auf dem richtigen Weg.

Ein letztes gefundenes Fehlverhaltensmuster, „systematisches Suchen“ genannt, erwies sich allerdings als sehr problematisch. Dabei hat der Besucher es aufgegeben, über die Bedeutung der Links nachzudenken, sondern probiert (genervt!) systematisch alle Links der Reihe nach durch. Es wäre verfehlt, dieses Verhalten analog zu gezieltem Verhalten zu untersuchen. Bei diesem Verhalten treten eine Häufung von Problemstellen, Klicks und „Zurück“-Klicks, sowie kurze Verweildauern auf. Zusammen mit einem Maß für die nötige „Lesezeit“ konnten wir schließlich eine parametrisierte Heuristik aufstellen, die dieses Fehlverhaltensmuster in den meisten Fällen erkennt und damit eine Verfälschung der Analyseergebnisse verhindert.

3 Fallstudie

Als Fallstudie wurde eine existierende Website (www.dlrg.de) in WeCaSo nachgebaut, Stand: 19.02.2013. Zu diesem Zeitpunkt bestand der Auftritt aus 543 Unterseiten mit 646 internen Links, sodass ein realistisch großes Versuchsobjekt vorliegt. Es wurden insgesamt 15 Navigationsaufgaben definiert, die so ausgewählt wurden, dass sehr verschiedene und auch verschieden tiefe Bereiche des Auftritts besucht werden mussten. Insgesamt haben 50 Versuchspersonen das RCS-Experiment durchgeführt. Als globales Ergebnis wurde ermittelt, dass die Lösungsquote bei 74% lag, wobei es große Unterschiede zwischen den einzelnen Aufgaben gab (s. Abbildung oben). So wurde die Aufgabe „Unfallversicherung Taucher“ von über 73% der Teilnehmer, "Einsatztauchen" aber nur von knapp 44% der Teilnehmer gelöst. Weitere Tabellen zeigen, auf welchen Seiten die Testpersonen „zu lange“ überlegt haben oder vermehrt falsch "abgebogen" sind. Auch Informationen dazu (wie auf der

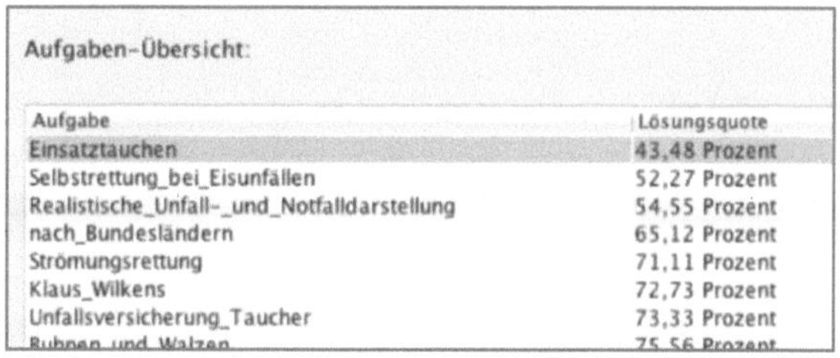
Aufgaben-Übersicht:

Aufgabe	Lösungsquote
Einsatztauchen	43,48 Prozent
Selbstrettung_bei_Eisunfällen	52,27 Prozent
Realistische_Unfall-_und_Notfalldarstellung	54,55 Prozent
nach_Bundesländern	65,12 Prozent
Strömungsrettung	71,11 Prozent
Klaus_Wilkens	72,73 Prozent
Unfallsversicherung_Taucher	73,33 Prozent

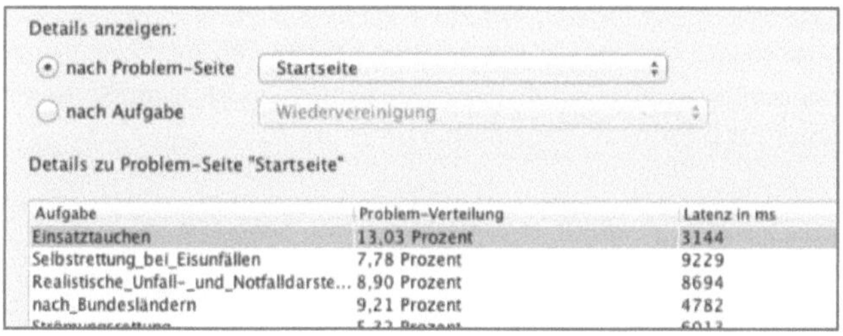
Details anzeigen:

nach Problem-Seite: Startseite

nach Aufgabe: Wiedervereinigung

Details zu Problem-Seite "Startseite"

Aufgabe	Problem-Verteilung	Latenz in ms
Einsatztauchen	13,03 Prozent	3144
Selbstrettung_bei_Eisunfällen	7,78 Prozent	9229
Realistische_Unfall-_und_Notfalldarste...	8,90 Prozent	8694
nach_Bundesländern	9,21 Prozent	4782

vorigen Seite gezeigt), inwieweit eine bestimmte Seite zu bestimmtem Fehlverhalten beigetragen hat, kann abgerufen werden. Hier sieht man etwa, dass die Startseite in rund 13% der Fälle zum Nichtauffinden der Seite „Einsatztauchen“ beigetragen hat.

4 Schlussbemerkungen

Das vorliegende Paper zeigt die Möglichkeiten der Auswertung von RCS-Experimenten anhand einer realistisch großen Fallstudie auf. Das Verfahren wurde softwaremäßig implementiert und mit einer signifikant großen Zahl von Versuchspersonen erprobt. Es ist allerdings nur ein erster Schritt, da viele Fragen noch offen bleiben. Zum einen ist es eine Kernfrage zur Rechtfertigung des gesamten Ansatzes, ob mit RCS die gleichen Probleme gefunden werden, wie mit "echten" Usability-Tests am realen Webauftritt. Die visuelle Gestaltung der Webseite beeinflusst entscheidend die Wahrnehmung aller Elemente, auch der Links, und damit den Navigationserfolg. Die Repräsentation aller Links als neutral gestalteter, gleich aussehender Buttons ist demgegenüber unnatürlich. Auch die Tatsache, dass die Versuchspersonen streng ebenenweise durch die Hierarchie geführt werden, entspricht nicht der gängigen Praxis in realen Webauftritten. Die Methode hat aber den großen Vorteil, dass die IA viel früher getestet und dann auch modifiziert werden kann, und es gibt deutliche Hinweise, dass es eine erhebliche Überschneidung gefundener Probleme zwischen RCS- und Usability-Test gibt (Zhao 2013).

Literaturverzeichnis

Barbula, A. (2011). Integration hierarchischer Sortierung, Multiple-Insert und Reverse-Card-Sorting in eine klassische Card-Sorting-Applikation. Bachelorarbeit. Institut für Informatik. Paderborn.

Brumberg, D. (2013). Entwicklung einer Java-Anwendung zur Auswertung von Reverse-Card-Sorting-Versuchen. Bachelorarbeit. Institut für Informatik. Paderborn.

Optimal Workshop (2012): Treejack. Information Architecture Validation Software. Online verfügbar unter http://www.optimalworkshop.com/treejack.htm, zuletzt geprüft am 6.3.13.

Schilb, S.: C-Inspector. A tool for information architecture testing. Steffen Schilb, Köln. Online verfügbar unter http://www.c-inspector.com/index.php, zuletzt geprüft am 6.3.13.

Uzanto Consulting (Hrsg.): Game-like Elicitation Methods. Online verfügbar unter http://www.themindcanvas.com.

Vdovkin, A. (2009). Entwicklung einer webbasierten Card-Sorting-Applikation. Bachelorarbeit. Institut für Informatik. Paderborn.

Zhao, H. (2013). Vergleichende Untersuchung von Navigationshierarchien mit Reverse Card Sorting und Benutzertests. Masterarbeit. Institut für Informatik. Paderborn.

M. Koch, A. Butz & J. Schlichter (Hrsg.): Mensch und Computer 2014 Tagungsband, München: Oldenbourg Wissenschaftsverlag, 2014, S. 299-302.

Automatisierte 3D-Modellierung für individualisierbare Massenprodukte

Simone Braun[1], Sifeddine Mouaouya[2], Kirsten Siekmann[2], Ramona Wallenborn[2], Markus Westphal-Furuya[1], Peter Wolf[1]

CAS Software AG[1]
mobile media & communication lab, Fachhochschule Aachen[2]

Zusammenfassung

Personalisierte Produkte werden gerade im Konsumgüterbereich immer mehr nachgefragt. Additive Manufacturing (3D-Druck) bietet hier neue Perspektiven um den Kundenwünschen zu begegnen. Die Mitgestaltung des Endkunden ist jedoch ohne 3D-Modellierungskenntnisse nur begrenzt möglich. Der hier vorgestellte Ansatz ermöglicht es auch einem nicht technisch und gestalterisch versierten Kunden im Rahmen von Freiheitsgraden ein Grundmodell zu individualisieren.

1 Einleitung

Im Bereich der Konsumgüter wird die Individualisierung von Massenprodukten (auch als „Mass Customization“ bekannt) immer beliebter. Kunden können z.B. auf Webseiten wie My Muesli ihre eigene Müslimischung zusammenstellen, mit NIKEiD Schuhe individuell gestalten oder auf Mykea mit Klebefolien IKEA-Möbel neu dekorieren[1]. Diese sind jedoch meist darauf beschränkt, dass der Kunde aus einer Palette von Modulen, Farben oder Materialien seine Kombination auswählen kann.

Neuerdings verbreitet sich zunehmend das Additive Manufacturing (ugs. 3D-Druck) als Produktionsverfahren von individualisierten Produkten wie Smartphone-Hüllen (Wohler's Report 2013). Online 3D-Druck-Plattformen[2] wie Shapeways, Ponoko und i.materialise erlauben den Nutzern ihre eigenen 3D-Designs hochzuladen, zu drucken und zu verkaufen. Bestehende Portale bieten Laien eine eher eingeschränkte Unterstützung mit minimalen Personalisierungsmöglichkeiten (Gebhardt 2014, Hu 2013, Rayana et al. 2014, Rosenstock & Wirt 2013). Shapeways ermöglicht eine automatische Modellerstellung bzw. Modellindividualisierung mit Hilfe von Online-/Offline-Apps. Eine App bezieht sich auf genau ein Pro-

---

1 http://www.nike.com/de/de_de/c/nikeid, http://www.mymuesli.com, http://thisismykea.com

2 http://www.shapeways.com, https://www.ponoko.com, http://i.materialise.com

dukt mit bestimmten Funktionen und Personalisierungsmöglichkeiten. So kann der Nutzer z.B. ein Bild hochladen, aus welchem anschließend ein 3D-Modell erzeugt wird, einem Ring eine Gravur hinzufügen oder eine Vase modifizieren. Diese Apps haben sehr unterschiedliche Benutzeroberflächen, sodass sie sich in der Handhabung unterscheiden. Zudem müssen manche Tools installiert werden, wodurch der Endkunde auf bestimmte Endgeräte und Betriebssysteme beschränkt wird. Portale wie ponoko oder i.materialise verweisen auf externe 3D-Werkzeuge wie z.B. Rhinoceros 3D, Autodesk Inventor oder Blender. Diese Tools erfordern Fachkenntnisse der 3D-Modellierung und sind für Laien ohne aufwändige Einarbeitung kaum zu verwenden. Werkzeuge wie Sketchup oder 123dapp fokussieren zwar eine einfache Bedienung, dennoch kann es für Laien schwierig sein, abstrakte Ideen zu konkretisieren; z.B. fehlen Funktionen wie komplexere Transformationen oder Operationen auf Knoten, Kurven und selektierte Flächen oder Unterstützungen durch Anker- oder Orientierungspunkte. Auch fehlt zumeist eine automatische Prüfung der Modelle auf ihre Druckbarkeit.

Ziel des hier vorgestellten Ansatzes ist, einem nicht technisch und gestalterisch versierten Kunden die Möglichkeit zu geben, das 3D-Modell eines Massenprodukts auf einfache Weise zu personalisieren. Dazu wurde eine mobile Applikation für Tablet-PCs entwickelt, genannt „Kiosk", mit der Endkunden ihr Produkt innerhalb bestimmter Freiheitsgrade individualisieren können. Ein spezielles Software-Modul der Applikation überprüft das modifizierte 3D-Modell automatisch auf seine Druckbarkeit, sodass fehlerfreie Druckdateien erzeugt werden. Die Individualisierung innerhalb von Freiheitsgraden setzt deren Erstellung in der vorangehenden Phase der Produktentwicklung voraus. Spezielle Modellierungswerkzeuge unterstützen Designer Freiheitsgrade auf einem 3D-Grundmodell zu definieren. Zudem erfordert die Sicherstellung der Druckbarkeit eines individualisierten 3D-Modells ein Regelwerk zur Definition, welche Parameter zulässig sind und welche zu fehlerhaften Druckdaten führen würden. Dazu wurde das Konfigurationspunkte- und Validierungspunkte-Konzept entwickelt.

2 Konfigurations- und Validierungspunkte-Konzept

Die Erstellung individualisierbarer Massenprodukte, die schon bei der Individualisierung automatisch auf ihre Druckbarkeit überprüft werden können, erfordert eine vorgelagerte Bestimmung gewisser Freiheitsgrade für den Endkunden. Das Konfigurationspunkte-Konzept ermöglicht es Designern mit einem Modellierungs-Tool bestimmte Lösungsräume auf einem 3D-Modell anzulegen, innerhalb derer anschließend eine Anpassung durch den Kunden geschehen kann. Personalisierungsoptionen werden durch sog. Konfigurationspunkte (KP) abgebildet, die auf Bereiche von 3D-Objekten angewendet werden können. Ein vom Designer aufgebrachter KP definiert einen Aspekt des 3D-Grundmodells, der später im Kiosk durch den Kunden weiter personalisiert werden kann; z.B. der im 3D-Modellierungsprogramm verfügbare KP „Text" für einen aufbringbaren Schriftzug ermöglicht dem Endkunden innerhalb des Kiosks, seinen eigenen Namen einzugeben. Somit stellt ein KP die Verbindung zwischen dem 3D-Modellierungsprogramm und dem Kiosk dar. Die KPs werden von parametrischen Python-Funktionen definiert, die später mit den Werten aufgerufen werden können, die der Kunde am Kiosk setzt. Diese Funktionen operieren dann auf der Blender-API um Modellierungsabläufe in Blender zu automatisieren. Ein Beispiel für einen

KP zur Rotation ist die Python-Methode „rotateMesh(meshId, axis, angle)", wobei die Konfigurationsparameter meshId, axis und angle im Kiosk vom Kunden belegt werden. Die Belegung erfolgt für den Kunden über einfach zu bedienende UI-Komponenten wie Textboxen und Slider. Nachdem der Kunde die Werte gesetzt hat, wird die Methode ausgeführt. Ihre Python-Implementierung automatisiert alle in Blender notwendigen Schritte um eine Rotation des mit meshId bezeichneten Objektes durchzuführen.

Nach Eingabe der Parameter durch den Kunden und Anwendung der KPs erfolgt eine automatische Prüfung der Druckbarkeit durch Validierungspunkte (VP). Die VP operieren analog zu den KP und erlauben eine unmittelbare Rückmeldung. Dabei wird zwischen allgemeinen und konfigurationspunktbezogenen VP unterschieden. Erstere prüfen das 3D-Modell auf allgemeine Voraussetzungen und Anforderungen des 3D-Drucks und werden immer ausgeführt. Zu prüfen ist, dass: a) das Modell ein kompaktes Volumenmodell ist bzw. seine Oberfläche eine minimale druckbare Wandstärke besitzt, b) das Modell geschlossen und zusammenhängend ist, c) die Kanten des Modells nicht zu mehr als zwei Flächen gehören, d) die Größe in Abhängigkeit der 3D-Druckmaschine zulässig ist, e) die Oberflächennormalen korrekt ausgerichtet sind. Wird eine dieser Eigenschaften verletzt, ist eine Modellkorrektur notwendig. KP-spezifische VP werden bei belegtem KP ausgeführt; z.B. überprüft der VP „BoundingBox", ob bestimmte Modellinhalte innerhalb definierter 3D-Räume liegen. Durch diesen Mechanismus kann auch nach komplexen KP-Transformationen sichergestellt werden, dass z.B. keine Teile eines Schriftzugs über die Grundmodellfläche hinausragen.

3 Blender Plugins & Kiosk

Um den Designer im Produktentwicklungsprozess beim Aufbringen der KP und VP zu unterstützen, wurden spezielle Werkzeuge in Form von GUI-Elementen als Plugins für das 3D-Modellierungstool Blender entwickelt. Abb. 1 zeigt die Dialogbox, mit der Designer die Einstellungen für einen KP zum Aufbringen eines Logos vornehmen kann. Dies sind hier der KP-Name, Logoname, Extrusionswert und Pfad zum Speicherort der Logos. Auf Basis der gesetzten KP und VP werden später die UI-Elemente im Kiosk für den Kunden gestaltet, z.B. für das Aufbringen eines Logos eine Upload-Möglichkeit, mit welcher der Kunde sein persönliches Logo hochladen kann. Diese Informationen werden in XML gespeichert und bilden zusammen mit dem eigentlichen 3D-Modell den Datensatz für den Kiosk.

Mit dem Kiosk lassen sich Produkte einfach individualisieren. Er bietet dem Kunden die Möglichkeit hinterlegte Muster anschauen, in eine nähere Auswahl zu übernehmen sowie einzelne Muster zu personalisieren und deren Druck zu beauftragen. Entscheidet sich der Kunde ein Muster zu personalisieren, werden die Bedienelemente wie z.B. Textboxen und Slider auf Basis der in XML beschriebenen KP und VP erzeugt. Mit diesen kann dann die Individualisierung, z.B. Logo aufbringen, skalieren oder rotieren, durchgeführt werden. Die 3D-Vorschau des individuell gestalteten Produkts wird mit WebGL gerendert. Die 3D-Daten werden dabei von einem server-seitigen Software-Modul durch Ausführung der KP und VP mit Blender und Python-Skripten erstellt. Da ein 3D-Modell nicht anhand seiner Knoten, Kurven und Flächen direkt editiert werden muss, entfallen für den Kunden diese komplexen

Arbeitsschritte. Ist die Individualisierung abgeschlossen, werden die Druck-Daten im STL-Format an den AM übermittelt.

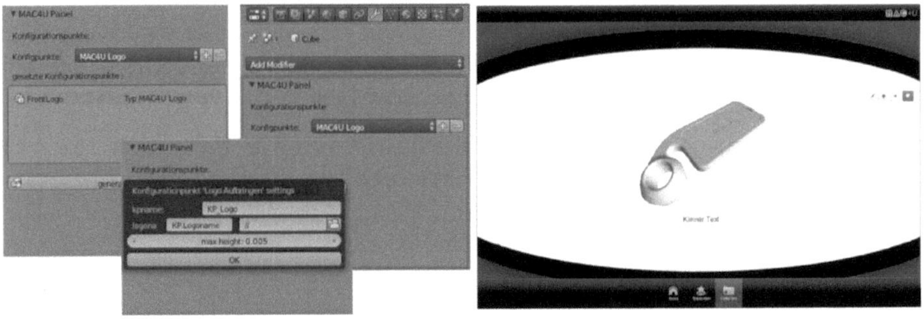

Abbildung 1: Blender-Plugins & Kiosk

4 Zusammenfassung

Das vorgestellte Konzept der Konfigurations- und Validierungspunkte ermöglicht eine Automatisierung der Individualisierung von Massenprodukten auch ohne 3D-Modellierungskenntnisse und stellt dabei sicher, dass die Individualisierung nicht zu fehlerhaften 3D-Modellen führt und die Druckbarkeit erfüllt wird. Die Blender-Plugins ermöglichen es dieses Konzept in die Produkterstellung zu integrieren und schaffen die Verbindung zum 3D-Grundmodell des Massenprodukts für die spätere einfache Individualisierung. Der Kiosk bietet eine kundengerechte Schnittstelle zur Wahrnehmung der Individualisierungsmöglichkeiten und die automatische Anwendung der KP und VP in Kombination mit den Kundeneingaben auf das 3D-Modell sowie die unmittelbare Feedback-Generierung für den Kunden. Eine erste Evaluation des Prototypen mit einem Additive Manufacturer und weiteren Probanden brachte positives Feedback hervor.

Danksagung

Dank an das BMWi-geförderte Projekt „MAC4U – Mass Customization für individualisierte Produkterweiterungen“ (Ref. Nr. 01MS12022A, http://www.mac4u-projekt.de).

Literaturverzeichnis

Hu, S. J.(2013). Evolving Paradigms of Manufacturing: From Mass Production to Mass Customization and Personalization. In: *Procedia CIRP,* vol. 7, 3-8.

Rosenstock, F. & Wirth, M. (2013). 3D-Druckereien in Europa – Eine Marktanalyse. CEDIFA Arbeitsbericht 2, Forschungszentrums CEDIFA

Rayana, T., Striukova, L. & Darlington, J. (2014). The Role of Online 3D Platforms in Open Innovation with Customers. In: *Proc. DDMC 2014*, Berlin, Germany.

Wohler's Report (2013), Additive Manufacturing and 3D printing, State of the Industry Annual Worldwide progress Report, Wohler's Associates, Inc

M. Koch, A. Butz & J. Schlichter (Hrsg.): Mensch und Computer 2014 Tagungsband,
München: Oldenbourg Wissenschaftsverlag, 2014, S. 303-306.

Computer im Grünen: IT-Systeme zur Unterstützung urbaner Gärten

Oliver Stickel, Thomas Ludwig, Volkmar Pipek

Universität Siegen

Zusammenfassung

Urbane Gemeinschaftsgärten stellen einen aktuellen Trend in der Bottom-Up Kultur dar, der zur ökologischen Nachhaltigkeit beiträgt und den wir derzeit beforschen. Wir präsentieren erste Ergebnisse unserer ethnografischen Untersuchungen und fokussieren dabei auf Problemfelder, mit denen urbane Gärten konfrontiert sind, wie z.B. Koordinations- oder Awareness-Herausforderungen. Aufbauend auf dieser ersten Analyse stellen wir einen Entwurf sowie erste Design-Mockups für unterstützende IT-Systeme vor, die auf im Garten verbleibenden, solarbetriebenen und per Funk angebundenen stationären Geräten und Sensoren, sowie einer mobilen App samt web-basierter Infrastruktur beruhen.

1 Einleitung

Urbane Gemeinschaftsgärten (UGG) sind üblicherweise relativ kleine Räume in städtischen Gebieten (oft auf ungenutzten Brachflächen), in denen lokale Gemeinschaften auf Nutzpflanzen fokussierte, nichtprofessionelle Agrikultur betreiben, welche sich positiv auf gesunde Ernährung, urbanes Mikroklima sowie Nachhaltigkeit auswirken (Brown & Jameton, 2000). UGG stehen jedermann offen und sind basisdemokratisch strukturiert, vergleichbar zu anderen Bottom-Up-Aktivitäten wie z.B. Makerspaces (Avram et al. 2013; Lawson, 2005). Fragen hinsichtlich der Praktiken und Strukturen, die solche Gemeinschaften ausbilden sind derzeit noch wenig beforscht, daher arbeiten wir im Moment ethnografisch daran, UGG in ihren Praktiken und Herausforderungen zu verstehen und dem Vorgehen der *Design Case Studies* (Vorstudie, Konzept, Implementierung, Evaluation in situ, Wulf & Rohde, 2011) folgend, unterstützende IT-Systeme zu entwickeln, von denen wir glauben, dass sie die geeignet sind, die gefundenen Probleme und Herausforderungen zu lösen. Hierzu führten wir explorativ eine Vielzahl informeller Interviews mit UGG-Aktivisten sowie teilnehmende Beobachtungen in einem örtlichen UGG durch und nahmen beobachtend an einer landesweiten UGG-Sitzung teil. Derzeit befinden wir uns in den ersten Schritten zur Analyse der ethnografischen Ergebnisse in Richtung Designkonzept. In diesem Beitrag möchten wir diese Ergebnisse sowie erste Entwürfe und Mockups vorstellen.

2 Ein IT-fokussierter Blick auf UGG

Auf den ersten Blick mag ein IT-fokussierter Blickwinkel auf oft technologisch niederkomplex gehaltene UGG-Aktivitäten nicht intuitiv erscheinen. Durch unsere ethnografischen Arbeiten sowie die Literatur (Avram et al., 2013; Avram, 2013) wird jedoch deutlich, dass sich hier mehrere Herausforderungen ergeben, die in besonderem Maße geeignet sind um durch IT-Systeme gelöst zu werden. Die zentralen Herausforderungen sind:

Kommunikation und Koordination: Durch die (von den Gärtnern begrüßte) völlige Offenheit des UGG sind Aktivitäten verschiedener Gruppen asynchron, was zu Problemen hinsichtlich Kommunikation und Koordination führt (z.B. die Absprache von Bepflanzungsplänen oder finanzielle Entscheidungen unstrukturiert über viele Kanäle).

Fachwissen: Auch wenn die Mitglieder des UGG durchweg enthusiastisch und motiviert sind, ist das gärtnerische Fachwissen stark heterogen, was oft zu Unsicherheiten und Problemen führt, z.B. bei Fragen wie welche Pflanze wie anzuzüchten ist.

Awareness und Gemeinschaftsbildung: Gärtner sind sich meist aus der Ferne nicht im Klaren darüber, was in "ihrem" Garten derzeit geschieht und ob jemand aus der Gemeinschaft dort ist. Gerade für Gärtner mit Fokus auf soziale Aspekte ist diese Frage jedoch von zentraler Bedeutung. Dies hemmt Begegnungen und Gemeinschaftsbildung.

Status-Überwachung und Automation: Oft werden z.B. beim Gießen oder Düngen optimale Level nicht erreicht, was auf mangelnde Koordination, Dokumentation und heterogene Anwesenheit im UGG zurückgeht („Hat schon jemand das Beet hier gedüngt?"). Auch Sicherheitsüberwachung und allgemeine Automatisierung, insbesondere der aufwändigen und enorm wichtigen Bewässerung kommen regelmäßig zur Sprache.

Außendarstellung: "Unsere" lose Gemeinschaft von Gärtnern hat Probleme mit ihrer Außendarstellung, da sich oft niemand motiviert fühlt, PR-Aktivitäten zu unternehmen. ("Ich gärtnere lieber als vor dem PC zu hängen und zu schreiben").

3 Stand der Garten-IT und UGG-Besonderheiten

Die untersuchte UGG-Initiative setzt bereits IT ein (Blog, Wiki, Mailingliste). Leider sind diese Systeme recht inkohärent, wenig integriert, setzen unterschiedliche Maße an IT-Vorwissen voraus und werden heterogen genutzt. Weiterhin berichten die Teilnehmer, dass z.B. Mailinglisten schnell verwirrend werden können und kein positives Nutzungserlebnis bieten. Mobiler Zugriff (in situ aus dem UGG) ist angesichts der verstreuten Systeme ebenfalls problematisch. Die Gestaltung von IT für UGG ist ein herausforderndes Feld, denn diese verfügen üblicherweise nicht über Strom- und Internetanschluss und durch Ideologie sowie die hohe Vandalismusgefahr müssen entsprechende Systeme so günstig und nachhaltig wie möglich sein. Weiterhin ziehen UGG-Aktivisten oft Befriedigung daraus, Arbeiten manuell zu erledigen, die Literatur deutet aber an, dass maßgeschneiderte, unterstützende Systeme positiv angenommen werden können (Avram, 2013).

4 „GardenApp“ – Ein IT-System für UGG

Das System, das wir vorschlagen, besteht aus drei Hauptkomponenten: 1. Einer zentralen Webplattform, deren API gleichzeitig als Backend der anderen Komponenten dient, 2. dauerhaft im Garten verbleibenden Geräten und Sensoren (ULV oder Ultra Low Voltage-Geräte), sowie 3. einer mobilen “Garten-App” (s. Abb. 1).

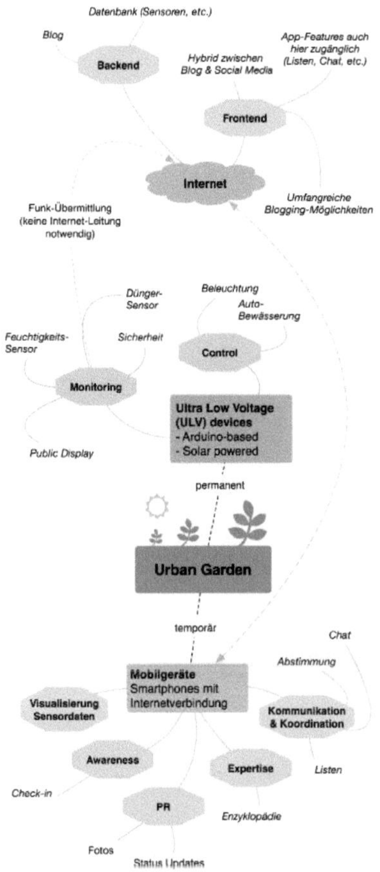

Abb. 1: Systemarchitektur

Garten-Zentraleinheit: Eine Solar-betriebene und z.B. Arduino-basierte Zentraleinheit im UGG kann Informationen von einfachen Sensoren (z.B. Bodenfeuchtigkeit) sammeln und gleichzeitig weitere Automatisierungssysteme (z.B. Bewässerung) steuern. Die Internetanbindung dieser Einheit wäre allerdings über GSM teuer und komplex, wofür sich jedoch in der Vergangenheit eine Lösung findet: Funktransmitter. Sehr günstige (und noch legale) Transmitter können eine Reichweite von zwei Kilometern haben, was in einer urbanen Umgebung üblicherweise ausreichend ist, um einen Empfänger zu erreichen, der bei einem Mitglied des UGG zuhause ans Internet angebunden ist. Dieses Teilsystem würde den ganzen UGG im Prinzip einen sprechenden Teil eines „Internet of Things“ werden lassen.

Mobilgeräte: Viele der beschriebenen Probleme lassen sich im Rahmen einer einfach zu bedienenden mobilen App lösen (s. Abb. 2). Wir konnten beobachten, dass ein Großteil der Gärtner bereits Smartphones besitzen und dieser Trend wird sich vermutlich nur verstärken. Kommunikation und Koordination können über ein informelles, unstrukturiertes *Chat*-System sowie *Listen* (Arbeitsbezeichnung) erfolgen. Listen sollen Datenstrukturen sein, die sich auf ein spezifisches Thema beziehen und Texte, Medieninhalte sowie Checklisten und Kommentare erlauben. Nachrichten aus dem Chat sollen in neue Listen transformiert werden können oder aber an bestehende angehängt werden können, so dass als wichtig angesehene Aspekte aus dem laufenden Chat verstetigt und diskutiert werden können. Unterstützend soll ein einfacher *Abstimmungsmechanismus* verteilte Entscheidungen ermöglichen. Weiterhin soll die App eine *Enzyklopädie* beinhalten, die als statische Referenz für dringend benötigte Expertise wie z.B. die Frage, wann welche Pflanzen gesetzt werden können, dienen soll sowie (über QR-Codes am Beet) Kontext-Informationen über Pflanzen liefern kann. Die App soll außerdem *Status-Updates* und *Check-Ins* unterstützen, die ähnlich funktionieren sollen wie man es aus anderen Sozialen Netzwerken kennt und die die Gärtner-

Gemeinschaft in spielerischer, motivierender Konversation nach innen und nach außen (PR) unterstützen sollen sowie Awareness-Probleme (z.B. Frage nach aktueller Anwesenheit im Garten) lösen sollen. Als letztes Feature soll die App die Daten der Zentraleinheit im Garten abfragen und übersichtlich darstellen können.

Internet-Plattform: Für die Vernetzung der Teilsysteme wird ein webbasiertes Backend benötigt, das Funktionen wie z.B. die Verteilung der Sensordaten aus dem UGG vornimmt. Weiterhin soll es eine Website speisen, die ähnlich wie ein klassischer Blog aufgebaut sein soll, deren ausführliche Artikel aber durch dynamische Bereiche für Status-Updates, Check-Ins sowie die Überwachungsdaten des UGG ergänzt werden. Auch Partizipation am Chat sowie an Listen und Abstimmungen soll für angemeldete Nutzer möglich sein.

5 Ausblick

Wir planen, das System, beginnend mit der App (interaktiver, nicht-funktionaler Prototyp) sowie der Basisstation (funktionaler Prototyp) in situ zusammen mit den Gärtnern weiterzuentwickeln. Zusätzlich werden wir unsere ethnografischen Arbeiten ausweiten um die Praktiken und Probleme der UGG besser verstehen zu können. Das Projekt wird begleitend auf www.gardenapp.de dokumentiert.

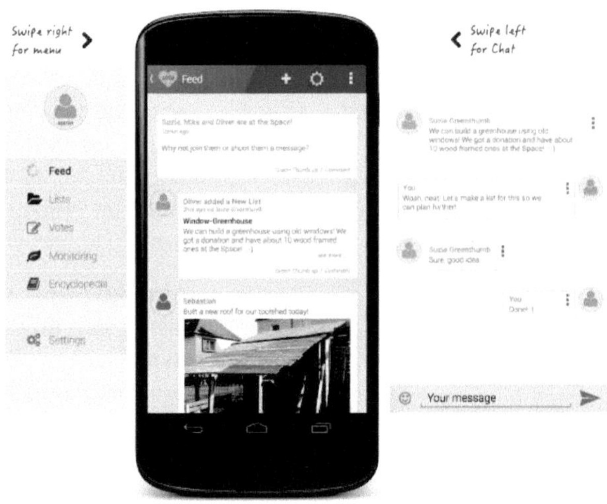

Abb. 2: Mockup Garden App

Literaturverzeichnis

Avram, G. (2013). Starting a Garden , Caring for It , Growing with It - a Study on Collective Practices in Urban Gardening. Proc. ECSCW 2013, Cyprus, Greece.

Avram, G., Boden, A., Posch, I., & Stevens, G. (2013). Do-It-Yourself Sustainable Living: Opportunities and challenges for DIY communities. Proc. CHI 2013, Paris, France.

Brown, K., & Jameton, A. (2000). Public Health Implications of Urban Agriculture. Journal of Public Health Policy, 21(1), 20–39.

Lawson, L. J. (2005). City bountiful : a century of community gardening in America. Studies in the History of Gardens Designed Landscapes (Vol. 97, pp. 428–430).

Wulf, V., & Rohde, M. (2011). Engaging with Practices: Design Case Studies as a Research Framework in CSCW. Proc. CSCW 2011. Hangzhou, China.

M. Koch, A. Butz & J. Schlichter (Hrsg.): Mensch und Computer 2014 Tagungsband,
München: Oldenbourg Wissenschaftsverlag, 2014, S. 307-310.

Data Ocean

Dieter Meiller

Fakultät Elektro- und Informationstechnik,
Ostbayerische Technische Hochschule Amberg-Weiden

Zusammenfassung

Hier wird das Konzept für eine neuartige Benutzungs-Oberfläche vorgestellt, welche die Verwaltung von Daten-Beständen und die Suche von Informationen stark vereinfacht: Anstatt eines reaktiven Systems wird ein proaktives System vorgeschlagen. Als Ersatz für die Desktop-Metapher wird angeregt, die Daten als aktive Lebewesen aufzufassen, die sich auf dem Ökosystem Computer bewegen: ein Data Ocean.

1 Ausgangssituation

Als vorherrschende Benutzungs-Schnittstelle zur Bedienung von Personal Computern hat sich die Schreibtisch-Metapher durchgesetzt. Diese wird seit ihrer Erfindung in den 70er Jahren des 20. Jahrhunderts nahezu unverändert als die vorherrschende Metapher zur Suche und Verwaltung von Daten-Objekten, den Dateien, eingesetzt. Seitdem Apple den Desktop von Xerox auf den Macintosh übertrug und im folgenden Microsoft mit Windows das Konkurrenzprodukt dazu schuf, hat sich der klassische Desktop nur unwesentlich verändert (Reimer 2005). Andere Bedienkonzepte wurden verdrängt oder konnten sich nicht durchsetzen. Die vorher wichtigste Schnittstelle, die Tastatur für Texteingabe auf der Konsole, wurde verdrängt durch die die WIMP-Bedienung mit der Maus als Haupt-Eingabegerät (Herczeg 2006, 112f.). Jedoch gab und gibt es einige interessante Entwicklungen, beispielsweise das Zoomable User Interface (Cross 1994) oder Lifestreams (Freeman 1997). Beide Systeme nutzen keine Ordnerstruktur zur Organisation von Daten. Eine Strukturierung ergibt sich aus der räumlichen oder zeitlichen Anordnung der Objekte.

2 Problem und Ansatz

Durch das Aufkommen neuer, mobiler Geräte, die zunehmend den klassischen PC verdrängen, wird die klassische Methode der Computer-Bedienung immer öfter in Frage gestellt und nach Alternativen gesucht. Ein weiteres, drängendes Problem ist die stark ansteigende Zahl an Daten-Objekten, die ein Nutzer verwalten muss und auf die er Zugriff haben will. Bei bisherigen Systemen muss meist der Nutzer selbst auf die Suche gehen und sich zum Ort (Ordner) des jeweiligen Daten-Objektes begeben. Deshalb wird die Such-Funktion in modernen Betriebssystemen immer beliebter. Dort wird der Mechanismus umgekehrt: Die Datei kommt, bildlich gesehen, nach der initiierten Suche zum Nutzer. Die Herausforderung ist es also, eine Methode der Datei-Verwaltung zu finden, die den neuen Anforderungen und des sich deswegen verändernden Nutzerverhaltens gerecht wird. Der vorgestellte Ansatz baut auf Erkenntnissen aus unterschiedlichen Bereichen auf:

Künstliches Leben (AL): Die formale Beschreibung des Verhaltens und der Simulation von Lebewesen ist ein interdisziplinärer Forschungszweig. Ein Unterbereich befasst sich mit der Simulation und der Beschreibung von Schwarmverhalten und dessen übergeordneten Auswirkungen, der Emergenz (Mataric 1993).

Information Retrieval: Dieses Gebiet beschäftigt sich mit der Suche in Datenbeständen. Interessant ist insbesondere das Fuzzy Retrieval, welches die Suchterme oder die gefundenen Dokumente nach Relevanz gewichtet (Cross 1994).

3 Lösung

Das hier vorgestellte Konzept sieht keine Ordnerstruktur zur Verwaltung der Daten-Objekte vor, analog zum Zoomable User Interface. Jedes dieser Objekte soll bestimmte Merkmale besitzen, anhand derer es identifiziert werden kann. Dateien mit textuellem Inhalt können anhand des Volltextes identifiziert werden. Andere, vorhandene Merkmale wie das Erstellungsdatum oder das Datum des letzten Editiervorgangs, die Dateigröße, der Ort der Erstellung oder andere in den Dateien enthaltenen Metadaten können ebenso der Identifikation dienen. Zusätzlich soll bei diesem Konzept die Möglichkeit gegeben sein, die Daten-Objekte mit Tags (Schlagworten) zu versehen. Die Objekte sollen sich in einem Raum (Daten-Ozean) bewegen können. Die Dimensionalität und Struktur des Raumes könnte vorzugsweise ein 2½-D Raum sein. Das bedeutet, die Objekte sind im zweidimensionalen Raum angeordnet und man kann hinein und heraus-zoomen. Möglich wäre es auch, die Objekte in einem 3D-Raum anzuordnen. Die Objekte sollen sich wie Lebewesen in einem Schwarm verhalten, beispielsweise wie Fische oder Vögel. Für diese soll folgende Regel gelten: Objekte sollen auf ihnen ähnliche Objekte zusteuern. Andere Objekte, mit denen das jeweilige Objekt gemeinsame Eigenschaften aufweist, sollen anziehend auf dieses wirken. Je mehr gemeinsam ist, desto größer die Anziehungskraft. Auf diese Weise soll das System selbstorganisierend und emergent Gruppen aus verwandten Daten bilden. Da die Daten nicht in disjunkte Mengen einzuordnen sind, werden die Gruppen ineinander verwoben sein. Damit die Benutzer diesen Vorgang kontrollieren kann, ist es notwendig, dass diese die Merkmale gewichten können: Sie können so kontrollieren, welche Merkmale zu Gruppenbildungen führen.

Agilität und Lebendigkeit: Die Datenobjekte sollen eine bestimmte Agilität (Beweglichkeit) aufweisen, die mit steigendem Alter abnimmt. Alte, langsame Objekte könnten von bestimmten Fress-Objekten aus dem Raum entfernt, also gelöscht werden. Diese Fress-Objekte wären, analog zur Desktop-Metapher, so etwas wie aktive Papierkörbe. Denkbar ist auch, dass der Benutzer die Möglichkeit hat, diese Fress-Objekte zu öffnen, um den entfernten Inhalt wieder zurückzulegen. Der Anwender könnte durch Entfernen des Fress-Objektes die in diesem enthaltenen Objekte endgültig löschen. Die Agilität der Daten-Objekte könnte durch Fütterung derselben wieder erhöht werden, gefüttert werden könnte durch Betrachtung oder Editierung der Dateien. So würden lange nicht mehr benutzte Dateien schließlich veralten und letztendlich automatisch entfernt werden.

Suche und Nutzeraktionen: In herkömmlichen Desktop-Systemen muss sich der Nutzer zu den Daten-Objekten hin begeben, indem er durch die Dateibäume zu den Dateien navigiert. Dieses Prinzip soll hier umgekehrt werden: Die Dateien sollen angelockt werden und zum Nutzer kommen. Gelockt werden die Dateien durch die Aussicht auf Futter, also die Wahrscheinlichkeit, benutzt oder betrachtet zu werden. Als „Lockstoff" werden Attribute ausgestreut, welche die gesuchten Dateien haben sollen. Die Intensität der Lockstoffe kann über die Angabe von Gewichtungen eingestellt werden. Die am besten passenden Dateien werden am stärksten zu den Lockstoffen hingezogen (Abbildung 1). Zusätzlich werden die agilen Datei-Objekte, also die häufiger benutzten, schneller am Ziel sein. Lockstoffe könnten temporär zur spontanen Suche ausgestreut werden oder für längere Zeit als Anker dienen, um die sich die Daten bewegen. Der Nutzer könnte aus zwei Perspektiven auf diese Welt blicken: Von außen, also aus einer Beobacher-Perspektive oder von innen, quasi als Taucher im Daten-Ozean.

4 Zusammenfassung

Die Nutzer heutiger Geräte sind oft aufgrund der großen Datenmengen und der Tatsache, dass viele Systeme überhaupt keinen Zugriff mehr auf das Dateisystem ermöglichen, nicht mehr in der Lage, sich zurechtzufinden. Suchfunktionen sind intuitiv und schnell, und so werden diese bevorzugt für den Dateizugriff genutzt. Daher wäre eine Umkehrung des bisherigen Bedienkonzepts passender: In einem modernen System sollte nicht der Nutzer zur Datei navigieren, sondern die benötigten Daten sollten zum Nutzer kommen. Dies impliziert ein aktives Verhalten der Datenobjekte. Deshalb wird als Ersatz für den klassischen Desktop eine neue Metapher vorgeschlagen: Ein Ökosystem, in dem sich die Daten wie Lebewesen verhalten, sich selbst organisieren und vom Nutzer angelockt werden können. Nur weil sich bisher kein alternatives Konzept durchsetzen konnte, bedeutet das nicht, dass es keine Alternativen gibt (Lanier 2014, S.17). Jüngste Ankündigungen von HP für neue, auf Memristoren (Williams 2008) aufbauende Hardware mit passendem Betriebssystem ohne Datenhierarchien könnten in die gleiche Richtung wie das hier vorgestellte Konzept weisen.

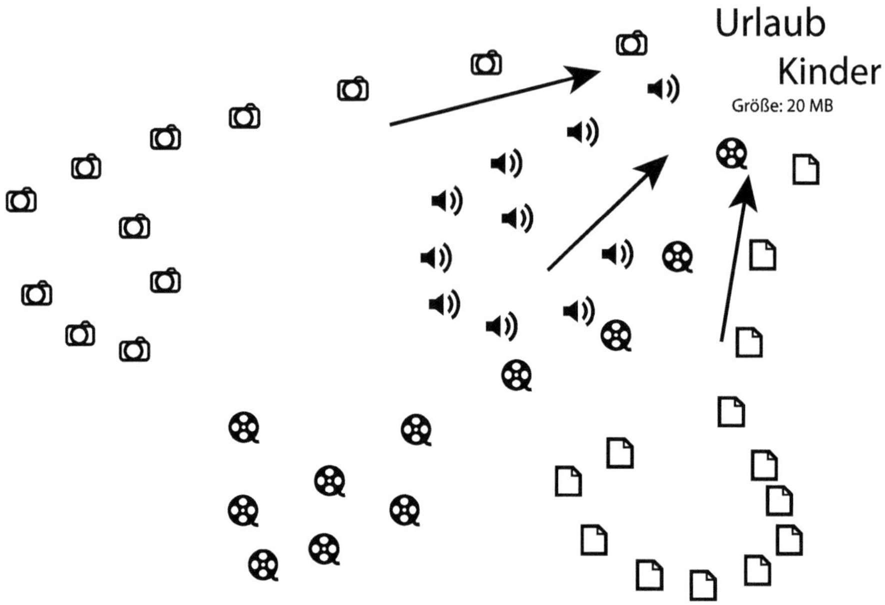

Abbildung 1: Visualisierung des Konzeptes

Quellen

Bederson, B. B. (2011). The promise of zoomable user interfaces. In: Behaviour & Information Technology, 30(6), 853-866.

Cross, V. (1994). Fuzzy information retrieval. In: Journal of Intelligent Information Systems, 3(1), S. 29-56.

Freeman, E. T. (1997). The lifestreams software architecture. Yale University.

Herczeg, M. (2006). Interaktionsdesign. Gestaltung interaktiver und multimedialer Systeme. Berlin, Boston: Oldenbourg Wissenschaftsverlag.

Lanier, J. (2014). Wem gehört die Zukunft? Hamburg: Hoffmann und Campe Verlag.

Mataric, M. J. (1993). Designing emergent behaviors: From local interactions to collective intelligence. In: Proceedings of the Second International Conference on Simulation of Adaptive Behavior (S. 432-441).

Reimer, J. (2005). A History of the GUI. arstechnica. com, May, 5.

Williams, R. (2008). How we found the missing memristor. In: Spectrum, IEEE, 45(12), S. 28-35.

Kontakt

Dieter Meiller, d.meiller@oth-aw.de

M. Koch, A. Butz & J. Schlichter (Hrsg.): Mensch und Computer 2014 Tagungsband,
München: Oldenbourg Wissenschaftsverlag, 2014, S. 311-314.

Der Einfluss des Geschlechts auf das Erleben von Self-Service Systemen

Christian Zagel

Friedrich-Alexander Universität Erlangen-Nürnberg

Zusammenfassung

In der vorliegenden Studie wird untersucht, inwiefern sich die Wahrnehmung von Frauen und Männern in Bezug auf das Erleben interaktiver, technologiebasierter Self-Service Systeme unterscheidet. Zum Einsatz kommt das zur Evaluation von Kundenerlebnissen entwickelte Service Fascination Research Model, welches subjektive und objektive Komponenten beinhaltet. Als Untersuchungsobjekt wird ein interaktives Schaufenster als konkretes, erlebnisbezogenes System durch 213 Probanden in Hinblick auf dessen funktionalen und emotionalen Nutzen bewertet. Die Ergebnisse zeigen, dass Frauen trotz geringeren Vertrauens in die Technologie das Erlebnis als positiver bewerten. Dies deckt sich mit den Erkenntnissen aus früheren Studien.

1 Einleitung

In der modernen Dienstleistungswirtschaft versuchen Unternehmen vor allem durch eine große Vielfalt von Dienstleistungen zu glänzen. Der Mensch als Service-Erbringer wird dabei zunehmend durch so genannte Self-Service Systeme ersetzt oder unterstützt, wodurch sich technologiebasierte Schnittstellen zwischen Unternehmen und Kunden ergeben (Meuter et al. 2000). Unternehmen haben den Nutzen von Self-Service Technologien (SST) nicht nur für Dienste im Internet (z.B. Online Shopping) erkannt, sondern auch für den Einsatz in physischen Geschäften, z.B. in Form von Kiosk Systemen. Diese werden oft mit technischen Innovationen versehen, um sich von Wettbewerbern abzugrenzen. Die Angebote sind dabei jedoch oft auf eine schnelle Umsetzung getrimmt, wodurch nicht selten generelle psychologische Aspekte im Design, insbesondere in Bezug auf Bedienbarkeit, Nutzererfahrung sowie der erlebten Freude, vernachlässigt werden. Dieser Mangel an nutzerzentrierten Entwicklungsmethoden führt nicht selten zu geringer Akzeptanz beim Anwender. Zur Generierung positiver Kundenerfahrungen (Customer Experiences) spielt darüber hinaus die Vermittlung einer Kombination aus utilitaristischem und emotionalem Nutzen eine entscheidende Rolle (Sandström et al. 2008). Das aktuelle Wissen zu der erlebnisbezogenen Wirkung einzelner Designaspekte technologiebasierter Service-Systeme, zu Evaluationsmethoden oder auch zu konkreten Umsetzungen ist jedoch begrenzt. In der Literatur wird deshalb vermehrt zur Forschung in diesem Bereich aufgerufen (Verhoef et al. 2009). Ziel des Beitrags ist es auf Basis des Service Fascination Research Models (Zagel et al., in Druck) die konkrete Umsetzung einer SST mit Fokus auf die Erzeugung von Customer Experience im Einzelhandel zu evaluieren. Es soll erforscht werden, ob und wie sich in der Wahrnehmung des Service-Designs geschlechterspezfische Unterschiede zeigen, um die Erkenntnisse zur Entwicklung zukünftiger Systeme einsetzen zu können.

2 Methode

2.1 Self-Service System

Als Anwendungsbeispiel dient ein interaktives Schaufenster eines großen Bekleidungsherstellers, welches über den Zeitraum von etwa zwei Monaten als Bestandteil der Ladenfassade installiert war. Ziel des Projekts war es, Kunden durch ein attraktiv gestaltetes System anzulocken und ihnen auch außerhalb der Ladenöffnungszeiten einen Einkauf über das persönliche Smartphone zu ermöglichen. Das Benutzerinterface war in zwei Bereiche aufgeteilt: ein interaktives Model in Lebensgröße auf der linken Seite, sowie ein virtuelles Kleiderregal auf der rechten Seite (vgl. Abbildung). Die Kunden konnten ihr Smartphone mit einer virtuellen Einkaufstasche koppeln und Produkte per „drag and drop" auf das Handy übertragen. Verwirklicht wurde das System über den Einsatz einer Displaywand, sowie einer großflächig auf der Glasscheibe aufgebrachten kapazitiven Touchfolie.

Abbildung 1: Interaktives Schaufenster

2.2 Durchführung der Evaluation

Die Evaluation des beschriebenen Systems fand innerhalb von zwei Wochen im laufenden Betrieb statt und wurde mit Endkunden bzw. Passanten durchgeführt. Insgesamt nahmen 213 Personen (135 weiblich, 78 männlich) an der Evaluation teil. Die Teilnehmer wurden während der Ladenöffnungszeiten befragt und waren zwischen 17 und 60 Jahre (M = 25,52; SD= 6,64) alt. Entsprechend des in Zagel et al. (in Druck) beschriebenen Vorgehensmodells wurden die Probanden kurz in das System eingeführt, während der Interaktion beobachtet und nach der Nutzung gebeten den Service Fascination Fragebogen auszufüllen.

2.3 Datenanalyse

Die demographischen Charakteristika wurden deskriptiv ausgewertet. Zur Analyse des Fragebogens (7er Likert-Typ) kam das in Zagel et al. (in Druck) vorgestellte Kausalmodell zum Einsatz. Dieses wurde mittels SmartPLS 2.0 über die Partial Least Squares Methode evaluiert. Während „Experiential Design" formative formuliert ist und sich aus Schmitt und Mangold's (2004) Erlebnisdimensionen (affektiv, kognitiv, verhaltensbezogen, sensorisch, sozial) zusammensetzt, sind alle anderen Komponenten reflektiv formuliert. Die Güte des Modells wurde entsprechend der Vorgaben für formative und reflektive Messmodelle validiert. Die aufgestellten Hypothesen sind in Abbildung 2 (links) veranschaulicht.

3 Ergebnisse

Tabelle 1 zeigt die Unterschiede der Bewertung durch Männer und Frauen inkl. Signifikanzwert (t-Test) und Effektstärke nach Cohen. Es zeigt sich, dass Frauen der Technologie signifikant weniger Vertrauen gegenüber bringen, die einzelnen Erlebnis-dimensionen jedoch besser bewerten. Der funktionale Nutzen (Perceived Usefulness) wird von beiden Geschlechtern annähernd gleich, jedoch insgesamt recht gering wahrgenommen. Die Ergebnisse entsprechen weitgehend den Erkenntnissen der gleichzeitig durchgeführten Beobachtung. Jedoch wurde das System unabhängig vom Geschlecht kaum durch Einzel-personen genutzt, was der geringen subjektiven Bewertung des sozialen Aspekts widerspricht.

		Frauen (N=135)			Männer (N=78)				
	Dimension	Median	Mean	SD	Median	Mean	SD	p	d
Experiential Design	Affective	5	5,11	1,40	5	5,09	1,20	0,370	0,015
	Cognitive	5	5,01	1,08	5	4,76	1,06	0,091	0,233
	Behavioral	4	3,97	1,42	4,5	3,93	1,61	0,833	0,027
	Sensory	5	5,09	1,25	5	4,74	1,15	0,041	0,288
	Social	4	4,00	1,45	4	3,62	1,30	0,057	0,272
Service Fascination	Experiential Design	5	4,83	0,96	5	4,56	1,07	0,064	0,270
	Technology Readiness	6	5,68	1,26	6	5,95	1,20	0,132	0,218
	Trust	2,5	2,84	1,58	4	4,01	1,75	0,000	0,712
	Perceived Usefulness	4	3,40	1,52	4	3,56	1,57	0,471	0,104
	Perceived Ease of Use	6	5,50	1,12	5,5	5,44	1,03	0,680	0,055
	Service Fascination	5	4,53	1,61	5	4,56	1,42	0,862	0,019

Tabelle 1: Evaluationsergebnisse Mittelwertvergleich nach Geschlechtern

Für das untersuchte System lassen sich bis auf H6 alle gegebenen Hypothesen bestätigen. Die beiden Zielkonstrukte Experiential Design (R^2=0,467) und Service Fascination (R^2=0,637) werden gut durch das Modell erklärt (vgl. Abbildung 2).

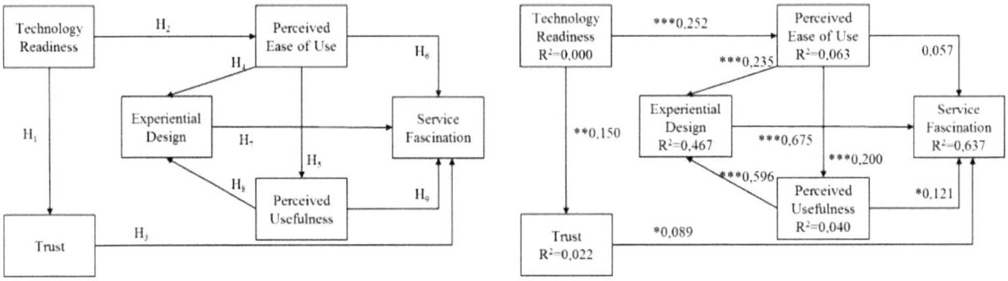

*Abbildung 2: Ergebnisse der PLS Analyse (*p<0.1, **p<0.05, ***p<0.01)*

4 Diskussion

Die geschlechterspezifischen Ergebnisse decken sich mit denen früherer Studien zu anderen Systemen (vgl. Zagel et al., in Druck). Frauen bewerten demnach trotz geringerem Vertrauen in die Technologie die Erlebnisdimensionen positiver. Im vorliegenden Fall entspricht jedoch insbesondere die Wahrnehmung des utilitaristischen Nutzens nicht der ursprünglichen Intention des Systems. Dies mag daran liegen, dass die Bewertung während der Ladenöffnungszeiten durchgeführt wurde. Die Kunden nutzten das System daher nicht zum Kauf, sondern lediglich aus Neugier. Der Kauf selbst fand im Ladengeschäft statt. Eine weitere Evaluierung nach Ladenschluss soll Aufschluss darüber geben, wie sich der veränderte Kontext auf die Wahrnehmung auswirkt.

Literaturverzeichnis

Meuter, M. L., Ostrom, A. L., Roundtree, R., & Bitner, M. J. (2000). Self-Service Technologies: Understanding Customer Satisfaction with Technology-Based Service Encounters. Journal of Marketing, 64(3), 50-64.

Sandström, S., Edvardsson, B., Kristensson, P., & Magnusson, P. (2008). Value in use through service experience. Managing Service Quality, 18(2), 112-126.

Schmitt, B., & Mangold, M. (2004). Kundenerlebnis als Wettbewerbsvorteil. Mit Customer Experience Management Makren und Märkte Gewinn bringend gestalten. Wiesbaden: Gabler.

Verhoef, P. C., Lemon, K. N., Parasuraman, A., Roggeveen, A., Tsiros, M., & Schlesinger, L. A. (2009). Customer Experience Creation: Determinants, Dynamics and Management Strategies. Journal of Retailing, 85(1), 31-41.

Zagel, C., Süßmuth, J., & Glomann, L. (in Druck). Assessing the influence of gender towards the adoption of technology-enabled self-service systems in retail environments. Gender-UseIT 2014 (#GUI'14), Berlin.

M. Koch, A. Butz & J. Schlichter (Hrsg.): Mensch und Computer 2014 Tagungsband,
München: Oldenbourg Wissenschaftsverlag, 2014, S. 315-318.

Enabling Natural Cross-Device Interaction in Personal Desktop Settings

Marius Brade[1], Steffen Buzin[2], Rainer Groh[1]

Chair of Media Design, Technische Universität Dresden, Germany[1]
SAP Research, SAP AG, Chemnitzer Strasse 48, 01187 Dresden, Germany[2]

Abstract

This work presents an easy to use approach for cross-device interaction using the scenario of having a laptop, desktop computer and mobile device co-located on a desk. A consistent user experience is created through enabling the use of any input device to interact with all co-located devices. The user can grab data from one device and move it to another one with the currently used input device. With this approach no manual setup of connections for data exchange is necessary. Instead this setup process is automated and invisible to the user.

1 Use Case

In business as well as in private life mobile multi touch devices, laptop or desktop computers are placed beside each other for sync or exchange (see Figure 1). Furthermore users want to stay alert for notifications on a mobile device to answer a message or call while working on other devices.

Using current systems concerning these tasks, the user has to switch his present interaction device, e.g. keyboard and mouse regarding laptop or desktop computers as well as undocking and touching a respective mobile device. Thereby the user has to keep in mind or find out which keyboard or mouse is attached to which screen, thus having to interrupt the flow of interaction with his actual task at hand and to think about input devices instead.

Figure 1: Typical use case scenario including laptop, PC and smartphone on the same desk

2 Related Work

When bringing different kinds of devices physically and virtually together, several evolutionary steps of related research affect the proposed approach. These topics include controlling different desktops, coupling them, exchanging and displaying data from mobile devices on big screens.

Regarding controlling different desktops, remote desktops and virtual machines [2] are integrating the guest screen like a native window improving data exchange between the systems by drag and drop. They usually focus on a single interaction device, thus not offering a solution for multiple co-located devices.

Regarding the coupling of co-located devices current approaches are either restricted to only the same type of device having to put it physically together [4] or expert configuration is needed for setup [5]. Cross-device interaction between mobile devices and large screens or computers is realized with different approaches, including gestures [1] and proxemics interaction [3]. Concepts for natural interaction between and seamless integration of co-located mobile devices, desktop and laptop computers in existing work environments are missing.

We asked twelve users – all are using co-located devices – several questions. First we asked if they wanted to move their mouse pointer to another co-located device for data exchange and recognized that it didn't work in the past, which was the case for seven users. Current workarounds employed by all participants are to use USB-devices, cloud services or establish other network connections for exchanging pieces of texts, files or other data.

3 Preliminary Study

We asked questions to twelve users – all are using co-located devices. Current workarounds employed by all participants are to use USB-devices, cloud services or establish other network connections for exchanging pieces of texts, files or other data. These manual and additional interactions to a task are reducing efficiency, effectiveness and satisfaction – as we found out in our questionnaire –, which are the main factors in user experience [6]. Seven users tried to move their mouse pointer to another co-located device for data exchange in the past and recognized that it didn't work.

4 Natural Cross-Device Interaction Concpet

We propose a *Natural Cross-Device Interaction* (NCDI) concept to speed up the process by enabling the use of any input device to interact with all co-located devices. Natural implies working as expected in our case. No prior manual setup is required and the devices detect their relative screen positions automatically. Thus it is not necessary to change physical input devices like keyboard or mouse. We demonstrated our concept to thirteen users and twelve found the approach easy to use and that it worked as expected. Three remarked that they find it tricky at the beginning for smartphones. One stated that it might be especially useful for all text based tasks. The new solution enables any keyboard or indirect pointing device – regardless to which computer it is attached – to be used across any computational device (see Figure 2) without manual configuration. This includes using an external keyboard or mouse on a mobile device.

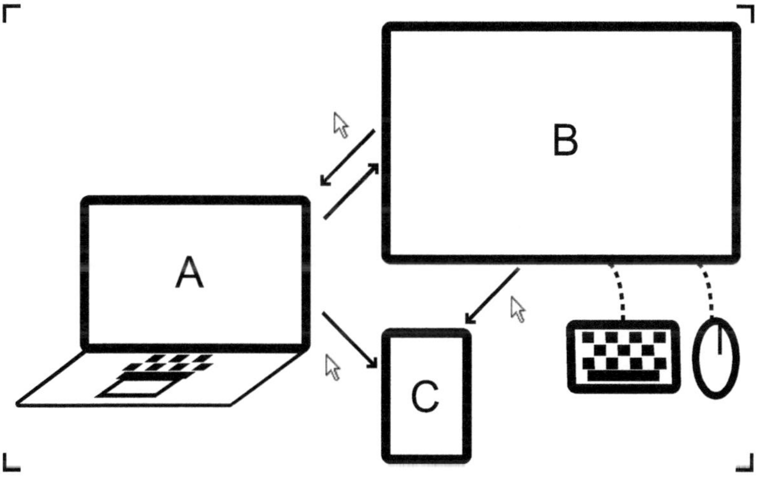

Figure 2: Any keyboard or indirect pointing device can be used across any computational device.

Figure 2 illustrates all possible interactions across co-located computational devices: Using the mouse connected to a desktop computer (B), the cursor can be moved over to the laptop screen (A) or the smartphone (C). Respectively the touchpad or pointing stick from a laptop (A) can be used to move the cursor to other device's screens (B, C). Depending on the cursor position or on an application being in focus any keyboard can be used. This way a keyboard from the laptop can be used together with the mouse from the PC or vice versa, if a mouse is attached to the laptop. Mobile devices are used additionally while working on other devices to stay alert for notifications and to answer a message or call. Occasionally data from a mobile device is required on a PC or laptop. For example a user has taken a note from the conversation with a colleague and needs the respective information for his current work at the PC. Instead of undocking the mobile device, mailing the respective text via e-mail or other workarounds to himself, the proposed approach allows the user to directly get the text with the current mouse and keyboard at hand. The same way he can answer messages on the phone.

5 Conclusion and Future Work

We identified the need for a more natural cross-device interaction between co-located computational devices in workplace settings. With our approach users can grab data from one device and move it to another one with the currently used input device. Our work reveals another way of thinking about devices – not as isolated – but rather as part of a unified user's information space. Different devices can be seen as just different views on this information space. To make the input devices available across all coupled devices the remote desktop approach is partially used. For coupling and locating different devices as well as exchanging data between them, technologies like broadband connection, NFC and RFID are used. Our approach offers a solution for moving a cursor from a laptop or PC to a mobile touch device, but interacting the other way round is a challenge not solved by our current concept. This limitation will be addressed in future work.

References

1. Dachselt, R., and Buchholz, R.: Natural Throw and Tilt Interaction between Mobile Phones and Distant Displays. *CHI '09.* ACM, New York, NY

2. Popek, G.J., and Goldberg, R.P. Formal requirements for virtualizable third generation architectures. Commun. ACM 17, 7 (July 1974), 412-421.

3. Marquardt, N., Diaz-Marino, R., Boring, S., and Greenberg, S. The proximity toolkit: prototyping proxemic interactions in ubiquitous computing ecologies. In *Proceedings of UIST'11.* ACM, New York, NY, USA, 315-326. DOI=10.1145/2047196.2047238

4. Tandler, P., Prante, T., Müller-Tomfelde, C., Streitz, N., and Steinmetz, R. Connectables: dynamic coupling of displays for the flexible creation of shared workspaces. In *Proceedings of UIST '01.* ACM, New York, NY, USA, 2001, pp. 11-20. DOI 10.1145/ 502348.502351

5. Synergy: Overview, 2012. Retrieved April 12, 2012, from Synergy: http://synergy-foss.org

6. ISO 9241-210, Ergonomics of human-system interaction -- Part 210: Human-centred design for interactive systems: http://www.iso.org/

Contact Information

Marius Brade: marius.brade@tu-dresden.de / Steffen Buzin: steffen.buzin@sap.com

M. Koch, A. Butz & J. Schlichter (Hrsg.): Mensch und Computer 2014 Tagungsband,
München: Oldenbourg Wissenschaftsverlag, 2014, S. 319-322.

Evaluating user preference on touch screen tablets by a complex tapping task with multiple targets

Thorsten Stark[1], Stefan Schade[2], Melanie J. C. Stade[3]

Informatik und Medien, Beuth Hochschule für Technik Berlin[1]
Psychologie Neuer Medien und Methodenlehre, Technische Universität Berlin[2]
Kognitionspsychologie und Kognitive Ergonomie, Technische Universität Berlin[3]

Abstract

The aim of this study was to investigate objective data indicating preferred areas of a touch screen tablet. Participants had to tap one of several colored targets arranged in theoretical sections. We assume that the sections with the highest number of touches indicate preference and "comfort zones". We found that the middle right section is the most preferred area on the tablet screen regardless of tablet orientation (portrait vs. landscape) and posture (single vs. both handed).

1 Introduction

With the prevalence of personal digital assistants (PDAs) and smartphones several studies in the past decade have been conducted to evaluate target positions and sizes for one handed thumb tapping on mobile small screen devices. In general, participants were instructed to hold their devices with one hand and use the thumb of the same hand for tapping targets varying in size and position. However, results of previous studies dealing with small screen devices could not be transferred to heavier and larger touch screen based tablet computers because (1) these devices are not held and used with the same hand, (2) people use the index (or middle) finger and thumb of their preferred hand as well as the thumb of the non-preferred hand, and (3) tablets are used in different orientations. Furthermore, the referred studies measured "preference" of target positions by (debatable) subjective ratings of participants in post-session questionnaires (e.g., Perry 2008). In addition, previous studies with a single-target/single-tap task approach did not consider that in real life scenarios there is usually more than one possible target available. Moreover, the interaction between user and tablet is an interplay between perception and reaction. Experiments with single-target/single-tap tasks did not consider visual search, information processing and attention allocation of the real world. Finally, in case of tablets only one posture (landscape, both handed) was analysed (e.g., Odell et al. 2012, Oulasvirta et al. 2013). Thus, we chose an alternative approach to investigate whether preferred areas exist on tablet computers and how these preferred areas correspond to tablet orientation and posture. We assume that users have preferred areas (*"comfort zones"*) on the screen and that these areas can be reached with a minimal amount of physical effort. For example, Young and colleagues (2012) showed that normal tablet usage causes a greater head and neck flexion especially compared with desktop computer usage. Contrary to previous approaches, we want to investigate the preference of different areas of the tablet computer based on objective tapping parameters (number of touches) in different conditions. Identifying comfort zones of tablet usage may help to establish new guidelines for designing tablet computers in order to reduce the amount of uncomfortable postures and gestures.

2 Methods

Participants. Overall twelve right handed subjects between 13 and 14 years of age (mean age=13.7; sex=4 female) of a German grammar school participated in the experiment. All participants received a standardized instruction, were unaware of the purpose of the experiment, and reported having normal/corrected-to-normal color vision and visual acuity. *Apparatus and stimulus.* For the experiment a mobile tablet computer by Apple (iPad 3; 2048×1536 Pixel; Apple A5X 1GHz dual-core, 1024MB RAM; see Figure 1, left) was used. Figure 1 (middle) illustrates an example screen in one experimental trial. On the 9.7" screen 54 grey discs were equally spaced on a virtual matrix in every trial. All discs were displayed with a radius of 44 pixels.

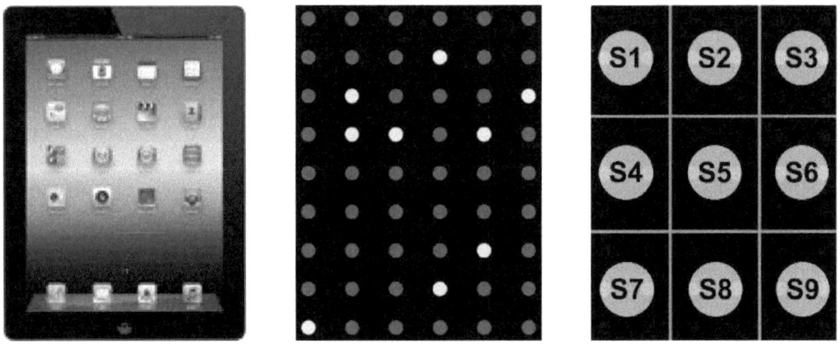

Figure 1: Left: mobile table computer (Apple iPad 3) in portrait orientation used in the experiment. Middle: example screen in one trial (portrait orientation). Right: Sectioning of the screen into nine (invisible) sectors for analysing preferred screen regions.

The 9.7" screen was divided into an imaginary three-by-three grid resulting in nine possible tapping sectors, each containing six discs (Figure 1, right). In every sector (S1 to S9) one of the grey discs turned into one of five target colors, while the remaining discs left grey. The targets were spaced at intervals of about 1.6° visual angle (horizontal and vertical) with an assumed viewing distance of 50 cm. The distance to the edge was about 0.46° visual angle for each exterior target position in both format conditions. *Task, procedure and design.*

Participants were instructed to tap one of the nine colored targets as fast and accurate as possible. We realised a two-by-two repeated measures design consisting of the factors *tablet orientation* (portrait vs. landscape) and *tablet posture* (single handed vs. both handed). In single hand posture the tablet is held with the non-dominant hand while the tapping task was performed with the dominant hand. In both handed postures the tablet is held with both hands while the display was tapped with the thumbs (100 trials per condition with varied condition sequence). The nine targets (one per sector) were colored for 1.000 ms or until participants touched a colored target. After 1.000 ms or as success feedback, all 54 target positions were displayed in grey for 1.000 ms (darker grey in case of success). The experiments were performed sitting in a darkened room with low level of brightness.

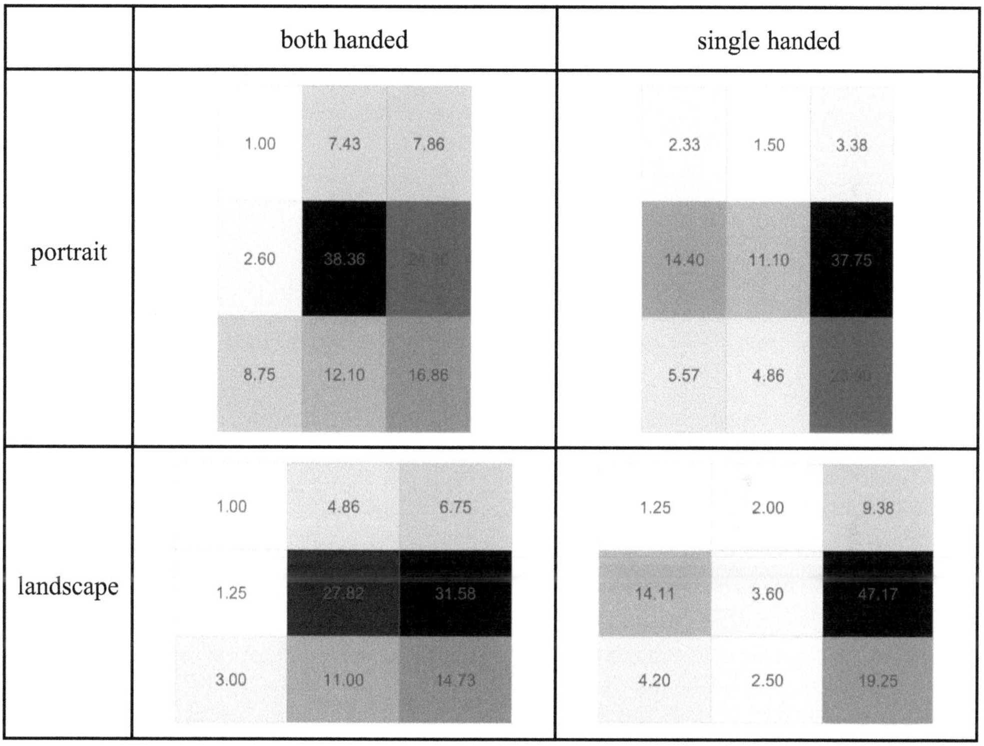

Figure 2: Heatmaps for all conditions indicating the mean absolute numbers of target taps by coloring from white (small numbers) to black (high numbers).

3 Results

The dependent variable was the *target hits*. Figure 2 illustrates the mean number of target taps by heatmaps indicating the comfort zones for the four conditions of the experiment. The descriptive analysis shows that users preferred – as expected – sectors on the right side of the tablet irrespective of the tablet orientation. In the both handed posture it seems that there is a tapping shift of the comfort zone to the centre of the screen although subjects were free in tapping.

4 Prospect

Several questions are relevant in the interaction between users and mobile devices:

1. How do visual stimuli on the screen, physical parameters of the user and surrounding distraction influence changings of the comfort zones?
2. Is there a left shift of comfort zones for left-handed subjects?
3. How does the tablet usage interact with eye tracking parameters?
4. How does a more realistic setting including movement and other subpopulations (e.g., elderly people, users with physical or psychological disorders) influence the mobile device usage?
5. What are implications for designing user-friendly devices, e.g. individual layout adjustment?

References

Odell, D., & Chandrasekaran, V. (2012). Enabling comfortable thumb interaction in tablet computers: a Windows 8 case study. Proceedings of the Human Factors and Ergonomics Society Annual Meeting, 56(1), 1907–1911. doi:10.1177/1071181312561278

Oulasvirta, A., Reichel, A., Li, W., Zhang, Y., Bachynskyi, M., Vertanen, K., & Kristensson, P. O. (2013). Improving Two-thumb Text Entry on Touchscreen Devices. In Proceedings of the SIGCHI Conference on Human Factors in Computing Systems (pp. 2765–2774). New York, NY, USA: ACM. doi:10.1145/2470654.2481383

Perry, K. B., & Hourcade, J. P. (2008). Evaluating One Handed Thumb Tapping on Mobile Touchscreen Devices. In Proceedings of Graphics Interface 2008 (pp. 57–64). Toronto, Ont., Canada, Canada: Canadian Information Processing Society.

Young, J. G., Trudeau, M., Odell, D., Marinelli, K., & Dennerlein, J. T. (2012). Touch-screen tablet user configurations and case-supported tilt affect head and neck flexion angles. Work, 41(1), 81–91. doi:10.3233/WOR-2012-1337

Kontakt:
stark@beuth-hochschule.de[1]; stefan.schade@tu-berlin.de; melanie.stade@tu-berlin.de

[1] The work of Thorsten Stark was supported in part by the ERDF funded R&D project MoMo of Berliner Senatsverwaltung Bildung, Jugend und Wissenschaft, Project no.: EFRE 20072013 2/51.

M. Koch, A. Butz & J. Schlichter (Hrsg.): Mensch und Computer 2014 Tagungsband,
München: Oldenbourg Wissenschaftsverlag, 2014, S. 323-326.

Evaluation des UEQ in einfacher Sprache mit Schülern

Andreas Hinderks[1], Martin Schrepp[2], Jörg Thomaschewski[3]

RMTSoft GmbH & Co. KG[1]
SAP AG[2]
Hochschule Emden/Leer[3]

Zusammenfassung

Kinder und Jugendliche sind eine relevante Zielgruppe für viele Produkte. Etablierte Fragebögen zur Messung der User Experience werden in der Regel mit Erwachsenen entwickelt und validiert und setzen daher ein gewisses Ausmaß an Sprachverständnis und Abstraktionsvermögen voraus. Bei der Anwendung mit Kindern und Jugendlichen können sich hier Probleme ergeben. Für den User Experience Questionnaire (UEQ) wurde deshalb eine spezielle Version für Kinder und Jugendliche erstellt. Diese wurde bisher aber nur mit studentischen Teilnehmern validiert. Wir beschreiben die Evaluation dieser Variante des UEQ mit Schülern. Die Ergebnisse zeigen, dass die verwendeten Items ab einer gewissen Altersstufe ausreichend gut verstanden werden. Allerdings konnten auch einige potentiell problematische Items identifiziert werden.

1 Einleitung

Kinder und Jugendliche sind für viele interaktive Produkte eine wichtige oder sogar die primäre Zielgruppe. Beispiele sind soziale Netzwerke (Facebook, Myspace, oder Youtube), Kommunikationsdienste (Skype, WhatsApp) oder Web-Angebote mit unterstützendem Unterrichtsmaterial für Schüler (Lernplattformen von Schulen, kommerzielle Lern- oder Nachhilfeangebote).

Es ist wichtig die User Experience solcher Produkte für Kinder und Jugendliche sinnvoll messen zu können. Etablierte Fragebögen zur Messung dieser Produktqualität wurden aber in der Regel mit Daten von Erwachsenen entwickelt und validiert. Da Kinder und Jugendliche über einen eingeschränkteren Wortschatz und eine geringere Abstraktionsfähigkeit verfügen, ist der Einsatz solcher Fragebögen in dieser Zielgruppe oft mit Problemen verbunden.

Für den User Experience Questionnaire (kurz UEQ, Laugwitz et al., 2006; 2008) wurde daher eine spezielle Version des Fragebogens für Kinder und Jugendliche erstellt (Hinderks et al., 2012). Der UEQ besteht aus 26 gegensätzlichen Begriffspaaren (z.B. langweilig/

spannend, kompliziert/einfach, kreativ/phantasielos), die die User Experience eines Produkts auf den 6 Dimensionen *Attraktivität*, *Effizienz*, *Durchschaubarkeit*, *Steuerbarkeit*, *Stimulation* und *Originalität* messen. Für die Version in einfacher Sprache wurden Fremdwörter bzw. für Jugendliche ungebräuchliche Begriffe durch einfachere Begriffe ersetzt. Auch gebräuchliche Begriffe, deren Übertragung auf die Bewertung eines Produkts ein hohes Abstraktionsvermögen erfordert, wurden entsprechend ersetzt.

Diese vereinfachte Version, die zusammen mit der Originalversion und verschiedenen Sprachversionen auf www.ueq-online.org frei zur Verfügung steht, wurde bisher mit studentischen Teilnehmern validiert (Hinderks et al., 2012 oder Schrepp et al., in press) und zeigte in diesen Untersuchungen eine gute interne Konsistenz der Skalen. Ziel dieses Beitrags ist es, die vereinfachte Version mit der eigentlichen Zielgruppe zu validieren. Es soll also überprüft werden, ob die verwendeten Begriffspaare für Kinder und Jugendliche ausreichend verständlich sind.

2 Evaluation mit Schülern

Zur Evalulation der vereinfachten Version wurden Schülerinnen und Schüler der 5., 6. und 7. Klasse der IGS Emden (www.igs-emden.de) im November 2012 befragt. Als Testobjekt standen Youtube und Wikipedia zur Auswahl, die zu Beginn des Fragebogens von den Teilnehmern zur Bewertung ausgewählt wurden. Insgesamt haben sich 15 Teilnehmer für Wikipedia und 87 für Youtube entschieden. Ziel der Evaluation war es, unverständliche Items zu identifizieren. Daher wurden die Schülerinnen und Schüler instruiert, ihnen unverständliche Items nicht zu beantworten, sondern diese im Fragebogen zu unterstreichen. Wird ein Item häufig auf diese Art markiert, gibt dies Hinweise auf Verständnisprobleme bei diesem Item.

3 Ergebnisse

Abbildung 1 zeigt für die drei Klassenstufen (5. – 7. Klasse) den prozentualen Anteil der Fälle, in denen einer der beiden Begriffe eines Items als unverständlich markiert wurde.

Die Daten zeigen deutlich, dass in der Klassenstufe 5 noch viele der Items nicht ausreichend gut verstanden wurden. In den Klassenstufen 6 und 7 geht die Zahl der unverständlichen Items dagegen zurück. Hier sind nur die drei Items *unberechenbar/voraussagbar*, *vorhersagbar/unvorhersagbar* und *ineffizient/effizient* offenbar noch kritisch. Allerdings hat hier möglicherweise das Testobjekt Youtube einen Einfluss auf die Interpretation der ersten beiden genannten Items. Die auf Youtube bereitgestellten Videos sollen den Nutzer unterhalten, das bedeutet, dass der Inhalt sowohl überraschend als auch unvorhersagbar sein kann. Dies hat evtl. die eigentliche Interpretation der Items als *die Bedienung der Video-Plattform ist vom Nutzer gut kontrollierbar* erschwert.

Der Focus der Untersuchung lag auf der Verständlichkeit der Items. Da die Teilnehmer instruiert waren, Items bei denen einer der Begriffe unverständlich war, nicht zu bewerten, und die Stichprobe eher klein war (N=102), lassen sich aus den Daten keine Bewertungen zur internen Konsistenz der Skalen ableiten.

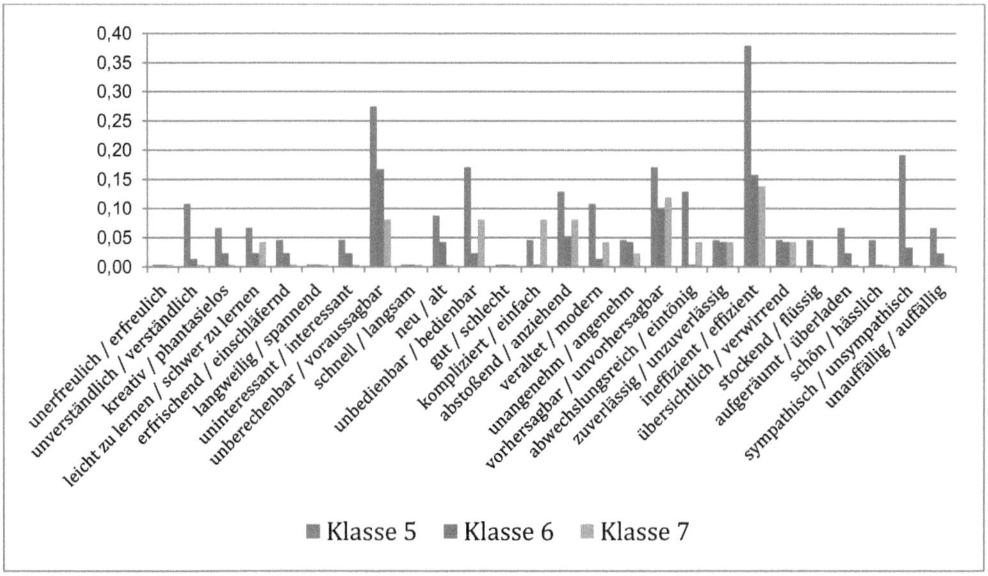

Abbildung 1: Verständlichkeit der Items in den drei untersuchten Klassenstufen. Die Y-Achse zeigt den prozentualen Anteil der Schüler, die einen der Begriffe des Gegensatzpaares als unverständlich markiert hatten.

4 Diskussion

Die UEQ Skalen bestehen aus je 4 Items für Effizienz, Durchschaubarkeit, Steuerbarkeit, Stimulation und Originalität, bzw. 6 Items für die Attraktivität. Ein nicht verstandenes Item hat einen, wenn auch begrenzten, Einfluss auf den gemessenen Skalenwert eines Teilnehmers. Zwar kann die Korrelation der Items einer Skala ein Indikator für eine Skaleninkonsistenz sein, aber nur, wenn das betreffene Item signifikant anders bewertet wurde. Die Häufigkeit von als unverständlich markierten Items ist also ein besserer Indikator dafür, ob der Fragebogen für die entsprechende Zeilgruppe angewendet werden kann.

Die Daten dieser ersten Evaluationsstudie mit Schülern zeigen klar, dass die speziell für Kinder und Jugendliche konstruierte Version des UEQ ab einem gewissen Mindestalter sinnvoll angewendet werden kann.

Für Schüler der Klassenstufe 5 waren offenbar noch viele der verwendeten Begriffe nicht ausreichend klar. Für diese Altersstufe scheint die Anwendung der vereinfachten UEQ Version daher noch nicht sinnvoll zu sein. Für Schüler der höheren Klassenstufen 6 und 7 waren die Items dagegen bis auf wenige Ausnahmen verständlich (wurden von weniger als

5% der Schüler als unverständlich markiert), d.h. ab diesem Alter respektive diesem Sprachverständnis kann man diese Version anwenden.

Drei der verwendeten 26 Items scheinen noch problematisch. Hier sollten evtl. Alternativen gesucht werden, die die Verständlichkeit weiter verbessern. Allerdings hat hier evtl. der Kontext der bewerteten Web-Seiten (Youtube) einen Einfluss, d.h. vor einer vorschnellen Ersetzung dieser Items sind weitere Untersuchungen sinnvoll.

Wegen der geringen Teilnehmerzahl und dem Focus auf die Verständlichkeit der Begriffe, konnten keine sinnvollen Kennwerte zur Reliabilität der einzelnen Skalen gerechnet werden. Hier muss in einer Folgeuntersuchung mit größerer Teilnehmerzahl weitere Information gesammelt werden, wobei die vorliegenden Studien mit studentischen Teilnehmern auf eine zufriedenstellende Reliabilität der Skalen hinweisen (Hinderks et al. 2012).

Literatur

Hinderks, A.; Schrepp, M.; Rauschenberger, M.; Olschner, S.; Thomaschewski, J. (2012). Konstruktion eines Fragebogens für jugendliche Personen zur Messung der User Experience. In: Brau, H.; Lehmann, A.; Petrovic, K.; Schroeder, M. (Eds.); *Usability Professionals 2012* S. 78 – 83, 2012.

Laugwitz, B.; Schrepp, M. & Held, T. (2006). *Konstruktion eines Fragebogens zur Messung der User Experience von Softwareprodukten.* In: A.M. Heinecke & H. Paul (Eds.): Mensch & Computer 2006 – Mensch und Computer im Strukturwandel. Oldenbourg Verlag, S. 125 – 134.

Laugwitz, B., Schrepp, M. & Held, T. (2008). Construction and evaluation of a user experience questionnaire. In: Holzinger, A. (Ed.): USAB 2008, LNCS 5298, S. 63-76.

Martin Schrepp, Andreas Hinderks, Jörg Thomaschewski (in press). Applying the User Experience Questionnaire (UEQ) in different evaluation scenarios. HCII 2014 Proceedings.

UEQ-Online: www.ueq-online.org (zuletzt besucht 02.05.2014).

Danksagung

Wir danken Herrn Moritz Tietjens, Schulleiter Herrn Günter Kottkamp sowie den Lehrerinnen und Lehrern der Integrierte Gesamtschule Emden für ihre Unterstützung bei der Durchführung der Untersuchung.

Kontaktinformationen

Andreas Hinderks: andreas@hinderks.org, Martin Schrepp: martin.schrepp@sap.com, Jörg Thomaschewski: joerg.thomaschewski@hs-emden-leer.de

M. Koch, A. Butz & J. Schlichter (Hrsg.): Mensch und Computer 2014 Tagungsband,
München: Oldenbourg Wissenschaftsverlag, 2014, S. 327-330.

Geschlechterunterschiede bei computerbezogenen Attributionen

Adelka Niels[1], Sascha R. Guczka[2], Monique Janneck[1]

[1]Fachhochschule Lübeck, [2]Universität Hamburg

Zusammenfassung

Computerbezogene Attributionen charakterisieren die Ursachenerklärungen, die Menschen für Ereignisse finden, die in der Interaktion mit Computern auftreten, sowie die Kontroll- und Einflussmöglichkeiten, die sie für sich wahrnehmen. In dieser Studie wurden geschlechtsspezifische Unterschiede im Attributionsverhalten untersucht. Männer und Frauen zeigten grundsätzlich dieselben Attributionsstile, unterscheiden sich aber in deren Ausprägung und Häufigkeit. Anders als in der Literatur berichtet zeigten Frauen dabei jedoch kein ungünstigeres Attributionsverhalten als Männer.

1 Grundlagen und Methodik

Attributionsprozesse umfassen die *Ursachenerklärungen*, die Menschen für Ereignisse finden, sowie *die Kontroll- und Einflussmöglichkeiten*, die sie für sich selber wahrnehmen (vgl. z. B. Försterling 2001). Dabei sind v.a. die folgenden Dimensionen bedeutsam: *Lokalisation* (wird die Ursache für ein Ereignis bei sich selbst oder externen Einflüssen gesehen?), *Kontrollierbarkeit* (welche Einflussmöglichkeiten schreibt man sich selber zu?), *Stabilität* (werden das Ereignis und seine Ursache als einmalig oder zeitlich stabil empfunden?) sowie *Globalität* (wird von einem spezifischen Ereignis auch auf andere Vorkommnisse geschlossen?).

Auf der Basis einer Typologie computerbezogener Attributionsstile (Janneck & Guczka 2013, Tab. 1) wurden *Geschlechterunterschiede* im Hinblick auf computerbezogene Attributionen untersucht. Die Erhebung der Attributionsstile fand im Rahmen von *Usability-Tests* statt. Die Probanden bearbeiteten verschiedene Aufgaben, die entweder auch mit wenig Erfahrung möglichst einfach lösbar (Erfolgssituation – Bsp.: Suchen Sie die Öffnungszeiten des Stadtteilbüros in der Innenstadt auf der Webseite www.luebeck.de) bzw. schwierig oder sogar unlösbar gestaltet waren, ohne dass die Probanden dies wussten (Misserfolgssituation – Bsp.: Suchen Sie die Bauverordnung für den Stadtteil Lübeck-Schlutup auf der Webseite www.luebeck.de). Nach jeder Aufgabe füllten die Probanden einen kurzen Attributionsfragebogen aus (vgl. Janneck & Guczka 2013). Zudem wurden Alter, Geschlecht, Ausbildung, Computerkenntnisse und -Nutzung erhoben.

Stile	
Erfolg	*„Realistische"* – „Manchmal habe ich Erfolg, manchmal nicht"
	„Bescheidene" – „Ich habe dieses Mal einfach Glück gehabt"
	„Glückspilze" – „Alles was ich anfasse gelingt"
	„Selbstbewusste" – „Ich bin kompetent und für meinen Erfolg selbst verantwortlich"
	„Boss" – „Der Erfolg beruht auf dem System, aber ich habe die Kontrolle darüber"
Misserfolg	*„Realistische"* – „Diesmal hat es nicht geklappt – nächstes Mal funktioniert es besser"
	„Achselzuckende" – „Keine Ahnung, woran es lag – jeder Misserfolg ist einzigartig"
	„Selbstbewusste – „Ich hab's verbockt, aber beim nächsten Mal mache ich es besser"
	„Resignierte" – „Ich verstehe nie, wie Computer funktionieren"

Tabelle 1: Typologie computerbezogener Attributionsstile (Janneck & Guczka 2013)

2 Ergebnisse und Diskussion

Insgesamt nahmen 58 Personen an der Untersuchung teil (48% weiblich, 52% männlich). Das Durchschnittsalter betrug 34 Jahre (Range: 17-75 Jahre). Das Bildungsniveau ist eher hoch. Frauen schätzten ihre Computerkenntnisse signifikant schlechter ein als Männer. Insgesamt wurden im Rahmen der Studie 340 Situationen erfasst, davon 177 Erfolgssituationen und 163 Misserfolgssituationen. Die Daten der Attributionsfragebögen wurden mittels Clusteranalyse ausgewertet (Bacher et al. 2010, vgl. Janneck & Guczka 2013).

Hinsichtlich der *Erfolgssituationen* wurden die Attributionsstile *„Realistisch"*, *„Bescheiden"* und *„Selbstbewusst"* repliziert (vgl. Tab. 1). Personen in Cluster A („Realistische") empfinden die Ursache für ihren Erfolg zeitlich eher instabil und bereichsspezifisch, während Personen in Cluster B („Bescheidene") die Ursache für ihren Erfolg eher im System sehen und diese auch für unkontrollierbarer halten. Personen in Cluster C („Selbstbewusste") attribuieren zeitlich stabiler und nehmen die Ursache für ihren Erfolg als situationsübergreifender wahr. Sie sehen die Ursache für ihren Erfolg von allen drei Clustern am ehesten bei sich.

Für die *Misserfolgssituationen* konnten für die drei Attributionsstile *„Realistisch"*, *„Selbstbewusst"* und *„Resigniert"* Ähnlichkeiten zu den vorherigen Studien gefunden werden (vgl. Tab. 1). Personen in Cluster D („Realistische") attribuieren von allen drei Clustern zeitlich am instabilsten und halten die Ursache für kontrollierbar und bereichsspezifisch. Personen in Cluster E („Selbstbewusste") weisen die höchsten Internalitätswerte auf, fühlen sich also verantwortlich für ihren Misserfolg, schreiben sich aber gleichzeitig auch Kontrollmöglichkeiten zu. Personen in Cluster F („Resignierte") empfinden zeit- und situationsübergreifend kaum Kontrolle, was sich als ein Gefühl des Ausgeliefertseins beschreiben lässt.

Geschlechtsspezifische Attributionsstile in Erfolgssituationen

Die geschlechtsspezifische Auswertung der Clusteranalysen zeigt ebenfalls die drei Attributionsstile „Realistische", „Bescheidene" und „Selbstbewusste". Männer und Frauen unterscheiden sich jedoch teilweise bei der Ausprägung der Attributionsdimensionen (Abb. 1). Die weiblichen „Realisten" (Cluster A) sehen die Ursache für ihren Erfolg zeitlich signifikant instabiler (p=0,003). Außerdem schreiben sie die Ursache für ihren Erfolg tendenziell eher sich selbst zu. Sie attribuieren also etwas souveräner und selbstbewusster, die Unterschiede sind jedoch nicht signifikant. Den Attributionsstil „Realistisch" zeigen mehr Männer als Frauen. Bei den „Bescheidenen" (Cluster B) zeigen sich keine signifikanten Unterschiede. In der Tendenz attribuieren die weiblichen Probanden zeitlich etwas stabiler. Das Geschlechterverhältnis ist ausgeglichen. Bei den „Selbstbewussten" (Cluster C) lassen sich kaum Unterschiede feststellen. Die Frauen sind hier in der Überzahl.

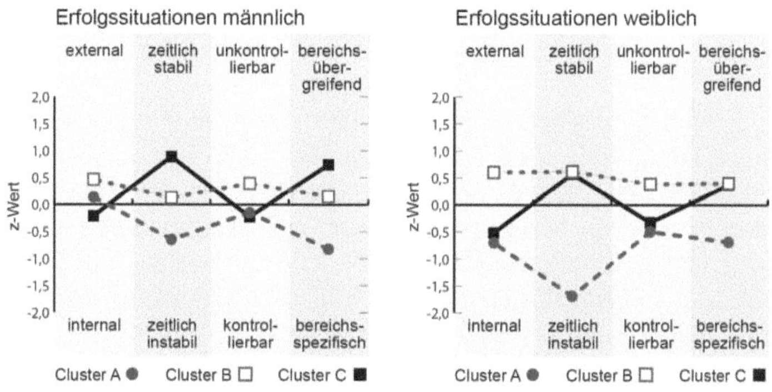

Abbildung 1: Attributionsstile in Erfolgssituationen nach Geschlecht

Geschlechtsspezifische Attributionsstile in Misserfolgssituationen

Auch bei den Misserfolgssituationen lassen sich bei beiden Geschlechtern die drei Attributionsstile „Realistisch", „Selbstbewusst" und „Resigniert" wiederfinden. Die Kurvenverläufe weisen jedoch insbesondere bei Cluster E recht große Unterschiede auf, sodass bei den Männern von E' gesprochen wird (Abb. 2).

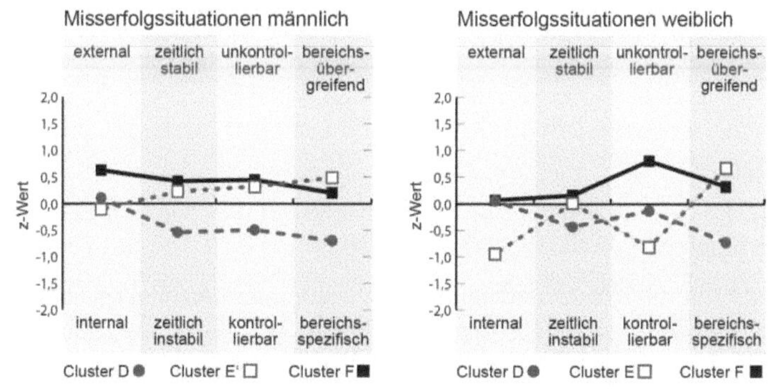

Abbildung 2: Attributionsstile in Misserfolgssituationen nach Geschlecht

Probanden beider Geschlechter aus Cluster D (Realistische) weisen keine signifikanten Unterschiede auf. Auch das Geschlechterverhältnis ist nahezu ausgeglichen. Die größten Unterschiede zeigen sich bei den „Selbstbewussten" (Cluster E/E'): Die männlichen Probanden empfinden die Ursache für ihren Misserfolg signifikant weniger kontrollierbar (p=0,024) und nähern sich hier den Werten der „Resignierten" an. Zudem verorten die männlichen Probanden die Ursache eher external (im System), die Frauen dagegen eher internal (bei sich selbst). Die Unterschiede sind jedoch nicht signifikant. In diesem Cluster sind gleich viele Männer und Frauen vertreten. Auch im Hinblick auf Cluster F (Resignierte) gibt es keine signifikanten Unterschiede, jedoch attribuieren die männlichen Probanden etwas externaler und halten die Ursache für etwas kontrollierbarer als die weiblichen. Die Männer sind in diesem Cluster in der Überzahl.

Diskussion und Ausblick

Wenngleich bei Frauen und Männern grundsätzlich dieselben Attributionsstile gefunden wurden, sind einige interessante Unterschiede sichtbar, v.a. bei *Misserfolgssituationen*: So sehen Männer über alle Stile hinweg eher *externale* Ursachen für ihren Misserfolg, was früheren Studien entspricht, die Männern einen eher „entlastenden" und selbstwerterhaltenden Attributionsstil attestieren (z.B. Sølvberg 2002). Allerdings zeigen sich in unserer Untersuchung nur tendenzielle Unterschiede, die nicht statistisch signifikant ausfallen, was möglicherweise in der Stichprobengröße begründet liegt. Im Widerspruch zu bisherigen Studien steht das Ergebnis, dass Männer aus dem Cluster der „Selbstbewussten" deutlich weniger Kontrolle über die Situation empfinden als die weiblichen Probanden in diesem Cluster und damit ein eher ungünstiges Attributionsmuster zeigen. Die Charakterisierung als „Selbstbewusste" erscheint damit nicht mehr als passend. Auch im Hinblick auf die Geschlechterverhältnisse innerhalb der Cluster bestätigen unsere Ergebnisse nicht die vorherrschende Meinung, dass Frauen eher ungünstige Attributionsstile zeigen (z.B. Sølvberg 2002): Bei den „Resignierten" finden sich mehr Männer als Frauen, während umgekehrt mehr Frauen einen „realistischen" Attributionsstil bei Misserfolgen aufweisen. Auch in Erfolgssituationen sind Frauen, was den günstigen „selbstbewussten" Attributionsstil anbelangt, in der Mehrzahl. Ob sich diese – von bisherigen Studien abweichenden – Ergebnisse replizieren lassen, bleibt abzuwarten. Interessant wäre zu überprüfen, ob beispielsweise Generationsunterschiede eine Rolle spielen. Insgesamt sehen wir in der Erfassung von Attributionsstilen mit einem differenzierten Instrumentarium einen vielversprechenden Ansatz, Geschlechterunterschiede bei der Computernutzung zu analysieren und zu bewerten, ohne Stereotype zu reproduzieren.

Literaturverzeichnis

Bacher, J., Pöge, A., Wenzig, K. (2010). *Clusteranalyse: Anwendungsorientierte Einführung in Klassifikationsverfahren*, 3. Aufl. München: Oldenbourg.

Försterling, F. (2001). Attribution. An introduction to theories, research and applications. Hove, East Sussex: Psychology Press.

Janneck, M., Guczka, S. R. (2013). The Resigned, the Confident, and the Humble: A Typology of Computer-Related Attribution Styles. *Proc. SouthCHI 2013*. Heidelberg: Springer, 373-390.

Sølvberg, A. M. (2002). Gender differences in computer-related control beliefs and home computer use. *Scandinavian Journal of Educational Research 46* (4), 409-426.

M. Koch, A. Butz & J. Schlichter (Hrsg.): Mensch und Computer 2014 Tagungsband,
München: Oldenbourg Wissenschaftsverlag, 2014, S. 331-334.

Geschlechtsstereotype bei der Interaktion mit virtuellen Agenten

Svetlana Nowak[1], Benjamin Weiss[2], Dietrich Manzey[3]

Fachgebiet Psychologie Neuer Medien und Methodenlehre, TU Berlin[1]
Quality and Usability Lab, TU Berlin[2]
Fachgebiet Arbeits-, Ingenieur- und Organisationspsychologie, TU Berlin[3]

Zusammenfassung

Im Rahmen einer laborexperimentellen Studie wurde die Bedeutung von Geschlechtsstereotypen bei der Interaktion mit virtuellen Agenten untersucht. Probanden interagierten mit einem weiblichen oder männlichem Embodied Conversational Agent (ECA), der ihnen bei einer Proxyinstallation assistierte, und beurteilten ihn anschließend in Bezug auf Geschlechtsattribute und Benutzerzufriedenheit. Bei gleichzeitiger Bearbeitung einer Zweitaufgabe zeigte sich ein kontrastereotyper Effekt in Bezug auf die stereotyp weiblichen Attribute. Zudem wurde der weibliche ECA weniger natürlich wahrgenommen als der männliche ECA. Da der ECA kein speziell weibliches Verhalten zeigte, werden die Ergebnisse darauf zurückgeführt, dass der weibliche ECA durch Widersprechen des Geschlechtsstereotyps auffiel und somit zum kontrastereotypen Effekt beitrug.

1 Einleitung

Nass und Kollegen (1994) konnten in zahlreichen Experimenten zeigen, dass Menschen auf Computer sozial reagieren, wenn diese Charakteristika enthalten, die mit Menschen assoziiert werden (= Computers are Social Actors bzw. CASA, Nass et al. 1994). Embodied Conversational Agents (ECAs) besitzen mehrere menschenähnliche Charakteristika (die antropomorphe Darstellung, die natürlich sprachliche Interaktionsform und das nonverbale Verhalten) und können somit potenziell auch sozialpsychologische Effekte auslösen (Übersicht siehe Krämer 2008). Experimente konnten z.B. bereits aufzeigen, dass geschlechtsstereotype Informationen unterschiedlich bewertet werden, je nach Geschlecht des virtuellen Agenten, der diese Information präsentiert (Lee 2003). Bei Beurteilungen von ECA-Bildern zeigen sich außerdem stereotype Effekte der Ethnizität, der Attraktivität und des Alters (z.B. Cowell & Stanney 2005, Khan & Angeli 2007). Es sind keine Studien bekannt, die die Auswirkungen des Geschlechtsstereotyps auf die Wahrnehmung des ECA-Verhaltens untersucht haben. Die zusätzliche Verhaltenskomponente sollte zu einer stärkeren Vermenschlichung und somit zu stärkeren sozialpsychologischen Effekten führen als in Situationen ohne Interaktion mit dem ECA. In der vorliegenden Untersuchung haben Probanden mit einem Assistenzsystem interagiert, welches entweder durch einen männlichen oder weiblichen ECA repräsentiert wurde. Es wurde vermutet, dass bei identischem ECA-Verhalten dem männlichen ECA stärker stereotyp männliche Attribute (= Kompetenzattribute, z.B. „durchsetzungsfähig") und dem weiblichen ECA stärker stereotyp weibliche Attribute (= Wärmeattribute, z.B. „weichherzig") zugeschrieben werden. Außerdem wurde die Hypothese aufgestellt, dass bei einem geschlechtsstereotypen Aufgabenkontext (= Assistenz bei einer Computeraufgabe) der männliche ECA besser in Bezug auf die Benutzerzufriedenheit beurteilt wird als der weibliche ECA. Stereotype sparen kognitive Energie und werden somit bei einer geringen Verarbeitungstiefe angewendet (Augoustinos et al. 1995). In der vorliegenden Untersuchung wurde eine Zweitaufgabe (Reaktionszeitaufgabe) benutzt, um die Verarbeitungstiefe zu manipulieren. Es wurde angenommen, dass Geschlechtsstereotype stärker zum Tragen kommen, wenn eine Zweitaufgabe bearbeitet werden muss.

2 Methode

Insgesamt 39 Versuchspersonen ohne Fachkenntnisse in Informatik und Computertechnik nahmen an der Untersuchung teil. Die Aufgabe bestand darin, einen Proxy zu installieren und zu konfigurieren. Das Assistenzsystem wurde anhand eines ECAs dargestellt, welcher den Probanden Instruktionen gab. Die Probanden wurden einer von vier Gruppen zufällig zugeordnet. Die Gruppen ergaben sich durch die zwei unabhängige Faktoren ECA-Geschlecht (männlich vs. weiblich, siehe Abbildung 1) und Verarbeitung (tief/ohne Zweitaufgabe vs. flach/mit Zweitaufgabe). Das Geschlecht der Probanden wurde innerhalb der vier Gruppen ausbalanciert.

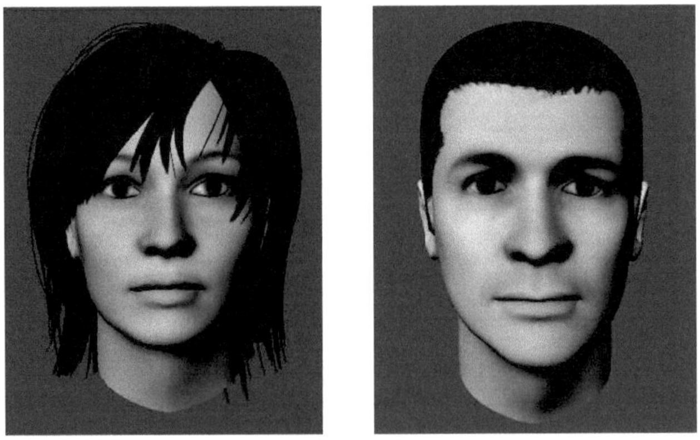

Abbildung 1: weiblicher und männlicher ECA

Nach der Interaktion haben die Probanden den ECA anhand geschlechtsstereotyper Kompetenz- (männlich) und Wärmeattribute (weiblich) beurteilt, die der Geschlechtstypizitätsskala entnommen wurden (Altstötter-Gleich 2004). Neben der Einschätzung des Alters und der Attraktivität des ECAs wurde die Benutzerzufriedenheit anhand der Conversational Agents

Scale erhoben (CAS, Wechsung et al. 2013), die aus den Unterskalen Helpfulness, Naturalness, Trust, Perceived Task Difficulty, Likeability und Entertainment besteht.

3 Ergebnisse und Nacherhebung

Alle statistischen Analysen wurden anhand einer 2 (Geschlecht) x 2 (Zweitaufgabe) ANOVA durchgeführt. Die Einschätzung der ECAs in Bezug auf Alter und Attraktivität unterschieden sich nicht signifikant. Für die Kompetenzattribute zeigten sich keine signifikanten Hauteffekte und keine signifikante Interaktion. In Bezug auf die Wärmeattribute wurde der Haupteffekt der Zweitaufgabe nicht signifikant. Der Haupteffekt ECA-Geschlecht erreichte Signifikanz ($F(1,35) = 5.07$, $p = 0.031$, $\eta^2 = 0.13$). Allerdings wird dieser Haupteffekt von einer signifikanten Interaktion Zweitaufgabe x ECA-Geschlecht überlagert ($F(1,35) = 4.28$, $p = 0.046$, $\eta^2 = 0.11$). Sie geht darauf zurück, dass Probanden erst bei gleichzeitiger Bearbeitung der Zweitaufgabe dem weiblichen ECA im geringeren Maße Wärmeattribute zugewiesen haben als dem männlichen ECA. Es zeigten sich aber keine Unterschiede in der Beurteilung der Wärmeattribute, wenn die Probanden die Zweitaufgabe nicht bearbeiten mussten. In Bezug auf die Benutzerzufriedenheitsskala CAS zeigte nur die Unterskala Naturalness einen signifikanten Haupteffekt des ECA-Geschlechts ($F(1,35) = 4.25$, $p = 0.047$, $\eta^2 = 0.11$). Der weibliche ECA wurde geringer in Bezug auf Naturalness eingestuft als der männliche ECA. Alle anderen Unterskalen zeigten keine signifikanten Effekte. Um der Frage nachzugehen, ob der kontrastereotype Eindruck erst durch die Interaktion oder bereits durch das Bildmaterial erzeugt wird, wurden die beiden ECA-Bilder ohne die Verhaltenskomponente beurteilt. Bei dieser Nacherhebung nahmen insgesamt 44 Probanden teil, die keine Fachkenntnisse in Informatik und Computertechnik besaßen. Sie bekamen entweder den männlichen oder den weiblichen ECA zu sehen und sollten ihren Eindruck anhand der Geschlechtsattribute wiedergeben. Die Daten wurden anhand von t-Tests für unabhängige Stichproben analysiert. Sowohl für die Wärmeattribute als auch für die Kompetenzattribute zeigten sich keine signifikanten Unterschiede in Bezug auf das ECA-Geschlecht.

4 Diskussion und Ausblick

In der vorliegenden Untersuchung zeigten sich weder bei der Betrachtung der ECA-Bilder (Nacherhebung) noch als Konsequenz einer Interaktion zwischen Nutzer und ECA Effekte, die auf die Anwendung von Geschlechtsstereotypen auf die Beurteilung von virtuellen Agenten schließen lassen. Entgegen den Erwartungen kam es sogar zu einem umgekehrten Effekt, der sich darin wiederspiegelte, dass dem weiblichen ECA in geringerem Maße Wärmeattribute zugeschrieben wurden, als dem männlichen. Der Befund, dass die ECA-Bilder keinen stereotypen Effekt zeigen, widerspricht den Untersuchungen zur bildbasierten Beurteilung von ECAs (z.B. Cowell & Stanney 2005). Dies könnte daran liegen, dass die ECA-Bilder in anderen Untersuchungen karikaturenhafter sind und somit eine geringere Auflösung zur sozialen Beurteilung bieten als es bei stark realistischen Bildern der Fall ist. Je weniger detailgetreu eine Darstellung ist, desto stärker verlässt man sich auf Stereotype. Der kontrastereotype Effekt kann wiederum erst durch die Hinzunahme der ECA-Stimme, des sprachlichen Verhaltens oder des Kontextes (Aufgabe) in Kombination mit dem ECA-Geschlecht erklärt werden. Die ECA-Stimme ist maschinenhaft und relativ tief (auch bei der Frau), das ECA-Verhalten ist sehr direktiv und die zu erfüllende Aufgabe ist dem Bereich der Informatik und Computertechnik entnommen. Durch die Zweitaufgabe treten diese Aspekte noch deutlicher hervor (durch die visuelle Ablenkung und die stärkere Arbeitsbelastung). Dadurch fällt beim weiblichen ECA die Diskrepanz zwischen Geschlecht und Verhalten stärker auf, was sich in der Beurteilung niederschlägt. Diese Diskrepanz führte wahrscheinlich auch dazu, dass der weibliche ECA als weniger natürlich beurteilt wurde. Die Ergebnisse zeigen, dass das ECA-Geschlecht durchaus die ECA-Beurteilung entsprechend dem CASA-Paradigma beeinflussen kann. Weitere Untersuchungen könnten mehrere weibliche und männliche ECAs gegeneinander testen um den Geschlechtereffekt mit anderen ECA-Merkmalen in Beziehung zu setzen. So könnte z.B. untersucht werden, ob eine höhere Abstraktion der ECA-Gestaltung den Grad der Stereotypisierung verstärkt. Wenn sich diese Annahme bestätigen lässt, könnte als nächster Schritt untersucht werden, wie die stereotype Wahrnehmung von ECA-Bildern mit verschiedenen Verhaltensaspekten interagiert. Entsprechende Erkenntnisse könnten einen Beitrag für die Gestaltung von ECAs liefern.

Literaturverzeichnis

Altstötter-Gleich, C. (2004). Expressivität, Instrumentalität und psychische Gesundheit. *Zeitschrift für Differentielle und Diagnostische Psychologie*, *25*(3), 123–139.

Augoustinos, M., Walker, I. & Donaghue, N. (1995). *Social cognition: An integrated introduction*: Sage.

Cowell, A. J. & Stanney, K. M. (2005). Manipulation of non-verbal interaction style and demographic embodiment to increase anthropomorphic computer character credibility. *International journal of human-computer studies*, *62*(2), 281–306.

Khan, R. & Angeli, A. de (2007). Mapping the demographics of virtual humans. In Tom Ormerod & Corina Sas (Hrsg.), *Proceedings of the 21st British HCI Group Annual Conference on People and Computers: HCI... but not as we know it-Volume 2* (S.149–152). British Computer Society.

Krämer, N. C. (2008). *Soziale Wirkungen virtueller Helfer: Gestaltung und Evaluation von Mensch-Computer-Interaktionen*. Stuttgart: W. Kohlhammer Verlag.

Lee, E.-J. (2003). Effects of 'gender' of the computer on informational social influence: The moderating role of task type. *International journal of human-computer studies*, *58*(4), 347–362.

Nass, C., Steuer, J. & Tauber, E. R. (1994). Computers are social actors. In Beth Adelson, Susan Dumais, & Judith Olson (Hrsg.), *Proceedings of the SIGCHI conference on Human factors in computing systems* (S. 72–78). ACM Press.

Wechsung, I., Weiss, B., Kühnel, C., Ehrenbrink, P. & Möller, S. (2013). Development and Validation of the Conversational Agents Scale (CAS). In *Proceedings Interspeech 2013*.

Kontaktinformationen

svetlana.nowak@campus.tu-berlin.de

M. Koch, A. Butz & J. Schlichter (Hrsg.): Mensch und Computer 2014 Tagungsband, München: Oldenbourg Wissenschaftsverlag, 2014, S. 335-338.

Hands-on-Activities als Werkzeug im Participatory Design mit Senioren

Julia Käfer, Martin Stein, Johanna Meurer

Institut für Wirtschaftsinformatik und neue Medien, Universität Siegen

Zusammenfassung

Dieser Beitrag beschreibt, wie die Idee der Hands-on-Activities (HoA) dazu beitragen kann, ältere Menschen auf aktive und konstruktive Weise in Prozesse des Participatory Design (PD) zu integrieren. Er reflektiert die Erfahrungen aus einem Workshop zur Entwicklung einer iTV-Applikation für ein Mobilitätsinformationssystem. Dabei konnten Potentiale und Grenzen der Technologie exploriert werden, was das Konzept der HoA zu einem geeigneten Instrument macht, um mit technikferneren Teilnehmern einen gemeinsamen Gestaltungsraum zu eröffnen.

1 Einleitung

Im Zuge des demographischen Wandels nimmt die HCI-Forschung den älteren Menschen mit seinen spezifischen Eigenschaften und Bedarfen zunehmend in den Blick. Informations- und Kommunikationstechnologien durchdringen nahezu jeden Aspekt unseres Lebens und können besonders älteren Menschen einen Mehrwert bieten. Damit diese Technologien für die Altersgruppe bedienbar sind, sollten Designer sich gezielt mit deren Perspektive beschäftigen. PD-Methoden stellen mächtige Werkzeuge dar, um Nutzern ein Mitspracherecht bei der Technikentwicklung einzuräumen. Senioren haben jedoch oft wenig Erfahrung mit neuen Technologien, wodurch aktive Partizipation erschwert wird. Es stellt sich also die Frage, wie man ältere Nutzer mit geringer Technikerfahrung dazu befähigen kann, sich als Co-Designer kritisch und konstruktiv in den Gestaltprozess neuer IKT-Systeme einzubringen. Im Folgenden wird gezeigt, wie das Konzept der HoA im Gestaltungsprozess mit älteren Nutzern eingesetzt wurde und welche Potentiale und Herausforderungen sich daraus ergaben.

2 Stand der Forschung

Mehrere Forschungsarbeiten über PD mit Älteren berichten von deren Schwierigkeiten, sich neue Technologien vorzustellen (Lindsay et al. 2012) und raten dazu, diskutierbare Artefakte und Praxen anzubieten (Massimi & Baecker 2006; Güldenpfennig & Fitzpatrick 2013). Rice

& Alm (2008) experimentieren mit neuen Visualisierungsmethoden wie dem interaktiven Theater, um Ideen in einer greifbaren Form zu präsentieren. Davidson & Jensen (2013) befürchten, dass eine geringere Technikerfahrung Ältere zu weniger effektiven Co-Designern macht. Ein Technikworkshop vor der eigentlichen PD-Sitzung kann hier die nötige Erfahrung vermitteln, um Potentiale und Grenzen der Technologie zu erfahren (Ellis et al. 1999). Eisma et al. (2003) berichten von positiven Erfahrungen mit Hands-on-Sessions. Hier bildet das direkte Erfahren der neuen Technik eine Diskussionsbasis und eröffnet dem Nutzer einen Gestaltungsraum, der ihn zur Teilnahme am Co-Design befähigt. Bisher ist allerdings nichts über den praktischen Einsatz dieses Tools im iTV-Design bekannt. Dieser Beitrag soll daher zeigen, ob mithilfe von HoA Nutzer ohne jede Erfahrung mit der Technologie dazu ermächtigt werden können, einen wertvollen Beitrag im Designprozess zu leisten.

3 Projektkontext und Methodik

Im Kontext des dreijährigen Forschungsprojekts „Sehr Mobil" entsteht in enger Zusammenarbeit mit Nutzern der Zielgruppe 60+ eine Plattform zur Erhaltung ihrer Mobilität, welche Informationen zu ÖPNV, Fahrdiensten und Mitfahrtgelegenheiten bündelt. Der gewählte Living-Lab-Ansatzes ermöglicht die Entwicklung nutzerzentrierter Innovationen in engen Austausch mit den Nutzern und die Evaluation in realen Lebenskontexten (Müller et al. 2013). So entstanden bereits eine Smartphone-Applikation und eine Internetpräsenz. Der nächste Schritt ist die Entwicklung einer TV-Anwendung, mit der die Nutzer das Angebot auch am TV mithilfe einer Google-TV-Box nutzen können. Die Hands-on-Session fand mit neun Nutzern im Rahmen eines Workshops zur Generierung von Anforderungen und Entwürfe für die iTV-App statt. Die Teilnehmer sind zwischen 60 und 84 Jahre alt und im Vergleich zu anderen Nutzergruppen als eher technikfern einzuordnen, obwohl die meisten von ihnen bereits Erfahrung im Umgang mit einem Computer oder einem Mobiltelefon haben. Die Technologien Smartphone und iTV waren den meisten aber zu Projektbeginn gänzlich unbekannt. Im Rahmen des Living Labs nehmen die Nutzer seit etwa zwei Jahren regelmäßig an verschiedenen Studien und Schulungen teil, sodass sie sowohl mit der PD-Methodik, als auch mit uns Forschern und den anderen Teilnehmern gut vertraut sind. Zudem nutzen alle im Zuge des Projekts ein eigenes Smartphone, wodurch sie sich ein Grundverständnis dieses Medium sowie einen Überblick über technische Realisierungsmöglichkeiten im Mobilitätskontext angeeignet haben (Meurer et al. 2013). Zu Beginn des Workshops reflektierten die Nutzer ihre Einstellung zum Medium TV, dann wurden in einem szenario-gestützten Brainstorming Anwendungsideen von iTV in Bezug auf Mobilitätsunterstützung diskutiert. Anschließend explorierte die Gruppe in einem wohnzimmerähnlichen Setting die Google-TV-Umgebung. Anhand verschiedener Apps (Videoportal, Nachrichten, ÖPNV-Verbindungen) erprobten die Teilnehmer den Umgang mit der Fernbedienung, das Navigieren und Selektieren von Inhalten und Texteingabe. Dabei erhielten sie die Aufgabe, ihre Eindrücke auf vorbereiteten Karten mit den Themen „Mir gefällt/mich stört", „Ich wünsche mir", „Ich finde überflüssig" und „Es fällt mir leicht/schwer" festzuhalten. Zum Schluss wurden aus den gesammelten Ideen Designentwürfe mittels Stift und Papier visualisiert.

4 Lessons learnt

Im Folgenden wird auf die wichtigsten Vorteile und Herausforderungen eingegangen, die sich bei der Anwendung der Hands-on-Activities gezeigt haben.

4.1 Fokussierung und Lenkung

Der offene, explorative Charakter der Session und der tendenziell große Redebedarf dieser Nutzergruppe sorgen für eine kreativ-chaotische Atmosphäre, in der der Moderator die Gruppe immer wieder auf das Thema fokussieren muss. Die Aufgaben sollten daher klar und prägnant sein und wiederholt werden, um thematische Verfehlungen zu vermeiden. Hier zeigt sich ein Vorteil der Karten darin, dass das Feedback im Gegensatz zu Fragebogentechniken direkt eingesehen und ggf. nachgefragt werden kann. Zudem regt das offene Ausfüllen die Teilnehmer untereinander zur Technikdiskussion an.

4.2 Technikeinstellung und Kritikvermeidung

Die Teilnehmer wurden gebeten, von jedem Kartentyp mindestens einen auszufüllen, sodass sie gleichermaßen positive wie negative Aspekte reflektierten. Dies wirkte der Tatsache entgegen, dass sich viele Ältere davor scheuen, Technik zu kritisieren (Eisma et al. 2003). Obwohl die Karten merklich zur Kritik ermutigten, fielen häufig kritische Äußerungen, die die Teilnehmer aber erst auf Nachfrage des Moderators für „aufschreibenswert“ hielten. Viele Teilnehmer gaben sich selbst die Schuld an einem Bedienproblem oder formulierten positive Aussagen nur unter der Bedingung, zuvor eine Bedienungsanleitung gelesen zu haben.

4.3 Soziale Aspekte

Vertrauensbildung wird häufig als Erfolgsfaktor für PD-Projekte mit Älteren angesehen (Massimi & Baecker 2006). Dies war in unserem Setting durch die Einbettung in ein Living Lab gegeben. Die Vertrautheit der Teilnehmer fördert die gemeinsame Exploration der Technologie, brachte aber auch neue Probleme mit sich. Die unterschiedlichen Grade an Technikaffinität unter den Nutzern übten auf die Unerfahrenen den Druck aus, sich vor den anderen nicht blamieren zu wollen. Unerfahrene gaben daher den Controller oft an Nutzer mit vermeintlich höherer Expertise ab, wenn sie selbst auf ein Nutzungsproblem stießen. Hier sollte der Moderator eine positive Umgebung des zwanglosen Explorierens schaffen, in der sich alle Nutzer gleichermaßen an der Interaktion beteiligen.

4.4 Öffnen neuer Möglichkeitsräume

Während einige Teilnehmer zunächst den Nutzen einer iTV-App anzweifelten, war während der Session eine gewisse Öffnung für die Technologie zu bemerken. Das praktische Erfahren und das bewusste Formulieren positiver Aspekte vermittelten die Stärken des Geräts eindrucksvoller, als es eine bloße Beschreibung oder Abbildung des Mediums vermochte. Umgekehrt konnten die Nutzer in der anschließenden Designphase gezielt auf die zuvor erfahrenen Schwächen Bezug nehmen. Entgegen der Befürchtung, die vorherige Exploration einer ÖPNV-App könne eine gewisse Designfixation mit sich bringen (Davidson & Jensen 2013), half die App viel mehr dabei, den Gestaltungsraum der Technologie besser zu begreifen und leistete einen eher inspirierenden Beitrag zum späteren Design.

5 Zusammenfassung

Obwohl das Durchführen von Hands-on-Sessions mit Älteren viel Aufwand und Disziplin erfordert, erweist sich dieses Werkzeug als hilfreich, um Nutzern eine unbekannte Technologie nahezubringen und ihnen eine kritische Stimme im PD-Prozess zu verleihen. Es hilft beim Überwinden von Skepsis, eröffnet einen gemeinsamen Gestaltungsraum und befähigt Ältere, einen wertvollen Beitrag zur Entwicklung zielgruppengerechter IKT-Lösungen zu leisten.

Referenzen

Davidson, J.L. & Jensen, C. (2013). Participatory Design with Older Adults: An Analysis of Creativity in the Design of Mobile Healthcare Applications. In Proc. of CC'13. ACM: New York. [S. 114–123].

Eisma, R., Dickinson, A., Goodman, J., Mival, O., Syme, A., & Tiwari, L. (2003). Mutual inspiration in the development of new technology for older people. In Proc. of Include '03. Helen Hamlyn Institute: London. [S. 252-259].

Ellis, R. D. & Cochran, D. L. (1999). Practices to encourage participation of older adults in research and development. In Ext. Abstracts of CHI '99. ACM: New York. [S. 39–40].

Güldenpfennig F. & Fitzpatrick G. (2013). Towards Rapid Technology Probes for Senior People. In: Holzinger A., Ziefle M., Hitz M., Debevc M. (Hrsg). Human Factors in Computing and Informatics. Springer: Berlin. [S. 664–671].

Lindsay, S., Jackson, D., Schofield, G. & Olivier, P. (2012). Engaging older people using participatory design. In Proc. of CHI '12. ACM: New York. [S. 1199 – 1208].

Massimi, M. & Baecker, R. (2006). Participatory Design Process with Older Users. In Proc. of the UbiCoomp2006 Workshop on future media.

Meurer, J., Stein, M. & Stevens, G. (2013). Living Labs zur Gestaltung innovativer Mobilitätskonzepte für ältere Menschen. In: Boll, S., Maaß, S. & Malaka, R. (Hrsg.), Mensch & Computer '13 - Workshopband. München: Oldenbourg Verlag. [S. 95-102].

Müller, C., Neufeldt, C., Jakobi, T. & Wulf, V. (2013). Ankerpunkte für das Participatory Design mit älteren Menschen. In: Boll, S., Maaß, S. & Malaka, R. (Hrsg.), Mensch & Computer '13 - Workshopband. München: Oldenbourg Verlag. (S. 347-354).

Rice, M. & Alm, N. (2008). Designing new interfaces for digital interactive television usable by older adults. Computers in Entertainment, 6(1).

M. Koch, A. Butz & J. Schlichter (Hrsg.): Mensch und Computer 2014 Tagungsband, München: Oldenbourg Wissenschaftsverlag, 2014, S. 339-342.

Illuminated Ring – A Wearable Display to Support Fluid Intake

Bengt Lüers[1], Thomas Crone[1], Veronika Strokova[1], Jutta Fortmann[1], Wilko Heuten[2], Susanne Boll[1]

[1]University of Oldenburg, Germany,
[2]OFFIS-Institute for Information Technology, Germany

Abstract

Insufficient drinking remains a widespread problem. Reminder signals help to remind a person to drink, but are often experienced as obtrusive and impractical in everyday life. We designed Illuminated Ring, a wearable display that supports fluid intake in that it displays the time elapsed since the last drink via single point lights. In a user-centered design process, we developed an interactive ring, which we evaluated in an exploratory field study. Initial results show that Illuminated Ring is perceived as an unobtrusive display which can help to drink sufficiently.

1 Introduction

Sufficient liquid consumption is essential to the human body's health. Nutritionists advise to drink up to 2 liters a day (EFSA, 2011), but only few people actually meet their drinking needs. In many cases, making people aware of their drinking behavior can already have a positive effect. As drinking is an everyday task and happens in various situations, a system for making its user aware needs to work properly yet discrete in various situations.

In this work, we propose Illuminated Ring: a display of single point lights discreetly integrated into a ring. Illuminated Ring displays feedback on the user's drinking behavior in an unobtrusive and always accessible way, while being small and pervasive at the same time.

2 Related Work

Ring displays aim to improve everyday tasks by miniaturizing traditional displays to the size of a ring. Smarty Ring[1] displays notifications of a smartphone as illuminated icons on a ring.

---

1 http://smartyring.com

Ring Clock[2] displays the time by illuminating the corresponding numbers engraved in a ring. While these indicator displays keep the visualization simple, their discrete visualizations do not resemble the level of a person's fluid intake, which has a progressive character. There are several wearable devices that serve as drinking reminders. Ah!Qua[3] is a fashionable wristband that prompts a user to have a glass of water by gently vibrating. The W+Plus anti-dehydration monitor concept[4] displays a configurable countdown on four ring-mounted seven-segment displays. While these systems tackle the issue of insufficient drinking, none of them supports continuous awareness because they trigger to a designated time and don´t show a progression.

To fill this gap, we propose Illuminated Ring: a light-based wearable display integrated into a ring that unobtrusively supports daily fluid intake.

3 Design

The following section presents the design process of Illuminated Ring. We describe a survey, the implementation of two prototypes, and a user study in which we evaluated the designs.

Survey
In order to reveal the users' needs and expectations, we conducted an online survey in which 53 people took part (Males: 21, Age: from 16, most in range *21–25*). 62% of the participants stated they would like to drink more. Most of the participants were students from Germany and Russia.

54% of the participants opted for a notification interval of 1-2 hours. 15 participants found green and blue LEDs most intuitive. We gave the participants the choice between different design features: The ring could have one or several LEDs on the inner or outer side of the palm. The LEDs could blink, fade or change color. The button to enter a drink could be on the opposite or same side as the LEDs. The participants did not show preference to either of these choices.

Implementation
As there were no clear preferences according to the ring and light design, we built two ring prototypes with four different light designs. We used silver ring blanks that were about 3 mm wide and had a platform of about 1 cm in diameter on top. The triple-LED ring had three blue SMD-LEDs and a button underneath (Fig. 1). The single-LED ring had one 5-mm Duo-LED (blue and green) on the bottom side (Fig. 3) and a button on the top side (Fig. 2). The light designs for the single-LED ring were two blue to green gradients, one in a linear and one in an exponential fashion (Fig. 4 top left and top center). The two light designs for the triple-LED ring were a countdown switching the blue LEDs off one by one and a runlight

2 http://www.ringclock.net/

3 http://www.ahqua.at/

4 http://www.folkwang-uni.de/de/home/hochschule/projekte/vollanzeige/?projektid=176&showdetails=1&%20backlink=268&cHash=e6c0373

orbiting the finger at increasing speed (Fig. 4 top right and bottom). We connected the ring via a flexible cable to a wristband that carried a lithium-polymer battery, a voltage regulator circuit and an Arduino LilyPad microcontroller as they would not have fitted on the ring.

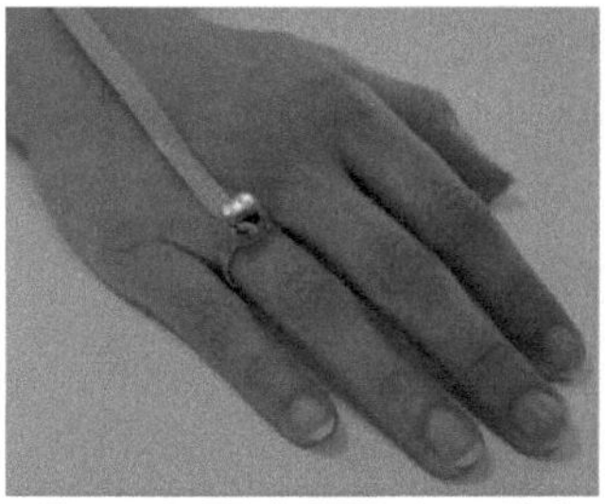

Figure 1: Triple-LED ring with 3 LEDs and a button underneath

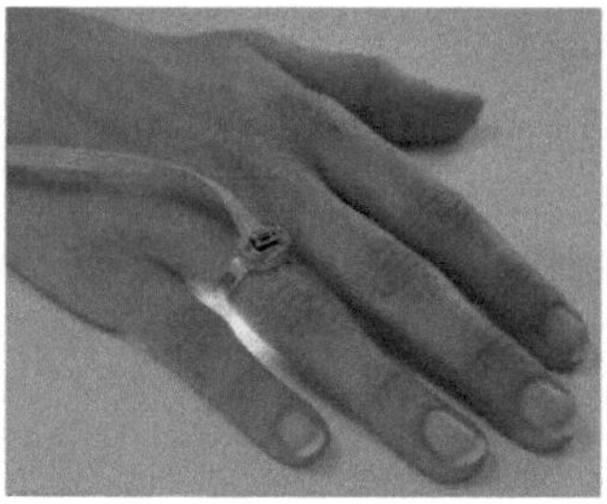

Figure 2: Single-LED ring (top side with button)

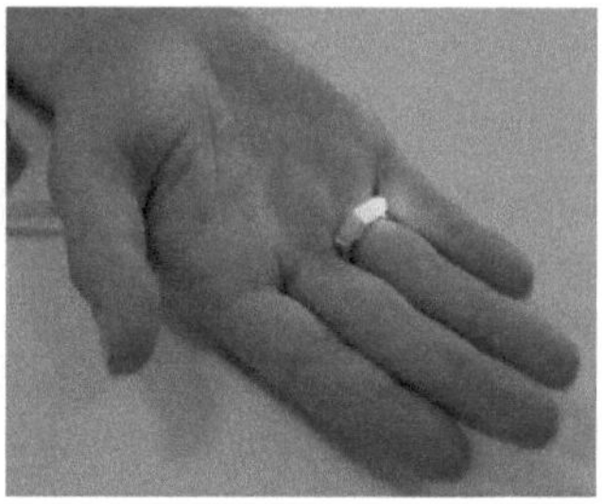

Figure 3: Single-LED ring (bottom side with LED)

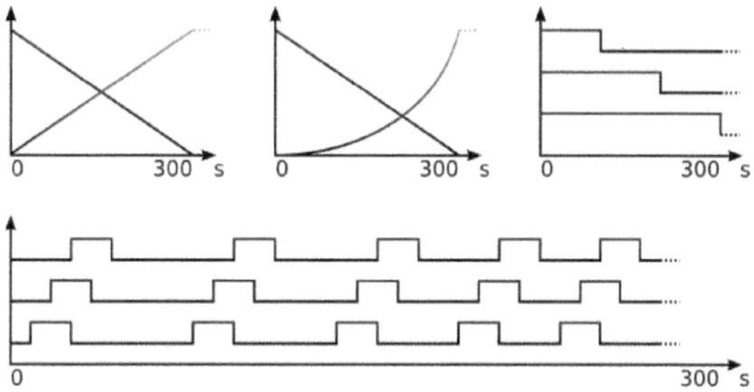

Figure 4: Light designs – line color indicates if LED is on (blue or green) or off (black), ***top row****: blue to green linear, blue to green exponential, countdown;* ***bottom row:*** *runlight*

User Study in the Lab

The following section describes the laboratory user study we conducted to find usability issues and to determine which design features our participants preferred.

We programmed the LilyPad so that the four light designs were displayed in random order and for 5 minutes each. Based on the "framework for evaluating ubiquitous computing applications" (Scholtz & Consolvo, 2004), which covers e.g. "Application Robustness" and "Appeal", we prepared interview questions about each light design, each ring and the wristband. The user study was conducted with 6 participants (Males: 5; Age: 21 to 32, M: 26, SD: 3.4). Two study conductors met separately with each participant in a well-lit and quiet room. The participant got handed out an informational sheet, signed a written approval and got verbal introduction. The participant was given the task to build with Lego bricks for 5 minutes while wearing the wristband and the ring which displayed the light designs. This activity should simulate an everyday, manual task. It ensured that the ring moved in the user's field of view, but hindered the user to focus it for longer than a glance. After 5 minutes, the participant was interviewed. This process was repeated for each ring and light design. At the end the participant could give additional feedback.

The participants were always able to fulfill their task. Most felt that a small ring is suitable to show information on drinking behavior. Many participants wanted to drop the wristband or the ring, forcing all electronics in one component. Single participants criticized the light as being too bright. The triple-LED with the countdown light design was liked most. The LEDs were favored to be on the inner side of the hand and the button to be on the opposite side.

4 Field Study

The following section describes an exploratory field study we conducted to evaluate the practicability of the revised prototype when used in real life situations.

Based on the results of the user study, we built a revised prototype with three blue LEDs facing inward opposing a button. The light design period was set to 90 minutes because that was the preferred drinking interval in the survey. The LEDs' brightness was lowered to 25%. The field study was conducted in Oldenburg, Germany, with 11 participants (Males: 5; Age: 22-83, M: 42, SD: 22), which we gathered from personal circles of acquaintances. When we met the participants at their homes, we introduced the study, handed out an informational sheet and let the participant sign a written consent. Participants were equipped with the revised Illuminated Ring and instructed to use it in their daily life and to push the button once each time they took a drink, which would (re-)start the period of the light design. We then left the participant with the system for a full day and met again for an interview.

The revised prototype was perceived as a suitable display for fluid intake. Although we had lowered the brightness since the initial implementation, it was still subject to criticism. Many participants estimated they drank more when wearing the ring, e.g. a participant said: "Even though I am aware of my drinking behavior, I drank more using the ring."

5 Conclusion

In this paper we presented Illuminated Ring, a light-based wearable display to support fluid intake. In a user-centered design process, we designed two ring prototypes covering alternative designs, evaluated them in a user study and based on the results built a revised prototype. We tested it in an exploratory field study and found it to be a suitable display for fluid intake. Further improvements we would like to make are to lower the brightness further or even adapt the brightness dynamically to ambient lighting conditions. In the next step we want to conduct a field experiment to investigate Illuminated Ring's effect on a user's drinking behavior.

References

EFSA Panel on Dietetic Products, Nutrition and Allergies (NDA)(2011). *Scientific opinion on the substantiation of health claims related to water and maintenance of normal physical and cognitive functions.* EFSA Journal 9, 4, 2075.

Scholtz, J., Consolvo S. (2004).*"Toward a framework for evaluating ubiquitous computing applications."*. Pervasive Computing, IEEE 3.2: 82-88

M. Koch, A. Butz & J. Schlichter (Hrsg.): Mensch und Computer 2014 Tagungsband,
München: Oldenbourg Wissenschaftsverlag, 2014, S. 343-346.

Intermodal personalized Travel Assistance and Routing Interface

Stefan Schaffer, Norbert Reithinger

DFKI GmbH, Projektbüro Berlin, Alt-Moabit 91c, 10559 Berlin

Abstract

An increasing amount of available data sources and intermodal travelling pose a challenge for the design of mobility apps. This paper examines the concept of an interface for intermodal personalized travel assistance and routing. The analysis of two central use cases *intermodal routing* and *personalization* revealed pitfalls and gaps for the design of mobility apps.

1 Introduction

The market of mobility applications underwent a strong growth over the last years. Besides the well-known transit solution by Google (Ferris et al. 2010), more and more app-based mobility services emerge (Weissman & Villalobos 2012). Standard functionalities include stating departure/arrival time, origin, and destination, finding the nearest transport stations, computing the shortest way between them and giving information about departure times, connections, lines involved and total travel time. In addition to this basic feature, each app usually offers some unique feature like e.g. augmented reality (Borgia et al. 2012), real-time information on the quality of service or route planning between special points of interests (Inglesant & Sasse 2007). At the same time, especially for big cities, an increasing amount of data sources is getting available. This includes static data like public transport routes as well as dynamic data like real-time information about weather and road traffic (Leitsch 2002). Future mobility apps will offer situation-related routing proposals by incorporating various kinds of data as well as combinations of transportation modes. The intermodal trip planner of the MOLECULES project e.g. calculates routes considering electro mobility and public transportation (Belinchón Rubio 2014). The number of available data sources together with the possibilities of intermodal transportation result in a large number of options regarding the personalization of routing requests. This development poses a challenge for the design of mobile applications, as the complexity of interfaces usually increases with the number of options. In this paper we reflect a concept of a mobility app supporting citizens in finding environment friendly routes. As a basic principle within the app, gamification will be integrated in a way that users can earn "green leaves" for choosing "green" connections.

Following a user centred approach, we discuss two central use cases, namely *multimodal routing* and *personalization*, and deduce implications for system and interface design.

2 Use Case Analysis

The use cases are depicted with the help of a functional mock-up (Figure 1). "Functional" means that the illustrated functionalities are supposed to be integrated into a GUI. Further interface and interaction design works will be carried out in a later development process.

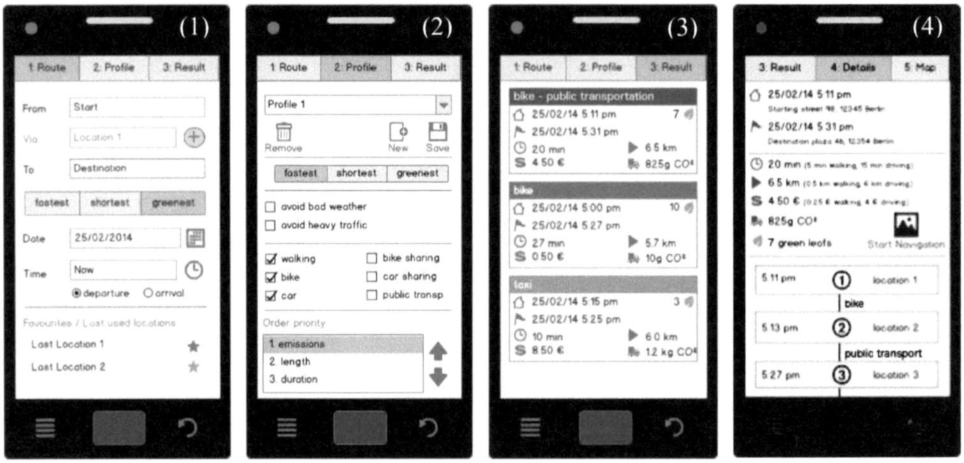

Figure 1: mock-up screens from left to right: (1) basic routing information, (2) personalization by options and routing preferences, (3) routing results, (4) navigation details for the selected result.

2.1 Intermodal Routing

Use case: A citizen is using the mobility app for planning a trip. Routing proposals are calculated and listed with the app. Amongst others, the app is offering an intermodal route comprising bike and public transportation. Both, an acceptable travel time at this particular time of the day, and the chance to be rewarded with "green leave" credits for choosing an environmentally friendly option convince the user to go for the intermodal option.

Implications: The basic routing information for intermodal routes on screen 1 does not differ substantially from common routing interfaces. The horizontal radio buttons, *fastest/shortest/ greenest*, allow the user for the prioritisation of routing proposals. The actual purpose of green mobility is taken into account by including an option for green routes. Last connections are displayed in a favourites list. The routing results are presented on screen 3. The intermodal route within the red routing proposal is clearly distinguishable as the different traffic modes are listed. The system provides information about CO_2 emissions and earnable points for "green" routes. Screen 4 shows details regarding traffic modes and the gamification information.

2.2 Personalization

Use case: A citizen is using the mobility app for planning a trip. Having access to the user profile, the App is proposing to take a public transport connection. The App is taking into account actual and forecasted weather and traffic situation. As rain is forecasted and the traffic situation between origin and destination is bad due to various construction sites and a heavy traffic load, modes "bike" and "car" were disregarded.

Implications: Personalization options are shown on screen 2. At the top of the screen a means to save profiles is integrated. For the *fastest/shortest/greenest* option a default can be set. Considering the integration of real-time data, options to *avoid bad weather* and *avoid heavy traffic* can be checked. The inclusion of traffic modes can be configured. At the end of the screen a means to order the priority of routing proposals is included.

3 Discussion

Intermodal routing only marginally affects the elements within the GUI. The task of gathering fundamental routing information is basically the same as for classical routing. However intermodal routing has to be particularly considered, if routing proposals and proposal details are displayed. Consequences for the GUI can arise, if the modal split within the proposed routes is high. If the number of transport modalities increases, the presentation of routing proposals within a list may have to be adapted in such a way that the information is still easy to process for a user. The gamification aspect of the mock-up only slightly affects the GUI so far. Displaying "green leaves" in the upper right corner of a routing proposal logically separates the gamification information from the routing data. On the proposal details screen "green leaves" are displayed as the last item within a list of detail information. When further developing the interface design, the way of presenting this information should be rethought, to optimally fit the users needs. Personalisation must provide means to store information about the users personal travel preferences, common start and end locations and information related to the usage of the app, including gamification behaviour. It has to be determined, which exact information has to be used and stored. It is also to be determined, whether the users profile information, including personalization options, will reside locally on the user's device, or centrally, on a server. However, processing requirements may call for at least a local copy. Data protection requirements also have to be examined, to find a viable solution. The profile data is the basis for the user adaptive intermodal routing. As can be seen, some of the personal preferences like *avoiding bad weather* require the inclusion of external services in the process of personalizing a route for the user. The data collected from the user's interactions, should be stored in a user history. This history can be used to create suggestions, increase the quality of the routing, and to advise users about their CO_2 footprint. Intermodal travelling and data sources produce more options for the user. Depending on the number of options, reconstruction of the personalization screen should be taken into account.

If more options have to be integrated, users could lose the track of the GUI. Limiting the number of options may be able by focusing on a specific user group or purpose of the app.

4 Conclusion and Future Work

The aim of this paper was to examine the concept of an interface for intermodal personalized travel assistance and routing. By analysing two central use cases, *intermodal routing* and *personalization*, pitfalls and gaps of the actual concept were revealed. Regarding the GUI design, valuable solutions for the presentation of the modal split within a routing proposal have to be found. We expect that a logical separation of functions related to utility and gamification functions improve the usability of an application. With respect to an increasing number of personalization options, resulting from available data sources and intermodal travelling, we recommend to focus on specific user groups or app purpose. Future work of this project will include interface and interaction design, development of a gamification concept, integration of speech interaction and system evaluation.

Acknowledgements

This research was supported by the European Union Seventh Framework Programme (FP7/2007-2013) under grant agreement 608991, project STREETLIFE.

Literaturverzeichnis

Belinchón Rubio, S. (2014). *MOLECULES - D3.2 Reference architecture and principles*. EU Project, 297244.

Borgia, F., De Marsico, M., Panizzi, E., & Pietrangeli, L. (2012). ARMob-Augmented Reality for Urban Mobility in RMob. In *Proceedings of the International Working Conference on Advanced Visual Interfaces* (pp. 258-261). ACM.

Ferris, B., Watkins, K., & Borning, A. (2010). Location-aware tools for improving Public transit Usability. *IEEE Pervasive Computing*, 9(1), 13-19.

Inglesant, P., & Sasse, M. A. (2007). Usability is the best policy: public policy and the lived experience of transport systems in London. In *Proceedings of the 21st British HCI Group Annual Conference on People and Computers: HCI... but not as we know it-Volume 1* (pp. 35-44). British Computer Society.

Leitsch, B. (2002). A Public-Private Partnership for Mobility-Traffic Management Center Berlin. In *9th World Congress on Intelligent Transport Systems*.

Weissman, D. & Villalobos, M. (2012). *Mobility Apps*. UC Berkeley: Institute of Urban and Regional Development.

Kontaktinformationen

stefan.schaffer@dfki.de

M. Koch, A. Butz & J. Schlichter (Hrsg.): Mensch und Computer 2014 Tagungsband,
München: Oldenbourg Wissenschaftsverlag, 2014, S. 347-350.

Is OntoWiki useful as Collaborative Working Tool for Engineers?

Selver Softic, Alexander Stocker, Manfred Rosenberger, Jürgen Zernig and Michael Schmeja

Area Information and Process Management, Virtual Vehicle Research Center, Inffeldgasse 21/A/I, Graz, Austria

Abstract

In this work we examined whether OntoWiki[1] can be used as collaborative working tool for engineers. We used a specific domain related ontology PROTARES (PROject TAsks RESources)[2], created in our previous work on collaboration modelling (Softic et al. 2013) from a real world use case, to adapt OntoWiki for the case study. With this example we want to test to which extent, semantically driven customized applications can support monitoring, reflection and decision making in engineering collaboration scenario.

1 Motivation

Intensive changes on product within engineering working process need a high communication and consolidation effort (Müller et al. 2012). This is still carried out in meetings and does not interact directly with engineering artefacts affected by these decisions. Our work aims to overcome some aspects of this problem by offering a collaborative working tool based upon collaboration model ontology PROTARES (PROject TAsks RESources) which we defined and created in our previous efforts on this topic (Softic et al. 2013). As collaborative tool for our model we used a OntoWiki. Our solution allows creation, editing, tracking and visualizing of data about tasks, depending requirements and goals, persons involved ,components and resources used, particularly during the planning and development phase of the product. With this case study we want to demonstrate the usefulness of OntoWiki as enabler tool for the purposes of collaborative working in the engineering environment.

---

[1] http://ontowiki.net

[2] http://purl.org/protares/ns/1.0/

2 Related Work

Semantic Web technologies fit well for designing complex models and relations. Their flexibility regarding changes in information model as well inference potentials are outlined earlier in research efforts like (Wache et al. 2001). Recent research (Jun et al. 2007, Matsokis & Kiritsis 2010) has shown that ontology based approach of modelling information in product design and development offers more flexibility on context changes than any other method applied so far. Those benefits, in particular for the segments of product life cycle, have been outlined by the work of (Young 2007). OntoWiki is a Wiki based collaborative environment application for maintenance and creation of semantically modelled data, originally developed to support distributed knowledge engineering scenarios (Auer et al. 2007, Frischmuth et al. 2010). It is extensible and it may also serve as development framework for knowledge based applications, as well as user interface for arbitrary RDF knowledge graphs.

3 OntoWiki as Collaboration Tool

We decided to reuse domain ontology named PROTARES (PROject TAsks RESources) created in our previous work (Softic et al. 2013). PROTARES is a light-weight ontology, which covers essential context of collaboration between engineers and project manager, on tasks level for development of racing car. The ontology combines own concepts, as well widely used vocabularies like FOAF (Friend of A Friend)[3] to describe persons, and Requirements Management Ontology[4],defined by the OSLC (Open Services for Lifecycle Collaboration) initiative, to describe requirements. In Figure 1 we see an example of visualization plug-in and editing interface in OntoWiki with PROTARES instances. This example shows the tree like visualization of a collaboration task with all related information. The visualization allows further on click expansion of linked concepts and uses colour schema to distinguish entities. OntoWiki enables user to get a fast overview over related resources, persons, and components related to this part of the work as well to monitor and edit changes on tasks, requirements, goals and deadlines.

[3] http://xmlns.com/foaf/spec/

[4] http://open-services.net/ns/rm/

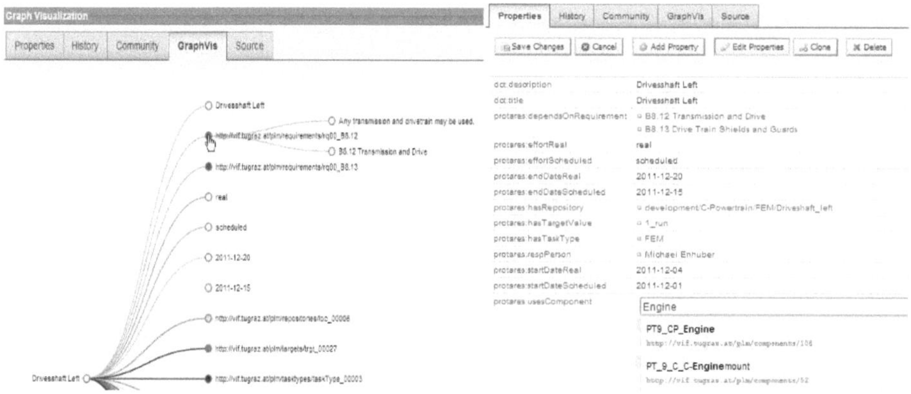

Figure 1: Visualisation and editing of collaboration task in OntoWiki

4 Evaluation and Conclusion

Our use case aims particularly on knowledge and information exchange in collaboration. We evaluated our prototype with Knowledge Management Approach (KMA) method firstly introduced by (Vizcaino et al. 2005). The KMA method analyse six aspects of the knowledge management process, which are: *Knowledge creation*, *Knowledge accumulation, Knowledge sharing*, *Knowledge utilization*, *Knowledge internalization* and *Knowledge integration*. This is done by evaluating based upon a checklist with questions regarding each of six aspects. According to results presented in Figure 2 our prototype supports fully the aspects of: *Knowledge integration*, *Knowledge accumulation*.

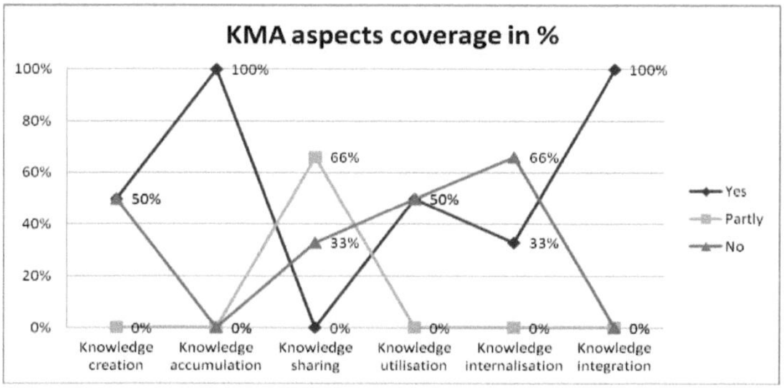

Figure 2: Positive, partial, and negative feature coverage in % for six aspects of KMA.

Evaluation of partial feature coverage depicted in Figure 2 reveals that aspect of *Knowledge sharing* is not covered yet. Negative feature coverage reveals the aspect *Knowledge internalisation* as not supported as well. Features for aspects like *Knowledge creation* and Knowledge *utilisation* are covered up to 50%. The preliminary evaluation we made implicitly confirmed observations showing that the tool can contribute strongly to

Knowledge integration, *Knowledge accumulation*, partially good to *Knowledge creation* and *Knowledge utilisation*, as well with some additional effort in the future also very intensively to Knowledge *sharing*.

Acknowledgements

The authors would like to acknowledge the financial support of the "COMET K2 - Competence Centres for Excellent Technologies Programme" of the Austrian Federal Ministry for Transport, Innovation and Technology (BMVIT), the Austrian Federal Ministry of Economy, Family and Youth (BMWFJ), the Austrian Research Promotion Agency (FFG), the Province of Styria and the Styrian Business Promotion Agency (SFG).

References

Auer, S., Dietzold, S., Lehmann, J., & Riechert, T. (2007). OntoWiki: A tool for social, semantic collaboration. In *Proceedings WWW 2007 Workshop on Social and Collaborative*. Banff, Canada.

Frischmuth, P., Martin, M., Tramp, S., Riechert, T., & Auer, S. (2013). Ontowiki-an authoring, publiccation and visualization interface for the data web. *SemanticWeb Journal (SWJ).*

Herskovic, V., Pino, J. A., Ochoa, S. F., & Antunes, P. (2007). Evaluation methods for groupware systems. In *Proceedings of the 13th International Conference on Groupware: Design Implementation, and Use. CRIWG'07*. Berlin, Heidelberg: Springer-Verlag, p. 328–336.

Jun, H., Kiritsis, D., & Xirouchakis, P. C. (2007). A primitive ontology model for product lifecycle meta data in the closed-loop plm. In *Enterprise Interoperability II*, Springer, p. 729–740.

Matsokis, A. & Kiritsis, D. (2010). An ontology-based approach for product lifecycle management. *Computers in Industry, Semantic Web Computing in Industry*, 61(8): 787–797.

Müller, P., Pasch, F., Drewinski, R., Bedenbender, H., Hayka, H., & Stark, R. (2012). Study on collaborative product development and digital engineering tools. In *PLM*, p. 389–399.

Softic, S., Rosenberger, M., Denger, A., Fritz, J., & Stocker, A. (2013). Semantically based visual tracking of engineering tasks in automotive product lifecycle. *In Proceedings of the 13th International Conference on Knowledge Management and Knowledge Technologies, ACM.*, p. 36.

Vizcaino, A., Piattini, M., Martinez, M., & Aranda, G. (2005). Evaluating collaborative applications from a knowledge management approach. In *Enabling Technologies: Infrastructure for Collaborative Enterprise, 2005. 14th IEEE International Workshops*, p. 221–225.

Wache, H., Vögele, T., Visser, U., Stuckenschmidt, H., Schuster, G., Neumann, H., and H¨ubner, S. (2001). *Ontology-based integration of information — a survey of existing approaches. In IJCAI–01 Workshop: Ontologies and Information Sharing*, p. 108–117.

Young, R., Gunendran, G., Cutting-Decelle, A., & Gruninger, M. (2007). Manufacturing knowledge sharing in plm: A progression towards the use of heavyweight ontologies. *International Journal of Production Research*, 45(7):1505–1519

Contact

Selver Softic, Area Information and Process Management ,Virtual Vehicle Research Center

Inffeldgasse 21/A, Graz, Austria, selver.softic@v2c2.at

M. Koch, A. Butz & J. Schlichter (Hrsg.): Mensch und Computer 2014 Tagungsband, München: Oldenbourg Wissenschaftsverlag, 2014, S. 351-354.

Kann man Website-Usability schnell valide mit Screenshots erfassen?

Meinald T. Thielsch[1], Ronja Engel[1], Gerrit Hirschfeld[2]

Institut für Psychologie, Westfälische Wilhelms-Universität Münster[1]
Deutsches Kinderschmerzzentrum, Vestische Kinder- und Jugenklinik Datteln[2]

Zusammenfassung

Um die Frage zu beantworten ob sich Website-Usability schnell valide anhand von Screenshots beurteilen lässt, wurde die wahrgenommene Usability mit objektiven Maßen der tatsächlichen Leistung verglichen. Insgesamt beurteilten 57 Probanden die Usability nach der unterschiedlich langen Darbietung von Screenshots (50 ms, 500 ms und 10 s) sowie nach der interaktiven Nutzung von Testwebsites. Es zeigte sich, dass die Beurteilungen anhand von Screenshots für alle Darbietungszeiten weder mit den Urteilen nach der Interaktion noch mit den objektiven Maßen der Benutzerfreundlichkeit signifikant korrelierten. Stattdessen hängen die Usability-Beurteilungen anhand von Screenshots sehr stark mit der Ästhetik-Bewertung zusammen. Nur die Usability-Bewertungen nach einer Interaktion mit der Website korrelieren hoch signifikant mit objektiven Maßen wie Bearbeitungsdauer oder Aufgabenlösung und zeigen keine signifikante Korrelation zu Ästhetik-Einschätzungen. Usability-Bewertungen, die allein auf Basis von Screenshots gemacht werden, sind durch die wahrgenommene Ästhetik beeinflusst und als alleinige Basis für Usability-Tests kritisch zu sehen.

1 Theoretischer Hintergrund

Usability ist ein Kernkonstrukt der Mensch-Maschine-Interaktion (Hornbaek, 2006) und definiert sich über die Effektivität, Effizienz und Zufriedenheit mit der Benutzer mit einem interaktivem System vorgegebene Ziele erreichen können (ISO, 2010). Website-Usability ist demnach nicht alleine die Eigenschaft einer Website, sondern entsteht durch die Interaktion mit dieser in einem bestimmten Kontext. Es existieren unterschiedliche Ansätze diese zu erfassen von formal-analytischen Verfahren, bei denen Experten anhand festgelegter Kriterien die Usability bewerten, bis hin zu Fragebogeninstrumenten und „Think-aloud"-Usability-Tests (vgl. Gediga & Hamborg, 2002; Salaschek et al., 2007). In verschiedenen Studien, insbesondere bei der Erfassung des Ersteindrucks, wird Website-Usability anhand von Screenshots untersucht. Hierbei wurde festgestellt, dass Urteile über die Usability nach 50 ms Darbietungszeit eines Screenshots sehr hoch mit denen nach 500 s korrelieren (Lindgaard et al., 2011). Aufgrund der fehlenden Interaktionsmöglichkeit stellt sich jedoch die Frage worauf die Probanden ihr Urteil basierten. So ist anzunehmen, dass verwandte Konstrukte wie Ästhetik (vgl. Moshagen & Thielsch, 2010) diese Ersteindrucksurteile beeinflussen (vgl. Tractinsky et al., 2000).

Zentrale Frage unserer Studie ist, ob pre-use Usability-Urteile auf Basis von Screenshots mit denen nach einer interaktiven Auseinandersetzung mit der Webseite vergleichbar sind. Außerdem soll geprüft werden, inwieweit die wahrgenommene Usability mit objektiven Maßen zusammenhängt und durch die wahrgenommene Ästhetik beeinflusst wird.

2 Methodisches Vorgehen

2.1 Stichprobe

An der Studie nahmen 57 Personen im Alter von 19 bis 32 Jahren ($M = 23.09$; $SD = 2.79$) teil, 70.2 % (n = 40) waren weiblich. Die Teilnahme war freiwillig und anonym.

2.2 Versuchsmaterial

Die Stimuli bestanden aus 50 Screenshots von Webseiten aus zehn Website-Kategorien, die auf Basis bestehender Testsets zusammengestellt wurden. Um Einflüsse der Bekanntheit auf die Ergebnisse zu vermeiden, wurden gezielt unbekannte Websites ausgewählt.

2.3 Versuchsablauf und erfasste Variablen

Die Datenerhebung fand in kleinen Gruppen von bis zu acht Personen statt. Nach einer einführenden schriftlichen Instruktion folgten die Bewertungen der Websites als Screenshots in drei verschiedenen Zeitbedingungen und als vierter Block die Interaktion.

Die Usability wurde jeweils anhand einer sechsstufigen Likert-Skala von „gar nicht benutzerfreundlich" bis „sehr benutzerfreundlich" gegeben. Jede Bewertung wurde abgegeben nachdem ein Screenshot für eine fest definierte Zeitspanne (50, 500 oder 10.000 ms) präsentiert wurde. Jeder Block bestand aus 50 Trials, sodass jede der 50 Webseiten in randomisierter Reihenfolge einmal pro Block präsentiert wurde.

Anschließend sollten sich die Teilnehmer interaktiv mit einer Webseite auseinandersetzen, bevor sie erneut Urteile über die Usability abgaben. Für die interaktiven Aufgaben wurde aus jeder Kategorie eine der fünf Webseiten des Gesamtsets ausgewählt (eine Darbietung des gesamten Versuchssets hätte eine zu große zeitliche Belastung für die Probanden dargestellt). Bei der Formulierung der Fragen wurden möglichst mittelschwere Aufgaben angestrebt, so dass alle Aufgaben mit drei bis vier Klicks zu lösen waren. Als Antwort wurden jeweils fünf Alternativen im Multiple-Choice Format vorgegeben von denen immer eine richtig war und drei als Distraktoren dienten. Die fünfte Alternative lautete immer „Ich habe mich bemüht, die Antwort jedoch nicht gefunden". Als objektive Maße wurden die bei der Aufgabenbearbeitung benötigte Zeit und Korrektheit der Lösung erfasst.

3 Ergebnisse

Die subjektiven Usability-Bewertungen auf Basis von Screenshots die 50 ms präsentiert wurden korrelieren sehr hoch mit den Bewertungen nach 500 ms ($r = .89$, $p < .05$) und nach 10 s Präsentation ($r = .87$, $p < .05$). Keine dieser Bewertungen korrelierte signifikant mit den Bewertungen nach der Interaktionsbedingung und den objektiven Maßen (siehe Tabelle 1).

Es zeigt sich allerdings, dass die subjektiven Usability-Bewertungen in den verschiedenen Screenshotbedingungen sehr hoch mit Ästhetikeinschätzungen korrelieren (siehe Tabelle 1).

Usability-Bewertung in der Bedingung…	**Bearbeitungs-dauer**	**Aufgaben-lösung**	**Ästhetik-bewertung**
Screenshot für 50 ms	.08	.19	.75**
Screenshot für 500 ms	-.11	.07	.75**
Screenshot für 10 s	-.19	-.07	.84**
Nach Interaktion mit Website	-.86**	.62*	.05

*Tabelle 1: Korrelation der subjektiven Usability-Bewertungen mit den objektiven Usability-Maßen Bearbeitungsdauer und Aufgabenlösung sowie der subjektiven Ästhetikbewertung; * = $p < .05$; ** = $p < .01$*

4 Diskussion

Die Daten legen nahe, dass schnelle Usability-Bewertungen auf Basis von Screenshots vor allem die subjektive Ästhetik widerspiegeln. Um Website-Usability valide zu erfassen, das heißt mit Ersteindrucksmessungen die auch prädiktiv für tatsächliche Performanz sind, müssen die Befragten zuvor mit der Website interagieren können.

Diese Ergebnisse stehen im Einklang mit Studien, die eine sehr schnelle Verarbeitung ästhetischer Reize annehmen (vgl. Thielsch & Hirschfeld, 2012) und die von einem Halo-Effekt von Ästhetik- auf Usability-Urteile ausgehen (vgl. Hassenzahl & Monk, 2010). Bei der Interpretation von Studien, die die Usability ausschließlich anhand von Screenshots bewerten, ist nach unseren Ergebnissen Vorsicht geboten. Die vorliegenden Befunde untermauern nicht nur die Forderung von Hornbaek (2006) gleichzeitig objektive und subjektive Usability-Indikatoren zu erfassen. Noch mehr legen sie nahe, Webusability-Tests auf echten Interaktionen zu basieren. Die Idee in einzelnen Studien, dass Probanden allein auf Basis von Screenshots anhand von Cues wie Suchfeldern oder Navigationsbenennungen Usability valide einschätzen können, scheint aus unserer Sicht nicht haltbar.

Literaturverzeichnis

Gediga, G., & Hamborg, K. (2002). Evaluation in der Software-Ergonomie: Methoden und Modelle im Software-Entwicklungsprozess. *Zeitschrift für Psychologie*, *210*(1), 40–57.

Hassenzahl, M., & Monk, A. (2010). The Inference of Perceived Usability From Beauty. *Human-Computer Interaction*, *25*(3), 235-260.

Hornbaek, K. (2006). Current practice in measuring usability: Challenges to usability studies and research. *International Journal of Human-Computer Studies*, *64*(2), 79–102.

ISO (2010). *Ergonomics of human-system interaction - Part 210: Human-centred design for interactive systems (ISO 9241-210:2010)*. Geneva: International Organization for Standardisation.

Lindgaard, G., Dudek, C., Sen, D., Sumegi, L. & Noonan, P. (2011). An exploration of relations between visual appeal, trustworthiness and perceived usability of homepages. *ACM Transactions On Computer-Human Interaction*, *18*(1), 1-30.

Moshagen, M. & Thielsch, M. T. (2010). Facets of visual aesthetics. *International Journal of Human-Computer Studies,* 68, 689-709.

Salaschek M., Holling H., Freund P.A. & Kuhn J-T. (2007). Benutzbarkeit von Software. Vor- und Nachteile verschiedener Methoden und Verfahren. *Zeitschrift für Evaluation, 2*, 1-30.

Thielsch, M. T. & Hirschfeld, G. (2012). Spatial frequencies in aesthetic website evaluations – explaining how ultra-rapid evaluations are formed. *Ergonomics, 55* (7), 731-742.

Tractinsky, N., Katz, A. S. & Ikar, D. D. (2000). What is beautiful is usable. *Interacting With Computers*, *13*(2), 127-145.

M. Koch, A. Butz & J. Schlichter (Hrsg.): Mensch und Computer 2014 Tagungsband,
München: Oldenbourg Wissenschaftsverlag, 2014, S. 355-358.

M3I: A Framework for Mobile Multimodal Interaction

Andreas Möller[1], Stefan Diewald[1], Luis Roalter[1], Matthias Kranz[2]

Distributed Multimodal Information Processing Group, Technische Universität München[1]
Lehrstuhl für Informatik mit Schwerpunkt Eingebettete Systeme, Universität Passau[2]

Abstract

We present *M3I*, an extensive multimodal interaction framework for mobile devices, which simplifies and accelerates the creation of multimodal applications for prototyping and research. It provides an abstraction of information representations in different communication channels, unifies access to implicit and explicit information, and wires together the logic behind context-sensitive modality switches by a rule-based approach. In this paper, we present the structure and major features of our framework, and show exemplary implementations of interaction modalities with help of *M3I*.

1 Introduction and Motivation

Multimodality denotes the usage of more than one modality (simultaneously or sequentially) for input and output (Oviatt 1999). Particularly in mobile settings, individual unimodal interaction modes can suffer from limitations (e.g., the *small screen* problem when only the visual channel is used). Multimodality is considered to be more efficient (Oviatt 1999) and more natural (Jokinen & Hurtig 2006). While mobile multimodal systems have been investigated in research (Möller et al. 2012a, Möller et al. 2012b, Schuster et al. 2011), the adoption of multimodality in the real world is still cautious, both from user and programmer side. With the *M3I* (*M*obile *M*ulti*M*odal *I*nteraction) framework, we aim to foster the development of multimodal applications and the system-wide use of multimodal interaction on mobile devices. We respect two notions of multimodality: context-based selection of output modalities, and novel multimodal input methods. To the best of our knowledge, *M3I* is the first approach that satisfies all of the following requirements:

- Holistic support of modeling, prototyping and implementation of multimodal behavior in mobile systems (often, only individual stages, such as prototyping, are supported)
- Support of multimodal input *and* output (other approaches focus either on the interpretation and fusion of input events, or on output modality switching by tasking applications)

- Support of context-driven multimodality (existing approaches are either pure context toolkits, or focus on multimodal interaction without integrating context, at least not using context for both in- and output)
- Applicability in standard development environments, without compiler adaptations (Schuster et al. 2011), and with state-of-the-art mobile operating systems (earlier approaches are dedicated to legacy or desktop platforms providing limited context support)
- Autonomous operation, without server-based evaluation or control through the cloud as e.g. in *Code in the Air* (Ravindranath et al. 2012)
- Definition of multimodal behavior based on *rules,* which is close to the human understanding of automated switching (approaches that use automata, state machines, etc., might comply less with the human mental model of such systems)

2 Mobile Multimodal Interaction Framework

M3I is implemented in Java as Android library. Figure 1 shows, on a conceptual level, the structure of the framework and its basic components. The key elements for realizing rule-based evaluation are `Statements` and `LogicalExpressions`, which describe explicit and implicit events, and `Triggers`, which describe a behavior of the system. Examples for statements are "the user is at home" or "the battery is charged more than 50%". They consist

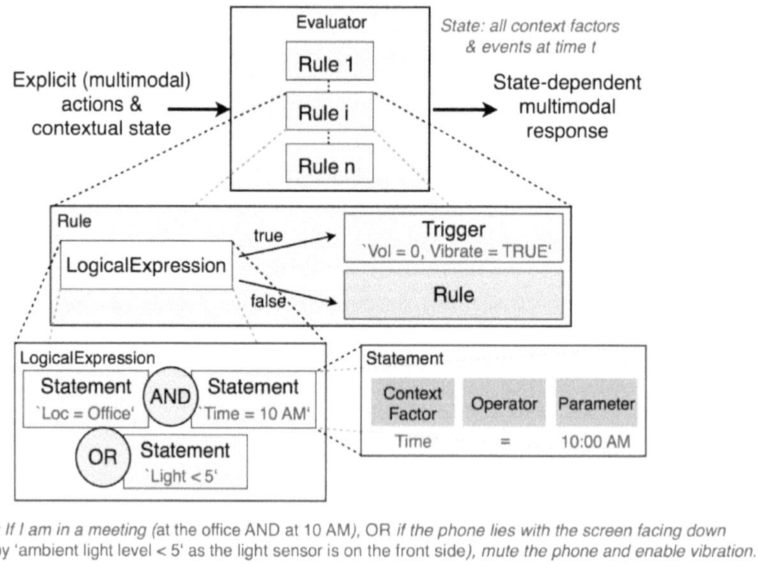

Figure 1: General Structure of the M3I *Framework. Rules define the system's behavior in response to explicit user actions and/or to implicit context factors and events. Thereby* M3I *realizes context-dependent modality changes or novel interaction methods involving different modalities.*

of a `ContextFactor` referring to the subject of the statement, and of an `Operator`, which allows numeric comparisons, within-range-tests, or regular expressions. `Rules` associate the events described by a `LogicalExpression` with appropriate `Triggers` that define what happens if the rule is true or false. Statements can be combined with, e.g., AND, OR, XOR, and NOT to logical expressions, and by recursively nested rules. The set of active rules is evaluated in the framework's `Evaluator` in regular intervals, which are variable to account for time-critical sensor data as well as for battery-conserving location updates.

The rule-based wiring and evaluation mechanism allows defining multimodal in- and output with consideration of context information. Under context, we subsume implicit information, such as the user's current location or activity that impact the choice of output modalities, but also explicit user actions like (e.g., accelerometer-detected) motion gestures, which are themselves part of an interaction. *M3I* formalizes such information as `ContextFactors` and supplies their current value by context methods. *M3I* economizes and simplifies accessing contextual information for the programmer, as it saves the overhead for initializing system services, for creating event listeners etc., and makes all functionality accessible by homogenous interfaces. Basic activity recognition and classification routines abstracting from pure sensor readings are included. *M3I* currently integrates over 50 context factors regarding, e.g., location, ambient noise and light level, device orientation, or proximity information.

Novel interaction methods that incorporate multiple modalities can be realized by linking data from different `Statements` using `LogicalExpressions`. Like this, explicit interactions, such as physical button presses or touch interactions can be intercepted and combined with implicit contextual information. *M3I* also unifies synchronous information and asynchronous information (making underlying *push* or *pull* paradigms transparent). By combination of validity settings and event timestamps, both parallel and sequential actions (e.g. for multi-step motion gestures) can be evaluated.

On output side, `Triggers` realize modality switches and thereby abstract how information should be represented. One notification can be provided, e.g., as visual, haptic or auditory response. States or contexts can be announced system-wide through an Android content provider. That way, each app can provide its own adaptations to state changes, accounting for the fact that interaction modes are often task-specific. An application can, e.g., offer a user interface with larger touch controls that are easier to hit when the user is on a walk.

M3I can easily be extended by feeding results of any method or callback into the framework's decision logic. Triggers are likewise not limited to predefined modalities or actions: a `MethodTrigger` allows implementing custom functionality by calling self-implemented methods. Unlike other frameworks, *M3I* is not focused on or built around an individual use case, but from scratch designed for a broad range of application areas.

3 Exemplary Implementations of Modalities

To prove *M3I*'s suitability for rapid prototyping, we implemented three exemplary multimodal interaction methods (see Figure 2). With *Raise&Call,* the user can bring the phone to the ear to start a call, combining a device motion gesture and speech as input modalities. With *Press&Shoot*, the camera app is started by pressing the volume button in upright position (motion gesture and button press), and *Pinch@Home* launches the maps application by mimicking a pinch-to-zoom gesture on the home screen (motion gesture, touchscreen). These three input methods were implemented with *M3I* in straightforward manner by a few simple rules (e.g., involving the accelerometer pose as implicit sensor reading and the button press as explicit action for the *Press&Shoot* method). *M3I*'s built-in abstractions (predefined device poses like "upright", "lying on the table", "display up/down") additionally accelerated the development of the *Raise&Call* and *Press&Shoot* methods.

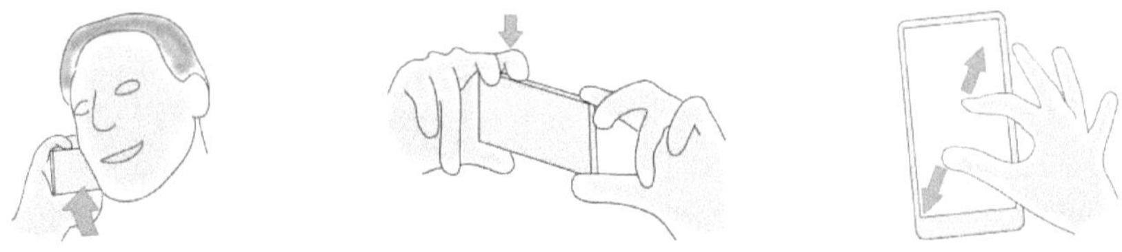

Figure 2: Exemplary interaction methods implemented with M3I*:* Raise&Call, Press&Shoot, *and* Pinch@Home

Future work will investigate automated deduction of desired modalities. When a user e.g. mutes the device every week at a certain location and time (probably because of a weekly meeting), *M3I* could proactively suggest this action. Unlike classical supervised learning where the learned model is not visible to the user, the rules to be created could be edited and reviewed to establish transparency about an application's multimodal behavior.

References

Jokinen, K., and Hurtig, T. (2006). User expectations and real experience on a multimodal interactive system. *Proc. INTERSPEECH.*

Möller, A., Diewald, S., Roalter, L., and Kranz, M. (2012). MobiMed: comparing object identification techniques on smartphones. *Proc. NordiCHI,* 31-40, ACM.

Möller, A., Kray, C., Roalter, L., Diewald, S., Huitl, R., and Kranz, M. (2012). Tool support for prototyping interfaces for vision-based indoor navigation. *Proc MobiVis at Mobile HCI.*

Oviatt, S. (1999). Ten myths of multimodal interaction. *Communications of the ACM,* 42(11), 74-81.

Ravindranath, L., Thiagarajan, A., Balakrishnan, H., and Madden, S. (2012). Code in the air: simplifying sensing and coordination tasks on smartphones. *Proc. HotMobile '12*, ACM.

Schuster, C., Appeltauer, M., and Hirschfeld, R. (2011). Context-oriented programming for mobile devices: JCOP on Android. *Proc. COP '11*, ACM.

Contact Information

{andreas.moeller, stefan.diewald, roalter}@tum.de, matthias.kranz@uni-passau.de

M. Koch, A. Butz & J. Schlichter (Hrsg.): Mensch und Computer 2014 Tagungsband,
München: Oldenbourg Wissenschaftsverlag, 2014, S. 359-362.

Movin'Klee – die neue Möglichkeit, beim Spielen mit Augmented Reality im Kunstmuseum zu lernen

Xiaomeng Jiang

Hochschule Augsburg

Zusammenfassung

In diesem Artikel wird untersucht, wie man durch Einsatz der Applikation Movin' Klee das Lernen beim Spielen mit Augmented Reality in einer Kunstausstellung verwirklichen kann; wie man mit neuer Technik museale Inhalte auf originelle Art und Weise zugänglich machen kann und ob die Verknüpfung von Augmented Realtiy und Smartphone tatsächlich das Museum- und besonders das Lern-Ergebnis des Besuchers verbessert – insbesondere des jüngeren und nicht klassischen Publikums im Kunstmuseum. (Besucher mit nur wenigen Kunstvorkenntnissen)

1 Einleitung

Lernen ist eine grundlegende Fähigkeit, die aus dem instinktiven Bedarf des Menschen kommt. Seit Jahren untersuchen zahlreiche Pädagogen Möglichkeiten mit dem einzigen Ziel, die effektivste Lern-Methode zu entwickeln. Bis heute gibt es allerdings keine übereinstimmende Meinung darüber. Trotzdem hat man übereinstimmend feststellen können, dass der Mensch durch Spaß beim Lernen den besten Lerneffekt erzielt.

Auf Basis der Lern-Theorie nach Falk und Dierking, gehört das Museum zu den besten Orten, Lernen und Spaß zu verbinden. Gegenüber der Besucheranzahl ist das Lern-Ergebnis des Besuchers trotzdem gering, nicht nur in diesem Kunstmuseum, sondern auch in vielen berühmten Kunstmuseen wie dem Louvre Paris; mehr als 80 Prozent der Besucher, die sich die bekannte Mona Lisa angesehen haben, hatten keine Geduld, die zahlreichen wertvollen Kunstwerke im restlichen Museum zu begutachten.

Motiviert von der Idee, ein steigendes Besuchererlebnis für ein Kunstmuseum zu schaffen, wurde die Verknüpfung von Augmented Reality und Smartphone in die Realität umgesetzt. Die neue Technik Augemented Reality besitzt die Fähigkeit, die reale und virtuelle Welt zu verbinden, wodurch es dem Besucher ermöglicht wird, beim Spielen mit AR sogar etwas zu lernen. In diesem Artikel steht die App Movin'Klee als der Vertreter für diese neue Methode.

Während die Anwendung in der „Paul Klee - Mythos Fliegen"-Ausstellung in dem Augsburger Museum H2 integriert und von den Besuchern genutzt wurde, ist eine Studie über den Lern-Effekt der App durchgeführt worden. Die Studie basiert auf Befragungen von 16 Test-Personen aus dem Usability Test, insgesamt 171 Befragten und der passiven Beobachtungen von Besuchern während der Ausstellung. Das Resultat zeigt einen positiven und vor allem effektiven Einfluss der App Movin'Klee. Die App faszinierte nicht nur die Zielgruppe, sondern beeinflusste auch den Lernerfolg positiv.

2 Die App Movin'Klee

Im folgenden Abschnitt wird die App Movin'Klee vorgestellt sowie ihre Funktionsweise und deren technische Umsetzung beschrieben. Außerdem wird ein Blick auf die Ausstellungsarchitektur geworfen.

2.1 Ziel der Applikation

Hauptsächlich ging es dem Kurator der Paul-Klee-Ausstellung Shahab Sangestan darum, mit einer mobilen Applikation Kinder und Jugendliche für die Ausstellung zu gewinnen. Während der Recherche-Phase stellte man fest, dass auch das Louvre in Paris mit dem Problem der fehlenden und jüngeren Zielgruppe zu kämpfen hat. Hier fehlt es an der Verbindung zwischen Kunstwerk und einem gewissen Unterhaltungsfaktor. Unter dem Aspekt des spielerischen Lernens wurde Movin'Klee entworfen. Der Benutzer soll nicht nur einen wissenschaftlichen, sondern auch einen spielerischen Zugang zu den Werken von Paul Klee erhalten, der wiederum das Interesse für den Künstler und dessen Kunst weckt.

2.2 Funktionsweise

Die App Movin'Klee baut grundsätzlich auf eine wesentliche Funktion auf. Über den deutlichen gekennzeichneten Start-Button gelangt der Anwender in die Kameraansicht seines Smartphones und damit in den Augmented-Reality-Bereich. Kurz darauf lädt die App die Inhalte für die dargestellten Animationen aus dem Internet herunter. Dabei greift sie auf Server des verwendeten Plug-Ins Junaio zu, dass vom Unternehmen Metaio bereitgestellt wird. Richtet der Nutzer seine Kamera nun auf eines von elf ausgewählten Paul-Klee-Bildern, startet automatisch eine Animation, die das Kunstwerk zum Leben erweckt. Es gibt drei Sorten von Animationen, 2D Animation, 3D Model und 3D Animation. Beispielsweise tanzen die Blumen aus dem Gemälde „ Blumen Garten von Taora". (siehe Abbildung 1)

Abbildung 1: Movin'Klee in der Paul Klee Ausstellung

2.3 Technische Umsetzung

Movin'Klee besteht aus einer nativen Applikation sowie einem Junaio-Plugin, dass die Schnittstelle zu Augmented Reality bildet. Dabei sind die nativen Apps in den jeweiligen Programmiersprachen für Android und IOS geschrieben. Der Augmented-Reality-Teil, der in diesem Fall den auf dem Junaio-Server befindlichen Channel darstellt, wurde anfangs in den Programmiersprachen PHP, HTML, AREL und jQuery entwickelt. Um eine bessere stabile Tracking-Datei bekommen zu können wurde der Channel über den Metaio-Creator 3.2 erstellt. Dieser Channel stellt eine Art Browser dar, in dem die Augmented-Reality-Objekte (Animationen) geladen und abgespielt werden. Die Umsetzung der Animationen und 3D-Objekte erfolgte in den Programmen Adobe After Effect, Flash, Autodesk 3D Studio Max, Maya 2012, das für die nachträgliche Bearbeitung benutzt wird.

2.4 Ausstellungsarchitektur

Der Ausstellungsraum im Museum wurde durch zwei unterschiedlich große Einbauten in zwei Bereiche bzw. Themen aufgeteilt. In diesen zwei Räumen, White Cube und Black Cube, sind Originalkunstwerke, Objekte und Persönliches von Paul Klee zu sehen. Außerhalb der Einbauten befinden sich die Garderobe, die Pädagogik, der Kiosk, die Cafeteria und die zwei App-Bereiche (siehe Abbildung 2).

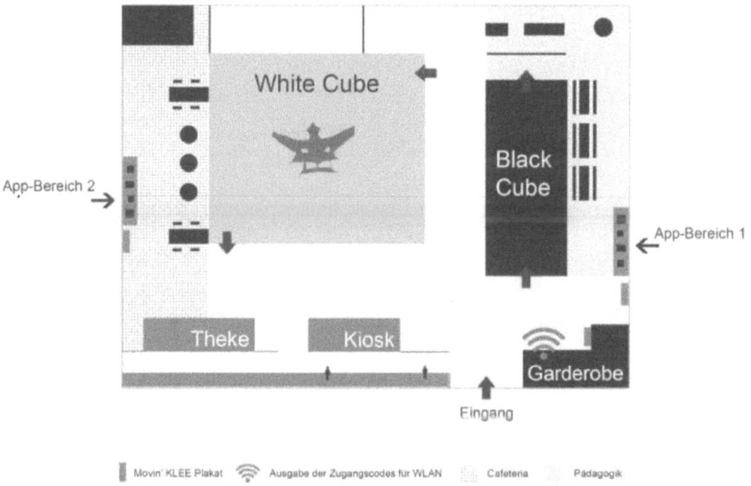

Abbildung 2: Ausstellungsarchitektur der Paul Klee Ausstellung

Die beiden App-Bereiche wurden von der eigentlichen Ausstellung ausgesondert, weil die Kunstwerke zum einen nicht fotografiert werden dürfen – richtet der Nutzer nun sein Smartphone auf eines der Original-Kunstwerke, könne das Aufsichtspersonal nicht sofort erkennen, ob die App benutzt oder ein Foto geknipst wurde. Aus diesem Grund wurden zwei Bereiche neben der Ausstellung geschaffen. Dort befinden sich auf einer Art Fensterbank insgesamt elf Reproduktionen von Paul Klee mit Informationstafeln sowie einem Stein mit ID-Marker.

Der Zugangscode zum kostenlosen WLAN kann sich der Besucher an der Garderobe abholen. Die Ausstellung beginnt im Black Cube und endet im White Cube. Wenn sich der Besucher vom Movin'Klee-Plakat angesprochen fühl, gibt es zwei Möglichkeiten. Entweder benutzt er die App bevor er in den Black Cube geht oder nach dem White Cube.

3 Evaluation und Zusammenfassung

Während der Ausstellung wurden die drei Untersuchungsmethoden Usability Test, Beobachtung und Befragung mit Hilfe eines Fragebogens durchgeführt, um schlussendlich die Wirkung und den Lerneffekt der App zu testen. Das Ergebnis des Usability Tests zeigt, dass alle Tester durch das neuartige Erlebnis motivierter durch die Ausstellung gehen. Mit der Methode des Beobachtens wurde ersichtlich, dass Besucher mittels der App Kunstwerke genauer und länger betrachten. Die Befragung von insgesamt 171 Teilnehmern verdeutlicht zudem, dass die App einen wesentlichen Einfluss auf den Lerneffekt hat. Anhand des zweiteiligen Fragebogens, indem nicht nur die Kunst-Vorkenntnisse, sondern auch der Lerneffekt innerhalb verschiedener Alters- und Personengruppen getestet wurde, zeigt, dass bei jüngerem Publikum mit wenig Kunstvorkenntnissen ein effektiverer Lerneffekt mittels der App erzielt werden kann.

Lernen ist ein andauender Prozess bzw. ein kontinuierlicher Vorgang, der nur in regelmäßigen Tests genau erforscht werden kann. Um den Lerneffekt der App „Movin'Klee" noch detaillierter zu messen, sollten deshalb weitere Untersuchungen in verschiedenen Zeitabständen durchgeführt werden. Auch wenn die Untersuchungsmethoden in der Paul Klee Ausstellung nicht perfekt waren, konnte anhand der Befragung ein erstes und aussagekräftiges Ergebnis erzielt werden. So zeigen die positiven Reaktionen und Untersuchungsergebnisse von Movin'Klee, dass die Technik Augmented Reality zweifelsohne zur Steigerung des Lernergebnisses beiträgt. Mit der stetigen Weiterentwicklung wird es in naher Zukunft viele weitere Möglichkeiten für den Einsatz von Augmented Reality im pädagogischen Lernumfeld geben.

Danksagung

Ich danke dem Team von Movin'Lab, da es ohne ihren motivierten Einsatz Movin'Klee niemals gegeben hätte. Ich danke Professor KP Ludwig John für die Beteuerung meiner Masterarbeit und der Hochschule Augsburg für die Chance hier studieren zu können. Außerdem danke ich meiner Familie und meinem Freund für die tatkräftige Unterstützung.

Kontaktinformationen

Xiaomeng Jiang,
E-Mail: jxmemilia@googlemail.com, Tel: 004917641545819
Adresse : Vinnhorster Weg 75 30419 Hannover Deutschland

M. Koch, A. Butz & J. Schlichter (Hrsg.): Mensch und Computer 2014 Tagungsband,
München: Oldenbourg Wissenschaftsverlag, 2014, S. 363-366.

Playful, collaborative approaches to 3D modeling and 3D printing

Thomas von Rekowski[1], Alexander Boden[2], Oliver Stickel[1], Dominik Hornung[1], Gunnar Stevens[1]

Universität Siegen[1], Fraunhofer FIT St. Augustin[2]

Abstract

Cheaper and more prevalent 3D printing technology offers new and emerging opportunities for non-experts to make and produce their very own physical items and products. However, most 3D modeling software is still geared towards experts and not as inclusive as the printing technology itself. At the same time, tools are usually limited in their possibilities for collaboration. Against this backdrop, we are conducting qualitative studies with children in Germany and Palestine on practices of co-constructive 3D modeling in virtual worlds. We aim to understand how children negotiate and cooperate on joint projects and how to lead non-experts playfully into 3D modeling. For this, we utilize the game Minecraft as well as the similar browser-based tool Cubeteam. In this paper, we present first results as well as design implications for co-constructive 3D modeling tools.

1 Introduction and State of the Art

Recently, there has been a growing proliferation of 3D printers and similar digital fabrication technologies. Due to sinking prices and progress in the availability and usability of such machines, new trends and opportunities for self-production are emerging. This goes along with a spread of related structures like Fab Labs and other, similar DIY oriented communities (Gershenfeld, 2007; Tanenbaum, Williams, Desjardins, & Tanenbaum, 2013). Given the potential of those technologies for fostering user-driven innovation as well as self-expression and creativity, it is prudent to carefully think about how to educate people in their usage from an early age in order to enable their participation in digital fabrication.

However, common tools for 3D modeling such as AutoCAD or 3Ds Max pose huge entrance hurdles since they are mostly geared towards experts and require training to be used properly. Hence, new interfaces and new HCI strategies are needed to democratize the 3D modeling process further (Sadar & Chyon, 2011). One such strategy is the utilization of playful 3D environments to playfully educate children in 3D modeling and to keep their motivation up. Such environments offer opportunities for collaboration in virtual worlds, which fits very well in established computer related learning theories such as constructionism (Harel & Papert, 1991). One of the most popular games in this fashion is Minecraft (https://minecraft.net), an open world game which places the player in a virtual environment resembling a fantasy world in which she or he can build almost anything easily from small cubes. Minecraft is increasingly being used in educational settings (e.g. Short & Short, 2012) and offers a co-constructive and co-creative, immersive, virtual environment. Tools such as Mineways (www.mineways.com) allow to export Minecraft creations to 3d printable models. Cubeteam (www.cubeteam.io) is a similar tool that is browser-based, needs no local installation / infrastructure and is expressly geared towards 3D printing.

In our ongoing work, we explore the viability of such playful tools for early education towards digital fabrication. Through the research project *Come_IN*, we have access to well-established (running for ten years) computer clubs, which are located in elementary schools in Germany, as well as two such clubs in refugee camps in Palestine. The clubs are geared towards constructionist, collaborative learning around the computer, ranging from programming with Scratch through basic electronics up to 3D printing.

2 Methodology

The majority of our study up until the time of writing was conducted for six months in one of the come_IN computer clubs hosted by a secondary school in Bonn, Germany. The club is part of the school's curriculum and for the 30 pupils aged twelve to fourteen, weekly participation in the club was obligatory. The kids received a basic introduction to 3d printing and were allowed to design whatever they desired (usually house-like structures such as castles) in groups of 4-5. We attended all sessions, being able to interact with the children and observe social interactions in situ. We also used remote monitoring to map onscreen interactions with real life situations. Photos, videos and field notes were taken and compiled into detailed protocols at the end of each session (28 so far). These were supplemented by server logs (player's activities, chats and evolution of the world). Furthermore, two group interviews (25 and 45min) regarding the children's experiences were conducted and transcribed. Analysis was done following a pragmatic Grounded Theory approach (Strauss & Corbin, 2008). The basic research questions were how children used the game for co-constructive practices, how they negotiated common projects in terms of communication and coordination and how their cooperation emerged over the course of the project.

At the time of writing, two of our researchers are at the come_IN club in Palestine with a 3D printer and will carry out a similar study there. This will hopefully yield highly contrastive results given the very different social background in the Middle East, and more specifically, a hard and threatened life as a refugee, supplementing and broadening our findings. Other 3D-printing and Maker-related work in hard social surroundings has proved valuable in the past (e.g. Dlodlo & Beyers, 2009; Mikhak et al., 2002). Our researchers will utilize the browser-based Cubeteam instead of Minecraft because the local infrastructure is limited and our intention to explore a wide variety of playful modeling tools. In doing so, they will pursue similar research questions as in the first study in Germany.

3 Findings and corresponding design implications

In this section, we present some of our most central findings and map them to possible design challenges for educational, non-professional 3D modeling and printing software tools.

On a technical level, Minecraft turned out to be surprisingly efficient for creating simple 3D models collaboratively. Despite some initial problems with learning the basic control functions of the game such as moving the avatar around, placing blocks in the game world and orienting in a 3d environment, all groups learned quickly how to use the game and were able to produce models suitable for 3d printing with very little instructions by the tutors. At the same time, it became apparent that the game lacked sophisticated coordination and awareness features other than a simple chat, which limited possibilities for in-game negotiation considerably. Especially for complex projects, more sophisticated mechanisms for coordination and awareness seem sensible (e.g. discussions mapped to specific structures or ownership signifiers for constructions through automatic color or signs). Furthermore, Minecraft does not take technological 3D printing limitations like difficulties in printing overhanging or floating structures as well as interior voids and cube size / scaling into account as of now which can become problematic during the printing process in some cases.

On the social level, we found that a lot of coordination work happened around the use of the game. In this regard, several practices emerged in the groups: *Instruction* (Children with advanced skills instruct others to build something according to given specifications), *Orientation* (Children use the in-game chat feature to allocate the position of team mates, certain building sites or even their own position), *Support* (in case of problems with certain tasks, children request support from tutors or use the chat to ask other players for help) and *Arbitrating* (some children take a stand for arbitrating in in-game conflict situations). Based on these patterns, we thus can identify a number of social roles that the children took on in the context of their activities: *Leader* – give instructions, experienced in the game, are asked for decisions on buildings. *Executive* – familiar with game controls, like to build according to instructions of the creative or leaders. *Creative* – assume creative activities (planning, personalization, giving creative advice and input, etc.). *Beginner/learner* – still in the process of appropriation of controls, ask others for help or 'work/tasks'. Like the technical aspects, the social ones should be reflected in the modeling tool. One example would be a video-game-inspired system which supports different roles as well as different stages in expertise and maps both aspects to specific tools, e.g. for support, for arbitration or for leading (in other games, leaders can e.g. get access to tools like birds' eye maps for better coordination).

4 Discussion and Outlook

Our analysis resulted in findings regarding *technical* and *social* aspects for playful, educational 3D modeling tools to facilitate early participation in digital fabrication. This includes – but is not limited to – coordination and awareness support features as well as the video-game inspired support for different roles children take on during collaborative 3D modeling as well as their learning and appropriation progress. Our results until now mostly concern *Minecraft,* embedded in western socio-cultural/political backgrounds and will be conveyed into more in-depth implications for design for 3D modeling/printing tools. This research will be supplemented by experimentation with different playful 3D modeling tools. Furthermore, we will continue our contrastive research in the Middle East - It will be interesting to see how the different context there influences practices regarding interaction, roles and choice of projects. Our superordinate goal is to broaden and ground our findings and design implications in a manner appropriate to the, global, spreading and increasingly important Maker culture which empowers and connects people around the world.

References

Dlodlo, N., & Beyers, R. N. (2009). The Experiences of South-African High-School Girls in a Fab Lab Environment. In Proceedings of WASET 2009.

Eisenberg, M. (2007). Pervasive Fabrication: Making Construction Ubiquitous in Education. In 5th ann. IEEE conf. on pervasive computing (PerComW'07) (pp. 193–198).

Gershenfeld, N. (2007). Fab: The Coming Revolution on Your Desktop--from Personal Computers to Personal Fabrication. Basic Books.

Harel, I., & Papert, S. (1991). Constructionism (p. 518). Ablex Publishing.

Mikhak, B., Lyon, C., Gorton, T., Gershenfeld, N., Mcennis, C., & Taylor, J. (2002). Fab Lab: An alternate Model of ICT for Development. In Development by Design.

Sadar, J. S., & Chyon, G. (2011). 3D Scanning and Printing As a New Medium for Creativity in Product Design. In Proc. of the 2nd conf. on Creativity and Innovation in Design (pp. 15–20). Eindhoven, Netherlands: ACM New York, USA.

Short, D., & Short, B. D. (2012). Teaching scientific concepts using a virtual world - Minecraft. In Teaching Science: J. of the Australian Science Teachers Ass. 58, 55–58.

Strauss, A., & Corbin, J. (2008). Basics of Qualitative Research. Basics of Qualitative Research: Grounded Theory Procedures and Techniques (Vol. 3).

Tanenbaum, J. G., Williams, A. M., Desjardins, A., & Tanenbaum, K. (2013). Democratizing technology: pleasure, utility and expressiveness in DIY and maker practice. In Proceedings of CHI 2013 (pp. 2603–2612). Paris, France.

M. Koch, A. Butz & J. Schlichter (Hrsg.): Mensch und Computer 2014 Tagungsband, München: Oldenbourg Wissenschaftsverlag, 2014, S. 367-370.

Product Experience Wall: A Context-adaptive Outfit Recommender System

Christian Zagel

Friedrich-Alexander Universität Erlangen-Nürnberg

Abstract

This paper presents research in progress and describes the concept and prototype of the so called "Product Experience Wall", an interactive and context-adaptive outfit recommendation system for retail fashion stores. The goal is to design an experiential system that serves both, functional and hedonic needs. Context adaption allows pro-actively approaching the user and recommending products based on the respective user context. Next to face detection algorithms, we use RFID sensors and interfaces to external data sources (e.g., weather information) to create a unique customer experience. This experience is furthermore supported by displaying product combinations on virtual, life-size avatars. The core functionality of the concept is based on the findings of qualitative interviews performed amongst 6 experts and 80 customers.

1 Introduction

Supported by the technological change, the use of self-service systems at the point of sale is considered being able to impinge upon the perceived value and quality of services (Verhoef et al. 2009, 31-41). It has already been proven that technology can make stores more interesting, trustworthy and attractive, thus affecting the brand's perception and image (Pantano & Naccarato 2010, 200-204). The provision of experiential, value-added services is regarded an appropriate means to differentiate from competitors (Merkle & Kreutzer 2008, 21). However, while general design principles for self-service systems have been assessed and communicated in the past (Magurie 1999, 263-286), practitioners often still neglect basic psychological aspects when developing self-service systems, especially the ones regarding usability, user experience, and joy of use.

Using the example of the textile industry, this paper presents a newly developed system that uses context adaptivity (Soylu et al. 2009, 992-1013) not only to support the users in their shopping task, but to also create a positive overall experience. Using sensor technology and third party data, the goal is to start a context-based and system-initiated interaction in order to realize an interactive outfit recommendation system. The service encounter therefore is personified by using a digital avatar. Focus on the experiential dimensions by Schmitt and

Mangold (2004) during development furthermore supports the delivery of emotional and functional value to the user. Figure 1 visualizes the vision of the final realization.

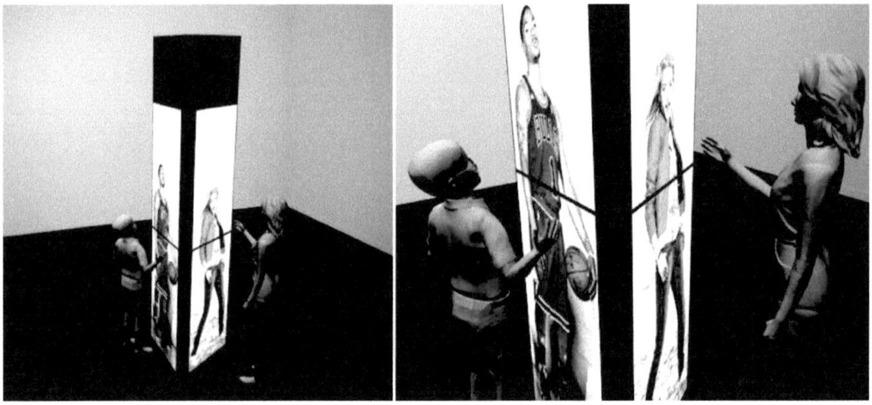

Figure 1: Product Experience Wall Concept

Based on 6 expert interviews and a qualitative study (semi-structured interview) performed amongst 80 customers (38 female, 42 male, aged 14 to 32) of retail fashion stores, aspects affecting the satisfaction in regards to utilitarian and emotional values during shopping were identified. Next to the fact that basically all fashion stores seem to offer the same experience, three main categories for improvement through technology were identified: products should be presented as outfit combinations, not individually (62 mentions), store staff is often not present or is not well informed (53 mentions), and missing product information (75 mentions). These aspects provide the foundation for the concept and prototype presented.

2 Prototype and Interaction Concept

The presented system implements context adaptivity by using several sensors and interfaces to external data: an RFID system allows the detection of products taken in front of the terminal and connecting to open source weather information services enables weather-based product recommendations. Nevertheless the core of the interaction is realized through a face detection engine that recognizes gender, age, and mood of the user or user group approaching the device. This approach allows the automatic adoption of the user interface by applying personalized content (e.g., colors). Next to adapting the product offers based on the gender, age, or mood detected, the sensors can also act as a trigger for a system-initiated interaction with the user. In our concept this happens through a life-size digital avatar representing a virtual store assistant. With this approach, a more personal, individual, and human-like interaction with the self-service system can be realized. As soon as a person approaches the system and his/her face is detected, the system initiates a conversation. Next to an automatic filtering of the products presented (e.g., based on gender), the facial features are used to steer the conversation and trigger an optimized interaction, thus making the interaction natural and immersive. The virtual store assistant is currently realized through short video clips which are either triggered through the sensors or through interaction of the user. While the avatar in the first case acts as a digital contact person, it can also be dressed up and used to present outfit combinations.

Predominant literature on face detection algorithms mainly focuses on verifying the identity of persons in the context of biometric identification (Huang et al. 2001, 617-638). Little research has been conducted so far on applying the technology outside the area of biometrics or security. The use for marketing purposes or human-computer interaction (HCI) seems to be promising, but concrete practical examples hardly exist. Focusing on the creation of positive customer experiences by addressing utilitarian (e.g., pre-filtering of the products) as well as emotional factors (e.g., system-initiated interaction), the concept is realized using the Fraunhofer SHORE SDK[1] (Kueblbeck & Ernst 2006, 564-572). The prototype as well as the UI are shown in Figure 2. A projector displays the image on a large acrylic-glass back-projection wall, equipped with a capacitive multi-touch foil. The size of the wall allows displaying human avatars in real-life size. All sensors are mounted behind the glass, realizing an unobtrusive representation of the technology. In order to achieve a high detection rate of the RFID tags, multiple antennas are mounted in different angles.

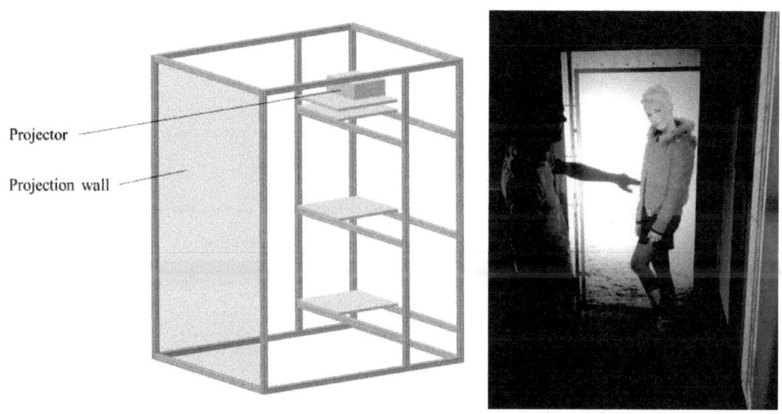

Figure 2: Prototypic Implementation (left: prototype construction, right: user interface with digital avatar

3 Conclusions and Outlook

First user tests show that both, the context-adaptivity as well as the real-life size avatar provide enormous potential for creating experiences. As the context adaption happens on a subconscious level, users get surprised if they received individualized content without having

[1] For additional information also see http://www.iis.fraunhofer.de/de/bf/bsy/fue/isyst.html.

to tell the system their needs. Further evaluations will provide a deeper insight into the utilitarian and emotional effects. Special emphasis will be put on the aspects of flow and immersion occurring through this new interaction concept. Next to finalizing the system as described above, additional functionality is planned. By applying image processing technologies, product recommendations will be given based on skin tone or hair color of the customer. The camera can furthermore be used to detect the heart rate of the user (Poh et al. 2010), allowing to draw inferences on emotions arising through interacting with the device or the products recommended. Furthermore, the outfit combinations will be visualized on the customer's personal avatar previously captured through a body scanner. In contrast to an augmented reality application, this also allows a more realistic visualization of drape and fit of the garment. Finally, using an animated avatar instead of linked video clips allows more flexibility in regards to product presentation and interaction. This provides additional functionality and positively influences the perception of the products (Suh et al. 2011).

Acknowledgements

We would like to thank the "HansFrisch-Stiftung", who supported this research.

Literature

Huang, T.; Xiong, Z. & Zhang, Z. (2011). *Face Recognition Applications*. In Li, S. Z. & Jian, A. K., (Eds.): Handbook of Face Recognition. Wiesbaden: Springer. 617-638.

Kueblbeck, C. & Ernst, A. (2006). Face detection and tracking in video sequences using the modified census transformation. *Image and Vision Computing 24*(6):564-572.

Magurie, M. C. (1999). A review of user interface guidelines for public information kiosk systems. *International Journal of Human-Computer Studies 50*(3):263-286.

Merkle, W. & Kreutzer, R. (2008). *Emotion, Leidenschaft und Begeisterung - Ein (noch immer) unterschätzter Erfolgsfaktor im Marketing*. In Kreutzer, R. & Merkle, W., (Eds.): Die neue Macht des Marketing. Wiesbaden: Gabler. 21-48.

Pantano, E. & Naccarato, G. (2010). Entertainment in retailing: The influences of advanced technologies. *Journal of Retailing and Consumer Services 17*(3):200-204.

Poh, M., McDuff, D. & Picard, R. (2010). Non-contact, automated cardiac pulse measurements using video imaging and blind source separation. *Optics Express 18*(10):10762-10774.

Schmitt, B. & Mangold, M. (2004). *Kundenerlebnis als Wettbewerbsvorteil: Mit Customer Experience Management Marken und Märkte Gewinn bringend gestalten*. Wiesbaden: Gabler.

Soylu, A., Causmaecker, P. & Desmet, P. (2009). Context and Adaptivity in Pervasive Computing Environments: Links with Software Engineering and Ontological Engineering. *Journal of Software 4*(9): 992-1013.

Suh, K., Kim, H. & Suh, E. (2011). What if your avatar looks like you? Congruity perspectives for avatar use. *MIS Quarterly 35*(3): 711-729.

Verhoef, P., Lemon, K., Parasuraman, A., Roggeveen, A., Tsiros, M. & Schlesinger, L. (2009). Customer Experience Creation: Determinants, Dynamics and Management Strategies. *Journal of Retailing 85*(1): 31-41.

M. Koch, A. Butz & J. Schlichter (Hrsg.): Mensch und Computer 2014 Tagungsband,
München: Oldenbourg Wissenschaftsverlag, 2014, S. 371-374.

Simulation and Digital Prototyping of Tangible User Interfaces

Stefan Diewald[1], Andreas Möller[1], Luis Roalter[1], Matthias Kranz[2]

[1] Distributed Multimodal Information Processing Group, Technische Universität München
[2] Lehrstuhl für Informatik mit Schwerpunkt Eingebettete Systeme, Universität Passau

Abstract

Physical prototyping is an important part in research and development of tangible user interfaces (TUIs). On the way from the idea to a working prototype, hardware prototypes usually have to be crafted repeatedly in numerous iterations. However, this can be very time- and cost-intensive when non-standard, expensive hardware components are part of the design. This brings us to think about digital prototypes that exhibit the same functionality as a physical TUI, but reduce the amount of resources that have to be spent. For that reason, we present a middleware-based process that allows developing and testing fully functional implementations of a tangible user interface as a digital device in a 3D virtual environment.

1 Introduction

The development and evaluation of prototypic tangible user interfaces (TUIs) (Ishii & Ullmer 1997) consumes a lot of effort and time due to iterative design and debug processes on some kind of hardware. Starting from I/O cubes, to tabletops and various augmented everyday objects, each TUI consists of individual hardware that has often to be built from scratch. In order to reduce the development time for initial prototypes, hardware frameworks, such as *Blades & Tiles* (Sankaran et al. 2009) or *Pin & Play* (Van Laerhoven et al. 2003), are used by developers. However, still a lot of work has to be spent on the hardware before a running prototype can actually be used for evaluating user interaction and HCI-related aspects. This is especially the case for TUIs that are based on novel hardware that is not yet available or cannot be realized within reasonable expenditure.

Hence, a prototyping approach allowing the simulation of tangible user interfaces at an early stage, e.g. to evaluate novel interaction concepts before building any kind of hardware, could extremely shorten the overall development time.

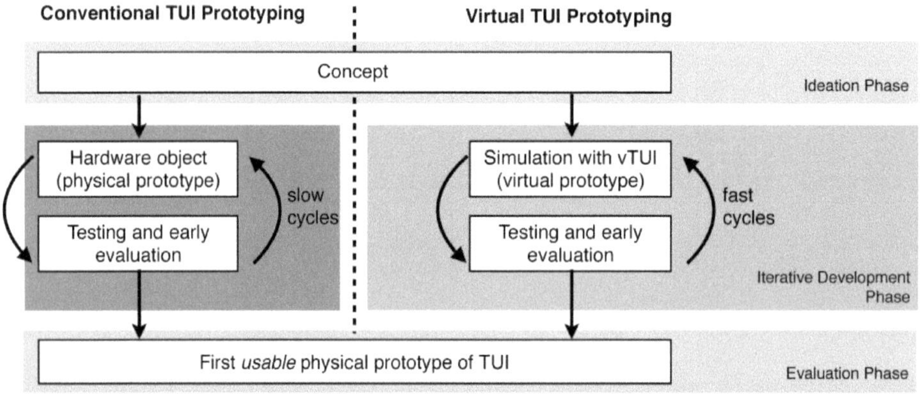

Figure 1: Comparison of the prototyping with physical (left) and digital (right) devices from the idea to the first physical prototype that can be used for a user evaluation. As potentially multiple physical prototypes are needed when prototyping with physical hardware, development cycles are faster with digital prototyping.

In this paper, we introduce a toolkit for TUI simulation that allows shifting the early prototyping process into a high-fidelity 3D virtual environment. That way, shapes of objects for a new TUI and/or new interaction concepts can be evaluated before an actual hardware prototype needs to be built (Holleis et al. 2005). The proposed toolkit is based on a middleware that can be used for digital as well as for physical TUIs. For that reason, interactions between real *and* simulated components are possible. Moreover, the transition from the digital to the physical prototype does not entail significant changes from software side.

2 Middleware-based Digital TUI Prototyping

Based on the results from Roalter et al. with intelligent and smart environments (Roalter et al. 2011), we assembled a toolkit that allows a complete virtual representation of a TUI. As presented in Fig. 2, we can create high-fidelity virtual prototypes that look almost identical to subsequently developed physical prototypes.

2.1 Requirements for a Digital TUI Simulation Environment

A simulation environment for TUIs needs to fulfill several requirements in order to enable a complete evaluation of the system at an early stage and to fulfill the key properties of TUIs as described by Kim and Maher (Kim & Maher 2008). Since tangible user interfaces are based on the linkage of the digital and physical domain, it is important that the simulation can simulate any kind of physical object, especially rigid body objects that are commonly used in many activities of daily living (ADL). A physics engine has to ensure that the digital objects behave like real physical ones. Besides the support for modeling objects of any arbitrary shape, it should further allow the use of realistic textures. Simple geometric shapes as well as complex TUIs should be supported. In order to allow an intuitive evaluation by the

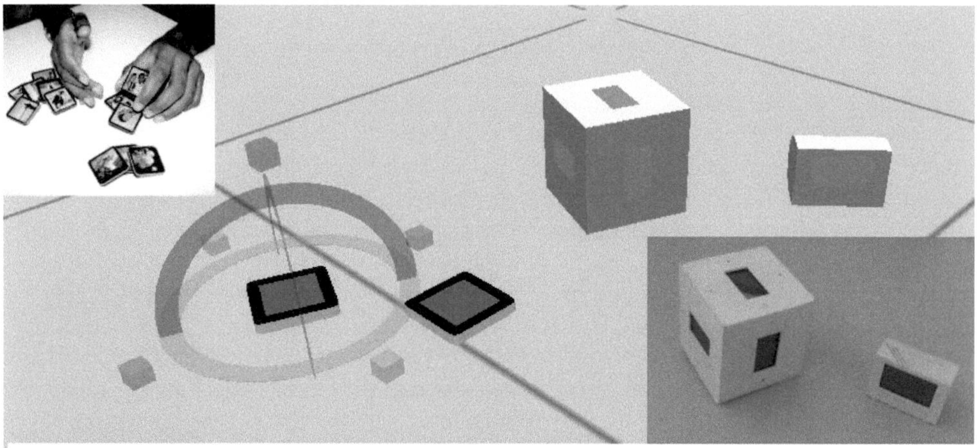

Figure 2: Digital TUIs (from left to right: two Sifteo cubes, an I/O cube and a ubiquitous presence system) and their real counterparts (images in the top left and bottom right corners). The left digital TUI is currently manipulated through the GUI. Gazebo allows for manipulation in all 6 degrees of freedom by applying force to the object.

user, it has to offer a user-friendly 3D interface with the possibility to interact with the simulated objects and to explore the virtual environment. Another important factor is the connection of the simulation environment to a middleware that can actively support the TUI development. It would be useful to choose one that can be used for the virtual simulation as well as afterwards for a physical implementation.

2.2 The ROS Middleware as TUI Middleware

Based on the requirements analysis, we have chosen the *Robot Operating System (ROS)*[1] as middleware. ROS is one of the major middleware systems in the domain of robotics. Thus, an advantage of this middleware is that a huge set of drivers and applications is already available. The middleware already provides us with basic messages and communication protocols to transfer any kind of data between different nodes. For the digital development process, ROS does not depend on existing hardware. The integrated 3D visualization tool *Gazebo* allows evaluating the digital prototype in a high-fidelity virtual environment with realistic physical properties. The physical elements for the simulation can be modeled with all common 3D modeling tools, such as *Blender*[2] or *Cinema4D*. Gazebo's functionality can be easily extended through a well-documented API, which allows, e.g., adding new kinds of virtual sensors and actuators. User interaction is possible via a graphical user interface (GUI).

---

1 http://www.ros.org/, last accessed Mar. 27, 2014.

2 http://www.blender.org/, last accessed Mar. 12, 2014.

3 Examples of Digital Prototypes

A collection of digital TUIs is depicted in Fig. 2. It shows (from left to right) two virtual *Sifteo cubes* (Merrill et al. 2012), a digital I/O cube and a digital TUI for a ubiquitous presence system (Kranz et al. 2006). The meshes have been created with the free 3D modeling software *Blender*. In order to allow physical simulation, the centers of gravity have been set to the objects' centers. Sizes and masses correspond to the respective physical objects. All of these TUIs are equipped with virtual accelerometers and virtual displays. The *Sifteo cubes* further have virtual proximity sensors and touch-sensitive screens (cf. Fig. 2 left). The communication system is based on the ROS middleware's communication infrastructure that can also be used by physical TUIs. The left *Sifteo cube* in Fig. 2 is selected for manipulation in Gazebo. The blocks and circles around the virtual object represent the six degrees of freedom (6DoF) that can be manipulated via the GUI. Besides mouse and keyboard input, the manipulation can also be performed with six-degrees-of-freedom (6DoF) technology such as *3Dconnexion*'s *SpaceNavigator*. This allows for a more realistic interaction with the 3D scene.

References

Diewald, S., Roalter, L., Möller, A., & Kranz, M. (2011). Towards a Holistic Approach for Mobile Application Development in Intelligent Environments. *Proc. MUM,* ACM, pp. 73-80.

Holleis, P., Kranz, M., Gall, M., & Schmidt, A. (2005). Adding Context Information to Digital Photos. *Proc. ICDCSW,* IEEE, pp. 536-542.

Ishii, H., & Ullmer, B. (1997). Tangible Bits: Towards Seamless Interfaces Between People, Bits and Atoms. *Proc. CHI*, ACM, pp. 234-241.

Kim, M. J., & Maher, M. L. (2008). The Impact of Tangible User Interfaces on Spatial Cognition During Collaborative Design. *Design Studies, 29*(3), 222-253.

Kranz, M., Holleis, P., & Schmidt, A. (2006). Ubiquitous Presence Systems. *Proc. SAC*, ACM, pp. 1902-1909.

Merrill, D., Sun, E., & Kalanithi, J. (2012). Sifteo Cubes. *CHI EA,* ACM, pp. 1015-1018.

Roalter, L., Möller, A., Diewald, S., & Kranz, M. (2011). Developing Intelligent Environments: A Development Tool Chain for Creation, Testing and Simulation of Smart and Intelligent Environments. *Proc. IE,* ACM, pp. 214-221.

Sankaran, R., Ullmer, B., Ramanujam, J., Kallakuri, K., Jandhyala, S., Toole, C., & Laan, C. (2009). Decoupling Interaction Hardware Design Using Libraries of Reusable Electronics. *Proc. TEI*, ACM, pp. 331-337.

Serrano, M., Nigay, L., Lawson, J.-Y. L., Ramsay, A., Murray-Smith, R., & Denef, S. (2008). The OpenInterface Framework: A Tool for Multimodal Interaction. *CHI EA*, ACM, pp. 3501-3506.

Van Laerhoven, K., Villar, N., Schmidt, A., Gellersen, H.-W., Hakansson, M., & Holmquist, L. (2003). Pin&Play: The Surface as Network Medium. *IEEE Communications Magazine, 41*(4), 90-95.

M. Koch, A. Butz & J. Schlichter (Hrsg.): Mensch und Computer 2014 Tagungsband, München: Oldenbourg Wissenschaftsverlag, 2014, S. 375-378.

Steuerung von Audiosoftware mit einem Musikinstrument

Karl-Arnold Bodarwé, Florian Echtler

Universität Regensburg, Lehrstuhl für Medieninformatik

Zusammenfassung

Auf Basis eines Szenarios im Home-Recording stellen wir ein System vor, welches die zur Aufnahme verwendete Software direkt über mit dem verwendeten Instrument gespielte Töne steuert. Das Ziel ist es hierbei, dem Musiker beim Aufnehmen von Musik die Bedienung des Aufnahmeprogramms soweit zu erleichtern, dass er die Hände nicht vom Instrument nehmen muss. Die Untersuchung mittels Nutzertests am Beispiel der Audiobearbeitungssoftware *Audacity* in Verbindung mit einer Gitarre zeigt, dass die vorgeschlagene Methodik funktioniert und von erfahrenen Gitarrenspielern akzeptiert wird.

1 Einleitung

Ziel dieses Projekts ist es, Musikern beim Aufnehmen in heimischer Umgebung und ohne Aufsicht eines Technikers oder ähnlichen Helfern (sog. „Home Recording") die Interaktion mit einem Aufnahmeprogramm zu erleichtern. Speziell sollte es den Musikern möglich sein, das Programm zu bedienen, ohne dabei das jeweilige Instrument aus der Hand zu legen.

Üblicherweise erfolgt die Steuerung der Aufnahmesoftware am Computer durch konventionelle Eingabegeräte wie Maus und Tastatur. In jedem Fall muss zumindest eine Hand vom Instrument genommen werden, um mit dem Aufnahmeprogramm zu interagieren. Je nach Instrument bedeutet das eine Neupositionierung oder auch weitere Schritte bei besonders sperrigen Instrumenten, bevor weitergespielt werden kann.

Im Gegensatz dazu sollen Benutzer des vorgestellten Systems in der Lage sein, mittels ihres Musikinstruments elementare Befehle an ein Aufnahmeprogramm zu senden, um damit das Greifen nach Maus und Tastatur zur Bedienung des Programms überflüssig zu machen. Ebenfalls sollte die Haltung am Instrument nicht so geändert werden müssen, dass das Spiel dadurch gestört würde. Auf diese Weise soll ein flüssiger Ablauf des Aufnehmens gewährleistet werden, der Musiker in ihrer kreativen Entfaltung nicht beeinträchtigt.

Eine mögliche Variante wäre eine Modifikation des Instruments, um Schalter oder zusätzliche Tonabnehmer zur Übertragung der Befehle zu benutzen. Jedoch können Musikinstrumente für professionelle Anwender Preise von mehreren tausend Euro überschreiten.

Jede Modifikation könnte den Wert, die Funktionalität oder auch den Klang des Instruments beeinträchtigen. Daher sollten mechanische Eingriffe am Instrument unbedingt vermieden werden und die Umsetzung keinerlei Änderungen am Instrument erfordern, sondern komplett außerhalb erfolgen. Das System besteht daher im wesentlichen aus zwei Komponenten: einem Fußschalter mit einem einzelnen Knopf, der den zwischen den zwei Modi „Aufnahme" und „Befehle" wechselt, und einem Plug-In für das Aufnahmeprogramm, das die Verarbeitung der Töne und das Auslösen entsprechender Befehle ermöglicht. Da sich das Projekt ausschließlich auf eine Erkennung der Tonhöhe stützt, ist das Plug-In grundsätzlich mit allen Instrumenten kompatibel, die in der Lage sind, den für den jeweiligen Befehl festgelegten Ton zu spielen.

Für die prototypische Realisierung des Projektes wurde die elektrische Gitarre als Instrument gewählt, welche durch die integrierten Tonabnehmer eine direkte Aufnahme des Signals am Instrument ermöglicht. Da außerdem das „Home Recording" vornehmlich in den Musikbereichen Rock, Pop und Jazz betrieben wird und die E-Gitarre dort sehr verbreitet ist, wurde für dieses Instrument der größte Nutzen sowie die höchste Wahrscheinlichkeit vermutet, für die Evaluation erfahrene Testpersonen zu finden.

2 Stand der Forschung

Es existiert eine Vielzahl von Projekten, die „traditionelle" Musikinstrumente in einen digitalen Kontext bringen. Der Fokus liegt hierbei oft ebenso auf der Gitarre, die durch ihre weite Verbreitung in der zeitgenössischen Musik zu den am häufigsten eingesetzen Musikinstrumenten zählt. Z.B existiert eine Vielzahl von Systemen, welche das Instrument mit zusätzlichen Sensoren versehen, um Daten über den Spielvorgang aufzuzeichnen oder die Möglichkeiten zur Tonerzeugung digital zu erweitern. Ein umfangreiches Beispiel für diesen Ansatz bietet die *GXtar* (Kessous et al., 2006), welche eine reguläre E-Gitarre als Basis verwendet und mit diversen alternativen Eingabemöglichkeiten (Joystick, Drucksensor usw.) versieht. Ebenfalls in diesen Kontext fallen kommerzielle System wie MIDI-Gitarren, welche direkt aus dem Spielvorgang MIDI-Signale erzeugen oder Instrumente wie die Gitarre *Firebird X* der Firma Gibson, die über eingebaute Effekte verfügt, die sich über Schalter am Instrument sowie eine Bluetooth-Verbindung steuern lassen.

Ein verwandter Ansatz erweitert nicht das Instrument mit Sensoren, sondern Hilfsmittel wie z.B. das Plektrum (*The MIDI Pick*, Vanegas, 2007) oder den Spieler selbst mit Hilfe eines Armbands (Matsushita & Iwase, 2013). Jedoch haben alle diese Ansätze gemeinsam, dass sie entweder ein spezielles Instrument erfordern oder dem Benutzer einen u.U. komplexen „Installationsprozess" vor dem Spielen abverlangen. Beide Nachteile werden vom hier vorgestellten Konzept vermieden, welches mit existierenden, unmodifizierten E-Gitarren einsetzbar ist und einen direkten Einstieg ins Spiel ermöglicht.

3 Umsetzung

Im Prototypen wird die Open-Source-Audiosoftware *Audacity* eingesetzt und mit einem Plug-In erweitert, welches laufend eine Fast-Fourier-Transformation (FFT) auf die eingehenden Audiodaten anwendet, dadurch die gespielten Töne analysiert und bei gedrücktem Fußschalter die Ergebnisse als Programmbefehle interpretiert. Die ausgewählten Töne und ihre Lage auf dem Griffbrett sowie die dazugehörigen Befehle (Aufnahme starten, Aufnahme abspielen, neue Spur hinzufügen, Spur löschen) sind in Abbildung 1 illustriert. Die Befehle wurden auf Basis einer Online-Vorstudie ausgewählt, in der 14 erfahrene Musiker über die in Aufnahmesoftware am häufigsten benutzten Kommandos befragt wurden.

Sobald der über USB angebundene Fußschalter gedrückt wird, wird nun eine möglicherweise laufende Aufnahme unterbrochen und stattdessen die FFT-Komponente aktiviert. Solange der Fußschalter gedrückt ist, kann der Musiker nun einen zum Befehl passenden Ton spielen. Wenn der Fußschalter losgelassen wird, wird der Befehl ausgeführt. Mit den 4 vorliegenden Befehlen ist der Musiker in der Lage, grundsätzliche Aufnahmeszenarien auszuführen, ohne eine Hand vom Instrument nehmen zu müssen. Das System verfügt über kein dediziertes grafisches Interface, da alle Handlungen und Befehle am Instrument vorgenommen werden.

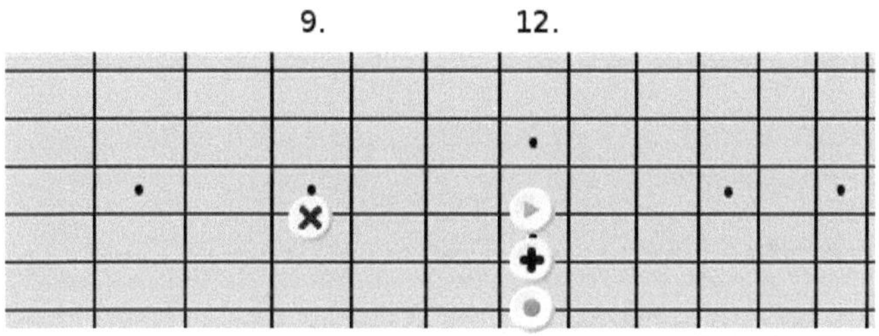

Abbildung 1. Lage der Befehlstöne auf dem Griffbrett als Tabulatur

4 Evaluation

Um das System zu testen und Feedback zu erhalten, wurde eine Evaluation in Form eines Usability-Tests durchgeführt. Hierbei sollte vor allem festgestellt werden, ob das System von verschiedenen Nutzern problemfrei bedient werden kann und ob Musiker durch dieses System unterstützt werden können.

Für die Evaluation wurden Testpersonen gesucht, die das Instrument Gitarre spielen konnten, sowie möglichst schon mit dem Programm Audacity gearbeitet hatten. Jede Testperson wurde gebeten, das eigene Instrument mitzubringen. Nach Unterzeichnen einer Einverständniserklärung wurden die Nutzer über die üblichen Vorgehensweisen in Nutzertests informiert, so z.B. das „Think-Aloud"-Prinzip. Anschließend wurden den Testpersonen vier Aufgaben gestellt, die sie mit dem Prototyp durchführen sollten. Die Aufgaben umfassten das Starten einer Aufnahme, das Abspielen, das Erstellen einer neuen Spur mit einer 2.

Stimme und das Löschen der letzten Spur. Zuletzt wurden die Nutzer gebeten, einen AttrakDiff-Fragebogen auszufüllen, um ihre Zufriedenheit mit dem Produkt zu messen.

Insgesamt nahmen 4 Personen an diesem Test teil, allesamt im Alter zwischen 25 und 30 Jahren. Sie wiesen mehrere Jahre Erfahrung mit dem Instrument Gitarre und im „Home Recording" auf. Keiner der Probanden hatte Probleme bei der Durchführung der Aufgaben, alle Aufgabenstellungen wurden verstanden und konnten umgesetzt werden. Da alle Testpersonen ihre eigenen Gitarren benutzten, wurde mit vier verschiedenen Instrumenten von vier unterschiedlichen Herstellern getestet. Die Auswertung des AttrakDiff-Fragebogens ergab durchweg positive Ergebnisse zur Qualität des Prototypen, sowohl bezüglich pragmatischer als auch hedonischer Qualität. Aufgrund der geringen Zahl der Teilnehmer ist es hier zwar nicht möglich, statistisch belastbare Aussagen zu treffen, jedoch ist aus diesen Ergebnissen trotzdem abzulesen, dass unser System dem Nutzer einen Mehrwert bringen kann.

5 Ausblick

Im Laufe dieses Projekts wurde ein funktionsfähiges System erstellt, das es einem Gitarristen erlaubt, das Aufnahmeprogramm Audacity zu steuern, ohne die Hände vom Instrument zu nehmen. Das Konzept wurde in einer Evaluation als sinnvoll bestätigt - eine kombinierte Steuerung über Fußschalter und Instrument ist möglich und kann von Nutzern ohne Probleme durchgeführt werden. In einer künftigen Studie sollte untersucht werden, wie sich der vorgestellte Ansatz gegenüber einem System aus mehreren Fußschaltern verhält.

Für die weitere Forschung relevant ist die Idee, eine Tonerkennung mittels FFT zur Steuerung von Programmen zu verwenden, um neuartige Benutzerschnittstellen zu entwickeln. Gerade im Bereich der Audiobearbeitungssoftware, oder in einer anderen, für Musiker entwickelten, Software ist hier ein Nutzen erkennbar. Mögliche Erweiterungen des Systems beinhalten einen Indikator, der dem Nutzer anzeigt, ob der gespielte Ton erkannt wurde und welcher Befehl dadurch ausgeführt wird, zusätzliche Befehle mit Konfigurationsmöglichkeit sowie eine interaktive Darstellung der Tabulatur.

Literaturverzeichnis

Loic Kessous, Julien Castet, and Daniel Arfib. '"GXtar", an Interface Using Guitar Techniques'. In Proceedings of the 2006 Conference on New Interfaces for Musical Expression, 192–95. NIME '06. Paris, France, France: IRCAM; Centre Pompidou, 2006. doi:10.1145/1142215.1142262.

Soichiro Matsushita and Daisuke Iwase. 'Detecting Strumming Action While Playing Guitar'. In Proceedings of the 2013 International Symposium on Wearable Computers, 145–46. ISWC '13. New York, NY, USA: ACM, 2013. doi:10.1145/2493988.2494345.

Roy Vanegas. 'The MIDI Pick: Trigger Serial Data, Samples, and MIDI from a Guitar Pick'. In Proceedings of the 7th International Conference on New Interfaces for Musical Expression, 330–32. NIME '07. New York, NY, USA: ACM, 2007. doi:10.1145/1279740.1279812.

M. Koch, A. Butz & J. Schlichter (Hrsg.): Mensch und Computer 2014 Tagungsband,
München: Oldenbourg Wissenschaftsverlag, 2014, S. 379-382.

The potential of smart glasses for smart homes

Ben Dauber, Philipp Meyer, Martin Christof Kindsmüller

Human-Computer Interaction, Fachbereich Informatik, Universität Hamburg

Summary

The intended contribution of this paper is to discuss the suitability of smart glasses for smart homes. Four different solutions currently used in smart homes were redesigned for the usage of smart glasses as the primary interaction device. An evaluation of the prototypes according to five design principles proposed by Norman (2002) suggests that smart glasses can be a valuable addition to existing smart home concepts.

1 Introduction

The idea of a home that intelligently supports its inhabitants through autonomic control of heating and lighting has been captivating people's minds since decades (Aldrich 2003). Though, mostly due to the lack of corresponding technology, smart homes in the past could not live up to the expectations (Trevennor 2012). With the ongoing advances in technology and the further miniaturization, the centralized access to smart home functionalities has been placed into the hands of the user in the form of smartphones and tablets. Although the concept of augmented reality has already been depicted long ago (Mann 2013) and multiple types of smart glasses are available on the market, only the comparatively recent development of Google Glass has been able to shift broad media attention on this category of smart devices. The aim of this research project has been to consider these fields of research jointly and evaluate the suitability of smart glasses as a controlling device for smart homes. To obtain a first impression of the relevance of this research area, a broad methodological approach was chosen to generate a widespread feedback within a limited period of time.

2 Methods & Material

In order to determine the state of art in smart homes, four prototypical solutions from different smart home areas were selected. The main intention of each solution was then extracted and reengineered for being used with Google Glass, resulting in four mockups that are briefly introduced below.

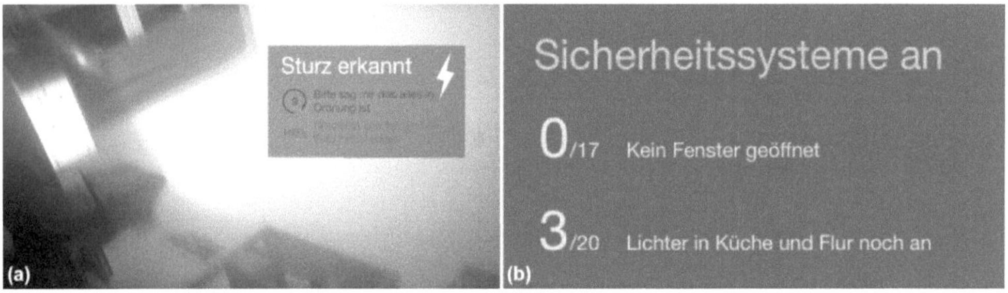

Figure 1: Prototypes of a fall detection (a) and a security (b) application for smart glasses

The example in the area *Healthcare* is a fall detection app (Figure 1(a)) that relies on the built-in acceleration sensor of the smart glass. As soon as a fall is detected, a predefined emergency routine that calls nearby relatives, nursing staff or the ambulance can be started.

The *Security* solution aims to ensure that when nobody is at home all security relevant settings are enforced, e.g. the windows are closed, lights are turned off and alarm system and presence detectors are turned on. The smart glass is able to detect when the wearer is about to leave the house and shows a Security-Card that gives a summary of all security relevant devices of the smart home (Figure 1(b)). Systems that have an actuator built-in can be controlled directly through the smart glasses using voice commands.

The overall goal of the *Energy* solution is to reduce energy consumption by detecting and switching-off unused electronic systems such as lights, TVs or hobs and display this information on the smart glasses. Through the subtle reminder the user is made aware of these systems and can directly turn them off.

The *Comfort* example allows the inhabitant to control e.g. window blinds through gestures. Using indoor navigation by intelligently combining the build in sensors and e.g. (off-board) pattern recognition of the video stream, the smart glasses are able to automatically detect the specific blinds the user is looking at. By moving the finger up or down the blinds can be operated.

All prototypes were evaluated against five design principles for human-computer interaction proposed by Norman (2002), namely *affordances, constraints, mappings, visibility*, and *feedback*. *Affordance* describes to what degree an object offers the user how she or he can interact with it. The term *constraints* refers to the intended limitation of the set of available actions. Whereas *visibility* indicates if a user is able to detect and understand the current status of the system, *mapping* is the relationship between control elements and the internal status of the system. *Feedback* describes the way the system reacts towards user interactions. These principles were initially derived by analyzing the interaction with everyday things and are now widely used to evaluate the usability of systems that offer user interaction.

The prototypes were evaluated by the authors in cooperation with a group of twelve students. All of them were experienced in the development of interactive systems and familiar with Norman's design principles. Prior to the evaluation, all students were introduced to the concepts of smart homes and smart glasses. After presenting each prototype, the findings were discussed in groups of two and submitted as group rating on a 5-point Likert scale (sample size $n = 7$ groups for *Comfort* & *Energy*, sample size $n = 1$ groups for *Healthcare* & *Security*). The sample size for the evaluation of the prototypes for *Healthcare* & *Security* was reduced in favor of inducing a broader and more qualitative feedback through a group discussion process instead of mere Likert scale ratings.

A combined quantitative and qualitative approach was chosen to deliver both a first rough estimate on the suitability of our concrete solutions as well as new and complementary solutions by fostering a more general discussion among the evaluators. We regarded Norman's design principles as suitable for analyzing smart homes because they were originally inspired by successful/failed interaction with everyday things (e.g. at home) and last not least because our evaluation experts were familiar with them.

3 Results

Figure 2 presents the results obtained from the quantitative evaluation of the four prototypes. It can be seen, that *mapping* received by far the best rating with results averaging at 4.5 points (prototypes weighted equally) and ranging only between 4 and 5 points. On the contrary, *affordance* was rated with an average score of 2.11 points (range: 1 to 4). Whereas the assessment of *visibility* tended to be positive (4.23 points), *constraints* and *feedback* were conceived rather poorly (3.67 and 3.33 points).

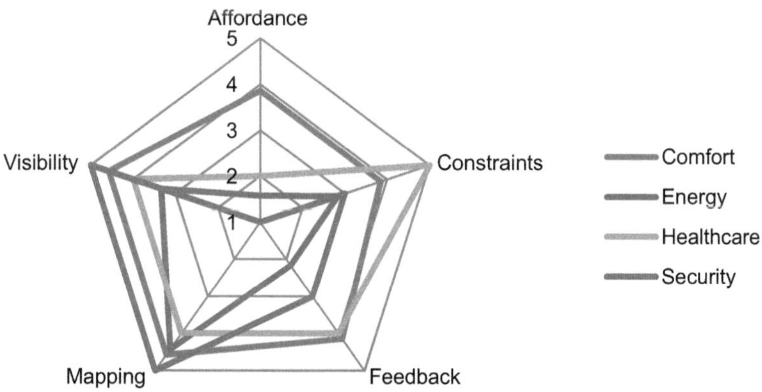

Figure 2: Results of the evaluation (verbal labels: (5) very good, (4) good, (3) medium, (2) poor, (1) very poor)

Whilst few themes that emerged throughout the qualitative feedback were specific to individual prototypes, a number of issues were identified that are of a more general nature. Whereas most evaluators perceived subtle notifications as helpful, some worried about constant interruptions. A common concern amongst the evaluators was that smart glasses might not be carried throughout the entire day, which is particularly crucial in the case of fall detection. Another recurrent theme in the discussion was the potential loss of privacy and the risks induced by poor data security.

4 Interpretation and Conclusion

The results of the evaluation were predominantly positive and revealed the general feasibility of smart glasses as a control unit for different elements in a smart home. Especially the *mapping* between the operated action and the status of the system, as well as the *visibility* of the status of the smart home system proved to be sufficient. However, the developed prototypes did not provide an adequate *affordance*, as most types of interactions were not obvious to the user but had to be trained (e.g. the specific voice commands). Likewise, the *feedback* seemed poor in the evaluation. This criterion however is not as important, as additional feedback is given directly through the addressed smart home component (e.g. the curtain closes).

The findings from this study indicate that smart glasses have the potential to be a valuable contribution for existing smart home environments. Through intelligent use and integration of the various components of smart glasses, a useful and powerful control element can be created. Further research with a larger and more representative sample size needs to be done though, to ensure the generalizability of these results.

Bibliography

Aldrich, F. K. (2003). Smart Homes: Past, Present and Future. In R. Harper (Ed.), *Inside the Smart Home* (pp. 17 – 39). London, UK: Springer.

Mann, S. (2013): Wearable Computing. In: M. Soegaard & R.F. Dam (eds.). *The Encyclopedia of Human-Computer Interaction, 2nd Ed.* Aarhus, DK: The Interaction Design Foundation. Available online at http://www.interaction-design.org/encyclopedia/wearable_computing.html

Norman, D. (2002). *The Design of everyday things*. New York, NY: Basic Books.

Trevennor, A. (2012). *Practical AVR Microcontrollers*. New York, NY: Apress.

Contact information

Martin Christof Kindsmüller, Human-Computer Interaction, Fachbereich Informatik, Universität Hamburg. mck@informatik.uni-hamburg.de

M. Koch, A. Butz & J. Schlichter (Hrsg.): Mensch und Computer 2014 Tagungsband, München: Oldenbourg Wissenschaftsverlag, 2014, S. 383-386.

Today, you walk! – When Physical Fitness Influences Trip Planning

Stefan Diewald[1], Andreas Möller[1], Luis Roalter[1], Matthias Kranz[2]

Distributed Multimodal Information Processing Group, Technische Universität München [1]
Lehrstuhl für Informatik mit Schwerpunkt Eingebettete Systeme, Universität Passau [2]

Abstract

Technology-based self-tracking of physical activity is a new trend. However, monitoring one's own behavior does not automatically motivate one to increase physical exercising. For that reason, we propose a concept that uses the tracked data for providing fitness routes in everyday trip planning, which are tailored to the users' needs, personal preferences, and fitness levels. We argue that utilizing the monitored data for directed exercising during daily routines can add value to the quantified-self movement.

1 Introduction and Background

Do you know what you did today, one year ago? You don't? – Some people do. And they can even tell you where they were, for how long, and with whom. The so-called *Quantified-Selfers* (Choe et al. 2014) track many kinds of data about themselves. With the support of self-tracking technologies, they diligently record their lives and collect large amounts of data that are often stored and processed by cloud systems. Besides those extreme users that track everything in their lives, there is also a broader trend of carrying fitness trackers around. Those trackers are either realized as small gadgets, such as the *Fitbit One*, *Nike+ FuelBand*, or *Jawbone UP*[1], or apps for smartphones, such as *Moves* or *Runtastic Pedometer*[2]. In contrast to sports trackers that are normally only carried and used during exercising (Möller et al. 2012), the fitness trackers are carried the whole day and continually measure steps taken, stairs climbed, overall physical activity intensity, distance traveled, hours slept, and quality of sleep. After uploading the data into the cloud, modern dashboards present activity and sleep graphs as well as abstract numbers of summed up steps and floors for each day, week, month, or overall.

Although having those numbers in black and white allows analyzing shortcomings (e.g., missing the 10,000 steps a day to meet minimum physical activity guidelines, cf. Le-

1 https://www.fitbit.com/one, http://www.nike.com/us/en_us/c/nikeplus-fuelband, https://jawbone.com/up
2 http://www.moves-app.com/, https://www.runtastic.com/en/apps/pedometer, last accessed May, 7, 2014

Masurier et al. 2003), it is not motivating most people to change their long-term behavior without further incentives (Swan 2013). The sole fact of using such a tracking system only influences short-term behavior (Hawthorne effect, cf. Leonard & Masatu 2006). In order to create long-lasting effects, the tracking platform providers offer incentives in the form of virtual badges or physical rewards as well as setting goals or sharing achievements on social platforms (Munson & Consolvo 2012). However, even those extrinsic rewards fail for most users after some time (Walsh & Golbeck 2014), as the desired behavior change (e.g. take more steps) is not triggered by a measure that can be well integrated in the people's daily lives.

For that reason, we propose a novel concept that includes the tracked daily fitness data in standard trip planning. By setting a daily physical activity goal, location preferences and special needs (such as barrier-free access) as well as standard trip parameters, the trip planning application calculates a route with walking segments so that the set physical activity goal (e.g., a certain amount of steps) can be reached.

2 Concept and Prototype of Fitness-based Trip Planning

Our concept primarily aims at users that need to increase their daily physical activity. This can, for example, be the case for certain medical indications, such as type 2 diabetes, obesity, or lack of exercise (Sigal et al. 2004). In that cases, patients often get prescribed a certain amount of steps per day, for example, 10,000 steps/day for healthy 'active' adults (Le-Masurier et al. 2003). The step count is normally tracked by standard mechanical or electronic pedometers.

Our concept allows embedding exercising in daily trips. This is enabled by coupling the current step count and the step history with a trip planning application. In order to be able to respond to the individual needs of the users, each user has to create an account and specify exercising goals as well as special needs. The goal can either be a specific step count that shall be reached on average per day, or a training program that gradually increases the exercise intensity to rise the initial daily step count average to the specified goal. Special needs define whether a user needs barrier-free access (e.g., no steps, max. inclination, even

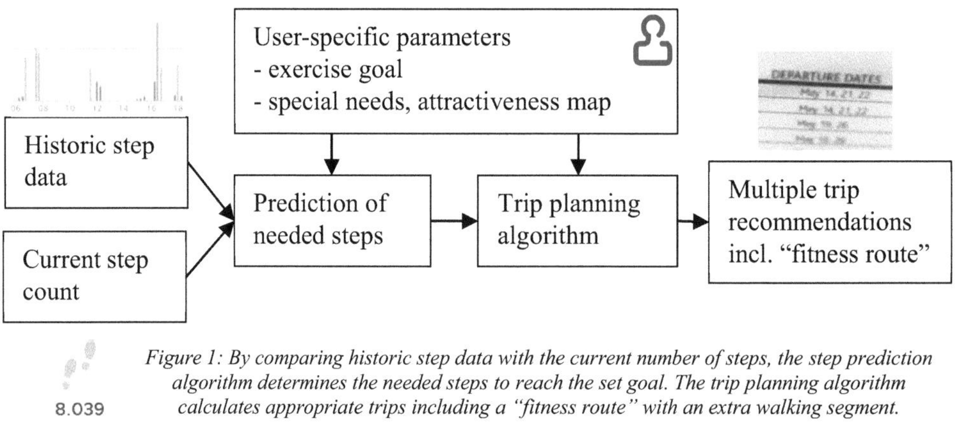

Figure 1: By comparing historic step data with the current number of steps, the step prediction algorithm determines the needed steps to reach the set goal. The trip planning algorithm calculates appropriate trips including a "fitness route" with an extra walking segment.

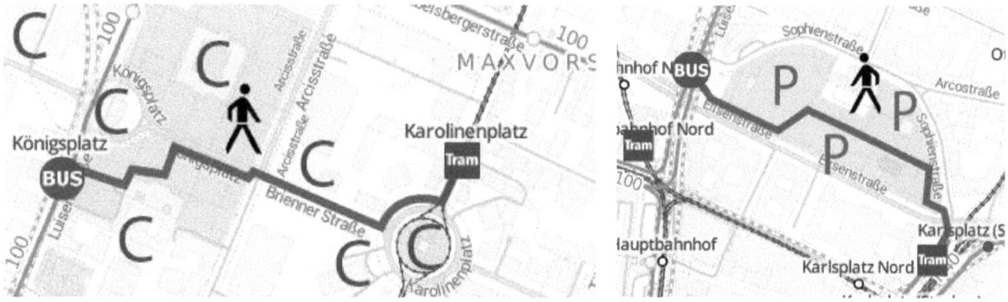

Figure 2: The algorithm uses a user-dependent attractiveness map to determine where the most enjoyable walking segment can be included in the "fitness route". The left image illustrates a walking segment in a cultural environment (C indicates cultural sites). In the right image, a walking segment in a park environment is depicted (P indicates park area). Walking segments are often inserted when transferring between different modes of transport. Map data: © OpenStreetMap contributors; Tram and bus logos: Munich Transport and Tariff Association

floor surfaces) or needs to transport something (e.g., walking aids or a stroller).

Users can further specify preferred training environments, such as cultural sites (e.g., historic, arts), parks, or shopping areas.

When a user wants to plan a new trip, the user opens the trip planning application and logs in into their personal account. The current step count of the user is fetched via the application programming interface (API) from a user specified cloud-based fitness tracking platform. By comparing the current step count with historical patterns, the trip planning platform calculates an estimation of steps that are needed to reach the specified goal on that day. Together with the defined needs, preferences, and entered trip parameters, the platform calculates several appropriate trip recommendations including a so-called "fitness route" with an additional walking segment so that the step count can be reached (cf. Fig. 1).

As users are more motivated when exercising is diversified but done in environments users are feeling well in (Munson & Consolvo 2012), an attractiveness algorithm creates an attractiveness map for each user by comparing the environment nearby the standard routes with user preferences (see Fig. 2). The attractiveness map is adapted after each trip such that often visited places get lower attractiveness values and new walking segments are returned for next similar route recommendations. In future, the attractiveness values can also be adjusted by giving feedback after a trip or by including recommendations of similar users.

Our current prototype is based on the open source trip planning platform OpenTripPlanner (Hilsman & Barbeau 2011) and uses OpenStreetMap data (Haklay & Weber 2008) for calculating the routes. Schedules for public transportation are imported from GTFS (General Transit Feed Specification) files provided by the public transportation agencies. The attractiveness map is implemented statically and only distinguishes between cultural sites, parks and shopping areas. These maps are generated from the density of entries in the respective categories from OpenStreetMap data. The OpenTripPlanner platform performs a multi-factor optimization with user-dependent constrains (Dibbelt et al. 2012) to allow for barrier-free access when needed, and to minimize trip duration and number of transfers. The optimization also takes into account our contributed algorithms to maximize attractiveness and to reach the determined step count. The historic and current step count is retrieved from the hline-online.com platform that allows real-time data gathering from coupled pedometers.

3 Conclusion and Future Work

We proposed a trip planning concept that includes physical activity data for helping users to reach defined fitness goals, and presented the setup of our first prototype. We argue that by embedding self-tracking information into everyday trip planning, users can more easily reach daily activity goals. We currently develop a mobile application that simplifies access to the trip planner (Diewald et al. 2012). As future work, we will add dynamic attractiveness maps and perform a comparison study with our implemented fitness trip planning platform.

Acknowledgements

This work was supported in part by the German Federal Ministry of Education and Research (BMBF, project PASSAge, funding number 16SV5748). Further information on the project PASSAge can be found on http://www.passage-projekt.de

References

Choe, E.K., Lee, N.B., Lee, B., Pratt, W., and Kientz, J.A. (2014). Understanding Quantified-Selfers' Practices in Collecting and Exploring Personal Data. *Proc. CHI,* ACM, pp. 1143-1152.

Dibbelt, J., Pajor, T., and Wagner, D. (2012). User-Constrained Multi-Modal Route Planning. *Proc. ALENEX,* Society for Industrial and Applied Mathemathics, pp. 118-129.

Diewald, S., Möller, A., Roalter, L., and Kranz, M. (2012). MobiliNet: A Social Network for Optimized Mobility. *Adjunct Proc. AutomotiveUI,* ACM, pp. 145-150.

Haklay, M., and Weber, P. (2008). OpenStreetMap: User-Generated Street Maps. *Pervasive Computing,* 7(4), 12-18.

Hillsman, E.L., and Barbeau, S.J. (2011). *Enabling Cost-Effective Multimodal Trip Planners through Open Transit Data.* Tampa, FL, USA:National Center for Transit Research.

Le-Masurier, G.C., Sidman, C.L., and Corbin, C.B. (2003). Accumulating 10,000 Steps: Does this Meet Current Physical Activity Guidelines? *Research Quarterly for Exercise and Sport,* 74(4), 389-394.

Leonard, K., and Masatu, M.C. (2006). Outpatient Process Quality Evaluation and the Hawthorne Effect. *Social Science & Medicine,* 63(9), 2330-2340.

Möller, A., Roalter, L., Diewald, S., Scherr, J., Kranz, M., Hammerla, N. Olivier, P., and Plötz, T. (2012). GymSkill: A Personal Trainer for Physical Exercises. *Proc. PerCom,* IEEE, pp. 213-220.

Munson, S.A., and Consolvo, S. (2012). Exploring Goal-setting, Rewards, Self-monitoring, and Sharing to Motivate Physical Activity. *Proc. PervasiveHealth,* IEEE, pp. 25-32.

Sigal, R.J., Kenny, G.P., Wasserman, D.H., and Castaneda-Sceppa, C. (2004). Physical Activity/ Exercise and Type 2 Diabets. *Diabetes Care,* 27(10), 2518-2539.

Swan, M. (2013). The Quantified Self: Fundamental Disruption in Big Data Science and Biological Discovery. *Big Data.* 1(2), 85-99.

Walsh, G., and Golbeck, J. (2014). StepCity: A Preliminary Investigation of a Personal Informatics-based Social Game on Behavior Change. *CHI EA,* ACM, pp. 2371-2376.

M. Koch, A. Butz & J. Schlichter (Hrsg.): Mensch und Computer 2014 Tagungsband,
München: Oldenbourg Wissenschaftsverlag, 2014, S. 387-390.

UPnP-Serviceplattform für Ambient Assisted Living Dienste

Volker Schürmann, Christian Weidauer

Lehrgebiet Softwaretechnik, Hochschule Bochum – Campus Velbert/Heiligenhaus[1]

Zusammenfassung

Dieser Beitrag stellt eine UPnP-Serviceplattform für Ambient Assisted Living Dienste vor. Der Fokus liegt dabei auf einer einheitlichen Sensor-/Aktuatorschnittstelle und der Einbeziehung von eventuell vorhandenen Geräten aus anderen Anwendungsdomänen, wie z.B. der Gebäudeautomatisierung, zur Reduzierung von Aufwand und Kosten bei der Realisierung von AAL-Lösungen.

1 Einleitung

Der demografische Wandel führt dazu, dass es immer mehr ältere Personen und Menschen mit gesundheitlichen Einschränkungen gibt, die dennoch möglichst lange eigenständig in ihren Wohnungen leben möchten. AAL (Ambient Assisted Living)-Lösungen unterstützen die ambulante Betreuung dieses Personenkreises. Die Industrie hat auf diesen Bedarf reagiert und in den letzten Jahren eine Vielzahl von Produkten, wie zum Beispiel Armbänder zur Überwachung von Vitalfunktionen oder Sensoren zur Sturzerkennung auf den Markt gebracht. Solche sind jedoch in der Regel proprietär und folgen keinen Normen oder Standards, da diese im AAL-Bereich bisher auch noch nicht existieren.

Einem Umstand, dem auch die Deutsche Normungs-Roadmap AAL (VDE 2012) Rechnung trägt, um den zukünftig erwarteten steigenden Bedarf an AAL-Anwendungen zu begegnen.

Das in diesem Beitrag vorgestellte Projekt OptAAL (Optimierung der Entwicklung von Ambient Assisted Living Lösungen) folgt den Empfehlungen der Roadmap und zielt dabei insbesondere auf eine Vereinheitlichung der Schnittstelle zur Sensor-/ Aktuatorebene und die Einbeziehung von eventuell vorhandenen Geräten aus anderen Anwendungsdomänen, wie z.B. der Gebäudeautomatisierung zur Reduzierung von Aufwand und Kosten ab.

2 Stand der Technik

Es gab in der Vergangenheit bereits einige Forschungsprojekte zum Thema AAL-Middleware. Die wesentlichen stellt dieses Kapitel kurz vor.

SOPRANO Ambient Middleware/openAAL

Die in (Balfanz et al. 2008) beschriebene Middleware für AAL-Anwendungen hat den Anspruch das gesamte Anwendungsumfeld von AAL-Systemen zu integrieren. Grundlage bildet ein OSGi (Open Services Gateway initiative)-Framework, in das die einzelnen Geräte als Services integriert werden.

Die Anbindung von Sensoren und Aktuatoren oder auch von Gebäudeautomatisierungskomponenten an das OSGi-Framework ist nicht Gegenstand des Projekts.

Ein ähnlicher Ansatz wird auch in (Palumbo et al. 2013) beschrieben. (Eichelberg et al. 2010) sieht zudem noch eine spezielle proprietäre Abstraktionsschicht für die Anbindung der Sensorik und Aktuatorik vor.

A Middleware for Self-Organising Distributed Ambient Assisted Living

Vom Grundsatz her verfolgt die Lösung aus (Schaefer 2010) einen ähnlichen Ansatz wie die zuvor beschriebenen Projekte mit OSGi-Basis. Allerdings ist die Anbindung von Sensorik und Aktuatorik integraler Bestandteil des Konzepts.

Für Geräte ohne eigene OSGi-Schnittstelle existiert eine Implementierung mit DDS (Data Distribution Service) als Abstraktionsschicht. Als weitere mögliche Technologien für diese Abstraktionsschicht werden DPWS (Device Profile for Webservices) und UPnP (Universal Plug&Play) genannt, da diese bereits von vielen Geräten im Anwendungsfeld unterstützt werden und somit eine OSGi-Anbindung mit relativ geringen Aufwand möglich ist.

3 Serviceplattform für AAL-Dienste

Die bisher entwickelten und in Kapitel 2 beschriebenen Lösungsansätze zielen vornehmlich auf die Bildung einer Serviceinfrastruktur ab. Die Anbindung von Sensorik und die Integration bereits bestehender Systeme werden nur am Rande behandelt. An dieser Stelle setzt der vorliegende Beitrag an und verfolgt dabei den Ansatz einer durchgängigen und einheitlichen Serviceplattform für AAL-Dienste unter Berücksichtigung des in (Schürmann & Weidauer 2012) dargestellten Konzepts. Dabei wird das Ziel einer weitgehenden Entkopplung der AAL-Dienste von der verwendeten Sensorik und Aktuatorik angestrebt. Um dieses zu erreichen, bildet die Serviceplattform sämtliche Sensoren und Aktuatoren auf eine einheitliche Schnittstelle ab.

Diese Schnittstelle erfüllt die folgenden Anforderungen:

1. Die Schnittstelle gestattet eine IP-Adressierbarkeit sämtlicher Geräte und bietet eine Web-Schnittstelle für die AAL-Dienste.

2. Sie soll möglichst einem etablierten Standard entsprechen oder sich an einem solchen orientieren.
3. Es sollten idealerweise Spezifikationen für möglichst viele Sensor- bzw. Aktuatortypen bereits vorhanden sein.
4. Für spezifische Gerätetypen muss die Möglichkeit zur Erstellung eigener Spezifikationen bestehen, vorzugsweise als einheitliches XML-Format.
5. Die Kommunikation zwischen AAL-Dienst und Sensor bzw. Aktuator soll sowohl zyklisch als auch Event-basiert möglich sein.

Eine Technologie, die weitestgehend über diese Eigenschaften verfügt, ist UPnP (UPnP 2008). In UPnP ist die Verwendung von Web-Schnittstellen Standard. Auch Spezifikationen für den Einsatz in der Gebäudeautomation sind bereits vorhanden. Für andere Anwendungsfelder können eigene Spezifikationen in einem standardisierten XML-Dialekt verfasst werden. Darüber hinaus unterstützt UPnP sowohl zyklische als auch Event-basierte Kommunikation. Damit ist UPnP in der Lage als einheitliche Abstraktionsschicht für spezifische AAL-Geräte und Geräte aus der Gebäudeautomation zu fungieren, siehe Abbildung 1.

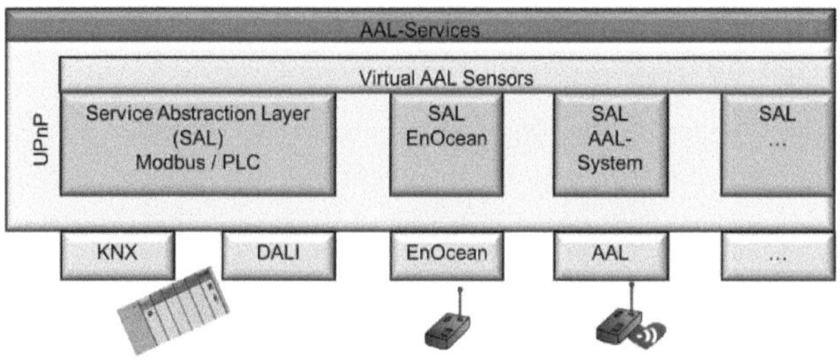

Abbildung 1:AAL-Serviceplattform

3.1 Anbindung der Gebäudeautomation

Moderne Gebäudeautomatisierungssysteme sind mittlerweile weit verbreitet, was dazu führt, dass heutzutage oft schon eine Vielzahl von unterschiedlichen Sensoren in einer Wohnung installiert ist.

Durch eine geschickte Auswertung der Sensordaten lassen sich prinzipiell die gleichen Informationen gewinnen wie durch spezielle AAL-Produkte. Die meisten Gebäudeautomatisierungstechnologien sind jedoch in sich geschlossene Systeme ohne Schnittstellen nach außen. Insbesondere das Weiterreichen von Events, wie das Betätigen eines Lichtschalters, ist i. d. R. nicht vorgesehen.

Daher wurde ein Modbus-UPnP-Gateway in Java entwickelt, dass von Automatisierungsgeräten ausgelöste Events in einer Web-Infrastruktur verbreiten kann.

3.2 Anbindung spezifischer AAL Sensorik und Aktuatorik

Die Anbindung AAL-spezifischer Sensorik und Aktuatorik erfolgt analog zu den Gebäudeautomatisierungsgeräten. Auch hier ist die Erstellung eines gerätespezifischen Service Abstraction Layers für die jeweilige Kommunikationstechnologie notwendig. Das Spektrum reicht von USB über Ethernet mit TCP/IP bis hin zu umfangreichen Datenbankschnittstellen. Bei Sensoren, die der Anwender direkt am Körper trägt, trifft man auch vermehrt auf kabellose Technologien wie Bluetooth und WLAN.

4 Fazit und Ausblick

Die hier vorgestellte Lösung bietet die Möglichkeit nahezu beliebige Sensorik und Aktuatorik in eine IP-basierte Kommunikationsinfrastruktur zu integrieren und sie dadurch auch mit anderen Geräten aus unterschiedlichen Anwendungsdomänen zu kombinieren. Auf diese Weise können die Werte für verschiedenste Dienste aus dem AAL-Umfeld genutzt werden, ohne dass diese sich auf die Details der Anbindung fokussieren müssen.

Zukünftig ist zudem die Spezifikation und Implementierung virtueller UPnP-AAL-Sensoren geplant. Dieses umfasst in erster Linie die Erstellung UPnP-kompatibler XML-Gerätebeschreibungen. Ein solcher virtueller Sensor könnte z.B. ein UPnP-Event erzeugen, wenn an einem physikalischen Bewegungssensor über einen längeren Zeitraum keine Bewegung festgestellt wurde, und so auf ein mögliches Problem hinweisen.

Literaturverzeichnis

Balfanz, D., Klein, M., Schmidt, A. & Santi, M. (2008). *Partizipative Entwicklung einer Middleware für AAL-Lösungen – Anforderungen und Konzept am Beispiel SOPRANO*. Köln: GMDS

Eichelberg, M., Hein, A. Busching, F. & Wolf, L. (2010). *The GAL middleware platform for AAL*. Lyon: 12th IEEE International Conference on e-Health Networking Applications and Services

Palumbo, F., Barsocchi, P., Furfari, F. & Ferro, E. (2013). AAL Middleware Infrastructure for Green Bed Activity Monitoring. *Journal of Sensors 2013*, ID 510126

Schaefer, J. (2010). *A Middleware for Self-Organising Distributed Ambient Assisted Living Applications*. Lyon: 12th IEEE International Conference on e-Health Networking Applications and Services

Schürmann, V., Weidauer, C. (2012). *Usage of Building Automation Infrastructure for Health-Care and Ambient Assisted Living Applications*. Orlando: IIIS Conference ICTA 2012

UPnP Forum (2008). *UPnP Device Architecture – Version 1.1*. UPnP Forum: USA

VDE (2012). *Die Deutsche Normungs-Roadmap AAL*. VDE: Frankfurt

M. Koch, A. Butz & J. Schlichter (Hrsg.): Mensch und Computer 2014 Tagungsband,
München: Oldenbourg Wissenschaftsverlag, 2014, S. 391-394.

Websitedesign: Was ist ästhetisch und was bleibt im Gedächtnis?

Maria Douneva[1], Rafael Jaron[2], Meinald T. Thielsch[1]

Institut für Psychologie, Westfälische Wilhelms-Universität Münster[1]
Nordlight Research GmbH, Hilden[2]

Zusammenfassung

Die vorliegende Studie untersucht, inwiefern sich verschiedene Designstile von Unternehmenswebsites nach kurzer Präsentation (5 sec) im Hinblick auf die ästhetische Bewertung und der Erinnerungsleistung bezüglich zentraler Seitenmerkmale unterscheiden. In einem Online-Expertenvortest mit zehn Teilnehmern wurde die folgende Einteilung von Websitedesigns bestätigt und weiter untersucht: SCOFA (strong colours of one colour family), LAPIC (large pictures) und SAPAT (same amount of pictures and text). Die Ergebnisse der Hauptstudie mit 458 Teilnehmern zeigen, dass von SAPAT-Seiten am meisten Merkmale erinnert werden sowie diese Seiten, zusammen mit LAPIC-Seiten, als deutlich ästhetischer eingeschätzt werden als SCOFA-Seiten. Diese Ergebnisse liefern praktische Hinweise, wie Designer Websites gestalten sollten, sodass diese nicht nur als ästhetisch empfunden, sondern auch schon nach flüchtiger Betrachtung durch die Nutzer gut erinnert werden.

1 Einleitung

Der erste Eindruck zählt, und zwar nicht nur im Umgang mit Menschen, sondern auch im Umgang mit Websites. Bereits bei der Präsentation einer Website für nur etwa 50 ms entscheiden Nutzer, ob sie eine Website ansprechend finden (u.a. Lindgaard et al. 2006; Tuch et al. 2012). Selbst wenn Aspekte wie zum Beispiel die Glaubwürdigkeit einer Seite beurteilt werden sollen, werden dafür nur wenige Sekunden benötigt (Robins & Holmes 2008). Für den ersten Eindruck spielt also weniger der Inhalt, sondern vielmehr das Design bzw. die Ästhetik einer Website eine entscheidende Rolle.

Websitedesigns sind sehr vielfältig, trotzdem lassen sich bestimmte Einteilungen vornehmen und diejenigen Merkmale identifizieren, welche die ästhetische Einschätzung beeinflussen, zum Beispiel die farbliche Gestaltung (u.a. Reinecke et al. 2013) oder das Verhältnis von Grafiken zu Text (Lin et al. 2013). Darauf aufbauend wurden im Vorfeld dieser Studie Unternehmenswebsites auf der Basis ihrer salienten Designmerkmale durch einen der Autoren in drei Kategorien eingeteilt: SCOFA (**s**trong **c**olours of **o**ne colour **fa**mily; vorwiegend farbige Flächen aus einer Farbfamilie), LAPIC (**la**rge **pic**tures; vorwiegend Bilder) und SAPAT (**s**ame **a**mount of **p**ictures **a**nd **t**ext; gleicher Anteil von Bildern und Texten). Analysen mit Adobe Photoshop untermauern diese Einteilung.

Das Ziel der vorliegenden Analyse ist es, diese Kategorisierung auf Unterschiede bezüglich der ästhetischen Einschätzung und der Anzahl erinnerter Seitenmerkmale nach einer Präsentationsdauer von nur fünf Sekunden zu untersuchen[1]. In vielen Studien werden objektive Usabilitykriterien oder subjektive Ästhetikeinschätzungen untersucht (z.B. Lindgaard et al. 2006, Reinecke et al. 2013). Hier wird beides erhoben, um validere Aussagen treffen zu können. Wir erwarten signifikante Unterschiede zwischen den Kategorien; aufgrund der explorativen Natur der Untersuchung stellen wir jedoch keine Hypothesen über die Richtung dieser Unterschiede auf.

2 Methoden

2.1 Websites und Probanden

Als Material wurden insgesamt 12 Websites verwendet (vier in jeder Kategorie). Inhaltlich stammen sie aus den Bereichen Finanzdienstleistungen, Versicherungen, Telekommunikation und Stromanbietern. Die Studie wurde online mithilfe von EFS Survey 8.0 durchgeführt.

Die Teilnehmer wurden über das Online-Panel PsyWeb (https://www.uni-muenster.de/PsyWeb) per E-Mail rekrutiert. Die Stichprobe bestand aus 458 Teilnehmern (52.2 % weiblich, 47.8 % männlich), die im Durchschnitt 39 Jahre alt waren (SD = 15) und seit 13 Jahren das Internet nutzten (SD = 4.4). Jeder Teilnehmer bewertete eine Seite, sodass sich drei Unterstichproben (unterteilt nach den Designkategorien) ergaben mit $n_{SCOFA} = 157$, $n_{LAPIC} = 153$ und $n_{SAPAT} = 148$.

2.2 Ablauf

Nachdem die Teilnehmer demographische Angaben gemacht und Fragen zu Ausschlusskriterien (Farbfehlsichtigkeit, Browsernutzung, Bildschirmgröße) beantwortet hatten, wurden sie zufällig Version A oder Version B der Studie zugeordnet.

In Version A wurde zuerst fünf Sekunden lang zufällig die Startseite einer der 12 Websites angezeigt. Direkt im Anschluss mussten die Teilnehmer mehrere Gedächtnisaufgaben beantworten, in die folgende Auswertung gehen diese drei Aufgaben ein: „Wie hieß das Unternehmen, dessen Webseite Sie gesehen haben?“ (offene Auswahl), „Wo war das Logo des Unternehmens platziert?“, „Wo war der Navigationsbereich/die Navigationsleiste zu finden?“ (multiple choice mit jeweils vier Optionen sowie „weiß nicht“).

[1] Eine umfassende Darstellung dieser Studie findet sich derzeit in Begutachtung (Douneva et al., under review), hier wird über die vorliegende Analyse hinaus der Ersteindruck mittels Reaktionszeiten bezüglich verschiedener websiterelevanter Attribute untersucht. Im Rahmen dieses Beitrags fokussieren wir insbesondere auf die zwei Variablen Ästhetik und Erinnerungsleistung.

Die visuelle Ästhetik wurde mithilfe des Fragebogens VisAWI (Visual Aesthetics of Websites Inventory, 18 Items auf siebenstufigen Likertskalen; Moshagen & Thielsch 2010) abgefragt, während die Teilnehmer die Webseite beliebig lange betrachten konnten. Im Anschluss mussten die Teilnehmer erneut die gleichen Gedächtnisaufgaben beantworten wie zu Beginn.

Version B unterscheidet sich von Version A dahingehend, dass die Teilnehmer lediglich am Ende die Gedächtnisaufgaben beantwortet haben, also nur einmalig statt zweimalig. Durch diesen Versuchsaufbau lassen sich zusätzliche Fragestellungen untersuchen, beispielsweise ob die Dauer der Website-Interaktion Einfluss auf deren ästhetische Beurteilung hat.

3 Ergebnisse

Die Auswertung erfolgte mithilfe von multivariaten Varianzanalysen (MANOVA), wobei *Designkategorie* die unabhängige Variable mit drei Stufen darstellt. Die abhängigen Variablen sind *Gedächtnisleistung* (Anzahl richtiger Antworten am Anfang in Version A bzw. am Ende in Version B, siehe Tabelle 1) und *Ästhetik* (Gesamtpunktwert von 1-7 im VisAWI).

In *Version A* ist die Anzahl richtiger Antworten (0-3) auf LAPIC- und SCOFA-Seiten etwa gleich, auf SAPAT-Seiten jedoch signifikant höher als auf SCOFA-Seiten ($F(2, 248) = 7.58$, $p = .001$) und höher ($p = .056$) als auf LAPIC-Seiten. In *Version B* zeigt sich dasselbe Muster, außer dass auf SAPAT-Seiten nun im Vergleich zu beiden anderen Kategorien signifikant mehr erinnert wird ($F(2, 204) = 3.48$, $p < .05$).

Zusätzlich zeigt sich, dass Teilnehmer, die länger mit der Seite interagiert haben (Version B), signifikant mehr Fragen richtig beantworten ($t(456) = -3,88$, $p < .001$, $d = 0.36$).

	Version A: Fragen am Anfang ($n = 231$)	Version B: Fragen am Ende ($n = 227$)
LAPIC	1.36 ± 0.90	1.60 ± 0.96
SCOFA	1.14 ± 0.91	1.74 ± 0.90
SAPAT	1.69 ± 0.97	2.04 ± 0.93
Gemittelt	1.42 ± 0.95	1.76 ± 0.94

Tabelle 1: Anzahl richtiger Antworten (M und SD) in Version A und B getrennt nach Designkategorie und gemittelt

Bezüglich der Ästhetik sind sich diesmal LAPIC- und SAPAT-Seiten sehr ähnlich, jedoch werden SCOFA-Seiten insgesamt als signifikant unästhetischer eingestuft (3.83 ± 1.17 vs. 4.32 ± 1.10 und 4.36 ± 1.07), $F(2, 401) = 9.70$, $p < .001$.

4 Fazit

Die vorliegende Studie nimmt, basierend auf ersten Eindrücken, eine neue Einteilung von Designs auf Unternehmenswebsites vor und untersucht Unterschiede zwischen ihnen bezüglich subjektiven (ästhetisches Urteil) und objektiven Faktoren (Gedächtnisleistung). Dabei zeigt sich, dass Seiten mit einem ausgewogenen Verhältnis zwischen Bildern und Text sowohl als ästhetisch empfunden werden als auch das Behalten relevanter Seiteneigenschaften deutlich begünstigen. Im Gegensatz dazu werden Seiten, die durch den starken Einsatz von Farben aus einer Farbfamilie auffallen, als vergleichsweise unästhetisch eingestuft und es wird relativ wenig Information behalten. Von Seiten mit hohen Bildanteilen wird ebenfalls relativ wenig behalten, sie werden allerdings als ästhetisch eingeschätzt.

Aus diesen Ergebnissen leitet sich für die Gestaltung von Websites die Empfehlung ab, besonders Wert auf die Balance zwischen Bildern und Text sowie den Einsatz von Farben zu legen. Das ist nicht nur im Hinblick auf den ersten Eindruck wichtig, sondern entscheidet auch mit darüber, ob sich Benutzer überhaupt daran erinnern können, wessen Website sie vor kurzem betrachtet haben. Ob der durch bestimmte Designmerkmale bedingte Erinnerungsvorteil länger anhält, eventuell sogar über mehrere Tage, sollte künftig mithilfe von Längsschnittstudien untersucht werden.

Literaturverzeichnis

Douneva, M., Jaron, R., & Thielsch, M. T. (under review). Effects of different website designs on first impressions, aesthetic judgments, and memory performance – an explorative online study with short presentation times.

Lin, Y., Yeh, C., & Wei, C.. (2013). How will the use of graphics affect visual aesthetics? A user-centered approach for web page design. *International Journal of Human-Computer Studies, 71*, 217-227.

Lindgaard, G., Fernandes, G., Dudek, C. & Brown, J. (2006). Attention web designers: You have 50 milliseconds to make a good first impression! *Behavior & Information Technology, 25(2)*, 115-126.

Moshagen, M. & Thielsch, M. T. (2010). Facets of visual aesthetics. *International Journal of Human-Computer Studies, 68*, 689-709.

Reinecke, K., Yeh, T., Miratrix, L., Mardiko, R., Yuechen, Z., Liu, J., & Gajos, K. Z. (2013, April-May). *Predicting users' first impressions of website aesthetics with a quantification of perceived visual complexity and colorfulness*. Paper presented at CHI, Paris.

Robins, D. & Holmes, J. (2008). Aesthetics and credibility in web site design. *Information Processing and Management, 44*, 386-399.

Tuch, A. N., Presslaber, E. E, Stöcklin, M., Opwis, K., & Bargas-Avila, J. A. (2012). The role of visual complexity and prototypicality regarding first impression of websites: Working towards understanding aesthetic judgments. *International Journal of Human-Computer Studies, 70*, 794-811.

Programmkomitee

Programmkomiteevorsitz

Prof. Dr. Michael Koch, Universität der Bundeswehr München

Programmkomiteemitglieder

Prof. Dr. Mirjam Augstein, University of Applied Sciences Upper Austria
Prof. Astrid Beck, HS Esslingen
Prof. Dr. Klaus Bengler, Technische Universität München
Prof. Dr. Udo Bleimann, Hochschule Darmstadt
Prof. Dr. Birgit Bomsdorf, Hochschule Fulda
Prof. Dr. Andreas Breiter, Universität Bremen
Prof. Dr. Angelika Bullinger-Hoffmann, Technische Universität Chemnitz
Prof. Dr. Andreas Butz, Ludwig-Maximilians-Universität
Dr. Simon Caton, Karlsruhe Institute of Technology
Prof. Dr. Raimund Dachselt, Technische Universität Dresden
Prof. Dr. Markus Dahm, Fachhochschule Düsseldorf
Dr.-Ing. Anke Dittmar, Universität Rostock
Tanja Döring, Universität Bremen
Dr.-Ing. Jens Drummer, Sächsisches Bildungsinstitut
Prof. Dr. Maximilian Eibl, Technische Universität Chemnitz
Prof. Dr. Peter Forbrig, Universität Rostock
Prof. Dr.-Ing. Frank Fuchs-Kittowski, HTW Berlin
Prof. Dr. Jens Geelhaar, Bauhaus-Universität Weimar
Thomas Geis, ProContext Consulting GmbH
Prof. Dr. Paul Grimm, Hochschule Fulda
Prof. Dr. Tom Gross, Universität Bamberg
Prof. Dr. Barbara Grüter, Hochschule Bremen
Prof. Dr. Jörg Haake, Fernuniversität Hagen
apl. Prof. Dr. Kai-Christoph Hamborg, Universität Osnabrück
Dr. Rüdiger Heimgärtner, Intercultural User Interface Consulting
Prof. Dr. Andreas M. Heinecke, Westfälische Hochschule
Dr. Niels Henze, Universität Stuttgart
Prof. Dr. Michael Herczeg, Universität zu Lübeck
Dr. Eelco Herder, Leibniz Universität Hannover
Prof. Dr. Thomas Herrmann, Universität Bochum
Dr. Paul Holleis, DOCOMO Communications Laboratories Europe GmbH
Prof. Dr.-Ing. Eva Hornecker, Bauhaus-Universität Weimar
Dr.-Ing. Tim Hussein, Universität Duisburg-Essen

Prof. Dr. Heinrich Hussmann, Ludwig-Maximilians-Universität München
Prof. Dr. Isa Jahnke, Umea University
Prof. Dr. Monique Janneck, Fachhochschule Lübeck
Dr. Hans-Christian Jetter, University College London
Prof. Dr. Reinhard Keil, Universität Paderborn
Prof. Dr. Andrea Kienle, Fachhochschule Dortmund
Dr. Martin Christof Kindsmüller, Universität Hamburg
Prof. Dr. Gudrun Klinker, Technische Universität München
Prof. Dr. Michael Koch, Universität der Bundeswehr München
Dr.-Ing. Dennis Krannich, Universität Bremen
Prof. Dr. Matthias Kranz, Universität Passau
Prof. Dr. Heidi Krömker, Technische Universität Ilmenau
Prof. Rolf Kruse, Fachhochschule Erfurt
Prof. Dr. Ulrike Lechner, Universität der Bundeswehr München
Andreas Lehmann, lemisoft
Prof. Dr. Jan-Marco Leimeister, Universität Kassel
Prof. Dr.-Ing. habil. Ulrike Lucke, Universität Potsdam
Dr. Stephan Lukosch, Delft University of Technology
Prof. Dr. Susanne Maaß, Universität Bremen
Prof. Dr. Rainer Malaka, Universität Bremen
Prof. Dr. Peter Mambrey, Universität Duisburg-Essen
Prof. Dr. Thomas Mandl, Universität Hildesheim
Prof. Dr. Maic Masuch, Universität Duisburg-Essen
Prof. Dr.-Ing. Gerrit Meixner, Hochschule Heilbronn
Dr. Florian Michahelles, Siemens Corporation
Prof. Dr. Kathrin Möslein, Universitaet Erlangen-Nuernberg
Prof. Dr. Jörg Müller, Technische Universität Berlin
Prof. Dr. Karsten Nebe, Hochschule Rhein-Waal
Prof. Dr. Verena Nitsch, Universität der Bundeswehr München
Prof. Dr. Horst Oberquelle, Universität Hamburg
Dr.-Ing. Hansjürgen Paul, Institut Arbeit und Technik
Dr. Martin Pielot, Telefonica Research
Prof. Dr. Niels Pinkwart, Humboldt-Universität zu Berlin
Prof. Dr. Volkmar Pipek, Universität Siegen
Prof. Dr. Bernhard Preim, Universität Magdeburg
Dr. Michael Prilla, Ruhr-Universität Bochum
Prof. Wolfgang Prinz, Fraunhofer FIT
Prof. Dr. Jochen Prümper, HTW Berlin
Prof. Dr. Ralf Reichwald, Technische Universität München
Prof. Dr. Harald Reiterer, Universität Konstanz
Dr. Christoph Rensing, Technische Universität Darmstadt
Dr. Alexander Richter, Universität Zürich
Dr. Andreas Riener, Johannes Kepler Universität Linz
Prof. Dr. Michael Rohs, Universität Hannover
Prof. Dr. Enrico Rukzio, Universität Ulm

Prof. Dr. Martin Rumpler, Hochschule Trier, Umwelt-Campus Birkenfeld
Prof. Dr. Gabriele Schade, Fachhochschule Erfurt
Prof. Thomas Schlegel, Technische Universität Dresden
Prof. Dr. Johann Schlichter, Technische Universität München
Univ.-Prof. Dr.-Ing. Ludger Schmidt, Universität Kassel
Prof. Dr. Andreas Schrader, Universität Lübeck
Prof. Dr. Ulrik Schroeder, RWTH Aachen
Prof. Dr. Petra Schubert, Universität Koblenz-Landau
Prof. Dr. Gerhard Schwabe, Universität Zürich
Prof. Dr. Jürgen Singer, Hochschule Harz
Prof. Dr. Stefan Smolnik, FernUniversität in Hagen
Prof. Dr. Christian Spannagel, Pädagogische Hochschule Heidelberg
Prof. Dr. Christian Stary, Universität Linz
Dr. Jürgen Steimle, Max Planck Institut für Informatik
Prof. Dr. Gunnar Stevens, Universität Siegen
Dr. Alexander Stocker, Virtual Vehicle Research Center
Prof. Dr. Markus Stolze, Hochschule für Technik Rapperswil
Dr. Friedrich Strauß, Landeshauptstadt München
Prof. Dr. Gerd Szwillus, Universität Paderborn
Dr. Dian Tan, Robert Bosch GmbH
Prof. Dr. Manfred Thüring, Technische Universität Berlin
Prof. Dr. Stephan Trahasch, Hochschule Offenburg
Prof. Dr. Manfred Tscheligi, Universität Salzburg
Prof. Dr. Rainer Unland, Universität Duisburg-Essen
Prof. Dr. Hartmut Wandke, Humboldt Universität zu Berlin
Prof. Dr. Gerhard Weber, Technische Universität Dresden
Prof. Dr. Michael Weber, Universität Ulm
Dr. Martin Wessner, Fraunhofer IESE
Prof. Dr. Christian Wolff, Universität Regensburg
Christian Wolters, Universität zu Lübeck
Prof. Dr. Christa Womser-Hacker, Universität Hildesheim
Dr. Wolfgang Wörndl, Technische Universität München
Prof. Dr. Jürgen Ziegler, Universität Duisburg-Essen

Autoren

Bei Fragen zur Produktsicherheit wenden Sie sich bitte an:
If you have any questions regarding product safety,
please contact:

Walter de Gruyter GmbH
Genthiner Straße 13
10785 Berlin
productsafety@degruyterbrill.com